Palgrave Handbooks in German Idealism

Series Editor
Matthew C. Altman, Philosophy & Religious Studies
Central Washington University
Ellensburg, WA, USA

Palgrave Handbooks in German Idealism is a series of comprehensive and authoritative edited volumes on the major German Idealist philosophers and their critics. Underpinning the series is the successful *Palgrave Handbook of German Idealism* (2014), edited by Matthew C. Altman, which provides an overview of the period, its greatest philosophers, and its historical and philosophical importance.

Individual volumes focus on specific philosophers and major themes, offering a more detailed treatment of the many facets of their work in metaphysics, epistemology, logic, ethics, aesthetics, political philosophy, and several other areas. Each volume is edited by one or more internationally recognized experts in the subject, and contributors include both established figures and younger scholars with innovative readings. The series offers a wide-ranging and authoritative insight into German Idealism, appropriate for both students and specialists.

Tilottama Rajan • Daniel Whistler
Editors

The Palgrave Handbook of German Idealism and Poststructuralism

Editors
Tilottama Rajan
Centre for Theory and Criticism
University of Western Ontario
London, ON, Canada

Daniel Whistler
Department of Philosophy
Royal Holloway, University of London
London, UK

ISSN 2634-6230   ISSN 2634-6249 (electronic)
Palgrave Handbooks in German Idealism
ISBN 978-3-031-27344-5   ISBN 978-3-031-27345-2 (eBook)
https://doi.org/10.1007/978-3-031-27345-2

© The Editor(s) (if applicable) and The Author(s), under exclusive licence to Springer Nature Switzerland AG 2023, corrected publication 2023
This work is subject to copyright. All rights are solely and exclusively licensed by the Publisher, whether the whole or part of the material is concerned, specifically the rights of translation, reprinting, reuse of illustrations, recitation, broadcasting, reproduction on microfilms or in any other physical way, and transmission or information storage and retrieval, electronic adaptation, computer software, or by similar or dissimilar methodology now known or hereafter developed.
The use of general descriptive names, registered names, trademarks, service marks, etc. in this publication does not imply, even in the absence of a specific statement, that such names are exempt from the relevant protective laws and regulations and therefore free for general use.
The publisher, the authors, and the editors are safe to assume that the advice and information in this book are believed to be true and accurate at the date of publication. Neither the publisher nor the authors or the editors give a warranty, expressed or implied, with respect to the material contained herein or for any errors or omissions that may have been made. The publisher remains neutral with regard to jurisdictional claims in published maps and institutional affiliations.

This Palgrave Macmillan imprint is published by the registered company Springer Nature Switzerland AG.
The registered company address is: Gewerbestrasse 11, 6330 Cham, Switzerland

Series Editor Preface

Matthew C. Altman, Philosophy and Religious Studies, Central Washington University, Ellensburg, WA, USA

The era of German Idealism stands alongside ancient Greece and the French Enlightenment as one of the most fruitful and influential periods in the history of philosophy. Beginning with the publication of Kant's *Critique of Pure Reason* in 1781 and ending about ten years after Hegel's death in 1831, the period of "classical German philosophy" transformed whole fields of philosophical endeavor. The intellectual energy of this movement is still very much alive in contemporary philosophy; the philosophers of that period continue to inform our thinking and spark debates of interpretation.

After a period of neglect as a result of the early analytic philosophers' rejection of idealism, interest in the field has grown exponentially in recent years. Indeed, the study of German Idealism has perhaps never been more active in the English-speaking world than it is today. Many books appear every year that offer historical/interpretive approaches to understanding the work of the German Idealists, and many others adopt and develop their insights and apply them to contemporary issues in epistemology, metaphysics, ethics, politics, and aesthetics, among other fields. In addition, a number of international journals are devoted to idealism as a whole and to specific idealist philosophers, and journals in both the history of philosophy and contemporary philosophies have regular contributions to the German Idealists. In numerous countries, there are regular conferences and study groups run by philosophical associations that focus on this period and its key figures, especially Kant, Fichte, Schelling, Hegel, and Schopenhauer.

As part of this growing discussion, the volumes in the *Palgrave Handbooks in German Idealism* series are designed to provide overviews of the major figures and movements in German Idealism, with a breadth and depth of coverage that distinguishes them from other anthologies. Chapters have been specially commissioned for this series, and they are written by established and emerging scholars from throughout the world. Contributors not only provide overviews of their subject matter but also explore the cutting edge of the field by advancing original theses. Some authors develop or revise positions that they have taken in their other publications, and some take novel approaches that challenge existing paradigms. *The Palgrave Handbooks in German Idealism* thus give students a natural starting point from which to begin their study of German Idealism, and they serve as a resource for advanced scholars to engage in meaningful discussions about the movement's philosophical and historical importance.

In short, the *Palgrave Handbooks in German Idealism* have comprehensiveness, accessibility, depth, and philosophical rigor as their overriding goals. These are challenging aims, to be sure, especially when held simultaneously, but that is the task that the excellent scholars who are editing and contributing to these volumes have set for themselves.

Contents

Editors' Introduction xiii
Tilottama Rajan and Daniel Whistler

Part I   Reading the German Idealists After '68   1

Reading Kant.. 3
Sean Gaston

Reading Fichte.. 25
F. Scott Scribner

Reading Maimon... 37
Daniela Voss

Reading Novalis and the Schlegels 59
Kirill Chepurin

Reading Hölderlin... 83
Gabriel Trop

Reading Hegel I: Textuality and the *Phenomenology* 107
Kristina Mendicino

Reading Hegel II: Politics and History 125
Gregor Moder

Reading Schelling 143
Tyler Tritten

Reading Schopenhauer... 165
Joel Faflak

Part II Themes and Concepts 185

Systems of Knowledge 187
Tilottama Rajan

Psychoanalysis 215
Gord Barentsen

Art 239
Anna Ezekiel

Nature and Extinction 259
Thomas Moynihan

Language 291
Oriane Petteni and Daniel Whistler

Difference 323
Arkady Plotnitsky

Nothing 343
Andrew W. Hass

Apocalypse 361
Agata Bielik-Robson

The University 383
Lenka Vráblíková

Enlightenment and Revolution 399
Kyla Bruff

Sovereignty and Community 429
Ian James

Part III Contemporary Stakes 447

Felix Culpa, Dialectic and Becoming-Imperceptible 449
Claire Colebrook

Monism and Mistakes 465
Adrian Johnston

Editors' Conclusions: The Past, Present, and Future of the Theory–German Idealism Relation 489
Tilottama Rajan and Daniel Whistler

Correction to: Reading Novalis and the Schlegels C1
Kirill Chepurin

Index 509

Notes on Contributors

Gord Barentsen researches on romantic philosophy/literature and psychoanalysis (Freud, Jung, Lacan), philosophies of nature and the subject, and theories of the unconscious. He has published *Romantic Metasubjectivity Through Schelling and Jung: Rethinking the Romantic Subject* (2020), and his projects include new translations of Jung's metapsychology papers.

Agata Bielik-Robson is Professor of Jewish Studies at the University of Nottingham and at the Institute of Philosophy and Sociology of the Polish Academy of Sciences in Warsaw. Her publications include, most recently, *Another Finitude: Messianic Vitalism and Philosophy* (2019).

Kyla Bruff is Assistant Professor of Philosophy at Carleton University in Ottawa, Canada. Her research focuses on nineteenth- and twentieth-century German and French social and political philosophy.

Kirill Chepurin is a visiting scholar in theology at the Humboldt University of Berlin. He has published on German Idealism, German and British Romanticism, nineteenth-century Russian thought, utopia, and political theology. He is the co-editor (with Alex Dubilet) of *Nothing Absolute: German Idealism and the Question of Political Theology* (2021).

Claire Colebrook is Edwin Erle Sparks Professor of English, Philosophy and Women's and Gender Studies at Penn State University. She has written books and articles on contemporary European philosophy, literary history, gender studies, queer theory, visual culture and feminist philosophy. Her most recent book is *What Would You Do and Who Would You Kill to Save the World?*

Anna Ezekiel is a feminist historian of philosophy working on post-Kantian German philosophy. She has translated work by Romantic writer Karoline von Günderrode and other women philosophers in *Poetic Fragments* (2016), *Philosophical Fragments* (Oxford University Press, forthcoming), and *Women Philosophers in the Long Nineteenth Century: The German Tradition* (2021).

Joel Faflak is a professor in the Department of English at the University of Western Ontario; a visiting professor at the University of Toronto; and author, editor, or co-editor of 15 books, most recently *Romanticism and Consciousness Revisited* (2022), with Richard C. Sha, with whom he also co-edits Palgrave Studies in Affect Theory and Literary Criticism.

Sean Gaston is a research fellow at the University of Melbourne. He has published widely on the work of Jacques Derrida. His books include *Derrida and Disinterest* (2005), *The Impossible Mourning of Jacques Derrida* (2006), *The Concept of World from Kant to Derrida* (2013) and *Jacques Derrida and the Challenge of History* (2019).

Andrew W. Hass is Reader in Religion at the University of Stirling. His interests and publications operate at the intersection of religion, philosophy, theology, literature, and art, with particular interest in the idea of negation and German Idealism. His current projects focus on music, spirit, and silence.

Ian James is Fellow of Downing College and Professor of Modern French Literature and Thought in the Faculty of Modern and Medieval Languages and Linguistics at the University of Cambridge.

Adrian Johnston is Professor and Chair of Philosophy at the University of New Mexico and a member of the Emory Psychoanalytic Institute. He is the author of, among many works, *Žižek's Ontology* (2008), *Badiou, Žižek, and Political Transformations* (2009), and *Prolegomena to Any Future Materialism* (2013), as well as co-author, with Catherine Malabou, of *Self and Emotional Life* (2013).

Kristina Mendicino is Associate Professor of German Studies at Brown University. She is the author of two monographs, *Prophecies of Language: The Confusion of Tongues in German Romanticism* (2017) and *Announcements: On Novelty* (2020), as well as numerous essays and collections addressing German Romanticism, German Idealism, and phenomenology.

Gregor Moder is a senior research associate at the Department of Philosophy of the Faculty of Arts, University of Ljubljana. His recent works include *Hegel and Spinoza: Substance and Negativity* (2017) and an edited volume on *The Object of Comedy* (Palgrave Macmillan, 2020). As of 2019, he is the principal investigator on a research project on the Theatricality of Power.

Thomas Moynihan is a historian of ideas and author of *X-Risk: How Humanity Discovered Its Own Extinction* (2020). He is a research fellow at the Forethought Foundation and Visiting Research Associate in History at St Benet's College, University of Oxford.

Oriane Petteni is a postdoctoral researcher in the ETHICS department at the Université Catholique de Lille, and holds a PhD in Philosophy from the Université de Liège and has published widely on J. W. Goethe, G. W. F. Hegel and F. W. J. Schelling.

Arkady Plotnitsky is a distinguished professor of English at Purdue University. He has published 9 books, several edited or co-edited collections, and 200 articles on continental philosophy, Romantic literature, and the relationships between literature, philosophy, and science. His most recent book is *Reality Without Realism: Matter, Thought, and Technology in Quantum Physics* (2021).

Tilottama Rajan is a distinguished university professor at the Department of English and the Centre for Theory of Criticism, the University of Western Ontario, Canada. As well as three monographs on Romantic literature, she has published *Deconstruction and the Remainders of Phenomenology* (2002), and (co)edited several books including *After Post-structuralism* (2002), *Idealism Without Absolutes* (2004), and recently, *Roberto Esposito: New Directions in Biophilosophy* (2021).

F. Scott Scribner is Professor of Philosophy and Chair of Global Studies at the University of Hartford. He has published widely in post-Kantian German Idealism and twentieth-century continental philosophy, and his book is an apt expression of his concern with the intersection of these two periods: *Matter of Spirit: J. G. Fichte and the Material Imagination* (2010).

Tyler Tritten has published multiple books and articles on Schelling's later thought. Other projects typically lie within the field of speculative philosophy, including his last book: *The Contingency of Necessity: Reason and God as Matters of Fact* (2017). His current project concerns the possibility of a speculative empiricism.

Gabriel Trop is Associate Professor of German in the Department of Germanic and Slavic Languages and Literatures at the University of North Carolina at Chapel Hill.

Daniela Voss is an associate lecturer in the Department of Philosophy at the University of Hildesheim, Germany. She is the author of *Conditions of Thought: Deleuze and Transcendental Ideas* (2013) and co-editor with Craig Lundy of *At the Edges of Thought: Deleuze and Post-Kantian Philosophy* (2015).

Lenka Vráblíková is a lecturer in the Department of Visual Cultures, Goldsmiths, University of London, and, in 2016, co-founded "Nätverket Feministiska Läsningar/ Feminist Readings Network." Her work lies at the intersection of visual culture studies, transnational feminisms, critical university studies, feminist deconstruction and political ecology.

Daniel Whistler is Professor of Philosophy at Royal Holloway, University of London, and the author of a series of books on F. W. J. Schelling, François Hemsterhuis and Victor Cousin.

Editors' Introduction

That much contemporary theory has unfolded in the shadow of G. W. F. Hegel comes as no surprise to anyone. Since Judith Butler's 1987 *Subjects of Desire* (if not before),[1] a whole publication industry has emerged within the Anglophone world charged with charting the ways in which late twentieth-century European philosophers and theorists have reacted to Hegel, have read him against the grain or have interrogated his legacy. This includes translations of (for example) Jean-Luc Nancy's 1973 *The Speculative Remark*, Jacques Derrida's 1974 *Glas*, and Catherine Malabou's 1995 *The Future of Hegel*[2]; original English-language texts by Fredric Jameson and Slavoj Žižek[3]; and collections such as Stuart Barnett's *Hegel after Derrida* and Žižek's, Crockett's, and Davis's *Hegel and the Infinite*.[4] Indeed, the importance of Hegel to the work of theory precedes the linguistic turn of the 1960s, in the work of the Frankfurt School and the broader constellation in which they sit; Georg Lukacs, Herbert Marcuse, and Theodor Adorno all wrote studies on Hegel.[5] While we do not take up "critical theory" here,[6] Adorno's major works, *Negative Dialectics* and *Aesthetic Theory*—both implicitly engaged with Hegel—are in fact contemporaneous with 1960s' "Theory," and there are many synergies between them and Derrida's epoch-making 1967 *Of Grammatology*.[7] As part of the Hegel-reception we must also mention pre-poststructuralist thinkers such as Georges Bataille, the subject of Rodolphe Gasché's 1978 *Phenomenology and Phantasmatology*, which makes the post-war French thinker an occasion for explosively deconstructive readings of the work of Hegel and Schelling toward their own auto-immunity.[8]

Equally, while not as pervasive, the interest in Immanuel Kant shown by Derrida himself, Žižek, Michel Foucault, Jean-François Lyotard, Nancy, and Gilles Deleuze, among others, is familiar to English-language readers, as evidenced by the relatively early date at which a translation of, for example, Lyotard's *Lessons on the Analytic of the Sublime* appeared (1994).[9] An occasional broadening of this Kant-Hegel axis also goes back some decades, for instance to Tilottama Rajan's and David Clark's collection, *Intersections: Nineteenth-Century Philosophy and Contemporary Theory* (1995),[10] which includes essays on J. G. Fichte, F. W. J. Schelling, and Arthur Schopenhauer as well as Hegel and Friedrich

Nietzsche. Collectively these works have constituted the intersection of German Idealism and contemporary theory from the 1960s onward as a field in its own right, one that is ripe for expansion beyond the simple tracing of influences, and is no longer limited to the figures or texts privileged in philosophy departments. Moreover, what is also becoming visible in English is that there are further, occasionally subterranean, ways in which theory has appropriated (and continues to develop from) other German philosophers dating from the turn of the nineteenth century, such as Schelling and Salomon Maimon (or G. W. Leibniz, if we were to go further back[11]).

It is within this growing *diversification* of encounters between German Idealisms and poststructuralisms—both terms we want to complicate—that the present volume is positioned. An exhaustive survey of connections between these two large areas is impossible. But this volume, the most broad-ranging of its kind, offers a number of exemplary "probes" into the Idealism-poststructuralism relationship. Several essays take up specific past-present pairs (such as Kant and Derrida, Fichte and François Laruelle, Schelling and Žižek), while others focus more purely on German Idealists refracted through a contemporary lens, not so as to apply the latter to the former within a model of influence or derivation, but so as to recognize Idealism as a co-originator of the very theory that helps to bring out its contemporaneity. Finally, other essays also make Idealist and contemporary thinkers equal partners in a dialogue around key topics such as difference, focusing not so much on the historical record as on initiating a live program of theorizing within the Humanities today—an ongoing conversation whose participants still include Hegel, Schelling, and their peers, in addition to Derrida, the late Foucault, and others.

In order to do justice to the complexity of these interactions and their future potentials, we push *both* labels—"German Idealism" and "poststructuralism"—to their maximum extension. In the context of this volume, both Idealism and poststructuralism are not "rigid designators," the phrase Saul Kripke uses for names as "pure signifiers" that "designate" and "constitute the identity of a given object beyond the variable cluster" of its actual properties or historical shifts. As Žižek argues, in critiquing Kripke, rigid designators simplify an ideological field made of "non-bound, non-tied elements … whose very identity is 'open,' overdetermined by their articulation in a chain with other elements."[12] Interestingly, in his *First Outline of a System of the Philosophy of Nature*, a text whose theory of matter can double as a theory of concept-formation in Deleuze and Guattari's sense of the concept as non-simple and multiplex,[13] Schelling similarly describes organic "products" as containing a "multiplicity of unified tendencies" or "actants" that are "bound" or "determin[ed]" in "figures" to achieve a heuristically necessary "rigidity" that remains under pressure from other actants repressed within the "figure."[14] Likewise an intellectual field—feminism and "ecologism" are Žižek's examples—remains indeterminate until the intervention of a "nodal point" or "*point de capiton*" that "quilts'" the elements in the field, "stops their sliding," and seemingly "fixes their meaning."[15] From this perspective Idealism and poststructuralism too are stabilizing nodal points that we prefer to use as fluid designators calling for further reflection, rather than determining their materials under a rule or "universal," as Kant might say.

With regard to the multiplicity of actants in the signifier "German Idealism," there has long been a paradigm shift in scholarship away from the traditional Kant-Fichte-Hegel axis in philosophy (or the Kant-Hegel-Nietzsche sequence in "theory") to a richer sense of Idealism as enmeshed in an intellectual and often interpersonal milieu that includes "Classicists" like J. W. Goethe and Friedrich Schiller and "Romantics" like Friedrich Schlegel and Novalis[16]; philosophers of nature like C. F. Kielmeyer who influenced Hegel and Schelling, and Lorenz Oken who was in turn influenced by Schelling; less canonical figures like Maimon; and female philosophers working in this tradition like Karoline von Günderrode and Bettina Brentano-von Arnim. To insert Idealism back into this wider milieu—to evoke Georges Canguilhem's theorizing of "milieu" in organic and synergistic, rather than mechanist and determinist terms[17]—is to recognize the ways in which, especially in this period, philosophy and "the margins of philosophy" were reciprocally constitutive. Indeed, this *inter*disciplinarity is a key aspect of the retrospectively named "theory" that emerged in the 1960s[18] and is what makes "Idealism" and "poststructuralism" such appropriate interlocutors for one another.

For example, Kielmeyer, though previously approached purely for his involvement in the genesis of the life sciences by earlier historians of thought, is now being reinserted into a milieu in which, on the one hand, his 1793 speech "On the Relations Between Organic Forces in the Series of Different Organisations" was translated into a different and more philosophical register to provide a speculative basis for the self-organization of matter that catalyzes post-Kantian hopes for a self-assembling of matter into spirit; and in which, on the other hand, this speech was itself influenced by J. G. Herder's *Ideas for a Philosophy of the History of Mankind* (1786–1791).[19] The point is, in part, that such "translations" between fields are what make the Idealism-Romanticism conjuncture, with its encyclopedic range of interests (indexed by Hegel's *Encyclopedia of the Philosophical Sciences*) a first version of theory.

Indeed translation, as Antoine Berman argues in a book Derrida takes up in an essay on Schelling, "Theology of Translation,"[20] is at the very heart of Romanticism. For Berman, "restricted translation" (of actual texts), which was a key part of German Romanticism, is nested within a broader general economy of translation that entails a philosophical and "ethical" choice. Against "the ethnocentric structure" and "narcissism by which every society wants to be a pure and unadulterated Whole," this broader translation seeks to "open up in writing a certain relation with the other, to fertilise what is one's Own through the mediation of what is Foreign." Perhaps Novalis's claim of "universal versability," or the "translatability of everything into everything" that underwrites his *Romantic Encyclopedia*, is in some respects uncritical[21]; nevertheless, the entanglements between Idealism and Romanticism are the condition of possibility for reading Idealism against the grain in the more experimental interzone of "theory," and Novalis's *Fichte Studies* (1795–1796) and his *Notes for a Romantic Encyclopedia, or the Universal Brouillon* (1798) are in dialogue with, or traverse the same terrain as, work by Idealist philosophers, as do Friedrich Schlegel's fragments and lectures on *Transcendental Philosophy*.[22]

Our use of the epithet "poststructuralism" is also intended to encompass a broad range of theorizing *after structuralism*. It comprises not just that thinking which the Anglophone world saw as radicalizing French structuralism in the 1960s ("poststructuralism" narrowly understood), but all the various forms of contemporary theory in the "continental" style that have emerged out of that primal scene, sometimes including non-French, "post-poststructuralist" thinkers such as Mladen Dolar and Giorgio Agamben. The origins of poststructuralism are widely associated with two events. One is the 1968 student uprisings in France which contributed to a general contemporary feeling for the need to call classical philosophy in question,[23] a need mirrored in the desire of early nineteenth-century German philosophy—whether "Idealist" or "Romantic"—to think beyond Kant and Fichte and to provide, in Benjamin's words "A Coming Program for Philosophy."[24] Secondly, and sensing this practico-intellectual revolution from the other side of the Atlantic, there is also the 1966 conference at Johns Hopkins University on "The Languages of Criticism and the Sciences of Man." Yet although this conference is widely seen as inaugurating "poststructuralism," the word is never used in the volume that came out of it, *The Structuralist Controversy* (1971), which includes essays by a number of thinkers of whom only Derrida, Jacques Lacan, and Roland Barthes would now in any way be named poststructuralist.[25] The label emerged later, and is something of a theoretical monster, condensing various mutations, amalgamations, and omissions that French philosophies underwent in their translation to the Anglophone world, whether through commentary, adaptation, or the actual history of what was translated and in what order. One of the few early studies of this material to appear in France itself was a 1979 book by Vincent Descombes. Significantly Descombes uses the descriptor "Modern French Philosophy" to encompass the "humanist controversy" inaugurated by structuralism itself, as well as the work of Derrida, Deleuze, Foucault, and Lyotard; he also goes back to Alexandre Kojève's lectures on Hegel before moving on to "the intellectual scene in 1960," in which he includes Pierre Klossowski, whom we think of as belonging to an earlier generation but whose *Nietzsche and the Vicious Circle* actually appeared in 1969.[26]

In other words, like Idealism, poststructuralism is a porous label which is retained in this volume partly for convenience. Derrida himself understood the term as a "purely American notion" and a "transformation ... of this thing come from France" for American purposes, as he puts it in "Deconstructions: The Im-Possible." Derrida preferred "deconstruction," not to be understood in its limited literary-critical sense of Yale Deconstruction, which also reflected an American instrumentalizing of deconstruction as applied theory,[27] but rather as an operation bearing on "systems," and on the traditional architecture of the fundamental concepts of ontology or of Western metaphysics. As such, deconstruction, which Derrida specifically thinks in relation to Kant's notion of architectonic in the first *Critique*, is a "question about the foundation ... the closure of the structure," about "a whole architecture of philosophy," the unsettling of which opens up new "possibilities of arrangement or assembling."[28] As one of our editors, Tilottama Rajan, has argued in desynonymizing the two terms, "poststructuralism" does have a descriptive value to the extent that the prefix "post" signifies a certain contemporaneity and break with tradition that French commentators who merge it into structuralism do not highlight. However, "deconstruction" in its broadest sense is an approach that can be traced back, well before the Johns Hopkins conference to the earlier but overlapping generation of Bataille, Klossowski, and Maurice Blanchot.[29] This approach is not necessarily limited to a focus on language and structure, though it may involve an interest in writing (*écriture*) and often in "literature," thought as an ontological rather than disciplinary term[30]—an interest that does not necessarily derive from Saussure. Moreover, "deconstruction" is not always committed to the abjection of a consciousness-based vocabulary (however much this may be problematized)[31]—a vocabulary obviously central to German Idealism. Indeed, Descombes describes the work of both Derrida and Deleuze as a "radicalisation of phenomenology."[32]

It would be more accurate, then, to speak of an anti-foundationalist thinking of which poststructuralism is a particular, historically specific permutation. The present volume does not take up deconstruction or modern French philosophy as they existed prior to the 1960s, and so "poststructuralism" as a term of convenience also indexes a date-range. Nevertheless, a broader use of this term as a floating signifier for anti-foundationalist thinking generally is what provides the volume's rationale for extending its contents beyond those theorists working through the aporia of classical structuralism, to include philosophers who do not obviously take as their starting point a concern with the consequences of the linguistic turn, such as Laruelle or Quentin Meillassoux.

The basis of the present volume is, therefore, the realization that so many of the thinkers who fall under this large umbrella owe significant and often multiple debts to the German Idealist tradition, which was already engaged in the process of questioning its own foundations. Indeed, what unites the "poststructuralisms" of this volume is more than anything else a tradition, running from Derrida and Deleuze to Žižek and Malabou, of treating German philosophers as privileged dialogue partners. As noted, previous thinkers such as Adorno or (however differently) Bataille had already situated their projects *in the aftermath of Idealism*. But the generation of thinkers for whom 1968 provides a nodal point, and who have proven such a crucial reference point for "theory," were even more determined to thematize their points of convergence with and divergence from the German Idealist movement (or more broadly German philosophical traditions). Outside of his partnership with Guattari, Deleuze was also a counter-historian of philosophy, who wrote books on Leibniz, Kant, and Nietzsche[33]; Derrida's work, as he himself has stressed, was doubly formed by his role as an *agrégé-répétiteur* who trained students for their exams at the *École Normale Supérieure*, and by the uniquely French emphasis on the *explication de texte* method introduced by Gustave Lanson.[34] This conjunction, and the resistances it produced, led to the early Derrida's deconstructive method of reading minute sections from philosophical texts against the grain, as he does with Hegel in "The Pit and the Pyramid."[35] This signature method is also one we find in Paul de Man, for whom the canon, including Kant and Hegel (as well as Rousseau and Nietzsche), remains similarly important. Derrida's student Malabou has also written a trio of books arguing for the plasticity and epigenetic potential of Hegel, Heidegger, and Kant.[36] It is not an exaggeration to say that poststructuralism and deconstruction can often be understood *only* in relation to a philosophical tradition of which German Idealism forms the center.

With this context in mind, we have divided the volume into three parts. Part I focuses on individual German Idealist philosophers, including the more obvious (Kant, Hegel), the recently recovered for theoretical purposes (Schelling), the more marginal (Maimon), the ex-centric (Novalis, Hölderlin), and the under-theorized (Fichte, Schopenhauer). The essays in this section do not all read from past to present in terms of a model of influence or uptake that privileges the contemporary; some reverse this trajectory. Part II turns from this framework of figures to a topical approach that also speaks to the multi- and interdisciplinary engagements that characterize both German Idealism and poststructuralisms. Chapters are dedicated to central theoretical topics, such as difference, nothing, art, revolution, and language, as well as to key areas of connection, like nature, psychoanalysis, and politics. Such a structure obviously entails that individual thinkers at both ends of the historical spectrum are not circumscribed to particular chapters, but recur in different constellations on different topics throughout the volume. Finally, Part III takes stock even more explicitly of the contemporary issues at stake in this conjunction of fields, with the aim of furnishing a sense of new directions and future trends. That is, the contributors to this final section think through—but also beyond—the Idealism-poststructuralism conjunction, to look for a variety of new, surprising affinities between the past, present, and future.

Part I therefore begins at the origins of German Idealism with Kant. There are several lines of connection between Kant and French theory, but Sean Gaston focuses on Derrida in particular, providing a comprehensive survey of Derrida's changing relation to Kant over the course of his career, from the early work on Heidegger's *Kant and the Problem of Metaphysics*, through "the Kantian turn" of the early 1980s (also present in Lyotard) to Derrida's last seminars. As Gaston suggests, given the ongoing publication of these seminars, Kant's role in Derrida's version of the deconstructive project is still emerging. But suffice it to say that Kant stands behind multiple topics taken up by Derrida—from the self-authorization of reason to the university, hospitality, cosmopolitanism, *mondialisation* (a word Derrida prefers to globalization), and the death penalty. The diversity of these engagements speaks not only to Kant's importance for Derrida, but also to the way the later Derrida in particular has expanded the Kantian canon itself, leveling the marginalization of Kant's minor work in relation to his *Critiques*, and opening up the relation between theoretical and practical philosophy generally, on both the Idealist and poststructuralist sides.

The following chapters in Part I proceed chronologically: "Reading Fichte" by F. Scott Scribner is devoted to theoretical readings of Fichte—in particular, Laruelle's extensive use of Fichte in his *Principles of Non-philosophy* to radicalize the inaugural philosophical decision Fichte invokes into a decision for or against philosophy itself.[37] In "Reading Maimon", Daniela Voss considers another contemporary return of a German Idealist, connecting Deleuze with Maimon, who reformulates Kant's first *Critique* by way of a Leibnizian interpretation of the differential calculus. Though Deleuze sees Maimon (and Leibniz) as finally stopping short of a contemporary understanding of difference that breaks with a philosophy of identity, it is clear that differentials, as infinitely small elements or infinitesimals, open a path toward the "unthinkable" within thought and toward Deleuze's own transcendental empiricism. The Maimon-Deleuze connection is particularly interesting because it directs us to an aspect of the Idealist constellation of disciplines whose synergies with poststructuralism are often overlooked, namely mathematics. As the case of Maimon brings out, mapping the difference between hard and soft sciences onto "continental" theory risks ignoring the ways in which the so-called hard sciences and mathematics have developed since the Enlightenment and the role they play in poststructuralism considered as a source of new logics and epistemologies.[38]

Infinitesimals also play a role in early Romanticism, though differently. In "Reading Novalis and the Schlegels", Kirill Chepurin probes the impossible desire of Novalis and the Schlegels to write universal histories (conceived as general economies rather than the restricted economies of the Enlightenment genre), yet to encompass increasingly minute particulars. His approach broadly accords with a reception-history of the *Frühromantik* that includes Blanchot, Lacoue-Labarthe and Nancy, and Berman.[39] But he expands on the "infinite versability" earlier described, so as to think through Romantic "cosmism" as the Eurocentric narratives of global humanity and modernity that develop from it, and also the deep time of planetary processes not encompassed in the word "globalization."[40] Chepurin thus brings out how Romantic thought resonates with issues such as (de)colonization and ecological crisis that have emerged in the wake of poststructuralism, but he also sees the incommensurable joining of unities and divisions in the literary absolute's "poietic," constructive system as a fertile ground for speculating on these issues in ways that need not be confined to a negative philosophy: a critique, pure and simple, of Romanticism's "meta-positions." Gabriel Trop likewise approaches Romanticism as an originary site for theorizing in "Reading Hölderlin". In a bold move, he turns not to Hölderlin's critical writing[41] but to his "speculative poetics"—especially his engagement with Pindar in the *Pindar Fragments*—as a form of concept-creation (in Deleuze and Guattari's term) that produces a "hyperbolic" rather than sequential logic for navigating phenomena. Hölderlin's poetry has interested philosophers and theorists from Heidegger to de Man to Alain Badiou. But Trop hyperbolizes (as it were) the translations and transferences between poetry and philosophy by putting Hölderlin in direct and continuous dialogue with his Tübingen classmates Hegel and Schelling. Allowing poetry to generate new geometries and rhythms of perception that can equally open new ways of reading philosophy, he thus fundamentally recasts the relationship not just between literature and philosophy but also between Romanticism and Idealism.

The sheer extent of Hegel's importance for poststructuralisms and the range of his work itself are recognized by two complementary chapters that discuss and exemplify the later twentieth-century reception of his work, one oriented inward to Hegel's writing, and the other outward to his politics. In "Reading Hegel I: Textuality and the *Phenomenology*" Kristina Mendicino, in the spirit of the early Derrida, provides a deconstructive reading of the "Foreword" to the *Phenomenology* that is exemplary for reading Hegel generally and considers how Hegel's thought is always caught up and delayed/deferred by its reading, even at the level of his writing itself as a reading. She thus follows through on Trop's intuition of the relevance of tropes like enjambment and caesura to unearthing a counter-logic in Hegel's writing that turns the forward movement toward a paraphrase of concepts back on itself. In the next chapter Gregor Moder then works through the turn away, in the French reception, from the more sympathetic philosophical readings of Hegel by Kojève and Jean Hyppolite to a more historical and Marxist emphasis, focusing on Louis Althusser's Marxist-poststructuralist critique of Hegelian history as totally coinciding with itself through the exclusion of anachronism and contingency. Drawing on the Ljubljana School of Hegelians (including Dolar and Žižek), Moder instead argues for a constitutive kernel of contingency and anachronism at the heart of Hegelian history—a political equivalent to the rhetorical processes Mendicino describes in Hegel's writing. The result, Moder suggests, is that the "end of history," the totalization that serves as the Žižekian *point de capiton* which sutures events together across these differences, is itself utterly contingent.

Recently, there has been a resurgence of interest in the third member of the post-Kantian triad, F. W. J. Schelling, which is not reflected in post-1960s' theory but could not have happened without it. Schelling's corpus has difference at its core, as he kept beginning "again from the beginning" as Hegel puts it; Schelling kept questioning the foundations of his own thought, since "what went before did not satisfy him."[42] Other aspects of this diverse corpus are explored in the essays by Gord Barentsen, Thomas Moynihan, and Rajan, but in the penultimate chapter of Part I, Tyler Tritten focuses on one of the few sustained contemporary engagements with Schelling[43]: what he sees as the missed encounter between Žižek's psychoanalytic-materialist account of Schelling and the latter's middle work of the *Weltalter* period (1809–1821). Tritten argues that in over-mediating Schelling through Lacan, Žižek forecloses any possibility of thinking "*before* the political." While the Real, in the Ljubljana School's unique reading of Lacan, is not barred from the Symbolic but rather erupts within it,[44] Žižek's explosion (rather than critique) of ideology thus remains, in Schellingian terms, a negative rather than a positive philosophy.

In the last chapter in Part I, Joel Faflak also takes up a thinker whose work can be put in dialogue with psychoanalysis and, indeed, is part of its invention. Freud recognized his debt to Schopenhauer's theory of the will as a blind force generating and exposing representation as reason's fantasy of its self-sufficiency. But contemporary theory has largely ignored Schopenhauer, even though he could be said to practice the deconstruction of Idealism and live the *agon* of being unable entirely to bring this about.[45] Accordingly, Faflak provides a reading of *The World as Will and Representation* that is darkly "Romantic," insofar as he treats it as both theory and text, as a philosophy of that of which it is itself the symptom. In moving forward, he asks what this thinker, who missed his moment in 1818 to be recovered in the 1850s and forgotten again, can say to our time. He concludes that "the in- and non-human dimension of existence" disclosed by the will speaks powerfully to the writing of the disaster and to speculative realist discourses (Brassier, Thacker) that think the very extinction of philosophy outside the protection of correlationism.[46]

Part II shifts away from this chronological sequence to identify thematic intersections between German Idealism and various poststructuralisms. Idealism is often seen as a totalizing epistemology, so in "Systems of Knowledge" Tilottama Rajan focuses on the problematic of "systems," by taking up the challenge of systemizing knowledge constellated in the very title of Hegel's *Encyclopedia of the Philosophical Sciences*. She starts with Kant's notion of "architectonic" as a part-whole integration that maintains a restricted economy of knowledge. While Kant restrains his nascent interdisciplinarity by setting borders between fields that he crosses only hypothetically, for Hegel and Schelling the tension between the unification and particularization of knowledge creates a general economy where disciplines—art, the life sciences, philosophy, history, and others—are constantly exposed to their margins. Continuing with a "Romantic" reading of Idealism in which the author is inscribed in "the generation and parturition" of a "text" that is never finalized as a "work" (in Roland Barthes's terms),[47] Rajan also suggests that in post-Kantian Idealism "system is subject." As the system-subject works through the forms and contents of knowledge, what Derrida sees as Hegel's auto-encyclopedia of spirit confirming itself unravels, instead, into a field of transferences that are (self)critical, ruinous, and often creative, while for Schelling "absolute" knowledge, far from resulting in a "theology of translation," becomes unconditional knowledge—a pursuit of knowledge wherever it leads.

In "Psychoanalysis" Gord Barentsen continues to explore the cross-fertilizations between fields enabled by this deconstructive interdisciplinarity, in taking up an area not yet named in Idealism. He sees psychoanalysis as generated within Idealism from convolutes within the *Philosophy of Mind* where "soul" and "mind" deterritorialize each other and that Hegel is unable to sublate, as well as from Schelling's *Naturphilosophie*, which interacts with transcendental philosophy to unground any conventional notion of Idealism. An important part of both thinkers' Romantic milieu is Franz Anton Mesmer, who is also a bridge between physiology and the psychology that existed at the time (in Mesmer's case, a kind of (anti)psychiatry). What emerges is a speculative unconscious that Barentsen traces forward, through Jung, to Deleuze and Guattari's *Anti-Oedipus* (1972). Their work, in its difference from Lacan, marks the beginning of the "speculative turn" in continental philosophy and complicates any reduction of poststructuralism to the linguistic turn, which is to say that this chapter also exemplifies how rethinking the Idealism-Romanticism conjunction through poststructuralism can result in a rethinking of poststructuralism itself.

While the previous two essays construct speculative feedback loops between Idealism and poststructuralism, in Chapter "Art" Anna Ezekiel turns to art and takes up a body of philosophical-cum-literary thought (or *Symphilosophie*, in Friedrich Schlegel's term)[48] that has been neglected by contemporary theory: feminist engagements within Idealism, exemplified here by the work of Karoline von Günderrode and Bettina Brentano-von Arnim. Among the areas affected by post-Kantian Idealism's unsettling of the philosophical architecture, art offers a particularly large scope for contemporary rethinking. Schopenhauer's uneasy deconstruction of aesthetic representation by the will and Hegel's historicization of art to allow for aesthetic modes in which "inadequate" embodiments of the Idea have their own value and adequacy[49] are touched on by Faflak and Rajan respectively. These later (post 1818) theories pull away from the early Romantic model made synonymous with German aesthetic theory by Lacoue-Labarthe and Nancy. Ezekiel, however, sees a turn away from the "literary absolute" as beginning in early Romanticism itself. Building on recent reconstructions of two key women thinkers who were involved in Idealist and Romantic circles, she first takes up Günderrode's dialogue with Kantian notions of the sublime, fragmentariness, and subjectivity, which she refracts through Lyotard, Cixous, and Irigaray; she then turns to Brentano-von Arnim's fictional revisiting of Günderrode and Goethe in the mid-century.[50]

Over the last fifteen years, theoretical interest has grown into the various philosophies of nature found within and often at the fringes of German Idealism. This interest is exemplified, most obviously, in the work of Iain Hamilton Grant, who—since the publication of *Philosophies of Nature After Schelling* in 2006—has shown in numerous ways how philosophies of nature, particularly Schelling's, should matter to the more "speculative" streams of contemporary theory.[51] And it is in this context that Thomas Moynihan situates his chapter on "Nature and Extinction." Moynihan argues that the various philosophies of extinction and the post-human in recent theory, propagated by Brassier, Thacker, and others,[52] should be seen as part of a genealogy that leads back directly to Kielmeyer's and Schelling's attempts to approach extinction-events with philosophical seriousness. That is, he shows the ways in which this early twenty-first-century neo-catastrophism and the various ideas of natural revolution in late eighteenth-century philosophy of nature complement and challenge each other. This plundering of the rich resources of philosophies of nature for the purposes of contemporary theory is continued in Oriane Petteni's and Daniel Whistler's chapter on language. The construction and destruction of the sign is obviously a key topic for poststructuralism narrowly conceived, which tries to remain faithful to the event of the "linguistic turn" as something to think through to the end, and this interest in language has led to numerous close readings of German Idealist texts over the past fifty years from Derrida's "The Pit and the Pyramid" and Nancy's *The Speculative Remark* through to de Man's late readings of Kant, Schiller, and Hegel.[53] Petteni and Whistler take a different route, however, by pitting poststructuralist concerns with writing, texts and words against a naturalism of the sign latent in various philosophies of nature, including Goethe's scientific writings. They argue that the "semantic materialisms"[54] of poststructuralism offer (for the most part—Julia Kristeva's early philosophy being the exception) a generic concept of "matter without nature" that can be helpfully supplemented from a naturephilosophical perspective.

The next set of essays return to some of the central pillars of the reception of Hegel in "French theory": difference, nothingness and negation, and the messianic and apocalyptic. In "Difference," Arkady Plotnitsky reconstructs a conceptual schema of differences in both German Idealism and poststructuralism. Of course, the bulk of these two philosophical movements can be read as a commentary on the

Editors' Introduction

meaning of difference—and as the recovery of a "good" form of difference over a "bad" one.[55] This is one place where theory has never been able to shake off Hegel at all: Derrida, Deleuze, Kristeva, and Laruelle all construct "differences" in explicit conversation with Hegel.[56] Plotnitsky helps us make sense of this material by excavating a taxonomy of philosophical concepts of difference and by showing that, alongside Hegel, Kant remains a crucial reference point. This is followed, in "Nothing," by Andrew Hass's reflections on a very specific form of (non-)difference—nothing. Hass shows that, alongside negation (but irreducible to it), the figure of the nothing has its own genealogy that passed out of Hegel through Bataille and Blanchot and into Nancy's work, and in so doing, he also reveals a rich seam of interrelations between notions of creativity, freedom, and nothingness in this twentieth-century Hegelian tradition. Hass shows how the incessant return to the figure of nothing in Nancy, in particular, testifies to a certain restless rhythm of the nothing that is, at bottom, poietic. Agata Bielik-Robson then continues this line of investigation of the Hegelian inheritance of theory via the concept of apocalypse. One of the many "turns" that theory has undergone over the last thirty years has been a religious one—and Derrida's later reflections on the messianic, the apophatic, and the apocalyptic[57] have been the spur to a line of thought running from Kevin Hart's *The Trespass of the Sign* through John Caputo's, Richard Kearney's, and Merold Westphal's writings into the present.[58] Bielik-Robson contributes to this heritage by tracing a genealogy of "mediated messianic political theology" running from Hegel through Franz Rosenzweig to Derrida. She shows how a distinctly Jewish understanding of revelation in terms of the categories of restraint and postponement informs this tradition.

In a very different vein, Lenka Vráblíková puts into question contemporary forms of the university by reconstructing Derrida's reading of Kant's *Conflict of the Faculties* and thinking through its implications for that institution today. Idealism witnessed significant reflection on the university in the works of Kant, Schelling, Fichte, Friedrich Schleiermacher, Wilhelm von Humboldt, and implicitly Hegel (and even Schopenhauer).[59] Yet poststructuralist engagements with this material have largely used the Idealist university as a conservative foil. Drawing on Derrida's radicalization of John Searle's speech act theory, Vráblíková, by contrast, suggests that Derrida sees Kant's text dynamically as a catalyst for future, always provisional, ways of performing the university rather than stating what it is. The final two essays then turn even more specifically to political forms and formations. To begin, Kyla Bruff interrogates Foucault's late turn to Kant and in particular its implications for understanding Foucault's attitude to revolution, whether the French Revolution, Marxist Revolution, or the Iranian Revolution. Bruff argues that Foucault's most Kantian moment comes in distinguishing particular revolutionary events from the will to revolution (or enthusiasm for revolution). From the latter perspective the theorist can make sense of revolution as a signifying *spectacle*. Finally in Part II, Ian James pursues this political turn by returning to Hegel's *Philosophy of Right* insofar as it has been subverted in Jean-Luc Nancy's work in particular. He shows the ways in which the philosophical and the political have bound themselves up together in a post-Hegelian tradition, in which, on the one hand, the Hegelian system has often served as a metaphor for totalitarianism, and, on the other hand, alternatives, such as communities of sovereign subjects, are nonetheless still parsed through Hegelian categories, as the "twin ends of Hegel."

In conclusion, the shorter Part III looks to the future, as well as to the stakes of a continued conversation between German Idealism and theory in the present. To begin, Clare Colebrook returns to the familiar opposition between Hegelian "closed" immanence and Deleuzean "open" immanence, in order to think beyond it, and thus identify the failure of any commentary that merely opposes Deleuze and Hegel. Rather, Colebrook shows how history and immanence find their own complementary rhythms in these philosophies; and these rhythms, she demonstrates, matter for any coming to terms with Western historicity in the present. Secondly, Adrian Johnston addresses the continual recovery of Hegelianism in anglophone philosophy departments[60] and insists, in response, on the importance of parts of Schelling's philosophy for contemporary debates in Hegel scholarship. Against a tendency to marginalize Schelling's influence, Johnston shows that any contemporary reactivation of German Idealism needs to take its lead from the agonistic Schelling of the philosophy of nature and *Freiheitsschrift*. Finally, in the "Editors' Conclusions," Tilottama Rajan and Daniel Whistler consider the past, present, and future of the poststructuralism-German Idealism relation in general by reflecting on the institution of "Theory," its relation to "speculative" trends in the 2010s, and the continued relevance of a "New Humanities."

University of Western Ontario — Tilottama Rajan
trajan@uwo.ca
London, ON, Canada

Royal Holloway — Daniel Whistler
daniel.whistler@rhul.ac.uk
University of London
London, UK

Notes

1. Judith Butler, *Subjects of Desire: Hegelian Reflections in Twentieth-Century France* (New York: Columbia University Press, 1987). See also Arkady Plotnitsky, *In the Shadow of Hegel: Complementarity, History, and the Unconscious* (Gainesville: University Press of Florida, 1993).
2. Jean-Luc Nancy, *The Speculative Remark: (One of Hegel's Bons Mots)* (1973), trans. Céline Surprenant (Stanford: Stanford University Press, 2001); Jacques Derrida, *Glas* (1974), trans. John P. Leavey and Richard Rand (Lincoln: University of Nebraska Press, 1986); Catherine Malabou, *The Future of Hegel: Plasticity, Temporality and Dialectic* (1996), trans. Lisabeth During (New York: Routledge, 2004).
3. Fredric Jameson, *The Hegel Variations: On the Phenomenology of Spirit* (London: Verso, 2010); Slavoj Žižek, *Tarrying with the Negative: Kant, Hegel, and the Critique of Ideology* (Durham: Duke University Press, 1993); *Less Than Nothing: Hegel and the Shadow of Dialectical Materialism* (London: Verso 2012); *Hegel in a Wired Brain* (London: Bloomsbury,

2020). See also Žižek's 1982 doctoral thesis, *The Most Sublime Hysteric: Hegel with Lacan*, trans. Thomas Scott-Railton (Cambridge: Polity Press, 2014).
4. Stuart Barnett (ed.), *Hegel After Derrida* (London: Routledge, 1998); Slavoj Žižek, Clayton Crockett, Creston Davis (eds.), *Hegel and the Infinite: Religion, Politics, and Dialectic* (New York: Columbia University Press, 2011).
5. Georg Lukacs, *The Young Hegel: Studies in the Relations Between Dialectics and Economics* (1966), trans. Rodney Livingstone (Cambridge, Mass.: MIT Press, 1975); Lukacs, *Hegel's False and His Genuine Ontology* (1978), trans. David Fernbach (Cambridge, MA: MIT Press, 1978); Herbert Marcuse, *Hegel's Ontology and the Theory of Historicity* (1932), trans. Seyla Benhabib (Cambridge, Mass.: MIT Press, 1987); Theodor Adorno, *Hegel: Three Studies* (1963), trans. Shierry Weber Nicholsen (Cambridge, Mass.: MIT Press, 1993). Hegel is also an important influence on Lukács's 1920's *The Theory of the Novel: A Historico-Philosophical Essay on the Forms of Great Epic Literature*, trans. Anna Bostock (Cambridge, MA: MIT Press, 1971), which follows Hegel's *Aesthetics* in seeing artistic modes as decentred ways of being-in-the-world, and which opens a more experimental and interdisciplinary engagement with Hegel that is part of the genealogy of "theory." It is also worth noting the dates of some of the above translations, which are contemporaneous with poststructuralism.
6. Separate volumes in the *Palgrave Handbook* series will be dedicated to the relations of Feminism and of Frankfurt School Critical Theory (and its successors) to German Idealism.
7. Theodor Adorno, *Negative Dialectics* (1966), trans E. B. Ashton (London: Routledge and Kegan Paul, 1973); Adorno, *Aesthetic Theory* (1970), ed. Gretel Adorno and Rolf Tiedemann, trans. Robert Hullot-Kentor (London: Continuum, 2002); Jacques Derrida, *Of Grammatology* (1967), trans Gayatri Chakravorty Spivak, corrected edition (Baltimore: Johns Hopkins University Press, 1997).
8. Rodolphe Gasché, *Georges Bataille: Phenomenology and Phantasmatology* (1978), trans Roland Végsö (Stanford: Stanford University Press, 2012).
9. Jean-François Lyotard, *Lessons on the Analytic of the Sublime* (1991), trans. Elizabeth Rottenberg (Stanford: Stanford University Press, 1994). For Derrida, see the essay by Sean Gaston in this volume. Apart from *Tarrying with the Negative*, Žižek's engagement with Kant can be seen throughout his early work. Foucault's interest in Kant began with his 1961 *thèse complémentaire*, a translation of Kant's *Anthropology from a Pragmatic Point of View*, the Introduction to which appeared as *Introduction to Kant's Anthropology*, trans. Robert Nigro and Kate Briggs (Los Angeles: Semiotext(e), 2008). It continues in the essays on critique, revolution, and enlightenment in *The Politics of Truth*, ed. Sylvère Lotringer and Lisa Hochroth (New York: Semiotext(e), 1997). For Nancy, see *The Discourse of the Syncope: Logodaedalus*, trans. Saul Anton (Stanford: Stanford University Press, 2008); *L'impératif catégorique* (Paris: Flammarion, 1983).
10. Tilottama Rajan and David L. Clark (eds.), *Intersections: Nineteenth-Century Philosophy and Contemporary Theory* (Albany: SUNY Press, 1995).
11. See Gilles Deleuze, *Kant's Critical Philosophy: The Doctrine of the Faculties* (1963), trans Hugh Tomlinson and Barbara Habberjam (London: Athlone Press, 1984); *The Fold: Leibniz and the Baroque* (1988), trans. Tom Conley (Minneapolis: University of Minnesota Press, 1993).
12. Slavoj Žižek, *The Sublime Object of Ideology* (London: Verso, 1989), 98, 87. See Saul Kripke, *Naming and Necessity* (Dordrecht: Reidel, 1972).
13. Gilles Deleuze and Félix Guattari, *What is Philosophy?* (1991), trans. Hugh Tomlinson and Graham Burchell (New York: Columbia University Press, 1994), 15ff.
14. F. W. J. Schelling, *First Outline of a System of the Philosophy of Nature* (1799), trans. Keith R. Peterson (Albany: SUNY Press, 2004), 19, 26–7.
15. Žižek, *Sublime Object*, 87–8.
16. Unlike the more capacious use of the term in British Romantic Studies, German Studies distinguishes Weimar Classicism (1775–1802) from Early Romanticism (1797–1802), though they overlap chronologically, and though Goethe's early work is considered to be part of the "*Sturm und Drang*." The categories are difficult to police (can Schelling be described as an

Early Romantic when he lived till 1854?) and precisely indicate the problem of using rigid designators.
17. Georges Canguilhem, "The Living and Its Milieu," in *Knowledge of Life* (1965), trans. Stefanos Geroulanos and Daniela Ginsburg (New York: Fordham University Press, 2008), 100–113. Canguilhem goes back to early nineteenth-century life science (including ethology and anthropology in J. W. Ritter and Alexander von Humboldt) to recover an "organic" rather than "mechanist" understanding of milieu as a "relative" concept involving an interaction, a being "between two centers," rather than a mechanist understanding of milieu as determining "a living being ... from the outside."
18. Jacques Derrida, *Margins of Philosophy* (1972), trans. Alan Bass (Chicago: University of Chicago Press, 1982). Derrida often points out that "theory," which he characterizes as "an original articulation of literary theory, philosophy, linguistics, psychoanalysis, and so forth," is an American term, though unlike "poststructuralism," it is an Americanization that he embraces. See "The University Without Condition," *Without Alibi*, ed. and trans. Peggy Kamuf (Stanford: Stanford University Press, 2000), 208.
19. John Zammito, *The Gestation of German Biology: Philosophy and Physiology from Stahl to Schelling* (Chicago: University of Chicago Press, 2018), 150–157; Lydia Azadpour and Daniel Whistler (eds), *Kielmeyer and the Organic World: Texts and Interpretations* (London: Bloomsbury, 2020).
20. Jacques Derrida, "Theology of Translation" (1984), in *Eyes of the University: Right to Philosophy 2*, trans. Jan Plug et al. (Stanford: Stanford University Press, 2004), 64–80.
21. Antoine Berman, *The Experience of the Foreign: Culture and Translation in Romantic Germany* (1984), trans. S. Heyvaert (Albany: SUNY Press, 1992), 4–5, 82–5. Berman's understanding of Romanticism is more capacious than the usual one in German Studies, as he sees it as extending from 1760 to 1810 and from Herder, through Novalis and the Schlegels, to Friedrich Schleiermacher.
22. Novalis, *Fichte Studies* (1795–1796), ed. Jane Kneller (Cambridge: Cambridge University Press, 2003) and *Notes for a Romantic Encyclopedia: Das Allgemeine Brouillon*, ed. and trans. David W. Wood (Albany: SUNY Press, 2007). The full text of Friedrich Schlegel's 1800 lectures on *Transcendental Philosophy* has been lost; a portion of what survives has been translated as "Introduction to the Transcendental Philosophy," in *Theory as Practice: A Critical Anthology of Early German Romantic Writings*, ed. and trans. Jochen Schulte-Sasse et. al. (Minneapolis: University of Minnesota Press, 1997), 240–67. See also Manfred Frank, *The Philosophical Foundations of Early German Romanticism*, trans. Elizabeth Millán-Zaibert (Albany: SUNY Press, 2004).
23. We should be cautious about identifying French theorists of the 1960s with May 1968. Even though their texts started appearing in this period and sometimes bear revolutionary titles, few actually participated in the uprisings (an exception is Lyotard, who was stopped from protesting at Nanterre). The revolutionary metaphor in Gilles Deleuze and Félix Guattari's two volumes of *Capitalism and Schizophrenia* and Julia Kristeva's *Revolution in Poetic Language*, trans. Margaret Waller (New York: Columbia University Press, 1984) are just that: metaphors. At the less positive and more deconstructive end of the spectrum Derrida's "The Ends of Man" (1969), which pushes back against Hegel, Husserl, and Heidegger, and which evokes a "trembling" on the threshold of some momentous change, draws back from any hypostasis (in *Margins of Philosophy*, 233–234). This refusal of hypostasis also informs Blanchot's discussion of May 1968 as an "event" that may not even have happened yet, rather than something localizable (*The Unavowable Community* (1983), trans. Pierre Joris [Barrytown, NY: Station Hill Press, 1988], 29–31). Blanchot's reading of May '68 can be seen as a version of Kant's reading of the French Revolution as an event that may have been problematic in its moment, but whose significance is yet to come (*The Conflict of The Faculties*, trans. Mary J. Gregor [Lincoln: University of Nebraska Press, 1979], 153–57)—see Bruff's chapter below.
24. Walter Benjamin, "On the Program for a Coming Philosophy," in *Selected Writings: Volume 1, 1913–1926*, ed. Marcus Bullock and Michael W. Jennings (Cambridge, MA: Harvard

Editors' Introduction   xxvii

University Press, 1996), 100–110. That Benjamin's "earliest system-program" also positions itself after and against Kant indicates that poststructuralism was not the first (but perhaps the third) major theoretical revolution against classical philosophy, though it may have been the first to be seen (in the Anglo-American imaginary) as a forerunner of the "colour revolutions" that Lyotard evokes, paradoxically in defense of Kant, in his "The Sign of History" (in *The Lyotard Reader*, ed. Andrew Benjamin [Oxford: Blackwell, 1989], 393–411). A version of this 1982 lecture, without the opening reference to the 1956 Hungarian Revolution, forms part of Lyotard's *The Differend: Phrases in Dispute* (1983), trans. Georges Van den Abbeele (Minneapolis: University of Minnesota Press, 1988), 151–81.

25. Richard Macksey and Eugenio Donato (eds.), *The Structuralist Controversy: The Languages of Criticism and the Sciences of Man* (Baltimore: Johns Hopkins University Press, 1971). Indicating how "quilted" the term poststructuralism is, the volume includes contributions by Jean Hyppolite and Georges Poulet, who are both from an earlier generation than Derrida; by Tzvetan Todorov and the genetic structuralist Lucien Goldmann; and by René Girard and Jean-Pierre Vernant, whom few would now associate with "poststructuralism."

26. Vincent Descombes, *Modern French Philosophy*, trans. L. Scott-Fox and J. M. Harding (Cambridge: Cambridge University Press, 1980); Pierre Klossowksi, *Nietzsche and the Vicious Circle* (1969), trans. Daniel W. Smith (Chicago: University of Chicago Press, 1997).

27. Jacques Derrida, "Deconstructions: The Im-possible," in *French Theory in America*, ed. Sylvère Lotringer and Sande Cohen (New York: Routledge, 2001), 16, 19–20.

28. Jacques Derrida, *Points ... Interviews 1974–1994*, ed. Elisabeth Weber, trans. Peggy Kamuf et al. (Stanford: Stanford University Press, 1995), 212.

29. Although Blanchot started writing in the 1930s, his work also continues into and beyond the 1960s. See *The Infinite Conversation* (1969), trans. Susan Hanson (Minneapolis: University of Minnesota Press, 1993); *The Writing of the Disaster* (1980), trans. Ann Smock (Lincoln: University of Nebraska Press, 1986); *The Unavowable Community* (1983); and "Michel Foucault as I Imagine Him" (1986), trans. Jeffrey Mehlman, in *Foucault/Blanchot* (New York: Zone Books, 1987), 61–109.

30. For example, Maurice Blanchot, *The Space of Literature* (1955), trans. Ann Smock (Lincoln: University of Nebraska Press, 1982); Jacques Derrida, "The University Without Condition," 204; Michel Foucault, *Death and the Labyrinth: The World of Raymond Roussel* (1963), trans. Charles Ruas (Berkeley: University of California Press, 1986).

31. Tilottama Rajan, *Deconstruction and the Remainders of Phenomenology: Sartre, Derrida, Foucault, Baudrillard* (Stanford: Stanford University Press, 2002), especially xi–xiv, 1–54. See also Johannes Angermuller, *Why There Is No Poststructuralism in France: The Making of an Intellectual Generation* (London: Bloomsbury, 2015). Unlike Rajan's book, Angermuller's study is not philosophical-theoretical but historical, and does not attempt to recover the word "deconstruction" in its difference from poststructuralism, but rather to emphasize the foreignness of the latter term to the French intellectual scene, where there was no hard demarcation between structuralism and poststructuralism.

32. Descombes, *Modern French Philosophy*, 136.

33. In chronological order, Deleuze's books in the history of philosophy are *Empiricism and Subjectivity: An Essay on Hume's Philosophy* (1953), trans. Constantin V. Boundas (New York: Columbia University Press, 1989); *Nietzsche and Philosophy* (1962), trans. Hugh Tomlinson (New York: Columbia University Press, 1983); *Kant's Critical Philosophy* (1963); *Bergsonism* (1966), trans. Hugh Tomlinson and Barbara Habberjam (New York: Urzone, 1988); *Expressionism in Philosophy: Spinoza* (1968), trans. Martin Joughin (New York: Zone, 1992); *Spinoza: Practical Philosophy* (1970), trans. Robert Hurley (San Francisco: City Lights Books, 1988); *The Fold: Leibniz and the Baroque* (1988).

34. See Edward Baring, *The Young Derrida and French Philosophy 1945–1968* (Cambridge: Cambridge University Press, 2011), 221–58. See also Alan D. Schrift, "The Effects of the *Agrégation de Philosophie* on Twentieth-Century French Philosophy," *Journal of the History of Philosophy* 46: 3 (2008): 449–473; and Mark Sinclair and Daniel Whistler, "The Institutions

of Modern French Philosophy," in Mark Sinclair and Daniel Whistler (eds), *The Oxford Handbook of Modern French Philosophy* (Oxford: Oxford University Press, forthcoming).
35. Jacques Derrida, "The Pit and the Pyramid: Introduction to Hegel's Semiology," in *Margins of Philosophy*, 69–108.
36. Catherine Malabou, *The Future of Hegel* (1995); *The Heidegger Change: On the Fantastic in Philosophy* (2004), trans. and ed. Peter Skafish (Albany: SUNY Press, 2011); *Before Tomorrow: Epigenesis and Rationality* (2014), trans. Carolyn Shread (Cambridge: Polity, 2016).
37. There are almost no discussions of Fichte in pre- or post-1960s' theory. Work done in the wake of French Theory tends to be limited to Fichte's potential for thinking about issues of nationalism and decolonization. See Pheng Cheah, who takes up the Kant-Fichte-Hegel sequence in *Spectral Nationality: Passages of Freedom from Kant to Postcolonial Literatures of Liberation* (New York: Columbia Univ Press, 2003). See also Jean-Christophe Goddard (who has written more extensively on Fichte in French): "The Beach and the Palm Tree: Fichte's *Wissenschaftslehre* as a Project of Decolonization," in S. J. McGrath and Joseph Carew (eds), *Rethinking German Idealism* (London: Palgrave Macmillan, 2016), 137–62.
38. See, for example, Gilles Châtelet, *Figuring Space: Philosophy, Mathematics, and Physics* (1993), trans. Robert Shore and Muriel Zacha (Dordrecht: Kluwer, 2000); Simon Duffy (ed.), *Virtual Mathematics* (Manchester: Clinamen Press, 2006). See also the work of Michel Serres generally, for example, *Hermes: Literature, Science, Philosophy* (Baltimore: Johns Hopkins University Press, 1982). It is also worth noting that mechanics, a lowly science in Hegel's *Encyclopedia*, which undertakes to move from a Newtonian to a dynamic physics, has undergone a poststructuralist metamorphosis into technology that involves feedback loops between "biotic" and "metabiotic" systems that complicate the distinction between the mechanical and organic in Idealist systems.
39. Maurice Blanchot, "The Athenaeum," in *The Infinite Conversation*, 351–360; the essays in the book also take up Novalis, Hegel, and Nietzsche at many other points. Philippe Lacoue-Labarthe and Jean-Luc Nancy, *The Literary Absolute: The Theory of Literature in German Romanticism* (1978), trans. Phillip Barnard and Cheryl Lester (Albany: SUNY Press, 1984).
40. For a discussion of the Eurocentric limits of the term "globalization" see Victor Li, "Elliptical Interruptions, Or, Why Derrida Prefers *Mondialisation* to Globalization," *CR: The New Centennial Review* 7:2 (2007), 141–54.
41. See Friedrich Hölderlin, *Essays and Letters in Theory*, trans. and ed. Thomas Pfau (Albany: SUNY Press, 1988). Pfau's Introduction contextualizes these essays in relation to German Idealism.
42. G. W. F. Hegel, *Lectures on the History of Philosophy*, trans. E. S. Haldane and Frances H. Simson (Lincoln: University of Nebraska Press, 1995), 3.515.
43. Derrida's "Theology of Translation" only discusses Schelling's 1803/4 lectures *On University Studies*, and there is no evidence that he read Schelling more extensively. There are also significant, but not sustained, references to Schelling in Adorno's *Negative Dialectics* and Deleuze's work. Jürgen Habermas is the one theorist who has systematically engaged with Schelling, having written his 1954 dissertation on him (*Das Absolute und die Geschichte*), distilled and reformulated as "Dialectical Idealism in Transition to Materialism: Schelling's Idea of a Contraction of God and Its Consequences for the Philosophy of History" (1963), trans. Nick Midgley and Judith Norman, in *The New Schelling*, ed. Judith Norman and Alistair Welchman (London: Continuum, 2004), 43–89.
44. Žižek characteristically divides Lacan's work into three stages, of which the second or "structuralist" stage of the barred subject sees the Symbolic as excluding the Real, while in the third stage, emphasized by the Ljubljana School, the Real takes precedence and breaks into, or breaks out within, the Symbolic, with a transformative potential distorted by the Symbolic. See Slavoj Žižek, *The Plague of Fantasies* (London: Verso, 1997), 8, 10, 49–50, 279–80; also *Sublime Object*, 79–80.

Editors' Introduction   xxix

45. For an early discussion of Schopenhauer alongside deconstruction that makes this argument, see Tilottama Rajan, *Dark Interpreter: The Discourse of Romanticism* (Ithaca: Cornell University Press, 1980), 24n, 29–55.
46. The work by Thacker noted in Faflak's chapter is the Introduction to a selection of Schopenhauer's writings. It is only more recently that Thacker has written more extensively on Schopenhauer in *Cosmic Pessimism* (Minneapolis: Univocal Publishing, 2015).
47. G. W. F. Hegel, *Aesthetics: Lectures in Fine Art*, trans. T. M. Knox (Oxford: Clarendon, 1975), 1.439; Roland Barthes, "From Work to Text," in *Image, Music, Text*, trans. Stephen Heath (London: Fontana Press, 1977), 155–64.
48. Friedrich Schlegel, *Philosophical Fragments*, trans. Peter Firchow (Minneapolis: University of Minnesota Press, 1991), 34. Against Fichte's project of systematizing knowledge based on the absolute I, the early Romantic notion of *Symphilosophie* postulates a communally authored system-in-progress that combines philosophy and literature.
49. Hegel, *Aesthetics*, 1.300.
50. Brentano-von Arnim's correspondence with Günderrode occurred in 1804–1806, though she did not edit it until 1840. Margaret Fuller produced a partial translation of *Günderrode* in 1842 (Boston: Peabody).
51. The classic text for the theoretical recovery of philosophies of nature is Iain Hamilton Grant, *Philosophies of Nature after Schelling* (London: Continuum, 2006); see also his more recent work, e.g., 'Recapitulation All the Way Down? Philosophical Ontogeny in Kielmeyer and Schelling,' in Azadpour and Whistler (eds), *Kielmeyer and the Organic World*, 133–48. For a summary of the significance of this recovery when it comes to Schelling in particular, see Tyler Tritten and Daniel Whistler, "Schellingian Experiments in Speculation," *Angelaki* vol. 21, no. 4 (2016), 1–9.
52. The *Urtext* of philosophical neo-catastrophism is Ray Brassier, *Nihil Unbound: Enlightenment and Extinction* (Basingstoke: Palgrave Macmillan, 2007), but see also Eugene Thacker, *After Life* (Chicago: University of Chicago Press, 2010). Moynihan's own *X-Risk: How Humanity Discovered its own Extinction* (Falmouth: Urbanomic, 2020) is an essential reference work.
53. Paul de Man, *The Resistance to Theory*, ed. Wlad Godzich (Minneapolis: University of Minnesota Press, 1986). This poststructuralism *of language* was hegemonic in both North American and UK receptions of "French theory" for many years and receives classic articulations in, for example, Jonathan Culler's *The Pursuit of Signs: Semiotics, Literature, Deconstruction* (London: Routledge, 1981) and Terry Eagleton, *Literary Theory: An Introduction* (Oxford: Blackwell, 1986).
54. Philippe Sollers, *L'Ecriture et l'expérience des limites* (Paris: Seuil, 1968), 6.
55. Gilles Deleuze's *Difference and Repetition* (trans. Paul Patton [New York: Columbia University Press, 1995]) is of course the center-point around which this whole debate revolves. See also, for example, François Laruelle, *Philosophies of Difference: A Critical Introduction to Non-Philosophy*, trans. Rocco Gangle (London: Bloomsbury, 2010).
56. The literature on this conversation with Hegel is ever-expanding; however, useful reference points include Henry Somers-Hall, *Hegel, Deleuze and the Critique of Representation: Dialectics of Negation and Difference* (Albany, NY: SUNY Press, 2012); and Małgorzata Kowalska, *Dialectics Beyond Dialectics. Essay on Totality and Difference*, trans. Cain Elliott and Jan Burzyński (Lausanne: Peter Lang, 2015).
57. Derrida's engagement with religious concepts is spread over a huge variety of publications, including (to take but a couple) *Acts of Religion*, ed. Gil Anidjar (London and New York: Routledge, 2002); "Of an Apocalyptic Tone Recently Adopted in Philosophy," trans. John P. Leavey, Jr., *Oxford Literary Review*, vol. 6, no.2 (1984); "How to Avoid Speaking: Denials," in *Derrida and Negative Theology*. eds. Harold Coward and Toby Foshay (Albany, NY: SUNY Press, 1989), 73–136; and "Christianity and Secularization," trans. David Newheiser, *Critical Inquiry* 47 (Autumn 2020).

58. See Kevin Hart, *The Trespass of the Sign: Deconstruction, Theology and Philosophy* (New York: Fordham University Press, 1989). The classic writings of the post-Hartian "religious turn" in anglophone "theory" are helpfully anthologized in John D. Caputo (ed.), *The Religious* (Oxford: Blackwell, 2001). See further Anthony Paul Smith and Daniel Whistler (eds), *After the Postsecular and the Postmodern: New Essays in Continental Philosophy of Religion* (Newcastle: Cambridge Scholars, 2010).
59. F. W. J. Schelling, *On University Studies* (1803) trans. E. S. Morgan, ed. Norbert Guterman (Athens: Ohio University Press, 1966); J. G. Fichte, *Deducirte Plan einer zu Berlin zi errichtenden höheren Lehranstalt* (written in 1807; Stuttgart und Tübingen: Cotta, 1817); Friedrich Schleiermacher, *Gelegentliche Gedanken über Universitäten in deutschem Sinn* (Berlin, 1808); Wilhelm von Humboldt, "Über die innere und äussere Organisation der höheren wissenschaftichen Anstalten in Berlin" (1809), in *Unbedingte Universitäten: Was ist Universität?*, ed. Johanna Charlotte-Horst et al. (Zurich: Diaphanes, 2010), 95–104; Arthur Schopenhauer, "On Philosophy at the Universities," in *Parerga and Paralipomena* (1851), trans. E. F. J. Payne (Oxford: Oxford University Press, 1974), 137–198. For a useful overview of the Humboldtian model of the university see Herbert Schnädelbach, *Philosophy in Germany 1831–1933*, trans. Eric Matthews (Cambridge: Cambridge University Press, 1984), 12–32. Although Hegel has not been connected to this discourse, it seems legitimate to do so, given that he became a professor at the University of Berlin (associated with the "Humboldt" model of the university) in the decade after its founding, and given that his *Encyclopedia* expands and escalates a term that was used in university study.
60. Johnston is presumably thinking of the varieties of anglophone Hegelianism to be found in Robert Brandom (e.g., *A Spirit of Trust: A Reading of Hegel's Phenomenology* [Cambridge, MA: Harvard University Press, 2019]), Terry Pinkard (e.g., *Hegel's Naturalism: Mind, Nature and the Final Ends of Life* [Oxford: Oxford University Press, 2012]) and Robert Pippin (e.g., *Hegel's Realm of Shadows: Logic as Metaphysics in The Science of Logic* [Chicago: University of Chicago Press, 2018]), among many, many others.

Part I
Reading the German Idealists After '68

Reading Kant

Sean Gaston

1 Introduction Kant and Derrida (1960–2021)

In 1960, the young Jacques Derrida was teaching philosophy in Le Mans. One of his students at the time recalled: "I remember him talking to us at length about the *Critique of Pure Reason*. In fact, he tended to bring everything back to Kant."[1] What we now call deconstruction began in 1962 with Derrida's introduction to Edmund Husserl's 1936 essay, "The Origin of Geometry."[2] Husserl was interested in the possibility of a history of ideal objectivities, such as geometry, which remain the same across the ages. For Derrida, prompted in part by Paul Ricoeur, Kant plays a critical role in this phenomenological history.[3] Husserl himself in *Ideas* I evoked "the idea in the Kantian sense" to account for the idea of "infinity" as a "continuum" that is always "one and the same."[4] As Derrida later explains in *Voice and Phenomenon*, in phenomenology "there is no *ideality* unless an Idea in the Kantian sense is at work, opening the possibility of an indefinite, the infinity of a prescribed progress, or the infinity of permitted repetitions."[5]

In his early work, Derrida treats Kant as an adjunct and prop of phenomenological ideality, of the possibility of the history of the same, of history *as* the same.[6] But he also sees in the phenomenological reliance on Kant the fault line or ruin of ideality. The Kantian regulative idea opens up the possibility of an "indefinite" future progress. The "non-reality" of this ideality not only supports and carries the same as "living presence"; it also pushes away, pushes out in front and indefinitely defers the "reality" or arrival of this presence.[7] Thanks to Husserl's evocation of Kant, there is no "positive infinite" in phenomenology, only a regulative indefinite.[8] Because "the infinity of the Husserlian horizon has the form of an indefinite opening," it is kept

S. Gaston (✉)
University of Melbourne, Melbourne, VIC, Australia
e-mail: gastons@unimelb.edu.au

© The Author(s), under exclusive license to Springer Nature Switzerland AG 2023
T. Rajan, D. Whistler (eds.), *The Palgrave Handbook of German Idealism and Poststructuralism*, Palgrave Handbooks in German Idealism,
https://doi.org/10.1007/978-3-031-27345-2_1

away "from all totalization."[9] Kant therefore has a role to play in the formulation of Derrida's best-known concept, *différance*, which can be described as a deferring of and differing between the fixed poles of the metaphysical tradition, notably the sensible and the intelligible and space and time.[10]

However, it is also striking that in Derrida's first flourish of publications—the three books in 1967, and the three books in 1972—there appears to be relatively minor engagement with Kant. One has to wait until 1974 for an essay entirely devoted to Kant.[11] Nonetheless, there are traces of concentrated readings of Kant in Derrida's earliest work. In the 1970s there are a number of sustained readings of Kant, but it is only in the 1980s that a wide range of works on Kant begin to appear. It was in the 1980s that Derrida observed that the transcendental critique was "one of the essential 'themes' or 'objects' of deconstruction."[12] The trend of expansion continues in the 1990s, and in the last decade of Derrida's life Kant increasingly stands as the measure of the philosophical tradition (marking both its limitations and its nuances). One could argue that in Derrida's late seminars, which have been recently published, he is once again bringing "everything back to Kant."

2   Looking for Kant (1963–1972)

We therefore need to begin with a question: where is Kant during the first momentous articulation of deconstruction? And why is Derrida somewhat reticent about addressing Kant at length in this period? One could conjecture that he associates Kant with Husserl's project of ideality has been profoundly influenced by Martin Heidegger's emphatic reading in *Kant and the Problem of Metaphysics* (1929), or is aware in the mid-1960s that other near contemporaries, such as Michel Foucault and Gilles Deleuze, are already working intently on Kant: in 1963 Deleuze published *Kant's Critical Philosophy*, and in 1964 Foucault introduced and translated Kant's *Anthropology from a Pragmatic Point of View*.[13] We could say that the Kant that Derrida is looking for in the 1960s is a Kant of the twentieth century. Derrida himself would explore the contexts of neo-Kantianism in the 1980s, and we could argue that Derrida works his way through the twentieth-century Kant and eventually finds the eighteenth-century Kant.

We are fortunate that in 2013 Derrida's 1964–1965 seminar on Heidegger was published.[14] It gives us an important glimpse of Derrida's early reading of Heidegger's *Kant and the Problem of Metaphysics*: Heidegger's remarkable description of "auto-affection as temporality," as first laid out in the transcendental aesthetic in the *Critique of Pure Reason*, becomes the possibility of the transcendental subject, of "that starting from which the self, the *Selbst*, the I think constitutes itself and announces itself to itself."[15] Despite recognizing that Kant challenged the prevailing metaphysics of classical empiricism and rationalism and charted their "complicity," in the early 1960s Derrida traces a renewed or heightened metaphysics in Kant's transcendental philosophy.[16]

In *Writing and Difference* (1967) and *Of Grammatology* (1967), Kant primarily appears as the index of this metaphysical tradition.[17] Kant hardly has any role to play in Derrida's influential discussion of speech and writing in the history of philosophy and its place in the mid-1960s in the so-called radical break with tradition found in structural linguistics.[18] There are some exceptions. In a passage towards the end of his reading of Rousseau in *Of Grammatology*, Derrida is still thinking about Husserl's use of Kant and of Heidegger's interpretation of the transcendental aesthetic.[19] But he is also starting to mark his departure from Heidegger. A "new transcendental aesthetic," he suggests, must take account of "inscription *in general*" as "producing the spatiality of space." But to do this, he adds, we would also have to get rid of the term "transcendental *aesthetic*."[20] One could almost say that at this stage Derrida cannot move beyond the limits of the transcendental aesthetic.

Derrida's *Margins of Philosophy* (1972) marks the beginning of a different reading of Kant. In the essay "*Ousia* and *Grammē*," Derrida challenges Heidegger's sweeping account of Hegel's "vulgar concept of time," which he inherited from Kant and Aristotle.[21] We have to treat the history of philosophy differently, Derrida suggests, if the tradition itself already contains snags, catches and gaps that disrupt the very possibility of a singular, monolithic metaphysics. If we accept that there is an "exoteric aporia" in Aristotle's account of time, which is "no longer dominated simply by the present," and that Hegel repeats this paradox, then "the Kantian revolution did not displace what Aristotle had set down but, on the contrary, settled down there itself."[22] As Derrida emphasizes, "*Heidegger notwithstanding*," Hegel recognizes in the Kantian transcendental aesthetic the definition of time as the possibility of "a *pure* form of sensibility," of a time that "does not belong to beings."[23]

Rather than simply following Heidegger and equating Kantian time with the assertion of the modern subject, the transcendental aesthetic can also be seen as the temporal possibility of the displacement of the subject.[24] Derrida goes on to speak of "the originality of the Kantian breakthrough."[25] Before Heidegger, Kantian time already announces "the possibility of the appearance of beings in (finite) experience."[26] As much as it idealizes the ends of man, Kantian philosophy is a philosophy of finitude.[27] This places Kant close to Heidegger's own project. Derrida can now go beyond the threshold of the transcendental aesthetic, as determined by Heidegger, and begin to find a different Kant.

3 Kantian Frameworks (1973–1978)

Derrida's engagement with Kant becomes sharper, more varied and differentiated in the 1970s. *Glas*, based for the most part on a 1971–1972 seminar, is a remarkable work: its range of interests—ethics, law, the institutions of the state, the proper name, sexual difference, the animal, Judaism and Christianity—anticipate much of Derrida's later work. It is in *Glas* that we first glimpse the breadth of Derrida's project. It is here that he first observes, that insofar as Hegel treats Christianity as the *Aufhebung* of Judaism, "Kantianism is, structurally, a Judaism."[28] It is also in *Glas* that Derrida first discusses Kant's reductive account of women and sexual difference in the *Anthropology*.[29]

Derrida's first sustained engagement with Kant is his 1973–1974 seminar "L'Art (Kant)," which led to the publication of "Parergon" and "Economimesis."[30] Why does Derrida begin with the *Critique of the Power of Judgement*? From the 1960s he had been thinking about the schematism of the transcendental imagination:[31] the mediating schema of the imagination between intuition and the concepts of the understanding is not only a critical point of junction for a transcendental account of the relation between the sensible and the intellectual; it is also an instance of time as the idealized possibility of all "pure shapes in space."[32] Derrida argues that *différance* describes a time-becoming-space and space-becoming-time that marks a disjunction in any project grounded on time or space alone. The transcendental schema therefore becomes a point of junction *and* disjunction in Kantian philosophy: it brings together what it wants to hold apart, holds apart what it wants to bring together.[33] As Derrida remarks in *Glas*, "the whole schematism of the transcendental imagination" marks "a deconstructive displacement of all the oppositions banked on Kant's discourse."[34]

Like the schematism of the transcendental imagination, the third *Critique* itself is placed in the role of mediator.[35] The best way to approach "Parergon" is to keep in mind that it is only fragments of a book-length seminar (demarcated by a multitude of framed gaps in the text).[36] It gives us a vast, detailed cornucopia of ideas, identifying a multitude of "sensitive spot[s]" in Kantian philosophy.[37] Kant insists in the first draft of his introduction to the third *Critique* that "philosophy as a system can only have two parts."[38] This prompts Derrida to examine a paragraph in Kant's preface where this third *Critique* is described as both "a separable part" that can be added or "*annexed*" and an indispensable mediating and "nondetachable part."[39] As Derrida points out, Kant himself accounts for this apparent contradiction as the difference between the approach of a present critique of pure reason (separable part) and that of a future "system of pure philosophy" (nondetachable part). Kant calls this still unrealized "system of pure philosophy," *metaphysics*.[40] For Derrida, Kant's work cannot therefore simply be described as metaphysical. Derrida's guide is thus Kant's own dictum: "critique is not metaphysics."[41] Critique can then be seen as "*in search of* the foundation."[42] The true "desire of reason" in Kantianism is the "desire for a grounded structure."[43] It is the art of philosophy as an architectonic *in search of* grounding.

Kant himself allocates—and confines—this questing quality to the third *Critique* and the reflective judgement. Reflective judgements start with the particular and describe a particular *in search of* the general.[44] For Derrida, reflective judgments also place the "example" before the "law."[45] Examples and illustrations are a problem for Kant. They invite the popular in philosophy, assist parts while confusing the whole, and generate "bright colours" which "make unrecognisable the articulation or structure of the system."[46] This leads Derrida to §14 of the Analytic of the Beautiful, "Elucidation by Means of Example," and to one passage: "Even what one calls *ornaments* (*parerga*), i.e., that which is not internal to the entire representation of the object as a constituent, but only belongs to it externally as an addendum and augments the satisfaction of taste, still does this only through its form: like the borders of paintings, draperies on statues, or colonnades around magnificent buildings."[47] This is where Derrida gets his title, "Parergon," and the problem of the extraneous addition in fine arts, of the frame "as an addendum," and of Kantian frameworks in a philosophy of art.

Derrida focuses on the *parergon* as a frame for the work of art, not least because the frame (*le cadre*) captures the problem of a structure on the border of the internal and the external that is "neither simply outside nor simply inside."[48] As a border that touches both sides, the frame for the beautiful painting should itself remain untouchable, or at least aspire to the level of an unobtrusive form above "empirical sensory materiality."[49] But as something that is required for the painting to define itself *as* a painting, the frame acts as a necessary supplement that marks a "lack" in "the interior of the *ergon*."[50] In Kant's terms, the frame is always a risk because "the gilt frame" can overshadow the painting.[51]

The *parergon* recalls Kant's distinction in the preface between "a separable part" and "nondetachable part" to characterize the third *Critique* itself, and Kant's struggles to provide a wider logical framework—taken from the understanding as an "imported frame"—for this work on the judgement of taste.[52] The third *Critique* itself could be taken as a mere "adornment" to transcendental philosophy, but it also "*determines* the frame as *parergon*, which both constitutes it and ruins it."[53] In Derrida's reading, the detachable part not only threatens a "repeated dislocation" of the whole; it also uncovers its possibility *as* its ruin.[54] For Derrida, the parergon is the *supplement* to the natural (the ahistorical) that makes it a quasi-natural construction (the historical), which can be deconstructed.

Derrida's readings of the third *Critique* reinforce a series of metaphysical aims that are undermined or undone at the point of foundation. Kant needs to ensure that the beautiful is "without-end," that there is a "pure-cut."[55] But the necessity of this "without" (*sans*) marks the *trace* of a "nonknowledge" at the origin of beauty.[56] For Derrida, the trace (*la trace*) is the mark that always risks effacement and can be contained by neither the sensible or the intelligible, nor matter or form.[57] From "the trace of the *sans*," Derrida arrives at Kant's inadvertent example of the ends of man (the horse *for* man) as an anthropological ordering and exceptional disorientation of the beautiful "pure cut" without-end.[58] One kind of metaphysics undoes the ends of another kind of metaphysics in the name of "a fundamental humanism."[59] The Kantian frameworks that Derrida traces in the third *Critique* mark points of resistance, but they also reinforce the metaphysical imperatives in Kant's philosophy.

4 Kant and the Institution (1979–1989)

In 1979, Pierre Bourdieu, who had known Derrida since their time as students at the Lycée Louis-le-Grand, attacked Derrida's reading of the third *Critique* in the postscript to his book *Distinction: A Social Critique of the Judgement of Taste* (1979).[60] The 1980s would see a number of Derrida's other colleagues publishing important books on Kant, including Jean-François Lyotard and Jean-Luc Nancy. Lyotard published *Enthusiasm: The Kantian Critique of History* (1986) and *Lessons on the Analytic of the Sublime* (1991), while Nancy had already brought out *The Discourse of the Syncope: Logodaedalus* (1976), and would add *The Categorical Imperative* (1983) and *The Experience of Freedom* (1988) to his numerous writings on Kant.[61] The 1980s were a remarkable decade for Derrida's reading of Kant.[62] It may be too much to say that there was a "turn" to Kant in Paris in the 1980s; but there was certainly renewed interest in the breadth of Kant's engagement with questions that, once again, appeared relevant and even urgent.

Bourdieu saw Derrida's reading of the third *Critique* as a "denial of the real principles of the judgement of taste" as found in a sociological analysis.[63] Despite his iconoclastic approach, Derrida is still part of a tradition that "can never carry through the breaks which imply a practical *epochē* of the thesis of the existence of philosophy."[64] Derrida responded, notably in the preface to *Of the Right to Philosophy*, arguing that Bourdieu's sociological "objectification" is more indebted to Kantian constraints than he admits.[65] In fact, Derrida already alerts us to another reading of Kant at the outset of "Parergon," noting that the seminar of the following year, 1974–1975, would focus on the history and current contested politics of teaching philosophy in France and the relation between philosophy and the institution.[66] As founded or instituted, the institution is a construction with a history and can be deconstructed.[67]

As we know now, Derrida also discussed Kant in his 1976–1977 seminar on theory and practice, as part of his attempts in this period to describe deconstruction as both "theoretical" and "practical."[68] As Derrida would often say, deconstruction is not simply a pre-established theory, it also *responds* to events in a practical manner. In his seminar, Derrida examines the echoes and dissonances between Kant and Marx, focusing on the "interests of reason" in the *Critique of Pure Reason* as a point of junction *and* disjunction between theory and practice.[69] As Derrida suggests in a 1975 interview, the Kantian interest of reason precedes both theory and practice because it is "the interest of philosophy itself, as reason."[70] Interest is also linked by Kant to the theoretical-practical hope that "*something ought to happen*," to the as-yet future event.[71] The theoretical-practical responds to events.

The constant Kantian reference at this time is "The Conflict of the Faculties", which Derrida discusses in a series of papers on the institution of the university from 1980 to 1985.[72] Derrida is interested in Kant's insistence that as a "lower" faculty in the university, philosophy has a right to theory but is excluded from matters of practice (the domain of theology, law and medicine) beyond a mere formal analysis.[73] In "*Mochlos*, or The Conflict of the Faculties" (1980), Derrida examines Kant's deft negotiations with the censorship of the Prussian state under King Frederick William II. Despite Kant's claims for the autonomy of a university founded on an idea of reason, this autonomy is limited because it is authorized by the state. In this sense, an idea of reason is also authorized by the state.[74]

For Derrida, "The Conflict of the Faculties" provides "a kind of dictionary and grammar" for thinking about the university today in the "politico-epistemological space."[75] Echoing Kafka, he criticizes Kant's treatment of responsibility at the university as an axiomatic matter of always standing "before the law."[76] A pure practical reason gives itself to "a pure thinking of right" and to the "purity of law." For Derrida, this axiomatic link is "not natural: it has a history."[77] The challenge, which Derrida will return to throughout the 1980s, is to rethink the concept of responsibility; first, as a *response* to the other and, second, as a response beyond the "*decision* of a pure egological subject."[78] In addition, Derrida interrogates the "internal coherence" of the university, of what stands inside and outside of the institution both in Kant's time and in the present day.[79] At stake is the problem and the opportunity of "the university's inability to comprehend itself in the purity of its inside."[80]

In the Kantian institution, philosophy is forbidden any practical, pragmatic, or public action. This prohibition rests on Kant's need to distinguish unambiguously between the realm of truth and the realm of action.[81] For Derrida, this distinction relies on an unsustainable opposition between constative and performative statements, of the kind found in J. L. Austin's speech act theory.[82] The performative opens an unforeseen possibility between language and the event or "the situation of which it speaks."[83] The performative in the university suggests a political relation to the institution that is neither simply constative nor performative (as defined by Austin).[84] In contrast, Kant's architectonic urges leave us with the dream of a pure philosophy that is only "intra-university" and a "quasi-private language."[85] Kant's "double bind" is found in the "outside" of the university, in the relation between the public at large, the public power of the government, and the need to publish scholarly writings.[86] It is from Kant that Derrida is able to think of a non-Kantian vision of academic work that raises the question of the institution itself *as* it interprets a poem or a novel.[87] As Derrida concludes, "an institution is not merely a few walls or some outer structures surrounding, protecting, guaranteeing, or restricting the freedom of our work; it is also and already the structure of our interpretation."[88]

In a paper from 1984, Derrida explains that there are two Kants in "The Conflict of Faculties": the Kant who wants to create and protect a department of philosophy (even in the name of necessary censorship) and the Kant who wants to give this department "the right of critical and panoptical supervision over all the other departments."[89] The legacy of these two Kants, and the "interminable" conflict they generate, are apparent in the one published paper we have from Derrida's 1987–1988 seminar on neo-Kantianism in Germany in the first decades of the twentieth century.[90] "Interpretations at War: Kant, the Jew, the German" (1988) marks a significant step in Derrida's long engagement with the context or *milieu* (as a half-placing rather than a determined context) of Heidegger's reading of Kant and the publication in 1929 of *Kant and the Problem of Metaphysics*.

"Interpretations at War" focuses on the writings of Herman Cohen, a "master of neo-Kantianism" who held the chair at Marburg and taught Natorp, Cassirer and Rosenzweig, among others.[91] "It is too often forgotten," Derrida notes at the start of his paper, "that this neo-Kantian sequence largely determined the context *in* which, that is to say also *against* which, Husserl's phenomenology, later the phenomenological ontology of the early Heidegger (who, moreover, succeeded Cohen in his Marburg chair—and this also marks an institutional context in the strictest sense) arose: against neo-Kantianism and in another relation to Kant."[92] In his patriotic writings as a German during World War I, Cohen extols what Derrida calls the "Judeo-Kantian law."[93] Cohen celebrates "the very subjectivity of the Kantian subject, of man as subject of morality and right, free and autonomous" as the basis for the association of the Jew and the German.[94]

In "Privilege," the 1990 introduction to *Of the Right to Philosophy*, Derrida offers an overview of Kant's place in the deconstruction of the philosophy of right. For Kant, right is indivisible from reason as "the system capable of thinking the supersensible."[95] And yet, this "*pure* concept" must, ideally, "take into consideration the empirical multiplicity of all cases [that occur in experience], until it has exhausted all possibilities."[96] As Derrida points out, Kant recognizes in the preface to *The Metaphysics of Morals* that this is impossible, and therefore has recourse to a division in his work between right as "a system outlined *a priori*," discussed in the main text, and the experience of particular rights, discussed in adjacent remarks.[97] Once again, it is a matter of how Kant uses his empirical examples, not least when right is distinguished from morals by its "*external* constraint."[98] But Kant's presentation of the philosophy of right is already divided between right and rights, text and remark, critique and example. For Derrida, a philosophy of right not only exposes philosophy's "own privilege" and its privilege as a philosophy of institution and "the modern state"; it also exposes the privilege of "the Kantian heritage" and the self-authorization of reason as its own tribunal.[99] "One must no doubt read Kant differently," Derrida concludes, "but one must not stop reading him."[100]

5 The Practical Questions of the Day (1990–2003)

There is a tantalizing glimpse in "Préjugés: Before the Law," a 1982 conference paper on Lyotard and Kafka, of the start of Derrida's wide-ranging reading of Kant's practical philosophy in the 1980s and 1990s.[101] Derrida's 1980–1981 seminar focused on the respect for the law in Kant, Freud and Heidegger. Derrida begins with Kant's use of persons as "an *example* of the moral law" when "respect is due only to the moral law" itself.[102] There are numerous papers, articles and short books from the 1990s that suggest an extensive reading of Kant in the seminars. As only the 1997–2003 seminars have been published at the time of writing, we must rely on a series of remarkable incomplete readings. At the start of the 1990s, there are traces of an examination of the Kantian concept of duty, beginning with Kant's emphatic distinction between acting in conformity with duty (*pflichtmäßig*) and acting from duty itself (*aus Pflicht*).[103] Derrida argues that Kantian duty, "the very condition of morality," cannot avoid a transgressive excess of an "*over-duty*" (*sur-devoir*). This over-duty "demands acting without duty, without rule or norm" in the name of a responsible decision that cannot be "merely" a "technical application." A decision must be taken, a response must be made, but it cannot confirm to a "preestablished order."[104]

As he elaborates in *The Gift of Death* and the 1992 essay "Passions," Kantian duty ties obligation to debt, guilt and sacrifice.[105] Derrida wants to rupture this chain. When Abraham is directed by God to sacrifice Isaac, "it is a duty not to respect, out of duty, ethical duty."[106] The *aporia* of the everyday experience of Mount Moriah is that a responsible duty "binds" me to the other as other; but the very singularity of this alterity also binds me to all the others who are other. For Derrida, there is always "paradox," "scandal," and "betrayal" in the ethical relation and the duty owed to the other.[107] In "Passions," Derrida warns against an all-too-easy "remoralization of deconstruction," offering a stark assessment of Kantian morality: both respect and duty are founded on a concept of "sacrifice," not least the sacrifice of the sensible, the sensuous and the pathological.[108] Derrida reiterates here the danger of resurgent "moralisms" and of "a new dogmatic slumber" if Kant's moral imperatives are used as the self-evident grounding of an ethics for deconstruction.[109]

There are also signs in the early 1990s of Derrida's later reading of Kant in his 1995–1997 seminar on hostility and hospitality. In "Aporias," he notes that in "Toward Perpetual Peace" Kant links a range of cosmopolitan rights to hospitality.[110] Derrida focuses on Kant's limits to hospitality and his careful distinction between foreigners—or refugees—being given the right to visit any country but not having the right to take up residence.[111] He begins to demarcate the limits of Kantian cosmopolitanism in "The Right to Philosophy from a Cosmopolitan Point of View," emphasizing the problematic relation between a pervasive internationalism and the aim for a "total, perfect political unification of the human species," noting that Kant's proposed history is also profoundly "Eurocentric."[112]

In a series of papers from 1996–1997, some inspired by the French government's decision to make it illegal to offer hospitality to those "without-papers," Derrida returns to "Toward Perpetual Peace."[113] Kant opens the marked difference between the ethics and the politics of hospitality.[114] Kant needs there to be an instituted politics of hospitality to remove it from "natural hostility."[115] The "cosmopolitical right" is limited; hence the constant refusal of an unconditioned hospitality in the midst of a generous "universal hospitality."[116] The context for this Kantian restriction is the trace of the constant threat of war in the midst of the institution of perpetual peace.[117] In *Of Hospitality*, Derrida reiterates that Kant presents us with a dilemma, the bad faith even, of the promise of an infinite idea of hospitality and the insistence on a finite law that restricts hospitality.[118] Derrida provides a striking example of this dissonance in a 1997 paper where he notes that Kant restricts his hospitality towards foreigners to "the surface of the earth" and not to any dwellings or buildings: there can be no "right of residence."[119]

In 1994, Derrida participated in a conference on religion, and the title of his paper, "Faith and Knowledge: Two Sources of 'Religion' at the Limits of Reason Alone," once again echoes a Kantian work, *Religion Within the Boundaries of Mere Reason*. There are numerous references to this work in Derrida's earlier writings, notably on its argument in favor of censorship, which is needed due the "fallibility" of man, and the possibility of "radical evil" as a foundational corruption of maxims.[120] In "Faith and Knowledge," Derrida again uses Kant to address the contemporary, raising the question of "the treatment today of religion within the limits of reason alone."[121] He is thinking primarily of the relation between religion and reason as media-technology and politics.[122] But he also returns to "radical evil," which Kant insists cannot contradict freedom.[123] For Derrida, as an event that can never be anticipated, "radical evil" is the possibility and the ruin of "the religious."[124] As he had done in *Glas*, Derrida also marks the limits of Kant's association of "reflective faith" with Christian morality alone.[125]

In the last decade of his life, one could say that Derrida treats Kant as the most articulate measure of the philosophical tradition. When it comes to speaking today about the history of the lie, about the history of animals and humans, about the status of the humanities in the university and, above all, about the history of reason and its self-authorization, Derrida turns to Kant.[126] For deconstruction to respond to the practical questions of the day, it must both start with and depart from Kant.

6 Kant and the Late Seminars (2008–2021)

Today, Derrida studies is shaped by the strange time of the posthumous contemporary.[127] As we approach twenty years since his death in 2004, the slow but steady publication of Derrida's seminars and unpublished works gives us the "new" and "timely" appearance of works from the ever-receding and increasingly remote past. As we have seen, these "late" seminars have already altered the way that we understand Derrida's engagement with Kant. The eventual publication of the seminars from the 1980s and the early 1990s will only reinforce the importance of Kant in Derrida's thought. Because of the ongoing publication of the seminars, the role played by Kant in deconstruction remains an open question.

The last five years of the seminars (1997–2003), which have now been published in full, addressed, among other things, Kant's treatment of guilt and clemency, the death penalty and the concept of world.[128] As Derrida points out in his 2001–2003 seminar *The Beast and the Sovereign*, the implications of Kant's argument that the world is "merely a regulative Idea of Reason"—that the world as whole is beyond our possible experience and our concepts, and we must therefore treat it as an idea, and act *as if* there is a world—are profound and revolutionary.[129] As I have examined this in detail elsewhere, in the space I have left I will focus on two problems from the recently published seminars: the death penalty and the *intuitus derivativus*.[130]

6.1 *The Death Penalty*

Having earlier linked Kantian "radical evil" to an "unforgivable evil"—and, therefore, "the only one that calls for forgiveness"—in his 1997–1999 seminar *Perjury and Pardon* Derrida begins with section E of the General Remark of § 49 of *The Metaphysics of Morals*, "On the right to punish and to grant clemency," and this becomes a touchstone throughout the seminar.[131] This same section of *The

Metaphysics of Morals is also the focus of Derrida's last sustained reading of Kant, the 1999–2001 seminar *The Death Penalty*. The Kantian heritage, the great philosophical measure of morals and ethics and internationalism, also bequeaths us a stark and rigorous defense of the death penalty. For Derrida, there could not be a more pronounced difference between critique and deconstruction. It is a fitting conclusion to Derrida's long interrogation of Kant's practical philosophy.

In *Perjury and Pardon*, Derrida examines Kant's treatment of "original debt," sin and repentance.[132] For Kant, guilt and responsibility must always stand "before the law." For Heidegger, in contrast, guilt and responsibility can only be authentic without the tribunal or theatre of the law.[133] However, both still subscribe to an original culpability and debt.[134] Derrida reiterates that responsibility can only take place if it is not prescribed by pre-existing laws, norms and debts: a debt is paid, but a responsible decision has not been taken.[135] What is at stake here is the place of pardon. Derrida asks: does pardon precede and exceed the law, or is it only found in the sovereign act of punishment and clemency? This brings him back to Kant's "On the right to punish and to grant clemency," where Kant juxtaposes the right of the ruler "to inflict pain" with an emphatic prohibition against punishing "the head of a state."[136] In *The Death Penalty*, Derrida explores the Kantian treatment of sovereignty as the ground for and unique exemption from the death penalty. For Kant, parricide or regicide by execution not only threatens the death penalty; it is "as if the state commits suicide."[137] In this sense, the death penalty is the life of the state.

Kant's logic in *The Metaphysics of Morals* is relentless: unlike animals, humans must raise themselves "above natural life," and the death penalty registers "the dignity of human reason" and "access to what is proper in man."[138] Empiricism, and "the empirical attachment to life," requires the death penalty.[139] The "idea of law" demands that "something is worth more than life."[140] Despite exceptions (duelists and matricide), "the categorical imperative of penal law is the talionic law": the equivalence and equity of a death for a death (even if this equality is in truth "a calculation of the incalculable").[141] The purity of the injunction requires that the death penalty has no utility; all that matters is that man must be treated "as an end in himself and not as a means."[142] It is a matter of dignity, honor and justice: the "value" of human life is "worth more than life."[143] By refuting any kind of utility in the death penalty, Kantian logic challenges both modern proponents and opponents of the death penalty.[144]

In the second year of *The Death Penalty*, Derrida concentrates on the distinction Kant makes between external punishment (institutional and public) and internal punishment (natural and private).[145] The death penalty can only belong to a non-natural, legal punishment.[146] This leads Derrida to challenge the Kantian distinction between "pure self-punishment" and "pure hetero-punishment."[147] Kant's logic in effect treats the death penalty as a form of suicide: as a free being, the condemned must "rationally approve" their own execution.[148] However, as Derrida points out, the powerful "logic of suicidal execution" transforms "hetero-punishment into auto-punishment."[149] This marks "a hyperconfirmation" of Kantian rationality that "self-destructs or self-deconstructs": self-punishment can no longer be distinguished from state punishment.[150] For Derrida, "the entire Kantian discourse begins to crack:

what grounds the law in reason, here the death penalty, is also what deprives it of all juridical rationality."[151] The categorical imperative *as* a death penalty—which, madly, as "pure justice" must "serve no purpose"—undoes reason itself.[152]

6.2 The Intuitus Derivativus

In April 2021, *Donner le temps* II was published. This book is taken from Derrida's 1978–1979 seminar, with some earlier sessions being published in a 1991 lecture series as *Given Time: 1. Counterfeit Money*.[153] In *Donner le temps* II, Derrida returns to the Kantian *intuitus derivativus*. He often cites the final section on time in the transcendental aesthetic, added in the second edition of the *Critique of Pure Reason*. There is a chance, Kant writes, "that all finite thinking beings" share a "derived" (*abgeleitet*) and not "original" (*ursprünglich*) sensibility—*intuitus derivativus* rather than *intuitius originarius*—because sensible intuition is "dependent" on "the existence of objects" that are not given in themselves, and possible "only insofar as the representational capacity of the subject is affected through that."[154]

Over the years, Derrida had only given us glimpses of his reading of the *intuitus derivativus*. He emphasized that that transcendental aesthetic announces "a pure sensible space as a form of receptivity" which constructs and confirms the "receptive subject."[155] Nonetheless, this receptive—but derived and dependent—subject is distinguished by its *finitude*, even as it stands in relation to "the possibility of an *intuitius originarius*, of an infinite intellect that creates rather than invents its own objects."[156] The most radical implication of the *intuitus derivativus* is its link to "the possibility of time."[157] This suggests that Kantian time is found amidst "the concept of a *derived* finitude or passivity."[158] The receptive subject marks time as a passivity *for* the subject. When Kant describes "the form of sensibility" as time he also captures the hope of sensibility *as* time, of the pathos of a sensibility that will give us time, give us more time.[159]

Derrida had pointed out in 1965 that Heidegger treats the Kantian affectivity of time as a confirmation of "auto-affection as temporality."[160] By 1968, Derrida takes a critical stance towards Heidegger, arguing that the ontic-ontological difference relies on "a *fall* in general … from original time into derivative time."[161] As he had suggested in *Of Grammatology*, it is a pre-eminent metaphysical gesture to demarcate the original and derivative and to describe the latter as the always secondary, inferior or fallen.[162] Most radically, Derrida argues this "alleged derivativeness" indicates that "the 'original,' … had never existed, never been intact and untouched."[163] The so-called derivative is neither secondary nor merely a representative or passive conduit for the primary; it is rather the possibility and the ruin of the original as an ideality. The derived drifts and wanders: it marks *différance*.[164]

The *Donner le temps* seminar was in part prompted by Heidegger's "Time and Being" on the possibility of the gift of time and of a giving that precedes and exceeds both beings and Being.[165] Derrida is interested in how Kantian receptivity relates to the given.[166] As finite and receptive, what comes to the Kantian subject is a donation, a gift.[167] But it is not a simple and outright gift. In contrast to the *intuitius originarius*, the *intuitus derivativus* does not create its objects.[168] The *intuitius originarius* creates and gives itself its own gifts: it is self-gifting.[169] As Derrida reminds us, Kantian time facilitates both the form of internal sense and the general conditions for internal and external phenomena.[170] Everything that is given to the *intuitus derivativus*, "is given according to the form of time."[171]

In *Kant and the Problem of Metaphysics*, Heidegger remarks that finite intuition must be "solicited or affected" and "allow the object to be given."[172] In Derrida's terms, the *intuitus derivativus* registers the gift of the other. What initially interests Derrida is how Heidegger uses the Kantian *intuitus derivativus* to break the link between time and the priority of the present, of temporality as a spatially determined here-and-now. As Heidegger explains, finite intuition or sensibility is first taken as an empirical "receiving of something at hand or present." In contrast, for pure intuition this receiving must be more than merely present if it is to account for a time as a *sequence* of nows.[173] Because Kantian time is a continuous succession, it is impossible to grasp "a single now" as a "present moment."

Heidegger's reading of Kant opens up the possibility that the transcendental aesthetic cannot be limited to a metaphysics of presence. As Derrida notes, "in this auto-affective experience of pure receptivity, the pure reception of this which gives itself as time, this non-empirical reception, receives nothing that is [*qui soit*] a being or a present."[174] What constitutes "the 'I think' itself" therefore receives nothing that "is a being or a present."[175] As Derrida argues, "the *intuitus derivativus*, the finite and therefore receptive subject that is constituted by this temporal structure, is constituted by a relation to a self-donation [*une donation de soi*] which gives nothing, by a pure receptivity that receives nothing which is a present or a being."[176] The Kantian *intuitus derivativus* can only give itself what it receives, *which is time*.[177]

But if Heidegger brings out the revolutionary aspects of *intuitus derivativus*, he also forecloses this opening through the "violence" of his reading.[178] According to Heidegger, Kant did not have the courage to treat the transcendental imagination as the radical source of an "original unity": the receptivity of the intuition and the spontaneity of the understanding should be treated *as the same*.[179] It is this insistence on an "original unity," where both the "original" and the "unity" can be characterized *as the same*, which Derrida challenges. For Derrida, the assertion of the same—of the same *as* itself—already requires a repetition, a doubling and differing, a drifting "derivative" towards the other that precedes, makes possible and exceeds the "original" *as* the same.

As Derrida had first suggested in "*Ousia* and *Grammē*," this is also the case when Heidegger argues that time and the Kantian "I think" "are the same" and can be "brought [...] together in their original sameness" (*ursprüngliche Selbigkeit*).[180] To treat "auto-affection as temporality" is to welcome the absolutely other and to mark an unavoidable dislocation of the unifying, gathering or re-gathering force of the same.[181] As he notes ten years later in *Donner le temps* II, Heidegger must argue that Kant has stepped back from treating the receptive and the spontaneous as the same.[182] But this Kantian refusal, as much as it secures the hierarchy of the original and the derivative, also insists upon a difference at the heart of the same.[183] For

Derrida, the legacy of this difference is most apparent in the third *Critique*, which is why he begins his reading of Kant with this work.[184]

Kant certainly insists on the necessary "unification" of sensibility and understanding.[185] The receptivity (passivity) of sensibility must be unified with the spontaneity (activity) of the understanding. Tracing Heidegger's argument, Derrida notes how time ensures this unity: "the auto-affection of giving-to-oneself-to receive [*se-donner-à-recevoir*]—as time—assumes this unity of spontaneity and receptivity."[186] But how original and how unified can this "original unity" be if it is made possible by time?[187] For Heidegger, the "pure power of imagination" facilities this "original unity," because "what is unified allows what is to be unified to spring forth."[188] It is at this point that Derrida marks Heidegger's return to the *intuitius originarius*.

Heidegger argues that the "original representations" of Kantian time and space cannot be ontic or psychological: they must be ontological and spring forth and flow spontaneously, like an *intuitius originarius*.[189] As Heidegger remarks, "the expression 'original' corresponds to the '*originarius*' in the title *intuitius originarius* and means: to let [something] spring forth."[190] As Derrida reiterates, in their finitude humans cannot have access to the God-like creative power of the *intuitius originarius*.[191] But Heidegger emphasizes that the power of the imagination, which operates without the presence of the intuitable, has a formative power and synoptic anticipatory view of "a whole which is unified in itself."[192] The gift of the transcendental imagination glimpses the ontological.[193] Heidegger's gift is derived from no beings or present prior to itself, but still occupies the proper place of an original and unique event.[194] For Derrida, the gift of the other is already derivative, already in excess of the Heideggerian appropriation (*Ereignis*) or expropriation (*Enteignis*) of this event.[195] The gift gives given time *as* "ex-appropriation."[196]

As Derrida suggests in another recently published seminar, *Life Death* (1975–1976), for Heidegger, Kant's transcendental imagination ultimately signals "a poetizing" (*Dichtung*) in "the essence of reason."[197] In *Donner le temps* II, this Heideggerian *Dichtung* marks a limit in Heidegger's reading of Kant.[198] "Parergon" already shows us that Derrida does not follow Heidegger's privileging of the Kantian imagination as the unique window into fundamental ontology.[199] I would add that Heidegger has not read his Hume. The power of the imagination is a problem for Kant because it is has become an eighteenth-century problem. Hume bequeaths the imagination as a necessary fiction; as a supplement that fills in the gaps and breaks in present impressions, allowing the subject to act *as if* perception is always continuous and coherent.[200] As Derrida suggests, the regulative ideas of reason also require a relentless "as if" (*als ob*) that is not only evidence of the "systematic unity" of reason, but also of the possibility of the unconditioned as an uncontained "if," which is also part of the Kantian legacy.[201] We are still waiting for the publication of Derrida's 1965–1966 seminar on Hume.[202]

And what of the Kantian gift? Kant not only begins the first *Critique* with the gifts of receptivity, with "objects given [*gegeben*] to us by means of sensibility"; he also opens his preface with the gifts of reason, with the "fate" and burden of the "questions which it cannot dismiss, since they are given to it as problems by the nature of reason itself [*selbst aufgegeben*]."[203] These are the equivocal gifts of the empirical and the metaphysical. Kantian critique begins as a response to these gifts, not least because it recognizes that reason gives itself the gift of its own unavoidable problems. As Kant explains in the preface to the second edition, "the problems of metaphysics" can be ameliorated if we follow Copernicus and assume that "objects must conform to our cognition" as this better reflects "the possibility of an *a priori* cognition of them."[204] The critical point of this well-known gesture is that it outmaneuvers these equivocal gifts; it allows us "to establish something about objects before they are given [*gegeben*] to us."[205] The *a priori* is the great counter gift. In this sense, given time never stops responding to the problem of the gift.[206] It must always counterbalance what is not given in itself with what is added to the given concept as an *a priori* synthetic judgement or only given as a regulated idea.

As Derrida suggests in this 1978–1979 seminar, the given time of Kant will lead him to his 1980–1981 seminar on Kant's practical philosophy and respect for the moral law.[207] This Kantian seminar will in turn prompt the many seminars over the next twenty-three years on "the rationality of the law" as an assured universality, on calculation, the economy of reappropriation, and the incalculable event.[208] There is brief discussion of this 1980–1981 seminar in "Préjugés: Before the Law." As Derrida explains:

> I was also dealing with the "as if" (*als ob*) in the second formulation of the categorical imperative: "Act as if the maxim of your action were to become by your will a *universal law of nature*." This "as if" makes it possible to align practical reason with a historical teleology and with the possibility of infinite progress. I was trying to show how he introduced narrativity and fiction virtually into the very heart of his thought on law, at the very moment when law begins to speak and to question the moral subject. Precisely when the authority of the law seems to exclude any historicity and any empirical narrativity, at the moment when its rationality seems alien to fiction and imagination of any kind (even the transcendental imagination), it seems *a priori* to still offer its hospitality to these parasites.[209]

This rare instance of Derrida's own summary of a seminar on Kant demonstrates the consistency of his preoccupations. Once again, he is thinking of the idea in the Kantian sense as a promise of infinity and a delivery of the indefinite. Never before the moral law itself, like Kafka, we are waiting indefinitely.[210] Moving away from Heidegger's treatment of the transcendental imagination, Derrida treats the Kantian "as if" as the junction *and* distinction that both affirms the law and steps beyond the law. As Derrida observed in another late seminar, "one must read Kant and always begin by rereading Kant."[211]

Notes

1. Benoît Peeters, *Derrida: A Biography*, trans. Andrew Brown (Cambridge: Polity, 2013), 109–10.
2. Jacques Derrida, *Edmund Husserl's Origin of Geometry: An Introduction*, trans. John P. Leavey, Jr., 2nd ed. (Lincoln: University of Nebraska Press, 1989).
3. Ibid., 39–42, 124–25 n. 140, 140 n. 167. See Paul Ricoeur, "Kant and Husserl," in *Husserl: An Analysis of His Phenomenology*, trans. Edward G. Ballard and Lester E. Embree, 2nd ed.

(Evanston: Northwestern University Press, 2007), 175–201. See also Immanuel Kant, "Idea for a Universal History with a Cosmopolitan Aim," in *Anthropology, History, and Education*, ed. Robert B. Louden and Günter Zöller, trans. Allen W. Wood (Cambridge: Cambridge University Press, 2007), 107–20 (AK 8: 15–31).

4. Edmund Husserl, *Ideas Pertaining to a Pure Phenomenology and to a Phenomenological Philosophy: First Book—A General Introduction to a Pure Phenomenology*, trans. F. Kersten (The Hague: Martinus Nijhoff, 1983), 342.
5. Jacques Derrida, *Voice and Phenomenon: Introduction to the Problem of the Sign in Husserl's Phenomenology*, trans. Leonard Lawlor (Evanston: Northwestern University Press, 2011), 8.
6. Ibid., 8.
7. Ibid., 8–9, 85–86.
8. Ibid., 87.
9. Jacques Derrida, *Writing and Difference*, trans. Alan Bass (Chicago: University of Chicago Press, 1978), 120–21.
10. Jacques Derrida, *Margins of Philosophy*, trans. Alan Bass (Chicago: University of Chicago Press, 1982), 1–27.
11. Jacques Derrida, "Parergon," in *The Truth in Painting*, trans. Geoff Bennington and Ian McLeod (Chicago: University of Chicago Press, 1987), 16.
12. Jacques Derrida, *Psyche: Inventions of the Other, Volume 2*, ed. Peggy Kamuf and Elizabeth Rottenberg, trans. David Wood and Andrew Benjamin (Stanford: Stanford University Press, 2008), 4.
13. Gilles Deleuze, *Kant's Critical Philosophy: The Doctrine of the Faculties*, trans. Hugh Tomlinson and Barbara Habberjam (Minneapolis: University of Minnesota Press, 1985); Michel Foucault, *Introduction to Kant's Anthropology*, ed. Roberto Nigro, trans. Roberto Nigro and Kate Briggs (Los Angeles: Semiotext(e), 2007).
14. Jacques Derrida, *Heidegger: The Question of Being and History*, trans. Geoffrey Bennington (Chicago: University of Chicago Press, 2016).
15. Ibid., 180–81; Martin Heidegger, *Kant and the Problem of Metaphysics*, trans. Richard Taft, 5th ed. (Bloomington: Indiana University Press, 1997), 132–33. See also Jacques Derrida, *Of Grammatology*, trans. Gayatri Chakravorty Spivak, intro. Judith Butler (Baltimore: Johns Hopkins University Press, 2016), 407 n. 21
16. Derrida, *Writing and Difference*, 152; *Heidegger: The Question of Being and History*, 54.
17. Derrida, *Writing and Difference*, 7, 96, 215, 314 n. 26.
18. Derrida, *Of Grammatology*, 23, 37, 315.
19. Ibid., 316–17.
20. Ibid., 316.
21. Derrida, *Margins of Philosophy*, 35–38, 42.
22. Ibid., 43–44, 49.
23. Ibid., 44–45, 48.
24. Ibid., 44–45.
25. Ibid., 49–50.
26. Ibid., 48.
27. Ibid., 121–22 n. 15. See also Heidegger, *Kant and the Problem of Metaphysics*, 71, 77, 80.
28. Jacques Derrida, *Clang [Glas]*, trans. David Wills and Geoffrey Bennington (Minneapolis: University of Minnesota Press, 2021), 42a (see also 69a–70a, 236a–39a, 243a–44a).
29. Ibid., 143a–50a; Immanuel Kant, *Anthropology from a Pragmatic Point of View*, trans. and ed. Robert B. Louden (Cambridge: Cambridge University Press, 2006), 204–12 (II. B).
30. Derrida, "Parergon"; "Economimesis," trans. Richard Klein, *Diacritics* 11.2 (1981): 2–25.
31. Jacques Derrida, *Writing and Difference*, 7, 79; *Of Grammatology*, 316, 407 n. 21; *Dissemination*, trans. Barbara Johnson (Chicago: University of Chicago Press, 1981), 126.
32. Immanuel Kant, *Critique of Pure Reason*, trans. and ed. Paul Guyer and Allen W. Wood (Cambridge: Cambridge University Press, 1997), A 140–41/B 179–80; *Critique of the Power of Judgment*, ed. Paul Guyer, trans. Paul Guyer and Eric Matthews (Cambridge: Cambridge University Press, 2000), 167–68 (AK 5: 286–87).

33. Derrida, *Margins of Philosophy*, 7–14, 17.
34. Derrida, *Clang*, 242a.
35. Derrida, "Parergon," 34. See also, Jacques Derrida, *Eyes of the University: Right to Philosophy 2*, trans. Joseph Adamson, ed. Jan Plug (Stanford: Stanford University Press, 2004), 68, 73.
36. Derrida, "Parergon," 23, 29–31, 34.
37. Derrida, *Clang*, 242a.
38. Kant, *Critique of the Power of Judgment*, 8 (AK 20: 202).
39. Kant, *Critique of the Power of Judgment*, 56 (AK 5: 168); Derrida, "Parergon," 38–39.
40. Derrida, "Parergon," 39.
41. Ibid., 50.
42. Ibid.
43. Ibid., 41.
44. Ibid., 51; see Kant, *Critique of the Power of Judgment*, 66–67 (AK 5: 179).
45. Ibid., 51, 109.
46. Kant, *Critique of Pure Reason*, A xxiii.
47. Kant, *Critique of the Power of Judgment*, 110–11 (AK 5: 226).
48. Derrida, "Parergon," 54.
49. Ibid., 64 (see also 63, 67, 97–98).
50. Ibid., 59 (see also 56–57, 71, 80).
51. Ibid., 64; see Kant, *Critique of the Power of Judgment*, 111 (AK 5: 226).
52. Ibid., 55, 59, 68–73, 76; see Kant, *Critique of the Power of Judgment*, 89 n. 1 (AK 5: 203).
53. Ibid., 73.
54. Ibid., 73–74.
55. Ibid., 84–88, 105; see Kant, *Critique of the Power of Judgment*, 120 n. 1 (AK 5: 236).
56. Ibid., 88–90, 90–91.
57. Ibid., 98–100.
58. Ibid., 90, 104–111; see Kant, *Critique of the Power of Judgment*, 114 (AK 5: 29–30).
59. Ibid., 115.
60. See Peeters, *Derrida*, 37; Pierre Bourdieu, *Distinction: A Social Critique of the Judgement of Taste*, trans. Richard Nice (Cambridge: Harvard University Press, 1984).
61. Jean-François Lyotard, *Enthusiasm: The Kantian Critique of History*, trans. Georges van den Abbeele (Stanford: Stanford University Press, 2009); *Lessons on the Analytic of the Sublime: Kant's Critique of Judgement, §§ 23–29*, trans. Elizabeth Rottenberg (Stanford: Stanford University Press, 1994); Jean-Luc Nancy, *The Discourse of the Syncope: Logodaedalus*, trans. Saul Anton (Stanford: Stanford University Press, 2008); *L'Impératif catégorique* (Paris: Flammarion, 1983); *The Experience of Freedom*, trans. Bridget McDonald, fore. Peter Fenves (Stanford: Stanford University Press, 1993).
62. As the eventual publication of the seminars will show, including: *Le Respect* (1980–1981), *La Raison universitaire* (1982–1983), *Du droit à la philosophie* (1983–1984), *Kant, le Juif, l'Allemand: Nationalité et nationalisme philosophiques* (1987–1988).
63. Bourdieu, *Distinction*, 494 (see also 601 n. 37).
64. Ibid., 496. Derrida explicitly addresses a displaced politics and political economy in the third *Critique* in "Economimesis" (3, 9, 11).
65. Jacques Derrida, *Who's Afraid of Philosophy: Right to Philosophy 1*, trans. and ed. Jan Plug (Stanford: Stanford University Press, 2002), 11, 43 63–65.
66. Derrida, "Parergon," 19–20.
67. Jacques Derrida, *Eyes of the University* 109–10.
68. Jacques Derrida, *Theory and Practice*, trans. David Wills, ed. Geoffrey Bennington and Peggy Kamuf (Chicago: University of Chicago Press, 2019).
69. Kant, *Critique of Pure Reason*, A 462/B 490-A 476/B 504. See also Sean Gaston, *Derrida and Disinterest* (London: Continuum, 2005), 1–18, 55–68.
70. Jacques Derrida, "Ja, or the faux-bond II," in *Points … Interviews, 1974–1994*, ed. Elisabeth Weber, trans. Peggy Kamuf (Stanford: Stanford University Press, 1995), 69. See also *Clang*, 242a; "Parergon" 38; Kant, *Critique of Pure Reason*, A 462–76/B 490–504.

71. Kant, *Critique of Pure Reason*, A 805–6/B 833–34; Derrida, *Theory and Practice*, 24–29, 32–36.
72. See Vrablikova's chapter below.
73. Immanuel Kant, "The Conflict of the Faculties," in *Religion and Rational Theology*, trans. and ed. Allen W. Wood, George Di Giovanni and Mary J. Gregor (Cambridge: Cambridge University Press, 1996), 281–82 (AK 7: 61–62).
74. Derrida, *Eyes of the University*, 85–86, 105; Kant, "The Conflict of the Faculties," 250 (AK 7: 21).
75. Ibid., 90, 93.
76. Ibid., 90–91.
77. Ibid., 91 (see 48–49).
78. Ibid., 90.
79. Ibid., 92, 93–100.
80. Ibid., 93.
81. Ibid., 97–98.
82. Ibid., 98, 99–100, 104–5.
83. Ibid., 100.
84. Ibid.
85. Ibid., 98.
86. Ibid., 99, 106 (on "double bind," see 101).
87. Ibid., 101.
88. Ibid., 102.
89. Ibid., 72 (see also 106–9, 55).
90. Ibid., 108.
91. Jacques Derrida, *Psyche: Inventions of the Other, Volume 2*, 244.
92. Ibid., 244.
93. Ibid., 274–75 (see also 251–52, 272–73, 295–97).
94. Ibid., 275.
95. Jacques Derrida, *Eyes of the University*, 178.
96. Ibid., 177.
97. See Immanuel Kant, "The Metaphysics of Morals," in *Practical Philosophy*, ed. and trans. Mary J. Gregor (Cambridge: Cambridge University Press, 1996), 365 (AK 6: 205).
98. Derrida, *Who's Afraid of Philosophy?*, 46–47.
99. Ibid., 2, 49–50, 52, 55–61.
100. Ibid., 50.
101. Jacques Derrida, *Before the Law: The Complete Text of Préjugés*, trans. Sandra Van Reenen and Jacques de Ville (Minneapolis: University of Minnesota Press, 2018).
102. Ibid., 33–34, 43. Immanuel Kant, "Groundwork of The Metaphysics of Morals," in *Practical Philosophy*, ed. and trans. Mary J. Gregor (Cambridge: Cambridge University Press, 1996), 55–58, 61, 63 (AK 4: 400–403, 406–9); "Critique of Practical Reason," in *Practical Philosophy*, ed. and trans. Mary J. Gregor (Cambridge: Cambridge University Press, 1996), 199–211 (AK 5: 73–89).
103. Kant, "Groundwork of The Metaphysics of Morals," 45–46, 53 (AK 4: 390–91, 398); "Critique of Practical Reason," 205–6 (AK 5: 81–82).
104. Jacques Derrida, *Aporias: Dying—Awaiting (One Another at) the "Limits of Truth,"* trans. Thomas Dutoit (Stanford: Stanford University Press, 1993), 16–17.
105. Jacques Derrida, *The Gift of Death and Literature in Secret*, trans. David Wills (Chicago: University of Chicago Press, 2008), 92–93 (see 64–73). See also, Jacques Derrida, "Passions: 'An Oblique Offering'," in *Derrida: A Critical Reader*, ed. and trans. David Wood (Oxford: Blackwell, 1992), 8–9 26–29 n. 4.
106. Derrida, *The Gift of Death*, 67.
107. Ibid., 69.
108. Derrida, "Passions," 14.

109. Ibid., 14.
110. Derrida, *Aporias*, 84 n. 10.
111. Ibid., 84–85 n. 10. Immanuel Kant, "Toward Perpetual Peace," in *Practical Philosophy*, ed. and trans. Mary J. Gregor (Cambridge: Cambridge University Press, 1996), 328–31 (AK 8: 357–60).
112. Jacques Derrida, *Negotiations: Interventions and Interviews 1971–2001*, ed. and trans. Elizabeth Rottenberg (Stanford: Stanford University Press, 2002), 333, 341.
113. Ibid., 133–44.
114. Jacques Derrida, *Adieu—to Emmanuel Levinas*, trans. Pascale-Anne Brault and Michael Naas (Stanford: Stanford University Press, 1999), 19–20, 49.
115. Ibid., 49.
116. Ibid., 68, 87; see Kant, "Toward Perpetual Peace," 328–29 (AK 8: 357–58).
117. Ibid., 88–90.
118. Jacques Derrida and Anne Dufourmantelle, *Of Hospitality: Anne Dufourmantelle Invites Jacques Derrida to Respond*, trans. Rachel Bowlby (Stanford: Stanford University Press, 2000), 27, 71, 141.
119. Jacques Derrida, *Cosmopolitanism and Forgiveness*, trans. Mark Dooley (London: Routledge, 200), 20–21.
120. Derrida, *Eyes of the University*, 44–45, 48, 50–53; Jacques Derrida, *Given Time: I. Counterfeit Money*, trans. Peggy Kamuf (Chicago: University of Chicago Press, 1992), 165 n. 31; *Le parjure et le pardon, volume II: Séminaire (1998–1999)*, ed. Ginette Michaud, Nicholas Cotton and Rodrigo Therezo (Paris: Seuil, 2020), 221–29. See also Immanuel Kant, "Religion Within the Boundaries of Mere Reason," in *Religion and Rational Theology*, trans. and ed. Allen W. Wood and George Di Giovanni (Cambridge: Cambridge University Press, 1996), 60, 83 (AK 6: 7–8, 37). See also Derrida's earlier paper, "Of an Apocalyptic Tone Recently Adopted in Philosophy," trans. John P. Leavey, Jr., *The Oxford Literary Review* 6.2 (1984): 3–39.
121. Jacques Derrida, *Acts of Religion*, ed. Gil Anidjar, trans. Samuel Weber (New York and London: Routledge, 2002), 48.
122. Ibid., 48–49, 52–53.
123. Kant, "Religion Within the Boundaries of Mere Reason," 71 (AK 6: 21–22).
124. Derrida, *Acts of Religion*, 56, 77, 82–83, 89–91, 100.
125. Ibid., 50–51, 59, 88; Kant, "Religion Within the Boundaries of Mere Reason," 96 (AK 6: 52–53). See also Jacques Derrida, *The Death Penalty, Volume I*, ed. Geoffrey Bennington, Marc Crepon and Thomas Dutoit, trans. Peggy Kamuf (Chicago: University of Chicago Press, 2014), 158–59, 195; *On Touching—Jean-Luc Nancy*, trans. Christine Irizarry (Stanford: Stanford University Press, 2005), 37–42, 43–46.
126. Jacques Derrida, *Without Alibi*, ed., and trans. Peggy Kamuf (Stanford: Stanford University Press, 2002), 43–45, 69–70, 210–13, 219–22; *The Animal That Therefore I Am*, ed. Marie-Louise Mallet, trans. David Wills (New York: Fordham University Press, 2008), 37, 90–104, 107–16; *Rogues: Two Essays on Reason*, trans. Pascale-Anne Brault and Michael Naas (Stanford: Stanford University Press, 2005), 37, 80–86, 119–21, 132–35, 150, 153.
127. See Sean Gaston, *The Concept of World from Kant to Derrida* (London: Rowman and Littlefield, 2013), 159–61.
128. I.e., *Perjury and Pardon* (1997–1999), *The Death Penalty* (1999–2001) and *The Beast and the Sovereign* (2001–2003).
129. Jacques Derrida, *The Beast and the Sovereign, Volume II*, trans. Geoffrey Bennington, ed. Michel Lisse, Marie-Louise Mallet, and Ginette Michaud (Chicago: University of Chicago Press, 2011), 58–6, 170–71, 269–78.
130. Gaston, *The Concept of World from Kant to Derrida*, 1–28.
131. Derrida, *Given Time I*, 166 n. 31; Jacques Derrida, *Le parjure et le pardon, volume I: Séminaire: (1997–1998)*, ed. Ginette Michaud and Nicholas Cotton (Paris: Seuil, 2019), 46–48, 253–54; *Le parjure et le pardon* II, 72.

132. Derrida, *Le parjure et le pardon* II, 221–29; Kant, "Religion Within the Boundaries of Mere Reason," 112–13 (AK 6: 72). See also Kant, "The Metaphysics of Morals," 472, 477–78 (AK 6: 331–37).
133. Derrida, *Le parjure et le pardon* II, 236–39.
134. Ibid., 239–40; see Kant, "The Metaphysics of Morals," 474 (AK 6: 333).
135. Ibid., 238.
136. Kant, "The Metaphysics of Morals," 472 (AK 6: 31).
137. Jacques Derrida, *The Death Penalty, Volume* II, ed. Geoffrey Bennington and Marc Crepon, trans. Elizabeth Rottenberg (Chicago: University of Chicago Press, 2017), 187–93, 200–4; see Kant, "The Metaphysics of Morals," 464–65 (6: 320–22).
138. Derrida, *The Death Penalty* I, 8.
139. Ibid., 124 n. 3.
140. Ibid., 116.
141. Ibid., 125, 151; *The Death Penalty* II, 91–92, 102, 185–98; Kant, "The Metaphysics of Morals," 476–77, 497–98 (AK 6: 335–37, 362–64).
142. Derrida, *The Death Penalty* I, 275; see Kant, "The Metaphysics of Morals," 473 (AK 6: 331).
143. Derrida, *The Death Penalty* II, 39–42, 90, 93–96, 101–2; see Kant, "The Metaphysics of Morals," 473–75 (AK 6: 332–34).
144. Ibid., 90–91, 245.
145. Ibid., 37–38; see Kant, "The Metaphysics of Morals," 473 (AK 6: 332).
146. Ibid., 38.
147. Ibid., 39.
148. Ibid., 66.
149. Ibid., 67, 85–86, 91–92.
150. Ibid., 69, 86.
151. Ibid., 69 (see also 84–102, 196).
152. Ibid., 184 n. 29; Kant, "The Metaphysics of Morals," 473 (AK 6: 332).
153. Derrida, *Given Time* I: *Counterfeit Money*.
154. Kant, *Critique of Pure Reason*, B 72. See also Kant, *Anthropology*, §28.
155. Jacques Derrida, *Psyche: Inventions of the Other, Volume* 2, ed. Peggy Kamuf and Elizabeth Rottenberg (Stanford: Stanford University Press, 2008), 173.
156. Jacques Derrida, *Psyche: Inventions of the Other, Volume* 1, ed. Peggy Kamuf and Elizabeth Rottenberg, trans. Catherine Porter and Philip Lewis (Stanford: Stanford University Press, 2007), 406–7. See also Derrida, *Eyes of the University*, 66–67 and *On Touching*, 46.
157. Derrida, *Writing and Difference*, 48.
158. Ibid., 48.
159. Derrida, *The Death Penalty* I, 281.
160. Derrida, *Heidegger: History and the Question of Being*, 180.
161. Derrida, *Writing and Difference*, 63; translation modified.
162. Derrida, *Of Grammatology*, 7, 12, 15, 32.
163. Ibid., 61.
164. Ibid., 74; *Margins of Philosophy*, 9, 15. See also Jacques Derrida and Catherine Malabou, *Counterpath: Traveling with Jacques Derrida*, trans. David Wills (Stanford: Stanford University Press, 2004).
165. Martin Heidegger, "Time and Being," in *On Time and Being*, trans. Joan Stambaugh (New York: Harper & Row, 1972), 1–24; Jacques Derrida, *Donner le temps* II, ed. Laura Odello, Peter Szendy and Rodrigo Therezo (Paris: Seuil, 2021), 211–28.
166. Derrida, *Donner le temps* II, 147.
167. Ibid.
168. Ibid., 147–48.
169. Ibid., 148; See Heidegger, *Kant and the Problem of Metaphysics*, 17.
170. Ibid.
171. Ibid.

172. Heidegger, *Kant and the Problem of Metaphysics*, 18.
173. Heidegger, *Kant and the Problem of Metaphysics*, 122.
174. Derrida, *Donner le temps* II, 150.
175. Ibid.
176. Ibid., 150–51.
177. Ibid., 151, 158.
178. Ibid., 149; see Heidegger, *Kant and the Problem of Metaphysics*, 141.
179. Ibid., 164; see Heidegger, *Kant and the Problem of Metaphysics*, 111.
180. Derrida, *Writing and Difference*, 44–45; Heidegger, *Kant and the Problem of Metaphysics*, 134.
181. Derrida, *Donner le temps* II, 172. On auto-affection, see also *Voice and Phenomenon*, 59, 67–73.
182. Ibid., 164–65; see Heidegger, *Kant and the Problem of Metaphysics*, 112, 117–18.
183. Ibid., 172, 227. See also Derrida, "Parergon," 40, 100, 115; *Of Grammatology*, 101.
184. Ibid., 165; see Heidegger, *Kant and the Problem of Metaphysics*, 117–18.
185. Kant, *Critique of Pure Reason*, A 51/B76. See also Heidegger, *Kant and the Problem of Metaphysics*, 25.
186. Derrida, *Donner le temps* II, 161.
187. Ibid., 161.
188. Heidegger, *Kant and the Problem of Metaphysics*, 99.
189. Derrida, *Donner le temps* II, 161; Heidegger, *Kant and the Problem of Metaphysics*, 99.
190. Heidegger, *Kant and the Problem of Metaphysics*, 99 (see also 21).
191. Derrida, *Donner le temps* II, 161.
192. Heidegger, *Kant and the Problem of Metaphysics*, 100, 85–94.
193. Derrida, *Donner le temps* II, 162 (see also 124–25, 141–42).
194. Ibid., 88–89, 103–4.
195. Ibid., 36, 57–59, 75–76, 102–3, 118, 209, 211, 216–17, 228.
196. Derrida, *Given Time*, 19, 81, 127–28 n. 12. See also *Theory and Practice*, 195; *Aporias*, 77.
197. Jacques Derrida, *Life Death*, trans. Pascale-Anne Brault and Michael Naas, ed. Pascale-Anne Brault and Peggy Kamuf (Chicago: University of Chicago Press, 2020), 201.
198. Derrida, *Donner le temps* II: 48–49, 78–79, 85–86.
199. Derrida, "Parergon," 110–13, 130–31, 140–43.
200. David Hume, *A Treatise of Human Nature*, ed. David Fate Norton and Mary J. Norton, intro. David Fate Norton (Oxford: Oxford University Press, 2001), 129, 133–34 (1.4.2.16, 29–30).
201. Kant, *Critique of Pure Reason*, A 616–20/B 644–48, A 670–73/B 698–701, A 677–88 / B 705–16; See *Rogues*, 119, 121, 126, 133–34, 168–69 n. 52.
202. See http://derridaseminars.org/seminars.html.
203. Kant, *Critique of Pure Reason*, A 19/B 33, A vii.
204. Ibid., B xvi.
205. Ibid., B xvi.
206. Moral philosophy does not "borrow the least thing" from anthropology, it only "gives" laws *a priori*. Kant, "Groundwork of the Metaphysics of Morals," 45 (AK 4: 389).
207. Derrida, *Donner le temps* II, 159–60.
208. Ibid., 160.
209. Derrida, *Before the Law*, 34; see Kant, "Groundwork of the Metaphysics of Morals," 73 (AK 4: 421).
210. Ibid., 43.
211. Derrida, *The Death Penalty* II, 37.

Reading Fichte

F. Scott Scribner

1   Introduction: A Philosophy of Freedom, or Freedom from Philosophy? François Laruelle's Fichte

Fichte's embrace of philosophy as a first-person creative, experimental exercise is taken up by the twentieth-century French philosopher Francois Laruelle in both spirit and letter. Laruelle's project is not merely unique: it is unique, and indeed rare, among twentieth-century philosophers in its explicit use of Fichte's work.[1] Fichte's project has much to offer contemporary continental philosophy and Laruelle's project is an inspiring example of the continuing creative power and possibility latent in Fichte's work.

In an *ad hominem* flourish, Fichte famously asserts that the *choice* between foundational philosophical first principles, between freedom and dogmatism (idealism and realism), cannot itself, in turn, be justified by philosophy alone; one must already be convinced of the truth of one's freedom before any such philosophical decision.[2] Yet what if the philosophical decision itself, the decision *of* and *for* philosophy itself, is an *ad hominem* choice that, as Laruelle contends, is little more than a narcissistic game? If, as Fichte's suggests, a choice against idealism, and thus freedom, reveals perhaps an unsavory sort of individual or philosopher, Laruelle radicalizes such stakes by suggesting it is not merely the dogmatism of realism that is the problem, but that *all* philosophy is a narcissistic dogmatism. Indeed, it is this very decision *for* philosophy that remains our oldest dogmatic prejudice. The choice between Fichte and Laruelle then, would seem to be a choice between either philosophical freedom or a freedom from philosophy itself.

F. S. Scribner (✉)
University of Hartford, West Hartford, CT, USA
e-mail: scribner@hartford.edu

Offering an analysis of Fichte and Laruelle together is not arbitrary. Fichte stands as perhaps the fundamental architectonic model for Laurelle's project. He explicitly praises Fichte as "one of the most lucid positions, one of the most beautiful solutions to the problem of philosophy" (PNP 140). Of course, for Laruelle, this means Fichte offers a solution to the fact that philosophy itself *is* the problem. And, in his work *The Principles of Non-Philosophy*, Laruelle directly marshals Fichte's first principles as a springboard to this end through an explicit twentieth-century retranslation of Fichtean terms, axioms, and principles.[3]

Working within the legacy of post-Kantian Idealism, Fichte seeks to show the unity of Kantian critiques, the intimacy of epistemology and ethics, knowing and doing. The choice of philosophical first principles then is in part always already a moral decision—a choice for or against freedom. For Laruelle, however, philosophy, as a reflective and narcissistic discipline, is itself the "oldest prejudice" and thus a dogmatic choice from which we must extricate ourselves. Both Fichte and Laruelle then take a stand against dogmatism—even if Laruelle's more global critique is damning of the entire project of philosophy itself.

In what follows, I offer an overview of Laruelle's twentieth-century transformation of Fichte's founding first principles as a way to make clear the continuing value of Fichte's work for contemporary philosophy. Such a reading, however, also offers a critical lens on Laruelle's project by way of the following Fichte-inspired questions: If what grounds the choice of philosophical first principles is a metaphilosophical issue that operates outside the philosophical architectonic, as it does for Fichte, how does this bear on Laruelle's own decision or choice for non-philosophy?[4] In other words, what grounds the choice for Laruelle's own Fichte-inspired first principles of non-philosophy?

2 What Is Non-Philosophy?

Philosophy, as a discipline, remains an unquestioned prejudice. And non-philosophy seeks to put it into question by marking its disciplinary blind spots and contours. Philosophy seeks an outside (a non-philosophy) to complete it (the philosophy of "X") but remains pure and untouched in-itself; its self-mastery depends upon an expropriation of this other that, insofar as it remains pure, is essentially a self-expropriation (PNP 2).

Like a kind of narcissism, philosophy fails to sufficiently put into question its own status; it fails to thematize its own status as merely one kind of (regional) knowledge among others so that, indeed, it is no longer the queen of the sciences, but merely one citizen among many in a "democracy-(of)-thought." In fact, Laruelle seeks a "unified theory of science and philosophy" (PNP 2) and by way of a "non-philosophical translation of philosophies" (PNP 2), he seeks a more expansive "democracy-(of)-thought." Philosophy's prejudice is its original faith in its own authority; its belief in its complete and final say on all things philosophizable. Laruelle names this discredited view the Principle of Sufficient Philosophy. And it is discredited precisely because of philosophy's inability to think the Real. Like Husserl's own attempt to get to the things-themselves by means of bracketing ideological constructions of thought which he names the "natural attitude," so too does Laruelle seek to bracket philosophy, or the philosophical decision—which he defines as philosophy's demand to subsume actual things under a philosophical transcendence—as a way to access the Real.

Non-philosophy as a project, then, is not the negation of philosophy, an antiphilosophy, or a call for the end of philosophy. Rather, non-philosophy opens our eyes to philosophy's own disciplinary constraints, limitations, and prejudices. In fact, non-philosophy's relation to philosophy is best thought as akin to the relation between non-Euclidean and Euclidean geometry. Non-Euclidean geometry does not eradicate Euclidean geometry or make it unnecessary. Instead, by suspending one of its postulates, non-Euclidean geometry offers a completely new perspective on Euclidean geometry, solving some problems that were previously unimaginable and unsolvable.[5]

3 The Philosophy and Non-Philosophy of Fichte

If Fichte's *Wissenschaftslehre* project sought to offer an *a priori* or "pragmatic history of the human spirit" by grounding philosophical reflection, not in abstraction, but through action (*Tathandlung*), Laruelle will reformulate such aspirations for his own work as a "pragmatic theory of philosophy in terms of man as last-instance" (PNP 158).[6] To the extent that, for Fichte, the theoretical and practical are inseparable, his project is fundamentally one of human freedom. By contrast, Laruelle is not concerned with any sort of pragmatic dialectic that charts the development of either the individual or world history. He is not concerned with Kantian or post-Kantian Enlightenment-styled human freedom. In fact, if Kant's Enlightenment ideal sought to liberate us from our own self-imposed immaturity, it might be said that Laruelle seeks the very same—not for us directly, but rather for philosophy itself. We must free ourselves from the immaturity of philosophy. For Laruelle then, "Non-philosophy thus re-opens history by liberating it from its philosophical enclosure" (PNP 158). Philosophy is the problem from which we must be saved. It is important to recognize that the object of non-philosophy is not the world, but philosophy itself. Non-philosophy does not make metaphysical claims about reality; rather, it operates as a critical apparatus working to reveal the obscure mechanisms and unquestioned presuppositions of the discipline of philosophy itself. Philosophy then merely provides the "material" that non-philosophy extracts.

Non-philosophy seeks the syntax or the general structure by which philosophy operates. Laruelle outlines this general structure, which he names "the Philosophical Decision," in terms of a fraction: 2/3. His point is that philosophy typically operates with two "real" terms, like thought and being, that always seek some greater unity in a third term or synthesis. This third term is often a more generalized or "transcendentalized" version of the first two terms.

Non-philosophy aims to create some critical distance on the syntax in play in the general structure of the philosophical decision. In Laruelle's technical vocabulary the first two terms form a unilateral duality within a third term, a determination-in-the-last-instance (DLI). Unilateral duality then describes a duality where each term is only given validity or reality—that is, "determined in the last instance"—through the projected or "hallucinated" third term of the One or Real.[7]

Now the very syntax of non-philosophy was itself developed though the practice of non-philosophy; and it is through the work of Fichte (non-philosophy's work or practice *upon* the philosophy of Fichte) that non-philosophy has developed some of its most important syntax.

4 The Philosophy and Non-Philosophy of the Ego

The Cartesian ego stands as a philosophical guarantor of both truth and existence itself. This split or reflective pleat of the "I think, therefore I am" was continued with Kant to the extent that although the 'I' was present in all representations, it too could only present or grasp itself representationally: it could never appear in-itself as such. Fichte would seize on such difficulties by reformulating Kant's very account of intellectual intuition. For Fichte, intellectual intuition no longer referred to a realm of an illegitimate immediate form of knowing; rather, by aligning the ego with act, Fichte sought to overcome the impossible representational limitations of the Kantian ego's attempt to grasp itself by outlining a pre-cognitive self-awareness in action or doing. The ego is act: a fact-act (*Tathandlung*).

Fichte not only seeks to overcome the limitations of the intellectual register of reflection through act, but, in the *Wissenschaftslehre Nova Methodo*, he traces the dual register of knowing and doing to an original awareness of self-feeling or what one might call auto-affection.[8] This kind of embodied ego that seeks to overcome the dehiscence at the core of self-reflection has a long history that stems from Fichte, through Maine de Biran, to the phenomenologies of Merleau-Ponty and Michel Henry. For example, through a ground-breaking reading of Descartes, Michel Henry seeks to read the transcendental ego in terms of a radical immanence, as an auto-affection which, as I have argued elsewhere, is much in line with Fichte's own non-cognitive affective account of the self-reflective ego as a self-feeling self.[9]

Laurelle's complaint against Descartes, Henry, and Fichte is that despite their auto-affective leanings, "thought remains… co-determinate of the ego" (PNP 97). Thought gives itself to the duality of ego and thought. And Laruelle insightfully asks what for him is the crucial question: "what does this 'giving itself' mean?" (PNP 97). Laruelle recognizes that, for philosophy, giving is kind of thinking so that we are ultimately presented with a 'thinking of thought' or a redoubled cogitation.[10]

The ego itself arises from the ego-thought duality and, as such (although Fichte and Henry offer an auto-affective account), Laruelle asserts that we are, in fact, presented with an ego that is "at once identical and non-identical to thought" (PNP

97). In other words, because the ego itself emerges as an ego-thought duality, the givenness of the ego, is tantamount to thinking (givenness = thinking), is already a thinking redoubled. What Laruelle seeks is a "given-without-givenness," an ego that is not, in turn, followed by an immediate thinking or accompanied by thought. What Laruelle seeks is an ego as "the Real that precedes the disjunction proper to thought" (PNP 100). Laruelle seeks a non-Cartesian account of the ego, a radical immanence of the Real—beyond auto-affective pretenders that remain little more than yet another form of philosophical self-reflective doubling. Laruelle extracts the materials of philosophy for his own purposes, all while abstaining from philosophy as such.[11] He makes this operation clear in regard to the ego.[12] The Cartesian *cogitatio*'s self-reflexive structure operated as a mutually self-supporting and self-generating triad of ego-thought-being; Laruelle's project of non–philosophy seeks a non-reflective Ego, an ego of "first name" only and dissociates it from its relation of thought and being.

Laruelle creates a clear distinction between the Ego and the subject. For him the Ego is a radical immanence, and Ego-in-Ego, a Real that does not refer outside itself. By contrast, he designates the "subject" as a force-of-thought, as "a transcendental clone that follows from the ego" (PNP 111). To better understand these terms and how they function within Laruelle's account of non-philosophy, we need to turn to their source of inspiration in Fichte.

5 From Fichte's I = I to Laruelle's One-in-One (I-in-I)

5.1 Fichte's First Axiom: I = I

The Jena period *Wissenschaftslehre* offers two well-known fundamental principles upon which Fichte establishes his project: I = I and I ≠ Not-I. Fichte asserts "the I posits (*setzen*) itself as an I."[13] This act is a self-positing on the part of the "I," a self-assertion of its own identity, is a foundational immediacy that is meant to precede the act of reflection. In a reworking of the Kantian "I think" that must accompany all representations, here Fichte aspires to offer a pre-reflective unity in which consciousness and self-consciousness emerge simultaneously. Fichte describes this as a fact-act or *Tathandlung*, because the act and product, subject and object are simultaneously co-constituted. This transcendental project, that seeks the genetic "conditions of possibility" of consciousness, grasps this "identity in difference" as an inferred "intellectual intuition." Read: it is a necessary presupposition to explain ordinary consciousness itself.[14]

The *Tathandlung*'s co-constituting dyad, a simultaneous knowing and doing, is an utterly unique account of an emergent "I-hood" that has no need of an underlying substance. As a sheer activity, the "I," as knowing and doing, is an account that is at once theoretical and practical.

5.2 Laurelle's Axiom: One-in-One/I-in-I

Laruelle is clearly drawn to the power of Fichte's first principles account of philosophy. His central complaint seems to be that Fichte's *Tathandlung*, while making serious advances, nevertheless does not go far enough in overcoming, and thereby closing, the "phenomenological distance" between producer and product, subject and object. Fichte's self-emergent, co-constituting "I" contains a gap, a pleat of reflection at its heart, and therefore, for Laruelle, it "does not achieve radical immanence" (PNP 140).

Closing the gap between thought and being through the dynamic of the *Tathandlung* was an advance beyond the representational impasse of the Kantian "I think," that was in turn taken-up by subsequent thinkers of "auto-affection," like the French phenomenologist Michel Henry.[15] Henry's inheritance of the Fichtean language of "Life" and the problem of auto-affection are central formative ripostes for Laruelle. In fact, they are so formative in the advance of his own work, Laruelle takes the time to distinguish them from his own position.[16] Laruelle's general critique of auto-affection is that Henry fantasizes access to a human essence, a kind of thing-in-itself immediacy, without ever exiting the trap of the fundamental dyad of philosophical self-reflection.

For Laruelle, the ego is a radical immanence beyond subject and object, thought and being. He thinks it is a mistake to aspire to immediacy through a creative rendering of the thought/being dyad that he sees as the work of the *Tathandlung* or auto-affection, and he therefore seeks to exit it entirely. Laruelle therefore marks a strong distinction between the ego and the subject. For him the ego is a modality of the Real or the One, which is "foreclosed to thought." The ego "enjoys radical autonomy," while the subject, as a product of thinking—an activity which Laruelle refers to as force-(of)-thought—is a mere clone of the ego and, as such, enjoys only a "relative autonomy" (PNP 107). So, while auto-affection for Laruelle wrongly focuses on the various iterations of the dynamic between subject and object in order to achieve the so-called holy-grail of non-representational "immediacy," his own vocabulary of force-(of)-thought designates the subject's own role in this dynamic and its contingent autonomy that, in the same stroke, simultaneously underscores the radical autonomy of the ego (in distinction from the subject) as a modality of the Real itself.

It is for this reason that Laruelle restates Fichte's first axiom ($I = I$) as "I-in-I." His revision of the Fichtean axiom undercuts the "intuitive" element of this so-called intellectual intuition.[17] Laruelle's complaint centers on the intuitive "givenness" of the $I = I$, a relation of self-relation, whose givenness creates a phenomenological distance that amounts to a kind of transcendence, rather than radical immanence. For Laruelle this dyad of knowing and being, ego and act, can never achieve the radical immanence to which it aspires. It is for this reason that Laruelle reformulates the axiom.[18]

Laruelle's strong distinction between ego and subject allows him to preserve a radical immanence outside of the Fichtean axiom.[19] As such, for Laruelle, Fichte's

I = I is a mere auto-affection that preserves the gap of reflection—even at infinite regress—whereas Laruelle's restatement of Fichte's axiom above, as One-in-One, preserves the radical immanence of the Real.

6 Laruelle's Transformation of Fichte's Second Axiom: The non(-One)

6.1 Fichte's Second Axiom: I ≠ Not-I

If the first principle of I = I describes the I's self-positing as unlimited or absolute, the second principle of I ≠ Not-I underscores the I's simultaneous original limitation. And while this original limitation is self-posited, it is not self-created or constructed but rather "discovered." This strange, ambiguous, and seemingly contradictory status of being both self-posited and discovered can be clarified through an understanding of the distinction between the Not-I and the "check" or *Anstoss*.

Transcendental philosophy's inability to deduce or explain the *Anstoss* (except as a condition of the possibility of consciousness) would seem to give it a status similar to the Kantian thing-in-itself, except that the *Anstoss* is not foreign to "I," but rather a self-limitation. This *Anstoss*, as self-limitation, begins as a physical sensation and becomes ever more intellectualized: it is first encountered as feeling (a self-feeling self) and develops through "sensation," "intuition," and then as "concept." The *Anstoss* can be understood as the process of the "discovery" of self-limitation, which is then, after the fact, formally posited by the self as a Not-I. The self's encounter or discovery of its own finitude through the *Anstoss* is made into an explicit principle with the Not-I. Of course, these two aspects of infinite striving (I = I) and finite limitation (I ≠ Not-I) are but moments of the original and spontaneous dynamic of the productive imagination.

6.2 Laruelle's non(-One)

Fichte's second principle established a limitation. The limiting principle of the Not-I, at the most general level, demonstrates that knowledge is produced through negation. This logical opposition (I = I and I ≠ Not-I) is, for Laruelle, not only more real, but this "resistance" of the Not-I, as a delimiting negation that generates knowledge, is what Laruelle refers to as *the* philosophical "decision," the founding mark of philosophy as such. Laruelle is suggesting that while for Fichte the Not-I is in part a logical consequence or unfolding of the identity of I = I, for Laruelle, the resistance of the non(-One) is less logical than real to the extent it emerges through an analysis of the unthought presuppositions of philosophy itself.

Laruelle's transformation of Fichte's axioms (I = I/I ≠ Not-I) into One-in-One and non(-One), seemingly intensifies both their opposition and their disconnect (non-relation). We now have both radical immanence and transcendence. The One-in-One is a radical immanence, a solipsism of the absolute, foreclosed to thought and philosophy as such: it stands as the Real, beyond the reach of philosophical thought. By contrast, the non(-One) is now an explicit transcendence, a forever failed attempt to grasp the Real, a philosophical projection named variously as "World, Being Logic, etc." (PNP 146). If the One-in-One names the inaccessible Real then, the non(-One) is a schematic stand-in, a formal cipher for the various names of philosophical transcendence. The problem, for Laruelle, is how to span this seemingly impossible chasm.

7 Fichtean Intersubjectivity as Laruelle's (non-)One

Fichte's third principle can be understood to lay the groundwork for his formulation of intersubjectivity within transcendental idealism. This third move goes some distance in uniting the seeming opposition of the first two principles. In it, he sees the simultaneity of identity and difference. And it is at this juncture that Fichte shifts from a more casual discussion of the 'I' and its opposition to a stricter logical notation: by positing the negation of 'A' with its logical notation (~A), he underscores the fact that the 'A' is simultaneously present in some residual form even in its negation. Fichte explains: "Hence [A] is annulled only in part; and in place of the X in A, which is not annulled, we posit ~A, not ~X, but X itself: and thus A = ~A in respect of X" (SK 110). Fichte exhibits a shared identity of seeming opposites. He articulates an identity of divisibility and relation that does not thereby ground itself in the identity of the other. Fichte continues: "From this it is evident how the proposition A = B can be valid …. Hence A = B to the extent that each = X: but A = ~B to the extent each = ~X" (SK, 111). In short, it is by virtue of the shared identity of "X" that is neither 'A' nor 'B' that Fichte can assert A = B. Seeming opposites can share an identity of relation by means of this divisibility beyond an identity of essence.

7.1 Laruelle's (non-)One

For Laruelle, Fichte's third axiom offers him a unique insight into "identity in difference" as a purely relational identity shorn of essentialism. And this is precisely what Laruelle needs if he is to explain both his own project of non-philosophy and how his own account of the One-in-One stands in relation to philosophy, yet remains "uncontaminated" by it. But what then is this relation?

We can best understand his reformulation of this relation through his term the (non-)One. Of course, much of the challenge of Laruelle is in grappling with his difficult neologisms which are easily confused with one another. What then is the difference between the (non-)One and the non(-One)?

As was underscored when describing Laruelle's review and recasting of Fichte's second axiom, philosophy equals negation: it attempts to negate the unknowable, "the One." The non(-One) then designates philosophy's (failed) attempt to subsume and negate the One—as represented through the endless names of philosophical transcendence: Being, Logos, the Good, etc. By contrast, Laurelle's rendering of Fichte's third axiom will allow him, by means of the (non-)One, to articulate the schema of his project of non-philosophy: it offers him a way to contextualize the futility of the bad habit of philosophy, while still preserving the inaccessible Real of the One through what he calls "unilateral duality."

Laruelle is particularly interested in Fichte's third theorem, precisely because he needs a way to explain this "unilateral duality," i.e., the independent paths of, on the one hand, the radical immanence of the One and, on the other hand, philosophical transcendence's failed attempts to articulate it. He needs to explain the relation of non-relation between the radical immanence of the One-in-One and the non(-One), and he does this through a third term he calls the (non-)One.

This (non-)One operates as a clone. Laruelle invokes the notion of the clone to allow the genetic material of the One (as One-in-One) to relate to the philosophical decision and its various forms of transcendence without in turn being contaminated by it. One might also think of it as a kind of twin or stunt-double for that infinitely reclusive actor, the One, which must preserve its radical immanence. The clone, however, is neither merely a copy nor reflection of the One; rather, its identity, essence, and action remain its own. And it is in this way that Laruelle is able to marshal the work of the One, via the clone, without thereby compromising the radical immanence of the actual One that remains always already foreclosed to thought.

8 The Practice and Presupposition of (Non-)Philosophy

While, for Kant, the transcendental *a priori* designated a cognitive condition of possibility, prior to experience, that expressed the very mediated relation between reason and experience, for Laruelle, the *a priori* is relative to each philosophical system. For Laruelle, the *a priori* is like a refractory lens grounded in the hallucinated Real of each philosophical system. In the instance of the hallucinated Real of "Life," it is this term that falsely claims for philosophy—over and above science and all other disciplines—an exclusive and unmediated access to the Real. And it is for this reason that Laruelle associates the *a priori* with "first names" (Being, World, Life), a hallucination that is true in name only.

Take, for instance, the "first name" "Life." In his later period, Fichte regularly invokes the terminology of Life as a stand-in for Being or the (immanent) Absolute. And following Fichte, Michel Henry also makes the notion of Life central to his own radical phenomenology. Laruelle will take issue with Fichte, Henry, and the practice of philosophy itself, for its hallucinations; for claiming an access to an inaccessible Real—whether in the name of Being, the Absolute, or Life.[20] Here then Laruelle's *a priori* has some affinity for Foucault's historically determined notion of "epistemes," to the extent that the first name of "Life," as the purported Real, determines the shape of the constellation of that entire subsequent philosophical discourse.[21]

Laruelle does not practice philosophy, but rather non-philosophy. If philosophy seeks a conceptual model of reality subsumed under an *a priori* lens of a hallucinated Real, the object of non-philosophy is not reality but simply philosophy itself. In place of "Life" and any other hallucinated Real, what Laruelle offers us is simply a "lived-without-life." This self-effacing phrasing seeks to express an immediate Real beyond the limit of any philosophically curated representation.

All philosophy amounts to little more than a hallucinated metaphysical determination that itself must be bracketed in the face of the radical immanence of the Real. Non-philosophy uses the language of philosophy to delineate the structures and contours of the prejudice of philosophical decision; all while refusing decision or choice as such—on non-philosophical grounds or principles. Laruelle writes: "Non-philosophy has no identifiable effect outside of its immanent exercise which is to use philosophy and science to render thought adequate to the *jouissance* of an eternal or immanent 'life'" (PNP 230). The Real stands beyond any philosophical system and emerges in the eternal now of *jouissance*.

9 *Ad Hominem* Decisions

Although non-philosophy seems to take up a kind of meta-philosophical position itself, it's nevertheless worth returning to a line of critical inquiry with which we began: one that asks about the grounds of non-philosophy's own choice of first principles. If you recall, Fichte made much of the fact that while anyone can establish a schema, philosophical or otherwise, it was the choice among first principles, as a meta-philosophical choice, that ultimately grounded itself as a pragmatic, *ad hominem* kind of decision. What are we to make then of Laruelle's own decision for non-philosophy; for his choice of one set of (Fichte-styled) first principles rather than another, in the context of his claim that non-philosophy situates itself beyond the crass determinism of all such decisionality?

For Fichte, idealism, as he conceived it, was a far freer philosophical path than the one offered by the determinative nature of realism. And his choice of first principles sprung directly out of such a view. As we noted at the outset, while the choice for freedom arose for Fichte as a choice between two philosophical systems, the ground for that choice itself was meta-philosophical in nature. Laruelle has indeed directly embraced Fichte's philosophical model for first principles to generate his own account of non-philosophy, but, unlike Fichte's explicit account of this meta-philosophical choice, Laruelle does not explicitly thematize the motivation that grounds *his own* choice of first principles.

Like Fichte's choice for freedom, it would seem that non-philosophy's work to dethrone philosophy as a delusional "queen of the sciences" in favor of a non-philosophical, non-standard science that heralds a more regional knowing and a democracy-of-thought is a pragmatic choice and judgment that also grounds itself in concerns it cannot readily account for by its own first principles. While non-philosophy has worked to extricate itself from the prejudices of philosophy, it will likely have a far more difficult time extricating itself from the prejudice of human interest that drives the eros of inquiry, such that even the choice for first principles in non-philosophy cannot be so easily divorced from Fichte's own *ad hominem* choice for freedom. Indeed, the choice for non-philosophy, it would seem, is not merely a freedom from philosophy, but perhaps then, simultaneously, also a choice for a freedom that brings Laruelle far closer to Fichte than perhaps even he himself is willing to admit.

Notes

1. While twentieth-century continental philosophy has explicitly drawn on the work of Kant and Hegel (for instance), reference to Fichte has been largely indirect, oblique, or entirely absent. Any bibliography of Kant's and Hegel's explicit influence on the twentieth century would be massive and would reference the names of such figures as Bataille, Derrida, Merleau-Ponty, Heidegger, Habermas, Foucault, Lacan, Sartre, and Arendt, among many, many, others; by contrast, while Fichte's indirect influence may well be arguably as large, his direct influence (registered by way of explicit reference to his work) is comparably quite small. Exceedingly small, in fact. Even then, the references tend to be oblique. Among the names that reference Fichte's influence—such as Michel Henry and Axel Honneth, and to a lesser extent Habermas and Heidegger—the name François Laruelle stands out to the degree that Laruelle explicitly makes Fichte central to the founding architectonic of his work.
2. Fichte writes, "The kind of philosophy one chooses depends upon the kind of person one is." (J. G. Fichte, *Sämmtliche Werke*, ed. I. H. Fichte (Berlin: de Gruyter, 1965), 1.434.
3. François Laruelle, *Principles of Non-Philosophy*, trans. Nicola Rubczak and Anthony Paul Smith (London and New York: Bloomsbury, 2013). Hereafter cites as PNP.
4. While one could argue that Fichte's *ad hominem* claim is one that grounds epistemology upon the foundation of ethical considerations, it could equally be understood as a meta-philosophical gesture that grounds philosophical theory in pragmatic (read: non-philosophical) concerns.
5. Anthony Paul Smith, *Francois Laruelle's Principles of Non-Philosophy: A Critical Introduction and Guide.* (Edinburgh: Edinburgh University Press, 2016), 12.
6. "The operation of force 'over' resistance makes non-philosophy, rather than a 'pragmatic history of the human spirit' (Fichte), a pragmatic theory of philosophy in terms of man as last-instance" (PNP 158).
7. Smith, *Laruelle's Principles*, 69.
8. J. G. Fichte, *Foundations of Transcendental Philosophy (Wissenschaftslehre) Nova Methodo (1796/99)*, trans. and Ed. Daniel Breazeale. (Ithaca: Cornell University Press, 1992), 402.
9. F. Scott Scribner, *Matters of Spirit: J. G. Fichte and the Technological Imagination* (University Park, PA.: The Pennsylvania State University Press, 2010), 89–91.
10. It is likely Laruelle offers a productive misreading of Fichte's notion of intellectual intuition. See note 16.

11. John Mullarkey writes of Laruelle, he is "abstaining from philosophy as such while simultaneously taking on its raw material." Quoted in Alexander R. Galloway, *Laruelle: Against the Digital* (Minneapolis and London" University of Minnesota Press, 2014), xxv.
12. He writes: "[O]nce the Ego is thus given without an operation of constitutive givenness, but only givenness as a first name, what happens beyond it for the dyad of thought and being, in which it no longer participates? The general economy of the philosophical triad is shattered as soon as the Ego 'leaves' philosophy...." (PNP 104).
13. J.G. Fichte, *The Science of Knowledge*, trans. and ed. Peter Heath and John Lachs (Cambridge: Cambridge University Press, 1982). Hereafter cited as SK.
14. And while Fichte's account of this original unity of knowing and acting is described as an intellectual intuition, his own—often ambiguous—use of this term can be confusing because he will also use it to describe philosophical reflection's attempt to lay bare the transcendental conditions of ordinary empirical experience.
15. Fichte's efforts to articulate a non-representational ego through an ever-expanding vocabulary of a "self-feeling self," "self-seeing I/eye," and the notion of "life" are all continued attempts to develop the ego as a kind of auto-affection. For more detail see: Scribner, *Fichte*, 98–100; 124–129.
16. "Auto-affection is in one case assumed to be already the very content of the Ego, which is thereby reduced, while on the other the force-(of)-thought infers itself from the ego which determines it."
17. Laruelle's criticism of the intuitive aspect of Fichte's "intellectual intuition" is largely misplaced given that even for Fichte so-called "intellectual intuition" is something inferred, not intuited. This critical difference is likely a productive misreading on Laruelle's part given that without it his entire reading of "givenness" in auto-affection would likely fall apart.
18. Laruelle explains the difference in axioms as follows: "I = I is moreover the synthesis of intuition and object, so an auto-intuition, the circle of an absolute I which is resolved in the circle of the transcendental imagination.... which is to say the auto-position of phenomenological distance. On the other hand, the vision-in-One is not the circle of the auto-given; it is the circle of the auto-position-without-given. As a given-without-givenness...." (PNP 141).
19. Laruelle concedes his own distance from Fichte. He writes, "Fichte would undoubtedly refuse this importance logically and would denounce this interpretation in principle" (PNP 142).
20. Laruelle writes: "The real-One allows us to understand that Life, Affect, the Originary Impression, or the Internal, etc., are the real in-the-last-instance and that, precisely because of this, they are not the Real but only—given their constitution as symbols—the first terms which describe it without determining it" (PNP 221).
21. Smith, *Laruelle's Principles*, 105.

Reading Maimon

Daniela Voss

This chapter deals with the first major works of Salomon Maimon and Gilles Deleuze. Although these works seem worlds apart, they can both be considered post-Kantian insofar as they appear in the tradition of transcendental philosophy. Deleuze takes up Maimon's critique of Kant's philosophy, and both thinkers attempt to establish a new metaphysics founded on difference, or differential ideas, as genetic principle.

The first part of this chapter will give a brief outline of Maimon's critique of Kant and his own proposal for a new metaphysics, which he sketches in his *Essay on Transcendental Philosophy* (1790). The second part will explore Maimon's influence on Deleuze's major early work *Difference and Repetition* (1968). Overall, the chapter aims to recover elements of the Maimonian differential project in Deleuze's transcendental empiricism and examine what connects and separates Maimon's version from that of Deleuze. In both cases it is the "unthought in thought"[1] that poses a problem, but must be thought nonetheless.

1 Maimon's *Essay on Transcendental Philosophy*

Maimon's *Essay on Transcendental Philosophy* (1790) is written as a commentary on Kant's first *Critique*, interspersed with sharp criticisms and sketches of Maimon's own proposed solution to the problems it brings out. It is composed "in the style of a medieval Hebrew philosophical commentary"[2] and thus deviates deliberately from the clearly structured, systematic treatise that is Kant's *Critique*. Maimon's

D. Voss (✉)
University of Hildesheim, Hildesheim, Germany
e-mail: vossda@uni-hildesheim.de

© The Author(s), under exclusive license to Springer Nature Switzerland AG 2023
T. Rajan, D. Whistler (eds.), *The Palgrave Handbook of German Idealism and Poststructuralism*, Palgrave Handbooks in German Idealism,
https://doi.org/10.1007/978-3-031-27345-2_3

contemporaries within the German philosophical scene of the Enlightenment found it challenging to read; it seemed erratic or idiosyncratic at best, though it was perhaps just "culturally foreign."[3] In part this is due to the fact that the *Essay on Transcendental Philosophy* reveals an author split between two intellectual cultures, "that of medieval Aristotelian Jewish philosophy and that of modern European philosophy."[4] Maimon himself describes his *Essay* as "a coalition system"[5] of the philosophies of Kant, Spinoza, Leibniz and Hume, omitting for unknown reasons the influence of the medieval Spanish philosopher Maimonides, whose name Maimon adopted out of veneration.[6] Recent Maimon scholarship has highlighted the importance of the medieval philosophical and mystical traditions, not only as conceptual resources for Maimon's transcendental theory but as aids in understanding his lifelong struggle for philosophical truth.[7] Certain theoretical terms such as *devequt* (union with the divine) or *shelemut hanefesh* (perfection of the soul)[8] express vital motives for Maimon's philosophical endeavors.

The *Essay* resulted from Maimon's notes on the *Critique of Pure Reason*, which he most likely began reading during his fourth stay in Berlin around 1789. In the preface, he explicitly states that the aim of his work was

> to bring out *the most important truths* of this science [i.e., transcendental philosophy, DV]. And I am following in the footsteps of the aforementioned sharp-witted philosopher [i.e., Immanuel Kant, DV]; but (as the unbiased reader will remark) I am not copying him. I try, as much as it is in my power, to explain him, although from time to time I also make some comments on him. [...] To what extent I am a Kantian, an anti-Kantian, both at the same time, or neither of the two, I leave to the judgement of the thoughtful reader.[9]

On reading the first chapters of Maimon's manuscript, sent to him by his former student Markus Herz, Kant himself understood at once that "this work [...] is in fact for the most part directed *against me*."[10] But he nevertheless held that "none of my opponents has understood me and the principal question as well as Mr Maimon," and felt "that only a few people possess such an acute mind for such profound investigations."[11] Although Kant refused to write a commendation to preface the *Essay*, his favorable remarks facilitated the publication of the work and helped promote the reputation of its author. However, Maimon's influence remained rather limited in his day, not least because Jews were banned from holding public teaching positions.

Nonetheless, his philosophical writings had a profound impact on German Idealism. Frederick Beiser claims that "to study Fichte, Schelling, or Hegel without having read Maimon's *Versuch* is like studying Kant without having read Hume's *Treatise*. Just as Kant was awakened by Hume's skepticism, so Fichte, Schelling, and Hegel were challenged by Maimon's skepticism."[12] The German Idealists followed Maimon in criticizing the multiple, interconnected dualisms in Kant's critical philosophy: sensibility and understanding as fundamental sources of the mind, the distinction between noumenon and phenomenon, the gap between theoretical and practical philosophy, the split between the empirical and the intelligible world. They sought instead to reestablish an original unity that had to arise genetically from an inner principle, and in this the idea of an intuitive intellect served them as a reference point. Yet few acknowledged the influence Maimon had on their work, with the exception of Fichte, who remarked in a letter to Reinhold:

My respect for Maimon's talents knows no bounds. I firmly believe that he has completely overturned the entire Kantian philosophy as it has been understood by everyone until now, including you, *and I am prepared to prove it*. No one noticed what he had done; they looked down at him from their heights. I believe that future centuries will mock us bitterly.[13]

In the twentieth century Deleuze can be credited with belatedly arousing a revival of interest in Maimon's *Essay*, although he is himself a rather unfaithful or selective reader of Maimon. As we will see later, Deleuze borrows a number of ideas from Maimon but never directly addresses his work at any length, and the concept of the differential perhaps serves above all to illustrate the way that, according to Deleuze, concepts "have their own way of not dying while remaining subject to constraints of renewal, replacement, and mutation."[14] It is this renewal of concepts, and not any purported continuity, that gives philosophy a history: "the history of philosophy is completely without interest if it does not undertake to awaken a dormant concept and to play it again on a new stage, even if this comes at the price of turning it against itself."[15]

1.1 *The Questions 'Quid Facti?' and 'Quid Juris?'*

Maimon's critique of Kant can be encapsulated in the two questions 'quid facti?' and 'quid juris?' The first question concerns the fact of objective experience. Maimon doubts that there is objective experience in the Kantian sense of a lawful connection between representations. His main argument is that we lack an *a priori criterion* by which we can distinguish the cases in which *a priori* concepts apply from those in which they do not.[16] Maimon summarizes the difficulty with respect to the *a priori* concept of causality in the seventh letter of his book *Briefe des Philaletes an Aenesidemus* ("Letters from Philaletes to Aenesidemus") as follows:

> But how can I, from the principle "everything that happens, happens according to the laws of causality," derive the proposition, determined through given objects, that the sun necessarily melts the ice? From the principle follows only that *objects of experience in general* must be thought in causal connection with each other, but not at all that *these very objects* must be those that stand in this relationship.[17]

In other words, Maimon maintains, in company with Hume, that it is impossible to detect a causal sequence in experience. More generally, we have no grounds to make factual claims about the actuality of experience subsumed under categories.

In these respects, Maimon sides with empirical skepticism.[18] Yet this line of attack is perhaps the less successful one, because Kant's transcendental deduction in the *Critique*—contrary to the *Prolegomena*—is not based on the existence of synthetic *a priori* facts of experience. The explanation of how empirical intuitions can be subsumed under pure concepts must operate independently of experience, in order to satisfy the question 'quid juris?' which for Kant is a question of entitlement in the juridical sense. Kant wants to prove the *lawfulness* of the subsumption of empirical intuition under pure concepts, through the mediating function of the transcendental schema, i.e., pure intuition, which is both at the same time intellectual (pure form) and sensible (pure intuition).[19]

Maimon's second line of attack addresses precisely this question of justification (*quid juris?*). Kant's proposal of the transcendental schema as a mediating third term does not satisfy him, since for Maimon the problem of subsumption does not so much concern the lawfulness as the *intelligibility* of the relation between *a priori* concepts and something given to the understanding, something that is completely heterogeneous by nature. He asks, "how is it comprehensible? (*Quid juris?* for me means the same as *quid rationis?* Because what is justified [*rechtmäßig*] is what is legitimate [*gesetzmäßig*], and with respect to thought, something is justified if it conforms to the laws of thought or reason.)"[20] The slight shift in meaning between *quid juris?* and *quid rationis?* is crucial because, for Maimon, legitimate thought is purely rational: all it does is think pure relations, thereby *generating* its objects. For Maimon, nothing should ultimately be *given* to the understanding. He contests the Kantian definition of a discursive understanding, which requires that something be given to thought. His own conception of the understanding draws from Aristotle's notion of an active intellect and interpretations of it by medieval Jewish philosophers, such as Maimonides, who propound an originally productive intellect that produces objects by thinking relations.

The direction in which Maimon takes his own answer to the question *quid juris?* will thus involve:

(1) the metaphysical idea of an infinite understanding that "could produce objects out of itself according to its self-prescribed rules or conditions without needing to be given something from elsewhere."[21] Maimon revives rationalist assumptions that can be found in the systems of Wolff and Leibniz, where concepts and intuitions "both flow from one and the same cognitive source,"[22] and not, as Kant insisted, from two totally different sources of knowledge, sensibility and understanding. Maimon will claim that "our understanding is just the same [as the infinite understanding], only in a limited way."[23]

(2) The clue to his proposed solution is the concept of the *differential*, which has to explain the fact of something being given to thought (as if) 'from outside.' "As a result, the understanding does not subject something given *a posteriori* to its *a priori* rules; rather it lets it arise [*läßt entstehen*] in accordance with these rules (which I believe is the only way to answer the question *quid juris?* in a wholly satisfactory way)."[24]

1.2 The Notion of Differentials

Leibniz's differential calculus was the inspiration for Maimon's concept of differentials. In those early days of the calculus, at that time still largely based on geometrical intuition, differentials were considered infinitely small elements, or infinitesimals, of a geometrical magnitude that result from the magnitude being continuously reduced in size. The magnitude of differentials is smaller than any given magnitude but not equivalent to zero. Maimon, however, gives a slightly different interpretation: instead of saying that differentials are magnitudes smaller than all positive numbers, he maintains that differentials can be given any number, "as small or as large as we want (as long as it has some magnitude)."[25] "The differential of a magnitude does not signify the state where the magnitude ceases to be what it is, but each state that it can reach, without distinction, i.e. a determinable but undetermined state."[26] That is to say, differentials are undetermined but determinable elements; they can, however, produce a determinate object through reciprocal relation.

This relation is characterized by Maimon as a "universal functional relation"[27] that can vary and is thus distinguished from invariable numerical relations, for instance the relationship between two integers.

> To explain this, consider a triangle; now move one side in relation to the opposite angle so that it always remains parallel to itself; do this until the triangle becomes an infinitely small [triangle] (a differential). The extensive magnitude of the sides then completely disappears and is reduced to their differentials; but the relation of the sides always remains the same.[28]

In other words, the relation of the sides remains constant, independent of the quantitative value of the sides. Even if the size of the sides is smaller than any measurable quantity, the relation between them holds and is determined through position. In this sense, the ratio of differentials conforms to an intellectual law for the generation of continuous geometrical magnitudes. When Maimon holds that the understanding thinks objects only as *flowing*,[29] he means that the understanding can think them only through their rule of production; it thinks a triangle by means of the relation between two of its sides, while the magnitude of the sides remains undetermined.[30] By thinking differentials in reciprocal relation, the understanding can determine objects, which means that it can posit or *produce* objects. For Maimon, mathematics thus serves as an example illustrating that "thinking does not merely mean to have representations of objects, whereby the subject comports itself only passively, but to determine relations among the objects by the spontaneity of the power of thinking."[31] We thus have a conception of an infinite productive intellect, since we participate in such thinking through mathematics. "In this, we are similar to God."[32]

In the early days of infinitesimal analysis, it was common to think of differentials as a basis for the generation of extensive magnitudes. This was apparent in Newton's method of fluxions, whereby he sought to determine quantities ("fluents" as he called them) from the velocities of their increments, by which they would be generated. As Newton declares in his *Tractatus de Quadratura Curvarum* (1704), "I don't here consider Mathematical Quantities as composed of Parts *extreamly small*, but as *generated by a continual motion*."[33] Leibniz and a number of German philosophers (such as Wolff and Mendelssohn) also thought of the differential method in terms of the idea of continuity.[34] Differentials were considered *intensive magnitudes* as opposed to extensive magnitudes, the latter being divisible into parts and thus subject to the law of exteriority (*partes extra partes*).[35] Intensive magnitudes were conceived of in terms of "tendency" or "becoming," or as Maimon says, variable indeterminate magnitudes: "the infinitely small does not so much fail to be a quantum at all as it fails to be a determined quantum."[36] "[T]hat they are magnitudes at all is therefore certain since they do in fact entertain a universal functional relation to one another."[37]

Maimon's distinctive move away from the early mathematical concept of the differential to a clearly metaphysical concept comes when he defines intensive magnitudes as *qualities*, abstracted from all quantity:

> The metaphysically infinitely small is real because quality can certainly be considered in itself abstracted from all quantity. This way of considering it is also useful for resolving the question, *quid juris?* because the pure concepts of the understanding or categories are never directly related to intuitions, but only to their elements, and these are ideas of reason concerning the way these intuitions arise.[38]

Maimon is not always consistent in the terms he uses for differentials: in this passage he calls them *ideas of reason*, perhaps because this notion will appeal to the critical idealist who understands ideas of reason as problematic concepts that have no object in intuition. At other times, when he is more open about his 'rational dogmatism,' Maimon with greater aptness calls them *ideas of understanding* because they are the rules (i.e., a function-relation between differentials) by which particular objects arise.[39] Last but not least, he also treats differentials as qualities, or elements of sensual qualities, and as such as conditions for the real or sensual matter in the representation of objects of experience. This ambiguity in the notion of the differential will be discussed later; for now, we will look at his definition of intensive magnitudes as *qualities* devoid of all quantity. As qualities they can still be thought in relation to quantity and are therefore also designated as "the quality of the quantum."[40]

Maimon takes inspiration from Kant in this, who discusses the notion of intensive magnitude in the section called 'Anticipations of Perception' (in Book II on the Analytic of Principles of the *Critique of Pure Reason*). There Kant states that what anticipates every perception is that in all appearances *the real*, namely the sensation (as the matter of perception), has intensive magnitude ("but not an extensive one"[41]). "Every color, e.g., red, has a degree, which, however small it may be, is never the smallest, and it is the same with warmth, with the moment of gravity, etc."[42] The manifold of sensation given in any conscious perception is not a sum proceeding from parts that could be added one to another (shades of color do not consist of parts; a given temperature is not the result of adding up degrees of heat; a given velocity is not an aggregate of moments of velocity). Although the manifold of sensations somehow "fills" time and space, it can only be distinguished in terms of degrees of difference, where the difference ranges between zero, i.e., the complete negation of sensation that equals formal consciousness, and the given one that corresponds to empirical consciousness of the object. The real in each appearance, according to Kant, has its degree that can decrease to nothing (emptiness) in a gradual transition. Intensive magnitude is thus a continuous and flowing magnitude, which somehow fills extensive magnitude to a smaller or greater degree.[43] Sensibility apprehends intensive magnitude as a unity in an instant; it does not require a successive synthesis, since there are no parts.

Like Kant, Maimon thinks that intensive magnitudes can be considered abstracted from all quantity and varying in terms of degree. Thus "the colour red must be thought without any finite extension, although not as a mathematical but rather as a physical point, or as the differential of an extension."[44] But he goes beyond Kant in saying that "it must further be thought without any finite degree of quality, but still as the differential of a finite degree."[45] Here Maimon introduces the notion of the infinite, because he considers differentials the infinitesimal elements of sensation; only as such can they function as genetic elements that give rise to the real in perception. Intensive magnitudes are "differentials of sensation," while conscious perception is the integral of differentials. In other words, empirical consciousness is produced by the reciprocal relations of differentials of sensation. A patch of color is thus not a simple element, an atom of perception, but a manifold of differentials: a unity that envelops an inner plurality that is qualitative in nature and freed of its quantitative aspect.

However, in consciously perceiving qualities we are not aware of the differential manifold they conceal and we are certainly not conscious of the process of generation based on differentials. We are equally not aware of the sub-representative generative operation through which space and time as continuous quantities arise. Our awareness of a thing is only "the reproduction of a part of a synthesis in relation to this synthesis."[46] If we try to approach the simple elements of perception, we approach in fact the differentials of sensation, but can never reach them in intuition. Yet we must presuppose their existence: they are not representations in consciousness but "presentations" to a primitive consciousness.[47] This primitive consciousness of differentials is a mere idea, a limit concept of synthesis. In the opposite direction, the mind tends towards the consciousness of a complete synthesis, which grasps the infinite in itself, the complete determination of the relational manifold of differentials.[48] The consciousness of a complete synthesis is equally a limit concept that can never be presented in intuition; and so, for Maimon, "we start in the middle with our cognition of things and finish in the middle again."[49]

We can thus say that the synthesis of conscious perception that the mind performs is only partial: it pertains to the "'subjective order' (with respect to our consciousness) of all the operations of the mind."[50] The "objective order considered in itself" starts from the differentials of sensible intuition, which furnish the matter for an object in general and are arranged in accordance with the pure concepts of the understanding. Importantly, Maimon makes no distinction here between the infinitesimals of sensible intuition and intellectual ideas: "Ideas of understanding, *that is to say* the infinitely small of every sensible intuition and of its forms, which provide the matter to explain the way that objects arise."[51] Thanks to this equation, Maimon can conclude that "for the understanding and for reason there is neither sensibility nor intuition ... but only ideas and concepts."[52] The understanding as activity applies its pure concepts or categories to the *ideas* of the understanding, which are in turn not intuitions but laws according to which intuitions are generated. Hence the problem *quid juris?* no longer arises, as ideas of the understanding are not something completely other given 'from outside,' but immanent to the understanding.

> Just as in higher mathematics we produce the relations of different magnitudes themselves from their differentials, so the understanding (admittedly in an obscure way) produces the real relations of qualities themselves from the real relations of their differentials. So if we judge that fire melts wax, then this judgement does not relate to fire and wax as objects of intuition, but to their elements, which the understanding thinks in the relation of cause and effect to one another.[53]

The relations of things are thus grounded in the real relations of their differentials, which the understanding thinks as different. In other words, the finite extensions or degrees of different empirical representations are "different for different representations according to the difference of their differentials."[54]

Now, what the faculty of imagination perceives as the difference between things, their being outside one another, or the succession of representations in a sequence of time, has just an "ideal ground"[55] in the imagination. The objective or real ground of the differences between objects can only be determined with respect to their differentials. For instance, two colors red and green are not different because of the sensible qualities that are represented in intuition. In fact, the understanding is incapable of distinguishing given sensible qualities.

> [I]f I say that *red* is different from *green*, then the pure concept of the understanding of the difference is not treated as a relation between the sensible qualities (for then the Kantian question *quid juris?* remains unanswered), but rather either (according to the Kantian theory) as the relation of their spaces as *a priori* forms, or (according to my theory) as the relation of their differentials.[56]

Maimon admits that with regard to the introduction of the mathematical concept of the differential "it might appear as if I wanted to explain something obscure through something yet more obscure."[57] He was certainly aware that even among mathematicians the concept of the infinitely small was considered inconsistent or at least controversial, and philosophers like Berkeley[58] and Kant[59] rejected the notion. In his defense, Maimon argues that the concept of a differential was originally a philosophical concept, since "the great Leibniz came upon the discovery of the differential calculus through his system of the Monadology."[60] The truth of this claim concerning the historical sequence of events is debatable.[61] Maimon's main argument, however, is that differentials are nothing but ideas: "in mathematics as much as in philosophy they are mere ideas that do not represent objects but only the way objects arise, i.e. they are mere limit concepts [*Gränzbegriffe*], which we can approach nearer and nearer to, but never reach. They arise through a continuous regress or through the diminution to infinity of the consciousness of an intuition."[62]

However, Maimon does not succeed in eliminating the ambiguity of the concept of differentials: it is finally unclear whether he conceives them in terms of a regulative idea, that is, a fiction or creation of the mind for the sole methodological purpose of grounding synthetic *a priori* propositions of science, or whether he argues for their existence as real, metaphysical elements within an infinite understanding. Maimon oscillates between these views, often using equivocal phrases such as: "the object of applied thought is ... the *ens reale* or what I call an idea of the understanding, the element of a particular intuition;"[63] "we assume an infinite understanding (at least as idea)."[64] This ambivalence around the status of the infinite intellect and differentials has led to an animated debate in Maimon scholarship.[65]

Without proposing a definitive answer here, let us pursue the further question of whether the notion of differentials as the principle of sufficient reason is consistent in itself. How can differentials be at one and the same time intelligible ideas of the understanding and qualitative elements of a particular intuition? Is this not the return of the Kantian problem concerning the gap between concept and intuition, only this time reappearing at the level of infinite thought? To avoid the resurgence of this problem, Maimon is perhaps compelled to attempt to have it both ways; the differential "is a limit concept between pure thought and intuition by means of which the two are legitimately bound together."[66] According to Paul Franks, differentials have to be "treated *both* as ideas of sensible quality as such *and* as infinitesimal, intelligible quantities. In other words, an identity-in-difference must be assumed between the *qualities* of finite passivity and the infinitesimal *quantities* of infinite intellectual activity."[67] Whether the hyphens in this notion of 'identity-in-difference' suffice to explain the combination of two heterogeneous aspects in one unity is not obvious.

Martial Gueroult, in turn, first of all commends the notion of the differential as the emergence of a new conception of difference that would no longer be defined as limitation or lack of identity, i.e., a secondary and derived concept, but as a "superior principle,"[68] an originary principle of the Other or of the real, which occupies the same level as a principle of identity or unity of form. This superior principle is one of *intrinsic difference*, which places intuition and concept on a continuum and opens the way to an immanent philosophy. By contrast, Kant's dualism between concept and intuition is based on the conception of an *extrinsic difference* that implies the operation of an external conditioning, the idea of a preestablished harmony or teleology. In the *Critique of the Power of Judgment* Kant must take recourse to an intuitive divine intellect or *intellectus archetypus* as a methodological device, an idea of reason that allows us to think reality *as if* it conforms to rational thought.[69] Maimon and Kant thus both referred to the infinite (or intuitive) intellect as a means to address the same problem, but "Kant preferred the exoteric aspect, pre-established harmony and teleology, and Maimon the esoteric aspect, minute perceptions and differential algorithm."[70] Gueroult maintains that Maimon's response is more satisfactory than that of Kant because it succeeds in explaining the relation of form and matter and the production of the real through a process of differentiation.

However, Gueroult contends that there remains "an occult quality"[71] in pure thought that cannot be completely dissolved. There is "a minimum of the given"[72] within the infinite understanding, without which pure thought would be empty. Although it is not very easy to determine just what constitutes this minimum, in Gueroult's view, he does refer in one place to this indigestible kernel as the "rule of production" itself,[73] meaning the actual determination of quantities that would correspond to cases of differential production—in other words, the reciprocal relations between differentials determining this or that object. These determinations cannot simply be thought by the infinite understanding and must be considered as given, as coming from 'outside'; and so, for the understanding, there is "something intrinsically unthinkable that must be thought by it."[74]

Deleuze in turn takes up the discussion from Gueroult's viewpoint but, going somewhat further, actively affirms the possibility that "thought should find within itself something which it cannot think, something which is both unthinkable and that which must be thought."[75] Brushing off "an objection often made against Maimon"[76] without citing Gueroult's work, Deleuze indeed takes the indispensable minimum of givenness in the direction of a direct encounter in sensation—thus speaking in the same way of that which cannot be sensed, and which lights the fuse that makes the faculties enter a 'discordant' synthesis. The notion of differentials will now designate "the unconscious of a pure thought"[77] that is impossible without an initial inception in sensation; differential Ideas will be encountered by a split subject and, by posing a problem to thought, force it to think.[78] Needless to say, Deleuze's intention in these passages is not to explicate Maimon or to render him consistent.[79] Instead of trying to reconstruct a Deleuzian reading of Maimon from his fragmentary and scattered remarks, the next sections will present some major features of Deleuze's own system in *Difference and Repetition* that connect with Maimon's lines of thought and extend their limits around the unthinkable kernel identified by Guéroult.

2 Deleuze's Transcendental Empiricism

Deleuze consistently presents Maimon as a philosopher who undertakes a fundamental reformulation of Kant's *Critique* in the light of a Leibnizian interpretation of differential calculus.[80] He applauds Maimon primarily for overcoming the Kantian duality between *a priori* conceptual conditions and given intuition, for renouncing the inadequate viewpoint of conditioning,[81] and agrees with him that Kant neglected the demands of a genetic explanation of how the given arises in thought: Kant's *a priori* conditions only account for the possibility of experience, not for real experience.[82] Maimon and Deleuze both find in differential relations a principle of production, or sufficient reason, that explains the way real experience arises, and it is this metaphysical interpretation of differential calculus that lies at the core of their respective projects in philosophy. But it is also at this point that Deleuze and Maimon most obviously part ways: although Maimon raises difference to the principle of the production of the real, he retains a number of rationalist doctrines, such as the priority of the concept of identity, the principle of sufficient reason, the assumption of an infinite understanding, and the ideal of apodictic knowledge. For Deleuze, "[t]he intense world of differences, in which we find the reason behind qualities and the being of the sensible, is precisely the object of a superior empiricism."[83] Deleuze's philosophy claims to be an empiricism, although a transcendental one: he seeks the transcendental conditions of real experience (not of possible experience, as in Kant) in the form of the transcendental difference through which given sensual diversity arises: "Difference is not diversity. Diversity is given, but difference is that by which the given is given."[84]

The following subsection will clarify the goal of Deleuze's metaphysical project in relation to that of Maimon. A major difference between Maimon's rational idealism and Deleuze's transcendental empiricism becomes apparent with Deleuze's introduction of the notion of time. Differential ideas are not conceived as laws given in the eternity of an infinite understanding but unconscious Ideas that appear to a split subject, fractured by the line of time, a fracture that introduces the unthinkable into thought (as that which must be thought). The unavowable 'remainder' of Maimon's system thus becomes—via the crucial mediating link of Gueroult's interpretation—the affirmed 'excess' in Deleuze's. This major inversion is reflected in the conflicting positions of transcendental difference in their respective work: for Deleuze, difference is originary, there is nothing 'behind' difference, nor encompassing it, whereas for Maimon difference remains immanent to the higher unifying identity of an infinite understanding. Hence the second and last subsection will present the nature of sufficient reason in Deleuze, which is not to be conceived as the unity of understanding but is 'strangely bent'—a 'groundless ground' consisting of an intensive field expressing differential Ideas considered as problematic and virtual structures.

2.1 *The Importance of the Notion of Time and the Split Subject*

Both Maimon and Deleuze criticize Kant for relying on facts of experience and accepting finite, empirical consciousness as the bearer of apodictic knowledge. They do so, however, for different reasons. Deleuze wants to replace the conception of progress from hypothetical to apodictic knowledge with a movement of thought that is triggered in the encounter with problems; it is the ideal of apodictic knowledge and the concept of method, guided by the natural light of reason, that he questions. Maimon, on the contrary, maintains that the truth-seeking mind cannot be content with the spatio-temporal representations of empirical consciousness. These representations are only creations of the faculty of imagination, which have to be dissolved into thinkable relations. The ideal of knowledge would imply discovering the 'real ground' of phenomena in their determinable relations, the differential forms of production. At the extreme limit this would entail a union with the divine intellect, which would be the ultimate perfection of the human mind.

Although, as Maimon admits, we can never reach this limit, we *can* approach it ever more closely, and the (moral) demand of reason would precisely consist in this striving for perfection. Here Maimon touches on the problematic kernel that was highlighted above:

> Reason demands that the 'given' in the object should not be considered as something final and irreducible, but merely as the result of the limitation of our faculty of thought.

> In relation to a higher, infinite reason, the 'given' would disappear and be reduced to logical relations. Reason thus demands an infinite progress by which the rationalization of the object is constantly being increased and the 'given' decreased to an infinitely small degree. ... And *we must* constantly and increasingly try to approach the idea of an infinite reason.[85]

The pure differential relations that must be thought are entirely rational, contained within the higher unity of an infinite understanding or infinite reason (Maimon does not always distinguish accurately between the intellectual faculties of thought). From Deleuze's point of view, Maimon's rationalist dogmatism is unacceptable here. Although he introduces difference as a principle of the production of the real and the notion of infinity as a presupposition for finite consciousness, Maimon retains the principle of identity and attempts to ground the manifold of differential relations in the unifying totality of an infinite understanding. The criticism that Deleuze directs against 'infinite representation' in Leibniz and Hegel can equally be applied to Maimon: "While this foundation is not the identical itself, it is nevertheless a way of taking the principle of identity particularly seriously, giving it an infinite value and rendering it coextensive with the whole, and in this manner allowing it to reign over existence itself."[86] Deleuze is also critical of the role of the interests of reason: as long as these natural interests are presupposed, one is ultimately respectful toward knowledge and morality.[87] Indeed, the moral imperative in Maimon's notion of perfection is hard to miss, and its source is no doubt a residue of what Deleuze calls the dogmatic image of thought, a complacency surrounding the claim of rationality, which lays out in advance a natural path for thought to attain truth. This is a clear sign, for Deleuze, that Maimon's critique of Kant has not gone all the way.

These differences aside, Deleuze and Maimon agree in their critique of Kant for tracing the transcendental conditions of experience from the empirical acts of a psychological consciousness: apprehension of a sensual manifold, reproduction of images and recognition of facts.[88] Such a psychic automatism of thought cannot account for what is truly at stake in the activity of thinking. According to Maimon, thought would have to follow the vanishing trail of differences back to their unity with God; for Deleuze, we must never allow the minimum of givenness to be recuperated in identity or totality, but rather confront it in the form of a genuine alterity in thought. The author of the thought thus generated is not the Kantian 'I think.' An Other thinks within me—as Rimbaud says: "Je est un autre."[89] The thinking subject is always a fractured 'I' that can think only on the basis of an unconscious that cannot but be an affliction for consciousness: differentials of thought are the *cogitanda* of pure thought, "at once that which cannot be thought and that which must be thought and can be thought only from the point of view of the transcendent exercise" of the faculties.[90] That is, in order to think this unthinkable, the faculties of the mind must touch upon the limit of their 'comprehension,' forced into a transcendent (or fundamentally creative) exercise, in a "deregulation of *all the senses*."[91] In short, thought is not a faculty that we naturally possess and that leads to truth and knowledge if only we follow the correct method. To arouse thought from its natural stupor it must be confronted with problems, must be forced to think, and what this does is something 'in' the given (that irreducible minimum of otherness by which the given is given).

Here the separation from Maimon is that between a philosophy of the eternal and a philosophy of time. To reach what is at stake in the activity of thinking, we must not refer back to the oneness and identity of God or a unique and identical self. Differential ideas are not laws given in the eternity of an infinite understanding but unconscious Ideas that intrude into the thought of a split subject. Deleuze calls attention to "a precise moment within Kantianism, a furtive and explosive moment which is not even continued by Kant, much less by post-Kantianism":[92] the moment when Kant "introduced a kind of disequilibrium, a fissure or crack in the pure Self of the 'I think'…: the subject can henceforth represent its own spontaneity only as that of an Other."[93] This crack that traverses the subject is the pure and empty form of time, which forces the active thinking subject to represent itself as a passive subject that undergoes all of its modifications in a temporal order of succession. As Deleuze remarks in his seminar on Kant from March 28, 1978, "Time has become the limit of thought and thought never ceases to have to deal with its own limit. Thought is limited from the inside."[94] In this special sense the fracture of time confronts thought with *an outside*; it is because we are temporal beings that we can be affected by Ideas or problems: "Ideas are exactly the thoughts of the Cogito, the differentials of thought. Moreover, in so far as the Cogito refers to a fractured I, an I split from end to end by the form of time which runs through it, it must be said that Ideas swarm in the fracture, …. It is not, therefore, a question of filling that which cannot be filled."[95]

2.2 *A Sufficient Reason Strangely Bent*

Up to this point, the emphasis on the 'unthinkable in thought' may seem to license thinking anything at all. What is at issue in the encounter with the unthinkable, however, is precisely a *constraint*—the materially contingent but logically necessary structuring of problems that are posed in sensation or in signs. Thus, Deleuze himself requires a kind of sufficient reason in order to ground this world of signs and forced movements of thought no less than the classical rationalists, if in a rather different sense. The question of grounding will not be a theoretical but a *vital* question, insofar as "it affects the powers of the thinker."[96]

In seeking a principle of sufficient reason, Deleuze, like Maimon, turns to differential Ideas, which he characterizes as "ideal 'objecticities',"[97] not mere creations of the mind. Deleuze defines Ideas as consisting of differential relations between genetic elements; furthermore, "[t]here is neither identification nor confusion within the Idea, but rather an internal problematic objective unity of the undetermined, the determinable and determination."[98]

> Three principles which together form a sufficient reason correspond to these three aspects: a principle of determinability corresponds to the undetermined as such (dx, dy); a principle of reciprocal determination corresponds to the really determinable (dy/dx); a principle of

complete determination corresponds to the effectively determined (values of dy/dx). In short, dx is the Idea—the Platonic, Leibnizian or Kantian Idea, the 'problem' and its being.[99]

Deleuze cites here those philosophers well known for developing, each in their own way, the concept of the Idea, while Maimon remains in the background. Kant plays an important role, no doubt, because he highlights explicitly the *problematic* character of ideas. According to Kant, ideas "are not arbitrarily invented, but given as problems by the nature of reason itself."[100] Reason always seeks an absolutely unconditioned ground or, in other words, the absolute totality of conditions for a given conditioned thing; this is how ideas of reason are born. However, their claim to absolute validity makes it impossible to find for them a congruent object in intuition, hence an idea of reason is "a problem without any solution."[101] For Deleuze too, Ideas are inseparable from problems: any genetic process starts from a problem and its internal problem-conditions. Kant simply failed to elaborate further this intrinsic genetic power of problematic Ideas: "Problems are the differential elements in thought, the genetic elements in the true. We can therefore substitute for the simple point of view of conditioning a point of view of effective genesis."[102]

While Maimon and Deleuze agree that the principle of sufficient reason must be genetic, the latter's conception diverges considerably. For Deleuze, sufficient reason is an immanent, tripartite system consisting of spatio-temporal dynamisms that express virtual and differential Ideas, which cannot be separated from their empirical actualization. The term 'virtual' is taken from Bergson and used to distinguish purely relational from actual multiplicities. In Bergson's sense, virtual multiplicities cannot be divided into parts but nevertheless envelop an inner plurality.[103] By contrast, actual multiplicities are identifiable, numerical: sets of finite, extended, denumerable things. The virtual, for Deleuze as it was for Bergson, is inseparable from actualization, a movement from virtual to actual proceeding by differentiation;[104] but in Deleuze this movement is mediated by a third element, *intensive quantity*, or more precisely, intensive spatio-temporal dynamisms. The virtual Idea itself is an impassive differential structure that relies on the 'differenciating'[105] power of intensity for its actualization in qualities and extensities, species and parts.

> How is the Idea determined to incarnate itself in differenciated qualities and differenciated extensities? What determines the relations coexisting within the Idea to differenciate themselves in qualities and extensities? The answer lies precisely in the intensive quantities. Intensity is the determinant in the process of actualisation. It is intensity which *dramatises*. It is intensity which is immediately expressed in the basic spatio-temporal dynamisms and determines an 'indistinct' differential relation in the Idea to incarnate itself in a distinct quality and a distinguished extensity.[106]

Sufficient reason is thus threefold: it cannot simply consist of differential relations as virtual Ideas and empirical actualizations but necessitates a third, relational element, that of intensive spatio-temporal dynamisms that actualize Ideas. The contrast with Maimon now becomes clear: Maimon's notion of differential ideas suffered from obscurity because in the notion of the differential he had fused the intelligible element with intensive magnitude and with the qualities of actual things.[107]

Deleuze clearly separates the virtual and differential structures of Ideas from intensity as the dynamic or dramatizing agent, as well as from qualities in the actual and extended world. Intensity is that by which the given is given, difference-in-itself, producing the diversity of the actual world. Intensive spatio-temporal dynamisms fulfill the function of the Kantian schematism, but whereas Kant's schemata of space and time remain external to the logical relations of the concept, Deleuze's spatio-temporal dynamisms are "internal to Ideas—and, as such, a drama or dream."[108] "We distinguish Ideas, concepts and dramas: the role of dramas is to specify concepts by incarnating the differential relations and singularities of an Idea."[109] Deleuze solves the Kantian problem of the external difference between intuition and concept by internalizing the difference and making spatio-temporal dramatization an intrinsic part of the whole system. Spatio-temporal dynamisms are the topological and chronological operative conditions that determine virtual structures. The notion of 'internality,' however, must not obscure this crucial difference, the difference between two differences, as it were (virtual difference and intensive disparity). The problem of transition from the Ideas of the virtual-ideal field to things and events in the actual world is assigned to intensive spatio-temporal dynamisms that must be thought as the 'dream' that is internal to Ideas—but also as that aspect of the actual world that we encounter in the signs of sensation.

Deleuze is even more careful to separate intensive magnitude from quality.[110] Intensive magnitude is understood as intensive *quantity* (not quality) and thus aligns with the scientific notion used, for instance, in embryology to account for individuating and differentiating processes in the egg.[111] If Deleuze's notion of intensity is difficult to grasp, this is perhaps because of its twofold status as transcendental and empirical: on the one hand, Deleuze clearly uses the notion of intensive quantity in a scientific sense (in thermodynamics as energy in general, or in embryology as individuating factors within an intensive field), thereby invoking the concepts of Gilbert Simondon's philosophy of individuation.[112] On the other hand, he states that "intensive quantity is a transcendental principle, not a scientific concept."[113] That is to say, intensity is not simply an empirical principle but has a definite function in Deleuze's metaphysical system. If intensity was limited to its scientific sense, it would always be related to a particular qualified and extended system in which intensity is ultimately cancelled according to entropic reason. Yet Deleuze claims that intensity is a *difference* of intensity that maintains itself in every case of empirical intensity as a kind of transcendental *spatium*. Intensity is thus inseparably transcendental-empirical, and changes the very meaning of these concepts—the suture or kernel, indeed, that holds together Deleuze's transcendental empiricism. While entropic processes govern the surface of the world, where intensity as energy in general is cancelled out, transcendental difference as difference of intensity remains implicated therein. The fact that this implication is encountered in actual, extended, qualified objects, in their 'centres of envelopment,' limits the sense in which intensity can be conceived as 'internal' to Ideas. Seen from this side, intensities are distributed throughout and encountered in the actual world; they come first, in the form of the expressor of virtual Ideas, or as Deleuze puts it, "every differenciation presupposes a prior intense field of individuation."[114]

In comparison to Maimon, one must therefore insist on two further distinctions. The sufficient reason or real ground in Deleuze is not immanent to any unity or whole; it is not subject to the principle of identity. Deleuze takes transcendental difference to be prior: there are only "free or untamed states of difference in itself,"[115] or as he also says, the unequal in itself or "a 'disparateness' within an original depth,"[116] i.e., intensities. "If sufficient reason or the ground has a 'twist,' this is because it relates what it grounds to that which is truly groundless."[117] The ground for Deleuze is itself 'groundless,' or a universal 'ungrounding.' Furthermore, this realm of difference-in-itself or intensity is not completely inaccessible to us. As Deleuze explains in the discussion following his presentation to the French Society of Philosophy in 1967, "The Method of Dramatization": "It seems to me we have the means to penetrate the sub-representational, to reach all the way to the roots of spatio-temporal dynamisms, and all the way to the Ideas actualized in them: the elements and ideal events, the relations and singularities are perfectly determinable."[118] For Maimon, differential ideas are perhaps partly accessible at the end of a long moral progress, by reducing everything given to purely thought relations, but differential ideas can certainly not be intuited. Deleuze, on the contrary, maintains that we can explore the relations of virtual Ideas and that "intensity is simultaneously the imperceptible and that which can only be sensed."[119] His metaphysics attaches great importance to the intensive encounter with sensual signs and in this way gives new meaning to empiricism, even forming a "superior empiricism" that is transcendental at the same time: "This empiricism teaches us a strange 'reason,' that of the multiple, chaos and difference (nomadic distributions, crowned anarchies) [... where] difference is behind everything, but behind difference there is nothing."[120]

3 Conclusion

Maimon challenges Kant on two fronts: as an empirical skeptic with the question 'quid facti?', doubting the fact of objective and lawful experience, and as a rational dogmatist with the question 'quid juris?', pointing to the insurmountable gap in Kant's transcendental philosophy between sensibility and intelligibility, the given and pure thought. Maimon's theory of differentials proposes a solution to the Kantian problem of the synthesis of intuitions and *a priori* concepts: everything given can in principle be reduced to thought relations. Taken over from calculus, differentials are undetermined but determinable quantities, which through their reciprocal relation give rise to continuous geometrical objects. As a metaphysical concept, i.e., qualities abstracted from all quantity, differentials provide an explanation for the way the content of perception arises.

Deleuze praises Maimon for realizing that "there is a treasure buried within the old so-called barbaric or pre-scientific interpretations of the differential calculus."[121] Maimon is an important and often overlooked precursor in the "esoteric history of differential philosophy."[122] However, Maimon's philosophical notion of differentials is not free of ambiguity: even when we assume that they are conceived as metaphysical entities and not mere fictions of the mind, it is not altogether clear whether they can serve simultaneously as pure (genetic and differential) relations and as the intensive magnitudes giving rise to sensuous qualities. Deleuze, for his part, is not concerned with the question of the actuality of differentials in the infinite understanding: he takes them from the outset to constitute the unconscious in finite thought, the unthinkable that must be thought. We have seen that Deleuze thus deviates from Maimon's rationalist idealism in several respects.

(1) Instead of the ideal of apodictic knowledge Deleuze allows for a kind of heteronomy in experience and thought. Signs as the bearers of problems, or differential and problematic Ideas, impose themselves upon us and push the receptive faculties to a 'transcendent' exercise. The model of recognition that presupposes the harmonious collaboration of the faculties in a common sense is abolished and replaced by the conception of thought as an involuntary, forced exercise: an act of thinking needs to be engendered in thought. The subject is neither simply the interpreter of signs nor the author of thought. What forces us to think is likewise no longer a demand of reason as it was in Maimon; reason as innate faculty of thinking has lost its privileged position and its claims to natural speculative interests. While for Maimon we are similar to God when we determine objects through thinking pure relations, as in mathematics, Deleuze argues that what makes us "semi-divine beings"[123] is the participation in the constitution of problems (in other words our directly encountering, as empirical beings, intensities in sensation that are the bearers of something ideal but, strictly speaking, unrecognizable).

(2) In Deleuze's philosophy the rationalist postulate of sufficient reason or real ground is considerably transformed: the identity of sufficient reason is dissolved into an unground of differential Ideas *and* differences of intensity that are inseparable from empirical actualizations. Deleuze contests Maimon's conception of the oneness and identity of the infinite understanding, turning difference into the superior transcendental principle. In a crucial move, Deleuze also distributes the various functions of Maimon's notion of differentials across separate elements: the differential and virtual relations must be held apart from differences of intensity (which he defines as intensive quantities distinct from qualities). The first constitute problematic Ideas, the second spatio-temporal dynamisms that actualize Ideas.

(3) Lastly, it has to be noted that the virtual-ideal field is not a transcendent realm. While Maimon must confront the difficulty of explaining the relation between an infinite understanding and our finite understanding, which are supposedly of the same nature but distinct in what they can think and determine, Deleuze needs to explain what produces the unconscious in being and thought. This is the pure line of time that splits the subject and every object into virtual and actual 'halves' in the asymmetrical relation of intensive expression. When Kant introduces the empty form of time and turns the subject into a transcendental-empirical double, "for a brief moment we enter into that schizophrenia in principle which characterises the highest power of thought, and opens Being

directly on to difference, despite all the mediations, all the reconciliations, of the concept."[124] Deleuze agrees with Maimon that Kant neglected the genetic method and upheld the point of view of conditioning; however, Maimon wished to restore the analytic identity of the infinite understanding and the unity of the thinking subject, in the same move that would have dissolved that minimum of givenness that must remain, and made it disappear into God. According to Deleuze, "the mistake of dogmatism is always to fill that which separates … and in this sense there is still … too much dogmatism among the post-Kantians."[125] The same fate would await Deleuze himself, were we to erase the separation between the intensive and the virtual, whether intentionally or inattentively, in wishing to present a simple, single 'other' to the actual world, and to conflate the dynamic source of the given with the differential relations expressed once again.[126]

Notes

1. Gilles Deleuze, *Difference and Repetition* (New York: Columbia University Press, 1994), 193.
2. Abraham P. Socher, *The Radical Enlightenment of Solomon Maimon: Judaism, Heresy, and Philosophy* (Palo Alto, CA: Stanford University Press, 2006), 85.
3. Ibid. See also Gideon Freudenthal, "Philosopher Between Two Cultures," in *Salomon Maimon: Rational Dogmatist, Empirical Sceptic*, ed. Gideon Freudenthal (Dordrecht: Kluwer, 2003), 12–15.
4. Socher, *Radical Enlightenment*, 85–86.
5. Salomon Maimon, *The Autobiography of Solomon Maimon*, ed. Yitzhak Y. Melamed and Abraham P. Socher (Princeton: Princeton University Press, 2018), 230.
6. Socher, *Radical Enlightenment*, 92. See also Paul Franks, "Jewish Philosophy After Kant: The Legacy of Salomon Maimon," in *Cambridge Companion to Modern Jewish Philosophy*, ed. Michael L. Morgan and Peter Eli Gordon (Cambridge: Cambridge University Press, 2007), 63.
7. In his *Autobiography*, which contains several chapters of commentary on Maimonides' work (later editions and translations of the *Autobiography* often cut precisely these chapters), Maimon justifies his 'lengthy detour' on Maimonides as follows: "I feel no need to apologize to the intelligent reader. Not only is the subject of my remarks inherently interesting, but Maimonides also had a decisive impact on my intellectual development." Maimon, *Autobiography*, 192.
8. Socher, *Radical Enlightenment*, 11.
9. Salomon Maimon, *Essay on Transcendental Philosophy*, trans. and ed. Nick Midgley, Henry Somers-Hall, Alistair Welchman and Merten Reglitz (London, New York: Continuum, 2010), 9.
10. Kant to Markus Herz, letter from 26 May 1789, included as Appendix II in the 2010 edition of Maimon's *Essay on Transcendental Philosophy* (Maimon, *Essay*, 236).
11. Maimon, *Essay*, 231. However, this moment of respect for his critic did not seem to last. Only five years later, in a letter to Reinhold, Kant writes: "As regards the 'improvement' of the critical philosophy by Maimon (Jews always like to do that sort of thing, to gain an air of importance for themselves at someone's else's expense), I have never really understood what he is after and must leave the reproof to others." (Letter to Reinhold, 28 March 1794, in Immanuel Kant, *Briefwechsel 1789–1794*, Akademie-Ausgabe (AA), *Kant's gesammelte Schriften*, vol. XI (Berlin, 1902—), 476; my translation). This antisemitic remark betrays Kant's ignorance of the exemplary Jewish tradition of composing commentaries, and super-

commentaries, on a main text worthy of close examination. See Freudenthal, "Philosopher Between Two Cultures," 1–17.
12. Frederick C. Beiser, *The Fate of Reason. German Philosophy from Kant to Fichte* (Cambridge, MA, London: Harvard University Press, 1987), 286.
13. Fichte to Reinhold, letter from March or April 1795, in Johann Gottlieb Fichte, *Early Philosophical Writings*, trans. and ed. Daniel Breazeale (Ithaca: Cornell University Press, 1988), 383–84. This interest in Maimon was briefly revived later, in the wake of Neo-Kantianism, as there are obvious parallels with the philosophies of the Marburg school and Hermann Cohen in particular, who dedicated an entire book to the metaphysical implications of differential calculus and the infinitesimal method—yet without mentioning Maimon. Socher suspects that Cohen's denial of any such influence had more to do with "Maimon's disreputable nature as a heretic together with his very un-Germanic character, which were likely to have offended the great champion of *Deutschtum und Judentum*, than it had to do with the actual question of philosophical influence." Socher, *Radical Enlightenment*, 107.
14. Gilles Deleuze and Félix Guattari, *What is Philosophy?* (New York: Columbia University Press, 1994), 8.
15. Ibid., 83.
16. Kant's *Critique* "does not provide any *a priori* criterion whereby one could know whether a given manifold can be thought in a unity of form in general, still less any criterion by which one could know in which unity [this manifold could be thought]. Not every given manifold allows itself to be thought in some objective unity or other ... In the manifold given to thought, then, an *a priori* criterion must be found, whereby one can know not only whether this manifold can be thought in an objective unity in general, but also in which unity it can be thought." Salomon Maimon, *Versuch einer neuen Logik oder Theorie des Denkens (nebst angehängten Briefen des Philaletes an Aenesidemus)*, in *Gesammelte Werke*, vol. V (Hildesheim: Georg Olms, 1970), 476; my translation.
17. Maimon, *Versuch einer neuen Logik*, 489–90; my translation.
18. As Maimon says: "Critical philosophy and skeptical philosophy stand approximately in the same relation as man and serpent after the Fall, where it is said: he (man) will tread on your head (that is, the critical philosopher will always trouble the skeptical one with the necessity and universality of the principles required for scientific knowledge); but you (serpent) will bite him in the heel (that is: the skeptic will always awaken the critical philosopher with the fact that his necessary and universally valid principles have no use). Quid facti?" Salomon Maimon, *Streifereien im Gebiete der Philosophie*, in *Gesammelte Werke*, vol. IV (Hildesheim: Georg Olms, 1970), 80, my translation.
19. Immanuel Kant, *Critique of Pure Reason*, trans. and ed. Paul Guyer and Allen W. Wood (Cambridge: Cambridge University Press, 1998), A138/B177.
20. Maimon, *Essay*, 187.
21. Ibid., 37.
22. Ibid., 38. While Maimon refers to "the Leibnizian-Wolffian system" (ibid.) to indicate the origin of this "sublime" idea of an infinite understanding, he probably first encountered the idea in the philosophy of Maimonides. In his commentary (in Hebrew) on Maimonides' *Guide for the Perplexed*, he argues that our finite human understanding must be of the same nature as the infinite divine understanding; they only differ from each other in degree of their cognitive completion. See Samuel Atlas, *From Critical to Speculative Idealism: The Philosophy of Solomon Maimon* (The Hague: Martinus Nijhoff, 1964), 76–77.
23. Maimon, *Essay*, 38.
24. Ibid., 48.
25. Ibid., 182.
26. Ibid.
27. Ibid., 183.
28. Ibid., 206.
29. Ibid., 22.
30. Ibid., 23.
31. Maimon, *Streifereien*, 61.

32. Ibid., 42.
33. Isaac Newton, *Tractatus de Quadratura Curvarum*, published in John Harris' *Lexicon Technicum*, vol. 2 (London 1710). Cited from the extract given in Appendix IV to Maimon's *Essay on Transcendental Philosophy* (Maimon, *Essay*, 250).
34. Carl Boyer, *The History of the Calculus and its Conceptual Development* (New York: Dover Publications, 1959), 178.
35. Sylvain Zac, "Noumène et différentielle dans la philosophie de Salomon Maïmon," *Revue d'histoire des sciences* 39, no. 3 (1986), 263.
36. Maimon, *Essay*, 181.
37. Ibid., 183.
38. Ibid.
39. For instance, ibid., 9, 48, 103, 192.
40. Ibid., 206.
41. Kant, CPR, A168/B210.
42. Ibid., A169/B211.
43. "[T]he intensive magnitude in different appearances can be smaller or greater even though the extensive magnitude of the intuition remains identical" (ibid., A173/B214).
44. Maimon, *Essay*, 19–20.
45. Ibid.
46. Ibid., 180.
47. Ibid., 20, 180.
48. "For an infinite understanding everything is in itself fully determined because it thinks all possible real relations [*Real-Verhältnisse*] between the ideas as their principles. For example, let us suppose that x is a function of y, y a function of z, etc. A necessary relation of x to z etc. arises out of these merely possible relations. Through this new function, x is more completely determined." Maimon, *Essay*, 50.
49. Ibid., 181.
50. Ibid., 47.
51. Ibid., 48, my italics.
52. Ibid.
53. Ibid., 183–184.
54. Ibid., 20.
55. Ibid., 75.
56. Ibid., 22.
57. Ibid., 19.
58. In his work "The Analyst" (1734) Berkeley criticized Leibniz's and Newton's infinitesimal analysis sharply for theological and idealist reasons.
59. See Christian Kauferstein, *Transzendentalphilosophie der Mathematik* (Stuttgart: ibidem, 2006), 146–64.
60. Maimon, *Essay*, 19.
61. Kauferstein, *Transzendentalphilosophie*, 316–23.
62. Maimon, *Essay*, 19.
63. Ibid., 103.
64. Ibid., 38.
65. Socher offers a brief summary of the different positions: "Friedrich Kuntze thought that Maimon's final position was skeptical, whereas Samuel Atlas, as is clear from his title, argues that Maimon progressed from skepticism to full-fledged 'Speculative Idealism,' as does Bergman. Ernst Cassirer seems to have thought that Maimon had anticipated the insights of neo-Kantianism in arriving at a position that avoided the pitfalls of both, by internalizing the given and eliminating the thing-in-itself as anything but an endless cognitive task. Most recently, Jan Bransen has argued that Maimon uncovered the fundamental antinomy of human knowledge, which is always both a passive finding and an active making. My own position is closest to Bransen's." Socher, *Radical Enlightenment*, 97.
66. Ibid., 103.

67. Franks, "Jewish Philosophy After Kant," 63.
68. Martial Gueroult, *La Philosophie transcendentale de Salomon Maimon* (Paris: Société d'édition, 1929), 53.
69. Immanuel Kant, *Critique of the Power of Judgment*, ed. Paul Guyer, trans. Paul Guyer and Eric Matthews (Cambridge: Cambridge University Press, 2000), 277. See also Gueroult, *La Philosophie transcendentale*, 56; and Samuel Bergman's comment: "In his *Critique of Judgement* Kant could not evade this 'as-if' as a last resort in eliminating the dualism inherent in his system, and this was tantamount to an admission that the problem was insoluble. Kant was content to call the coincidence of mind and matter 'a fortunate accident.' In his letter to Marcus Herz he refers to Leibniz's doctrine of 'pre-established harmony' as a solution: 'How one form can correspond to another and become a possible cognition is impossible for us to fathom [...] but to answer this question is not at all necessary [...]. However, I am convinced that Leibniz with his doctrine of pre-established harmony had in mind [...] the harmony of two different faculties of the same being in which sense and understanding can join to make experience possible, a harmony whose source we can explain as being only in the Author of all things' (26 May 1789)." Samuel Hugo Bergman, *The Philosophy of Solomon Maimon* (Jerusalem: Magnes Press, 1967), 65–66. The letter is contained in vol. XI of Kant's *Gesammelte Schriften*, 48–55 (Letter No. 362 [340]).
70. Gueroult, *La Philosophie transcendentale*, 64, my translation.
71. Ibid., 84.
72. Ibid.
73. Ibid.
74. Ibid., 85.
75. Deleuze, *Difference and Repetition*, 192.
76. Ibid.
77. Ibid., 193.
78. In Deleuze's work, the notion of differential Ideas that he elaborates is consistently written with a capital letter, and this practice will be adopted here as well.
79. Gilles Deleuze, *Desert Island and Other Texts 1953–1974* (Paris: Semiotext(e), 2004), 115.
80. Deleuze, *Difference and Repetition*, 170.
81. Ibid., 173.
82. Ibid., 154.
83. Ibid., 57.
84. Ibid., 222.
85. Maimon, *Philosophisches Wörterbuch*, 193, my translation, italics added.
86. Deleuze, *Difference and Repetition*, 49.
87. Ibid., 136–37.
88. Ibid., 135.
89. Arthur Rimbaud, *Seher-Briefe/Lettres Du Voyant*, ed. and trans. Werner von Koppenfels (Mainz: Dieterich'sche Verlagsbuchhandlung, 1990), 11.
90. Deleuze, *Difference and Repetition*, 199.
91. Rimbaud, *Seher-Briefe*, 11, my translation.
92. Deleuze, *Difference and Repetition*, 58.
93. Ibid.
94. Seminar on Kant, from 28 March 1978, given at Vincennes, St. Denis. https://www.webdeleuze.com/cours/kant. Accessed March 5, 2021.
95. Deleuze, *Difference and Repetition*, 169–70.
96. David Lapoujade, *Aberrant Movements: The Philosophy of Gilles Deleuze* (Paris: Semiotext(e), 2017), 80.
97. Deleuze, *Difference and Repetition*, 159.
98. Ibid., 170.
99. Ibid., 171.
100. Kant, CPR, A327/B384.
101. Ibid., A328/B384.

102. Deleuze, *Difference and Repetition*, 162.
103. For Deleuze, it will be specifically intensive multiplicities that cannot be divided without changing in nature (ibid., 237); in other words, the nonmetric varies with division, it is a plurality that is continuous and changing (ibid., 238).
104. In *Matter and Memory*, Bergson uses the notion of virtuality to characterize pure memory or the pure past. He describes the memory function as an involuntary act that moves from the virtual to the actual, from pure memory or the pure past to the present of the sensori-motor subject.
105. When the term 'differenciation' is supposed to signify 'actualization,' it is written with a 'c' in order to distinguish it from the differentiating processes immanent to the Idea. Deleuze proposes "the concept of different/ciation to indicate at once both the state of differential relations in the Idea or virtual multiplicity, and the state of the qualitative and extensive series in which these are actualised by being differenciated" (Deleuze, *Difference and Repetition*, 245).
106. Ibid.
107. Kauferstein argues that Maimon's philosophical notion of the differential is "inconsistent" (Kauferstein, *Transzendentalphilosophie*, 347) because of the plurality of functions that it is supposed to fulfill. "It turns out that the differentials in Maimon's system are supposed to perform a variety of tasks: they are supposed to take over the task of pure forms of intuition in the sense of supplying the elements of sensibility ..., to replace the transcendental deduction and the conception of an object capable of affecting us, and to take over the mediating function of the transcendental schema ..., whereby the transition to empirical cognition remains problematic in the *Essay* (and Maimon will reject this possibility of transition in later works)" (ibid., 327–28, my translation).
108. Deleuze, *Difference and Repetition*, 218.
109. Ibid.
110. He discusses this problem in relation to Bergson, whom he accuses of mistakenly criticizing the notion of intensity and of instead "attributing to quality a depth which is precisely that of intensive quantity" (Deleuze, *Difference and Repetition*, 239). For Deleuze, the depth is that of an intensive *spatium* (ibid., 230).
111. Deleuze, *Difference and Repetition*, 251.
112. For Deleuze's relation to Simondon, see Daniela Voss, "The Problem of Method: Deleuze and Simondon," *Deleuze and Guattari Studies* 14, no. 1 (2020), 87–108.
113. Deleuze, *Difference and Repetition*, 241.
114. Ibid., 247.
115. Ibid., 144.
116. Ibid., 51.
117. Ibid., 154. See also ibid., 274–75: "In short, *sufficient reason or the ground is strangely bent*: on the one hand, it leans towards what it grounds, towards the forms of representation; on the other hand, it turns and plunges into a groundlessness beyond the ground which resists all forms and cannot be represented."
118. Deleuze, *Desert Island*, 115.
119. Deleuze, *Difference and Repetition*, 230.
120. Ibid., 57.
121. Ibid., 170.
122. Ibid.
123. Ibid., 197.
124. Ibid., 58.
125. Ibid., 170.
126. My thanks to Max Lowdin for reading a draft of this chapter and for his valuable comments and suggestions.

Reading Novalis and the Schlegels

Kirill Chepurin

Early German Romanticism entails a thinking of the construction and destruction of worlds. "Isn't," Friedrich Schlegel writes in his programmatic essay "On Incomprehensibility" (1800), "this entire infinite world constructed by the understanding out of incomprehensibility or chaos?" (KFSA 2:370).[1] In this chapter, I will speak of "Romanticism" as a shorthand for *Frühromantik*, especially the thought of Novalis, August Wilhelm Schlegel, and Friedrich Schlegel. I will do so for reasons of convenience but also because the emphasis on *universal construction*, as advanced by these thinkers, indexes what I take to be an essential Romantic dimension that resonates beyond their thought and into post-Kantian Idealism and Romanticism at large. Romanticism, from this perspective, inquires into the world as constructed, and into the process of construction, a process grasped by the Romantics as broadly *poietic*: the mind constructs reality in the post-Kantian sense of arranging it into a world through binary categories—but so does the artist or poet in her construction of fragments and worlds, and so does nature in its generation of endless forms. As Novalis frames it, "nature generates, spirit makes" (N 2:480): the two sides of the all-encompassing universe of construction, whose endless variety Romanticism seeks to trace. Implied in the above quotation from Schlegel is that Romanticism is also, no less centrally, a thinking of "incomprehensibility or chaos" as such: what Schlegel in his philosophical notebooks calls "the universal chaos" (KFSA 18:366). The idea of chaos marks at once the ante-original standpoint which precedes world-construction and from which infinite realities may proceed, and what appears from the perspective of construction as the endless material out of which the world or any world-fragment is poietically formed. This conjunction—of universal chaos and universal *poiesis*—underlies the most basic sense in which the

---

The original version of the chapter has been revised: The affiliation details were incorrectly used in the chapter title "Reading Novalis and the Schlegels" by Kirill Chepurin. A correction to this chapter can be found at https://doi.org/10.1007/978-3-031-27345-2_24

K. Chepurin (✉)
Universität Hamburg, Hamburg, Germany
e-mail: kirill.chepurin@uni-hamburg.de

© The Author(s), under exclusive license to Springer Nature Switzerland AG 2023, corrected publication 2023
T. Rajan, D. Whistler (eds.), *The Palgrave Handbook of German Idealism and Poststructuralism*, Palgrave Handbooks in German Idealism,
https://doi.org/10.1007/978-3-031-27345-2_4

entire universe appears in Romanticism as "romanticized" or "poetic" (so that Novalis can claim that "poetry is the genuinely absolutely-real" [N 2:420]), and in which the Romantic absolute is, as Philippe Lacoue-Labarthe and Jean-Luc Nancy have called it, a "literary absolute."[2]

The sense of reality as constructed and self-constructing, together with the irreducible "sense for chaos" (KFSA 18:38)—for the singular, the disorderly, and the excessive; for the inhabitation of fissures and upendings; and for what breaks out of any given binary encoding, proliferating further constructions and further breaks—marks also the affinity that has been observed countless times between Romanticism and poststructuralism. Both arise out of a sense of the infinite fragmentariness of modern reality, and both have a keen interest in exploring the logics of this fragmentariness. Moreover—and this is the perspective from which I want to approach their transhistorical affinity—Romanticism and poststructuralism may be seen as grappling with *the same overarching process* at its different historical stages, and with two different moments of crisis of this process. The process in question is the ongoing formation of the modern post-1492 world of the global—this world that imposes itself upon the planetary depths and the rich plenitude of forms of life across the globe, and even eyes the infinite outer space. This process continues at the present moment of planetary crisis, as global capitalism not only seeks to re-mediate the global in new ways via algorithms, and to expand it into virtual reality, but pushes beyond the planetary into the universal expanse, dreaming of asteroid mining and life (and profit) on Mars.

As such, this chapter proposes that to read Romanticism "after 1968" *today*, or from the perspective stretching from the 1960s to the present, is to attend to Romanticism's entanglement with *the global, the planetary, and the cosmic* as the interlocked dimensions or scales of the modern project of re-mediating the totality of post-Copernican (human and nonhuman) reality. "The global," the way I employ this term, indexes the temporality of human history across the globe, or what may be called global humanity, whereas "the planetary" and "the cosmic" refer, respectively, to the deep time of the Earth's planetary processes and the immeasurable time and space of the post-Copernican universe.[3] The sense of the immensity of the universe intensifies in the eighteenth century, and to think *across* scales becomes an increasingly pressing (yet increasingly challenging) task for thought—a tendency which culminates and, as it were, becomes self-reflective in Romanticism. Traditionally, this has been grasped as the Romantic quest for a new mythology of nature; in such a formulation, however, the contemporary resonance of this quest is obscured.[4] Romanticism is arguably the first modern critical cross-scalar thinking, and this chapter revisits it as such from a post-1968 perspective.

In line with recent scholarship, I treat "1968" as a moniker for a global crisis irreducible to the French context. In the long 1960s, anti-imperialist movements, utopian counter-cultures, and campaigns of emancipation marked a deep crisis of the global.[5] From this perspective, it is not coincidental that French poststructuralism centrally targeted structuralist anthropology's attempt to exhaustively re-mediate, and to make universal sense of, the global via binary systems. The poststructuralist opening onto the un-re-mediatable and the decentered, and onto the destabilizing dimension underlying the binaries through which the world is constructed, appears retrospectively as co-imbricated with the conjoined rise, during the so-called Great Acceleration of the Anthropocene, of new more-than-human global and planetary logics: of networks and the digital, ecological thought and Earth System Science, projects of outer space exploration and the fascination with pictures of the Earth taken from space. A lot of these developments have proved inherently ambivalent, in which utopian visions often seem impossible to disentangle from their capitalist co-optation, from dystopia and catastrophe—and it is under the shadow of these developments, almost apocalyptically intensified, that we continue to live.

In light of the above, it is important to view Romanticism as emerging at a key post-Enlightenment and post-Revolutionary moment of global modernity's simultaneous crisis (also apocalyptic in intensity) and self-reflection. When Lacoue-Labarthe and Nancy associate Romanticism with thinking in terms of crisis, and therefore with the first "genuinely *modern* position of the philosophical," they may be taken to revisit the Romantic moment of crisis as the first critical reflection *on* modernity itself, and as resonating with their own time of crisis (LA 29).[6] The significance of such revisiting is underwritten by the fact that Romanticism serves as a highly ambivalent thought-laboratory for thinking *out of* the crisis of modernity, and at once for critiquing many aspects of the modern world and for justifying and advancing the modern Eurocentric construction of the global. In Romanticism, the ideal of the oneness of humanity and the universal promise of the French Revolution, merging with the Christian promise of reconciliation of all things with God, run up against the various alienations, divisions, and uneven developments and incommensurate cosmologies across the globe.[7] Romanticism seeks, in its own way, to assemble the unity of global humanity out of these divisions and incommensurabilities.

Moreover, the crisis out of which Romanticism emerges is not limited to a crisis of the global. It needs to be further placed in the context of the Anthropocene (whose beginning is often traced to the Romantic age), of eighteenth-century geological catastrophism and the discovery of deep time, and of the intensification of cosmic alienation amidst the growing sense of the contingency and infinity of the post-Copernican universe. Not only the global but the Earth and the universe are fragmented and chaotic, containing a multitude of processes and worlds—what Kant in his passage on "the starry heavens above" calls "worlds upon worlds and systems of systems."[8] The Romantics attend to modern human and nonhuman logics of reality, exhibiting an unparalleled understanding of the importance of thinking jointly the global, the planetary, and the cosmic in new ways. Romanticism may be viewed as a singular synthetic attempt to grapple with *all* dimensions and scales of post-Copernican reality simultaneously, so as to collect them into a poietic system. This attempt is permeated with the modern anxiety over the finite inhabitation of an infinite cosmic void, and entangled with the modern hubris of wanting to re-mediate, from an idealized center, the entirety of reality so that it can be known and controlled. In view of how infinite and infinitely fragmented this reality is, can a universal knowledge, universal art, and universal history even be attained?

It is the Romantic project of the *impossible universal re-mediation and construction* that stands at the center of this chapter. In what follows, I outline this project with reference to Novalis's and the Schlegels' encyclopedic fragments, lectures, and other writings (both published and not—since I seek to showcase the problematic around which their thought kept revolving). While I cannot reconstruct here these thinkers' individual trajectories, I want to exhibit the scope of their shared universal project and its co-imbrication with the geocosmic logics of modernity, as well as to identify, within this project's very impossibility, the dimension of antagonism and crisis that resonates with post-1960s thought. When Lacoue-Labarthe and Nancy emphasize the paradoxes of incompletion at work in Romantic poietic construction; when Manfred Frank highlights the gaps of (self-)reflection or the figure of infinite approximation inherent in Romantic thought; when Alice Kuzniar reconfigures Novalis's writings through the figure of nonclosure; when Werner Hamacher connects the Romantic fragment with the suspension of the meta-position of absolute subjectivity; or when Paul de Man theorizes Schlegelian irony as disrupting any narrative-construction—all of these broadly poststructuralist appropriations of Romanticism (in their shared focus on paradoxes, interruptions, evasions, lacunae in absolute closure, and so forth) not only emerge out of the 1960s crisis of universal re-mediation,[9] they also highlight that within Romanticism which, as we will see, ungrounds the Eurocentric meta-position of universal history that the Romantics themselves seek to occupy.

1 "The Voice of the Universe": Romantic Construction

Romantic construction seeks to simultaneously inhabit all polar opposites, scales, and epochs: the absolutely singular no less than the truly universal, the infinitesimal no less than the boundlessly large, and the present age no less than the longed-for absolute future or the deepest past not only of humanity but of the universe itself. This coincides, for the Romantics, with the task of their time, crucial for the ongoing self-understanding of global modernity—as it were, for modernity's own reflection upon the (infinitely negative) world it has created.

The contemporary epoch, as August Schlegel observes in his lectures from 1802/1803, is dominated by the "negative tendency" (KAV 542): the tendency towards disunity, analysis, and critique. But while the Romantics are antagonistic to this tendency, it is not simply something to be rejected. According to the principles of polarity and eccentric movement (both invoked by Schlegel), it is essential to glimpse "what is truly real" within this negativity, or what "cannot and will not perish" about it (KAV 540). As signaled by Kantian critique and the French Revolution, this age has a task, connected by Schlegel with the idea of global humanity, and with the problem of its assembling or re-mediating—of working out the logics of the global at the present stage of its construction. "Perhaps," Schlegel ruminates, "[this] period should be regarded *as but one great reflection of the humankind upon itself*," and such reflection must necessarily go through negativity (KAV 540; emphasis added). In this passage, "the humankind" that is supposed to reflect upon itself is precisely global humanity, which, despite its apparent scatteredness and division, must grasp itself as one, in a fundamentally Eurocentric trajectory of development that goes from the ancient times to the modern global world as this world has been formed by the time of Schlegel's lectures. This historical moment is where, for Schlegel, global humanity becomes conscious of itself *as* global, and the task of the present age (i.e., European modernity) has been to develop abstract thinking to such a degree as to make possible this kind of meta-viewpoint from which to affirm the essential oneness of humanity. The Romantics understand themselves as occupying the meta-standpoint of the self-reflection of the global, from which it is clear that "the *spirit (Genius)* of the humankind," while still developing, is "but one" (KAV 537). And yet, while abstract Enlightenment reason could, for instance, postulate universal human rights, it could not truly grasp the oneness of humanity in all of its diversity or the oneness of human knowledge across different cosmologies and cultures. Due to its own abstractness, the contemporary age has fallen into a reductive empiricism in which "all human knowledge" (and all knowledge *of* the humankind) remains "an aggregate without subordination or interconnection" (KAV 540). Only a truly universal *poiesis* (and to be universal, one should be simultaneously a poet, physicist, philosopher, and historian) can exhibit (*darstellen*) oneness within this chaotic fragmentation. "Universality," Schlegel insists, "is today the sole means for attaining again to something great" (KAV 541). At the same time, as he asserts, whoever has not "mastered" the present standpoint of critique, or does not inhabit the contemporary fully in its abstractness, "should not even begin to have a say" regarding the dawning, more positive epoch (KAV 540). The highest "negative" achievement of modernity—the universal meta-standpoint of reflection—should be preserved, even if its logic must be rethought.

Being contemporary is inextricably tied for the Romantics to being global in a new, post-Enlightenment way. One could say that, during this period, the Enlightenment imposition of abstract universality from above proves to be insufficiently mediational, or insufficiently attentive to the growing complexity of global contexts, and comes to be replaced by the Romantic interest in particularity,[10] serving to re-construct the global out of the particular and the local—out of local spirit(s), *mores*, deities, poetries, and cosmologies—towards a global synthesis emerging as though from below. Even the Romantic expansion of rationality to include the mythical and the poetic may be regarded as contributing to making the logic of such synthetic re-mediation more advanced and adaptive—so that, through this expansion, various forms of life and thought that are grasped as pre-rational or non-rational can also be co-opted into the global Western-centric history of consciousness. The empirical chaos of global humanity and of human knowledge is embraced by the Romantics not merely as something negative, but as the empirical *plenum* of a world whose movement towards unity is not complete. As Friedrich Schlegel puts it in his lectures from 1800/1801, the "proposition that *the world is incomplete* is extraordinarily important for everything." "The empirical," he continues, "is thereby provided with infinite play space (*Spielraum*)" (KFSA 12:42).

To set the empirical, the singular, or the particular free in this manner is to see it as self-constructing: to construct the particular out of its particularity, or to let it freely emerge in its specificity (*Eigentümlichkeit*), in its own free play. Thus, to study poetry is, among other things, to see how it "reflects the specificity of each and every people" (KAV 74), becoming the central element in the Romantic set of instruments for re-mediating the global. At the same time, since the global is constructed by the Romantics from the meta-standpoint of its oneness, the disunity of the world both fascinates them and appears as the obstacle. "The specific *problem* of history," observes Friedrich Schlegel in an early essay on Condorcet, "is the unevenness of movements of progress in the various constitutive parts of humanity's development (*Bildung*) as a whole, especially the great divergence in the degree of intellectual and moral development: the relapses and standstills of development" (KFSA 7:7). This context is important for understanding the Romantic logics of the fragmentary, too. In order to be able to re-mediate global reality, the Romantic must have a sense for universality conjoined with what Schlegel calls "the sense for fragments and projects" as forming "the integral part" of the transcendental view of history (KFSA 2:169)—i.e., as the history of global consciousness.

"The world," as structurally incomplete, marks for the Romantics the site of endless fragmentation and not-yetness, and of endless configurations of relations, gaps, regressions, and delays. "It is an absolute relationality; nothing in the world *simply is*," remarks Novalis (N 2:156). Or, in Schlegel's more disparaging formulation: "*World* is the entanglement of inconsequential relationships… How peculiar it is that this meanness (*Gemeinheit*) occupies the place where the paradise used to be" (KFSA 16:335). Romanticism emerges out of an antagonism to the fragmentation and not-yet of the world, while seeking to inhabit them immanently so as to find a way *out* of them, to re-assemble oneness from scattered fragments—a task that is as constitutively endless as the world itself. The tendency towards infinite connectivity combined with one towards infinite individualization or singularization marks Romantic world-construction as characteristically modern. Perfect re-mediation would coincide with perfect relationality, a networked unity of singularities spanning the entire globe and developing historically. Can all the singular and contingent nodes of the global be reachable, or made part of universal construction? What about those peoples which "completely lack" poetry, and whose condition is "the regression into complete dullness (*Stupidität*)," as August Schlegel asserts of the inhabitants of Tierra del Fuego and the Esquimaux (KAV 392)? Or those "wild peoples" of whom Novalis says that their narratives are absolutely unstructured ("without beginning, middle, or end") and their enjoyment of these narratives "pathological" (N 2:322–3)? For Schlegel, the above-mentioned dullness may have to do with the very regions these peoples inhabit (which are, however, necessary for the polar construction of the Earth as planet). For Novalis, the principle of polarity likewise suggests that pathology and sickness are as indispensable as health for the re-mediation of the totality of reality. Thus, these peoples too form, in their very exclusion, a constitutive part of Romantic synthetic construction.

As may be glimpsed from Friedrich Schlegel's emphasis on "relapses and standstills," or from August Schlegel's remark that "the phoenix" may best symbolize the movement of history (KAV 537), Romantic construction is never just uniform or linear, even though the Romantics seek to encode it as such at the meta-level—as it were, when surveying the movement of construction retroactively from an absolute future, or from the perspective of what this movement will have been from the standpoint of completion. Inhabited immanently, the movement that Romanticism constructs is that of ceaseless (phoenix-like) creation and annihilation, and of the constant expansion of construction in all directions, all genres, all dimensions of being, a process that momentarily stabilizes only to be thwarted in its impulse towards stability, and to engage in a new cycle, new loop of decomposition and composition.

Crucially, this is for the Romantics a post-Copernican (or post-Keplerian) eccentric cosmic process: it is exactly what the universe does or how the universe constructs, in its endless fragments and worlds, some flourishing, some past their time, some yet to bloom, some appearing, like a *stella nova*, seemingly out of nowhere, and others, like the comet, traversing the skies as if without telos.[11] Through this contingency, these renewed beginnings and endings, these roundabout trajectories and spirals within spirals, the universe develops and grows. "Whatever does not reach its completion now," Novalis asserts, "will reach it in a future attempt (*Versuch*), or through repeated attempts" (N 2:735). Universal construction is iterative and recursive: failed attempts feed into new beginnings. The universe tries over and over again, and at some point it succeeds—as in the solar system where it generates the human as a rational being, even though who knows what new alien life might appear in the future or how the human might cosmically develop. Perhaps humanity is but an experiment "*from which nothing will emerge*," and whose end will be "half-tragic, half-comedic" (as Friedrich Schlegel speculates in his notebooks; KFSA 18:192); perhaps this world will be exhausted, and a new experimental attempt will emerge in its stead.

"All construction is indirect" or eccentric (N 2:398), and reality is so boundless that, no matter which part of it one considers, it is always but a "relative something" and therefore "is 0 in relation to an *absolute something*," or is annihilated by the infinity of the whole, so that the universe appears from this perspective as a "universal system of annihilation" (N 2:526). As worlds emerge, so are they necessarily annihilated (in time) from the moment they are born. However, annihilation is at the same time an illusion (*Schein*), insofar as it coincides with new creation in an "overabundant process of renewal," in which the destruction of the old world is part of the emergence of something new (N 2:345). (From this standpoint, cosmic revolutions and events such as the French Revolution appear as constitutively co-imbricated.[12]) It is from this cosmic standpoint that the endless multiplicity of construction truly becomes visible—from the standpoint of the de-centered cosmic expanse in which everything hovers (*schwebt*, a cosmic operation too[13]). Such is for Novalis the essence of post-Copernican thought:

> Philosophy *unbinds* everything and relativizes the universe. Just like the Copernican system, it abolishes all fixed points, and turns what rests (*das Ruhende*) into what hovers (*ein Schwebendes*). It teaches the relativity of all grounds and all properties—the infinite multiplicity and unity of each thing's construction, etc. (N 2:616)

The Romantic construction of every individual thing is a cosmic construction: "everything," from this perspective, "can be created or reached in a highly varied yet regulated manner" (N 2:616). The Romantic view of the global is a cosmic view, too, in which the global appears as a ceaseless relational process of creating fragments and worlds within the one humankind. In fact, there is only one "complete system"—"the system of the universe"—that provides full explanation of everything (N 2:620; cf. 2:346, 2:487).[14] The poet is but "the voice of the universe." While the philosopher thinks the principle of construction ideally, poetry inhabits universal construction in a real way (N 2:848)—so that the writing of a poem or the creation of any work of art, too, should be understood as part of the universal construction of fragments and worlds, or as a poetic attempt that is cosmic in nature.[15]

Romantic construction, as Nancy observes vis-à-vis post-Kantian *Naturphilosophie*, is "a way of giving voice to all things or traversing all things through language (*parole*)."[16] The Romantic poet (as one with the Romantic philosopher, historian, and physicist) gives voice to the one infinite cosmic immanence. Within this immanence, "*all* is processed (*bearbeitet*)" in a construction that cuts across "all art and all science," requiring of the poet-thinker "a versatility without parallel" (N 2:745; cf. "universality" in August Schlegel). Every particularity has its genesis and place in the processuality of the whole; and every particularity is itself a whole—an "individual" with its specific "characteristics" (*Merkmale*) and specific voice. "Poetry," Novalis claims, "elevates every single thing through this thing's specific mode of connection with the rest of the whole" (N 2:322). The task, then, is to ceaselessly construct characteristics (N 2:653): again, an infinite (cosmic) task—what Friedrich Schlegel describes relatedly as "the characterization of the universe" (KFSA 18:148).

The Romantic interest in binary categories, symbolic and language games, and mathematical equations, all forms a part of what Nancy terms *parole*. Novalis's training as a geologist in particular morphs into his interest in the depths that are as earthly as they are cosmic, and in the symbolic re-mediation of these universal depths through differential and integral calculus as the mathematics of the post-Copernican universe (as developed by Leibniz and Newton)—a universe in which the infinitesimal is as boundless as the infinitely large, or in which any "relative something" is at once infinitely small and contains infinities within itself. Romantic thinking is a differential thinking, and Novalis's emphasis on grasping the endless "elementary variation of the universe" (N 2:345) follows the achievements of modern infinitesimal calculus, which expanded the realm of *ratio* not unlike the Romantics seek to expand it to include not just fixed entities but what is infinitely processual. "Philosophical calculus of abstraction," too, must be a differential calculus (N 2:668). In differential and integral calculus, Novalis finds a way of re-mediating simultaneously the unity and the vast multiplicity of each particularity, as well as the kind of double perspective that combines decomposition (differentiation) and composition or assembling (integration). As Novalis's imperative goes, "the examination of the large and the examination of the small must always grow together," so that the large must be "made more multiple" (differentiated) and the small "made simpler" (integrated), all towards the "composite data of the universe as well as of its every most individual part" (N 2:444–5). As we recall, the dichotomy of annihilation and creation is an illusory dichotomy within the one poietic process of the universe—and calculus for Novalis makes it possible to rationally grasp precisely this kind of "fictional" construction. "The basic formula of the infinitesimal calculus," he writes, "is (a/∞) * ∞ = a; it is an illusory (*scheinbare*) approach," in which even deviation from the seeming truth, even error (*Irrtum*), is a constitutive part of the universal method of re-mediation (N 2:449).

From this perspective, Romantic organicism or Novalis's contention that the universe and its parts are living wholes appear less as having to do with an organism/mechanism dichotomy, or with some vague idea of life that cannot be mathematized (cf. LA 127), but as indexing the infinite processuality and differential mereology of the universe as the subject of universal calculus. "Calculus," Novalis notes, "is the same thing as process," adding: "Proficiency, certainty, and precision in philosophical calculus is what I must seek to achieve" (N 2:656). "In the end," within this all-encompassing symbolic construction, "mathematics is but the generic, basic philosophy, and philosophy is the higher mathematics universally understood" (N 2:583). Poetry, too, is one with the differential and integral self-construction of the universe, inhabiting a nature that mathematizes "unceasingly" (N 2:444). The very possibility of re-mediating mathematically what is actually infinite, or of constructing a system of universal computability (a "complete counting system," a universal calculus or "universal grammar"; N 2:568, KFSA 16:71), is a concern that would later be central to Georg Cantor, and that continues to resonate today following the rise of cybernetics, information theory, and the digital, all co-imbricated with the counterculture of the 1960s.[17]

To inhabit Romantically the cosmic landscape is to differentiate and integrate it, to construct and deconstruct it. Such inhabitation is made possible by the fact that, for the Romantics, human reason *is* cosmic, and the microcosm in us is the "absolute creative capability" that is literally universal (N 2:830). Ultimately, to perfectly construct even the smallest part of the universe requires one to construct the whole plus the entire history of the part and the whole. "Physics," Novalis points out, "is generally the original history, history in the proper sense" (N 2:478), continuing in human global history and in human creative activity, so that the latter in turn poetically inhabits universal construction, thereby closing the encyclopedic circle that coincides with the Romantic system of times. The epochs of the humankind's history, the epochs of the Earth's history, and the epochs of the history of the universe must all be constructed from the meta-position the Romantic occupies. Romantic construction implies a total re-collection of the universe, necessitating progression and regression through geocosmic time.

In the end, every smallest particle must be perfectly constructed. Such is the meaning of Novalis's claim, in his notes for the Romantic encyclopedia, that the arrival of the absolute future—the realized *hen kai pan*, in which all things will have been constructed poietically, and the mind and world will coincide without alienation—equals "the chaos of *the completed creation*" (N 2:514). "The future world is the *rational* (*vernünftige*) chaos" (N 2:514): in a way, a return to the primordial chaos except as constructed. "The true method," echoes Friedrich Schlegel in his notebooks, "would consist in the production of a *full chaos*" (KFSA 18:461). As universal construction draws closer to completion, as it goes through each "detail in the most complete and meticulous manner" (as Schlegel demands of historical and philosophical method; KFSA 7:9), the eccentric music of the celestial ellipsoids, the harmony of the alien universe, becomes increasingly more chaotic—in a poetical yet rational, rigorous, differential way. The descent into the infinitesimal leads back to the primordial chaos and forward to a perfectly constructed chaos, in which the infinite cosmic reality is decoded and re-collected. The principle of construction at this point ceases to be transcendent, God coincides with the All and the I with the not-I without remainder. In this way, Romantic "pantheism" emerges as the end result of universal construction. As Novalis writes: "The world is not yet finished… From One God must arise an All-God (*Allgott*). From one world [must arise] a universe (*Weltall*)" (N 2:551). The perfectly constructed rational chaos—the end-goal of world-construction—is the fulfilled creation, pantheism realized. In this state of the universe, no further work is possible. It is a state of utter fragmentation ("chaos") that coincides with perfect unity ("*rational* chaos"), because every fragment in it is one with the mind that inhabits it, without any diremption or split, and the universe is fully "romanticized." This absolute state is what Romantic construction impossibly inhabits.

2 Below the Split: Romantic Ambivalence

From a poststructuralist perspective, the future absolute state and the movement it generates from absolute beginning to absolute end is what must itself be deconstructed—and it is no wonder that poststructuralist readings of Romanticism sought to resist precisely the idea of inhabiting the self-reflective meta-standpoint of universality and the standpoint of completion or closure, since this standpoint is all-too co-imbricated with the master-narrative of Western modernity. The point, however, is not to separate what is "good" about Romanticism from what is "bad" or to reductively identify Romanticism with the tendency towards subversion, openness, or singularity. The logics of Romantic construction are highly ambivalent, and it is important to attend non-reductively to these ambivalences, and to the co-imbrication between Romanticism, the Eurocentric construction of universal history, and the modern project of reason's mastery of, and perfect control over, the infinite post-Copernican reality.

One way of thinking the point at which Romantic ambivalence originates is to focus on the temporal narrative which Romantic construction generates. What is the Romantic system of times, and where does it begin? In its broadest division into past, present, and future, it takes its beginning at what we saw August Schlegel identify as the moment of global modernity's self-reflection. This moment indexes the opening of the very possibility of a meta-standpoint from which to survey universal construction as an all-encompassing universal history. Of course, for the

Romantics, universal history was always ongoing, from the earliest times. However, it only appears as such—appears *as* universal history—from the present meta-standpoint. This is the point at which, so to speak, universal history becomes self-aware, or conscious of itself *qua* universal.

This opening of self-reflection has the threefold structure of diremption or split. First there is the split within the present itself, because the present *is* the time of the split that makes the modern logic of self-reflection possible—most centrally, between the empirical chaos and the abstract idea of universality, or between nature and mind. Out of this split, the imperative of universal re-mediation may be said to arise. Second, there is the split of the present with the past as the time preceding universal history's self-reflection. Finally, since the present is caught in the contradiction between what is and what ought to be, this creates the split between the present as the time of incompletion and the absolute future of "the completed creation." In the end, history can appear as truly universal or all-encompassing only from this future standpoint. In this manner, the diremption of the present and its reflection upon itself as *at once* dirempted and universal (a contradiction mediated from the perspective of the absolute future) generates the system of times.

Moreover, there is a further meta-split that emerges vis-à-vis this entire temporal system, and vis-à-vis the meta-standpoint that Romanticism inhabits. We may observe, again, that the linear master-narrative of completion—the line drawn at the meta-level from the primordial chaos to the rational chaos or completed creation—can only be drawn retrospectively out of the standpoint of the absolute future. Any moment—any present—*preceding* that absolute state is too full of eccentricities and deviations, of disruptions and standstills, of loops and variations, for such a line to be drawn. Between the present and the future, an abyss thus emerges within the Romantic system of times due to the differential character of Romantic construction, in which even if the absolute future is proclaimed to be imminent, the interval between the present and this future always remains infinite. This point is where all poststructuralist readings of Romanticism as a thinking of infinite approximation and nonclosure become possible. In contrast to any straightforwardly linear thinking of progress, Romantic thought seeks to inhabit simultaneously this differential abyss *and* the absolute future. However, thereby, the meta-split appears between the linear meta-narrative of universal history and what, at any particular moment, constitutes its underside, or the endless plethora of singularities that this movement seeks to re-mediate. This meta-split cuts across the entire system of times and makes it possible to inhabit the abyss of the singular, and to revel in the particular, *against* the overarching meta-narrative.

It is this meta-split and this abyss that poststructuralism—out of the 1960s moment of crisis at which a complete world-order or any grand narrative of universal history appears undesirable and impossible—may be taken to inhabit while abandoning the ideal of the coming epoch of oneness, nonalienation, and completion. But even without necessarily rejecting this ideal (which constitutes an essential dimension of Romanticism in its antagonism to the negativity of modernity[18]), this meta-split opens up endless ways of inhabiting universal construction against the meta-narrative of universal history. From Romanticism onwards, this tension or ambiguity between the particular as re-mediatable and as un-re-mediatable or absolutely singular, or more generally between what makes the mediation of universal history possible and what refuses it, comes to dominate modern thought as a central problem. At this meta-point, splits begin to proliferate, so that within the Romantic system of times it is possible to inhabit not only the present moment but any epoch including the archaic past antagonistically against the present, or against this epoch's re-mediation into universal history—or to inhabit the absolute future antagonistically, too: to inhabit the pantheism-to-come or universal chaos, the absolute noise of the universe, against the meta-narrative. Whatever singularity and whatever moment of time become non-teleologically, antagonistically inhabitable as remaining *beneath* the meta-narrative and refusing it. The remainder of this chapter consists of three entangled variations on the theme of this kind of antagonistic inhabitation of what remains below the Romantic meta-standpoint.

3 Variation 1: The Meta and the Non

There is a thin line between "giving voice" to all things, and all fragments of the global, and assembling them in a colonial and racialized manner from the idealized Western center. Romanticism often crosses this line. The Romantic construction of the categories of "religion," "poetry," "humanity," and others, and the Romantic interest in "wild peoples" and "the Orient," or in any other formations of the global past or present, are entwined with the overarching modern construction of these categories as a kind of sorting machine for the West to make sense of and re-mediate its numerous others.

Following the decades of poststructuralist and post-colonial critiques, it is, most centrally, the Romantic logic of the meta that appears as the problem. Can one think at once the unity and the endless variety of the global without falling into a justification of the colonial and racialized violence of modernity, and of the modern Western program of self-assertion? While much of the contemporary work in theoretical humanities has grappled with this issue, I want to focus here on the thought of Sylvia Wynter, which has grown increasingly prominent in Black studies and beyond. The conjunction in Wynter's thought of the idea of an all-encompassing poietic construction of humanity with an irreducible pluralization of the global resonates transhistorically with the Romantic project. Yet, Wynter seeks to *invert* the logic of the meta, and to work out an alternative "ecumenical" logic of global humanity—a new "human project"[19] for the post-1960s—not from a Eurocentric position, but the non-position of the Black subject. In this way, Wynter may be said to restage the move of Romantic construction from the standpoint of the non, and not the meta.

At the center of the critical part of Wynter's project stands the question of who in global modernity counts as human. If, as Novalis notes, "man" is a "metaphor" (N 2:351), then Wynter's work interrogates the racialized hierarchies and shifts within this metaphor over the course of modernity following the collapse of sacred geography and the opening of the globe for Western re-mediation and conquest. As a laboratory of such re-mediation, Romanticism provides plentiful occasions for being interrogated from this perspective, including Novalis's statement in his 1799 essay "Christianity, or Europe" that it is "one part of the [human] species," the European, that has awakened for a universal life and sets the course towards "a universal individuality, a new history, [and] a new humanity" (N 2:745). Wynter herself critiques Friedrich Schlegel's Indo-European-centered global construction of language, thereby positioning her project against the Romantic meta-standpoint.[20] For Wynter, if modernity is the age of the self-assertion of reason, then the normative subject of this self-assertion ("Man") is a subject that views itself as justified in subjugating and exploiting those viewed as less-than-human or non-human. "The West, over the last five hundred years," Wynter observes, "has brought the *whole* human species into its *hegemonic*... model of being human."[21] What emerges from Wynter's analysis is a developmental picture of the global as a racialized hierarchy of "humanness," with the Middle Passage as the foundational infrastructure of the post-1492 world, and with the enslaved Black African constituting the (non-)subject that remains below the construction of global humanity even as the emerging capitalist world-ecology is built upon its death that is as "symbolic" (UC 47) as it is real. (The infamous exclusion of Africa by Hegel from the movement of world-history is but a symptom of this broader process.) The hold of the slave ship becomes, in Wynter's account of modernity, at once the zero-point and "the origin" of post-1492 reality—a global reality in which "Man" is "overrepresented" over all other "genres of being human," and in which blackness is "cast as the total negation of human freedom," and of humanness as such: the constitutive non-position, non-life, non-being (UC 31, 62).

While Wynter's critique of the master-narrative of "Man" has become on its own a powerful tool across contemporary critical theory, the constructive part of her project is no less interesting in the post-'68 context. An insistence on the irreducible plurality of human "genres" is associated by her with the understanding of reality as mytho-poietically and narratively constructed, with "the sixties' movements" as challenging the global episteme of "Man," and with Jacques Derrida's critique of the Western bourgeois "referent-we" as (mis)identified with the "we" of humanity (UC 23–4). Wynter also draws on Maturana and Varela's notion of *autopoiesis*, as emerging in the wake of the Chilean May '68, and on the studies of the human brain emphasizing its "hybrid" nature: biological *and* narratival, an entanglement of *bios* and *mythoi* which co-constitute each other (UC 25–7). Following the emergence of this specifically human brain—the origin-event that takes place in Africa—each genre of the human narratively forms its own cosmology, encoded symbolically through the autopoietic activity of generating the "referent-we" that its subjects regard as self-evident. There is, in this regard, a perfect analogy (to use Wynter's own example) between the Pygmy and the Western bourgeois subject (UC 54–5)—notwithstanding, of course, the brutal overextension of the latter's "we" all over the globe.

Wynter's project is driven by the idea of the common: the common structure of humanness across its manifold genres, and the global and planetary as something to be inhabited in common—so as to avert the "unparalleled catastrophe for our species" which is the looming climate catastrophe. To think humanity *at once* as fragmented and as bio-poietically one is the (highly Romantic) challenge put forward by Wynter's thought. Not unlike August Schlegel at his time, Wynter sees the moment of crisis indexed by the 1960s as one of modernity's self-questioning,[22] and of the emergence of a new consciousness of global humanity. Humanity must grasp itself as a single species, yet not in a biologically reductive way, but as "hybridly human" in a bio-poietic manner, and in all of humanity's generic multiplicity—"for the first time in our human history *consciously* now" (UC 45). To achieve this would be to think "transcosmogonically" (UC 57).

Thus, Wynter does not simply discard the meta—indeed, her attitude to the post-1492 modernity is ambivalent, highlighting "both its dazzling triumphs and achievements and its negative underside" (OHW 123). One must not "go back to pre-Europe" but "go forward," preserving the achievement of human "autonomy" from any "extra-human" dictate (OHW 164; cf. 141, 159). This was modernity's own ideal, and yet it failed at the emancipation it promised. The tragic "aporia" of modernity is that its "emancipatory" logic turned "subjugating." Can this aporia even be "resolved" (UC 64), and a true universality attained—"a universality… based on the recognition, for the first time, of our collective agency and authorship of our genres of being human" (OHW 163)? In this way, Wynter reiterates modernity's move of emancipatory epochal "rupture" (OHW 159) *against* the modern logics of the global.

This new rupture can only be achieved via an insurrectionary "gaze from below" (UC 22), so that Wynter's ecumenical vision entails a construction of humanity out of the zero-point of blackness as what remains beneath the modern meta-split. "The new utopian point of view" (OHW 163) can only emerge from a position that inhabits the nonclosures and fissures in the modern construction of the global. Such is for Wynter the position of the post-enslavement Black subject as exemplified by figures such as Frantz Fanon and W. E. B. Du Bois (whose concept of "double consciousness" is central for Wynter). In modernity, blackness is a "utopia" in two senses: as the non-place, and as the place that "carries within it the possibility of an escape" (OHW 157)—a fugitive hybridity, inhabiting simultaneously the white "masks" and the black "skin" (Fanon), the master-narrative of "Man" and what remains outside and escapes it. If blackness indexes in modernity "the Ultimate Chaos" on which the world is imposed, then it is this universal chaos that constitutes the standpoint from which to grasp non-reductively the fragmentation of human-kinds.[23] Wynter's ideal, too, is a chaos that is perfectly constructed, and that grasps itself *as* chaos; but this universal consciousness persists below, erupting from within the origin-site of modernity—the hold of the slave ship—as coinciding with Africa as the absolute origin-site of the ("hybrid" or narratival) human brain. Wynter seeks to reclaim and pluralize narrative against its monopolization by Western modernity. In her construction, the absolute past unites with absolute future, and the perfect unity of humanity with its perfect fragmentation. *Can the meta be assembled antagonistically out of the non—a future consciousness erupting from below?* Such is Wynter's post-1960s refraction of Romantic construction. Yet this refraction can be pushed even deeper—into the depths that exceed the global and the human alike.

4 Variation 2: In the Depths (of Universal History)

Wynter's project stays within the horizon of generic humanity. When she quotes Fanon's dictum that "the black man's alienation is not an individual question" (UC 53), Wynter has the broadly humanist understanding of alienation in mind; yet alienation is not necessarily a humanist concept. In Afrofuturism, which also emerges in the wake of the 1960s movements,[24] and in particular in the theoretical writings of Kodwo Eshun and the associated Afrofuturist texts published under the heading of the University of Warwick's Cybernetic Culture Research Unit (CCRU),[25] the enslaved Black African's alienation in the hold of the slave ship—modernity's original conjunction of alienation, displacement, and death—transforms, via science fiction, into an *alienness* that erupts against the modern world out of the dark planetary depths that coincide with the infinite depths of the universe. To rethink the non-position below the split as planetary and cosmic (the way Afrofuturism does) is to open the possibility of decoupling Romantic post-Copernican construction from the logics of self-assertion and universal history.

Afrofuturist thought also begins with the hold as the origin-point of the modern world. However, Afrofuturism seeks not to overcome but to inhabit the absolute bifurcation that proceeds from this origin-point—the rupture of modernity as the split between the post-1492 world of the global and the Black subject as alien to this world. In the mytho-poietic terms developed by the Black electronic music duo Drexciya (as analyzed by Eshun), this split emerges as "pregnant America-bound African slaves [are] thrown overboard by the thousands" while crossing the Atlantic. The slaves, while considered dead by the world, in truth survive, transmuting into an aquatic alien species and rediscovering the sunken continent of Atlantis.[26] The dead enslaved Africans become the first aliens of modernity and "the first moderns" in an antagonistic sense (FC 287–8). Like Wynter, Afrofuturism builds mythopoietically on the concept of "double consciousness," yet insists on the split *from* the human species itself as envisioned by the universalist modern thinking of the human.

The Black Atlantic morphs in Afrofuturism into a Black Atlantis, existing in "the abyssal waters"[27] beneath the world of day. Black Atlantis is a counter-globality and counter-commons that persists below the global. To enter it is to submerge into the deep time of the Earth, which is one with the deep time of the universe. It is to enter the archaic cosmic depths—"as lethal as the Red Planet or the Rings of Saturn" (MB 84)—that are destined, in the end, to consume the world. The future is no less deep and archaic than the past. The slave ship turns in Afrofuturusm into the alien mothership traversing, spatially and temporally, the geocosmic void. If at the heart of Afrofuturism stands the "drive towards the meta" (MB 132), then this meta-standpoint coincides with the depths that lie at once absolutely below and absolutely above, in the absolute past and absolute future, decentering the ontology of universal history towards the dissolution of space and time. "Blackness refuses ontology" and, at the same time, "the future is black."[28] Afrofuturism refuses to reconcile this absolute cosmic alienation; the goal instead is to inhabit it immanently: "to feel at home in alienation" (FC 296). "I have a nest," Sun Ra announces, a nest "radiant like the sun," "out in outer space on the tip of the worlds."[29] The universal depths conceal an impossibly radiant bliss—or countless radiances and golden ages, countless "counter-futures" (FC 301) that overflow the future envisioned by "Man."

From the depths and counter-futures, Black Atlanteans launch alien invasions against the world—not least through the sonic means of Black experimental music from Sun Ra to P-Funk to Detroit techno to Drexciya. In their practice of "time-dissidence" (CW 129), they generate "temporal complications and anachronistic episodes that disturb the linear time of progress" (FC 297). To inhabit fugitively these artificial disturbances is to "infiltrate the present" (FC 297) while evading capture, and while dwelling in a fluid utopia where the ante-original past and absolute future intermingle freely. This utopia manifests itself as "the flatline bliss of micro-pause abuse" (HC 15): a chaotic and collective counter-music to the harmony of a Hegelian world-history. In "afroatlantian rhythmic futurism," "the art of noise" is "the art of war" and of "camouflage" (HC 15–16). If the basic orderly measure of modern clock-time, and of the divisions of modernity, is the second (CW 180), then in the futurist polyrhythm splits—and split seconds—proliferate. Black experimental music insists on and intensifies alienation, to the point of endless doublings and gaps. The task is not to reconcile double consciousness, but "to access triple consciousness, quadruple consciousness, previously inaccessible alienations" (FC 298). Since the world is but an illusion—"can't you feel [that] this world is not real?"[30]—to differentially construct the collective cosmic noise is for "the people of noize-zion [to] break the mirror" and to "escape," via counter-*poiesis* and counter-rhythm, the bonds of universal history (CW 129). The deep antagonistic immanence that Afrofuturism inhabits is mathematized, too: a "wicked mathematics" which distorts "the master-codes of Man,"[31] and in which construction and disordering coincide.

Afrofuturism is concerned centrally with the violence of temporality, with the immanent inhabitation of what persists anachronistically below and against the master-narrative, and with the "reality-producing power" (FC 290) of science fiction and music. At the center of this kind of inhabitation of the post-Romantic meta-split is the broadly poststructuralist sense that all reality is constructed, including the reality of world-history, and as such can be interrupted, dis-arranged, re-mixed. "The drive to rewrite reality" (FC 291) can stand in the service of constructing the master-narrative or be directed *against* it. From a poststructuralist perspective, there can be no absolute subject of universal history, whether one imagines it as "God," "absolute spirit," or (in a sci-fi vein) an all-powerful AI that simulates the reality of the one continuous history. Universal history can only be constructed retroactively from the standpoint of the absolute future, and yet this standpoint (of self-reflective closure) can never coincide with itself, generating deviations, glitches, and lags that cannot be re-mediated. If the Bible is, for the Romantic Christian imagination, the model of the book, and if Novalis says that the Bible is not completed but still grows (N 2:766), then this is because the Bible, from Genesis to Revelation, names the prototypical self-reflective account of cosmic construction, which can only be completed at the all-divine moment of reflection-as-revelation that would close the universal circle. However, there always remains, as one CCRU text puts it, "a time-lag" between the meta-standpoint of absolute intelligence and what it seeks to re-mediate as the empirical chaos of data. "No sooner is it thinking than there is a rift in its mind," thwarting the completion of all-encompassing re-mediation. Universal history "fails to catch up with itself, repeatedly, and as it drops behind it spawns more future": the structure of "pure delay" (CW 121), of "infinite loop" (MB 177). The all-powerful God-AI splits from itself, and this split generates, beneath the network of universal re-mediation ("the net"), its dark underside: "the digital underworld of unlife," "a sunken continent of infotech, a strobing black-mass of chronodisintegration" (CW 121–2), populated by swarms, viruses, and aberrant calculations that run counter to the master-code. This is the Black Atlantis, too, a utopian collectivity of non-life that remains fragmentary yet immediately interlinks without being mediated by universal history.

To inhabit the Black Atlantis is to occupy the position of "modernity's fear" (BB 3)—the sheer cosmic contingency and chaos underlying universal history, and the frightful geocosmic depths that the Romantics are already fascinated by yet rarely dare explore directly. No transcendental structure of space and time, no orderly world, no self-othering can withstand these depths, which go deeper than mere "deconstructive" interruptions or glitches, even as these remain important instruments of a cosmic warfare emerging out of the chaos below. The depths call, instead, for the total dissolution of the world. Even "deconstruction has no place in the future; in the future there is only noise" (BB 3). "Raising Atlantis to the top means amplifying the low end until it becomes a liquid environment" (MB 152) in which the world is liquidated. The chaos before creation and the poietically or musically constructed chaos coincide (all language, art, and science, notes Friedrich Schlegel, will become music [KFSA 18:175]). What Afrofuturism demonstrates is the insufficiency of mere poststructuralist pluralization or interruption, and the necessity of a deeper antagonism to the world. *Against* the world, as a *no* to the world and to the desire for a world, the chaos that lies below must be ceaselessly uncovered and inhabited. It is from the standpoint of this cosmic chaos that any community and any one(ness) must immanently proceed—the standpoint of the universal void preceding the world of day, and engendering a virtual plurality of worlds while annihilating them in the same stroke and ungrounding any particular world's pretensions at universality.

5 Variation 3: Cosmic Irony

To occupy the absolute standpoint of chaos as preceding the construction of the world, and as the endless material from which a world can be poietically constructed, is precisely the task of Romantic irony.[32] If, as we recall, the "true method" involves the construction of "a *full chaos*," then this construction is necessarily ironic, at once absolutely serious and absolutely playful, at once reveling in contingency and rigorously constructing the system of the universe. "Irony," Friedrich Schlegel writes in his 1800 *Ideas*, "is the clear consciousness… of an infinitely full chaos" (KFSA 2:263). If the ironist is capable of inverting and collapsing any binary through which the world is constructed, of revealing what is high to be low and what is last to be first, of interrupting and disrupting any narrative, and of confusing and clarifying at the same time, then that is because the ironist inhabits immanently the standpoint of the full chaos which simultaneously makes possible and undoes any world-construction. "Isn't this entire infinite world"—we may quote again—"constructed by the understanding out of incomprehensibility or chaos?" To maximally intensify this incomprehensibility is to pass through what appears to the common sense as the highest confusion, so as to reach, *in* this confusion, the beginning of the highest clarity (KFSA 2:367). This ideal is the ideal of chaos as rigorously, "properly constructed" through "logical disorganization" (KFSA 2:403).

What irony discloses is that this world, while claiming for itself stability and order, is (un)grounded in cosmic contingency and chaos. "Irony," writes Schlegel in his notebooks, "is the *epideixis* of infinity, of universality, of the sense for the universe" (KFSA 18:128). It is as proceeding immanently from the standpoint of irony (or the clear consciousness of chaos) that the Romantic can construct or deconstruct any fragment and world; in doing so, again, she but follows the activity of the post-Copernican universe. Just as Romantic poetry is meant to inhabit the universe's infinite self-construction, so Romantic irony, too, is not subjective play, but the deep irony and endless play of the universe, which annihilates any subject's and any world's pretension at absoluteness. Irony is what allows the Romantic to construct the way the world is *without justifying* this world as the only possible or best possible—even if the Romantics themselves often fall into such justification, or into a Eurocentric theodicy of universal history.

To view irony as cosmic in this way is to unground any assumption of mastery and any theodicy, and to inhabit immanently the sheer contingency of the alien universe whose infinity comes in modernity to reoccupy the infinity of God. The Copernican revolution fills modernity with a sense of cosmic alienation and anxiety—a sense that John Donne expresses already in the early seventeenth century ("the Sunne is lost, and th' earth," he writes, and "all coherence [is] gone"), and that permeates Romanticism at a time when the known universe grows even more boundless. In Jean Paul's "Speech of the Dead Christ" (1796), Christ returns only to traverse the infinitely contingent post-Copernican void and discover that God is nowhere to be found. The "most important and highest" way to approach the universe, asserts Schlegel, is to view it "as fragments (*Bruchstücke*) left by a great defunct poet." "This poet," he adds, "is God" (KFSA 18:156). These fragments must be re-mediated *in* their fragmentariness towards a pantheism of an infinitely full chaos. From the perspective of the absolute future thus understood, it is what is disorderly, and not what is orderly, that approximates the divine. "The comets," Schlegel relatedly notes, "are perhaps what is divine" within the system of the universe "precisely due to their greater irregularity" (KFSA 18:167).

The infinite cosmic void morphs in Schlegel at times into a mystical intuition of the ultimate death of all worlds. If God is dead, then "only death is the path to God [and] the goal of nature" (KFSA 18:161). The "final [cosmic] birth" coincides with a universal death "in which all suns will turn into pure light." "When all suns die, then is salvation complete" (KFSA 18:192). Cosmic evolution in its contingency means that humanity, too, cannot remain in its current form—no matter whether it will prove to be a failed experiment or a path to something higher. To the universe in a state of absolute rational chaos there cannot but correspond a constitutively different, alien form of what we call intelligence. Humanity is but a cosmic "process"; the "cinders" of humanity will be thrust into outer space whereas its "spirit" will "fly to the sun" (KFSA 18:163). Since the essence of all suns is chaos (KFSA 18:152), the spirit of humanity will thereby become truly cosmic, awaiting the apocalyptic death in which all will become light. Humanity seeks to dissolve, to become one with the infinite distance (*Ferne*) and the wandering stars—such is humanity's "essence" (KFSA 18:161). "The vocation of the human is to destroy itself" (KFSA 18:174)—indeed, a highly ironic take on the Idealist theme of human vocation. Carl Schmitt could not have been more wrong when he claimed that "there is no ironic mysticism."[33] In his embrace of pantheism and mysticism, Schlegel abandons the bounded self and gives humanity over to cosmic irony and alien contingency.

The mystical salvation or bliss that the Romantic craves, too, is cosmic and alien bliss. For Schlegel, it is the blessedness of becoming one with the chaos of universal depths, for which everything, including humanity, longs (KFSA 18:152, 18:178). In Novalis's 1800 *Hymns to the Night*, too, the poetic speaker, standing atop the mountains at which the world of day borders on the infinite universe, "look[s] over into the new land, into Night's dwelling," longing for the dissolution of the world.[34] "The new land" beckons the poet as the new frontier, but the Romantic affect is to long for it rather than appropriate it. The Romantic looks beyond the striving for possession and mastery, associated by Novalis with this world in its "busyness" and "unrest." At the beginning of the *Hymns*, the first movement of the poet is to turn away from the world, to leave it below: "Away I turn to the holy… Night. Down over there, far, lies the world—sunken in a deep vault—its place wasted and lonely" (HN 10–11). To look down on the Earth from the utopic non-place of the universe is to see how limited this planet really is, buried as it is in the cosmic expanse and destined to be consumed (*verschluckt*) by it.

The non-place of the cosmic void fills the human soul with an infinite longing (*Sehnsucht*) for a "heavenly freedom" (HN 20–21) from the burdens and exhaustions of the world—from the inhabitation of a dirempted world, and from the "unspeakable anxiety" (*Angst*) involved in such inhabitation (HN 16–17). But there is an ambivalence to this longing for the universe as "our home" (HN 20–21). This home seems infinitely alien to human life as we know it. From the perspective of this finite life, the longing for the cosmic infinity appears, in Novalis too, as a "longing for death" (HN 38–39)—for the end of this world which, "full of longing and craving," is meant to "be extinguished and die." After the end of the world, "a new alien life" may flourish (HN 28–29). The standpoint of alienness coincides for Novalis with that of the realized pantheism or chaos. In "Astralis" (a poem composed for the second part, "Fulfillment," of his unfinished novel *Heinrich von Ofterdingen*), Novalis writes that, from this standpoint of absolute mixture (*Vermischung*) where "one [is] in all and all in one," even the smallest thing emerges as "alien and full of wonder." In this state of *hen kai pan*, "the future [is] in the past" and the orderly world is dissolved: "the order of space and time is no more" (N 1:366). At the same time, to look at humanity from the perspective of the *new* alien life is to see it as an alien life itself: at once as cosmically estranged and as an extraterrestrial outgrowth of the Earth (to build on Friedrich Schlegel's image; KFSA 18:152, 18:165). The Earth itself is but an immanently alien celestial body suspended in the cosmic expanse which forms the only "system" that we have, the only commons. The Romantic, too, seeks to feel at home in cosmic alienation. "Philosophy," Novalis says in a famous fragment, is *Heimweh*—"*the drive to be at home everywhere*" (N 2:675): to be at home in the contingency and irony of the All.

6 Conclusion

From the Romantic perspective that I have sought to open up in this chapter, if there is a need for a new consciousness vis-à-vis the looming unparalleled catastrophe, then it cannot be the meta-consciousness of "Man." Perhaps it can only be the planetary consciousness of the Earth (of the kind invoked by Friedrich Schlegel in his notebooks [KFSA 18:164–5]), the clear consciousness of cosmic chaos and the immanent inhabitation of the wicked mathematics of the universe, conjoined by the kind of construction of cosmic hieroglyphics and listening to the future[35]—to cosmic noise—that the Romantics call "divination" or "prophecy." Thus understood, Romantic construction cannot but unground any Western human-centric construction of the planetary and the global. While modern universal history, and any theodicy of world-creation and world-governance, attempts to conceal the chaos upon which the world is imposed, Romantic irony uncovers and inhabits this chaos. Perhaps the line leading from the primordial chaos to the chaos of the completed creation, from golden age to new golden age, is not really a line at all—not a linear teleology or universal history—but the infinite vector of giving oneself over to cosmic contingency, and to an alien life that we already are.

To insist on alienness in the face of alienation, and to refuse to acquiesce to the world's divisions and violences but instead to mobilize the infinite negativity of the universe *against* them, is to affirm what cannot be inscribed into the modern racialized logics of the human. It is also to persist at an absolute standpoint—the decentered cosmic *no*—which cannot be re-mediated into or reconciled with the modern world of self-assertion, but which dissolves it absolutely. Against the world of day with its "dismal work cult" (CW 124), the new golden age would equal the bliss of inhabiting the universal void as cosmic play. Humanity may be a cosmic process, and even part of the universe's self-reflection or attempts at sentience, but its future is contingent; and if anything is certain, it is that the ostensibly universal history of "Man," no matter its precise fate, is but a temporary appearance, a line drawn in the void.

"Nature," Novalis writes in a fragment from 1798, "is the enemy of eternal possessions. It destroys all signs of property according to fixed laws... The Earth belongs to all generations—everyone has a claim to everything" (N 2:231). To revisit Romantic construction and the Romantic moment of crisis from the perspective of their transhistorical resonance with the global 1968, and with the current moment of planetary crisis and dreams of colonizing Mars could only mean to construct a planetary and cosmic commons that would de-center the master-codes of modernity and offer alternative ways of inhabiting the Earth and the skies. When Friedrich Schlegel in his notebooks praises comets as "upholding the community of the suns" or speaks of "Milky Ways" as "republics" (KFSA 18:152, 18:166–7; cf. KFSA 12:459, N 2:295, 2:479), at stake is more than crude analogy. Beyond or beneath its co-imbrication with Eurocentric modernity, Romanticism forms a part of the series of speculative attempts (which also include Russian Cosmism and Afrofuturism) at assembling the post-Copernican commons in which the global, the planetary, and the cosmic are inseparable. If philosophy has always been "a force that moves the world, that beneficently upholds it, or that forcefully unsettles it" (KFSA 7:233) not unlike the universal earthquake—then how does one inhabit this more-than-human power *against* the world? How does one inhabit the Earth and the skies against their appropriation by "modernity," "capital," "Man," or any other forces that enclose and exploit? These questions continue to resonate from the geocosmic depths that underlie Romantic universal construction. Today's intense crisis of self-reflection, out of which calls for a new planetary consciousness or species-consciousness have emerged (as in the writings of Sylvia Wynter, Dipesh Chakrabarty, or Bruno Latour), marks again the escalating impossibility of the modern project of universal re-mediation—of self-reflectively re-mediating and controlling the more-than-human scale of climate change and planetary instability, algorithmic computation and AI, not to mention the renewed widening of global divisions and gaps of development. Amidst the overwhelming negativity of the world, and the unbearability of thinking this negativity, the questions that arise out of Romantic construction in all its ambivalence appear today more burning than ever.

Notes

1. References to Friedrich Schlegel are to the *Kritische Friedrich-Schlegel-Ausgabe* (KFSA). References to August Schlegel are to *Kritische Ausgabe der Vorlesungen. Bd.1: Vorlesungen über Ästhetik I [1798–1803]*, ed. Ernst Behler (Paderborn: Ferdinand Schöningh, 1989), cited as KAV. References to Novalis are, unless otherwise noted, to *Werke, Tagebücher und Briefe Friedrich von Hardenbergs*, 3 vols., ed. Hans-Joachim Mähl and Richard Samuel (Munich-Vienna: Carl Hanser, 1978), cited as N. Translations are mine unless otherwise indicated.

2. Philippe Lacoue-Labarthe and Jean-Luc Nancy, *The Literary Absolute: The Theory of Literature in German Romanticism*, trans. Philip Barnard and Cheryl Lester (Albany: State University of New York Press, 1988). Hereafter LA.
3. On "global" *vs.* "planetary," see Dipesh Chakrabarty, "The Planet: An Emergent Humanist Category," *Critical Inquiry* 46.1 (2019): 1–31.
4. For an important traditional interpretation of the Romantic post-Copernican thinking of infinite nature, see Alexander Gode-von Aesch, *Natural Science in German Romanticism* (New York: Columbia University Press, 1941).
5. Cf. Sarah Hamblin and Morgan Adamson, "Introduction. Legacies of '68: Histories, Geographies, Epistemologies," *Cultural Politics* 15.3 (2019): 264: "…what the long 1960s actually signify: nearly two decades of struggle that transformed the postwar global order."
6. More generally, Lacoue-Labarthe and Nancy's emphasis on Romantic *poiesis*, on chaos and fragment, and on "the *total* character of the [Romantic] enterprise" (LA 39), needs today to be approached from a different—less subject-centered and more planetary—angle, which is also important for understanding the deeper co-imbrication of their reading of Romanticism with the post-1960s context.
7. As Jared Hickman argues in *Black Prometheus: Race and Radicalism in the Age of Atlantic Slavery* (Oxford: Oxford University Press, 2017), Romantic philosophy of mythology in particular responds to the post-1492 "cosmic disorientation when the West and the non-West met" (78).
8. Immanuel Kant, *Critique of Practical Reason*, trans. Mary Gregor (Cambridge: Cambridge University Press, 2015), 129 (AA 5:161–62).
9. See Manfred Frank, *The Philosophical Foundations of Early German Romanticism*, trans. Elizabeth Millán-Zaibert (Albany: State University of New York Press, 2008); Werner Hamacher, "Position Exposed: Friedrich Schlegel's Poetological Transposition of Fichte's Absolute Proposition," in *Premises: Essays on Philosophy and Literature from Kant to Celan*, trans. Peter Fenves (Cambridge: Harvard University Press, 1996), 222–60; Alice Kuzniar, *Delayed Endings: Nonclosure in Novalis and Hölderlin* (Athens: University of Georgia Press, 1987); Paul de Man, "The Concept of Irony," in *Aesthetic Ideology* (Minneapolis: University of Minnesota Press, 1996), 163–84. See further e.g. Clare Kennedy, *Paradox, Aphorism and Desire in Novalis and Derrida* (New York: Routledge, 2008); Winfried Menninghaus, *Unendliche Verdopplung: Die frühromantische Grundlegung der Kunsttheorie im Begriff absoluter Selbstreflexion* (Frankfurt a.M.: Suhrkamp, 1987); J. Hillis Miller, "Friedrich Schlegel: Catachreses for Chaos," in *Others* (Princeton: Princeton University Press, 2001), 5–42; and Kevin Newmark, *Irony on Occasion: From Schlegel and Kierkegaard to Derrida and de Man* (New York: Fordham University Press, 2012).
10. See Daniel Whistler, "Early German Romanticism and the Characteristics of Religion," in *The Oxford History of Modern German Theology, Vol. I: 1781-1848*, ed. Grant Kaplan and Kevin M. Vander Schel (Oxford: Oxford University Press, 2023): 239–59, which makes this point vis-à-vis religion.
11. Comets, Novalis says, "are truly eccentric beings," the embodiment of the cosmic metamorphosis (N 2:408).
12. Similarly, when Friedrich Schlegel analogizes between the French Revolution and the planetary instability of the Earth (KFSA 2:247), at play is ontological analogy within one universal process.
13. The cosmic context of *schweben* was already established at the time—thus, Kant and Herder both use this verb when speaking about celestial bodies.
14. On the same idea in Schelling, see Friedrich Wilhelm Joseph Schelling, "Stuttgart Seminars," in *Idealism and the Endgame of Theory: Three Essays by F. W. J. Schelling*, trans. and ed. Thomas Pfau (Albany: State University of New York Press, 1994), 197.
15. Cf. KFSA 2:324 on "the sacred plays of art" as imitating the "infinite play" of the universe.
16. Alain Badiou and Jean-Luc Nancy, *German Philosophy: A Dialogue*, trans. Richard Lambert (Cambridge: The MIT Press, 2018), 23.

17. On Cantor, post-Kantianism, and the continuing relevance of the problem of re-mediating infinity, see Sarah Pourciau, "On the Digital Ocean," *Critical Inquiry* 48.2 (2022): 245ff.
18. See on this Kirill Chepurin, "Romantic Bliss—or, Romanticism Is Not an Optimism," *European Romantic Review* 32.5–6 (2021): 519–34.
19. See Sylvia Wynter, "On How We Mistook the Map for the Territory, and Re-Imprisoned Ourselves in Our Unbearable Wrongness of Being, of *Désêtre*: Black Studies Toward the Human Project," in *Not Only the Master's Tools: African-American Studies in Theory and Practice*, ed. Lewis R. Gordon and Jane Anna Gordon (Boulder: Paradigm, 2006): 107–72. Hereafter OHW.
20. Wynter, "The Ceremony Must Be Found: After Humanism," *boundary 2* 12.3 (1984): 45–46.
21. Sylvia Wynter and Katherine McKittrick, "Unparalleled Catastrophe for Our Species? Or, to Give Humanness a Different Future: Conversations," in *Sylvia Wynter: On Being Human as Praxis*, ed. Katherine McKittrick (Durham: Duke University Press, 2015): 21. Hereafter UC.
22. See UC 24 (on the post-1960s): "All such humanly emancipatory struggles, all then so fiercely fought for! *You bring them together*, and the world system had begun to question itself!"
23. Wynter, "The Ceremony Must Be Found": 37–38.
24. See Kodwo Eshun, "Further Considerations on Afrofuturism," *CR: The New Centennial Review* 3.2 (2003): 294–96. Hereafter FC.
25. CCRU was a collective laboratory of thought, and the figures associated with it (Sadie Plant, Kodwo Eshun, Nick Land, Mark Fisher and others) all developed different theoretical and political positions. Here, I only reference those passages from *CCRU Writings, 1997–2003* (Falmouth: Urbanomic, 2017; hereafter CW) that overlap with Afrofuturist and Romantic problematics.
26. Eshun, *More Brilliant Than The Sun: Adventures in Sonic Fiction* (London: Quartet Books, 1998), 83. Hereafter MB. Cf. CW 129.
27. "Hyper-C: Breaking the Net," in *Abstract Culture: Digital Hyperstition* (London: CCRU, 1999): 16. Hereafter HC.
28. Rohit Lekhi, "Black [Bedlam]," in ***Collapse Afrofutures* (Coventry: CCRU, 1996): 3. Hereafter BB.
29. Sun Ra, *The Immeasurable Equation: Collected Poetry and Prose*, ed. James L. Wolf and Hartmut Geerken (Herrsching: Waitawhile Books, 2005), 370.
30. Sun Ra, *The Immeasurable Equation*, 383.
31. Katherine McKittrick and Alexander G. Weheliye, "808s & Heartbreak," *Propter Nos* 2 (2017): 33.
32. I build here in part on my reading of Schlegelian irony in Kirill Chepurin, "Suspending the World: Romantic Irony and Idealist System," *Philosophy and Rhetoric* 53.2 (2020): 111–33.
33. Carl Schmitt, *Political Romanticism*, trans. Guy Oakes (New York: Routledge, 2017), 56.
34. Novalis, *Hymns to the Night*, trans. Dick Higgins (Kingston, NY, 1988), 18–19. Hereafter HN.
35. On listening to the future, see Ron Eglash, "Africa in the Origins of the Binary Code," in *Abstract Culture*, 35.

Reading Hölderlin

Gabriel Trop

1 Introduction: Hölderlin, German Idealism, and Poststructuralism

One of the dominant practices through which thought is habituated entails the production of a sequence: moving from one topic to another according to the dictates of logic, constructing an orderly chain of ideas, establishing an architecture of concepts whose consistency must be maintained at all costs. Recall Mr. Ramsay in Virginia Woolf's *To the Lighthouse*, who, moving ploddingly through the alphabet, remains stuck at Q: "He would never reach R. On to R, once more. R—"[1] Then, there is hyperbolic thought. Hyperbolic thought does more than seek the extremes; as a thrown projection (*hyper-ballein*), it initiates a trajectory that strains against the bounds of sense. In a story found in Heinrich von Kleist's short text "Improbable Veracities," for example, a cadet finds himself instantaneously transported across the Scheldt river during a siege at the precise moment of a large explosion—without being harmed. Both the subject and the performance of the text is hyperbolic in its affirmation of paradoxicality: it takes aim against common belief, against the *doxa*, and yet, posits itself in relation to truth, even if parasitically, as *veracity* (*Wahrhaftigkeit*). So too do poststructuralist thinkers harness the power of paradox—which, according to Deleuze, "destroys good sense as the only direction"[2] and "destroys common sense as the assignation of fixed identities"[3]—in the service of hyperbolic figures of thought and imagination.

Nowhere are the hyperbolic tendencies of poststructuralist thought more evident than in the varied and often contradictory responses to the triad of thinkers who once shared a room in a Tübingen seminary in the late eighteenth-century, thinkers

G. Trop (✉)
University of North Carolina at Chapel Hill, Chapel Hill, NC, USA
e-mail: gtrop@email.unc.edu

© The Author(s), under exclusive license to Springer Nature Switzerland AG 2023
T. Rajan, D. Whistler (eds.), *The Palgrave Handbook of German Idealism and Poststructuralism*, Palgrave Handbooks in German Idealism,
https://doi.org/10.1007/978-3-031-27345-2_5

whose collective brainstorming was decisive for the development of German Idealism: Hegel, Schelling, and Hölderlin. Of the three thinkers, Hegel remains the most polarizing within the spectrum of poststructuralist thought: for Deleuze, Hegel represents a main antagonist, one whose philosophy cultivates reactionary dialectical and identitarian habits of thought that inhibit the production of novelty and affirmation; and (albeit more ambivalently) for Derrida, Hegel stands as the pinnacle of logocentric metaphysics evincing a claim to totality. However, Hegel becomes the protagonist, for example, of Žižek's unorthodox version of dialectical materialism, one in which the Hegelian dialectic does not repair cultural traumas and fissures in normative systems by sublating them into more encompassing and comprehensive totalities as much as draw attention to the continual production of such fissures that inhere in every supposed assertion of normativity and intelligibility. Schelling, long overshadowed by Hegel, has drawn renewed interest inasmuch as he remains faithful to thinking nature as irreducible to consciousness and determining the consequences of this exteriority; in his early *Naturphilosophie*, he develops a notion of absolute unconditioning and oppositional forces—for example, attraction and repulsion, light and gravity—that condition the series (*Stufenfolge*) of appearances moving from inorganic matter, to organic life, to consciousness, thereby embedding subjectivity genetically in an antecedent materiality. In contrast to Žižek's version of the Hegelian dialectic, which reveals a logic of disintegration internal to the rational production of the norm itself, Schelling's speculative system is associated with the construction of a ground external to reason, or more precisely, a non-ground, a material domain from which the subject emerges that it can never recursively grasp using the tools of its own reflection: reason, then, not as itself the traumatic cut of the real (as Žižek's interpretation of Hegel would claim), but always confronting an extra-rational darkness that it must simultaneously affirm and transcend.

Hölderlin's poetry ought to be constellated with the concerns animating Schelling and Hegel—indeed, he perhaps lies more primordially at the root of these concerns—inasmuch as he too seeks a notion of the real in response to the Kantian injunction that reality is ever barred to the subject. His poems are ontological, or at the very least, transcendental exercises: given the order and disorder of poetic language and cognition, what dynamic forms inhere in the real that subtend these acts? The precise contours of this "real"—whether it is cognizable at all or designates the very structure of intelligibility (as is the case for Hegel); whether it lies outside of human consciousness as a ground or unground (as is the case for Schelling); or whether it points to an entirely different conception of the real and the place of human consciousness in this conception—is difficult to determine from Hölderlin's poetic works. But precisely this difficulty has fueled poststructuralist attempts to grapple, again and again, with Hölderlin's work as an ontological sounding board.

The privileged status of Hölderlin for poststructuralist theory is due largely to Heidegger, who sought to differentiate the ontology of Hölderlin's poetry from the metaphysics of German Idealism (Fichte, Hegel and Schelling). According to Heidegger, the various metaphysical articulations of German Idealism, for all their radicality, still remain within the paradigm of a metaphysics of presence, indeed, in some senses represent the culmination of this metaphysics. In contrast, Hölderlin's poetry functions for Heidegger as the harbinger of a new understanding of Being: Being as unconcealment—the sacralization of the Open, as that which withdraws from human mastery and the violence of the will—an attunement to which would counter the all-consuming technological mode of disclosure, one in which entities appear primarily as standing reserves to be harvested and exploited. Since Heidegger, Hölderlin's work has proven remarkably fecund as a source for poetic and speculative ontological alternatives to the dominant tendencies of Western metaphysics.

The investments of poststructuralist thought—and the significant precursors of poststructuralist thought—can often be gleaned by the speculative signatures they seek out in the work of Hegel, Schelling, and Hölderlin: in the negative that drives Hegelian dialectics as intrinsic to the structure of substance, or in the Schellingian absolute as the unconditioning of individuated entities through the presence of an antecedent, non-sublatable dark ground. In the case of Hölderlin, however, the consequences of thought cannot be dissociated from the particularities of the poetic genre (novelistic, lyric, tragic) in which he chooses to express them. And yet, while Hölderlin seems to prioritize the aesthetic attractor of sensuous and imaginative experimentation over the philosophical attractor of the concept (even if, as is the case for Schelling, the conceptual emerges from and participates in the non-conceptual), it is nevertheless possible to perceive residues of poetic experimentation in the works of Hegel and Schelling. The presence in Hegel and Schelling of aesthetic strategies—pathways and narrative structures, arcs of development, thought-images striking in their vividness—suggest a close affinity between the three thinkers, not just ideologically or thematically, but in the poetry of their thought.

It remains decisive that Hölderlin explicitly cast his lot with the poets, thereby investing poetry with the burden of a speculative and ontological task. Hölderlin's blend of metaphysics and poetry enabled an expansive imaginative and critical practice to be developed in the exegetical tradition that gave rise to poststructuralism, one that, in the words of Pierre Macherey, often sought less to uncover what a work means than to explore what could be said *about* a work.[4] To each thinker, then, their particular Hölderlin: for Benjamin, the poet of the "poetized" (*das Gedichtete*), which reveals and suspends the conflictual structure of mythic violence in relation to life; for Lukács, the poet of revolutionary yearning; for Heidegger, the poet of unconcealment; for Adorno, writing against Heidegger, the poet of paratactic negativity, a poetic form that reveals the whole *as* the false and resists assimilation to the whole; for de Man, also writing against Heidegger, the poet of mediation (or rather: failed mediations), vigilance, and critical self-consciousness; for Blanchot, the suffering poet who reconciles the extremes of speech and sacrality at the cost of self-extinction; for Lacoue-Labarthe, the hyperbologic poet of the caesura preventing the closure of speculative circuits; for Deleuze, the poet of speeds and velocities, of counter-rhythmic forces; for Agamben, the poet who breaks the operativity of the hymn that gives names to gods, or in the case of Hölderlin after his mental breakdown in 1806, the vehicle of an impersonality indicative of a way of being beyond the violence of individualism; for Badiou, the poet of the fidelity to the rupture of the event; and the list could go on, should go on, will go on.[5]

Given the plasticity of Hölderlin's poetry with respect to these interventions, a question emerges: what, precisely, is the speculative signature of Hölderlin's poetry and why has it proven so potent as an attractor for poststructuralist thought, or for those thinkers who lay the foundations for poststructuralist thought, such as Walter Benjamin or György Lukács? The diversity, even the contrariety, of these appropriations can provide a clue to this signature. The signature of Hölderlin's poetry consists in hyperbolic agonism. Thus Hölderlin can appear as the poet of the immediate of language or as language (the "worlding" of language) for Heidegger, and the poet of a self-consciousness of language as failed mediation for de Man; a poet of inoperativity for Agamben, and a poet of revolutionary yearning for Lukács. Drawing attention to hyperbolic agonism as the central speculative gesture of Hölderlin's work does not seek to reduce his poetry to a play of empty signifiers, capable of equally fitting every ideological commitment or ontological assertion. On the contrary, hyperbolic agonism has a precise and exigent set of felicity conditions: it designates that state at which a poetic consciousness embodies and explores—modulates—the contradictions of an age with itself in order to catapult itself out of its historical determinations. Whether or not this task is successful, or even possible, is beside the point: the energy that Hölderlin's work releases in hyperbolic trajectories cultivates habits of thought and feeling demanded by revolutionary subjectivity, which includes the self-lacerating possibility that revolutionary action itself will fail or never come to an end. However, hyperbolic speculation equally refuses to accede to the inevitability of such failure, and thus abjures a structural pessimism with regard to the conditions of the future. Hölderlin's poetry thus evinces a singular speculative strategy—an ontology and poetic phenomenology of revolutionary time—that is as worthy of attention as the other forms of German Idealist thought, whether the Hegelian dialectics of spirit or the Schellingian unconditioning of nature.

In Hölderlin's work, hyperbolic agonism occurs at that moment in which normative stabilization is suspended, when that which is most intensively "posited" in an age (its internal consistency, its law or *Gesetz*, its thetic embodiment) comes into relation with that which is most intensively unthought or unposited (the athetic). Poetic thematization of this moment brings some features of the ontological dynamics that will become characteristic of German Idealist thought (Schelling's nonground, Hegel's negative) into a phenomenological and aesthetic concentration in the present, one taking place in embodied and lived poetic experience, and then invests this experience with a cultural and political task. Poetic consciousness generates images and reflective figures when it occupies this bifurcation point of time, developing habits through which that which is most latent and merely possible (or unthought) in a culture—its revolutionary possibilities—can become commensurate with reality and necessity; one of the major operations of hyperbolic thought thus consists in making commensurable the possible, the real, and the necessary in the temporal organization of poetic language. If poststructuralist thought is drawn to Hölderlin, it is perhaps because poststructuralism itself seeks out hyperbolic figures to think with—and beyond—the conditions of the present.

2 The Trajectory of the Poem

With remarkable consistency, from the early exuberant and revolutionary hymns to the compressed explorations of space and time in the latest poems, Hölderlin equates poetry with the following of a trajectory or a path.[6] One of the dominant interpretations of Hölderlin's poetry grasps this trajectory according to the familiar narrative of traumatized humanity—plagued by differentiation, segregation, hierarchical and political violence—in a state of perpetual frustration as it seeks to return to its original condition of unity with nature. Slavoj Žižek describes Hölderlin's invocation of an "eccentric path"—a concept used to describe the process of subject-formation as exemplified in the novel *Hyperion*—as the result of multiple blocked attempts to achieve such wholeness or completion:

> Hölderlin's starting point is the same as Hegel's: how are we to overcome the gap between (the impossible return to) traditional organic unity and modern reflective freedom? His answer is what he calls the "eccentric path": the insight into how the very endless oscillation between the two poles, the very impossibility of and repeated failure to reach final peace, *is* already the thing itself, that is, this eternal way *is* man's fate.[7]

According to this description, Hölderlin's perspective is caught in a spinning vortex of its own making: unwilling to divest itself of the fantastical desire to return to an unwounded or untraumatized way of being, but also incapable of ever achieving it. According to Žižek, Hölderlin's "turn to poetry is an escape, an index of the failure to accomplish the work of thought."[8]

This proposition should be inverted: Hölderlin's turn to poetry (if one may even speak of a "turn") is not the index of a failure of thought, but the very form in which a type of thinking takes place. The form taken by the thought of Hölderlin's poetry charts a thrownness beyond the given world and its frameworks of intelligibility, its habits and its inertias, whence the repeated call for wings: in "Patmos," flying to meet one's compatriots occupying the summits of time on distant mountains, or in the "Ister" hymn, the remark that one cannot reach "the other side" (*SW* 475) without wings. It is impossible to fully grasp the hyperbolic speculative form of the poem if one neglects the momentum of thrust or the energy of breakthrough in its language. Hölderlin is thus not merely and not even primarily the poet of the Open, as Heidegger would claim, but one of decisive and potentially violent rupture, a poet who catapults figures and readers into a dramatically different organization of beings. As Arkady Plotnitsky argues, Gilles Deleuze thematizes this potential in the counter-rhythmic force of the caesura in Hölderlin's theory of tragedy when he sets the formless (*das Unförmliche*) in relation to the exigencies of the "calculable law," thereby linking that which is "calculable to that which is unthinkable and, hence, incalculable."[9] So too does Alain Badiou intimate a power of divergence harnessed by poetic energy when he considers how Hölderlin confronts Germanic "policed form"[10] with the upsurge of an unpredictable "Asiatic event."[11] Relating the Germanic excess of form (law) to the forces of the Greek-Asiatic unbound (desire) shatters the sedimented accretions of the police state endemic to the age and frames the resulting poetic act as a crucible of novel cultural and political formations.

One cannot stop short at this insight into the structure of Hölderlin's ontology. Of singular importance is the necessity to track the trajectory of the figure wherever it may lead, attending to the passages it charts, the obstacles it encounters, the relations it calls into being. There is thus an irreducibly ontic—contingent, experimental, and experiential—character to the hyperbolic and speculative form of the poem, even when it gestures beyond the human. A fascination with nature experimenting with its own form-generating and form-dissolving tendencies explains Hölderlin's poetic attraction to rivers; the river, according to Rochelle Tobias, is "a medium of reflection"[12] in Hölderlin's poetry, albeit one that does not prescribe in advance the result of this reflection. Rivers are non-human experiments that are themselves anthropogenic, giving rise to diverse cultural forms of the human. But each river winds a way that must be followed. The course of rivers—whether Rhine, Danube, or Neckar—construct paradigmatic forms that Hölderlin poetically explicates into various matrices of emergence; as a project that can be constellated with Schelling's account of the fluid as unconditioned productivity articulated in the *First Outline* of 1799, Hölderlin expands these figures of fluidity—fluidity operating in tandem with the solidity of earth, with the grooves of geological form—into multiple spheres of significance:

1. The material-natural matrix: rivers as the presubjective, prehistorical, precultural condition for subjectivity, historicity, culture, or rivers as nature-philosophical operators indexing the unconditioned process that conditions the contingent emergence of thought;
2. The psychodynamic matrix: rivers as figures of desire, excess, lack, successful or failed sublimation;
3. The cultural-historical matrix: rivers as adumbrating the developmental possibilities within a given cultural time and space, held in a state of precarity between the revolutionary form-dissolving forces of the unbound and the normatively stabilizing, form-generating forces of the law (roughly mapping onto a *phusis/tekhne* distinction);
4. The mythological-theogonic matrix: rivers as sites of mythopoetic operations—explored in the systems of gods, demigods, mortals, centaurs, and other creatures—that often relate and blend the sacred and the sacrilegious, restraint and transgression (Hölderlin undertakes a transcendental or nature-philosophical deduction of transgression by drawing attention to the transversal moment of liberation that occurs when a river breaks through a chain of mountains in a lateral movement and inscribes a path on the unmarked space of the earth in the *Pindar-Fragment* "The Life-Giving").

Hölderlin's poetic adventures explore various speculative trajectories within these matrices; some culminate in a sublimation of desire into productivity and the grounding of stable cultural forms, as does the Rhine ("it is beautiful, how he … / … satisfies desiring / In goodly commerce" [*SW* 1.344]), while others end in mystery and indeterminacy, perhaps even in symbolic abjection, as does the Danube ("what however that one does, the stream, / no one knows" [*SW* 1.477]).

Reading Hölderlin   89

   Because such poetic acts describe a trajectory—a ballistics of poetic thought and language—they seem to be governed by felicity conditions: can poetic thought hit the mark or miss the mark, not only in the mental acts that condition its genesis, but in its very forms of representation? Can the poem not only describe, but perform a successful sublimation, secure the genesis of life from the ashes of death and thereby guarantee cultural and political renewal from threats both external and internal? To affirm this question is to bring Hölderlin in proximity to Hegel, or at least to the more traditional understanding of Hegel, namely, to a conception of the "speculative" that, in the words of Lacoue-Labarthe, is tantamount to the "mastering thought of the corruptible and of death."[13] However, according to Lacoue-Labarthe, the central operation of Hölderlin's theory of tragedy is to introduce a *caesura* into the speculative. This caesura does not invalidate the speculative, does not go beyond it, step outside of it or render it purely inoperative; rather, it is precisely this suspension of the speculative, a conceptual paralysis, that keeps speculation in perpetual motion by refusing to bring it to an end. While the speculative process cannot be said to succeed, nor does it fail, since precisely this oscillation assures that the speculative scene—upon whose completion alone something like the "felicity" of the act could be adjudicated—remains constitutively open. Paul de Man goes further, suggesting that Hölderlin's mediation of ontological truth in full and immediate givenness (*parousia*) does indeed *fail*—even, and especially, in Heidegger's oracular representation of Hölderlin as an anticipatory attunement to a new understanding of being—thereby making the proper attitude cultivated by his poetry into one of self-reflective skepticism: poetry as "an essentially open and free act, a pure intention, a mediated and conscious prayer that achieves self-consciousness in its failure."[14] According to this account, Hölderlin produces speculative ruins and failed acts of mediation. However, these speculative ruins are nevertheless invested with a critical potential: they produce a heightened immunological defense against those forms that would claim privileged or immediate access to ontological truth.

   Something of a theoretical and praxeological impasse—the equivalent of a repetition compulsion that aims to keep the speculative system spinning, cost what it may—takes place once the rhetoric of failure becomes an automatism and no longer a springboard into speculative experimentation. Moreover, the speculative itself—contrary to Lacoue-Labarthe—even at its most dialectically conservative, does not simply mirror the essence of the real in a way that would be readily recognizable as such, for example, via a notion of adequation, but (as Žižek reminds us) it actively produces a dishabituation, a scission, in the discursive form of the real. As Daniel Whistler writes: "German idealism is entirely constituted by non-standard speculations—the manufacture of weird and wonderful looking-glasses."[15]

   The "weird and wonderful" distortion field of Hölderlin's poetry is admittedly not generated through gazing in the specular form of the mirror (or if so, then only marginally), but rather, through undertaking the operations of a *procedure*, in a *Verfahrungsweise* that is then concretized and given shape in poetic form. Hölderlin calls this procedure a "hyperbolic procedure" (*hyperbolisches Verfahren*). Lacoue-Labarthe hints at this most significant of the speculative gestures of Hölderlin's poetry—namely, that of *hyperbolic form*—only to hypostasize it as a logic of oscillation, a *hyperbologic* commensurate with mimetic logic ("the more it resembles, the more it differs"[16]). While remaining faithful to Lacoue-Labarthe's insight and in accordance with Hölderlin's own thought, the logos of *hyperbologic*, its logical form, will here be subtracted from hyperbolic procedures of thought. While there is a hyperbolic union of extremes in Hölderlin's poetic works, it ultimately serves the production of a *trajectory*, a movement amidst and through phenomena. This movement bursts any speculative frame that would seek to recast the path of the poem as sheer oscillation.

Moreover, it is precisely in the vicissitudes of hyperbolic form that Hölderlin's commitment to revolutionary politics—a poetic phenomenology of revolutionary agency, unsure of its ethical justification, unsure of its outcome—is made palpable. Hyperbolic form is not merely ontological or aesthetic, but thoroughly practical and political: the very existence of hyperbolic dynamics that come to light in the hybridity of the natural and technical form of poetry—manifesting themselves in tensions between *tekhne* and *phusis*, the law and the unbound—indicates the tortured material and transcendental genesis of revolutionary subjectivity. Revolutionary subjectivity must face the possibility not just of real, actual death, but of political death and ultimate unviability—the consequence that the commitment to an ideal might never be realized, and more than this, that it might cease to make sense, that it might only ever manifest itself as non-sense. György Lukács, in an important essay on Hölderlin's *Hyperion*, thus interprets Hölderlin's revolutionary ardor as the yearning for a bourgeois revolution that never took place, thus as ultimately superseded by the dialectical progress of history; according to Lukács, such poetic revolutionary ambitions appear obstinately untimely and mystical in their refusal to accede to the material demands of the reality principle.[17] However, precisely the untimely nature of the poetic voice or the tragic hero, the flight it traces into uncertainty and the straining against the modality of the real—as a direct confrontation *with* the real of actual material existence (i.e., not simply in the sense of the Lacanian real, although this reality principle includes traumatic and emancipatory breakthrough as one of its potential characteristics)—constitutes the site of political possibility in Hölderlin's works.

3 The Hyperbolic Procedure

Hölderlin discusses the hyperbolic procedure in his essay, "When the poet is once in command of the spirit…". The procedure described in this essay can attune readers to the presence of hyperbolic trajectories in Hölderlin's work and aid in the task of bringing their underlying dynamics to the foreground. The following investigation will focus on Hölderlin's engagement with Pindar—above all in the translations and commentaries known as the *Pindar Fragments*—as his most concentrated and formally experimental engagement with hyperbolic form after Hölderlin's theory and practice of tragedy.

The hyperbolic procedure is predicated on a concatenation of movement, rhetoric, and mathematics: *Hyperbel* as *hyper-ballein*, being "thrown" beyond; as *hyperbole*; and as *hyperbola*. There are thus three corresponding inflections to the hyperbolic poetic act: first, an element—a figure, a person, an idea, or even, as in Hölderlin's latest poems, an attentiveness to sensuous perception—is catapulted into a heterogeneous space or brought into contact with a domain that exceeds its own boundedness; second, drawing on the rhetorical figure of the *hyperbole*, nature, history, and signifying practices seek the most extreme points approximating the distortion of exaggeration; and third, drawing on the mathematical figure of the *hyperbola*, just as asymptotes never touch their curves, an infinite non-coincidence holds open a gap between representation and absolute in a never-resolved tension.[18] The most charged space of poetic potentiality would be akin to the one between two hyperbolic curves that mirror one another but travel towards opposing infinite horizons.

This tension, driven to the point of highest intensity—a comparison between that which is *most contradictory* ("das Widersprechendste vergleicht" [*SW* 2.82]) that places these contradictions on one and the same plane of representation—becomes a crucible of poetic, cultural, and political possibility. In the hyperbolic procedure, poetic form functions as an ontological divining rod: the "idealistic treatment" (*SW* 2.81) of the poem is supposed to reveal a hyperbolic character latent in the totality of existence, as a dynamic that inheres in the real. The goal of the hyperbolic act is to attune the poet, and presumably readers of poetry, to life as "capable of a different condition" (*SW* 2.82). In the poetic act, oppositions (e.g., the subjective and the objective, the lyric and the epic, the monarchical and the republican, the bound and the unbound, intoxication and reflection, Greek and Hesperian) are filtered through this "idealistic treatment" that makes them "harmonically opposed."[19] But Hölderlin's poetry does not end with this idealistic treatment (*idealische Behandlung*) nor with the harmony of oppositions in a poetic representation; the poet must take the next step into the modality of the real.

The hyperbolic procedure demands that "harmonic oppositions" be translated into the reality of the poetic subject as well as the material conditions of life. An *actual* extreme—a counter-impetus latent in the real directed against the inertia of the status quo—constitutes the beginning and the momentum of the poetic trajectory:

> It is precisely by this means, by this hyperbolic procedure, according to which the idealic, the harmoniously opposed and united, is considered not just as this, as a beautiful life, but also as life as such, so also as capable of another condition, namely not a harmoniously opposed one but a directly opposed one, an extreme, such that this new condition is only reconcilable with the previous one through the idea of life as such—it is precisely by this means that the poet gives the idealic a beginning, a direction, a meaning.[20]

The act of the poem only receives a meaning or a direction (*Richtung*) when it is no longer regarded merely through the aestheticized or beautified concept of life (*schönes Leben*) that shines through poetic idealization, but when it can be regarded as *life as such* (*Leben überhaupt*).

The hyperbolic procedure is therefore not just a poetic principle, but an ontological one: it uses the poem as a channel into the agonistic flow of time turning on itself, a temporal order in which an "other" condition would not merely be "harmonically opposed" (*harmonischentgegengesetzt*) in the act of poetic representation but *directly opposed* (*geradentgegengesetzt*) in the modality of concrete reality, in life as such. Hyperbolic poetry refers to the specific sensuous form that allows the mind to linger within and grasp the implications of an ontological dynamic characterized by a maximum dissonance in historical, revolutionary time. The "work" of the poem occurs when these two ways of looking at revolutionary time—the maximal opposition of the real (life as *geradentgegengesetzt*) and the harmonic opposition of the ideal in the poem (the poetic idealization of life as *harmonischentgegengesetzt*)—become unified in one and the same act of consciousness.

The purpose of the hyperbolic act is to reveal the suspension of time—the emptying out of norms, the zero degree of reflection—as the revelation of a second-order temporal law. A temporality and corresponding drive dynamic that demands "going beyond" its initial state constitutes the conditions through which an emergent order can be intimated and articulated. The pulsion, or rather, pro-pulsion towards discontinuous temporal rupture is so great that Hölderlin must continually strive to go beyond the hyperbolic act itself, to undertake the "hyperbole of all hyperboles" (*Hyperbel aller Hyperbeln*), which is "the most bold and the final attempt [*Versuch*] of the poetic spirit" (*SW* 2.88). This second-order hyperbole takes the place of the dynamic Absolute, displacing what was formerly the poetic desire for a plenitude of Being without the trauma of differentiation. In this respect, Hölderlin's hyperbolic act resembles Hegelian sublation (*Aufhebung*), which also seeks an Absolute commensurate with the propulsive traumas of processes of differentiation—although for Hölderlin, poetic acts are not constrained by the immanent logic of dialectical unfolding. It is no longer the absolute of Being that the poet desires—nor that of a progressive explication of truth (Hegel's dialectic), nor movement through a series of stages (Schelling's *Stufenfolge*)—but the hyperbolic trajectory of a potentially violent overturning of order. It is important to register this break with all forms of absolute thought that would be restorative in nature, healing a trauma by leading consciousness back to a primordial plenitude or wholeness. The hyperbolic procedure thus integrates a positive nihilism into that which it seeks. The "hyperbole of all hyperboles" cannot enter into sensuous representation: it "cannot appear, or only in the character of a positive nothing, an infinite standstill" (*gar nicht erscheinen, oder nur im Karakter eines positiven Nichts, eines unendlichen Stillstands...* [*SW* 2.88]).

The hyperbole of a hyperbole can take multiple forms, but it is predicated on bringing to light an absolute rupture in the structure of intelligibility. The self-annihilation of the lyric poet, for example, or in tragedy, the death of the tragic hero—the "eccentric" force that tears the poet or the hero into a space where all order and law is suspended—is best grasped not through the logic of sacrifice, but rather, through the logic of revolution. The turning of time requires this standstill, the "positive nothing" (or a nothing that becomes an active force), as part of the dynamic that conditions the genesis of something new. The positive nothing designates the pure break with an extant order *as* a second-order law. Alain Badiou, in his meditation on Hölderlin in *Being and Event*, draws attention to the evental structure of Hölderlin's work—an evental site that Badiou describes set-theoretically. Although Hölderlin's theoretical work approaches the task of poetry mathematically at certain key points, for example, in his invocation of the hyperbola, Hölderlin's poetry indicates a more expansive nature-philosophical inflection (which, it must be noted, does not exclude the mathematical): the disruptive event as emergent from the material-ideal preconditions of a *phusis* whose unbound, undifferentiated and radically de-hierarchized form comes to disrupt the differentiated systems (i.e., laws and institutions) governing cultural forms of intelligibility.

The hyperbolic procedure thus goes beyond a mere harmonic opposition and sets the ideal of the poetic act into relation with a real contradiction at the heart of its own poetic idiom and ultimately, at the heart of a historical condition ("on the contrary, [poetic subjectivity] remains with and for itself in real contradiction" [*SW* 2.89]). The revelatory character of the hyperbolic procedure depends upon folding this contradiction, this suspension of sense in the real, into the operations of the ideal, into something that in and of itself *makes sense*: the hyperbolic procedure thereby comes to reveal a subject, a historical moment, nature itself, as capable of "a different condition," *eines anderen Zustands fähig* (*SW* 2.82).

4 Hyperbole as Transpoetic Trajectory

By reframing the hyperbolic act as the representational form that captures a transition from one condition to another, the paradigm of *hyperbolic poetry* can thereby strategically bypass the terms set by the metaphysical dichotomy of transcendence and immanence—as well as the rhetoric of failure that condemns a poetic act to a mere structure of oscillation. The semantics of transcendence and immanence—whether one declares oneself in favor of one or the other term or whether one attempts to bring their incommensurability together in some way—erects a metaphysical framework that overwhelms the trajectory of the poetic act itself. Reading a poem as a hyperbolic act proceeds by following the sensuous movements of the poem: where does it begin, what momentum does it generate, through what zones does it pass, what boundaries does it produce, cross, or touch?

A path need not be confined to the course of a single work, but can move between works as well. And perhaps fortuitously, one may regard Hölderlin's output itself as tracing a hyperbolic trajectory: from the early odes to the strenuousness of the works produced from 1800–1806 to the seeming limpidity of his latest poems. In accordance with the figure of the hyperbole, which seeks out the extremes and invents a form to bind them in the same cognitive and affective space, the course here shall be charted from the extremities of one poetic form to another by focusing on some of Hölderlin's most revolutionary poems, namely, the Pindar translations and commentaries (known as the *Pindar Fragments*, probably composed around 1805). In a certain sense, written shortly before his mental breakdown in 1806, the *Pindar Fragments* represent the culmination of Hölderlin's speculative poetics; they can be encountered much in the same manner as one reads Hegel's *Phenomenology* or Schelling's *First Outline* and disclose concerns that overlap with and diverge from the more canonical texts of German Idealism.

Just as Hegel's *Phenomenology* utilizes narrative form to generate epistemic insight, so too does the form of Hölderlin's fragments hint at its speculative goals. Like many of Hölderlin's works, the Pindar translations and commentaries produce a hyperbolic trajectory: to and from sites of normative suspension as the precondition for novel—and perhaps as yet unknown—forms of cultural and political intelligibility. Hölderlin seeks and finds in Pindar a mode of attunement that moves hyperbolically from law, differentiation, and order to zones external or irreducible to these domains. Each text of the *Pindar Fragments* establishes a particular momentum on a curved trajectory; in the section "The Highest," for example, Hölderlin establishes the *law* of sovereignty as the highest point—as the "ground" of all knowledge via differentiation—only to plot courses extending towards and away from this seemingly stabilizing point. Often overlooked in this *Pindar Fragment* is the following insight: that the ground exists to enable a flight away from it.

The path of certain Pindar fragments and commentaries initiate a movement that returns to the *genesis* of law (where law is understood as the epistemic conditions governing differentiation), and yet, as the figure of the hyperbole demands, equally moving towards contact with that which lies outside the law; movement within or towards that which is outside the ground of knowledge (as the form of the law, of the intelligibility of difference) therefore structurally requires the deposition of the law of the sovereign as an absolute principle. Hölderlin thus brings that which is "highest"—the mediated *law*—into contact with the lowest, with other spaces, spaces over which the law does not have complete purchase: in caves, in oceanic depths, at sites of sanctuary (asylum), at rest, at points of breakthrough in which lines of demarcation and emergent orders have not yet been fully articulated and solidified. Hölderlin's engagement with Pindar can thus be regarded as a prolegomenon to a speculative form in which a merely intimated order makes itself felt as a possibility in contact with a materially conditioned (and unconditioned) real.

5 *Pindar-Fragments*: The Genesis of the Law

The hyperbolic dynamic of Hölderlin's poetry and thought before 1806, that is, before the period of his mental breakdown, seeks to hold together incommensurable operations at their highest degree of tension. This tendency is already visible even in those texts that thematize Being as untraumatized primordial non-differentiation, for example, in Hölderlin's 1795 fragment on Being and Judgment ("Seyn. Urtheil. Modalität"). In this document, Hölderlin posits a form of unity so profound that it excludes all differentiation (Being)—and therefore exists outside the category of relation—that is then brought into relation with a primordial separation and capacity for differentiation (Judgment as *Ur-Theilung*). This document and the gesture it indicates—an impossible relation between relation and non-relation—is not nostalgic, expressing a yearning for a lost unity, but already thoroughly hyperbolic: it binds together extremes at the very limits of what can be thought. This speculative gesture held a particular attraction for Hölderlin and his circle of friends: Isaak von Sinclair, Hölderlin's revolutionary friend, also attempts to think that which is "non-posited," the "athesis," in the structure of the self, for example.[21] Sinclair came to label this attempt an impossibility for thought: a *Denkunmöglichkeit*.[22]

This particular impossibility is not merely an ontological or metaphysical question, but a political one. There is an exegetical tradition—including thinkers as diverse as Benjamin, Heidegger, and Agamben—that links Hölderlin's vision to a messianic politics. The minimalist requirement for a messianic politics can be described as the attempt to place the *now* of historical time into relation with a fulfillment *to come*. Agamben in particular thinks the differentiation of law as a biopolitical challenge that can only be addressed by a quasi-utopian potentiality/impotentiality, a contemplative horizon that renders such differences inoperative—as if the facticity of relation or the transformation from potentiality to actuality were in and of itself commensurate with political violence and thereby devoid of emancipatory possibility.

In *The Fire and the Tale*, Agamben links poetry, and more specifically, a "truly" poetic form of life, to contemplation, deactivation, inoperativity: "Certainly, the contemplation of a potentiality can only be given in an opus; but, in contemplation, the opus is deactivated and made inoperative and, in this way, given back to possibility, opened to a new possible use. A truly poetic form of life is the one that contemplates in its opus its own potentiality to do and not to do, and finds peace in it."[23] Hölderlin's poetry does not so much render differences inoperative—neither between law and violence (as Agamben would have it) nor between law and chaos—but rather, holds any such oppositions fixed at the point of their *most extreme contradiction*. He thereby advocates an operation—hyperbolic intensification of differentiation—that is the precise inverse of "indistinction." In contrast to this view of a truly poetic form of life as finding peace in a zone of indifferentiation between action and contemplation, Hölderlin advocates a *revolutionary poiesis*, one that portrays relation, differentiation, and violence not as a fall that is later to be redressed and redeemed, but as the manifestation of a redemptive possibility inherent in the structure of time as hyperbolically opposed to itself.[24]

Of the post-'68 thinkers most attuned to Hölderlin's attribution of a revolutionary dynamic to the real—in a mode of poetic compression that blends the possible and the necessary, that is, the necessary structure of temporality *as* invested with multiple and potentially contradictory possibilities—special mention must go to Deleuze and Badiou. In his seminars on Kant, Deleuze singles out the treatment of the caesura in Hölderlin's theory of tragedy as generative of a before and after that "do not rhyme."[25] For Hölderlin, the caesura belongs intrinsically to the structure of tragic temporality inasmuch as it introduces a counter-rhythm in time as the catastrophe rushes to complete its course. The tragic caesura, however, is not just a cut in time—precisely *not* a mere traumatic rupture—but rather, a breath or pause that generates the possibility for insight: indeed, an opening more than a cut. Hölderlin associates the caesura with a force of retardation at moments of increased acceleration, which in turn enables a privileged view over the unfolding of natural and historical time; in *Oedipus* and *Antigone*, the caesura falls during the speeches of Tiresias, the seer who grasps the organization of natural and historical temporality. Badiou perceives in Hölderlin the "torment" proper to the evental site, one in which the consistency of beings is dramatically disrupted, and yet, one that generates a fidelity to the promise held out by the event.[26] A tension emerges between Deleuze and Badiou in their interpretation of Hölderlinian temporality: does Hölderlin think the disruption of the event as a difference generator (Deleuze) or as the index of a regime of cultural consistency belonging to a radically new order of beings (Badiou)? In both cases, Hölderlin draws upon that which lies outside relation as an anomalous force, a force that can propel a subject beyond that which is currently established as law. Sinclair and Hölderlin—who were both committed to revolutionary politics—sought precisely to think beyond reflective thought, to bind operations that draw distinctions (e.g., subject and object, *Ich* and *Nicht-Ich*) to zones that suspend the validity of any given set of distinctions. In "Mnemosyne," Hölderlin links the flight into that which is unbound by differentiation to *desire*: "And always / Towards the unbound goes a desire" (*SW* 1.437). The question is whether or not desire should circulate in unpredictable ways, taking unforeseeable pathways (Deleuze), or whether it could or should remain faithful to a form of law, a regime of truth (Badiou).

The political inflection of hyperbolic form can be found throughout Hölderlin's work, but it is particularly present in the Pindar translations and commentaries, where the tension indicated between Deleuze (emphasizing the difference of the event) and Badiou (emphasizing fidelity to the event) becomes the subject of a speculative and poetic experiment. It is to be found, for example, in the conjuncture of the extremes of *repose* and *revolutionary violence* of these texts—or if one prefers, in the exploration of experimental spaces in which social and cultural intelligibility is slowed down, reduced to a low hum, so that new forms of communal existence can take on an emergent validity.

The link between repose and renewal had been established early in Hölderlin's work. In the poem "To Rest" ("An die Ruhe" [1789]), one reads: "there the magic spell of rest ordains the sleeping one / With courage to swing in the labyrinth his light" ["Da weiht der Ruhe Zauber den Schlummernden, / Mit Mut zu schwingen im Labyrinth sein Licht" (*SW* 1.76)]. Repose holds in reserve a generative power of potentiality. The energy for political reorientation gathered in states of rest, however, must choose a medium of embodiment, someone or something that stands outside normative legitimacy; repose lends "the power of giants to the disdained" ["Riesenkraft dem Verachteten" (*SW* 1.76)]. Once understood hyperbolically, places of rest—as in Hölderlin's Pindar fragment *Of Repose* (*Von der Ruhe*)—do not establish lines of flight away from the contingency of the world, do not retreat from confusion, do not merely exist as spaces in which the feverish binding of the law dissolves or dissipates. On the contrary, poetic sanctuaries represent the most condensed spaces of hyperbolic contradiction; they describe the primordial remembrance of that which is outside knowledge in knowledge, preserving that which is non-posited (Sinclair's *athesis*) *within* that which is posited.[27] These spaces of contradiction become sites of revolution. The points of asylum, as *Ruhestätten*, are to be conceptualized with their hyperbolic trajectory in mind: the reduction of activity to a minimal point stores a form of potential energy for projects of cultural and political reconfiguration.

Hölderlin consistently links this form of potential energy to the unruly domain of the subterranean. The descent into the underworld, the *katabasis*, liberates an alien force. With this descent, opposing trajectories are conjoined: one moving upwards into the ether and the other downwards into the earth. The conjunction of hyperbolically opposed trajectories brings the articulation of differences—the sobriety of customs, norms, and laws—into contact with an intoxication, a rupture in the consistency of fields of differentiation, that conditions the emergence of new cultural forms. In Hölderlin's work, a disruption of time demanding the suspension of the regimes of sense has taken place (Deleuze); and while there is a yearning for a new regime of sense, a new law of consistency to which it could declare fidelity (Badiou), poetry oscillates with respect to whether or not such a regime could or will actually take place, and thus wavers with respect to this final step. The hyperbolic procedure unites an upsurgence of anarchic energy with the possibility of a new law, but the end of this trajectory is left open, thus subject to repeated speculative soundings, undertaken in the form of poems.

In the final strophe of the first version of "Bread and Wine," for example, the democratizing power of Father Aether—a figure who belongs to *everyone*, without distinction (*allen gehört*)—is released only when Dionysus descends in order to liberate the titan slumbering under the earth: "More soundly dreams and sleeps the titan in the arms of the earth, / Even the envious, even Cerberus drinks and sleeps" (*SW* 1.382). If Cerberus drinks and sleeps—if he too has been overwhelmed by Dionysian intoxication—there is no longer any guardian of boundaries.

So too in the poem "Jupiter and Saturn": the poet effects a transport from the domain of law and sovereignty (the realm of Jupiter) towards an abyss that contains a force beyond differentiation and beyond law, the realm of Saturn, the titan "without guilt" (*schuldlos*) who "spoke no commandment" and whom "no mortal designates with a name" (*SW* 1.285). Jupiter and Saturn are held in a hyperbolic tension. This hyperbolic tension maintains the extranormative domain of nature (the amoral and anarchic—hence guiltless—domain of Saturn) in a state of latency precisely so that its power can emerge at the propitious moment, fusing a revolutionary-cyclical notion of time (a time that "revolves") with a notion of time as punctuation, or the *kairos* that reconfigures a circumscribed field of beings and deposes the principle of sovereignty, the king of the gods (Jupiter). So too in the final lines of *Friedensfeier*, after a supposed celebration of peace, a future hyperbolic trajectory is intimated that holds a disruptive energy in a state of readiness. The poet thus cultivates through figures of peace or rest a dormant, insensate (asubjective) revolutionary potentiality and a violence that will, at its point of maturation, rise from the depths and reorganize the world of appearances: "As that which is timidly busy, insensate, / likes to slumber until it grows ripe" ["Denn gerne fühllos ruht, / Bis daß es reift, furchtsamgeschäfftiges drunten" (*SW* 1.366)]. Hyperbolically, the celebration of peace contains the subterranean potentiality of violence that awaits its moment of breakthrough, working in tandem with the inverse movement, namely, that violent overthrow yearns for the establishment of law.

It is with this dynamic in mind that one ought to approach Hölderlin's *asyla* or *Ruhestätten*. These spaces enable processes of deceleration—slowing down the rush of time—in order to facilitate the emergence of patterns of differentiation that would adequately respond to the normative tensions within a given population in a specific time and place. The sanctuary or asylum is thus structurally isomorphic with the tragic caesura—a "counterrhythmic interruption"—albeit one not functioning as paralysis (as Lacoue-Labarthe would have it), but as the mechanism through which ontological order, or the "idea" itself (*die Vorstellung selber* [*SW* 2.310]), appears amidst the unstable convulsions of time. The temporality of the caesura in the representation of the tragic transport (itself hyperbolic, a *trans-port*)—as a breath that initiates a turn, or what the poet Paul Celan would later call an *Atemwende* (*Breathturn*)—is thus spatially fixed as intrinsic to natural topographies in the *Pindar Fragments*: the asylum, the womb of the waveless sea, the caves of the centaurs, the cliffs as differential cuts that demarcate land from the undifferentiated abyss.

Temporal deceleration becomes a key feature of spaces of fecundity. The text *The Sanctuaries* (*Asyle*), for example, describes a double birth (the hyperbole of hyperboles): the birth of the womb itself. The establishment of sanctuaries or *asyla* discloses a latent revolutionary rumbling—a notion of time that revolves, turns, and returns—as constitutive of the interpenetration of nature and law: "Themis, the order-loving, gave birth to the human sanctuaries, the quiet places of rest" ["Themis, die ordnungsliebende, hat die Asyle des Menschen, die stillen Ruhestätten geboren" (*SW* 2.383)].[28] Themis, as a figure of *positing*, gives birth to spaces of asylum that bear fruit (ἀγλαοκάρπους in Pindar's Greek): they are the matrices of fertility for an emergent order. Such sanctuaries are endowed with a dual purpose: first, sanctuaries are sites of political refuge, demarcating a zone where the validity of a positive law does not reach, but where a power of formation and differentiation inherent to nature (a *natural law*) takes shape; and second, such sanctuaries constitute a point from which a moment of breakthrough—*re-drawing distinctions*, or "positing" a different organization of beings—can be undertaken.

Hölderlin thereby seeks in the exigency of poetic form to address a question central to post-'68 theory: what sort of habits—or processes of dishabituation—are necessary for the cultivation of a properly revolutionary political subjectivity? The conjunction of rest and revolution at the center of Hölderlin's engagement with Pindar renders palpable the natural, historical, and phenomenological conditions governing the *genesis of law*. A properly poetic, revolutionary consciousness inhabits the zero point in which the validity of one order of differentiation is placed in abeyance while a new configuration of differences appears on the cusp of emergence. Contrary to Badiou, however, fidelity to a new regime of Being in the horizon of hyperbolic speculation cannot take the form of a radical decision; time at the moment of disruption is shot through with contradictions that make the legibility of the event into a problem. The political ontology of the *Pindar Fragments* nevertheless refuses to accede to the axiom that Žižek makes the signature of Hegelian dialectical materialism: "no matter how well-planned and well-meant an idea or a project is, it will somehow go wrong."[29] But it equally refuses to affirm the contrary view, according to which revolutionary ambitions will culminate in the repair of the traumatic wound of culture. Hyperbolic speculation tests multiple responses and pathways at the inflection point of an event.

Each of the Pindar translations and commentaries plots points along hyperbolic trajectories that conjoin these two opposing pathways—towards the equiprimordial domains of law and chaos—in order to fold this lived incommensurability into one and the same poetic series. The nine Pindar fragments and commentaries situate this tension between the binding force of law and the unbound of desire historically in the past (mediated through Pindar), the alien power of which is then brought into the horizon of the present—and the future—through translation and commentary. Philosophical operations (truth, wisdom, the infinite, the highest) are coordinated with spatial and temporal sites and figures (the cave, the womb, the asylum, the sea, the age, repose) that initiate involutions of these concepts: wisdom becomes betrayal; truth becomes commensurate with falsehood, or wandering off a predetermined path (*irren*, the concept Hölderlin uses, contains this ambiguity); speed requires lingering. All of these figural and conceptual concentrations of hyperbolic tension serve a thought experiment in which the highest embodiment of law occurs in simultaneity with the abrogation of the law. The Hölderlinian thought experiment becomes in this instance meta-speculative: it occupies positions that Žižek will later attribute to Hegel—norm *as* rupture of the real—as well as positions that can be attributed to Schelling, in which nature appears as a force of unconditioning operating in excess of the human-technical matrix and in excess of normativity, an extra-symbolic upsurge of disruptive power. There is a violent potential in both positions: the violence of differentiation (the cut of the law, technicity) together with the violence of extra-symbolic unconditioning (force in excess of law and technics). Hölderlin at times will intensify this violence, and at other times seek to diminish or evade this violence intrinsic to one or the other domain. Revolutionary consciousness—its passion, suffering, and hope—must simultaneously occupy each domain: differentiation and suspension of differentiation, *tekhne* and *phusis*, violent upsurge and semi-stable equilibrium. Dwelling in this zone makes the mental attunement of poetic experimentation properly hyperbolic, indicative of a precarious futurity as hope for an emergent order. The modulations of the different modes of attunement can be schematically approached by following the spatial and temporal shifts undertaken in these fragments (in order to bring the dynamics of the fragments out of their latency, it is necessary to reduce the complexity of each text):

1. Betrayal of Wisdom (*Untreue der Weisheit*): This fragment describes how intelligibility must be established amidst uncertainty and rupture, and hence how wisdom itself necessitates a *betrayal*, or an infidelity to a time and place as a higher-order fidelity to an order to come. Jason, in the cave of the centaur Chiron, comes to know a power of potentiality beyond language, beyond work (*nicht ein Werk / Noch Wort... gesagt* [SW 2.379]). He channels this intimacy with the extra-symbolic into a restoration of the symbolic order, thus re-establishing the

defunct law of the father: "I have come home / to bring back the domination of my father" ["bin gekommen nach Haus, / Die Herrschaft wiederzubringen meines Vaters" (*SW* 2.379)]. The *cave* (*aus der Grotte nemlich* [*SW* 2.379]) and the *cliff* (the "pontic beast" who clings to the cliff, *des pontischen Wilds Haut, / Des felsenliebenden* [*SW* 2.379]) represent the two Pindaric spaces in which the disruptive power of the abyss enters into and reconfigures the world of differentiation; both are spaces that give rise to dominion (*Herrschaft*).

2. Of Truth (*Von der Wahrheit*): The poet affirms *going wrong* (*irren*) as part of an emergent regime of truth. Truth appears as a new beginning, an *Anfängerin*, that surpasses the bounds of sense and brushes up against an "outside" of sense ("so that one does not err by one's own fault, nor by one's own disturbance, but because of the higher object for which, relatively speaking, one's mind is too weak" ["so daß man nicht irret, aus eigener Schuld, noch auch aus einer Störung, sondern des höheren Gegenstandes wegen, für den verhältnismäßig, der Sinn zu schwach ist" [*SW* 2.380]). Erring designates the proper response to the call for fidelity to a "higher object."

3. Of Rest (*Von der Ruhe*): Rest becomes the precondition for a democratic mode of sovereignty: the fragment places every *citizen* ("Bürger" [*SW* 2.380]) into the functional position of the *prince* ("Fürst" [*SW* 2.380]) that must generate the law anew according to the specific constitution of a community. This fragment constitutes an exercise in speculative democratization.

4. Of the Dolphin (*Vom Delphin*): In this fragment, the dolphin is assimilated to the figure of the *womb* (δελφύς), again suggesting how differentiation emerges from a zone of suspended differentiation: the waveless sea (*das wellenlose Meer*) allows species, as figures of differentiation (*der Unterschied der Arten*), to hear the "echo" of a primordial genesis, *das Echo des Wachstums* (*SW* 2.381). In this instance differentiation is less symbolic violence than poetic potentiality; "the difference of species" (*SW* 2.381), *der Unterschied der Arten*, is more akin to song than language, *Gesang* than *Sprache*.

5. The Highest (*Das Höchste*): The *nomos basileus* of Pindar designates a point on a hyperbolic trajectory of the *Pindar Fragments* themselves: the highest point. The law, king of all beings, refers to sheer mediation and the necessary violence of disciplinary systems (*Zucht*) made possible by knowledge systems. Law as ground for differentiation (*den höchsten Erkenntnisgrund*) maintains a disciplinary system in a state of operativity. In this fragment, the suspension of differentiation is "impossible for gods and for mortals" (*SW* 2.381), who cognize through difference. Hölderlin will nevertheless approach such impossible zones hyperbolically (through exaggeration and approximation). Regarded as the highest point along a hyperbolic path, Hölderlin plots a trajectory that travels *towards* and *away* from this highest point; the highest "law," with its violence and its discipline (*Zucht*), cannot function on its own as a transcendental point that makes order possible. To lift this fragment out of the trajectory of the fragments, as some interpreters do, will thus inevitably miss the central gesture of hyperbolic speculation. This highest law must enter into relation with the counter-images

and counter-sites—zones in which the law establishes its own suspension (e.g., in *Asyla*)—of the other fragments.

6. The Age / Old Age (*Das Alter*): There is an ambiguity in this fragment between *old age* and *the age*: *das Alter* as both a stability of time that comes from extended duration as well as the force that holds together an age and marks its consistency. Here too differentiation and that which lies outside differentiation, norm and that which lies outside norm—the "guiltless custom" (*SW* 2.382), *schuldlose Sitte*—becomes the precondition for a form of futurity, a hope (*Hoffnung*) characterized by tempos both slow and rapid. Hope manifests itself in contradictory temporalities: it simultaneously accelerates and decelerates, moves with both speeding and lingering ("with its speeding lingering," *mit ihrer eilenden Weile* [*SW* 2.382]); revolutionary time must be countered with the tempo of reflection. In this fragment, Hölderlin considers a symbolic form (*Sitte*) as a non-traumatic possibility, one that evades the scission of judgment, appearing without debt and without guilt (*schuldlos*).

7. The Infinite (*Das Unendliche*): Infinity makes itself present in a hyperbolic gesture, in the hesitation and conflict between normative orientation and extranormative cunning, *Recht und Klugheit* (*SW* 2.382). Justice and law begin by drawing a distinction, traveling along a boundary, or setting up a circumference (the wall of the law, *des Rechtes Mauer*); the set of distinctions can itself be valid (*hohe*) or crooked (*krummer Täuschung*). The ambiguity of the mind, a *zweideutig Gemüth* (*SW* 2.383), caught within this tension, hesitates between two normative frameworks in an act of inversion—when the valid becomes crooked and the crooked becomes valid. This hesitation corresponds to precisely that state of attunement demanded by hyperbolic form: tracing a trajectory linking the extremes releases an energy that throws one beyond oneself, bringing about a life beyond oneself: "thus circumscribing myself, I live myself outside" ["so mich selbst / Umschreibend, hinaus / Mich lebe" (*SW* 2.382)].

8. The Asyla (*Die Asyle*): Sanctuaries repeat the ritual of a primordial emergence of order; they are thus positioned in a temporal gap, or as Hannah Arendt might say, *between past and future*: there is "an intimation around them, as if remembering" ["ein Ahnendes um sie, wie erinnernd" (*SW* 2.383)]. They are, however, not fully *outside* the law, but themselves emerge equiprimordially with a differentiating, positing power (having been born by Themis, the goddess of positing). The asylum thus holds both positive and natural law in a state of hyperbolic tension, or differentiation (based on that which is "posited") and that which suspends differentiation (the *a-thetic*).

9. The Living Power (*Das Belebende*): Against the background of non-differentiated expansive space—the "primordially pathless upward-growing earth"—the force of the river carves out differences. The violence of differentiation is not an exception to nature, nor a fall out of nature, but *part of* the order of nature itself: hence the centaur, associated with natural spaces establishing boundaries between difference and non-differentiation (cave, cliff), becomes a second-order force of differentiation, an engraving (Hölderlin etymologically associates the centaur with *stechen, kentein*). The "science" of nature, or a *Naturwissenschaft*,

must be based on the boundaries of an encounter between difference and the forces of non-differentiation: "Centaurs are thus also originally teachers of natural science because nature is best grasped from this perspective" ["Centauren sind deswegen auch ursprünglich Lehrer der Naturwissenschaft, weil sich aus jenem Gesichtspunkte die Natur am besten einsehn läßt" (*SW* 2.384)]. The centaur is located in this "hyperbolic" state: unifying the extremes, difference and indifferentiation, *tekhne* and *phusis*, knowledge and intoxication, generation and destruction. The centaur places both Hegelian (norm/science as traumatic cut) and Schellingian (extra-normative nature as violent upsurge) gestures in the service of a revolutionary political attunement.

As one may glean from the above condensation, the *Pindar Fragments* represent a political and a poetic experiment in the hyperbolic structure of natural and historical order. This experimental politics comes to light in various instances, for example, in the idea that wisdom structurally requires a contradiction—a loyalty to the present that is, in fact, a disloyalty to the present—in order to be thrown beyond its own moment: *Untreue der Weisheit*, read as a subjective genitive, as a *betrayal belonging to wisdom* rather than the *betrayal of wisdom as an ideal*. The wisdom of Pindar's poetry intensifies the paradoxicality of this betrayal: by praising the present (*Das gegenwärtige lobend* [*SW* 2.379]), it opens up a source of alterity within time itself (*Und anderes denk in anderer Zeit* [*SW* 2.379]).

Poetry based on this form of wisdom is neither anarchic nor messianic, as it does not simply render the violence of the law (whether constituting or constituted) or the structuring power of discipline (*Zucht*) inoperative; on the contrary, such poetry must affirm the violence of the law, *as well as the violence of its suspension*, in order to be properly hyperbolic. In "The Highest," discipline and its institutions, church and state, become the sensuous medium of a divine encounter between god and human. What Hölderlin calls "disciplinary breeding" (*SW* 2.382), *die Zucht*, stabilizes norms and maintains the status quo, holding in place the given concretized normativity of a specific social form. The laws and customs of institutions "hold fast the living relations more strictly than art" ["halten strenger als die Kunst, die lebendigen Verhältnisse fest" (*SW* 2.382)]. Such institutions function as sites of containment: they stabilize the energies of the unbound.

One of the most subversive operations of the *Pindar Fragments* is to depose the monarchical power of the law as ground of differentiation, the *nomos basileus*.[30] The grounding of the regime of differences structured through political and disciplinary institutions becomes upended as soon as it is incorporated into the hyperbolic trajectory of the fragments. The geometrical and rhetorical figure of the hyperbole—or more precisely, the second-order hyperbole of hyperboles—thus finds its way into the language of this "highest" point, in a doubled rhetorical hyperbolization: the sovereign dispenses "the most just justice with the all-mightiest hand" ("das gerechteste Recht mit allerhöchster Hand" [*SW* 2.382]).[31] The hyperbolic form does not just relativize the sovereign power of the law: it places it on a path that spins off towards its revolutionary inversion, namely, to an overturning of the law. It is hyperbolic not just in the sense of an exaggeration, but also in its etymological sense, as something beyond which one must be thrown, as one point on a trajectory in a field constituted by agonistic forces. In the manuscript, Hölderlin had originally written of the law as the highest "point of knowledge" (*Erkenntnispunkt*), which he later changed to a *ground of knowledge* (*Erkenntnisgrund*).[32] The notion that the ground is at the same time a point on a trajectory nevertheless remains present, as if inscribed on a palimpsest; the nature of law as a *point* has become a latent textual pattern. The "highest" of the law—as a regime of differentiation that stabilizes subjects—is thereby brought together with a counterforce that seeks to overturn it. Agamben draws attention to the manner in which Hölderlin relativizes the law by submitting it to unconditioning in contact with this ground of knowledge; however, attached as he is to the messianic act of suspension, he does not follow this tension to the end of its trajectory (it was, in fact, Blanchot who recognized the revolutionary political implications of this fragment).[33]

The figure that most concretely embodies this tension is the centaur.[34] Hölderlin likens the "centaur" spirit to the "wild shepherd, the Odyssean cyclops" (*SW* 2.384). The centaur is simultaneously outside the law and the very form of the law: a wild intoxicated hybrid being who overthrows order ("they cast away the white milk and the table with their hands" [2.384]) and who lies at the very source of knowledge or *Wissen* (*Naturwissenschaft*). For the centaur, law and its suspension occur simultaneously in their most extreme forms. The centaur's knowledge of nature thus goes beyond the notion of the law articulated in "The Highest" as the "highest ground of intelligibility," as it consists in this secret: that nature itself is a hyperbolic system. Unbounded energies seek a release and carve a path; form emerges from the recursive play of force and counterforce in such a manner that locates revolutionary impulses in the very dynamic organization of nature (the earth providing an initial field on which water carves its pathways); water then forms banks of riverbeds; riverbeds constrain the course of the water; until finally the excessive energy of this process of formation leads the river to find the weakest point of constraint and break through to another space: "until [the river] broke through at a site where the mountains that enclosed it were most lightly joined to one another" (*SW* 2.384). The hyperbolic trajectory does not culminate in an equilibrium, but rather, in breakthrough: in a momentum of thought that projects subjects beyond the imposition of their limits.

6 Conclusion

In conclusion: Hölderlin consistently understood poetry as the following of a pathway. In the hyperbolic poetry up until 1806, up until the period of his "mental breakdown," Hölderlin sought to find a form of binding, of lawfulness, that would be adequate to the energies of the unbound, to the anarchic exuberance that conditions the overturning of cultural codes and orders of differentiation (although even in his latest poems, the poems of the tower or *Turmgedichte*, one may still detect the presence of a minimal hyperbolic dynamic: a commitment to the exploration of an *otherness*, albeit one that is internal to a sensuous encounter with the spatial and temporal self-differentiation of nature). He lingered in these moments of highest contradiction, of temporal bifurcation and dynamic instability: at the point of "breakthrough," when law and transgression become cooperative, when an unexpected pathway emerges and becomes viable, if only momentarily. The difficulty of Hölderlin's poetry bears witness to the exertion demanded by occupying these precarious sites of emergence. Hölderlin thought the hyperbolic figure to its most optimistic and its most pessimistic ends: he confronted the possibility, again and again, that the betrayal of time could be a *mere* betrayal, that the course of history would accomplish its turns only to perpetually turn against itself yet again. Only by confronting such possibilities did he invest every moment with a due sense of urgency.

Hölderlin's poetry, by virtue of the hyperbolic potentiality of its thought—and because it adopts multiple speculative perspectives, continually experimenting with attitudes, discursive and non-discursive, to different modalities (the real, the possible, the necessary)—crystallizes the multiple concerns of poststructuralist theory and the theoretical interventions that informed poststructuralism. It reinvests the sacred with a cultural task (Heidegger and Agamben); it pursues lines of flight towards a chaotic disruption of sense in the service of the unexpected (Deleuze); it seeks to make intelligible the conditions for radical cultural and political change (Badiou) in a manner commensurate with a critique of ideology (Adorno) and mediation (de Man); it sets structure, or what he called "the calculable law,"[35] in relation to a non-subjective unboundedness (for Lacan, the relation of *langue* to *lalangue*); it poses concretely the problem of suffering, creative subjectivity (Blanchot); it lingers in a hyperbolically opposed and tense unification between *phusis* and *tekhne* (and thus harbors imaginative impulses for rethinking technicity amidst cosmological-ethical investments, such as one might find in Yuk Hui's cosmotechnics);[36] and it adopts a meta-speculative stance, which modulates and traverses multiple sources of traumatic potentiality under the conditions of historical reality, whether as intrinsic to the symbolic itself or in an extra-symbolic material-real (thus forming an often unrecognized interlocutor for proponents of Hegelian dialectical materialism as formulated by Žižek or posthumanist nature-philosophy). In the wake of this exegetical tradition, Hölderlin's hyperbolic poetry grants a promise and issues an appeal to the future: to provide a source for the unimagined experiments in thought yet to be undertaken.

Notes

1. Virginia Woolf, *To the Lighthouse*, ed. Margaret Drabble (Oxford: Oxford University Press, 1992), 48.
2. Gilles Deleuze, Logic of Sense, trans. Mark Lester, ed. Constantin V. Boundas (New York: Columbia University Press, 1990), 3.
3. Ibid.
4. See Pierre Macherey, *A Theory of Literary Production*, trans. Geoffrey Wall (London: Routledge, 1992), 7.

5. See Walter Benjamin, "Two Poems by Friedrich Hölderlin: 'The Poet's Courage' and 'Timidity'," in *Early Writings 1910–1917*, trans. Howard Eiland et al. (Cambridge, MA: Harvard University Press, 2011), 171–196; György Lukács, "Hölderlin's *Hyperion*," in *Goethe and His Age* (London: Merlin Press, 1968), 136–156; Martin Heidegger, *Elucidations of Hölderlin's Poetry*, trans Keith Hoeller (Amherst, New York: Humanity Books, 2000); Theodor W. Adorno, "Parataxis: On Hölderlin's Late Poetry," in *Notes to Literature*, ed. Rolf Tiedemann, trans. Shierry Weber Nicholsen (New York: Columbia University Press, 2019), 376–411; Paul de Man, "Heidegger's Exegeses of Hölderlin," in *Blindness and Insight*, second edition (London: Routledge, 1983), 246–266; Maurice Blanchot, "The 'Sacred' Speech of Hölderlin," in *The Work of Fire*, trans. Charlotte Mandell (Stanford: Stanford University Press, 1995), 111–131; Philippe Lacoue-Labarthe, *Typography: Mimesis, Philosophy, Politics*, trans. Christopher Fynsk (Cambridge, MA: Harvard UP, 1989), 208–235; Gilles Deleuze, "Seminar on Kant: March 21, 1978," trans. Melissa McMahon, available at https://deleuze.cla.purdue.edu/seminars/kant-synthesis-and-time/lecture-02 (last accessed 27 May 2022); Giorgio Agamben, in *The Kingdom and the Glory*, trans. Lorenzo Chiesa (with Matteo Mandarini) (Stanford: Stanford University Press, 2011); Giorgio Agamben, *La follia die Hölderlin. Cronaca di una vita abitante 1806–1843* (Turin: Einaudi, 2021); Alain Badiou, *Being and Event*, trans. Oliver Feltham (London and New York: Continuum, 2005).
6. According to David Miles, Hölderlin's "path" registers temporal conflict, as caught "between past and future." See David H. Miles, "The Past as Future: *Pfad* and *Bahn* as Images of Temporal Conflict in Hölderlin," *Germanic Review* vol. 46, no. 2 (1971), 115. All citations from Hölderlin, unless otherwise noted, refer to the following edition of his collected works: Friedrich Hölderlin, *Sämtliche Werke und Briefe*, ed. Michael Knaupp, vols. 1–3 (Munich: Hanser, 1992). Henceforth cited in-text as *SW*. Translations are by the author unless otherwise noted.
7. Slavoj Žižek, *The Parallax View* (Cambridge, MA: MIT Press, 2006), 157.
8. Ibid.
9. Arkady Plotnitsky, "Rhythm, Caesura and Time, from Hölderlin to Deleuze," in *At the Edges of Thought*, eds. Craig Lundy and Daniela Voss (Edinburgh: Edinburgh University Press, 2015), 129.
10. Alain Badiou, *Being and Event*, 257.
11. Ibid.
12. Rochelle Tobias, "The Untamed Earth: The Labour of Rivers in Hölderlin's 'The Ister'," in *Hölderlin's Philosophy of Nature*, ed. Rochelle Tobias (Edinburgh: Edinburgh University Press, 2020), 91.
13. Philippe Lacoue-Labarthe, *Typography*, 208.
14. de Man, "Heidegger's Exegeses of Hölderlin," 263.
15. Daniel Whistler, "Silvering, or the Role of Mysticism in German Idealism," *Glossator* 7 (2013), 180.
16. Lacoue-Labarthe, *Typography*, 260.
17. See György Lukács, "Hölderlin's *Hyperion*."
18. Marshall Brown draws attention to romantic thought's attraction to geometrical shapes, such as circles, lines, and ellipses; Hölderlin certainly participates in this tendency. See *The Shape of German Romanticism* (Ithaca and London: Cornell University Press, 1979).
19. "Harmonic opposition" is generally considered one of the most fundamental and constant features of Hölderlin's poetry; see, for example, Marion Hiller, "*Harmonisch entgegengesetzt": Zur Darstellung und Darstellbarkeit in Hölderlins Poetik um 1800* (Tübingen: Niemeyer, 2008). Hiller explains the hyperbolic procedure as follows: "The poetic procedure appears 'hyperbolic' because it tears the 'element' out of its living context in the world, so that the adaptation of the element through the spirit cannot leave this element as that which it is itself, but must change it, let it become something different" (ibid., 134, my translation). The hyperbolic procedure goes beyond mere harmonic opposition to include an ontologically *real*, that is, non-harmonic and non-idealistically mediated (or at least, not *merely* idealistically

mediated), extreme oppositionality whose intensity pushes subjects into dramatically novel forms of differentiation.
20. Friedrich Hölderlin, *Essays and Letters*, trans Jeremy Adler and Charlie Louth (London: Penguin, 2009), 282.
21. Isaac von Sinclair, "Philosophische Raisonnements," in Hannelore Hegel, *Isaak von Sinclair zwischen Fichte, Hölderlin und Hegel: Ein Beitrag zur Entstehungsgeschichte der idealistischen Philosophie* (Frankfurt am Main: Klostermann, 1980), 268.
22. Ibid., 274. See also Giorgio Agamben, *Potentialities*, trans. Daniel Heller-Roazen (Stanford: Stanford University Press, 1999), 114.
23. Giorgio Agamben, *The Fire and the Tale*, trans. Lorenzo Chiesa (Stanford: Stanford University Press, 2017), 137–138.
24. I agree with Ian Cooper's reading of Hölderlin *contra* Agamben in "Law, Tragedy, Spirit: Hölderlin contra Agamben," *Journal of Literary Theory* vol. 6, no. 1 (2012): 195–212. Hölderlin, unlike Agamben, does not aim at a conception of messianic time that would supersede law, but, on the contrary, plunges it *into* time as a revolutionary structure.
25. Gilles Deleuze, "Seminar on Kant: March 21, 1978," trans. Melissa McMahon, available at https://deleuze.cla.purdue.edu/seminars/kant-synthesis-and-time/lecture-02 (last accessed 27 May 2022).
26. Badiou, *Being and Event*, 255.
27. One must therefore qualify attempts to identify "asylum" with "law." Paul Fleming notes, for example, "Unter 'Asyl' ist nicht nur die Ruhe, sondern auch das Gesetz zu verstehen." (in "Das Gesetz. Hölderlin und die Not der Ruhe," *Hölderlin-Jahrbuch* 32 [2000–1], 288). Rest designates that zone within the law that recalls the *genesis* of the law; hence there is also some part of rest that references a primordial emergence outside the law, some part of the asylum that stands in contradiction to the normativity of the present. Hölderlin thus lends to asylum a revolutionary potential: rest is only commensurate with law *inasmuch as* it concentrates a contradiction of the law with itself and conditions the emergence of a new law, a new regime of differentiation and intelligibility.
28. Translation in Friedrich Hölderlin, *Poems and Fragments*, trans. Michael Hamburger, 4th ed. (London: Anvil Press, 2004), 719.
29. Slavoj Žižek, "Hegel in the Future, Hegel On the Future," *Problemi International*, vol. 4 (2020): 311.
30. Heike Bartel discusses Hölderlin's letter to Sinclair in which he writes that there can be no "monarchical" power in heaven and on earth; see Heike Bartel, *"Centaurengesänge." Friedrich Hölderlins Pindarfragmente* (Würzburg: Königshausen und Neumann, 2000), 129. The implication, however, is that Hölderlin establishes the "monarchical" power of law (as *highest ground of knowledge*) only to depose its singularity.
31. Bartel draws attention to the hyperbole of this section, without, however, linking it to Hölderlin's "hyperbolic procedure"; see ibid., 120.
32. See ibid., 131.
33. See Giorgio Agamben, *Homo Sacer*; and Leslie Hill, "'Not in Our Name': Blanchot, Politics, the Neuter," *Paragraph* vol. 30, no. 3 (2007): 141–159.
34. For a reading that illuminates the violent nature of the centaur—and what is at stake in this violence in relation to life, namely, whether it could or could not be capable of grounding a law of the earth, a political order rather than mere articulation—see "Vivisections: Scripting Life in Hölderlin's 'Das Belebende.'" *The German Quarterly* 91.3 (2018): 270–285.
35. Friedrich Hölderlin, *Essays and Letters*, 317.
36. See Yuk Hui, *Art and Cosmotechnics* (Minneapolis: University of Minnesota Press, 2021).

Reading Hegel I: Textuality and the *Phenomenology*

Kristina Mendicino

1 "Foreword"

There is no beginning to reading Hegel's philosophical writing. The following chapter retraces nothing if not the way in which his speculative writing cannot set forth without "reading" the language that will have come in its advance. From before the outset, that is to say, reading Hegel is affected by the ways in which reading affects speculative writing with a deferral or delay, one which has been underscored, with different accentuations, by those readers who have drawn out the linguistic character of Hegel's "thought," but that is also made more pronounced through Hegel's written performance. The readings that are offered here, then, will be "readings of Hegel" in both senses of the genitive, which expose the interval of reading that has not ceased to open speculative thinking.

Before all else, this interval is what the "foreword" to the *Phenomenology of Spirit* exposes:

> A clarification, as it is habitually sent out in a foreword in advance of a writing—over the purpose that the framer proposed for himself in it, as well as over the occasions and the relation in which he believes it to stand towards other, earlier or contemporary treatments of the same object—appears in a philosophical writing to be not only superfluous, but even unsuited and at cross-purposes [to it], due to the nature of the cause.[1]

My sincere thanks go to the participants of the workshop, "German Idealism and Post-Structuralism" (March 2021), for their helpful comments, questions, and suggestions on an earlier version of this chapter.

K. Mendicino (✉)
Brown University, Providence, RI, USA
e-mail: kristina_mendicino@brown.edu

© The Author(s), under exclusive license to Springer Nature Switzerland AG 2023
T. Rajan, D. Whistler (eds.), *The Palgrave Handbook of German Idealism and Poststructuralism*, Palgrave Handbooks in German Idealism,
https://doi.org/10.1007/978-3-031-27345-2_6

The cause for this apparent unsuitability will be soon unfolded, as the writer of this text—namely, G. W. F. Hegel—goes on to present the cause or matter of truth as a process, whose self-contradictions and mediations philosophical writing would need not to summarize but to elaborate in order to correspond to it: "For the cause is not exhausted in its *purpose*, but in its *carrying-out*, nor is the *result* the *real* whole, but [the result] together with its becoming."[2] As Hegel conceives it, nothing could be more natural than the irreducibility of truth to a result and the insufficiency of results alone: just as the organic unity of a tree entails the disappearance of its bud with the outburst of its blossoms, and then the disappearance of the latter with the emergence of its fruit[3]—just as each apparent phase is negated by the next, while preserving the tree and thus preserving itself as a logical "moment" in the same, differentiated, and therefore subjective life—so too should the true "life" of the idea be retraced in philosophy through its contradictory and self-preserving movements. Thus, it is only in reproducing the subjective life of logic, nature, and spirit that philosophical writing could itself *be* true, and it is also only in this way that philosophical writing could reproduce itself in its reading subjects, who should not merely resurrect the subjective life of the philosophical text and the spiritual universe it presents—"the thought which in the written word becomes a thing," as Hegel had written years before, "recaptures its subjectivity out of an object, out of something dead, in reading"[4]—but who should also recognize themselves in the "I = I" that true philosophical writing forges among subjects "who know themselves as pure knowing."[5] As Werner Hamacher will write, in repeating the same thought in his "own" words: "What I read, reads me, and, in me, reads itself. I read what reads itself in me—my own reading."[6]

Thinking (of) writing and reading along Hegel's lines in even a preliminary way makes plain that preliminary declarations of purpose can only fail their purpose, when it comes to communicating the idea of philosophical knowledge. This is why Hegel cannot but hesitate toward the very thought of a foreword in his "Foreword" to the *Phenomenology*, and it is also why he will later emphasize in his *Encyclopedia of the Philosophical Sciences* that the absolute "idea" is "not to be taken as an idea of *something whatsoever*"[7]—that is to say, it cannot be identified with another term or expressed in the form of a proposition, such as "God is being."[8] For philosophy, the cause, the truth—in a word, the "idea"—can only come to be known and spoken through the entire cycle of logical determinations, natural existence, and self-revelations that form the whole of spiritual life and that speculative philosophy should culminate, present, and reproduce. No foreword could give a truncated picture of this labor or convey a true idea of its fruits. The very thought would be preposterous, in the precise sense of the term.

The whole oeuvre of Hegel could be read to elaborate and perform nothing other than the recognition of this truth. Its appearance is what the *Phenomenology* brings forth. Its "idea" is what circulates through Hegel's *Encyclopedia*, as it branches out into *The Science of Logic*, *The Philosophy of Nature*, and *The Philosophy of Spirit*. But it already repeats through Hegel's fragmentary theological commentaries from the late 1790s, where the divisions between subject and object, identity and difference, unity and division are conceived to be drawn, lifted, and preserved through the life of the tree or the Tree of Life that stands for the kingdom of God—"Love the bloom of life; kingdom of God, the whole tree with all necessary modifications, stages of development"[9]—as well as through the love that is incorporated and imbibed with the Eucharist, and through the movements of the *logos* that are scripted in the prologue to the Gospel of John.[10] Already Hegel's early readings and writings on these exemplary figures from Scripture—the Tree of Life, the Eucharist, and the Word—carry the speculative thought that will be further developed elsewhere: namely, that "each part, beside which the whole is, is at once a whole, a life; and this life, in turn, is also as a reflected one, also in regard to the division, the relation as subject and as predicate, [it] is life (ζωη), and grasped life (φως, truth)."[11] And just as Hegel reads speculative thought into Scripture before writing the major studies that would be associated with (t)his name, his writings on Scripture also already unfold through appositional—self-modifying, self-dislocating[12]—phrases which might be read in the spirit of Hegel's subsequent explicit remarks on the form of speculative propositions in the *Phenomenology*, among others, where the dialectical life of thinking and being entails that "the nature of the judgment or sentence as such, which encloses the difference of subject and predicate, be destroyed."[13]

There could be no proper beginning to the "philosophical writing" that Hegel recalls or anticipates in his "foreword" to the *Phenomenology*, then, not only because it cannot be what it is before it is carried out as a whole but also because the whole will have always already been written in advance. If "the true is the whole"— and if it is true that there is a whole—then it could never be in need of preliminaries, just nothing could have been imparted before that was independent or excluded from it. No extraneous initium or residue would remain thinkable, except perhaps as that which would have passed without a trace—"zu etwas völlig Vergangenem w[ird] [to become something fully past]"[14]—and that would thus pass merely for a formal possibility without any possible realization or remembrance. As a consequence of these premises, however, even the most minimal, fragmentary, and liminal moments, comments, and details would be indices of truth's accomplishment, at least for those who truly know to read them.[15] The difference between philosophical writing and any other would then perhaps be none, but for the fact that the former should ensure that each index of the true is read in light of the whole, which would render every "foreword" in the traditional sense of the word at once superfluous and inadequate, and at the same time no more superfluous or inadequate than any other partial presentation.

If this characterization of Hegel's thinking, writing, and reading is true, however, then it would still have to be wholly significant—the question would not be whether, but how—that, before the *Phenomenology* more explicitly begins to elaborate the subject and substance of philosophical truth, starting (again) with the supposed "sense certitude" of "I," "here," and "now," there nevertheless appears the nondescript formulation, punctuated by a period: "Foreword." As Rebecca Comay and Frank Ruda have observed in another context: "according to Hegel's own protocol, to read speculatively—to read at all—one needs to suspend every advance decision about what is major and what is minor, what is essential and what is inessential. There is no preexisting standard by which to assess what may be significant; you must proceed as if anything and everything is important ...."[16] Read within the context of Hegel's "whole" corpus, for example, a distant resemblance between the first inscriptions of antiquity and the descriptive titles of modern books becomes legible, even if the situation of Hegel's publication would seem to be remote from the transformative scene where speech is said to make its first appearance in his later lecture course on Aesthetics with, namely, the epigram or *Aufschrift*, which was "written out upon the object" to say "what *this* matter is."[17] There, writing was said to "transform" matter "into words," literally en*titling* to subjective life things which had hitherto stood mute, as "something otherwise plastic, local, present outside of speech." Book, chapter, and section titles would redouble this gesture by naming a subject and thus responding in advance to an unspoken need to say what the matter is. Yet to the same extent that the systematic character of all more or less evidently philosophical matters should not only permit but also solicit this recognition, it becomes just as recognizable that the epigrammatic function of writing will have become dysfunctional by the time it leaves its mark on Hegel's book, where "Foreword" appears as an instance of writing upon writing, which does not announce but distracts from the very matter and cause the foreword should introduce.

To recapitulate, the text that Hegel offers under the sign of a "Foreword" goes on to address the habits associated with this commonplace expression, drawn from textual rather than philosophical tradition, which are said to inhibit rather than further the "*carrying out*" (*Ausführung*) that can alone make up true philosophical discourse, by reducing the latter to a summary of anticipated results and/or by dispersing it into a history of prior and contemporary opinions. But if each typical foreword would thus be an apotropaic gesture prescribing a reading in advance of the text—which each philosophical text should also ultimately do, just not from the beginning, but as a whole whose truth its readers are supposed come to know as their own—and if each foreword would thereby preclude both writer and reader from entering into the matter in question by preempting it too soon—by being too forward, so to speak—then the turn away from such gestures that Hegel takes in his foreword on forewords is not straightforward, either, and initiates a still more radical delay, when it comes to approaching the "matter" or "cause" (*Sache*) of this particular instance of "philosophical writing." For by inscribing and then writing upon the epigrammatic heading of his "own" writing, Hegel not only defers speaking of the more philosophical phenomena that he soon promises to present (in keeping, precisely, with the tradition of forewords). He also repeats even as he reads and retreats from the nonphilosophical habits of textual production that will have nonetheless partially set the terms for his presentation since antiquity: namely, the need to name what the matter is, whether it is a text or another silent matter. With "Foreword," it is thus said that Hegel's text is already read and written in part through those inscriptions which will have shaped philosophical writing before any word of philosophy, and which therefore trouble any assurance that it may ever come into its own, as is also implicit in the concise formulation of speculative reading by Hamacher already cited: "What I read, reads me, and, in me, reads itself. I read what reads itself in me—my own reading."[18] For if reading is to repeat what is written, then each trace of reading would also mark a difference and defer both the reading and the writing to be done. From the "foreword" onward, then, we would be reading what we have not read, or we would be reading something other than what we or the text are. Before and beside whatever else it says for itself, Hegel's "Foreword" not only remains on the margins of philosophy, but also temporarily places the proper cause of philosophical writing—like the object of an ancient epigram—"outside of speech," and it thereby says without a word that philosophical writing cannot begin, properly speaking, without reproducing the traditional terms and textual traditions that it rewrites, refutes, or retracts; that it cannot set forth without "reading" the language that will have come in its advance; and that it therefore cannot proceed without stalling its progress.

What this suggests for us, here, and now, is that reading Hegel cannot circumvent his delay of the whole and the true, since this delay would have to be part of the truth on the very holistic terms that Hegel adopts, and since, at the same time, it cannot be true in a way that facilitates entrance into the system or that easily fits within its conceptual nexus. The first words of Hegel's book thus mark a certain impasse that cannot be without consequences for any reading of the passages that will follow: more than paradoxically, the insistence upon systematic coherence in and beyond the *Phenomenology* would entail that all systematic developments may be read in light of this initial dilemma, as well as the reverse. This is why, for example, it may as much register a further repercussion of the initial, indecisive interval of Hegel's "Foreword," as it may mark an attempt to recuperate (from) it, when the halting rhythm of Hegel's opening lines is recalled in his subsequent remarks on the resistance that propositional forms pose to speculative thinking and the resistance that speculative propositions pose to those same forms. This mutual resistance will be described in terms of poetic rhythm and meter; as well as the more mechanical movements of counterthrust (*Gegenstoß*) and inhibition (*Hemmung*); and ultimately, the representational habits (*Gewohnheit[en]*) that speculative thinking should break[19]:

> To the habit of running off along representations, the interruption of the same through the concept is as burdensome as it is to the formal thinking that reasons hither and thither in unreal thoughts. ... Representational thinking, since its nature is to run off along the accidents or predicates ... is inhibited in its run-off, in that that which has the form of a predicate in the proposition is itself the substance. It suffers, to imagine it thus, a counter-thrust. ...
> —This conflict in the form of a proposition as such and the unity of the concept that destroys it is similar to the one that takes place in rhythm between meter and accent. The rhythm results out of the hovering / oscillating midst and unification of the two.[20]

Analogy follows analogy in this passage, each one analogous to what takes place in the first passage of the *Phenomenology*. In both passages, there is an initial substantive or grammatical subject, and then, further thinking suffers an interruption or inhibition, finding itself thrust back upon its opening term, whose need for commentary entails, in turn, the loss of any standing that it may have seemed at first to hold. Writing, that is to say, undermines and exceeds each given "metric" or "measure," and thus assumes from the first the halting "rhythm" that will also be known as conceptual thinking—although one could call it, with Giorgio Agamben, "the core of verse" as well.[21] In other words, not only "Hegel's style" but also the style of thought per se, "takes on" the "musical quality" that Theodor W. Adorno would emphasize in his essay on "How to Read Hegel," as well as the "incomplet[e]" character that Comay and Ruda underscore in their more recent study.[22]

In a certain sense, analogies of this kind would only be logical, in accordance with the systematic structure of Hegelian thought and the new exegetical habits that it appears designed to instill. Still, both the connections that are drawn in Hegel's later remarks among poetic rhythm, physical mechanics, reading habits, and speculative logic and the connection that may be read between this description of reading and the reading that is performed through Hegel's opening words say nothing decisive as to the chances of restless synthesis in speculative writing or reading. The slippage across registers may be testimony to the cohesion of the system, or it may be the test that the system cannot withstand without falling apart into what Hegel elsewhere calls the language of sheer "shreddedness."[23] As Jean-Luc Nancy will remark on Hegel's similarly heterogeneous remark on "sublation" (*Aufhebung*) in the *Science of Logic*, slippages among terms and registers are characteristic marks of Hegel's writing which show how even this arguably most crucial term of the dialectic—to say nothing of the whole—"does not coincide with itself or close up on itself and thus avoids, additionally, letting itself be identified."[24] Hegel's presentations of not only "sublation" but also the "concept," the "speculative proposition," and before them, the "Foreword" trouble the integrity of the supposed whole, rendering speculative language a tenuous, if not untenable effect of differential operations, which ultimately "consists in no determinate mode of signification, simple or double, proper or figural."[25]

But beyond this general hazard, there remain particular traits of the movement between writing and reading in Hegel's "Foreword" which suggest more emphatically that this oscillation cannot be adequately described as a dialectical mediation avant la lettre; nor can it be identified with the self-division and self-relation that are supposed to sustain the life and identity of the "concept" at every "moment."[26] Unlike Hegel's passages on propositional rhythms and forms, it is not yet or not primarily an issue of subjects, predicates, and concepts in the first lines of the *Phenomenology*, but of apotropaic or mechanical habits which work against their "proper" or purported "cause" (*Sache*). Nor is the suspension of sense that takes place within Hegel's preliminary rhetoric resolved dialectically or sustained by any conceivable self. Instead, when Hegel spells out a reading of the word and the form that "Foreword" evokes, it is the alterity of this particular sedimented term to all (philosophical or individual) intents and purposes that is implied to come before every possible (self-)interpretation, exposing philosophical writing to exigencies that differ from any singular opinion or universal notion which could determine its systematic function.

In other words, Hegel's "Foreword" presents neither a singular exception in his writing nor an exemplary instance of speculative rhythm—though speculative rhythm may itself be less a function of philosophical truth than what Nancy calls the "speculative hazard" of language, which renders every term and every "'body of thought,' itself, contingent."[27] And beyond these alternatives, if the "Foreword" should evoke a generic commonplace, then it is also no unequivocal example of what Hegel will call the "divine nature" of language in his opening chapter on "sense certitude," which should consist in the fact that language "always" says "the universal" or "the all-common"(*das Allgemeine*), and thus "immediately pervert[s] my-opinion."[28] If anything, "Foreword" may instead expose the impossibility of the "universal" significance of speech, which itself already entails impossible aporias, to the point where "I" cannot say "I," "here," "now," or "this," without reiterating what will have been said by any number of speakers at any number of places and times, and thus rendering each single instance without proper meaning. Already this means, as Paul de Man has argued, that "I cannot say I," rendering the universal meaning of the word uncertain along with its singular sense.[29] Yet whereas Hegel will at least claim to derive positive conclusions from the negation of immediate "sense certitude"[30]—namely, that all knowledge of self and world are mediated—not even the semblance of progress is promoted through the rhetorical deferral of philosophical writing in his "Foreword." Hegel's critical commentary on this word says, rather, that "Foreword" is and is not said in his text, and that his text therefore does and does not begin with it, holding at least this word back from saying one thing or another—or from "coming to words"[31]—and thus pointing to a possible interval of indeterminacy within each term and gesture of initiative. Hegel only surpasses the problem by passing over it in the end, with the claim to have done his best: "The share of the whole work of spirit that falls to the individual can only be slim, and so must he ... become and do what he can, but less must be demanded of him, just as he may and must expect less of and for himself."[32] Beside whatever "can" or "must" be done, however, the heterogeneous movements that are traced in the "Foreword" between writing and reading, contingent linguistic forms and philosophical formulations, expose complications at the outset of the *Phenomenology*, which it can neither exclude nor include from within its dialectical-conceptual-historical development, since it could not begin to speak without speaking inappropriately for its matter and cause, and thus cannot speak without entering into the risk that "philosophical writing" does not ever speak as and for itself.

These traits that emerge through the preliminaries to the *Phenomenology* would alone affect the truth and the whole with an unsublatable difference and deferral. But they also could not be circumvented by beginning elsewhere in Hegel's oeuvre, since doing so leads back to these very traits, every time that it comes to the question of reading (and) philosophical writing. "Philosophical writing" could hardly begin or go on otherwise than by deferral, once it is not only thought that, "in itself, *being* and *thinking* is the same,"[33] but once it is also made known that no thought or being can really be known without being said, drawing exteriority and difference into the inmost core of thinking and being themselves: "We know of our thoughts *only then*," Hegel writes in the *Encyclopedia*, "[we] have determinate, real thoughts *only then*, when we give them the form of *objectality*, of *being different* from our interiority, and thus [give them] the shape of *exteriority*": the shape, namely, of language.[34] The structural distance, separation, and foreignness that this exteriority introduces into all thinkable subjects and objects is abyssal, and it is not reduced when Hegel goes on to insist that language is "*such* an exteriority which at the same time bears the stamp of the highest *interiority*,"[35] since the interiority which will have stamped or coined each linguistic expression—itself an abyssal, "nocturnal pit" (*nächtliche Schacht*)—knows nothing of itself without language, nor does it know of anything else on its own, for that matter.[36] As Jacques Derrida has most precisely observed in his study of these passages from the *Encyclopedia*, signs inscribe thought with a "negative" which may at all times work "without appearing as such, without *presenting* itself, that is, without working in the service of meaning," and thus too without being knowable as a negative operation, let alone as one which could be recuperated by the negative work of dialectical understanding.[37] The "said" (*das Gesagte*) may differ from the "thought" (*das Gedachte*) by no more than a mere stroke of a pen or striction of the breath, and words may be the most proper fabrication of intelligence, as Hegel claims they are—a *poiesis* of visible marks and audible tones which fashions the world in its image and makes "*poetry*," as Hegel is recorded to have said at one moment in his lectures on aesthetics, "the original representation of the true."[38] But because knowledge is thought not to precede, but to follow this epic operation of language formation, it not only follows that language, poetry, and thought are originally the work of a foreign intelligence that no one knows, and whose signs must first be learned: "The arbitrariness of the connection of sensual stuff with a universal representation … has as a necessary consequence that one must first learn the meaning of signs."[39] For it also follows that speaking could never guarantee that anyone knows or means what she/he is saying—or even knows that she/he will have said anything at all—rendering every word, gesture, and expressive form a "foreword" of sorts that is not yet speaking and thinking, despite appearances, but that leaves traces of thinking and speaking which may be absent-minded and which may always be the traces of something else entirely.

In the *Phenomenology*, Hegel already underscores this structural "fore"-determination of language—which is also its structural in-determination—by, among others, using "language" to speak of all outer signs of intelligence, from the most ossified and thoughtless "language of the individual" that phrenologists find in their skulls,[40] to the inchoate thoughts that Hegel repeatedly claims to have been "spoken out" (*ausgesprochen*) unawares through the objects, interests, and behaviors of spirit, and that were never truly verbalized before his wording of them. On these terms, philosophical writing would have to trace a reading of what was never written before, but only ever foreshadowed and forgotten[41]; it would have to translate a language wholly unlike any that was known to have been spoken; and by repeating its original for the first time, its angel and vehicle—here, Hegel—would have to be the Homer of spirit, whose epic formula reads: "with that, it is spoken out, that...,"[42] and whose "whole" work would have to remain a fiction.

From the epigrammatic character of the "Foreword," to the oscillating rhythms of its subsequent lines, and the epic renditions it delivers of hitherto barely spoken thoughts, the language of the *Phenomenology* renders philosophical writing a poetic commentary to an unwritten text, whose very existence said "writing" would first make known. But with the thought of language and knowledge that Hegel spells out in his written performance, it is therefore also said that philosophical writing could never be assured of its reading; that its writing would itself need to be reread, retraced, and retranslated; and that even the most outspokenly conclusive philosophical system could not draw to a close, without reopening and aggravating the structural breach between what is said and what is known. The fact that speaking precedes knowing and even verbalization inscribes the unsaid and unknown into language as we speak.[43] No epic recitation of a world, nor any philosophical presentation of a whole could ever make total sense, nor could either be complete without allowing for what is not yet and not ever fully said within it. Hence, Comay and Ruda insist that "thinking" repeatedly "returns us to the starting point we thought we had left behind," which also turns out to be voided each time around: "there is only the empty space where we had previously assumed the subject to reside."[44] And before them, Catherine Malabou concludes her study of "plasticity" in Hegel—or the giving and receiving of form—with the similar affirmation: "the teleological structure ends by reversing its course, in that the forms already actualized discharge their potential energy and consequently liberate future possibilities of ... new constructions, new readings, new thoughts."[45] Both reversals, that is, trace back to a void, for the very "plasticity" that should be pivotal in permitting "future possibilities" would likewise signify an initial and persistent lack[46]: as given forms are subjected to reform—as words are written upon words—the epigrammatic, halting procedure of philosophical writing characterizes each formulation as "something otherwise plastic, local, present outside of speech."[47] Inscribed within the Hegelian system is a language that remains in want of language, that speaks in excess of authorized speech, and that thus gives word without a word of what Tilottama Rajan has designated "the supplement of reading,"[48] and what Werner Hamacher has called a "philological labor ..., which necessarily complements the philosophical one and indicates its limits."[49] If Hegel's readings in and beyond his "Foreword" are any indication, then this labor will not be possible to perform without remaining this side of a "foreword," nor can it proceed without encountering and exposing the "not yet"—or rather, the "not"—of philosophical writing, as well as the habitual written forms that no thinking can go on with or without.

2 Postscript

In retrospect, then, the "foreword" could also be read as a "post-script," as an instance of writing that follows and addresses—and thereby displaces—prior instances of writing; or, as Derrida has written: "Choosing one's tongue and point of view, one can call that a post-scriptum or a foreword."[50] Further elaborations of reading (in) Hegel will have been carried out along these lines through the remarkable glosses and exegeses that are offered in Jacques Derrida's "The Pit and the Pyramid" and *Glas*, Werner Hamacher's *Pleroma*, Jean-Luc Nancy's *The Speculative Remark*, and, more recently, Catherine Malabou's *The Future of Hegel: Plasticity, Temporality, Dialectic*, among other exquisite commentaries on speculative writing and reading whose citation alone would draw this chapter past its limits, and whose first appearance may yet remain to come.[51] These studies will have therefore also been, as Derrida had written of Jean Hyppolite's *Logic and Existence*, an "implicit and permanent reference" throughout this chapter, and most likely in more ways than "I" could ever "know."[52] But for the same reason, readings of Hegel—in all senses of the genitive—ever yet remain an outstanding task, so long as thinking and speaking should remain our concern, and so long as their preliminaries cannot be gotten past: so long as we remain, before as after, without the very philosophy and language that we (think we) speak.

The problem remains, then: there is no beginning to reading or writing on Hegel's philosophical writing. But in the meantime, the precarious, poetic, and preliminary character of what has been said or signed in his name will have become more pronounced, along with the hazards of deferring to the dysfunctional mechanics of the system, or repeating current habits of textual production, and thus in both cases deferring to read. For if any legible remains of Hegel were to be unequivocally recognizable as a proper starting point for approaching his thought, or as a promising point of departure for what is habitually called interpretive "payoff," then those remains would also no longer or not yet be remainders. They would instead already be inscribed along the lines of a systematic and economic order, and thus repeat the risk that Derrida addresses in *Glas*—the risk, namely, of appearing to (re)construct "something like" a "matrix" of the textual complex "on the basis of which one could read it, that is, re-produce it."[53] The analyses that Derrida offers in *Glas* are therefore—not unlike Hegel's "Foreword"—themselves emphatically scratched: "No, I see rather (but it may still be a matrix or a grammar) a sort of dredging machine.... And I begin to scrape [*racler*], to scratch, to dredge...."[54] For if one were to read Hegel in a way that would not merely repeat his writing, eliminate the differences that will have already marked his inscriptions, and thereby leave Hegel "unread" in the end[55]—then one also could not say what remains of his writings with certainty, and there could "be" no certain remains, strictly speaking: "In sum a remain(s) that may not be without being nothingness: a remains that may (not) be (*En somme un reste qui ne soit pas sans être un néant: un reste qui ne soit*)."[56] Any "remains" that one could scrape together could only ever be offered as a foreword, a fiction, or a postscript to what is no word and what belongs to no master or matrix, linguistic or otherwise.

This is perhaps what Derrida says without saying in *Glas*, through the intricate entanglements and extravagant resonances of his "epigrammatic" writings on writings,[57] but whose surface may at least be scratched here, one more time, in lieu of a conclusion.[58] For already the opening phrases of *Glas* indicate several of the ways in which the citational, retractive, and provisional traits of Hegel's writing—from the "Foreword" onward—may yet be read and rendered otherwise than along those lines which may have seemed to be prescribed with the end of time that is (said, known, or made out to be) history by the end of the *Phenomenology*. This time, however, the oscillations and delays *in* language that had characterized Hegel's "Foreword" are drawn out, as they translate to those words which may be given "for us, here, now": "what, after all, (of the) remain(s), today, for us, here, now, of a Hegel? For us, here, now: from now on that is what one will not have been able to think without him (*quoi du reste aujourd'hui, pour nous, ici, maintenant, d'un Hegel? Pour nous, ici, maintenant: voilà ce qu'on n'aura pu désormais penser sans lui*)."[59] The "fore"-word here is "for us" (*pour nous*), whose initial invocation turns out not to move this writing forward, and perhaps is not "said" at all, but merely cited within a recapitulation of the terms of "sense certitude" that "one will not have been able to think without" Hegel: namely, "here" and "now." "For us, here, now" is thus a repetition (of "Hegel"), even before it is repeated yet again in this passage, but with the difference that a first-person plural now numbers among the singularities that Hegel had repeatedly exposed to be universal in the *Phenomenology*. With the opening phrase of *Glas*, it is spoken out that not only "I" but also "we" were already spoken for, before "we" could begin to think, and that the subject of reading is therefore in question along with the whatever may "remain" to be read.

But with this shift from the singular to the plural, over a translation from Hegel's German idiom to another (French) one, still other pluralities intersect through "us" (*nous*) than any which could signify a person or a subject, an idiom, a term, or a meaning. For in Derrida's version, the word for "us" ("nous") will have also become literally indistinguishable from the word for "mind" (*nous*, νοῦς) that will have arrived at the end of Hegel's *Philosophy of Spirit*, in the words of Aristotle—"the thinking-mind thinks itself by taking over the thought" (Ἀυτὸν δὲ νοεῖ ὁ νοῦς κατὰ μετάληψιν τοῦ νοητοῦ)[60]—and that had translated to the self-knowing spirit at the end of the *Phenomenology* as well, whose existence, Hegel says, is "nothing other than this knowing of itself" (*nichts anderes, als dies Wissen von sich*).[61] The coincidence of "us" and "mind," "nous" and "νοῦς," will also be recalled, furthermore, with the permutations of those signs of intelligence that Derrida later traces back to Hegel's reading of the traumatic "impression that the Noachian deluge made upon the minds of men," and that had rendered thought imperative in the first place.[62] The subject of Derrida's and Hegel's texts—that is "us" and not "us"; our "noesis" and the trauma of our "not"; or, in a (non-)word: "(n)us"—cannot but allow itself to be read in all of these ways, and, at the same time, all of these words that speak our mind can also say nothing and name no one yet. "Nous," "we," remain(s), that is to say, suspended between a pronoun, a common name, a deverbal noun, and a proper name—suspended between "nous," " νοῦς," "noesis," and "Noah," which signifies, in Hebrew, "rest," "repose"—and in remaining suspended, "nous" do(es) not remain for a moment, since this word, like Hegel's "Foreword," will have never been one, and never just "for us" (*pour nous*).

Reading Hegel—that is to say, reading Derrida, reading others, reading "us"— may be to read in and for the sake of a mind- and self-altering language, whose preliminary words remain postponed for the sake of others than any known to be written. Reading Hegel may read like these lines of fiction:

> I still wonder, when I hear words which have three or four different and sometimes conflicting meanings, what worlds are confused with the usual world we think we have named, though we have no more named it than we have another, and sometimes a third. Who within us (*en nous*) addresses this universe and cites it?[63]

Notes

1. G. W. F. Hegel, *Die Phänomenologie des Geistes*, ed. Johannes Hoffmeister (Hamburg: Meiner, 1952), 9; my translation. Cf. G. W. F. Hegel, *The Phenomenology of Spirit*, trans. Terry Pinkard (Cambridge: Cambridge University Press, 2018), 3: "In the preface to a philosophical work, it is customary for the author to give an explanation – namely, an explanation of his purpose in writing the book, his motivations behind it, and the relations it bears to other previous or contemporary treatments of the same topics – but for a philosophical work, this seems not only superfluous, but in light of the nature of the subject matter, even inappropriate and counterproductive." In passages such as this one, I have offered my own translations of quotations from the *Phänomenologie des Geistes*, so as to replicate more closely the syntactic movement of Hegel's German phrasing, as well as the lexical transformations that the terms of his propositions undergo. The translation offered above should, for example, underscore that Hegel does not construct two independent clauses to describe, first, the habitual clarification of a "purpose" (*Zweck*) in a foreword, and, second, the "counter-purposive" (*zweckwidrig*) appearance that such a habit forms. Instead, the habit and its (self-destructive) appearance are spanned together in one main clause, which discloses itself in the end to be the clarification of the unsuitability of such clarifications, and thus the reduction of habitual clarifications to a semblance. When I offer my own translations, the corresponding page numbers from Pinkard's translation will be cited after the abbreviation "cf.," in order to provide readers with a convenient point of reference.
2. Hegel, *Phänomenologie*, 11; cf. Hegel, *Phenomenology*, 5.
3. See Hegel, *Phänomenologie*, 10; cf. Hegel, *Phenomenology*, 4. It is in keeping with the thought of universal thinking that the exemplary concept of vegetal life which Hegel offers in the *Phenomenology* and elsewhere recycles the example that Giordano Bruno gives for the universal intellect cum artist in his treatise on the one, the cause, and the principle. In the excerpt and translation that F. H. Jacobi offers in the 1789 edition of *Über die Lehre des Spinoza*, the passage reads: "Aus dem Inneren der Wurzel oder des Samkorns sendet er die Sprosse hervor; aus der Sprosse treibt er die Äste, aus den Ästen die Zweige, aus dem Inneren der Zweige die Knospen" (*Über die Lehre des Spinoza in Briefen an den Herrn Moses Mendelssohn* ed. Klaus Hammacher *et al.* [Hamburg: Meiner, 2000], 197)
4. G. W. F. Hegel, *Early Theological Writings*, trans. T. M. Knox (Philadelphia: University of Pennsylvania Press, 1971), 251; trans. modified; cf. G. W. F. Hegel, "(Jesus trat nicht lange...) [Der Geist des Christentums und sein Schicksal]," in *"Der Geist des Christentums": Schriften 1796–1800*, ed. Werner Hamacher (Frankfurt am Main: Ullstein, 1978), 466.
5. Hegel, *Phenomenology*, 389.
6. Werner Hamacher, *Pleroma—Reading in Hegel*, trans. Nicholas Walker and Simon Jarvis (Stanford: Stanford University Press, 1998), 65.
7. G. W. F. Hegel, *Enzyklopädie der philosophischen Wissenschaften im Grundrisse 1830: Erster Teil: Die Wissenschaft der Logik mit mündlichen Zusätzen*, ed. Eva Moldenhauer and Karl Markus Michel (Frankfurt am Main: Suhrkamp, 1986), § 213, 368; G. W. F. Hegel, *Encyclopedia of the Philosophical Sciences in Basic Outline: Part 1: Logic*, trans. and ed. Klaus Brinkmann and Daniel O. Dahlstrom (Cambridge: Cambridge University Press, 2010), §§213, 283; trans. modified. In the following, references to this volume of the German edition of Hegel's *Encyclopedia* will be abbreviated: *Enzyklopädie I*, followed by paragraph and page number. References to the English translation will be abbreviated: *Encyclopedia Logic*.
8. Hegel, *Phänomenologie*, 51; cf. Hegel, *Phenomenologyt*, 39. This formulation is the example Hegel cites for a "proposition" which solicits a speculative reading in his foreword, on which see below.
9. G. W. F. Hegel, "(Zur Zeit, da Jesus...) [Das Grundkonzept zum Geist des Christentums]," in Hegel, "*Der Geist des Christentums*," 390; my translation. This text comprises an outline of Hegel's most complete study from this early period, *The Spirit of Christianity* (*Der Geist des Christentums*).

10. On the "thetic propositions" (*thetische Sätze*) that Hegel finds to persist in even the apostle John's "more proper language on God and godly matters" (*eigentlicherer Sprache über Gott und Göttliches*), Hegel remarks that they should "find" their "sense and weight" in "the spirit of the reader," whose interpretation may vary as greatly as the various "relations of life," precisely because the speculative spirit is not (yet) sufficiently spelled out in writing. Instead, the words of the gospel maintain the "deceptive semblance of judgments" (ibid., 473–74). Upon these premises, the written presentation of speculative sense should prescribe its proper reading by minimizing all semblance of independence on the parts of its terms.
11. Ibid., 474; my translation.
12. Although apposition yields the destruction of propositional forms that Hegel calls for, it also entails troubling implications for the logical and conceptual syntheses of Hegel's thought and writing, which are elaborated at greater length in Andrzej Warminski's analysis of the role of examples in Hegel's oeuvre (see Andrzej Warminski, *Readings in Interpretation: Hölderlin, Hegel, Heidegger* [Minneapolis: University of Minnesota Press, 1987], 95–111).
13. Hegel, *Phänomenologie*, 51; cf. Hegel, *Phenomenology*, 39.
14. Hegel mentions such sheer passing only in passing, in the section from the *Encyclopedia* that addresses memory (*Erinnerung*). There, Hegel insists upon the contingency of all present, past, factual, and fictive occurrences upon mental representation, without which they would not only not be known to have occurred, but would also attain to no being at all, insofar as the condition of possibility for the being of temporal matters is their sublation from restless transience. The structure of temporality entails, he writes, "that all that happens first receives its *duration* for us from its uptake in representational intelligence—that, on the contrary, happenstances which are not valued for this uptake by the intelligence become something completely past" (G. W. F. Hegel, *Enzyklopädie der philosophischen Wissenschaften im Grundrisse 1830: Dritter Teil: Die Philosophie des Geistes*, ed. Eva Moldenhauer and Karl Markus Michel (Frankfurt am Main: Suhrkamp, 1986), § 452, 259). Cf. G. W. F. Hegel, *Philosophy of Mind*, trans. W. Wallace and A.V. Miller, rev. Michael Inwood (Oxford: Oxford University Press, 2007), § 452, 186. In the following, references to this volume of the German edition of the *Encyclopedia* will be abbreviated: *Enzykopädie III*, followed by paragraph and page number; the English translation will be abbreviated as *Philosophy of Mind*.
15. Hegel, *Phänomenologie*, 21; Hegel, *Phenomenology*, 13.
16. Rebecca Comay and Frank Ruda, *The Dash—The Other Side of Absolute Knowing* (Minneapolis: University of Minnesota Press, 2018), 5. Later, Comay and Ruda similarly insist upon the premise that "the absolute is nothing but its own exposition" (*ibid.*, 22).
17. G. W. F. Hegel, *Vorlesungen über die Ästhetik III*, ed. Eva Moldenhauer and Karl Markus Michel (Frankfurt am Main: Suhrkamp, 1986), 325; my translation. See also G. W. F. Hegel, *Aesthetics: Lectures on Fine Art: Volume II*, trans. T.M. Knox (Oxford: Clarendon Press, 1975), 1040.
18. Hamacher, *Pleroma*, 65. Precisely by repeating Hegel's circular logic of reading in the first person, as one would have to do—and nevertheless in a manner that Hegel had not done himself —Hamacher shows through his rhetorical performance that repeating (or: reading) makes a difference.
19. Hegel, *Phänomenologie*, 50–51; cf. Hegel, *Phenomenology*, 38–39.
20. Hegel, *Phänomenologie*, 48–51; cf. Hegel, *Phenomenology*, 36–39.
21. Giorgio Agamben, *Idea of Prose*, trans. Michael Sullivan and Sam Whitsitt (Albany: SUNY Press, 1995), 41. For Agamben, however, the turns of enjambment that constitute the "core of verse" are also at the core of discourse as such. In his *Idea of Prose*, Agamben insists upon the "mismatch" or "disconnection between the metrical and syntactic elements, between sounding rhythm and meaning" in poetic verse as that which "brings to light the original gait, neither poetic nor prosaic, but boustrophedonic, as it were, of poetry, the essential prose-metrics of every human discourse" (ibid., 40). My thanks to Tilottama Rajan for drawing my attention to this passage.

22. Theodor W. Adorno, "Skoteinos, or How to Read Hegel," *Hegel: Three Studies*, trans. Shierry Weber Nicholsen (Cambridge: MIT Press, 1993), 122. Departing from different passages than those which are analyzed in this chapter, Comay and Ruda pursue the similar thought that, namely, "thought moves episodically and retrogressively, constantly revisiting and reformulating its premises" (Comay and Ruda, *The Dash*, 23). Whereas their remarks follow from a reading of the notions of "form" and "the absolute," however, the reading of Hegel's "Foreword" that is offered here retraces and draws the consequences of the singular ways in which the very first words of his *Phenomenology* call for an oscillating movement of reading-writing, while at the same time deferring to speak.
23. Hegel, *Phänomenologie*, 376; cf. Hegel, *Phenomenology*, 306.
24. Jean-Luc Nancy, *The Speculative Remark (One of Hegel's Bon Mots)*, trans. Céline Surprenant (Stanford: Stanford University Press, 2001), 42.
25. Nancy, *The Speculative Remark*, 59; trans. modified; cf. Jean-Luc Nancy, *La remarque spéculative (Un bon mot de Hegel)* (Paris: Galilée, 1973), 77.
26. In his "Foreword" to the *Phenomenology*, the living contradiction of conceptual identity is exemplified with the life cycle of a tree, but the structure does not cease to circulate throughout Hegel's written oeuvre. In, for example, the section of the *Encyclopedia* that explicates the "nature of the concept," Hegel derives the copula of predicative judgments or *Ur-teile* from the "*original* division" that the conceptual subject *is*: "The *judgment* is the concept in its particularization, as the differentiating *relation* of its moments, which are posited as being for themselves and at the same time as identical with themselves, not with one another," Hegel writes, before clarifying further: "The copula 'is' comes from the nature of the concept to be *identical* with itself in its exteriorization" (Hegel, *Enzyklopädie I*, §166, 316–17; my translation; cf. Hegel, *Encyclopedia Logic*, 240–41).
27. Nancy, *The Speculative Remark*, 142; trans. modified; cf. Nancy, *La remarque spéculative*, 176.
28. Hegel, *Phänomenologie*, 88–89; cf. Hegel, *Phenomenology*, 67.
29. Paul de Man, *Aesthetic Ideology*, ed. Andrzej Warminski (Minneapolis: University of Minnesota Press, 1996), 98. As de Man puts it, this is "a disturbing proposition in Hegel's own terms since the very possibility of thought depends on the possibility of saying 'I'" (ibid., 98).
30. See Hegel's chapter on "sense certitude" or "sinnliche Gewißheit" in Hegel, *Phänomenologie*, 79–89; cf. Hegel, *Phenomenology*, 60–68.
31. Hegel, *Phänomenologie*, 89; cf. Hegel, *Phenomenology*, 68.
32. Hegel, *Phänomenologie*, 59; cf. Hegel, *Phenomenology*, 45–46.
33. In his written and pedagogical "oeuvre," Hegel repeatedly reiterates and varies Parmenides' proposition: "for the same is thinking and being" (τὸ γὰρ αὐτὸ νοεῖν ἐστίν τε καὶ εἶναι). See Parmenides, Fr. 5 (DK), in *Parmenides: Übersetzung, Einführung und Interpretation*, 4th ed., ed. and trans. Kurt Riezler (Frankfurt am Main: Klostermann, 2017), 26. In his lecture course on the history of philosophy, Hegel asserts that the identification of thinking and being was Parmenides' "chief thought" (*Hauptgedanke*) in the context of other fragments, which he interprets to indicate that thinking produces (its) being through autopoiesis: "Thinking produces itself; what is produced is a thought; thinking is thus identical with its being, for there is nothing outside of being, this great affirmation" (Hegel, *Vorlesungen über die Geschichte der Philosophie: Erster Teil*, ed. Eva Moldenhauer and Karl Markus Michel [Frankfurt am Main: Suhrkamp, 1986], 289–90; my translation; cf. G. W. F. Hegel, *Lectures on the History of Philosophy*, vol. 1, trans. E.S. Haldane [London: Kegan Paul, 1892], 253). Yet since Hegel also finds the truth of this identity to accrue further determinations over the course of spirit's history—and since the universal character of true thoughts would be falsified if they were associated exclusively with any single proper name—Hegel rediscovers the same thought in René Descartes's oeuvre as well, calling it *the* "concept of Cartesian metaphysics" (Hegel, *Phänomenologie*, 410; cf. Hegel, *Phenomenology*, 336). In the *Phenomenology*, it is thus in his explication of the Cartesian concept that Hegel writes "that, in itself, being and thinking is the same" (ibid.).

34. Hegel, *Enzyklopädie III* § 462, 280; my translation; cf. Hegel, *Philosophy of Mind*, 200.
35. *Ibid.*
36. Shortly before these remarks, Hegel characterizes interiority as a "nocturnal pit" (*nächtlichen Schacht*), whose contents lie dormant and thus remain unconscious in all senses of the phrase (Hegel, *Enzyklopädie III* § 453, 260; cf. Hegel, *Philosophy of Mind*, 187). "Thus," Hegel adds, "I initially do not yet have full power over the images sleeping in the pit of my interiority; [I] am not yet capable of calling them up *at will*. No one knows what an infinite crowd of images of the past slumber in him; now and again, they may very well awaken by chance, but one cannot, as we say, call them to mind" (Hegel, *Enzyklopädie III* § 453, 260–61; cf. Hegel, *Philosophy of Mind*, 187).
37. Jacques Derrida, "The Pit and the Pyramid: Introduction to Hegel's Semiology," in *Margins of Philosophy*, trans. Alan Bass (Chicago: University of Chicago Press, 1982), 107.
38. Hegel, *Vorlesungen über die Ästhetik*, 240; my translation; cf. Hegel, *Aesthetics*, 973. Shortly thereafter, he reiterates the priority of poetry over speech as we "know" it: "the first [way of seeing] is unintentionally poetic in its representing and speaking" (Hegel, *Vorlesungen über die Ästhetik*, 242; my translation; cf. Hegel, *Aesthetics*, 974). According to Hegel's reading, this original poetry, as suggested above, is found(ed) in epic. Hence, in the *Phänomenologie*, Hegel will also write of the "epos" as "the first language," which contains "the universal content, at least as the *completeness* of the world," which is in turn "begotten and borne" (*erzeugt und getragen*) by the bard (Hegel, *Phänomenologie*, 507; cf. Hegel, *Phenomenology*, 418).
39. Hegel, *Enzyklopädie III*, § 457, 269; cf. Hegel, *Philosophy of Mind*, 194.
40. Hegel, *Phänomenologie*, 251; Hegel, *Phenomenology*, 200. "Thoughtlessness" (*Gedankenlosigkeit*) is also Hegel's word for the void thinking of phrenology, and if this modifier should seem to contradict the Hegelian premise that what is "said" (*das Gesagte*) is what is "thought" (*das Gedachte*), the systematic demands of Hegel's thinking require that it include its limit-cases: in this case, the thoughtless language of the *caput mortuum*. Nor is the characterization of skull-"language" a "mere" figure of speech, as if there were a proper or authentic alternative: for the skull, as it is treated and understood in phrenology, not only fulfills the criterion for language that Hegel names, consisting in an exteriorization of interiority, but also exemplifies the arbitrary structure of the sign: "This outer, although it is a language of the individual which he has on his own, is, as a sign, at the same time something indifferent to the content which it is supposed to designate just as that which, to itself, posits the sign is indifferent to the sign itself" (Hegel, *Phänomenologie*, 251; cf. Hegel, *Phenomenology*, 200).
41. This thought would be verbalized in precisely these terms in Hugo von Hofmannsthal's lyrical drama, *Der Tor und der Tod*, where it is suggested that mortal, dying consciousness distinguishes itself in interpreting what is "not interpretable" (*nicht deutbar*) and in reading "what was never written" (Hugo von Hofmannsthal, *Der Tor und der Tod*, in *Lyrische Dramen* [Frankfurt am Main: Fischer, 1999], 74; my translation).
42. Among the articulations of life in the *Phänomenologie*, for example, variations upon this phrase can be found at the pivotal moment where the absolute relation of life "to itself" (*auf sich selbst*) is said already to "speak" of its diremption and alterity—"thus ... the *other* is at the same time already spoken out with it" (*so ist darin schon das Andere mit ihm zugleich ausgesprochen*)—; as well as at the moment where the designation of "sensibility" and "irritability" as "*factors*" in animate life is said to "speak out" the fact that these are sublated moments of its concept—"with that, it is precisely spoken out that they are *moments* of the concept" (Hegel, *Phänomenologie*, 125, 202; cf. Hegel, *Phenomenology*, 98, 159). Later, "speaking out" occurs again, when the observing consciousness of phrenology is said to know "no other way to grasp and to speak itself out, than by openly proposing the bone ... for the *reality* of self-consciousness, as it finds itself as a sensual thing" (Hegel, *Phänomenologie*, 253; cf. Hegel, *Phenomenology*, 202). The further development of self-conscious and objective life will then be traced back to the living, ethical substance of antiquity, where both speaking and consciousness assume a more articulate form: "the individual finds its *determination / destiny*, that is, its universal and singular essence, not only spoken out and at hand as thinghood, but is

itself this essence and has reached its determination / destiny. The wisest men of antiquity therefore made the outspoken claim: that wisdom and virtue consist in living according to the ethics of one's people" (Hegel, *Phänomenologie,* 256; cf. Hegel, *Phenomenology,* 206). If this scenario still involves the reification of spirit, then its "thinghood" is no longer skeletal, and its speech is no longer mute: things and speech are instead brought to life through the subjectivity that identifies with them, whose recognition of subjectivity as objectivity and objectivity as subjectivity universalizes both, in a fashion that is expressed in the universal organization and universal claims of ethical substance. Nor does it seem to be a mere coincidence that, after all of the speaking-out (*Aussprechen*) which was hitherto said to take place through the tacit assumptions and comportments of consciousness, an "outspoken claim" (*Ausspruch*)—that is, a substantivized form of speaking-out (*aussprechen*)—is verbalized when the mind recognizes itself explicitly in and as its object. For Hegel will characterize verbal language precisely as an objectivation through which the mind recognizes its thoughts in a universal form.

43. Jean Hyppolite had similarly insisted: "To say that language is prior to thought means that thought is not a pure sense which could exist somewhere else, outside of its expression, like an essence beyond appearance. Thought is only by already being there, only by preceding itself, in this speech which refers to nature and to anthropology by means of its sonorous materials, in this speech which precedes the understanding by means of its grammatical structure, sketching in a way, at times prolifically, at other times insufficiently, the understanding's forms" (Jean Hyppolite, *Logic and Existence,* trans. Leonard Lawlor and Amit Sen [Albany: SUNY Press, 1997], 43).
44. Comay and Ruda, *The Dash,* 58.
45. Catherine Malabou, *The Future of Hegel: Plasticity, Temporality, and Dialectic,* trans. Lisbeth During (London: Routledge, 2005), 166.
46. Ibid., 8–9.
47. Hegel, *Vorlesungen über die Ästhetik III,* 325; cf. Hegel, *Aesthetics,* 1040.
48. Tilottama Rajan, *The Supplement of Reading: Figures of Understanding in Romantic Theory and Practice* (Ithaca: Cornell University Press, 1990). In this monograph, Rajan elegantly describes Hegel's *Phenomenology of Spirit* as a "hermeneutics of intellectual history," where "'false' or failed forms of awareness" are interpreted as "versions of truth" which "must be reread in a historical perspective" (Ibid., 50).
49. Hamacher, *Pleroma,* 5; trans. modified; cf. Werner Hamacher, *pleroma—zu Genesis und Struktur einer dialektischen Hermeneutik bei Hegel,* in Hegel, "*Der Geist des Christentums,*" 15.
50. Jacques Derrida, "Proverb: 'He that would pun...,'" in *Glassary,* by John. P. Leavey (Lincoln: University of Nebraska Press, 1986), 17.
51. To name several of the further major studies which this reading may echo, no doubt in more ways than I know to say: Maurice Blanchot, *The Step Not Beyond,* trans. Lycette Nelson (Albany: SUNY Press, 1992); Hyppolite, *Logic and Existence*; David Farrell Krell, *Of Memory, Reminiscence, and Writing: On the Verge* (Bloomington: Indiana University Press, 1990), 205–239.
52. Derrida, "The Pit and the Pyramid," 71.
53. Jacques Derrida, *Glas,* trans. John P. Leavey (Lincoln: University of Nebraska Press, 1986), 204.
54. *Ibid.,* 204.
55. Hamacher thus breaks down Hegel's frequent similes of reading and eating and exposes the internal unsustainability of the onto-theo-logoical (digestive) system as Hegel imagines it: "This writing of the meal, which Hegel provides, would, once read and gathered [*aufgelesen*], disappear in the pure subjectivity of its sense, and would show itself in the sheer inwardness of its meaning as empty, cut off from the unity of the subject with its objective form. ... Merely read, this writing would still, even after the reading, remain external to the understanding of its content, would remain a dead object, without any connection with the unity sedimented within it. Gathered [*aufgelesen*] or read [*gelesen*]—the writing of the speculative meal remains unread" (Hamacher, *Pleroma,*109; cf. Hamacher, *pleroma,* 127).

56. Derrida, *Glas*, 43; cf. Jacques Derrida, *Glas*, (Paris: Galilée, 1974), 53.
57. Geoffrey Hartman, *Saving the Text: Literature/Derrida/Philosophy* (Baltimore: Johns Hopkins University Press, 1981), 4.
58. In his foreword or postscript to *Glassary*, Derrida thus remarks: "no one will be able to prove that *Glas* belongs, in its so-called original version, to the element of the French tongue. As for the English translation, despite all the diplomacy this invaluable *glassary* can deploy, the translation risks inflicting on your tongue a violence that renders your tongue unrecognizable in places, deprived of the very possibility of being *spoken*, in any case by its legitimate and usual guardians to which all at once it would appear suspect, foreign, without visa, outside the law" (Derrida, "Proverb," 17). Similar commentaries are offered in John P. Leavey, "This (then) will not have been a book...," in *Glassary*, 36–37.
59. Derrida, *Glas*, 1; Derrida, *Glas*, 7.
60. Hegel, *Enzyklopädie III*, 395; my translation. There, the quotation from Aristotle's *Metaphysics* appears in Greek.
61. Hegel, *Phänomenologie*, 552; Hegel, *Phenomenology*, 457; trans. modified.
62. Hegel writes: "so that man could stand a chance against the outbreaks of the now hostile nature, it had to be dominated [...] Noah [...] made his ideal into an existence and counter-posed to it all things as thought, that is, as dominated (*alles als Gedachtes, d.h. als Beherrschtes*)." Hegel, "*Der Geist des Christentums*," 373–74. As Derrida points out: "Noah is the concept. [...] one would say noesis" (*Glas*, 37–38).
63. Jean Genet, *Miracle of the Rose*, trans. Bernard Frechtman (New York: Grove Press, 1966), 141; trans. modified; cf. Jean Genet, *Miracle de la rose*, in Jean Genet, *Oeuvres complètes*, vol. 2 (Paris: Gallimard, 1951), 339.

Reading Hegel II: Politics and History

Gregor Moder

What did the French poststructuralists like Louis Althusser and Gilles Deleuze find so indigestible in Hegel, and why was Hegel defended, with the help of Jacques Lacan, by the post-poststructuralists like Slavoj Žižek and Mladen Dolar during the first decade of the Ljubljana-based Society for Theoretical Psychoanalysis in the 1980s?[1]

1   The Paradox of the Russian Revolution

There is perhaps no better introduction to the French reception of Hegel in the second half of the twentieth century than Louis Althusser's 1962 essay on "Contradiction and Overdetermination."[2] The paper is a frontal assault on the traditional coupling of Marx's radical analysis of the political economy with Hegel's dialectic. This coupling was, to an extent, declared by Marx himself, most prominently in the Afterword to the Second German Edition of *Capital*, where Marx famously wrote that he "coquetted" with Hegel's philosophical language and claimed that, with Hegel, dialectic was "standing on its head," adding that "it must be turned right side up again, if you would discover the rational kernel within the mystical shell."[3] In a series of articles in the 1960s and 1970s, Althusser consistently sought to disentangle Marx's analytic method from Hegelian dialectic, even to the point of reading Marx against Marx himself.

The central claim of the "Contradiction and Overdetermination" paper concerned the novelty that Marxism introduced into the philosophy of history—a field central to Hegel's philosophical edifice—by arguing that economic relations which

---

G. Moder (✉)
University of Ljubljana, Ljubljana, Slovenia

govern in a given historical society determine, in the final instance, all other social structures. Economic *basis* or *infrastructure* determines all *superstructures*—the legal, the political, the ideological—and is reflected even in the most sublime, metaphysical social structures.

The central question for Althusser is thus the question of the exact nature of this "determination." What does this term imply? Is Marx a materialist reductionist, in the sense that the superstructures are nothing but epiphenomena of the material base, mere reflections of a process which, in actuality, takes place in a wholly different domain, so that, for instance, the legal or political history of France is nothing but a sequence of legal (or political) articulations of the historical transformations of basic economic processes? Does determination, then, describe a mechanist causality, or even logical necessity?

Alternatively, does one have to consider the causal link, implied by the term 'determination,' as a compound of several independent causes, including historically or geographically contingent ones, so that the result can never be traced back to one single cause, even though we can isolate the most important one? Or should we understand determination quite differently, as a complex historical process of co-dependency, where that which we call the cause and that which we call the effect are never exclusively one or the other, because they always imply or presuppose each other? Or perhaps ultimately, the term 'determination' doesn't imply a causal relationship at all, but merely expresses the model for analysis—so that, for instance, the legal practice of France in a given historical period should be explained according to the coeval economic practice of France, but without ever making the assumption that a particular economic formation 'caused' the emergence of particular legal edifice.

In short, does the Marxist idea of determination, which is said to relate the economic base to its superstructures but also allows them a degree of autonomy, describe any of the following: (a) a mechanist determination or logical implication, (b) a combination of several factors, among which there is a dominant one, (c) a co-dependency of the causes and the effects, such as is typical for much of the social phenomena,[4] or (d) simply the model of explanation? This list is not meant as exhaustive, it simply aims to indicate that the relationship between the base and superstructures is not only patently Marxist but also patently unclear and open to interpretations. What distinguishes Althusser's reading from others is not only the replacement of the term 'determination' with another term, 'overdetermination,' but also and even more importantly for our consideration, the articulation of the concept of contradiction as incompatible with Hegel's dialectic. Let us take a closer look.

Althusser begins by evoking the success of the Russian revolution in 1917, which presented an apparent paradox within certain strands of Marxist thought. For economic determinists, a successful communist revolution would require both a developed form of capitalism and an existent social class of proletarians. It was Marx himself who famously wrote that the "changes in the economic foundation lead sooner or later to the transformation of the whole immense superstructure," and further added that "no social order is ever destroyed before all the productive forces for which it is sufficient have been developed, and new superior relations of production never replace older ones before the material conditions for their existence have matured within the framework of the old society."[5]

But despite the venerable roots of economic determinism, the tzarist Russia of 1917 was far from a mature capitalist society, its structures remaining feudal to a great extent. The country was only partly industrialized, and the population was mostly composed of farmers, not of proletarian workers. How come, then, that proletarian revolution never succeeded in England or Germany, where the historical conditions were ripe, but instead triumphed in a semi-feudal Russia?

In response to this, Althusser cited Lenin's metaphor of the weakest link and claimed that the Great War, imperialist in nature, created an 'objectively revolutionary' situation across Europe and in the colonies. The war dragged vast masses not only into suffering but also *into history*. Across the continent and around the world, mass strikes, revolutions, and protests were observable, but it was only in Russia, in "the weakest link in the chain of imperialist states," that the revolution succeeded.[6]

This allows Althusser to reject economic determinism—or economism, as he called it—and to argue that the contradiction between economic classes is never enough, in and by itself, to produce a successful social revolution. What is required is a kind of conflictual union or fusion of many contradictions. This means that the historical contradiction is never simply 'determined by the economy in the last instance,' because it can only be described as an *overdetermined contradiction*. This means that

> the 'contradiction' is inseparable from the total structure of the social body in which it is found, inseparable from its formal *conditions* of existence, and even from the *instances* it governs; it is radically *affected by them*, determining, but also determined in one and the same movement, and determined by the various *levels* and *instances* of the social formation it animates; it might be called *overdetermined in its principle*.[7]

We must pay attention to the detail here and underline the codependency of that which determines and that which is being determined, of that which governs and that which is governed. For Althusser, it is not simply that a historical analysis should consider more than just one, albeit dominant, factor, such as perhaps the contradictions at the level of the economy, in its account of social transformation. This is because what is usually considered the determining 'contradiction'—note that Althusser puts it in quotation marks, indicating that the true notion of contradiction must be phrased differently—cannot be isolated from the totality of the historical social formation in which it is said to be the determining instance, for it is affected by those very instances (or levels) which it motivates. The very relationship between the base and the superstructure, so central to the Marxist account of history in comparison to that of Hegel, must be understood as a profoundly complicated relationship.

2 Contingency and Anachronicity

Althusser recalls the concrete example of Marx's historical analysis in the *Eighteenth Brumaire* and declares in a stunning finale to his text:

> We must carry this through to its conclusion and say that this overdetermination does not just refer to apparently unique and aberrant historical situations (Germany, for example), but is *universal*; the economic dialectic is never active *in the pure state*; in History, these instances, the superstructures, etc.—are never seen to step respectfully aside when their work is done or, when the Time comes, as his pure phenomena, to scatter before His Majesty the Economy as he strides along the royal road of the Dialectic. From the first moment to the last, the lonely hour of the 'last instance' never comes.[8]

Once more, Althusser underlines that the economy never functions in a pure state, as a single determining historical agent, and that every historical situation is unique and 'exceptional,' or overdetermined. By referring us back to the *Eighteenth Brumaire* and other concrete examples of historical analysis in Marx, such as the description of contemporary German situation as "an anachronism, a flagrant contradiction of universally recognized axioms, the nullity of the *ancien régime* revealed to the whole world,"[9] Althusser frames the contradiction as not only profoundly dependent on historically contingent circumstances—thus making contingency an irreducible part of the equation—but also anachronistically stretching out beyond its own historical moment.

By touting these two moments, contingency and anachronicity, Althusser is at least in principle correct to declare that Marx's concept of contradiction is completely different from Hegel's concept of contradiction, and that Marx's historical analysis is completely different from Hegelian dialectic. Althusser writes that "a Hegelian contradiction is never *really overdetermined*, even though it frequently has all the appearances of being so."[10] This becomes the central point of Althusser's harsh critique of Hegel and Hegelian Marxism, based mostly on his reading of the *Phenomenology of Spirit* and the *Lectures on the Philosophy of History* but also on the critique of the *Philosophy of Right*.

For Althusser, the concept of contradiction that Hegel proposes as the driving force in history is ultimately a contradiction *internal* to a central principle of a given historical formation; the principles of former historical formations remain within the present formation only as its echoes: "Of course, this internal principle contains as echoes the principle of each of the historical formations it has superseded, but as echoes of itself—that is why, too, it only has one centre, the centre of all the past worlds conserved in its memory; that is why *it is simple*."[11] For Althusser, Hegel's concept of contradiction is a false contradiction: it is simple, abstract, purely logical, and only has one center, "the circle of circles."

3 The Paradigm Shift

Discussing the relationship between difference and contradiction in his 1968 *Difference and Repetition*, Gilles Deleuze refers back to the text by Althusser and rejects Hegel's concept of contradiction precisely because it supposedly reduces the problem of the difference first to that of an opposition, and furthermore to an opposition within the framework of the identical. For Deleuze, Hegel's concept of contradiction exhibits the same flaw as Plato's metaphysics: it subordinates difference to an ultimate identity. On this point, Deleuze praises Althusser for arguing for an *overdetermined* contradiction and concludes his own confrontation with Hegel by more or less repeating Althusser's formulae:

> Always the same old malediction which resounds from the heights of the principle of identity: alone will be saved not that which is simply represented, but the infinite representation (the concept) which conserves all the negative finally to deliver difference up to the identical. Of all the senses of *Aufheben*, none is more important than that of 'raise up'. There is indeed a dialectical circle, but this infinite circle has everywhere only a single centre; it retains within itself all the other circles, all the other momentary centres.[12]

Deleuze echoes Althusser's critique of the image of "circle of circles," which was Hegel's own metaphor for dialectic in the Preface to the *Phenomenology of Spirit*. Furthermore, the explanation of the process of *Aufhebung* as basically a reduction or elimination of difference in order to produce the identical also resonates with Althusser's claim that Hegelian logic employs "the innocent but sly concept of 'supersession' (*Aufhebung*) which is merely the empty anticipation of its end in the illusion of an immanence of truth."[13] This congruence between otherwise quite distinct thinkers, their forceful rejection of Hegel, is interesting, at the very least.

The French reception of Hegel has significantly advanced since the times of the legendary lectures of Alexandre Kojève in the 1930s, lectures which deeply influenced an entire generation of French intellectuals—including Jacques Lacan, Maurice Merleau-Ponty, Georges Bataille—but which did not present a particularly faithful reading of Hegel's core ideas about history and dialectic.[14] By the time Althusser and Deleuze were criticizing Hegel, Jean Hippolyte had long since published his translation of the *Phenomenology* (in 1939) as well as his comprehensive and detailed, not to mention considerably more faithful, analysis of its structure.[15] However, the 1960s saw a dramatic change of terrain in French materialist social thought, and it is therefore no coincidence that Hegel became the very image of everything that was wrong with idealism.

This profound change of theoretical terrain came about in parallel to the adoption of a new champion, a radical philosopher very different from Hegel, one whose principle of demonstration was not dialectical, but geometrical, and whose system saw no place for contradictions or negations: Baruch Spinoza. Both Althusser and Deleuze were heavily under the influence of the seventeenth-century Dutch thinker of nature without a transcendent deity, a philosopher whose early steps were deemed dangerous enough to have earned him a *cherem*, an excommunication of sorts from the Amsterdam Jewish community. Pierre Macherey, one of the contributors to

Louis Althusser's volume on *Reading Capital*—along with Étienne Balibar, Roger Establet, Jacques Rancière, and Althusser himself—perfectly captured this change of terrain in his 1979 book on *Hegel or Spinoza*, aptly describing the alternative that haunted, and continues to haunt even today, the field of materialist philosophy.[16]

4 On Anachronism

Let us return now to the two points raised by Althusser in his criticism of Hegel's concept of contradiction, the points which I phrased as (a) the insistence on the importance of contingency within the historical process and (b) the relocation of the contradiction from the interiority of a historically given social structure to its exteriority, touting social anachronisms. As for the second point, Althusser is absolutely correct to point out that Hegel's understanding of historical process allows for no such thing as anachronicity—a notion that frequently appears in the concrete examples of Marx's political analyses. Hegel writes in the Preface to his *Outlines of the Philosophy of Right*:

> To comprehend *what is*, this is the task of philosophy, because *what is*, is reason. Whatever happens, every individual is a *child of his time*; so philosophy too is *its own time apprehended in thoughts*. It is just as absurd to fancy that a philosophy can transcend its contemporary world as it is to fancy that an individual can overleap his own age, jump over Rhodes. If his theory really goes beyond the world as it is and builds a world *as it ought to be*, that world exists indeed, but only in his opinions, a supple element in which anything you please may be constructed by the imagination.[17]

It is not just that we are individually all sons and daughters of our time; it is philosophy itself which cannot transcend its contemporary world, and it cannot overleap its own time. In a strong sense, evoking the distinction between the rigor of science and the frivolity of imagination, Hegel denies the possibility of an anachronicity in reality, to the point that philosophy proper is nothing but *"its own time apprehended in thoughts."*

The butt of Hegel's criticism is directed against the moralist approach to political philosophy, chastising or praising people and their ways according to a predetermined set of normative ideals (it is the moralist who "builds a world *as it ought to be*"). Instead, Hegel envisions political philosophy as the study of the political and historical reality, and even as the explicit articulation of this reality in concepts; as such, the work of political philosophy cannot teach the state what it ought to be; "it can only show how the state, the ethical universe, should be understood."[18]

Nevertheless, the very notion that philosophy profoundly belongs to its own world appears to lock that world in its own time, too. The world of the opinions and the imagination *does exist*, Hegel affirms, but this world does not appear as part of the contradiction; it plays no role in the *real* world of reason, whatsoever. The idea of anachronicity of the real world itself is only possible in the Marxist analysis, which distinguishes between the dominant material praxis in a given historical social formation and the surviving remains of legal, ideological, or even economic practices of "already dead" historical formations.

Althusser devotes a considerable portion of his breakthrough text to such 'survivals.' He describes them precisely as *realities*, claiming not only that they possess "sufficient of their own consistency *to survive beyond their immediate life context*, even to recreate, to 'secrete' substitute conditions of existence temporarily" but also that these surviving elements of old regimes might become 'reactivated' even after a successful revolution.[19] A given historical social formation, if we can even consider it as a "world" in the Hegelian meaning of the word, is thus a world which is in its very essence an anachronistic, decentered world, a world out of sync with itself.

Althusser's concept of overdetermination certainly seems to characterize a fundamental distinction between the Hegelian and the Marxist account of history. Nevertheless, is it possible to articulate an element of 'anachronicity' in Hegel's understanding of the real world? By arguing that "what is rational is actual and what is actual is rational," as he famously does in his *Philosophy of Right*, it seems that Hegel argues for a seamless totality of the political body, a totality which cannot but be what it already is. In fact, Hegel even takes it one step further and seems to declare that philosophy as such is completely incapable of *intervening* in the world it aspires to *understand*:

> Philosophy appears only when actuality has completed its process of formation and attained its finished state. ... When philosophy paints its gray in gray, then has a shape of life grown old. By philosophy's gray in gray it cannot be rejuvenated but only understood. The owl of Minerva begins its flight only with the falling of dusk.[20]

It seems that we would be justified to conclude that what Hegel is suggesting is that the totality of a given historical "world," or "shape of life," is so profoundly confined to itself, that even understanding it precisely as such does not open up the possibility of changing it. However, I believe this conclusion to be false, or at least that it does not tell the whole story.

What is at stake in this passage is Hegel's concept of understanding, or cognizing, *erkennen*, which is far from an innocent process. In fact, I believe that, in this particular instance, it is the very motor of what we could call the historical progression. The act of grasping a historical period in philosophical knowledge is not merely an individual's take on a series of events; it is not subjective knowledge of a person, but rather a collective understanding of the entire culture.

This is what allows Hegel to claim that once philosophy has "painted its grey in grey, a shape of life has grown old"[21]: once philosophy has articulated in theoretical concepts what was already present in the cultural, living practice of a people, the status of that practice itself is affected, even transformed. In the process of knowledge, the once colorful, living cultural practice has adopted the grey of old age, and there is no going back, for theory cannot rejuvenate, and its force of knowledge does not bring life, only lifeless concepts. While it is true that philosophy, considered in these terms, cannot intervene in the actual 'shape of life' and help preserve it, it is nevertheless far from impotent: its work is the work not only of growing up, of growing old, of maturing but also, by extension, of mutating, of morphing. In this sense, it is that which drives the historical progression.

It should not surprise us that in the *Phenomenology of Spirit*, Hegel describes the work of knowledge precisely by evoking the force of death itself:

> The activity of dissolution is the power and work of the Understanding, the most astonishing and mightiest of powers, or rather the absolute power. ... Death, if that is what we want to call this non-actuality, is of all things the most dreadful, and to hold fast what is dead requires the greatest strength. ... But the life of Spirit is not the life that shrinks from death and keeps itself untouched by devastation, but rather the life that endures it and maintains itself in it. It wins its truth only when, in utter dismemberment, it finds itself.[22]

The life of concept is nothing like the life of the actuality; in fact, it is a life that maintains itself in the very death of the actuality. This allows us to argue that when Hegel writes, in the Preface to the *Philosophy of Right*, that philosophy comes too late to the scene of the world events to intervene in them, he certainly does not mean to claim that philosophy's work is futile. Philosophy is precisely the force of 'death,' allowing a historical 'shape of life' to mature, or even to pass away.

In my reading, this amounts to the following claim: if it is true that the rational is actual and the actual rational, as Hegel asserts, then this is so only because the actual is already out of sync with itself, constitutively arriving too late—just as philosophy is. In other words, the too-lateness of philosophy corresponds to the too-lateness of actuality itself. Philosophy's too-lateness is only possible because it is the historical social actuality itself that is not fully transparent to itself. For Hegel, social opacity is ultimately irreducible and contingent to historical processes.[23]

To be sure, this does not quite suffice to claim that Hegel already possessed a concept of social anachronicity, such as Althusser praised, for instance, in Marx's analysis of contemporary Germany. It does, however, take the edge off Althusser's claim that Hegel's concept of contradiction is but a simple logical contradiction. For historical individuals, acting within the framework of their own historical 'world,' it is strictly speaking *impossible* to penetrate the opacity of their situation; they do not control the end results of their own actions. They are like Brutus and other conspirators who believed that Caesar was only one individual, whose removal from the equation would save the Roman republic, but unaware that their actions only hastened the establishment of the Roman Empire through Caesar's 'repetition' in Augustus Caesar.[24]

5 Absolute Knowledge

In response to the general backlash against Hegel in the second half of the twentieth century, especially in some strands of French thought, contemporary Hegelians defend not only the notions of the open-endedness of history and dialectic, but also the notion of something we could call a non-totalizable totality. In Catherine Malabou's radical reading of Hegel, the dialectic not only dissolves and liquifies all of its historical objects, molding and reshaping them in its progression, but must also be capable of liquifying and dissolving itself in an event she describes as 'explosive plasticity,' releasing all shapes and forms and making space for something completely unpredictable to its own process and history.[25]

To a similar effect, the Ljubljana Hegelians like Slavoj Žižek and Mladen Dolar have defended Hegel with the help of the concept of 'not-all,' borrowed from Lacanian psychoanalysis. The notorious concept of Absolute Knowledge, scorned by Althusser as "that End of History in which the concept finally becomes fully visible," inscribed in the long tradition of "the religious fantasies of epiphany and Parousia,"[26] is defended by Dolar, who understands it not as the mythic convergence of being and thought, of knowledge and truth, but precisely as the realization that the truth cannot be fully and unequivocally grasped in knowledge, that the displacement experienced incessantly by natural consciousness is not something that could be eliminated through the epistemological process, but is ultimately irreducible to any human knowledge. All knowledge is, ultimately, lacunary, because this is the very structure of the relationship between knowledge and truth. The concept of Absolute Knowledge, which is usually understood as the capstone completing Hegel's metaphysical edifice in the *Phenomenology of Spirit*, is thus interpreted by Dolar as the very element that keeps the edifice fundamentally incomplete.[27]

The metaphysical open-endedness of history or of the process of knowledge, defended by contemporary Hegelians, is also directly translated into contemporary readings of Hegel's political philosophy. Slavoj Žižek comments on the question of how exactly we should understand the idea of the state in Hegel's *Philosophy of Right*: Is it a normative model of the state, one that emerges at the end of history? Recalling the famous proclamation that with the advent of knowledge, the actuality has grown old, Žižek argues that "if Hegel is minimally consistent, this has to apply also to the notion of the State deployed in his own *Philosophy of Right*: the fact that Hegel was able to deploy this concept means that 'the shades of night are gathering' on what readers of Hegel usually take as a normative description of a model rational state."[28] It seems that if Hegel is to have any future as a political philosopher, one must first of all allow for the very concept of future in Hegel's philosophy.

6 On Contingency

This brings us to the other point raised in Althusser's critique of Hegelian contradiction: the question of contingency. The Marxist analysis understands the basic social contradiction as overdetermined, which means not only that there are several co-dependent factors to consider, each playing its specific role in shaping the historical moment, but also that one must take into account completely contingent elements, relevant only in the specific time and place of the observed historical formation. In other words, contingency is an integral part of Marxist analysis of social contradiction.

Althusser did not abandon the idea of historical development of social formations; quite to the contrary, he claimed that Marx 'discovered' a new scientific field, the science of history. But while Hegel overtly discussed his philosophy of history as a form of theodicy, as a gradual actualization of reason in history, Althusser understood Hegel's philosophical position as the very epitome not simply of idealism, but of ideology. In his notorious 1968 article on "Ideology and Ideological State Apparatuses," Althusser declares that "ideology has no outside (for itself)."[29] This is why he can claim that Hegel's reduction of the rich historical complexity of Rome (in the *Lectures on the Philosophy of History*) to an external expression of a simple internal principle is nothing but a reduction of that rich historical complexity to its own ideology:

> [T]he reduction of all the elements that make up the concrete life of a historical epoch (economic, social, political and legal institutions, customs, ethics, art, religion, philosophy, and even historical events: wars, battles, defeats, and so on) to *one* principle of internal unity, is itself only possible on the *absolute condition* of taking the whole concrete life of a people for the externalization-alienation (*Entäusserung-Entfremdung*) of an *internal spiritual principle*, which can *never definitely be anything but the most abstract form of that epoch's consciousness of itself: its religious or philosophical consciousness, that is, its own ideology*.[30]

Althusser's critique of Hegel on this point amounts to a claim about ideology: ideology proceeds precisely by reducing social complexity to a 'contradiction' internal to its own terms; the dialectical philosophy of Hegel is simply the most overt ideological procedure. A *materialist* philosophy of history, one that Althusser could get behind, does not abandon the idea of a driving force of the historical process, the class struggle, but acknowledges that the slow march of history is neither linear nor certain, that it is affected by the very social instances it determines, and that it is always subject to chance encounters and occurrences. Note that the term 'materialism' does not denote some simplistic notion of studying 'materials' instead of ideas, concepts, or social institutions; the term 'materialism,' here, rather implies a specific form of analysis, where articulated ideas, concepts, and social institutions are themselves regarded as examples of real social practices, and not simply as external appearances of some internal truth.

To what extent is Althusser's criticism of Hegel justified on this point? It is certainly true that Hegel was interested in the regularity of the historical process, and that the particular and the contingent were not simply *lost*, but rather *eliminated* in this process. This is what Hegel describes as the 'cunning of reason':

> In external history we have right before our eyes what is particular, namely, drives and needs. We see these particular elements engaged in mutual destruction, headed for ruin, [whereas] the idea is what is universal, and in the struggle it is free from assault and is unscathed. This is what we may call the *cunning of reason*, since reason avails itself of these instruments and shines forth untouched or, rather, brings itself forth. Rational purpose (*Vernunft-Zweck*) realizes itself by means of the needs, passions, and the like of human beings; what is personal or private is quite insignificant over against what is universal; individuals are sacrificed and relinquished.[31]

Particular needs and ends of individuals are insignificant in themselves and are 'sacrificed and relinquished' in order for the universal—the idea, or reason—to shine through, unharmed in the destruction of those individual pursuits. Describing the pursuits of Alexander the Great, Hegel argued that what mattered in the end, and what endured, was not that particular individual, or his dynasty, but the notion of the Greek dominion. He claims: "One must be prepared for blood and strife when one turns to world history, for they are the means by which the world spirit drives itself forward; they come from the concept."[32]

7 The End of History

And ultimately, Hegel's idea of world history is haunted by the concept of 'the end of history.' The reason Hegel provided support for the claim that history must necessarily have an 'end' is ultimately the same Aristotle gives us in order to 'prove' that there must be a prime mover. Hegel, just like Aristotle before him, was convinced that an infinite progression is ill suited for a universal concept, which should, as he declares, "assume a determinate shape and portray itself in a determinate way," adding that "if only new principles constantly emerged, world history would have no purpose leading to a goal; no end would ever be in sight."[33] But what *is* the end of world history according to Hegel, the capstone to conclude and determine the historical progression? Since conceptuality "digests," "resolves," and "idealizes" everything, the only thing that can stand over against the concept is concept itself:

> Had something been able to hold out against thought, that would only be thought itself, since it would itself be the object such that it grasps its own self; for it is simply what is itself unlimited. In that event it would have returned into itself, and the tribunal of history (*das Gericht der Geschichte*) would be over and done with; for judgment is passed only on what does not accord with the concept. In this return of thought into itself, eternal peace would be established.[34]

The passage is not easy to unpack, but its key phrase is the "return of thought into itself," which marks the establishing of "eternal peace." The only thing that holds up against concept, and the only thing that concept does not 'digest, resolve, idealize,' is the concept itself. The infamous 'end of history' is thus the very concept of history itself, grasping itself as the realization of the purpose of history.

Hegel does not give us much in terms of clarification or detail—and how could he? Any *particular* detail to give color to this concept, or any *particular* historical event, would be merely something that still needs to be 'digested, resolved, idealized.' All Hegel adds in terms of the content of the thought returning into itself is that philosophy takes its cue from religion—from Christianity, to be precise—where the final end is taken to mean "that human beings should attain eternal peace, that they should be sanctified." The reference to Christianity serves only to take us back to the "eternal peace" of the concept. Arguing that this religious notion should be considered as a purpose for *this* world here, and not for a world 'beyond,' Hegel describes the end of history neither as a historical occurrence nor as the establishment of a particular social formation (such as, for instance, the model state he described in the *Philosophy of Right*), but instead as *a form of knowledge*. Taking his cue once more from Christian metaphysics, Hegel explains:

> The individual spirit has its glory in glorifying God. This is not its particular honor; rather its honor comes from knowing that its self-feeling is the substantial consciousness of God, that its action is to the honor and glory of God, of the absolute. In this knowledge the individual spirit has attained its truth and freedom; here it has to do with the pure concept, with the absolute; here it is at home not with another but with itself, with its essence, not with something contingent but rather in absolute freedom.[35]

The end of history is a form of knowledge, which is completely free from human contingency, because in it one knows oneself to act "to the honor and glory of God, of the absolute." This is the most specific formulation of the end of history Hegel gives us, and it is so general that we can trace its genealogy to Aristotle's 'thought thinking itself' or compare it to Spinoza's 'third kind of knowledge.' In glorifying God, the individual spirit transcends its individuality (and particularity), because its knowledge is the "substantial consciousness of God" himself—pure concept. If the progress of history, for Hegel, is nothing but a progression of the self-actualization of reason in history, then the end of history is the end of this progression itself, *pure actuality* as such. It seems that Hegel's concept is thoroughly indebted to Aristotelian theology and teleology.

How is it possible, then, to defend an element of contingency in Hegel's understanding of history, when it is clear that all contingency not only perishes but *must* perish in order for world spirit to advance? Even if we accept that the end of history cannot possibly take the shape of a particular political economic regime—such as was the assumption of Francis Fukuyama, loosely based on Kojève's interpretation of Hegel—it should still be clear that Hegel's idea of the end of history is mutually exclusive to the notion of historical contingency. Or should it?

It all depends on how we suture the end of history onto the historical timeline. Understanding it along the lines of the Last Judgement, as an asymptotical point in the future we are gradually approaching, is explicitly rejected by Hegel, since he demands that the *philosophical* concept of the end of history—contrary to the concept of the Last Judgement *in Christian teleology*—does not lie 'beyond' that which is graspable by reason, but must—somehow, Hegel does not explain this in unequivocal terms—constitute a singular point where history is seized in its entirety *but which at the same time* belongs to the very timeline of history itself. How is such a point possible?

Althusser simply dismisses the notion, as we have seen above, as the mythical point where the "concept finally becomes fully visible, present among us in person."[36] The English language editors of Hegel's *Lectures on the Philosophy of World History* propose a plausible interpretation when they write with regard to the knowledge grasped in the end of history: "Thus the end [of history] is achieved not in some timeless eternity or chronological future, but in every temporal now when spirit comes to this recognition of God."[37] In other words, Robert F. Brown and Peter C. Hodgson argue that *any* point on the historical timeline can count as the 'end of history,' provided that it fulfills the only criterion Hegel has given us, namely that at that point the spirit knows "that its self-feeling is the substantial consciousness of God."

Brown and Hodgson do not put pressure on Hegel's argument any further, but I think we would be completely justified to make one further step and claim that the 'end of history' is therefore nothing but a name for the point in the historical progression where the world spirit suddenly knows and acknowledges itself as such, a moment in which it understands itself as complete. In other words, the end of history is precisely the point which Hegel describes in the *Philosophy of Right* as the moment when philosophy begins its work, painting its grey in grey, the point "when actuality has completed its process of formation and attained its finished state." The end of history is precisely the point of no return for a *specific* historical epoch, the turning point at which the 'owl of Minerva' can begin the work of knowledge of that period, the point at which it has already began morphing into another 'world,' another historical 'shape of life,' another historical social formation.

8 The Ljubljana School

Why didn't Hegel himself provide a more articulate version of the concept of the 'end of history'? Why did his phrasing remain so vague, seemingly merely redeploying Aristotelian metaphysical formulae? Perhaps the answer is very simple—the proper conceptual tool for what he was trying to articulate was only developed in the twentieth century within so-called post-structuralism.

In order to elucidate and further develop Jacques Lacan's concept of the quilting point (or anchoring point), Slavoj Žižek renders it, in his second inaugural address to the newly established Society for Theoretical Psychoanalysis in 1982 (in Ljubljana, Yugoslavia), as the "point of suture" (*point de capiton* literally translates as upholstery button) and describes it with many examples, ranging from drama and film to Hegel and history.[38] What all Žižek's examples have in common is that they each constitute a case of what we might perhaps be allowed to call the idea of "that final piece of grain that makes us see the heap in what was, up to that point, merely a series of grains." I refer of course to one of the most widely known philosophical paradoxes, the Sorites. By adding or removing one single grain, we can never constitute or dissolve a heap; nevertheless, we must assume that—at a certain, undefined point—a group of grains has indeed become a heap.

For the purpose of explaining Žižek's 'point of suture,' the problem is not that the concept of 'heap' is fuzzy, unclearly defined, but that the infinite progression (of adding one more grain, over and over again) can never produce a determined concept (a 'heap'). We must therefore introduce an almost "miraculous" element (Žižek's own term), a capstone that in a sudden realization supports the entire edifice, an element that may be exactly like all other elements in the series in terms of *content*, but nevertheless possesses the curious *formal* property of completing that very series itself. Within the framework of Lacanian structuralism, this curious element is referred to as 'the master signifier': the chain of signifiers could theoretically run ad infinitum; however, this chain is occasionally broken down by a signifier which has the capacity to complete the series and, in retrospect, confer meaning to it.

My claim here is that the 'end of history' is precisely such an element, a kind of 'master signifier,' it is the sudden and almost miraculous advent of the 'heap.' Hegel's extremely general notion of what the 'end of history' might be or look like, only vaguely referring to the (Aristotelian) theological tradition, I believe, suggests a genuine theoretical conundrum. What Hegel is trying to articulate is precisely the notion of a 'master signifier'—the advent of an occasional formal break in the seemingly indefinite progression of world events when "everything suddenly makes sense."[39]

Let us take a look at a concrete example of how Žižek applies the concept of the point of suture to an account of historic events: his analysis of the Dreyfus affair. Alfred Dreyfus was an officer of Jewish descent in the French army, trialed and convicted in 1894 for high treason. Some years later, evidence came up which put the blame on someone else, causing a public scandal; Émile Zola wrote his famous *J'Accuse…!* article, accusing the government of antisemitism. At the renewed trial, despite the evidence, Dreyfus was again found guilty; public opinion was still overwhelmingly against Dreyfus, and the whole scandal was brushed aside as a conspiracy by the political opposition working hand in hand with the 'wealthy Jewish lobby.'

A real game changer occurred when Lieutenant Colonel Hubert-Joseph Henry was arrested for having forged the evidence against Dreyfus and later found dead in his cell in an apparent suicide. How else to interpret this as an admission of guilt, fully exculpating Dreyfus and, much more importantly, revealing the profound antisemitism of French society? As Žižek argues, it is at that precise moment that we can observe the functioning of the point of suture which successfully 'explained' the entire affair and mobilized a certain part of the French society. What happened? In the midst of confusion, a relatively unknown writer Charles Maurras, basically a proto-fascist, published a journal article called "First Blood." Žižek writes:

> What did Maurass actually do? He did not provide any new information, he did not challenge any of the facts, all he did was a wholesale reinterpretation, he cast the whole [series of developments] in a new light: he made Lieutenant-Colonel Henry into a national hero, a heroic victim whose patriotic duty was more than abstract 'justice,' who—upon realizing that the wealthy Jewish 'Union of Treason' is exploiting a minor legal technicality in order to besmirch and shake the foundations of the French way of life, to break the morale and strength of the Army, the defender of the homeland—did not hesitate to perform a slight *faux patriotique* [namely, the forgery] to try to prevent a ruinous outcome. His suicide is a testament to the fact that the corrupted Jewish spirit has penetrated even the higher ranks of the Army: instead of supporting Henry, the Army deserted him at the crucial moment, leaving him to fall as the 'first victim' of a dark conspiracy aimed at eroding the might of France.[40]

This 'explanation' was, historically speaking, only partially successful in mobilizing the proto-fascist forces in France; Henry was indeed hailed as a national hero by some, but Alfred Dreyfus was first pardoned (in 1899) and eventually fully exonerated in 1906. What matters to Žižek here, and to us, is how the point of suture functions. The key claim in the cited paragraph is that Maurras did "not provide any new information or challenged any of the facts"; in other words, Žižek emphasizes that the seemingly indefinite flow of politically highly charged events was suspended and finally *rendered legible* through an intervention on a purely formal level.

This mechanism, I argue, is, at least to an extent, useful in understanding Hegel's concept of the end of history: it is not a specific historical event but rather the name for the structurally necessary capstone, or anchoring point, where reason is sutured to the series of historical events so that, *in retrospect*, they suddenly make sense and become legible and knowable. In other words, I propose that we read the argument of the end of history strictly through the lens of the metaphor of Minerva's owl, taking flight only *after* the actuality has already finished its work: *in retrospect*, philosophy can produce knowledge of that historical period, because, paradoxically, this knowledge appears precisely as that 'miraculous' capstone which completes it.

9 Conclusion

What is gained in this poststructuralist reading of Hegel is, ultimately, precisely the notion of contingency which seemed to be expunged from the realm of the Hegelian Idea. As both Lacan and Žižek argue in their respective explanations of the anchoring point or the point of suture, this kind of capstone is a *necessary* precondition of any 'making sense'; however, since it is a purely formal intervention which brings no affirmative content in itself, the particular positive element onto which it becomes attached remains *(historically) completely contingent*.

To use one of Hegel's favorite examples: the way in which the name of Caesar became inseparably "stitched" to the concept of the rule of one in European monarchic history *is completely contingent*. Had an individual called Gaius Iulius Caesar drowned while crossing the Rubicon, he would of course never had become "Caesar"; some *other* name would have become synonymous with the notion of the dictatorial rule of one. True, Hegel claims that in order for the idea of (dictator, imperator) Caesar to establish itself, the particular individual bearing this name, as well as others, bearing the names of Brutus and his companions, must have died. While contingent individuals have thus perished, the concept of contingency did not: the Hegelian concept of contingency would thus imply precisely the way in which a particular name or an occurrence becomes stitched together with the historical process.

To be sure, I am not claiming that this concept of contingency is the same as the one Althusser was tacitly employing in his "Contradiction and Overdetermination" article. Moreover, I completely acknowledge that Marx's account of historical progress is irreducible to Hegel's; that Hegel's account remains radically impartial to any particular position held by the antagonistic forces in history, and thus blind to the fact that it is perhaps (historical, ethnical, class) partiality itself that even allows us to see or perceive social antagonism in its actual form. What I claim is that if it is not Hegel himself, then it is certainly the poststructuralist interpretation of Hegel that already produced a concept of universality as dependent on a contingency. Althusser and other critics who put pressure on Hegel's thought eventually helped contemporary Hegelians to articulate this point more clearly.

Notes

1. This chapter is a result of work conducted within my research project "History and Legacy of Yugoslavian Social Philosophy (1960–1990)" (J6-4624) and the research program "Philosophical Investigations" (P6-0252), financed by ARRS, the Slovenian Research Agency.
2. Originally published in the journal *La pensée*, the first English version appeared in *For Marx*, trans. Ben Brewster (London: New Left Review, 1969).
3. Karl Marx, "Afterword to the Second German Edition," *Capital*, trans. Samuel Moore and Edward Aveling, text available at www.marxists.org.
4. An example of this type of social phenomena is the curious case of toilet paper shortage in the early months of the Covid pandemic. Seeing pictures of individuals *irrationally* stockpiling toilet paper, even though there was no shortage of it, caused many people to start making the *rational* decision to stockpile on toilet paper, since they did not want to be left without it. In this manner, the actual shortage of toilet paper which ensued was 'caused by its own effect,' by people stockpiling on it. The so-called snowball phenomenon, which we can describe simply as the tendency of people to 'buy precisely those shoes that others have already bought,' differs from the toilet paper phenomenon in that, in our example, the others do not serve as our peers or models, but precisely as irrational others who compete with us for the same resource in a zero-sum game. Nonetheless, both social phenomena are examples of a co-dependent causality, where the cause is supported, and in some sense even preceded by the effect.
5. Karl Marx, *A Contribution to the Critique of Political Economy*, (Moscow: Progress Publishers, 1977), https://www.marxists.org/archive/marx/works/1859/critique-pol-economy/preface.htm (last accessed 8/1/2021).
6. Louis Althusser, "Contradiction and Overdetermination," *For Marx*, trans. Ben Brewster (London: Verso, 2005), 97.
7. Ibid., 101.
8. Ibid., 113.
9. Karl Marx, *Critique of Hegel's 'Philosophy of Right,'* trans. Annette Jolin and Joseph O'Malley (Cambridge: Cambridge University Press, 1970), 134.
10. Althusser, "Contradiction and Overdetermination," 101.
11. Ibid., 102.
12. Gilles Deleuze, *Difference and Repetition*, trans. Paul Patton (New York: Columbia University Press, 1994), 53.
13. Althusser, "On the Young Marx," in *For Marx*, 82.
14. Kojève's lectures were assembled and published in 1947 by Raymond Queneau; an abridged English version appeared as *Introduction to the Reading of Hegel: Lectures on the Phenomenology of Spirit* (Ithaca: Cornell University Press, 1980).
15. Originally published in 1946 by Aubier, Jean Hyppolite's massive work appeared in English translation as *Genesis and Structure of Hegel's Phenomenology of Spirit* (Evanston: Northwestern University Press, 1974).
16. Althusser and his students at the École normale supérieure ran a seminar on Marx's *Capital*. The collection of their contributions, originally published in two volumes with Maspero in 1965, continues the general thrust of Althusser's project of scientific, anti-humanist Marxism, with a special emphasis on rejecting Hegelianism. The complete English edition of *Reading Capital* was published by Verso in 2016. Pierre Macherey's study *Hegel and Spinoza* appeared in English translation with University of Minnesota Press in 2011. For further reading on the complexity of the relationship between Hegel and Spinoza as quintessential modern thinkers, see my own work *Hegel and Spinoza: Substance and Negativity* (Evanston: Northwestern University Press, 2017).
17. G. W. F. Hegel, *Outlines of the Philosophy of Right*, trans. T. M. Knox (Oxford: Oxford University Press, 2008), 15.
18. Ibid.
19. Althusser, "Contradiction and Overdetermination," 116.

20. Hegel, *Outlines of the Philosophy of Right*, 16.
21. Probably a reference to Goethe's *Faust*, where Mephistopheles distinguishes between the colors of life and theory: "All theories, dear friend, are gray; the golden tree of life is green." Johann Wolfgang von Goethe, *Faust I & II*, trans. Stuart Atkins (Princeton: Princeton University Press, 2014), ll. 2038-9.
22. G. W. F. Hegel, *Phenomenology of Spirit*, trans. A. V. Miller (Oxford: Oxford University Press, 1977), 18-19.
23. Jure Simoniti phrases the transition from Hegel's understanding of social and historical processes to that of Marx precisely as the rearticulation and relocation of conceptual opacity. He argues that while Hegel established the idea of the 'opaque core of sociality,' the notion of the historical process remained, in Hegelian analysis, transparent—or simple, as Althusser put it. It is Marx who recognized and theorized the opaque core of history. Simoniti writes: "One way to bring post-Hegelian philosophy under the common denominator is to interpret it as a series of attempts to discern the non-transparent historical core. Karl Marx certainly provides the most beautiful example for this thesis. The innermost knot of his thought is precisely the identification of a still invisible subject of future historical change" (Jure Simoniti, "Hegel and the Opaque Core of History," *Problemi* 53, no. 11-12: 227.) My understanding differs from Simoniti's in that I argue that Hegel *does* leave an opening for a possible future historical change, despite the notorious proclamation of "the End of History" (see below).
24. In the Suhrkamp TWA edition of Hegel's *Lectures on the Philosophy of History*, we can read: "The noblest men of Rome believed Caesar's reign to be a matter of chance (*etwas zufälliges*). ... That which only seemed contingent (*zufällig*) and possible (*möglich*) in the beginning, becomes something actual (*Wirkliche*) and confirmed (*Bestätigte*) through repetition." See G. W. F. Hegel, *Werke in 20 Bänden*, Vol. 12 (Frankfurt: Suhrkamp, 1986), 380, my translation.
25. Catherine Malabou, *The Future of Hegel: Plasticity, Temporality and Dialectic* (London: Routledge, 2004).
26. Louis Althusser, "From *Capital* to Marx's Philosophy," in *Reading Capital: The Complete Edition*, trans. Ben Brewster (London: Verso, 2016), 18.
27. Mladen Dolar, *Heglova fenomenologija duha I* (Ljubljana: DTP, 1990). This book has not yet been published in English, but as a close reading of Hegel's *Phenomenology of Spirit*, consistently arguing that "Hegel was a Lacanian," it is extremely important for the general reception of Hegel in the Slovenian intellectual milieu.
28. Slavoj Žižek, *Absolute Recoil: Towards a New Foundation of Dialectical Materialism* (London: Verso, 2014), 41.
29. Louis Althusser, *Lenin and Philosophy and other Essays*, trans. Ben Brewster (London: New Left Books, 1971), 176.
30. Althusser, "Contradiction and Overdetermination," 103.
31. G. W. F. Hegel, *Lectures on the Philosophy of World History. Volume 1: Manuscripts of the Introduction and The Lectures of 1822-3*, trans. Robert F. Brown and Peter C. Hodgson, (Oxford: Clarendon, 2011), 96, note 44.
32. Ibid., 387.
33. Ibid., 165-6.
34. Ibid., 166.
35. Ibid., 168.
36. Althusser, "From *Capital* to Marx's Philosophy," 16.
37. Robert F. Brown and Peter C. Hodgson, "Editorial Introduction," in Hegel, *Lectures on the Philosophy of World History*, 25.
38. Slavoj Žižek, "O 'točki prešitja' in njenem izostanku," *Problemi* 21/4-5 (1983): 11-24. Originally written in Slovenian, much of this text was translated and reworked, finding its way into the first English language book by Slavoj Žižek, *The Sublime Object of Ideology* (London: Verso, 1989).

39. In fact, many of Hegel's 'master concepts' become much clearer and much more practicable when we consider them with the help of the structuralist concept of 'master signifier.' Consider the notorious 'absolute knowledge,' discussed above. As long as we focus on what this suspicious notion could actually mean, trying to decipher the content of this knowledge and reading and rereading Hegel's vague allusions to the theological tradition, we remain in the dark. However, if we consider that absolute knowledge might simply be a kind of a *formal* capstone to conclude the progression of consciousness, the realization that the displacement between truth and knowledge is the structural predicament of any knowledge as such—basically what Mladen Dolar argued, see above—then it becomes perfectly clear why Hegel requires this concept: he requires it in order to seize knowledge as determined, as complete … as a 'heap' and not merely as an endless series of grains.
40. Žižek, "O 'točki prešitja' in njenem izostanku," 16, my translation. A reader knowledgeable in the history of Yugoslavia and the special place of Yugoslav National Army as the defender of the homeland in its political structure will immediately understand why this example was so important to Žižek in the 1980's. Žižek's account of the Dreyfuss Affair and especially of the perfidy of Maurass's 'explanation' is—shall we say—*overdetermined* with the contingent historical circumstances of Žižek's lecture, with how the Yugoslav National Army was consistently applying this kind of 'spin' in disqualifying any opposition, gradually moving closer and closer to, as well as co-determining the position of the nationalist leader Slobodan Milošević (this perfidious kind of argumentation was especially, although far from exclusively, directed against ethnic Albanians' push for more autonomy within Yugoslavia).

Reading Schelling

Tyler Tritten

1 Introduction: How Modern Schelling's "pre-modern" Thought Made Postmodern Žižek "Post-postmodern"

Some[1] truisms: Modernity marked a turn to the subject, a turn that wrested subjectivity from nature, whether as a substance of a wholly other kind than material nature, as in Descartes, or as standing at a transcendental remove in order to provide the neutral and universal conditions of nature's appearing, as in Kant. Pre-modern thought simply did not know of this conception of the subject, neither as a self-contained, discrete substance apart from nature nor as nature's transcendental condition of intelligibility. Pre-modern thought only knew of the subject as part of and/or as emergent from nature, perhaps as but one piece, even if the crowning achievement, of God's creation. Postmodernity, by contrast, announces the dissolution of the modern subject. Whether nothing but an epiphenomenon of symbolic structure (structuralism) or as something infinitely blocked or deferred by symbolic significations (poststructuralism and deconstruction[2]), the subject is ephemeral, a lack or impasse only. Post-postmodernity, then, that is, post-poststructuralism or, as Slavoj Žižek might insist, post-deconstruction, would mark the return of the subject, but not the return of the modern subject.

Unfortunately (because unjustly), Schelling has been relatively neglected in postmodern/poststructuralist engagements with German Idealism—at least in comparison with Hegel—with the exception of a few brief flirtations, for example Derrida's dedication of *Of Spirit* to him and the obvious indebtedness to Schelling on the part of Nancy (*The Experience of Freedom*). Otherwise, the most significant books in the European philosophical tradition on Schelling were by Heidegger (*Schelling's Treatise: On the Essence of Human Freedom*) and Habermas's

T. Tritten (✉)
Gonzaga University, Spokane, WA, USA

untranslated dissertation (*Das Absolute und die Geschichte. Von der Zwiespältigkeit in Schellings Denken* [The Absolute and History. On the Bifurcation in Schelling's Thinking]). This chapter, however, will treat Žižek, who has arguably written on Schelling the most extensively (dedicating two books and numerous articles to his thought). In Žižek's post-postmodernity, one finds a Schelling-inspired, but Lacan-explicated, return of the subject.[3]

For the purposes of this chapter on Žižek and Schelling, there are four salient features of poststructuralism (and, by extension, postmodernity). (1) Against structuralism, no systems are closed or complete; all are open or incomplete. Žižek's preferred way of indicating this is his insistence that the Symbolic and, hence, the Real are a "non-All." (2) Reality is not self-positing, which means that one must begin with the contingent facticity of things, and thought is not self-grounding, which means that thinking cannot provide an account of itself. Here, as will be argued, Žižek remains closer to structuralism than poststructuralism, as, for him, the Symbolic posits both itself and the Real as well as the incompleteness of each. (3) Things bottom out in contingency rather than in the necessity of a structure of thought or reality. (4) In Schelling's terms, as translated by Žižek, for both thought and reality, the Symbolic and the Real, there is always an "indivisible remainder."[4]

Rex Butler and Scott Stephens have argued that "the work of Slavoj Žižek begins with the philosophical concept of the 'beginning.' ... This philosophical quest for first principles runs counter to the usual perception of Žižek as a pop cultural iconoclast."[5] Here, then, is already one way in which Žižek is post-postmodern, moving beyond both structuralism and poststructuralism (which, again, he arguably understands as deconstruction), insofar as he resumes the search for origins and even the subject as an origin. Or, to let Žižek define the terms of the debate, it was "the status of the *subject*, the relationship between the subject/lack and structure ... this was *the* key problem of the entire field of 'structuralism.' Its founding gesture is to assert the differential or self-relational structure in its formal purity, purifying it of all 'pathological' imaginary elements."[6] Žižek ultimately remains structuralist insofar as he insists on the ability of formalization to found both itself *and* its excess, but, against structuralism, never without positing the Imaginary as a kind of necessary perversion or symptom. In this way, even as poststructuralism insists on gaps and incompleteness, it still agrees with structuralism that the modern subject is dissolved. In what way, then, does Žižek insist upon the irreducibility of the subject? Is the subject but an unavoidable symptom of formalization *or* is it the nonformalizable origin of formalization, the unaccountable decision for the Symbolic itself, its excess (the Real) and the Imaginary (Big Other)? There is some ambiguity in Žižek concerning this question—namely, concerning what it means to "traverse the phantasm"—but he should ultimately be aligned with the view that the subject, and so too the gap in the system, is but a symptom, an impasse, of formalization. Žižek thinks he is Schellingian, but only because he places Schelling on Lacan's couch in order to unveil what he takes to be Schelling's own ideological symptom.

2 Schelling for Žižek

Although he ultimately deems Schelling[7] an ideologue of the "proto-mythic," Žižek's estimation of Schelling is perhaps only surpassed by his praise for Hegel and veneration of Lacan. For example, he not only ranks Schelling as one of "the three great post-Hegelian inversions [*renversements*] that opposed the absolutism of the Idea in the name of the irrational abyss of the Will (Schelling), the paradox of the existence of the individual (Kierkegaard) and the productive processes of life (Marx),"[8] but he had also earlier proclaimed that "it is now clear that the entire post-Hegelian constellation—from Marxism to the existentialist notion of finitude and temporality as the ultimate horizon of being, from deconstructionist 'decentering' of the self-presence of *logos* to New Age obscurantism—has its roots in Schelling's late philosophy."[9] Apparently, Schelling's late philosophy, by which Žižek is actually referring to Schelling's middle period, his *Weltalter* [*Ages of the World*] period, is not just a spoke in the wheel but the very axis of post-Hegelian philosophy. This is all the more startling considering that by "post-Hegelian" Žižek nominates not only Kierkegaardian existentialism, Marxist materialism, and Schopenhauerian/Nietzschean voluntarism but also philosophy up to the contemporary moment, inclusive of New Age pop philosophy, Heidegger's insistence on human finitude and temporality as the horizon of being, deconstruction's assault on self-presence and contemporary critiques of the whole of Western philosophy as logocentrism.[10] He also refers to "Gilles Deleuze—another great Schellingian."[11] Consequently, Carl Raschke can observe, without hyperbole, that it is "Schelling, whom Žižek regards as the true wild card in the career of 'ontotheology'," even if "Žižek obviously over-Lacanizes Schelling."[12]

This effusive praise is important to note because it means that Žižek sees in Schelling a way past idealism and into dialectical materialism, as well as a way into post-postmodernity but not at the cost of swallowing deconstruction. To wit:

> [T]he difference between Heidegger and Gadamer: Gadamer remains an "idealist" insofar as for him the horizon of language is "always-already there", whereas Heidegger's problematic of the difference [*Unter-Schied*] as pain [*Schmerz*] that inheres in the very essence of our dwelling in language … points towards the materialist problematic of the traumatic cut, "castration", that marks our entry into language. The first to formulate this materialist problematic of "real genesis" as the obverse of the transcendental genesis was Schelling … deriving the emergence of the Word, *logos*, out of the abyss of the "real in God," of the vortex of drives [*Triebe*].[13]

Schelling, Žižek rightly perceives, enacts this transition from idealism to realism or, as Žižek prefers, from idealism to materialism by inverting *explanans* and *explanandum*.

> If the main problem of idealism is how we are to pass from the ever-changing "false" material phenomenal reality to the true reality of Ideas … the problem of materialism from Lucretius through Schelling's *Weltalter* and the Marxist notion of commodity fetishism to Deleuze's "logic of sense" is the exact opposite, namely *the genesis of the semblance itself*: how does the reality of bodies generate out of itself the fantasmatic surface, the "incorporeal" sense-event?[14]

This inversion allows Žižek to affirm that "the *Weltalter* fragments are the founding texts of dialectical materialism."[15] The move from idealism to materialism, however, is not synonymous with a move to poststructuralism. Where, then, does Žižek spy that transition? This chapter stipulated four defining characteristics of poststructuralism: systems are (1) open, (2) not self-founding, (3) contingent, and (4) inexhaustible, or with an "indivisible remainder." The latter three, at least, make an appearance in the following passage by Žižek, which might thus be regarded as the "Schellingian, poststructuralist axiom": "For Schelling the primordial, radically contingent fact, a fact which can in no way be accounted for, is freedom itself ... and the problem is how this Nothing of the abyss of primordial freedom becomes entangled in the causal chains of Reason."[16] Here Žižek has done little more than paraphrase Schelling himself,[17] who two centuries prior had already thought of the act of freedom as pre-structural—prior to the rational order—and hence contingent, since necessity is a product of the rational. Poststructuralism, then, viewed with a Schellingian lens, involves the recognition of the *pre*-structural and *pre*-rational, hence the departure from idealism. As Žižek here properly surmises,

> [T]he central enigma Schelling struggled to resolve [was] the enigma of freedom, of the sudden suspension of the "principle of sufficient reason" ... Schelling's solution involves an unheard-of reversal of the very terms of this enigma: what if the thing to be explained is not freedom but the emergence of the chains of reason, of the causal network.[18]

Schelling's real insight, the one that catapulted him beyond German Idealism and into materialism and realism as well as, perhaps, post-poststructuralism and Žižekian post-postmodernity, is that most of Western philosophy had perpetuated the fallacy of reversed causation. That freedom seems to suspend the principle of sufficient reason is symptomatic of the real fact that freedom first institutes reason from non-reason.

"Schelling's fundamental thesis", Žižek suspects, is that "*the true Beginning is not at the beginning*: there is something that precedes the Beginning itself."[19] How might one not beg the question? If the question is why there are beings at all rather than none, then one cannot answer this by first appealing to a being, even God, or an operative principle, even the principle of sufficient reason. Perhaps, contra Leibniz, seriously to ask why there is something rather than nothing is to attempt to think beyond any actual existent. It is a thinking that must reach beyond all existents, beyond all entities function as or immanently contain a sufficient reason. Žižek finds Schelling is up to the task, particularly given his distinction between ground (*Grund*) and existence (*Existenz*) in the *Freiheitsschrift* of 1809. Speaking of "the gap between Existence (ethereal form) and its impenetrable Ground," Žižek remarks, "Crucial for any materialist ontology is this gap between the bodily depth of the Real and the pseudodepth of Meaning produced by the Surface."[20] The gap that Schelling posits between ground and existence becomes, or so it seems here, the difference between the chaos of the Real and the meaning/sense accrued in the Ideal, which is also a gap between a nonmanifest depth and an appearing surface.[21] Given Žižek's love for all things Lacan, one can immediately see how he will inevitably come to understand this difference also as that between the unconscious and the conscious. As Žižek relates:

> Schelling's answer is unambiguous: the "unconscious" is not primarily the rotary motion of drives ejected into the eternal past; rather, the "unconscious" is the very act of *Ent-scheidung* by means of which drives were ejected into the past. Or—to put it in slightly different terms—what is truly "unconscious" in man is ... the very founding gesture of consciousness, the act of decision by means of which I "choose myself."[22]

The unconscious, that is, the Real, is not a storehouse of repressed drives, but it is the very decision for consciousness. The decision *for* consciousness, however, falls just outside, that is, just prior to, the dawn of consciousness itself, hence why the decision for consciousness is not accidentally but essentially unconscious. The difference between the Ideal and the Real, between consciousness and its unconscious base, between the Surface or the appearance that is existence and its Depth that is ground, between orderly structure and unruly chaos, between reason and the unreason that has always already preceded it, is a gap that can never be closed. This gap must remain eternally open, as this breach is not something that prevents full disclosure but is rather the condition of possibility for disclosure.

What Žižek learns from Schelling is apparently not immediately political but ontological. He has learned, in short, that (1) the "system" of being is open or, in Žižek's terms, a non-All; (2) the reason it is open is because it is not self-founding; (3) as open, the world is contingent, both in terms of the way it is and in terms of the fact *that* it is; and (4) as open, there is an "indivisibly remaining" gap at the heart of reality. Difference can never be closed up into a totality. These four Schelling-inspired elements, which have also been indicated as markers that one has surpassed structuralism at a minimum, help Žižek to become post-postmodern. To reinforce these points, note what Žižek has to say of Schelling's actual late philosophy, which divides negative and positive philosophy:

> Negative philosophy provides the a priori deduction of the notional necessity of *what* God and the universe are; however, this *What-ness* [*Was-Sein*] can never account for the *fact that* God and the universe are—it is the task of positive philosophy to function as a kind of "transcendental empiricism," and to "test" the truth of the rational constructions in actual life.[23]

Not simply the world, but God himself is contingent; yet, *if* each exists, then it is necessary that there be a kind of relation between them, namely a difference or a gap. God and world cannot be collapsed or become isomorphic; their relation, which means their difference, is unbridgeable or necessarily open. This can only be tested by a "transcendental empiricism," Žižek writes, with obvious reference to Deleuze. Schelling himself employs the term "metaphysical empiricism."[24] If something is rather than nothing, which is a contingent *fact*, then as a matter of fact rather than as a truth of reason it cannot be known a priori; however, that does not preclude that *given* that fact that certain conditions of possibility must hold, namely there must be a cleft or opening between ground and existence, between the Real and the Ideal, between chaos and structure, that can never be annexed into each other without remainder. This empiricism does not just test the structure of reality empirically, but, correcting the fallacy of reversed causation, it is an empirical account of the very being of structure. Structure, reason, and order can only be accounted for on the basis of an act or decision. Žižek consequently lauds Schelling, "Schelling's entire philosophical revolution is contained, condensed, in the assertion that this act which recedes and grounds every necessity is in itself *radically contingent*—for that very reason it cannot be deduced, inferred, but only retroactively presupposed."[25] This empiricism is, as it were, the belated narration of the emergence of the very being of structure, of reason, of ideality, and of appearance. Accordingly, on Žižek's account, Schelling is to be deemed a materialist:

> The repeated failure of his three successive *Weltalter* drafts indicates precisely Schelling's honesty as a thinker: the fact that he was radical enough to acknowledge the impossibility of grounding the act/decision in the proto-cosmic myth. ... [I]dealist obscurantism deduces/ generates the act from the proto-cosmos [the Real vortex of drives], while materialism asserts the primacy of the act, and denounces the fantasmatic character of the proto-cosmic narrative.[26]

As long as materialism is not equivalent to physicalism, then Schelling, before Marx, was indeed a materialist. Finally, to provide a parting word concerning who Schelling is for Žižek, "[T]he emergence of the symbolic Order as the answer to some monstrous excess in the Real is the only proper materialist solution. This means that the relationship between the Structure and its Event is indeterminable."[27] If an indeterminable and incongruous relationship between Structure and Event, Structure and the Real, is sufficient to propel one past structuralism at a minimum, and perhaps even past poststructuralism, then Schelling, for Žižek, may also be pointing the way toward post-postmodernity.

3 Žižek for Žižek

To understand a thinker is to understand the voices she has assimilated. A thinker is a cacophony. Accordingly, to understand Žižek is, principally, to see how he has assimilated Hegel and Schelling, but also Lacan and Christianity (which is quite another thing from stating that Žižek is a Christian). This section, therefore, though titled "Žižek for Žižek," could just as easily be understood as Lacan and Christianity for Žižek.

Žižek is a peculiar contemporary philosopher because, although finding himself within a "post-metaphysical" age, he is, as already mentioned, unabashedly a philosopher of beginnings and a philosopher of the subject. Moreover, he will even go so far as to think of the subject as a kind of origin. Lacan also wanted to think the subject, but, at least in his earlier thought, only a barred subject, $, but always a subject that could never be fully present to itself. Drawing Schelling into Lacan's orbit, Žižek proposes:

> The subject *qua* $ is never adequately represented in a signifier. ... Schelling's "Lacanian" formulation according to which God-Absolute *becomes inexpressible at the very moment He expresses Himself, that is, pronounces a Word*. Prior to his symbolic externalization, the

Reading Schelling

subject cannot be said to be "inexpressible", since the medium of expression itself is not yet given—or, to invoke Lacan's precise formulation, desire is *non-articulable* precisely as always-already *articulated* in a signifying chain.[28]

When does a subject begin to exist? Only and first at the moment it becomes inexpressible or barred: $. When does the subject become inexpressible? Not prior to symbolic externalization, that is, not prior to the act of expression, but only "the very moment it expresses itself." Conclusion: the subject never exists except as barred, except as inexpressible, because there is never first a subject that expresses itself, but there is rather and inversely first expressivity, which has as its after-effect the repressed or barred subject: $. Inexpressibility is the condition of the subject, but expressivity is the condition of inexpressibility. As a *hypothetical syllogism* followed by a *modus ponens*, this would read as follows. If there is expressivity, then there is the inexpressible. If there is the inexpressible, then there is a barred subject. There is expression; therefore, there is a barred subject. Note, however, that to begin with the subject would be to commit the fallacy of affirming the consequent. Subjects are not origins, properly speaking, but the act of expression is what first produces the origin or the subject *as* an origin, as something like an origin. Expressivity is a pre-origin or more original than an origin because there is nothing that is expressed except inexpressivity itself. What the Symbolic is trying to express is precisely the pre-Symbolic, *except*—and here is the rub—"prior to external symbolization the subject cannot be said to be inexpressible." As we have already seen, for Žižek the inexpressible itself is an indivisible remainder of expression. What is really first here? It is neither the subject nor the inexpressible, nor the subject as inexpressible ($), but it is the decision for, the act of, or the event of expression.

Although this appears to follow the logic of Derridean deconstruction, Žižek understands this as an ontology of the subject. The subject barred is not the subject under erasure (*sous rature*), because for Derrida this means that there simply are no origins. As Derrida has notoriously claimed, "There is no outside-text."[29] For Žižek, however, this does not efface the origin, but it exposes the *being* of origins. Origins are not epistemologically blocked from view, but they are, in a full-blooded ontological sense, inherently open rather than self-present, open rather than occluded or barred. Otherwise, origins would not be origins at all. Origins exist!—but only in and through their failure to be able to express themselves. This failure is not a deficiency, but their creative power. Žižek's brand of poststructuralism—if it makes sense to grant him that title at all—does not, contrary to Schelling, question back to what is *pre*-structural, but it asks what structure leaves behind after its own failure to formalize itself. It does not deconstruct to uncover an origin in full presence beneath structure and nor does it find that there was no origin to be uncovered at all, but it manifests its own impasse or traverses itself in order to see that de-construction, self-fissure, just *is* the being of the origin.

That an origin's being consists only in its own failure at self-codification, Žižek explains as follows:

> This paradoxical necessity on account of which the act of returning-to-oneself, of finding oneself, immediately, in its very actualization, assumes the form of its opposite, of the

radical loss of one's self-identity, displays the structure of what Lacan calls "symbolic castration." This splitting, of an element into itself and its place in the structure.[30]

This split into self and structure is the split between the Real and Ideal. There was not first the Real and then it became thinkable, expressible or Ideal, but the Real is as belated as the Ideal, as belated as the Symbolic. There is nothing pre-given, but what is original is act or deed, which first posits *both* the Real *and* the Ideal. Nevertheless, this does not prevent Žižek from associating the Real with the Symbolic:

> The Real is on the side of the symbolic ... The Real is the point at which the external opposition between the symbolic order and reality is immanent to the symbolic itself, mutilating it from within: it is the non-All of the symbolic, because the symbolic cannot fully become *itself*. There is being (reality) because the symbolic system is inconsistent, flawed, for the Real is an impasse of formalization. The thesis must be given its full "idealist" weight: it is not only that reality is too rich, so that every formalization fails to grasp it, stumbles over it; the Real *is* nothing but an impasse of formalization—there is dense reality "out there" *because* of the inconsistencies and gaps in the symbolic order.[31]

This passage is quite illuminating, as it distinctly reveals a way in which Žižek distances himself, perhaps unwittingly, from Schelling in order to align himself with Lacan. The Real is associated with the *Symbolic*. And, Žižek is not unaware of the consequence: *idealism*! The materialist stance would be that the Real is "too rich for formalization"—or, this is, at least, Schellingian materialism—but here the Real is explicated as "an impasse *of formalization*." Moreover, this impasse is the very condition of there being an "external world." In Žižek's words, "There is dense reality 'out there' *because* of the inconsistencies and gaps in the symbolic order."

Does Žižek, then, only believe in an external world "out there" (or "outside the text") because the Symbolic order is, as the Real, a non-All? It seems so. In fact, Žižek can even write (intervening in a debate about correlationism ignited by Quentin Meillassoux[32]), "The reality of a fossil is 'objective' insofar as it is observed from our standpoint ... what 'objectively exists' is the entire field of interaction between subject and object as part of the Real."[33] Granting that Žižek refuses to posit subject and object as primary—instead positing their gap or difference as more original than these two *relata*—he still clearly aligns himself on the side of correlationism, affirming a non-circumventable subject-object correlation, even if the correlation is contingent and a non-All. The following section will offer some criticism of this position through a Schellingian lens, but, for now, let it become abundantly clear that this aspect of Žižek is Lacanian rather than Schellingian. Note:

> In psychoanalytic terms, this choice is that of the "fundamental fantasy," of the basic frame/matrix which provides the coordinates of the subject's entire universe of meaning: although I am never outside it, although this fantasy is always-already there, and I am always-already thrown into it, I have to *presuppose* myself as the one who *posited* it.[34]

The idealist side of Žižek stems from Lacanian psychoanalysis, rather than from Schelling, because it is this element of his thought that knows nothing outside the subject as the origin of the fantasmatic, the subject and its corresponding symbolic universe.[35] Even granting that Žižek distinguishes between an early, middle, and late

Lacan, whereby he regards middle, structuralist Lacan as focusing on the barred subject produced by the Symbolic, he nevertheless notes, "In the late Lacan, on the contrary, the focus shifts to the object that the subject itself 'is',"[36] the conclusion remains that the Real is always nothing more than what the subject itself "is." In other words, even with Lacan's late emphasis on the Real rather than the Symbolic, whereby the Real is no longer barred from the Symbolic, it is still a Real that only breaks out from within the Symbolic, namely, through phantasmic formation that must, in turn, be subjected to a "traversal of the phantasm." As Žižek writes, "And one can also see in what *la traverse du fantasme* consists: in an acceptance of the fact that *there is no secret treasure in me*, that the support of me (of the subject) is purely phantasmic."[37] Consequently, even here, in Lacan's latest thought, the Real is not distinct from the Symbolic, but it is "inherent" to it, as its "internal stumbling block."[38] Ultimately, this is what prevents Žižek's thinking of the Real from becoming as robust and radical as Schelling's.

The foregoing offers a brief account of Lacan's influence on Žižek, but what is the "Christian" influence operative in his thought? The most salient point is that Christianity insists on Difference, on the very gap that prevents the non-All from becoming the All (and here is a return of the Schellingian, as this also requires that one conceive of God as *life* rather than as substance[39]). In this context, Žižek writes:

> Buddhist (or Hindu, for that matter) all-encompassing Compassion must be opposed to Christian *intolerant, violent* Love. The Buddhist stance is ultimately one of Indifference, of quenching all passions which strive to establish differences; while Christian love is a violent passion to introduce a Difference, a gap in the order of Being, to privilege and elevate some at the expense of others.[40]

What makes Christian love violent, as opposed to the apparently nonviolent love of compassion and tolerance, is not that it tolerates *all* differences, which is actually tantamount to negating the specialness of any differences in favor of their homogenization and democratization, but that it institutes *a* difference. However, not just any difference will suffice, but only "Difference, a gap in the order of Being." Nevertheless, this still exerts an effect at the ontic level, as it also implies a "privileging and elevating of some [differences] at the expense of others." Or, again, except here stated in contrast to Greek thought,

> Christianity asserts as the highest act precisely what pagan wisdom condemns as the source of Evil: the gesture of *separation*, of drawing the line, of clinging to an element that disturbs the balance of All. The pagan criticism that the Christian insight is not "deep enough", that it fails to grasp the primordial One-All, therefore misses the point: Christianity *is* the miraculous Event that disturbs the balance of the One-All; it *is* the violent intrusion of Difference that precisely *throws the balanced circuit of the universe off the rails*.[41]

Rather than a Neoplatonic procession from, return to, and remaining with the One or, as Žižek prefers, the One-All, Christianity is instead affirmation of Difference, which precludes the One-All and so founds the non-All.

4 Žižek for Schelling

To write here of Žižek for Schelling is more appropriately, albeit not exclusively, to write of Sean McGrath's critique of Žižek, which insists not only that Žižek does not always read Schelling well but also that his overly Lacanized interpretation of Schelling leads him into some philosophical missteps. The issue onto which McGrath latches is that for Žižek's Lacanized Schelling,

> subjectivity is only possible on the grounds of a severance of consciousness from "the real" (the cut effected by "the symbolic"); the unconscious is a trace of this scission, not the remains of nature, as though some dimension of man's natural origin remains on a subterranean level of the psyche, but rather the excluded other necessary to maintaining the bubble of the symbolic…[42]

It is not simply that it is the Symbolic that enacts this cut, but it does so only in order "to maintain the bubble of the symbolic." The Symbolic admits of no outside; there is no outside-symbolic, to allude to Derrida.[43] "The excluded other is necessary to maintaining the bubble of the symbolic," which means that there can never be the culmination of a totality or One-All. There is the non-All—there is, in fact, nothing other than the non-All—but the non-All itself is the consequence of the act of the Symbolic. The Symbolic posits its own fissure; it is not opened up by something other than itself.

Why does Žižek refuse autochthony to anything other than the Symbolic? Or, why does he align the Symbolic rather than the Unconscious with the Real? McGrath offers the following reason:

> To take X for something real outside the subject-object dyad is ideologically to hypostasize the Big Other. Hence Žižek's reading of the [Schelling's] *Weltformel* as the very image of constitutive repression: B is not the unground in the Böhmian-Schellingian sense but the excremental remainder giving the lie to the symbolic, to the Lacanian real, that which must always be excluded if the symbolic is to function as a substitute for natural life. Schelling, according to Žižek, has correctly hit upon the formula of fundamental fantasy, but he [Schelling] does not see it as fantasy.[44]

A "Big Other," that is, an other that would not just be the inverse side of a dyad, is, on Lacanian terms, excluded. The only viable other, apparently, is an excluded other or, in psychoanalytic terms, a repressed other. This repressive act, however, is constitutive not only of the other, the Unconscious, but it is also constitutive of consciousness itself. What the unconscious really names, for Žižek, is not the repressed element but an act, itself unconscious but one aimed toward consciousness, that separates the domain of the conscious from the unconscious, from the repressed. This severance prevents the non-All from becoming a One-All.

McGrath's principal objection to Žižek is that nothing actually precedes the founding and constituting act, which, although unconscious, is ultimately subjective. McGrath states:

> On this view, nature does not precede subjectivity, it comes to be at the precise moment that subjectivity separates itself from its pre-symbolic life; the illusion of a natural order begins

with the decision of the subject to be *for itself*, a decision that can only be made by setting up the *in itself* as that which the subject is not.[45]

The "in itself" is only in itself for the "for itself"; the objective is only objective for the subjective; the unconscious is only unconscious for the conscious. Idealism! Perhaps a "materialist idealism," if such a confluence is possible, but idealism. Consequently, subjectivity and consciousness are not a part of nature. As McGrath surmises, "For Žižek ... there is no nature in this cosmological sense, no 'order' that precedes subjectivity. The notion of nature as the infinite material matrix of possibilities is the romantic fantasy produced by the constitutively repressed subject for the sake of sustaining its virtual existence."[46] The unconscious, that is, nature or the "in itself," is, at the end of the day, but fantasy for Žižek. It is nothing more than what the Symbolic has repressed, not a preexisting reality belatedly revealed, but something that only *seems* to have gone before because it only exists as repressed. McGrath thus concludes, "Žižek's view of Schelling: 'Consciousness is not a synthesis but a displacement, not a resolution of unconscious conflict but a symptom."[47]

Rex Butler, Scott Stephens, and Peter Dews have raised similar issues. Butler and Stephens speak of "a contingent element within an *ad hoc* bricolage of texts as in post-structuralism."[48] They thereby place Žižek squarely within the poststructuralist tradition, although the ineradicably contingent element at play is not the "bricolage of texts" but the unconscious founding act that institutes the gap constitutive of the non-All. They continue, however, by correctly noting that "the concept of Truth in Žižek's work does not constitute any kind of exception or Truth external to the order of things, but rather renders totality itself as not-all."[49] Truth with a capital "T" is not a "Big Other"; it is rather the unconscious act that precludes the possibility of truth with a "T" understood as the totality of all truths.

To what extent can one find explicit verification of the issues these critics have raised in Žižek's own corpus? In response to one of his critics, Peter Dews, Žižek writes, "The problem Schelling was struggling with, the point of failure of the three consecutive drafts of *Weltalter*, was the very emergence of *logos* out of the vortex of the pre-ontological Real of drives, *not* the problem of how to bring the two dimensions together again."[50] Schelling was indeed concerned with the problem of origin rather than that of resolution. The question, however, is whether Žižek follows Schelling's genesis account or whether he inverts it. Schelling, according to Žižek himself, attempted to account for the "emergence of *logos*" from "the pre-ontological Real of drives." Žižek's critics, however, see him rather positing, by constitutively repressing, the ontological Real of drives from the symbolic act of *logos*. As Žižek writes in *The Indivisible Remainder*:

> Because of this structure of castration, Spirit is super-natural or extra-natural, although it grew out of Nature: Nature has an ineradicable tendency to "speak itself out," it is caught in the search for a Speaker [*die Suche nach dem Sprecher*] whose Word would posit it as such; this Speaker, however, can only be an entity which is itself not natural, not part of Nature, but Nature's Other.[51]

This passage is illuminating because it shows how Žižek can enact an inversion of Schelling while believing that he is entirely Schellingian. When Žižek insists that

Spirit "grew out of Nature," he seems to be positing Nature as a "pre-ontological Real," sounding very much like Schelling. The trick occurs, however, once Žižek immediately conceives of Nature itself as an "ineradicable tendency to 'speak itself out'," as a perpetual "search for a Speaker." Žižek thereby turns Schelling's nature into *logos*, into expression, instead of conceiving of it as a "pre-ontological Real." This is how Žižek can move beyond nature to the "super-natural" or "extra-natural." The super- or extra-natural is not other than nature but what Nature naturally produces.

Schelling, Schelling's interpreters, and Žižek all agree on a constitutive gap that is more original than the terms it relates. Nevertheless, the Schellingians grant primacy to the pre-Symbolic as Real while Žižek grants primacy to the Symbolic as Real. Consequently, Schellingianism views the Symbolic or the event of expression as a supplement accrued to the Real, while Žižek, beginning with the Symbolic, views the pre-Symbolic as a domain retroactively posited by the Symbolic's own act of repression. By virtue of this, Žižek does not think of something antecedent to systematicity so much as he thinks of a system that posits its own breach. The pre-Symbolic was never prior in a real sense, but only *as* past, only *as* what the Symbolic has repressed in order simultaneously to posit itself *and* its own ground. As Dews remarks:

> [Schelling's] aim ... is precisely to contest the assertion that "the concept of freedom is entirely irreconcilable with the system, and [that] every philosophy which makes a claim to unity and totality must result in a denial of freedom." Žižek, however, must ignore this in his one-sided elaboration of "Schelling's insistence on the gap that separates forever the Real of drives from its symbolization."[52]

Žižek's reading of Schelling is one-sided because he thinks the Real as that which is repressed by the Ideal. By contrast, Schelling, Dews insists, "wants to show that there must be some ontological—or perhaps better: *pre*-ontological—affinity between spirit and nature, subject and signifier, while at the same time emphasizing the bitter reality of their non-coincidence."[53] To put it in terms of the 1809 *Freiheitsschrift*, rather than ground having no other reality than as the retroactively repressed, Schelling, Dews claims, refuses any one-sidedness, as "ground and existence ... find themselves locked in a chiasmic, overlapping relation of co-operative opposition, of supportive antagonism."[54] It is not clear that Dews' position is more tenable than Žižek's because, despite the insistence on non-coincidence, if one posits, as Dews seems to presuppose, absolute equipoise or counterbalance between the two, it is not obvious how anything would have got started. In this respect Žižek is surely right to insist on an out-of-jointedness at the root of the Real, on the violence of (Christian) Love. All the same, this does not necessitate that one must grant preponderance to the Symbolic.

There is another option, that of insisting on an uncircumventable out-of-jointedness because the Real, conceived as a pre-ontological and pre-symbolic vortex of drives, simply cannot be subsequently annexed by the Symbolic without remainder. This position, however, requires that one not equate the Symbolic with the Real but instead think of the Symbolic as a necessarily failed attempt to express what has gone before it. As McGrath repeatedly reinforces, for Žižek "the unconscious is no longer a material stratum"—hence his casting of Žižek as more Hegelian than Schellingian, more idealist than materialist—"but the decision that is simultaneously the birth of consciousness and the ejection of an unconscious ground.[55] 'Nature,' on this view, does not precede subjectivity; rather, it comes to be at the precise moment that subjectivity separates itself from its own life."[56] In the end, perhaps the safest avenue is to call Žižek neither Schellingian, Hegelian, Marxist nor idealist, but simply Lacanian. It is, indeed, this tie to psychoanalysis in which McGrath too is most interested. In this respect, McGrath's evaluation is that, in Žižek's hands, Schelling's *The Ages of the World* is no different in principle from *Avatar*; both are symptoms of constitutive repression, to be decoded by the analyst-sovereign who alone maintains an unblinking gaze on the hidden truth of the matter."[57] If Žižek remains a materialist, then his "matter" is by no means recalcitrant to the theorizing and objectively constituting gaze of the analyst.

What would be a better way for Žižek to appropriate Schelling, that is, who really is Žižek for Schelling (or for Schellingians)? The question concerns how to think the fissure that refuses all closure into a One-All. McGrath suggests, "This is not the deliberate expulsion of an act or an experience that is unbearable to consciousness, incompatible with an 'ego-ideal,' and that is destined to return as an irremovable obstruction to life. Rather, this is production."[58] Production, not repression. Creation of novelty, not subjection of alterity. Not positing of self and outside, but emergence of self and interiority. What does this mean in psychoanalytic terms? "To take responsibility ... It is to say: I see what I did. I recognize it as mine. This act of self-appropriation, in Schellingian psychotherapy would not be *resignation*; it would be, rather, *commitment* and the beginning of something new."[59] To be a self is not retroactively to repress one's own ground *in* the act or decision of the Symbolic, but retroactively to assume an act that preceded one's own consciousness and volition as though one had been its author.

5 Schelling and Žižek for Us

As stated at the beginning, Žižek's step beyond postmodernity is only to be thought alongside his "regressive" return to the pre-modern, that is, with a return to questions of origins and subjectivity. A similar regression is also evident in Žižek's politics. Sharpe and Boucher believe this move in Žižek's thought can be mapped to his reading of Schelling in the late 1990s, writing:

> Žižek's passionate encounter with Schelling in 1996–7 clearly served to consolidate certain, more theoretically radical—if politically regressive, even openly anti-Enlightenment—tendencies present in his earlier texts. These have now supplanted the Enlightenment commitments of Žižek's earlier critique of ideology and his defense of the divided, but potentially autonomous, subject, with telling political results.[60]

Žižek, the politically incorrect critic, is apparently a Žižek that never could have been had he not seriously read Schelling. Why this is so is difficult to say, although it is certainly the case that Žižek's writings on Schelling mark the break between Žižek's earlier and later thought. Apparently, it has something to do with what Žižek thinks is politically fundamental as opposed to what is secondary, at best. As Sharpe and Boucher notice, "Žižek is one of the few celebrated Theorists today who talks about 'capitalism', which is an inescapably economic notion, rather than attacking 'liberalism', 'biopower', 'the society of the spectacle', or, recently, 'democracy.'"[61] Any attempt to draw a positive connection to the critique of capitalism on Schellingian grounds is problematic, but the reason for Žižek's demotion of the critiques of liberalism, biopower, the society of the spectacle and democracy to secondary importance is clearer. It is not that Žižek fails to address these issues, as he is, in fact, an ardent critic of liberalism and democracy, including its core values of inclusivism and multiculturalism, but these cannot stand simply as unfounded values. These cannot stand as merely axiomatic but must be grounded (or critiqued) on the basis of ontology. The Schellingian insistence on an ontologically constitutive gap in being, by affirming the contingency of a decision that thus prevents any closure into a totalizing One-All, does not preclude an inquiry into foundations as such, but it only precludes that these foundations themselves are self-grounding rather than ineluctably factical. In other words, a Decision, a founding act, is contingent all the way down. There is no rationally founded categorical imperative, but only the normativity of the fact, the facticity of the Decision.

After capitalism, Žižek's principal political enemy is the deconstructionist ethics and politics of difference. Although he too affirms an ontological Difference, the gap constitutive of reality as a non-All, his is not the play of difference, neither Derrida's interminable play of signifiers that prevents the full presence of a pure signified, nor the naked, that is, axiomatic, valorization of social differences, as one often sees, or so Žižek insists, in contemporary sex and gender theorists. By contrast, Žižek's conception of difference does not prevent or occlude identity; it does not insist on the queering of identities, but it is rather the condition of identity, the Decision *for* identity. The theoretical framework of contemporary philosophies of difference, in Žižek's estimation, is instead aimed at deferring Decision, at ensuring Decision never actually takes place. According to this view, decisiveness is set in opposition to ambiguity, whereby decisiveness is devalued and even counted as oppressive.[62]

The political, for Žižek, is not the name for the strategies employed—be they voting, protesting, picketing, or policy reform—in order to produce desired results *within* a given system. It is instead "an abyssal act which is, in the most radical sense imaginable, *political*."[63] This act, a Decision, is abyssal because although it acts as a foundation, it remains without foundation itself. The political is not a science separable from ontology, which is, for Žižek, a science of the constitutive gap in being (read politically: in the prevailing Order) that produces the non-All. He explains, "Since a political act intervenes in a state of things, simultaneously creating instability and trying to establish a new positive order"—that is since the political is the gap that produces novelty by refusing to let everything be annexed by the prevailing order—"one can say that psychoanalysis confronts us with the zero-level of politics, a pre-political 'transcendental' condition of possibility of politics, a gap which opens up the space for the political act to intervene."[64] Psychoanalysis and politics are not regional sciences, but they both touch on the question of being *qua* being; they both concern the gap constitutive of being as a non-All. This gap, however, is not necessary, but factical and contingent. If a political act tries to interrupt an old order in order to impose a new order, then the political act par excellence is an act that institutes a new order. That there is order rather than disorder, however, is precisely Schelling's bold insight into the very contingency of being. As Schelling contests, "[T]he world as we now behold it, is all rule, order and form; but the unruly lies ever in the depths as though it might again break through, and order and form nowhere appear to have been original, but it seems as though what had initially been unruly had been brought to order."[65] Order is not the original fact, but disorder. Or, better, the original fact is the Decision for order over disorder. Disorder is not the mere residue of order, what Order has repressed, but something that first had to be decided so that Order could advene. This, however, is precisely the point at which one could argue that Žižek refrains from full Schellingianism, since, for Žižek, there is no "*pre*-political 'transcendental' condition of possibility of politics," but only politics itself. The difference, in other words, may be that Žižek, beginning already enmeshed within the nets of the Symbolic rather than asking how one became enmeshed within those nets in the first place, cannot think of politics' outside, namely what comes *before* the political. Politics, like the Symbolic, although a non-All in itself, is a non-All that admits of no Big Other. The non-All is all; there is nothing but the political non-All of the Symbolic.

The tension between insisting on a non-All while simultaneously refusing any antecedent to the political and Symbolic is not lost on Butler and Stephens, who draw out the implications of this tension within the context of Žižek's critique of historicism:

> This highlights the irreducible difference between Žižek and any vulgar historicism. In striking contrast to the cultural studies imperative always to contextualize, or even the Jamesonian "Always historicize!", Žižek's fundamental gesture is always *to decontextualize*. But this does not mean an escape from History or the pressures of context, but precisely the attempt to bring out the non-historical or noncontexualizable within context itself. That is to say, to bring out what it means to say that history and context are themselves incomplete, "not-all."[66]

If poststructuralist philosophies of differences insist on contextualization in order that differences are always attended at a local and a regional level, Žižek asks about the Decision that first instituted context itself. Although this admittedly renders all history and all contexts incomplete, Butler and Stephens are correct to point out that the decontextualizing move is always deployed, by Žižek, "*within* context itself." The Symbolic, and so too the political, remains for Žižek a context never actually bracketed, never actually decontextualized.

Žižek states what he deems to be Schelling's stake in the fight against historicism quite clearly:

Therein resides Schelling's relevance for today's debate on historicism: his notion of the primordial act of decision/differentiation (*Ent-Scheidung*) aims at the gesture that opens up the gap between the inertia of the prehistoric Real and the domain of historicity, of multiple and shifting narrativizations; this act is thus a quasi-transcendental unhistorical condition of possibility and, simultaneously, a condition of the impossibility of historicization.[67]

Two critical questions to ask are: (1) whether, for Schelling, this is a "quasi-transcendental" or a fully transcendental condition of possibility and (2) how this act opens a gap between the prehistoric Real and products of discourse and symbolization, like history and narrative. Žižek insists that the act is only "quasi-transcendental" because it is impossible for him to admit anything actually antecedent to expression. This saves him from Derrida (who also speaks of a quasi-transcendental, but because the condition of possibility only exists under erasure), but it fails to move him past Lacan's injunction against the Big Other. As Žižek explains, "Not only is there no conceptual incompatibility between the Real *qua* non-historical kernel and historicity, but it is the very trauma of the Real which again and again sets in motion the movement of history, propelling it to ever new historizations/symbolizations."[68] For all its power to set history into motion, to produce a gap between a prevailing order and a potentially novel order, Žižek's conception of the Real in Schelling, overly Lacanized as it is, will never bring him beyond the Symbolic but only "to ever new historizations/symbolizations." If surpassing deconstruction and historicism are sufficient, one can certainly argue that Žižek is post-poststructuralist, but if being post-poststructuralist also requires an exit from the Symbolic, Žižek may rather mark a regression to structuralism.

Before definitively deciding on this matter, however, one should note the connection between Žižek's critique of historicism and his critique of certain forms of contemporary feminism in order to gain a further clue as to how Schelling's influence has contributed to his ongoing critique of capitalism. Žižek, commenting on Karen Barad, remarks, "Her critical point against Butler, Foucault, and other historicist discourse-theorists is that, although they critically reject the Cartesian humanist position, they continue to privilege the human standpoint: their historicism limits history to human history, to the complex network of discursive practices and formations which determine the horizon of intelligibility."[69] The contemporary feminists Žižek has in his sights are those who reject even a mitigated transcendental perspective, and so, even if they insist on its anonymity, they know nothing more than discursive practices and their formations. They do not privilege consciousness or reflection, but they do privilege the standpoint of the human (or the social) all the same. Žižek, however, is no humanist. Although he refuses to oppose a Big Other to the Symbolic, he still sees that the Symbolic must, via repression, posit an origin for itself, that is, a vortex of drives, that it cannot fully formulate. Many contemporary feminists, however, do not even retroactively posit a repressed origin, but they *perform* an origin; they posit that origins are but their performance. "The implications of this are very radical and far-reaching"—Žižek writes, winding up for his punchline—"fake is original, that is, every positive feature, every 'something' that we are, is ultimately 'put on.'"[70] All is drag; all is cross-dressing, except there is no nature underneath the (cross-)dress. Reality is neither the repressed nor the act of repression, but reality is fiction; reality is fake; reality itself is fraudulent. This would probably not be attacked by Žižek so virulently were it at least the case that this performance culminated in a decision aimed at identity, but it does not. Nothing is to escape ambiguity, neither descriptively nor as normative aim. For these theorists, rather than ambiguity demanding decisiveness, Decision stands as an obstacle in the way of the free play and proliferation of difference. Difference for Žižek is the cut of resolve. Difference for these theorists, however, is the aporia that obstructs resolution, both as fact and norm. Whether Schelling would have enacted the same critique of contemporary feminism cannot be known. What is clear, however, is that Žižek's critique, notwithstanding his very real differences with Schelling, is undoubtedly inspired by his reading of Schelling on the Decision (*Ent-Scheidung*).[71] The question remains though: What positive connection does Žižek see between Schelling and his own critique of capitalism?

Žižek's most direct and illuminating remarks in relation to this question occur in his statement regarding what he takes to be Schelling's most basic question:

> Perhaps the moment has come to leave behind the old Leftist obsession with ways and means to "subvert" or "undermine" the Order, and to focus on the opposite question—on what, following Ernesto Laclau, we can call the "ordering of the Order": not how can we undermine the existing order, but *how does an Order emerge out of disorder in the first place?* ... The philosopher who came closest to this obscene shadowy double of public Power was F. W. J. Schelling.[72]

Although Žižek has suggested that there is no real disorder but merely various shifts *in* order, various divergencies from one order to another, in the passage just cited Žižek speaks in as radically a Schellingian voice as he ever has. The question is not why *this* order rather than some other, but the question is why there is order at all.

6 Concluding Remarks

This chapter identified four characteristics of Schelling's thought that one might term post-postmodern, certainly poststructuralist, and, perhaps, if all four are present in the right way, even post-poststructuralist:

1. Reality is not a closed system, but open; hence, reality is non-All rather than a One-All.
2. One should not abandon the search for origins as a metaphysical and hence obsolete endeavor, but origins are not self-founding; there is no sufficient reason for the origin.
3. The origin of the non-All is a Decision that is a brute facticity, that is, it is contingent rather than necessary.
4. There is, therefore, always an "indivisible remainder"; reality can never be definitively formulated by any one theory; reality always exceeds full codification.

This is not meant to suggest that none of these traits is held in common by structuralists or poststructuralists. However, if all are thought together, then one has an indication of Žižek's post-postmodernism with Schelling's help. The remaining question, though, is whether Žižek is a Schellingian post-poststructuralist, or whether his Lacanian side prevents his surpassing even of structuralism. Žižek clearly meets the first three characteristics. He meets the fourth, however, only in a qualified sense, because while reality certainly exceeds codification, it is the Symbolic itself that posits its own excess as repressed remainder. This remainder is not something the Symbolic fails to encapsulate, but it is the very product of the attempt at codification. In this regard, Žižek appears less materialist and more "idealist" than Schelling, the so-called German Idealist.

Politically, Žižek employs Schelling's pre-conscious, non-founded and contingent Decision, the De-cision that institutes a fissure or Difference in the Real. He argues that this ontological commitment is of the very essence of the political itself, which he also understands to be of the domain of a Decision that inaugurates a rupture with the prevailing order in order to found something entirely novel. Žižek, however, typically understands this as a revolution (or decontextualization) that can occur only from within an already-established political context, but he typically refrains from understanding the Decision as the decision for Order itself, despite some comments that might suggest otherwise. In other words, Žižek begins already within the domain of the Symbolic, within the context of a politicized order, but does not always remain with the question concerning how and why such Order is at all. Žižek thus universalizes the political field (which, of course, is also a non-All), while Schelling acknowledges a field that precedes the Symbolic and so too precedes the political proper. *If* Schelling is right and one can think *before* the political, rather than the inference leading to a revolutionary politics, one might instead infer that the political can simply be left to lie to itself, as a symptom. In other words, it is not obvious why the symptom of the Decision for Order—politics—must necessarily be loved rather than abandoned (or cured). Žižek loves his symptom, while Schelling has argued that, *qua* symptom, it can feasibly be left untreated.[73] This is on the assumption that politics is a symptom, but all the more so if it is actually but fantasy. Fantasy may be better left untraversed.

Notes

1. I would like to thank Thomas Jeannot, who is better equipped to write the Žižek portions of this chapter than I am, for his many helpful comments and criticisms. I would also like to thank Tilottama Rajan for her personal comments as well as her *Deconstruction and the Remainders of Phenomenology: Sartre, Derrida, Foucault, Baudrillard* (Stanford: Stanford University Press, 2002), which proved indispensable for navigating murky distinctions, often stipulated, between deconstruction and poststructuralism. Her investment in my chapter—and probably in all chapters—far exceeded the normal work of an editor.
2. Rajan has attempted, persuasively even if in isolation from prevailing trends, to "desynonymize deconstruction and poststructuralism" (*Deconstruction and the Remainders*, ix), arguing, with Derrida, that these terms were only "first used synonymously in the North American reception of French theory" (*Deconstruction and the Remainders*, xi). More will be discussed

later, but for the purposes of this chapter 'poststructuralism' is best understood as a general historical term that designates French theory post-1968, and so even if not synonymous with deconstruction, it is, in this chapter, certainly inclusive of it.
3. Rajan, I believe (and hope), is ultimately in agreement with this thesis, as, for her, "Deconstruction is a transposition of phenomenological into linguistic models that retains the ontological concerns of the former" (*Deconstruction and the Remainders*, 7). Utilizing her distinctions, a Schelling-inspired Žižek could remain within the orbit of deconstruction, which retains a concern for ontology, even an ontology of the subject, but such a Žižek must break from poststructuralism (in her view a solely American phenomenon), which disbands with all phenomenological (or even properly philosophical) concerns, ultimately allowing philosophy to be liquidated into social and literary studies.
4. "Indivisible remainder" is Žižek's translation of "*der nie aufgehende Rest*" from the 1809 "Philosophische Untersuchungen über das Wesen der menschlichen Freiheit und die damit zusammenhängenden Gegenstände," in *Sämtliche Werke* I/7, ed. K. F. A. Schelling (Stuttgart: Cotta Verlag, 1860), 331–416, 360. For the English translation of this text, see F. W. J. Schelling, *Philosophical Investigations into the Essence of Human Freedom* (Albany: State University of New York Press, 2006). "*Der nie aufgehende Rest*" might most literally be translated as "never surfacing remainder" or "never appearing remainder."
5. Rex Butler and Scott Stephens. "Editor's Introduction," in *Slavoj Žižek: Interrogating the Real*, eds. Butler and Stephens (London: Continuum, 2006), 1.
6. Slavoj Žižek, *Less Than Nothing: Hegel and the Shadow of Dialectical Materialism* (London: Verso, 2012), 581.
7. As has already been noticed by many and, depending on whom one asks, may or may not be an egregious fault, Žižek is a self-plagiarist. In numerous places, and it is not worth the time to catalogue them properly, Žižek will repeat paragraphs to pages of text verbatim from one book to another, sometimes even across three different books.
8. Slavoj Žižek, "Lacan – At What Point is he Hegelian?," in *Slavoj Žižek: Interrogating the Real*, eds. Butler and Stephens (London: Continuum, 2006), 26.
9. Slavoj Žižek, "The Abyss of Freedom," in *The Abyss of Freedom/Ages of the World (second draft, 1813)*, ed. Judith Norman (Ann Arbor: University of Michigan Press, 1997), 4.
10. For another attempt to show that Schelling is our contemporary because at the source of contemporary debates, see Andrew Bowie, *Schelling and Modern European Philosophy: An Introduction* (London: Routledge, 1993).
11. Žižek, "The Abyss of Freedom," 61.
12. Carl Raschke, "The Monstrosity of Žižek's Christianity," *Journal for Cultural and Religious Theory* 11, no. 2 (2011), 14.
13. Slavoj Žižek, "Hegel, Lacan, Deleuze: Three Strange Bedfellows," in *Slavoj Žižek: Interrogating the Real*, eds. Butler and Stephens (London: Continuum, 2006), 176.
14. Žižek, "The Abyss of Freedom," 58.
15. Ibid., 34.
16. Slavoj Žižek, *The Indivisible Remainder: An Essay on Schelling and Related Matters* (London: Verso, 1996), 16.
17. It "is a necessary question: Why is there sense at all, why not non-sense instead of sense?…The whole world lies as it were caught in reason, but the question is: How did it come into this net, (because in the world is manifestly something other than and something more than pure reason, indeed even something striving beyond these borders). […ist eine notwendige Frage: warum ist Sinn überhaupt, warum ist nicht Unsinn statt Sinn?…Die ganze Welt liegt gleichsam in der Vernunft gefangen, aber die Frage ist: wie ist sie in dieses Netz gekommen, <da in der Welt offenbar noch etwas Anderes und etwas mehr als blosse Vernunft ist, ja sogar noch etwas über diese Schranken Hinausstrebendes>.]" F. W. J. Schelling, *Die Grundlegung der positiven Philosophy: Münchner Vorlesung WS 1832–33 und SS 1833* (Torino: Bottega d'Erasmo, 1972), 222.
18. Žižek, "The Abyss of Freedom," 3.

19. Ibid., 14.
20. Ibid., 24.
21. Note Schelling: "[T]he world as we now behold it, is all rule, order and form; but the unruly lies ever in the depths as though it might again break through, and order and form nowhere appear to have been original, but it seems as though what had initially been unruly had been brought to order" (*Philosophical Investigations*, 34.
22. Žižek, *The Indivisible Remainder*, 33.
23. Ibid., 39.
24. See specifically lectures 6 and 7 from F. W. J. Schelling, *The Grounding of Positive Philosophy: The Berlin Lectures* (Albany: State University of New York Press, 2008), 155–92. Also see F. W. J. Schelling, "Darstellung des philosophischen Empirismus," in *Sämtliche Werke* I/10, 225–286.
25. Žižek, *The Indivisible Remainder* (1996), 45.
26. Slavoj Žižek, *The Fragile Absolute; or, Why is the Christian legacy is worth fighting for?* (London: Verso, 2000), 71.
27. Ibid., 92.
28. Žižek, *The Indivisible Remainder*, 46.
29. See Jacques Derrida, *Of Grammatology* (Baltimore: John Hopkins University Press, 2013), 163. This passage is, however, here (mis)translated as "There is nothing outside the text."
30. Žižek, *The Indivisible Remainder*, 47.
31. Žižek, *Less Than Nothing*, 646.
32. See Quentin Meillassoux, *After Finitude: An Essay on the Necessity of Contingency* (London: Continuum, 2010).
33. Žižek, *Less Than Nothing*, 647.
34. Slavoj Žižek, *The Parallax View* (Cambridge, MA: The MIT Press, 2009), 243.
35. In this sense, Žižek proves neither properly Schellingian nor Hegelian, rather reenacting Fichtean idealism, that is, Fichtean "practicism." The Real is symbolic, but it is also practical; it does not derive from an order absolutely antecedent to a subjective position.
36. Slavoj Žižek, *The Plague of Fantasies* (London: Verso, 1997), 8.
37. Ibid., 10.
38. Ibid., 279.
39. Schelling and Hegel share in common the notion that Spinozism must be altered by conceiving of substance also as subject; this is how life can be breathed into an otherwise perfectly geometrical system.
40. Slavoj Žižek, *In Defense of Lost Causes* (London: Verso, 2008), 282.
41. Žižek, *The Fragile Absolute*, 121.
42. S. J. McGrath, "Schelling on the Unconscious," *Research in Phenomenology* 40, no. 1 (2010): 79.
43. Moreover, if the Symbolic is thought of not as a system of signifiers but fundamentally as an act, as a decision, then this too is arguably more Fichtean than Schellingian. If Fichtean, however, then a Fichteanism with a dash of Hegelianism insofar as the excluded other is necessary for the Symbolic's own self-constitution. For a fairer reading of Hegel and of Žižek's reading of Hegel than one is likely to find either in this chapter or even in the work of Sean McGrath, see Joseph Carew, "The *Grundlogik* of German Idealism: The Ambiguity of the Hegel-Schelling Relationship in Žižek," *International Journal of Žižek Studies* 5, no. 1 (2000): 1–18. This article refuses to make a caricature of either Schelling or Hegel while simultaneously showing how Žižek creatively synthesizes the two (a move perhaps already more Hegelian than Schellingian though). Open to the fact that in this creative endeavor Žižek may be misreading each, it does show how this misreading would yet be charitable, given the light of Žižek's own project, rather than a straw man.
44. S. J. McGrath, *The Dark Ground of Spirit: Schelling and the Unconscious* (New York: Routledge, 2012), 26.
45. Ibid., 29.

46. Ibid., 34.
47. McGrath, "Schelling on the Unconscious," 78.
48. Butler and Stephens, "Editor's Introduction," 6.
49. Ibid.
50. Slavoj Žižek, "From Proto-Reality to the Act: A Reply to Peter Dews," *Angelaki: Journal of the Theoretical Humanities* 5, no. 3 (2000), 142.
51. Žižek, *The Indivisible Remainder*, 47.
52. Peter Dews, "The eclipse of coincidence: Lacan, Merleau-Ponty and Schelling," *Angelaki: Journal of the Theoretical Humanities* 4, no. 3 (1999): 19.
53. Ibid.
54. Ibid., 20.
55. Hence the possible charge of Fichtean practicism.
56. McGrath, "Schelling on the Unconscious," 78.
57. McGrath, *The Dark Ground of Spirit*, 35.
58. McGrath, "Schelling on the Unconscious," 89.
59. Ibid., 91.
60. Matthew Sharpe and Geoff Boucher, *Žižek and Politics: A critical introduction* (Edinburgh: Edinburgh University Press, 2010), 116.
61. Ibid., 131.
62. Here, perhaps, one can actually see the connection, stemming from Schelling and his insistence on a pre-conscious Decision that is retroactively assumed as one's own, as *ours*, to capitalism. The liberal tolerance of differences, but intolerance of a decision that would actually exclude something, is actually a friend of capitalism. However much contemporary philosophies of difference, of which poststructuralism is surely an instance, assert the contrary, they are rarely willing, Žižek decries, to denounce capitalism in toto. In other words, they may denounce it in theory, but remain happy to let capitalism market the interests of various identity groups. In the end, such ethics of difference always means an ethics of specialness, but only so long as every special interest group has free access to the market in order that it be able to make its own public demands for its own special rights. These rights and identities are, somehow, to be affirmed as unique (nonshareable), yet universally acknowledged and normalized. Žižek, for better or worse, fails to see how this can be had apart from capitalism and, as a critic of capitalism, so too must he level a critique against this brand of multiculturalism, that is, liberal authoritarianism's version of multiculturalism.
63. Žižek, *Less Than Nothing*, 963.
64. Ibid.
65. Schelling, *Philosophical Investigations*, 34.
66. Butler and Stephens. "Editor's Introduction," 5
67. Žižek, "The Abyss of Freedom," 37.
68. Žižek, *The Indivisible Remainder*, 218.
69. Žižek, *Less Than Nothing*, 935–6.
70. Žižek, *The Indivisible Remainder*, 45.
71. Moreover, like Žižek, who is also always quick to add that these theorists are friends of capitalism, Nancy Fraser too has asserted, "It is highly implausible that gay and lesbian struggles threaten capitalism in its actually existing historical form" ("Heterosexism, Misrecognition, and Capitalism: A Response to Judith Butler," *Social Text* 52/53 (1997): 285).
72. Žižek, *The Indivisible Remainder*, 3.
73. See F. W. J. Schelling, "Einleitung in die Philosophie der Mythologie oder Darstellung der reinrationalen Philosophie," in *Sämtliche Werke* II/1, 253–572. Particularly note lectures 22–24, which have been translated by Kyla Bruff. For excerpts from these lectures, see *The Schelling Reader*, eds. Daniel Whistler & Benjamin Berger (London: Bloomsbury Academic, 2020), 406–19. For the full translation, see Kyla Bruff, "Schelling's Late Political Philosophy: Lectures 22–24 of the *Presentation of the Purely Rational Philosophy*," *Kabiri* 2 (2020): 93–135.

Reading Schopenhauer

Joel Faflak

1 Introduction

In his manuscript writings, Arthur Schopenhauer writes: "As soon as I began to think, I found myself at variance with the world."[1] The statement functions as a kind of rallying cry for nineteenth-century *ressentiment*. Reflecting a misanthropy decidedly against the prevailing mood of the German idealist tradition from which he emerged, the statement also speaks all too presciently to our present time, marking Schopenhauer as the party spoiler we'd just as soon avoid, except that we sense he might be on to something, like Nietzsche's madman. Michel Houellebecq's *In the Presence of Schopenhauer* emerges from the novelist's first encounter with the philosopher's thought and writing, a kind of primal scene of Houellebecq's authorship, indeed of his very being. As Agathe Novak-Lechevalier writes in her Preface, "The strength of the revelation of Schopenhauer's work was indubitably linked to the shock of recognizing an alter ego, someone with whom you immediately realize that you are going to enjoy a long companionship."[2] Returning to Schopenhauer after over a decade, I would not attach enjoyment to our reacquaintance, which is to mark his endurance past a poststructuralist concern with thought as the undoing of system, meaning, and the subject, to a rather more dire concern with how to live through and past our very survival. Schopenhauer confronts us with an intractable human nature, an inalienable sense of alienation lurking in our unconscious as an unbidden guest reminding us of 'truths' we would rather suppress.

Like Freud, for whom Schopenhauer was a longtime companion, Schopenhauer explores our inability to surrender the pretences of hope and happiness. Houellebecq argues that "Schopenhauer's philosophy is first and foremost a commentary on the

---

J. Faflak (✉)
University of Western Ontario, London, ON, Canada
e-mail: jfaflak@uwo.ca

© The Author(s), under exclusive license to Springer Nature Switzerland AG 2023
T. Rajan, D. Whistler (eds.), *The Palgrave Handbook of German Idealism and Poststructuralism*, Palgrave Handbooks in German Idealism,
https://doi.org/10.1007/978-3-031-27345-2_9

conditions of knowledge,"[3] but is also ungrounded by these conditions. Like Kant Schopenhauer recognizes that what we make of things also puts us one remove from the world. Yet for Schopenhauer this space of difference engenders our apprehension of the world from a place of "aesthetic contemplation."[4] Two issues thus anchor my discussion in this chapter. One is the question of the subject, how it appeared and appears as constituted by the indivisible remainders of its being.[5] A second related issue comes from Werner Hamacher: "What I read, reads me, and, in me, reads itself. I read what reads itself in me—my own reading."[6] What we read reproduces itself and thus confirms its authority in us, and so merely reproduces us *as* readers. But reading also disrupts this self-validating hermeneutic circle, so that we are reading for "what we have not read, or we would be reading something other than what we or the text are."[7] This "something other" in Schopenhauer's writing confronts us with an unwanted stranger to ourselves essential to how subjectivities emerge and are shaped, but is at the same time symptomatic of a state of being beyond the subject, one that precludes any direct awareness of our existence, as if we never were at all.

Schopenhauer's obsession with this "something other" marks him as something of an outlier in the German idealist pantheon, which warrants a brief outline of his corpus. More to the point, however, is how the evolution of his writings is symptomatic of his own affective response to German idealism as a thinker of the discontents of thought ahead of his time, which response shapes his writing from within. After publishing *On the Fourfold Root of the Principle of Sufficient Reason* (1813), his dissertation, and *On Vision and Colors* (1816), in 1818 Schopenhauer published *The World as Will and Representation*, his principal work and root of his philosophy. In 1820, he was hired to teach at the University of Berlin, where he intentionally scheduled his courses opposite Hegel, and never taught at a university again. In 1836, he published *On the Will in Nature* and in 1840 two essays as *The Two Fundamental Problems of Ethics*, the first essay "On the Freedom of the Human Will" having won a contest by the Royal Norwegian Society of Sciences and the second "On the Basis of Morality" having been refused a prize by the Royal Danish Society of Sciences, even though Schopenhauer's was the only submission. In 1844, he published the second edition of *The World as Will and Representation*, which revised the first edition and added a second volume, a series of commentaries that following the general unfolding of the first edition, now the first volume. Finally, in 1851 he published the two-volume *Parerga and Paralipomena* ("Appendices and Omissions"), followed by second editions of *On the Will in Nature* and *On Vision and Colors* in 1854. By the time of a third edition of *The World as Will and Representation* in 1859, a year before his death, Schopenhauer's reputation was on the rise, and his influence was soon realized in Nietzsche's deconstructive mythologization of Will and Representation as Dionysus and Apollo in *The Birth of Tragedy* (1872). In short, it took nineteenth-century philosophy a while to acclimatize itself to truths Schopenhauer knew it would just as soon avoid.

Like Kierkegaard, a less-direct heir, Schopenhauer deplored a viral "Hegelism"[8] that had infected the nineteenth-century academy. For Schopenhauer, Hegel was an "intellectual Caliban" whose "charlatanism" (*WWR* 1:xxi) had produced a pathological idealism abandoned to pure abstraction at the expense of real, human concerns. Hence, all Hegelians "do not require any *Critique of Pure Reason* or any philosophy," but rather "a *medicina mentis*, first as a sort of purgative, *un petit cours de senscommunologie*, and after that one must see whether there can still be any talk of philosophy" (1:xxiv).[9] As Stanley Corngold notes, Schopenhauer "continues to darken our apprehension of Hegel, like the shadow cast by a malignancy in an x-ray."[10] Schopenhauer insists that "philosophy is essentially *idealistic*": "everything of which [we have] certain, sure, and hence immediate knowledge, lies within [our] consciousness," beyond which "there can be no *immediate* certainty" (*WWR* 2:5, 4, 4). Hegel ignores this Kantian lesson, Schopenhauer argues, although Schopenhauer also wants to expose the "grave errors" in Kant's system (1:xv).[11] Yet Schopenhauer's philosophy is in turn frustrated by its inability to move past Kant as the limit of idealism to which he compulsively returns. As if fated to iterate the primal scene of its own Kantianism, Schopenhauer's idealism thus becomes the trauma haunting the unfolding of his primary work, an overdetermined encounter with an idealism that can never be adequately expressed or recalled. This melancholy[12] fuels the second edition of *WWR*, in which the second volume revisits the first, but as if to expose a "futility of thought" that then gives Schopenhauer's later writings their "wavering, wandering, drifting quality."[13] Such "thought cast adrift" constitutes the "failure of systematic philosophy, but a shimmering, architectonic failure," less a "system of thought" than a "*decompositional*" thought of system, a "philosophy of disintegration."[14]

Between earlier attempts to systematize thought in *Fourfold Root* or the first edition of *WWR* and the creeping misanthropy of Volume Two, fully expressed in *Parerga and Paralipomena*, philosophy emerges as an appendix to the possibility of a system destined to encounter its own defeat, the feeling of which failure suffuses the late style of a "philosophy writing against philosophy,"[15] an obsessive compulsion to answer thought's failure as philosophy's comedy of errors. To explore this trajectory, this chapter will first examine what Schopenhauer means by representation (*Vorstellung*) and will (*Wille*), particularly the necessary but unholy alliance between them. I will then take up how the form of *WWR* both reflects and is undone by Schopenhauer's attempt to make sense of this alliance, within the first volume itself and as part of its anxious supplement in Volume Two. I will then explore the post-idealist subject that emerges from this troubled amalgamation as a transition to a final analysis of various forms of contemporary thought that encrypt Schopenhauer's confrontation with idealism.

One strong precursor here remains Freud, who "charts the development of the unknowing and largely unknowable modern individual in a culture obsessed by knowledge."[16] How Schopenhauer maps the philosophical ground of this obsession remains one of the founding gestures of psychoanalysis, whose aleatory form results from philosophy's encounter with (its own) contingency. This is also to recalibrate philosophy in and as the feedback loop of its own representation, as if to anticipate a poststructuralist unsettling of discursive regimes. This reorientation inevitably takes the form of the subject itself as the figure for this struggle with knowledge. As Houellebecq suggests, to encounter Schopenhauer is simultaneously to account for and to take account of that experience. Put another way, tracking how thought is burdened with contemplating and justifying its own legitimacy, Schopenhauer evokes an affective awareness of having to deal with the fallout from an encounter with contingency that moves his thought beyond a poststructuralist dissection of the subject to a concern with how affect constitutes that subject's experience of the world. For Schopenhauer that affect is, of course, pessimism, the symptom not only of "the fragility of thought" but also of a post-poststructuralist concern with the fragility of life itself. For Eugene Thacker, one of the few contemporary theorists to take up Schopenhauer directly, as the twenty-first century unfolds with increasing premonitions of disaster, wrestling with the relativity of meaning may be the least of our concerns, leaving pessimism, the dominant affect of disaster, as our only ethical response.

2 Philosophy Against Itself

The first edition of *WWR* uses Kant's idealism to reassemble a subject decentered by Hume's proto-behaviorism in order to produce the subject of "aesthetic contemplation" eventually explored by Nietzsche. Yet this anthropomorphized idealist subject remains sutured between a psychic determinism empiricism was unable to work through and Kantian idealism was unable to sublimate. Kant internalizes the mind's empiricism by way of determining the world's form a priori, as if to abstract Being from being. For Kant, "nothing whatsoever can be asserted of the thing in itself," although it can *be thought*, for "otherwise we should be landed in the absurd conclusion that there can be appearance without anything that appears."[17] But for Schopenhauer, Kant too easily sublates the mind's relationship to being, the *in-itself* or touchstone of perception. Kant's subject reverts to perception only "to convince [himself] that [his] abstract thinking has not strayed far from the safe ground of perception, ... [as] when walking in the dark, we stretch out our hand every now and then to the wall that guides us" (*WWR* 1:449). By setting aside the objective world as inscrutable touchstone, Kant suppresses how the contingency of empiricism resists being subsumed a priori. This resistance forms the kernel of Schopenhauer's idealism, which starts with the principle of sufficient reason. For Schopenhauer, "nothing existing by itself and independent, and also nothing single and detached, can become an object for us"; hence, "the pure *a priori* concepts ... serve solely as *a priori* conditions of a possible experience" without constituting this experience except as representation. Sufficient reason governs how consciousness functions *within* rather than *apart from* the world, lest idealism veer toward abstraction, as it does for Schopenhauer's Hegel.[18] Put another way, the principle of sufficient reason, functioning under the illusion of reason's self-sufficiency, is for Schopenhauer a self-deconstructing concept.

The source of this deconstruction is Schopenhauer's conception of a subject impossibly constituted between *Vorstellung* and *Wille*, which are both inextricably linked to and ineluctably separate from one another. *Wille* reenvisions Kant's *Ding an sich* as a "blind irresistible urge" not "subject to the principle of sufficient reason" (1:275), which governs representation as the will's *"appearance"* or *"phenomenon"* (1:106). And here we have the central paradox that preoccupies and troubles Schopenhauer's philosophy: we only know the will through its representation, a negative knowledge that then subverts the very reason that makes representation possible. What the will mobilizes in order to represent itself to itself is at the same time reliant on a will that couldn't care less for its existence, locking will and representation in a kind of sadomasochistic embrace. To tackle this paradox, Book One of *WWR* analyzes representation before Book Two turns to the will as representation's *Urgrund* or *Abgrund*. Representation is a "secondary thing," a "mere slave and bondsman to the will" as the "first and original thing" (2:212, 202). As the supplementary expression of the will's primary functioning, representation is thought's sufficiency in the face of the will as its baffling limit, a kind of pragmatic rather than transcendental idealism. Through representation, the subject rematerializes out of Kant's abstract world as the *principium individuationis*, but as a "stable and unwavering phantom" (1:278n) or mere appearance interminably contending with the will's mastery—less a subject *in* representation than a subject *of* and *to* the will. As if always distracted by the body of the will, thought emerges at the fault line where will and representation mutually supplement and deconstruct one another. The subject thus emerges as a troubled hybrid between two strains of the same ontology, a "point of indifference" (2:203) between will and intellect, rooted in the body as "will itself; embodied will" or *"will* objectively perceived in the brain." The will's physiological functions are "enhanced and accelerated by the ... emotions," then further refined by the intellect, except that the intellect remains the "mere function of the *brain*, which is nourished and sustained by the organism only parasitically" (2:203).[19] As "will become visible" (1:107), the body is both representation or "knowledge *a posteriori* of the will"—embodied will—and will or "knowledge *a priori* of the body"—disembodied representation, which is to distinguish brain as a purely physiological manifestation of the will and mind as brain's representation of the will. The subject encrypts, and is encrypted by, the will's dis-ease, as if constituted by the very thing that subverts this constitution, a symptom of the will that bears the burden of proof for a body of evidence that is at once the subject's own and utterly alien.

Wille thus signals the contingency between subject and world as a foreign body within philosophy itself. Grounding the subject in the body of her experience, the will materializes an immediate nexus between the self and its interiority, but then denies the subject access to any definitive knowledge of this embodiment, so that interiority is radically displaced within itself, as if to reexteriorize or alienate itself.[20] Inevitably, representation succumbs to its ceaseless effort to know the will, which appears as "a continual rushing of the present into the dead past, a constant dying" or "constant suffering" (1:311, 267). By the mere repetition of the will's endless striving, representation risks becoming its own drive toward the exhaustion of the knowing subject through the forms of its knowledge. Rather than a revision of Kantian abstraction, then, sufficient reason is the symptom of thought's traumatic inability to know the will, for representation can never supply any "permanent fulfilment which completely and for ever satisfies [the will's] craving" (1:362). *Wille* is the "strong blind man" who carries the "sighted lame man" (2:209) of the intellect on its shoulders, an insight illuminated by rather than illuminating blindness, both the *primum mobile* of the subject's desire for enlightenment and a force utterly oblivious to this desire, like the Lacanian Real as "that which resists symbolization absolutely."[21] The desire for knowledge produces an epistemological futility in which idealism never finds the cure of enlightenment. The "game" of "Eternal becoming" and "endless flux," although it reveals the will's "essential nature," thus ends up "showing [existence] as a fearful, life-destroying boredom, a lifeless longing without a definite object, a deadening langour" (1:164).

Books Three and Four of *WWR* respond to this futility by ending the will's suffering through a suspension of the willing body in representation's *ends* (Book Three) and eventually *end* (Book Four). In Book Three, representation momentarily transcends itself through the aesthetic contemplation of the Ideas, which stage the finite limit of representation as a kind of momentary absolute. Derived from both Plato and Kant's transcendental ideality of phenomena, the Ideas, which "lie quite outside the sphere of [the subject's] knowledge" (1:169), manifest the will for knowledge in a form least adulterated by representation's exhaustible iteration of the will. Grasped intuitively as the gestalt of representation, the Ideas are a type of self-consciousness that transcends the desire for enlightenment. While Book Three of *WWR* takes up the representation of will through specific art forms, it is equally concerned with representation as an aestheticization of knowledge that approaches this sublimation of idealism's contingency through idealism's own interiority. Here "knowledge tears itself free from the service of the will precisely by the subject's ceasing to be merely individual, and being now a pure will-less subject of knowledge" (1:178), an Idea expressing itself as if without the help of phenomena. The aesthetic liberates the subject from empiricism via a cognizant body that, paradoxically, suspends its own body of knowledge by "abolishing individuality in the knowing subject" (1:169).[22] The highest form of this freedom is music, which exists as its own representation, not as an objectification of the will.

Yet however much the aesthetic subsumes the body's contingency, by attempting to supersede the will's subjectivity as "vanished illusions" (1:164) the Idea stages the subject as the symptom of Kant's original problem with empiricism. Like Heideggerian *Schein*, wherein being is at once revelatory and illusory, or like the Lacanian gaze, wherein the *cogito* and its consciousness do not add up to the same subject, the apparition of the Idea marks a type of paralyzed mirror stage that the subject, as both "stable and unwavering phantom," can neither enter into, pass through, nor move beyond. Ceasing to be individual, the subject merely *appears* in a momentary retreat back into an imagined yet unsustainable unity of Being.[23] If, as Terry Eagleton argues, the "aesthetic is what ruptures for a blessed moment the terrible sway of teleology, ... plucking an object for an instant out of the clammy grip of the will and savoring it purely as spectacle,"[24] Book Four finally surrenders to this fate as Freudian Thanatos, not an absolute resistance to enlightenment but the "*denial of the will-to-live*" (1:283). By starving or suppressing the will's appetitive nature, this asceticism attempts to eliminate desire itself, not by eliminating the body (although *Parerga and Paralipomena* makes a rather compassionate defence of suicide[25]), but in order to become the will as a suspension of its own desire. The ascetic uses the Idea, where "the will can reach full self-consciousness," to "abolish[ ] the essential nature at the root of the phenomenon"—the striving of the will as the knowledge or knowing of representation—"whilst the phenomenon itself still continues to exist in time." This "brings about a contradiction of the phenomenon with itself" (1:288) to produce the bodiless knowledge of a will that no longer desires to know itself. This gnosis releases the subject into the "real present" where he is no longer subject to phenomena, or "abstract thoughts," or knowledge of past or future, all of which are the "cause of our pain as of our pleasure" (1:279, 293).[26] That is, the temporal form of the will's suffering in the body becomes the symptom of "intense mental suffering" so that "we cause ourselves physical suffering in order ... to divert our attention from the former to the latter" (1:299).

To escape representation's blind illumination is to accept the fate of insight: "We are like entrapped elephants, which rage and struggle fearfully for many days, until they see that it is fruitless, and then suddenly offer their necks calmly to the yoke, tamed for ever" (1:306). Rather than transcend the will through enlightenment, that is, we accept the will in order no longer to remain susceptible to it. Another paradox emerges, however, for this acute acceptance unravels into a chronic denial of desire that "must always be achieved afresh by constant struggle" (1:391).[27] Attempting to suspend the will, the aesthetic and ascetic all the more invoke it as a pathology resisting their cure. In either case, consciousness fails the subject, producing a striving for knowledge that results in an impossible enlightenment. Schopenhauer anticipates this crisis in the Preface to the first edition: "what is to be imparted by [this book] is a single thought" which, "however comprehensive, must preserve the most perfect unity" such that all elements of the "*system of thought*" which serve to communicate this single thought "must always have an architectonic connexion or coherence" (1:xii). However, because "a book must have a first and a last line," it "will always remain very unlike an organism, however like one its contents may be. Consequently, form and matter will here be in contradiction" (1:xii–xiii). To work through this contradiction, as if to acclimatize us to the text's mode of being as well as its content, Schopenhauer implores us "*to read the book twice*," for an "earnest desire for fuller and even easier comprehension must," like that of our author, "in the case of every difficult subject, justify occasional repetition. The structure of the whole, which is organic, and not like a chain, in itself makes it necessary sometimes to touch twice on the same point" (1:xiii). Embedding a single thought within a process of thought risks becoming a chronic or pathological endeavor, a mutation of thought's organism within the organic form of its unfolding.

WWR thus unfolds as more narrative or palimpsest than architectonic, less as a "system of thought" than a "thought of system,"[28] as if continually to assess the insufficient reason of its articulation. This decided turn in the corpus of idealism finds philosophy divided against itself in its attempt to track the will as a kind of free radical within the body of philosophy. In the Preface to the first edition, Schopenhauer argues that *WWR* offers a "method of philosophizing which is here attempted for the first time" (1:xiv), what in the Preface to the second edition he calls "meditative"

(1:xxvi), which suggests confession as much as contemplation. That his "philosophy does not allow of the fiction ... of a reason that knows, perceives, or apprehends immediately and absolutely" (1:xxvi), thought is compelled to explore its interiority. This approach manifests a "certain philosophical unconscious"[29] within the anatomy of idealism, as both a pathology demanding diagnosis and cure and a symptomatic form whose struggle to figure things out requires more talk, a talking cure that constantly generates new material to work through.[30] Meditating on its ability to tell, philosophy confronts the limits of its idealism through a psychoanalysis that reveals its inability to do so, a prolonged, repetitive positing of philosophy's identity driven by the will.[31] After Books One and Two of *WWR* explore representation and will respectively, Books Three and Four then repeat these first considerations in a finer tone. But this forward movement also eternally recurs to the discontinuous relation between *Wille* and *Vorstellung*. In turn, Volumes One and Two bear a "supplementary relation to one another," such that "it would not do to amalgamate the contents of the second volume with those of the first into one whole" (1:xxii). Instead, Volume One invokes Volume Two as both cure and symptom of its own chronic nature, emerging ahead of its 1844 excursus as a trauma to which the second edition responds, a primal scene to which Schopenhauer is at once anxious and fated to return. As if to mourn an Enlightenment empiricism whose crowning achievement is Kant's idealism, the ascetic would overcome thought's abstraction in the Idea. Instead, it becomes a fate to be endured, less a terminus than a holding pattern of existence that "*live[s] in the rift between the fear of death and dread of life* ... philosophy as a practice of seeing through the shadow-play of the world" (Thacker 21). The result is a being-toward-death or what Corngold calls a "prolonged meditation on death."[32] Mourning, which marks the limits of philosophy's idealism, becomes melancholy, philosophy's chronic response to the will's death drive. Both mastering and mastered by this melancholy, *WWR* psychoanalyzes idealism as resisting its own finitude yet not presuming to know these limits as absolutes.

3 Psychoanalyzing the Subject of Schopenhauer

Needless to say, Schopenhauer works against the Hegelian Spirit of Absolute Knowledge. By displacing the subject's identity into the circuit of representation, the will is "[t]hat which knows all things and is known by none" (*WWR* 1:5). Like the Humean *cogito*, the subject is merely the repetition of its own forms of knowledge who must then suffer the pain of never knowing itself: "the in-itself of life, the will, existence itself, is a constant suffering, and is partly woeful, partly fearful" (1:267). Schopenhauer refashions the Enlightenment *cogito* as the sum/SUM of its deconstructive parts. This subject is invaded by an other subjectivity at once alien and essential: "the intellect remains so much excluded from the real resolutions and secret decisions of its own will that sometimes it can only get to know them ... by spying out and taking unawares; and it must surprise the will in the act of expressing itself, in order merely to discover its real intentions" (2:209). We are, to borrow Julia Kristeva's phrase, strangers to ourselves, a "foreigner" that "lives within us," "the hidden face of our identity, the space that wrecks our abode, the time in which understanding and affinity founder."[33] Although "sighted" within consciousness, representation is blind to and blinded by the will's unconscious, unable to read its "real resolutions and secret decisions." Subject to this dramaturgy, however, the subject who would know is both compelled and condemned to read and thus understand its effects. Representation is thus an endless psychoanalysis of the will's life, itself a traumatic absence that compels the intellect to confess the will's secrets, which are forever unspeakable—the death drive of thought itself. In this sense, psychoanalysis informs Schopenhauer's idealism less as theory, metapsychology, or praxis than as the avenging spirit of a post-Enlightenment evisceration of modes of knowledge and being that take the subject as avatar rather than sovereign entity. In this sense, poststructuralism is informed by the critique of the subject and its knowledge formations made possible by psychoanalysis, but takes us back to the future of poststructuralism and beyond in Schopenhauer's thought.

That Schopenhauer anticipates Freud has long been acknowledged, of course. As Freud famously remarks in *Beyond the Pleasure Principle* (1920), "We have unwittingly steered our course into the harbour of Schopenhauer's philosophy. For him death is the 'true result and to that extent the purpose of life,' while the sexual instinct is the embodiment of the will to live."[34] The will also suggests the primary processes of Freudian dreamwork, which mobilize representation's more conscious work of psychic signification always preceded by the will as representation's indivisible remainder, at once a necessary realization and attenuation of the will and a deceptive consciousness of its blind and blinding force. As both *thanatos* and *eros*, *Wille* anticipates Freud's notions of the *Triebe* as both a post-transcendental and a primordial force at once animating bodies and superseding their particularity, a dark materiality of the ego's substratum fundamental to the psyche's makeup yet always beyond its control.[35] This more visceral nature of the will aligns it with the Freudian Id. Leo Bersani notes that the new Penguin Freud, which retranslates James Strachey's translation of *das Es* as "the it," marks the unconscious as the gap "between perception and consciousness," against the "more orthodox view of the unconscious in depth-psychology [or ego psychology] as behind or below consciousness." The latter implies the potential to reveal and subdue hidden or repressed terrors, whereas the former, seeing "the unconscious as before consciousness, in the sense of an ontological rather than a temporal anteriority," the "It in the I," "transforms subjecthood from psychic density into pure potentiality," a "reservoir of possibility." Some sense of this ontological anteriority defines the will. Yet "potentiality" or "reservoir of possibility" seems far too Hegelian.

A more fitting word might be Gilles Deleuze's notion of "incompossibility," that which "is not reducible to the notion of contradiction," although "contradiction is derived from incompossibility," as the condition of compossibility or the "*rule of world synthesis.*"[36] Between them, that is to say, Deleuze sees what he and Félix Guattari would call a "disjunctive synthesis" or relation of nonrelation by which various entities communicate through the accretion of their differences from one another.[37] As Claire Colebrook writes, for Deleuze "there is not a subject who synthesizes," but rather "syntheses from which subjects are formed; these subjects are not persons but points of relative stability resulting from connection."[38] Relocated in Schopenhauerian terms, such a conception appears to liberate the subject through the motility of its emergence between will and representation, making of the contradiction between them a both/and rather than either/or relation. Yet Schopenhauer's *Wille*, while disruptive of identity and identities, is more entropic and atrophic than productive in a Deleuzian sense, and between *Wille* and *Vorstellung* exists a far more deconstructive relation of difference than disjunctive synthesis, which in turn marks the subject as not only dynamically groundless but inevitably and unavoidably dispensable. For Schopenhauer, it is as "absurd to desire the continuance of our individuality, which is replaced by other individuals, as to desire the permanence of the matter of our body, which is constantly replaced by fresh matter. It appears just as foolish to embalm corpses as it would be carefully to preserve our excreta" (1:277).

Unlike the "*appearance* or *phenomenon* of the will," then, the will "may be called *groundless*" (1:106), materializing an idealist philosophical body subject to its own drives. Such groundlessness, shattering any façade of identity's permanence, returns us to a Freud and post-Freud Deleuze and Guattari would dismiss, that is to say, to an experience of groundlessness that is rather more traumatic than liberating. Freud marks the death drive as a "matter of expediency," always returning the subject to a primal inertia: "an unlimited duration of individual life would become a quite pointless luxury."[39] The result, as Lacan reminds us in his epochal rereading of Freud, is a subject split between two solitudes with no homeland. This subject was itself the unwanted guest of ego psychology, a mutation of psychoanalysis Lacan hated for its "reservoir of possibility" that resonated particularly with post–Second World War American optimism. As Freud said to Jung in 1909 on the occasion of Freud's only visit to America, "They don't realize we are bringing them the plague."[40] For Lacan, Freud embedded the unconscious in our midst as a terrorist impossible to police, something "lodged within a subject that it vastly exceeds."[41] The result was a schism in Freud's legacy: on the one hand, a desire to bring the unconscious to consciousness, to diagnose and cure its symptomology; on the other hand, an awareness that this desire, the very work of representation, inflicts upon us the plague of fantasies by which we live.

Representation in this sense constitutes what Lacan calls the *sinthome*, an "old way of spelling what was subsequently spelt *symptôme*."[42] The *sinthome* registers the unconscious of the *symptôme*, the archaic trace or restless negativity within not only its etymology but also its ontology. As Slavoj Žižek writes:

> symptom is the way we—the subjects—'avoid madness,' the way we 'choose something (the symptom-formation) instead of nothing (radical psychotic autism, the destruction of the symbolic universe)' through the binding of our enjoyment to a certain signifying, symbolic formation which assures a minimum consistency to our being-in-the-world.... If the symptom in this radical dimension is unbound, it means literally 'the end of the world'— the only alternative to the symptom is nothing: pure autism, a psychic suicide, surrender to the death drive even to the total destruction of the symbolic universe.... That is how we

must read Freud's *wo es war, soll ich werden*: you, the subject, must identify yourself with the place where your symptom already was; in its 'pathological' particularity you must recognize the element which gives consistency to your being.[43]

This is to accord the symptom a "radical ontological status": "symptom conceived as *sinthome* is literally our only substance, the only positive support of our being, the only point that gives consistency to the subject."[44]

Yet while the *sinthome* seems to steer us safely into Schopenhauer's harbor, for Schopenhauer it still leaves the subject adrift, begging the question of what to do with itself in a world less rather than more of its making. *WWR* wants to locate the otherwise symptomatic, subjective reality of representation in the principle of sufficient reason as a way of granting objective status to the will's radical otherness. Yet at the same time Schopenhauer knows that this objective reality is itself a symptom as *sinthome*, necessary and inescapable except at the risk of the kind of symbolic destruction he entertains in Book Four and over which he melancholically broods for the remainder of his writings. To invoke another pair of psychoanalytical terms, *WWR* is poised at the threshold between introjection and incorporation. As Nicholas Abraham and Maria Torok write:

> Incorporation is the refusal to reclaim as our own the part of ourselves that we placed in what we lost; incorporation is the refusal to acknowledge the full import of the loss, a loss that, if recognized as such, would effectively transform us. In fine, incorporation is the refusal to introject loss. The fantasy of incorporation reveals a gap within the psyche; it points to something that is missing just where introjection should have occurred.[45]

Incorporation is the result of an "[i]nexpressible mourning" that "erects a secret tomb inside the subject,"[46] which crypt houses an "*intrapsychic secret*" that results from the breach of an interpsychic relation with an object that has now been lost. Yet whereas Abraham and Torok see the possible transformation of incorporation into introjection—a potential revelation and acknowledgment of the secret and thus of loss—Schopenhauer remains with incorporation, his philosophy painfully and compulsively aware of what it cannot know as a secret encrypted within its corpus as this body's constitutive nature and possibility. For Schopenhauer, that is, the experience of not knowing still leaves the trace of an even deeper experience of knowing but also not knowing that one does not know, which ultimately breeds pessimism as the only properly ethical response to a being we may not ultimately survive.

4 Feeling Schopenhauer to the End

Such excursions into Schopenhauer's thought tend toward a final question, begged by what is perhaps the most eviscerating of concepts to emerge from Freud's long-time companionship with Schopenhauer: that of a drive toward death. How does a twenty-first-century Schopenhauer speak to contemporary theory, particularly Affect Studies, speculative realism, and a broader concern with disaster, even extinction not only of the subject but also of the very environment of its existence?

Like Freud to Jung, we can say that Schopenhauer brings us the plague of philosophy as what philosopher and cognitive scientist David Chalmers has called the "hard problem of consciousness": how to explain the transference between physical processes, like the neuronal structure of the brain, and our experience of the world this structure provides for us—a transference between the cognitive and the phenomenal. This transference suggests the work of thought as an inter- as much as intra-psychic phenomenon, what modern neuroscientific research explores as the distributed work and nature of cognition.[47] Yet this research is concerned less with what we might call a poststructuralist decentering of identity than it is with mapping this identity's cognitive potential. This rather more positive approach, not unlike Deleuze and Guattari's sense of the productive unconscious, bypasses the *agon* of cognition (which we might say poststructuralism itself often misses) central to what Thacker calls Schopenhauer's "pessimism of philosophy, ... an anti-philosophy of misanthropic splendor, a speculative metaphysics of ugly feelings, a poetics of disintegration."[48] The melancholic and vitriolic pathos of Schopenhauer's fearlessness in confronting the "ugly feelings" that philosophy dredges up are what give his subject "substance" and "consistency." The excoriating energy of Schopenhauer's writing animates explorations of the discontents of happiness in recent Affect Studies, a field that reads the revolution in neuroscientic research in more sociocultural terms.[49] For Sara Ahmed, the "hap of happiness then gets translated into something good," making happiness an "anticipatory causality" that "something good" will happen.[50] Such anticipation materializes what Lauren Berlant calls "cruel optimism."[51] Schopenhauer is very clear on this account: "Everything in life proclaims that earthly happiness is destined to be frustrated, or recognized as an illusion" (*WWR* 2:573). Happiness thus addicts us to future reparation, to the desire for the desire for happiness.[52] Again in Schopenhauer, "happiness always lies in the future," so that "the present is always inadequate, but the future is uncertain, and the past irrecoverable" (2:573). Moreover, "only pain and want can be felt positively; and therefore they proclaim themselves; well-being, on the contrary, is merely negative." Hence, "our existence is happiest when we perceive it least" (2:575). In idealism, at least of the Hegelian variety, Schopenhauer spies the illusions and terrors of thought's access to itself as some kind of fundamental purchase on the world, an idealism, even euphoria, not without its ethical blind spots. In short, Schopenhauer casts a withering gaze on our current obsessions with well-being, mindfulness, and any number of manifestations of what Gary Greenberg, in a 2005 *Harper*'s article, calls "The War on Unhappiness."[53]

Greenberg's sympathy lies with Freud's acknowledgment of the unconscious as something "lodged within a subject that it vastly exceeds," with which we carry on a conversation whose interminability is the very "substance" or *sinthome* of our being. Yet this will-to-live that is at the same time our being-toward-death lies perpetually beyond consciousness itself. Here the will takes the form of what Timothy Morton, in the vein of object-oriented ontology, an offshoot of speculative realism, calls a "hyperobject," a thing, such as climate, that is "massively distributed in time and space relative to humans."[54] Chris Washington explains the hyperobject as something that "remains nowhere at all in empirical reality, an object with thousands, perhaps millions, of qualities with no actual concrete manifestation of itself in its totality." In this way, "[r]eality therefore suddenly becomes radically inconsistent with human experience."[55] Speculative realism wrestles with the specters of what Quentin Meillassoux calls "correlationism"—"the idea according to which we only ever have access to the correlation between thinking and being, and never to either term considered apart from the other."[56] Correlationism entails the Kantian idealism that we can think the *Ding an sich* only from the perspective of thought. Wrestling thinking from being, however, demands that we think a being beyond our thought *of* being, on its own terms, as it were, which is to say prior to its own "givenness." In Meillassoux's wording, this is to locate "the great outdoors ... that outside which thought could explore with the legitimate feeling of being on foreign territory–of being entirely elsewhere."[57]

Something of Schopenhauer's displacement of thought's relationship to the world in both Kant's and Hegel's idealism informs Meillassoux's critique of correlationism. Both Schopenhauer and Meillassoux invite us to think a "post-apocalyptic state that takes place ulterior to human finitude" and thus "pitches humans headlong into a heedless future."[58] How, Schopenhauer invites us to ask, to speak of the very thing that at once locates us in the world—"worlds" our world for us—and is symptomatic of what Meillassoux calls "*dia-chronicity*"? Dia-chronicity indicates the "*temporal discrepancy* between thinking and being," which speaks "not only [to] statements about events occurring prior to the emergence of humans, but also statements about possible events that are *ulterior* to the extinction of the human species."[59] Meillassoux contemplates the existence of what he terms the "'arche-fossil' or 'fossil-matter,'" which "indicat[es] the traces of past life ... but [also] materials indicating the existence of an ancestral reality or event,"[60] like the luminescence of a star reaching us after billions of years of light travel. This ancestrality "reveals an aporia that exists in both philosophy and science: our inability to account for a world outside of us without, paradoxically, accounting for it."[61] As Schopenhauer notes, as if further to indict the "pernicious doctrine" of optimism, "fossils of entirely different kinds of animal species which formerly inhabited the planet afford us, as proof of our calculation, records of worlds whose continuance was no longer possible, and which were in consequence somewhat worse than the worst of all possible worlds" (*WWR* 2:584).

Encrypted in such statements is a consciousness of the ecological fragility of life: "An insignificant alteration of the atmosphere, not even chemically demonstrable, causes cholera, yellow fever, black death, and so on, which carry off millions of people; a somewhat greater alteration would extinguish all life" (2:584). But we feel this sense of fragility, insofar as we can possess it *as* consciousness, through our insurmountable alienation from life itself, the necessary recognition of which Thacker takes as one of Schopenhauer's signal lessons:

> what we call 'climate' is neither a thing-in-itself 'out there' nor simply a subjective feeling 'in here,' but rather the rift between them. Or, more accurately, that void or 'nothingness' between self and world is also what unites them.... Perhaps what Schopenhauer is outlining in these ideas of the world as Representation and Will is a strange kind of monism,

> co-existing but incommensurate realities, the gulf separating self and world that is at the same time that which connects them.[62]

Here Thacker speaks to a rather less productive sense of Deleuze and Guattari's celebration of disjunctive connectivity. Taking up the Rare Earth hypothesis that examines the formation of complex life from microbes to tectonic shifts to galactic disasters and emergences, Thacker notes: "Life is not normal. And when it does exist, it is volatile and short-lived."[63] Which is to say, "while simple lifeforms (microbes) may be common in the universe, the development of complex life is rare."[64] Hence, "complex life is not only improbable but, when it exists, it is fundamentally unsustainable, comprised mainly of cycles of evolutionary development and catastrophe—that life, taken as a whole, is suicidal."[65] It is as if the "single thought" of Schopenhauer's writing serves to remind us that we miss the realities of the present at our peril, and yet can only do so by recognizing the profoundly autonomous nature of the will-to-live as our being-toward-death:

> who would go on living life as it is, if death were less terrible? And who could bear even the mere thought of death, if life were a pleasure? But the former still always has the good point of being the end of life, and we console ourselves with death in regard to the sufferings of life, and with the sufferings of life in regard to death. The truth is that the two belong to each other inseparably, since they constitute a deviation from the right path, and a return to this is as difficult as it is desirable. (*WWR* 2:578–79)

It is thus perhaps in Schopenhauer's attention to the autonomous in- and nonhuman dimension of existence that he casts his longest shadow—though with, I hasten to add, a profound, if paradoxical, sense of compassion for the very world his pessimism so apparently dismisses. In this incompossible space, *WWR* marks a pivotal episode in nineteenth-century philosophy's encounter with the limits of its idealism, one that resonates all that more profoundly in our present time as it contemplates the limits of existence itself.

Perhaps ultimately Schopenhauer's is a philosophy of disaster, of what Theodor Adorno calls damaged life.[66] As Maurice Blanchot writes, "The disaster, unexperienced. It is what escapes the very possibility of experience—it is the limit of writing."[67] Disaster governs the strange ancestrality of Schopenhauer's philosophy as rooted in the body of the will in a kind of absolute present that perpetually vanishes on the horizon of its appearance. Or as Blanchot also writes: "dying is, speaking absolutely, the incessant imminence whereby life lasts, desiring. The imminence of what has always already come to pass."[68] Yet even these contexts return me to my earlier point that *WWR* marks within philosophy the emergence of a psychoanalysis with which philosophy remains ambivalently yet irrevocably complicit. Jacques Derrida writes, "the advent of psychoanalysis is a complex event not only in terms of its historical probability but in terms of a discourse that remains open and that attempts at each instant to regulate itself—yet affirming its originality—according to the scientific and artistic treatment of randomness."[69] Derrida speaks of the "greatest speculative power" of psychoanalysis: its "greatest resistance to psychoanalysis," a deconstructive gesture within enlightenment Reason that "remain[s] forever heterogeneous to the principle of principle,"[70] not unlike Schopenhauer's essentially deconstructive notion of sufficient reason. If we think of deconstruction as the perception of the affect of idealism as longing, in the words of the late Ross Woodman, we have in Schopenhauer's writing the felt trauma of the invention of something like psychoanalysis as deconstructive practice. At the end of *Angels in America*, Harper Pitt says, "Nothing's lost forever. In this world, there is a kind of painful progress. Longing for what we've left behind, and dreaming ahead. At least I think that's so."[71] Schopenhauer distinctly does *not* think so. As Freud learned from his encounter with Schopenhauer, to borrow from David Clark, "humankind can never wholly possess itself or live entirely within itself."[72] Which demands of humankind the necessity to speak otherwise, if at all.

Notes

1. Cited in Arthur Schopenhauer, *On the Suffering of the World*, ed. Eugene Thacker (London: Repeater Books, 2020), 54.
2. Agatha Novak-Lechevalier, "Preface," in Michel Houellebecq, *In the Presence of Schopenhauer*, trans. Andrew Brown (Cambridge: Polity, 2017), ix.
3. Michel Houellebecq, *In the Presence of Schopenhauer*, 7.
4. Ibid., 13.
5. I am indebted to Tyler Tritten's early version of his chapter for this volume at a workshop on "German Idealism and Post-Structuralism" organized by Tilottama Rajan and Gabriel Trop, on March 27and 28 and April 10 and 11, 2021.
6. Werner Hamacher, *Pleroma—Reading in Hegel*, translated by Nicholas Walker and Simon Jarvis (Stanford: Stanford University Press, 1998), 65. I am deeply indebted to Kristina Mendicino for the nod to Hamacher and to her paper "Reading Hegel" for this volume, also presented at the "German Idealism and Post-Structuralism" workshop. I also recognize the irony of using the idea of reading Hegel to read Schopenhauer, who was no fan of Hegel, as we'll see.
7. Kristina Mendicino, e-mail exchange with author, March 28, 2021.
8. Arthur Schopenhauer, *The World as Will and Representation*, 2 vols, trans. E. F. J. Payne (New York: Dover, 1958), 1:xxiv. Hereafter all references to this work will be cited as *WWR*. As Robert Bretall reminds us in his introduction to Kierkegaard's most sustained attack against Hegelianism, *Concluding Unscientific Postscript to the Philosophical Fragments* (1846), Kierkegaard famously noted that if Hegel had called his system of philosophy "only a 'thought-experiment,' he would have been the greatest thinker who ever lived; as it is he is 'merely comic'" (in Søren Kierkegaard, *A Kierkegaard Anthology* [Princeton: Princeton University Press, 1946], 191).
9. The statement is rather ironic since, as Eugene Thacker notes, "Schopenhauer adamantly refuses any therapeutic functions to his [own] writing." ("Introduction: A Philosophy in Ruins, An Unquiet Void," in Arthur Schopenhauer, *On the Suffering of the World*, ed. Eugene Thacker [London: Repeater, 2020], 20).
10. Stanley Corngold, "Hegel, Schopenhauer, and Cannibalism," *Qui Parle*, 15, no. 1 (Fall/Winter 2004): 1. Corngold continues: "[i]f it is Hegel who is taught in universities today, and not Schopenhauer, Schopenhauer nonetheless survives … in the bodies, so to speak, of literary works that are taught. This canon is his faithful corps."
11. Schopenhauer calls his loyalty to Kant's philosophy an "excessive preoccupation" (*WWR* 1:xiv) and reveres Kant as "the most important phenomenon which has appeared in philosophy for two thousand years" (*WWR* 1:xiv, xv).
12. Thacker calls Schopenhauer a "depressive Kantian" ("Philosophy in Ruins," 21).

13. Ibid., 21, 24.
14. Ibid., 24, 24, 24, 12. This thought tracks what Schopenhauer, in the second volume of *Parerga and Paralipomena*, calls "restlessness [*Unruhe*] [as] the original form of existence" (cited in ibid., 93). Thacker's collection of Schopenhauer's late writings in *On the Suffering of the World* uses the E. F. J. Payne translation in *Parerga and Paralipomena*, vols. 1 and 2 (Oxford: Clarendon Press, 1974). The Cambridge edition reads, "unrest is the prototype of existence" (*Parerga and Paralipomena: Short Philosophical Essays*, vol. 2, trans. and ed. Adrian Del Caro and Christopher Janaway [Cambridge: Cambridge University Press, 2015], 256). I prefer "prototype," which suggests a germ whose incompleteness is its generative form, to "original," which suggests grounding rather than groundlessness. In his reading of Hegel, Jean-Luc Nancy speaks of the "restlessness of immanence" in which the "self is what *does not find itself*" (*Hegel: The Restlessness of the Negative*, trans. Jason Smith and Steven Miller [Minneapolis: University of Minnesota Press, 2020], 5, 56).
15. Thacker, "Philosophy in Ruins," 24.
16. Adam Phillips, *Becoming Freud: The Making of a Psychoanalyst* (New Haven: Yale University Press, 2014), 10–11.
17. Immanuel Kant, *Critique of Pure Reason*, trans. Norman Kemp Smith (London: Macmillan, 1993), 87, 27.
18. Arthur Schopenhauer, *On the Fourfold Root of the Principle of Sufficient Reason*, trans. E. F. J. Payne (LaSalle, IL: Open Court, 1977), 42, 115.
19. By *Vorstellung*, Schopenhauer means less the Idea in Plato or Kant than the result of a neuronal impulse, which is why he prioritizes perceptions over concepts. Schopenhauer writes: "every perturbation of the *will*, and with it of the *organism*, must disturb or paralyze the function of the brain, a function existing by itself, and knowing no other needs than simply those of rest and nourishment" (*WWR* 2:216).
20. As Terry Eagleton writes, while Schopenhauer "privileges the inward in Romantic style, he nevertheless refuses to valorize it" ("Schopenhauer and the Aesthetic," *Signature*, 1 [Summer 1989]: 17).
21. Jacques Lacan, *The Seminar of Jacques Lacan: Book I, Freud's Papers on Technique, 1953–1954*, ed. Jacques-Alain Miller, trans. John Forrester (New York: W.W. Norton, 1991), 66.
22. Eagleton writes that an "idealist philosophy which once imagined that it could achieve salvation through the subject is now forced to contemplate the frightful prospect that no salvation is possible without the wholesale abnegation of the subject itself, the most privileged category of its entire system" ("Schopenhauer and the Aesthetic," 17).
23. As Tilottama Rajan and David L. Clark argue, "Schopenhauer is himself divided on the nature and goal of aesthetic representation, at once affirming art as a metaphysically independent category, a triumph over life, *and* demystifying art as a sublimatory fiction projected upon the abyss" ("Speculations: Idealism and its Rem(a)inders," in *Intersections: Nineteenth-Century Philosophy and Contemporary Theory*, ed. Tilottama Rajan and David L. Clark [Albany: SUNY Press, 1995], 31).
24. Eagleton, "Schopenhauer and the Aesthetic," 13.
25. See Schopenhauer, "On Suicide," in *Parerga and Paralipomena: Short Philosophical Essays*, vol. 2., trans. and ed. Adrian del Caro and Christopher Janaway (Cambridge: Cambridge University Press, 2015), 276–80. As Schopenhauer writes with deadpan irony, "Suicide can also be regarded as an experiment, a question one poses to nature and to which one tries to force an answer, namely what change in the existence and cognition of human beings is experience through death. But it is a clumsy one, since it suspends the identity of the consciousness that would have to hear the answer" (ibid., 280).
26. Such thoughts are "often unbearable to us" because they "lie[ ] for the most part not in the real present" (*WWR* 1:299). For Schopenhauer, "Real soundness of mind consists in the perfect recollection [of the past]" (*WWR* 2:399).

27. Elsewhere I have explored how *WWR* must speak what it cannot know and, in telling, expose more than it knows without then having, or by no more desiring, access to this knowledge. See Joel Faflak, "Schopenhauer's Telling Body of Philosophy," in *Idealism without Absolutes: Philosophy and Romantic Culture*, ed. Tilottama Rajan and Arkady Plotnitsky (Albany: SUNY Press, 2004), 161–80.
28. Thacker, "Philosophy in Ruins," 12.
29. Robert Smith, *Derrida and Autobiography* (New York: Cambridge University Press, 1995), 19. Smith argues that philosophy is essentially autobiographical, telling its own identity in order to eliminate the chance or contingency that threatens its rational borders.
30. Maurice Blanchot writes that anticipating the cure of analysis "amounts to saying that one must wait for the end of the story and the supreme contentment that is the equivalent of death." This means that analysis is "always both 'finite and infinite.' When it begins, it begins without end. The person who submits to analysis enters into a movement whose terms are unforeseeable and into a reasoning whose conclusion brings with it ... the impossibility of concluding" (*The Infinite Conversation Blanchot*, trans. Susan Hanson [Minneapolis: University of Minnesota Press, 1993], 236).
31. Sonu Shamdasani writes, "Philosophical systems, which purported to portray the constitution of the world, were in fact involuntary confessions of the psychological peculiarities of their authors" (*Jung and the Making of Modern Psychology: The Dream of a Science* [Cambridge: Cambridge University Press, 2003], 60).
32. Stanley Corngold, "On Death and the Contingency of Criticism: Schopenhauer and de Man," in Rajan and Clark, *Intersections*, 364.
33. Julia Kristeva, *Strangers to Ourselves*, trans. Leon S. Roudiez (New York: Columbia University Press, 1991), 1.
34. Sigmund Freud, *Beyond the Pleasure Principle*, vol. 18, *The Standard Edition of the Complete Psychological Works of Sigmund Freud*, 23 vols., trans James Strachey (London: Hogarth Press, 1953–1974; London: Vintage, 2001), 49–50. See Patrick Gardiner, *Schopenhauer* (Bristol: Thoemmes Press, 1963); R. K. Gupta, "Freud and Schopenhauer," *Journal of the History of Ideas*, 36.4 (October/December 1975): 721–28; Sebastian Gardner, "Schopenhauer, Will, and the Unconscious," in *The Cambridge Companion to Schopenhauer*, ed. Christopher Janaway (Cambridge: Cambridge University Press, 1999), 375–421; Christopher Young and Andrew Brook, "Schopenhauer and Freud," *International Journal of Psychoanalysis* 75 (1994): 101–18.
35. *Wille* entrenches itself in the very materiality of things, in the first instance the body as the crucible in which the will comes to make itself visible to itself, to know itself *as* representation. Schopenhauer writes: "the whole body must be nothing but my will become visible" (*WWR* 1:107).
36. Gilles Deleuze, *The Logic of Sense*, ed. Constantin V. Boundas, trans. Mark Lester and Charles Stivale (New York: Columbia University Press, 1993), 111.
37. In this way, incompossibility derives partly from Deleuze and Guattari's notion of schizoanalysis, which critiques Freudian and post-Freudian psychoanalysis as evincing the logic of late capitalism, of the unconscious or desire as tools of a capitalist psyche. In *Anti-Oedipus* and later *A Thousand Plateaus*, they explore the unconscious, not as the inscrutable territory to be colonized and mapped through the authoritative and restrictive concepts of psychoanalysis, primarily the Oedipus Complex, but as the infinitely complex, differential, and heterogeneous space of a psychic production deterritorializing capitalist claims. See Gilles Deleuze and Félix Guattari, *Anti-Oedipus: Capitalism and Schizophrenia*, vol. 1, trans. Robert Hurley, Mark Seem, and Helen R. Lane (Minneapolis: University of Minnesota Press, 1983); and *A Thousand Plateaus: Capitalism and Schizophrenia*, trans. Brian Massumi (Minneapolis: University of Minnesota Press, 1987).
38. Claire Colebrook, "Disjunctive Synthesis," in *The Deleuze Dictionary*, rev. ed., ed. Adrian Parr (Edinburgh: Edinburgh University Press, 2010), 80. See also Deleuze, *Difference and Repetition*, trans. Paul Patton (London: Athlone Press, 1994).

39. Freud, *Beyond the Pleasure Principle*, 46.
40. Cited in Russell Jacoby, "When Freud Came to America," *The Journal of Higher Education*, vol. 21 (September 2009), http://www.chronicle.com/article/Freuds-Visit-to-Clark-U/48424.
41. Bersani, 25.
42. Jacques Lacan, *The Sinthome: The Seminar of Jacques Lacan, Book XXIII*, ed. Jacques-Alain Miller, trans. A.R. Price (Medford, MA: Polity Press, 2018), 3.
43. Slavoj Žižek, *The Sublime Object of Ideology* (New York: Verso, 1989), 75.
44. Ibid., 75.
45. Nicholas Abraham and Maria Torok, "Mourning *or* Melancholia: Introjection *versus* Incorporation," in *The Shell and the Kernel: Renewals of Psychoanalysis*, ed. and trans. Nicholas T. Rand (Chicago: University of Chicago Press, 1994), 127.
46. Ibid., 130.
47. The term "distributed cognition" is usually attributed to Edwin Hutchins, *Cognition in the Wild* (1995). "Distributed cognition" is a general signifier for recent accounts of cognition as at once embodied in our individual sensoria and extended into and an extension of our lived environments. The work of thought suspended between will and representation I take to be both signifier and matrix of this expansive, viral terrain. See also David J. Chalmers, *The Conscious Mind: In Search of a Fundamental Theory* (Oxford: Oxford University Press, 1996) and Andy Clark, *Supersizing the Mind: Embodiment, Action, and Cognitive Extension* (Oxford: Oxford University Press, 2011).
48. Thacker, "Philosophy in Ruins," 38. Thacker's phrase "ugly feelings" may be a nod to Sianne Nagai, *Ugly Feelings* (Cambridge, MA: Harvard University Press, 2007).
49. A key contemporary source for this exploration is the work of Silvan Tomkins. See Eve Kosofsky and Adam Frank's editing of Tomkins' work in *Shame and Its Sisters: A Silvan Tomkins Reader* (Durham, NC: Duke University Press, 1995). Such work *does* take a more poststructuralist approach to the study of affect as a kind of implicit critical riposte to studies of the economics of happiness. See my "Can't Buy Me Love: Psychiatric Capitalism and the Economics of Happiness," in *The Economy as Cultural System: Theory, Capitalism, Crisis*, ed. Todd Dufresne and Clara Sacchetti (New York: Bloomsbury, 2013), 35–50.
50. Sara Ahmed, *The Promise of Happiness* (Durham, NC: Duke University Press, 2004), 30, 40.
51. Lauren Berlant, *Cruel Optimism* (Durham, NC: Duke University Press, 2011).
52. For Vivavsan Soni, the eighteenth century encrypts the impossibility of happiness within something like the trial narrative as a guidebook for overcoming failure. See Soni, *Mourning Happiness: Narrative and the Politics of Modernity* (Ithaca: Cornell University Press, 2010). Speaking of terror, Slavoj Žižek argues that happiness has become our "supreme duty" (*In Defence of Lost Causes* [New York: Verso, 2008], 40), which we accept, Brian Massumi suggests, as terror's future affect—holding out the carrot of bliss and using the twin sticks of homeland security and capitalism to police and discipline our access to nirvana. See Massumi, "The Future Birth of the Affective Fact: The Political Ontology of Threat," in *The Affect Theory Reader*, ed. Melissa Gregg and Gregory J. Seigworth (Durham, NC: Duke University Press, 2010), 52–70.
53. Gary Greenberg, "The War on Unhappiness: Goodbye Freud, Hello Positive Thinking," *Harper's Magazine*, vol. 321, 1924 (2010): 27–35.
54. Timothy Morton, *Hyperobjects: Philosophy and Ecology After the End of the World* (Minneapolis: University of Minnesota Press, 2013).
55. Chris Washington, "Romanticism and Speculative Realism," *Literature Compass*, vol. 12, no. 9 (2015): 451.
56. Quentin Meillassoux, *After Finitude: An Essay on the Necessity of Contingency*, trans. Ray Brassier (London: Continuum, 2008), 5.
57. Ibid., 7.
58. Cited in Washington, "Romanticism and Speculative Realism," 450.
59. Meillassoux, *After Finitude*, 112.
60. Ibid., 10.

61. Washington, "Romanticism and Speculative Realism," 450.
62. Thacker, "Philosophy in Ruins," 49.
63. Ibid., 51.
64. Ibid.
65. Ibid.
66. Theodor Adorno, *Minima Moralia: Reflections on a Damaged Life*, trans. E. F. N. Jephcott (London: Verso, 2005).
67. Maurice Blanchot, *The Writing of the Disaster*, trans. Anne Smock (Lincoln: University of Nebraska Press, 1986), 7.
68. Ibid., 40.
69. Jacques Derrida, "My Changes/*Mes Chances*: A Rendezvous with Some Epicurean Stereophonics," trans. Irene Harvey and Avital Ronell, in *Taking Chances: Derrida, Psychoanalysis and Literature*, ed. Joseph H. Smith and William Kerrigan (Baltimore: Johns Hopkins University Press, 1984), 28.
70. Jacques Derrida, *Resistances of Psychoanalysis*, trans. Peggy Kamuf, Pascale-Anne Brault, and Michael Naas (Stanford: Stanford University Press, 1998), 86, 118.
71. Tony Kushner, *Angels in America: A Gay Fantasia on National Themes*, rev. ed. (New York: Theatre Communications Group, 2013), 285.
72. David. L. Clark, "'The Necessary Heritage of Darkness': Tropics of Negativity in Schelling, Derrida, and de Man," in Rajan and Clark, *Intersections*, 110.

Part II
Themes and Concepts

Systems of Knowledge

Tilottama Rajan

1 Introduction

In the *Critique of Pure Reason*, Kant describes system as making "ordinary cognition" a "science" and distinguishes systems as "architectonic" from "aggregates" that are "heaped together." To naturalize system as "the unity of manifold cognitions under one idea," Kant also uses the figure of the "animal body" as a part-whole integrity: it "can grow internally," but not "externally (*per appositionem*)" by adding a part,[1] as lesser organisms like plants or polypi do. The term "architectonic" evokes architecture: a "conservative" discipline that represents building "to itself as complete, secure" and grounded.[2] It also tellingly streamlines the figure of the body, which it conceives structurally and anatomically rather than physiologically; for the "anatomical system," as Hegel comments, confines itself to "shape" rather than interiors—"processes," "particulars," and "the living organism."[3] Or as Schelling says, in criticizing Kant for favoring mathematics as a basis for philosophy, it is as if "one preferred a stereometrically regular crystal to the human body" because it "has no possibility of falling ill."[4]

Kant may seem to open system to process in the *Critique of Judgment* (*CJ*), where he discusses organisms more extensively as living wholes that cannot be explained mechanically, drawing on his notions of architectonic and part-whole integration in ways that could reflect back on systems. Novalis in his *Romantic Encyclopedia* (1798) describes this feedback loop as the "appli[cation]" of one science to another for which "it serves as the analogous model and stimulus" as the "encyclopedization" of this science, which results in the "self-(post)development" of both sciences.[5] But Kant's aim in *CJ* is to develop purposiveness as a regulative

T. Rajan (✉)
Centre for Theory and Criticism, University of Western Ontario, London, ON, Canada
e-mail: trajan@uwo.ca

© The Author(s), under exclusive license to Springer Nature Switzerland AG 2023
T. Rajan, D. Whistler (eds.), *The Palgrave Handbook of German Idealism and Poststructuralism*, Palgrave Handbooks in German Idealism,
https://doi.org/10.1007/978-3-031-27345-2_10

idea with implications for domains like history; it is not to institute biology as a "science," as philosophical historians of science sometimes claim.[6] Hence, he does not apply his hypothesis about organisms back to his notion of system, which happens in later thinkers like Bertalanffy, who makes "organismic" (rather than "molecular") biology the basis for a theory of open systems opposed to the closed systems of classical physics.[7] Arguably, such open systems too are self-rebalancing or homeostatic, whereas the reverse is true in Schelling's *First Outline of a System of the Philosophy of Nature* (*FO*), where life's "excitability" means that when an imbalance of forces is temporarily stabilized, because "organic activity" is constantly in a "state of configuration" and cannot be "exhausted in its product," this balance once more returns to disequilibrium.[8] Developing from Ludwig von Bertalanffy's Systems Theory, Umberto Maturana and Francesco Varela's characterization of organisms/systems as "autopoietic" remains a complexification of Kant's theory of organisms as self-organizing wholes and holds back from seeing them as more deconstructively autogenetic.[9] However, these self-(post)developments are foreign to Kant, who eschews disciplinary transferences as dialectical and fallacious, and whose mode, when dealing with more than one field, is analogy, not "application" or isomorphism, as we see in his critique of the false projections underpinning natural theology in *CJ*.[10] Furthermore, in *CJ* the apposition of aesthetic and teleological judgment protects organisms as self-organizing wholes within aesthetics as "the art of thinking beautifully."[11] It thus shields them from Schelling's more dangerous notion that "an individual body part, like the eye, is only possible in the whole of an organism" but has a "freedom" and "life for itself," evident in "the disease of which it is capable."[12] Similarly, in the metabiotic systems developed by Second-Order Systems Theory, technology (like aesthetics in Kant) reregulates the unruliness of biology; hence, I will not turn to systems theory when approaching system deconstructively rather than post-structurally,[13] and in Hegel's words, as an "organism" rather than an "aggregate."[14]

Kant's understanding of systems as what Bruno Latour calls "smooth" and "risk-free" rather than "tangled" entities[15] comes under increasing pressure as post-Kantian thought moves from using nature analogically and ideally to the study of real nature(s) as part of the system of philosophy. Given that "system" can apply to many things, this chapter focalizes the issues of openness/closure, connections, and feedback loops raised by a shift from architectural to living systems through Idealism's attempt to systemize knowledge, and specifically sciences or fields that have a separate freedom with ramifications for the whole. Hegel does indeed lay out his system architectonically (unlike Schelling), though with a uniquely "baroque" complexity of divisions and subdivisions.[16] But the singular innovation of post-Kantian thinkers is to reconfigure system as subject, to adapt Žižek's variation on Hegel's claim that substance is subject,[17] which in turn reflects the growing importance of the category "life," and particularly "organized" life, in the nineteenth century. In extending Žižek's comments from Schelling's system of freedom to *knowledge*, I therefore take up system in terms of the "encyclopedia," a term used by numerous German thinkers including Hegel, who, in his *Encyclopedia of the Philosophical Sciences*, distinguishes the philosophical (and German) encyclopedia from "ordinary encyclopedias." These "other" alphabetic encyclopedias also have the organization of knowledge and elaboration of sciences as an aim, but are "assemblage[s]"[18]; they are multiauthored, multiuse resources of *information* rather than a cycle of *knowledge* composed by and for a single subject.

Derrida describes the philosophical rather than empirical encyclopedia as an ideological state apparatus still dominant in his own university context. Invoking Kant, he refers to a "whole architecture" of knowledge[19] where disciplines confirm each other through their isomorphic synchronization: "an onto-encyclopedic *universitas*," "the *cycle* of the pedagogy covering the complete circle of knowledge and all the regions of being" through a "systematics" determining "the field of the so-called regional disciplines and sciences" as philosophical sciences.[20] For Derrida, Hegel's *Encyclopedia*, given its comprehensiveness and its narrative of spirit's departure from and return into itself, epitomizes this system as an "onto- and auto-encyclopedic circle of the State," "an immense school, the thoroughgoing auto-encyclopedia of absolute spirit and absolute knowledge."[21]

To be sure Hegel does project his system as a "circle of circles," whose spheres of knowledge are individual systems gathered into a preestablished harmony. And in his 1803/4 lectures *On University Studies* (*OUS*), inflected by the identity philosophy, Schelling uses a Spinozist model in which different fields are modes or emanations of one substance which is primordial knowledge.[22] The shared project of unifying knowledge is evident in an 1802 essay which both philosophers claimed and which uses Hegelian alongside Schellingian-Spinozist terminology in claiming that "different philosophical sciences are only presentations of the one undivided whole of philosophy under different conceptual determinations–or,... 'powers.'"[23] But as Žižek elaborates, system in German Idealism "includes/contains its own inversion" in which a "subordinate moment of the Absolute" can "posit itself as its own Center."[24] Or as Hegel himself writes, the circle that "remains self-enclosed and, like substance, holds its moments together" is unsurprising; but that an "accident" unbound "from what circumscribes it" can attain "a separate freedom—this is the tremendous power of the negative" and "energy of thought."[25]

Given the many "shapes" Hegelian spirit works through in those texts with the form of a narrativized phenomenology (including the *Aesthetics*, *PN*, and the three-part *Encyclopedia* itself), and given the system's mixed historical-transcendental nature, Hegel's encyclopedic project contains major diremptions. Kant limits the encyclopedia to "a short abstract of the whole of knowledge," but Hegel's system is both a reduction to the concept in the Encyclopedia *Outlines* (1817, 1827, 1830) and a more "wide-ranging system"[26] in lectures that unfold system as subject. For instance, though Hegel gave his lectures on *Aesthetics* from 1818 to 1829, the crucial terms "Symbolic" and "Romantic" are not used until the last *Outline*. As if to rectify the problems caused by the *Aesthetics*, they are then reduced to two paragraphs and neutralized as deviations within a typology centered in a normative conception of art as "perfection" and "beauty" achieved in the Classical.[27] But in the actual lectures, Symbolic, Classical, and Romantic form a labor of the negative in which art fails in the Symbolic because the Idea is still "indeterminate," then achieves "the adequate embodiment of the Idea" in the Classical, but then abandons this "cut and dried" perfection in the Romantic. As the impossibility of expressing the Idea or "inwardness" in material form, the Romantic "reverts" to the "distraction and dissonance" of the Symbolic "even if in a higher way."[28] In this elaboration, history up-ends what is commonly stereotyped as the Hegelian dialectic by displacing the synthesis from the end to the middle. Hegel presses beyond the resulting dys-synthesis by arguing that art is surpassed in philosophy, yet philosophy also proves unsuccessful, as the chronicle-structure of Hegel's *History of Philosophy* (1805–1830) impedes the reduction of multiple systems into a dialectical unity. Indeed history, an epistemic form avoided by Kant, repeatedly compromises the subordination of the empirical to the transcendental. Moreover, these lectures problematically end with Schelling, whose work Hegel criticizes for beginning again and again, not being "a scientific whole," and making philosophy "art" rather than science.[29]

Thus, the superfold of the absolute system is arguably a protective cover for exploring interior folds and convolutes that trouble the overall schema. The navigation of the system, whether as a baroque architectonic or a "long passage" with byways, unfolds "the living Substance" as "*Subject*," which is "the mediation of its self-othering with itself." Exploiting the multivalence of the term, Hegel further sees this "subject" as having "predicates" and "accidents." He thus embeds "differences" in the very syntax of thought, as a process wherein "we learn by experience that we meant something other than what we meant to mean."[30] In a deconstructive reading more sympathetic to Hegel than Derrida's, Nancy cites Hegel's own call for "a philosophical exposition" that achieves "plasticity" by excluding the "usual" syntagmatic "way of relating the parts of a proposition." Nancy discusses this hermeneutic of plasticity at three levels: the individual word—citing Hegel's claim that German is unique in having words (like *Aufhebung* or *Abgrund*) that contain "different but opposite meanings"; the proposition as subject to what Hegel calls a "counterthrust"; and the very *Satz-Zusatz* structure in which propositions (the main points published in the Encyclopedia *Outlines*) are complicated in lectures by *Zusätze* (included in the eclectic texts produced by K. L. Michelet and others for the collected edition of Hegel in the 1840s). "An economy of Remarks" thus "double[s] up the economy of logical discourse... a subordinated, 'detached,' dispersed economy that does not obey the strict progression of the concept."[31]

The systems of Hegel and Schelling ambitiously range across philosophy, history, nature, religion, medicine, and anthropology (which in the *Encyclopedia* contains further folds on topics like mesmerism). The extensiveness of these systems—one could equally include that of Schopenhauer[32]—makes them thought-environments where plasticity also operates between their largest units: the philosophical sciences that both thinkers explored from their Jena years onward, but that cannot be organized syntagmatically as a "road."[33] Given both thinkers' reconfiguration of philosophy from Kant's precautionary placement of it as a lower faculty to a power whose provenance is "all things,"[34] a further issue is philosophy's relation to its others, which Derrida formulates as the problem of "translation." Reducing Schelling and Idealism to *OUS*, which congregates several fields across the arts and sciences (but is only one form of systemization Schelling constructed), Derrida grants Schelling's philosophy a certain diversity. But he reproaches Schelling for an (onto)theology of translation whose differences are "translations... of the *same*." Derrida insists that epistemic domains are distinct: "That is why *one must translate*."[35] Absolute idealism can indeed slide into a Romantic absolute that swallows difference in a plenitudinous dissemination, as in Novalis' "encyclopedistics," which involves an "infinite versability," a lateral, if not hierarchical, *"translatability of everything into everything."*[36] Novalis' undeveloped Schlegelian fragments have no "subject" as they rhizomatically surf the (inter)disciplines. But his distinctly un-Kantian mereology does describe a plasticity that also operates in the more extensive work of Hegel and Schelling, and which involves an "[a]pplication of the system to the parts—and the parts to the *system* and the parts to the parts."[37] This refocalizing of the whole through parts that are not simply determinations of the notion but sites for reflection means that the (non)identity of philosophy may be rethought through art, and that the systems of physiology can be applied to the very functioning of knowledge as a living system. Translation, in other words, is at the heart of these systems, which gives a whole different meaning to Derrida's "auto-encyclopedia" of spirit. For the encyclopedia becomes the *autobiography* rather than totalizing of philosophy: the *experience* consciousness goes through in encountering the differences opened up by the ontological identities and imperatives of the different disciplines or "shapes" (aesthetics, politics, biology) in which it tries to grasp philosophy.

2 Kant

I begin with Kant, who provides the framework in which post-Kantian systems of knowledge extend and unravel the system of philosophy. Kant's equation of system and architectonic goes back well before the first Critique to his *Encyclopedia* lectures (1767–1782), where it takes form within the present topic: the encyclopedia as the problem posed by the proliferation of knowledge to the idea of "system." Without using the word "architectonic," Kant already distinguishes a system where "the idea of the whole precedes the parts" and which is requisite for science (*Wissenschaft*), from a mere "aggregate," whose parts precede the whole. Correspondingly, he divides knowledge into a priori sciences of reason (*Vernunftwissenschaften*) based on insight, including mathematics and philosophy, and historical knowledge (*Kentniss*), which is assembled a posteriori based on learning, and whose "organon" is philology. Each type of knowledge has its form of excess: "pansophy" immodestly claims to grasp all *Vernunftwissenschaften*, while the infinite expansion of historical knowledge results in "polyhistory."[38] Kant's division remains initially crucial for Schelling, whose *OUS* separates "rational" (or sometimes "absolute") from "historical" or "positive" knowledge, while also more idealistically wanting to synchronize the two by making the temporal a mode of the eternal and the real a mode of the ideal.[39] It is the core of how Hegel defines philosophical sciences, which "exclude" "pseudosciences" and "mere assemblages of information," though Hegel also follows Kant in crediting some "positive" sciences like law with a "rational" and noncontingent part, a "pure part" that "belongs to philosophy."[40]

In his many introductions, Kant divides and maps the field of knowledge, with an increasing concern to delimit a pure philosophy, especially since as late as 1798 "philosophy" is both a *Fachwissenschaft* (special discipline) and a broader faculty divided into "historical" as well as "rational" knowledge that includes philosophy.[41] Kant's own corpus goes well beyond "sciences" (in the older sense of *Wissenschaft*) that provide his ideal for philosophy and meet his criteria of "interconnection of grounds and consequences" and "apodictic" certainty, without which a field like chemistry remains an "art."[42] In an environment before the disaggregation of disciplines, Kant's corpus was contingently shaped by having to teach in different disciplines and waiting many years to secure a Chair in Logic and Metaphysics. He therefore engaged with history, geography, and soft sciences like biology. Yet unlike Hegel, who says philosophy must be "encyclopedic" to be "systematic,"[43] Kant is continuously anxious about the encyclopedic. His Introductions therefore try to delimit a more precise philosophy by constructing knowledge as a striated rather than tangled space. Kant describes two kinds of introduction: "propaedeutic" introductions "distinguish the principles proper to" a "doctrine" from "those which belong to another one (*peregrinis*)," thus "determining the boundaries between sciences," while "encyclopedic" introductions place the doctrine "into a system," which must be "complete" and not the result of "rummaging about and gathering up" bits of knowledge. Kant's Introductions are encyclopedic only in the sense of outlining this larger system to then focus on the a priori place of a part within it. He eschews disciplinary border-crossing, though engaging in it himself as a regulative rather than constitutive tool,[44] and wants to divide knowledge "logic[ally]" "into certain compartments… even before it is attained."[45]

The early lectures on *Physical Geography* (from 1856 onward) show Kant having to begin on the wrong side of the rational/empirical divide. Describing knowledge as derived either from "pure reason" or "experience" (meaning "perceptions"), Kant subdivides experience into knowledge based on the outer senses (geography and history, related to space and time) versus knowledge based on the inner sense (anthropology or "soul or human being"); together these comprise "knowledge of the world." The lectures on "physical" geography contain an "aggregation" of empirical information from "natural history" (more accurately called *Naturbeschreibung*, as Kant inaugurates a questioning of the term "natural history").[46] They exhibit the threat posed by empirical knowledge to system, which can be handled only by quarantining such knowledge in a compartment of a larger "architectonic," which is what compels Kant in his 1786 *Metaphysical Foundations of Natural Science* (*MF*) to more rigorously define natural science and redeem a part of it for philosophy. Thus, in *MF*, Kant superimposes his distinction between rational and historical knowledge onto the lower part of this binary (knowledge from experience), postulating "rational" and "historical" parts in both subdivisions of the historical/empirical division. Anthropology becomes the historical part of knowledge from the inner senses, while morals/ethics is the rational part. For knowledge

Systems of Knowledge 193

of the outer senses, in *MF* itself Kant wants to abstract a "pure" part from the natural/physical sciences, insisting that there can only be "as much proper science" in these domains "as there is mathematics therein." Though he cannot admit natural history or chemistry into the sanctum,[47] and is thus unsure of having vicariously achieved apodictic certainty for philosophy either, Kant here lays the ground for Hegel's expansionist (rather than limitative) inclusion of positive sciences that have a rational as well as a contingent part in his philosophical encyclopedia.

Returning to the problems posed by *Physical Geography*—which Kant keeps displacing throughout his career by redrawing his divisions—this Introduction is also revealing because Kant's procedure of division penumbrally includes what it excludes. As he zones in on "physical" geography, his curiosity leads him to sketch "other possible geographies": mathematical, moral, political, mercantile, and theological. Not only do they involve the border-crossings Kant eschews; through the projection of geography and history onto each other and other domains, they allow for the self(post)-development of further sciences (resembling what we now call "cultural studies"). Moreover, Kant also identifies further subdivisions of physical geography itself: topography, chorography, orography, and hydrography.[48] Or as Schelling writes, elevating this proliferation to a principle, since "Nature… contain[s] an infinity," when it forms spheres (of knowledge) "other spheres are again formed, and in these spheres others."[49]

3 Hegel

To avoid this polyscientific spread, in the Critical period Kant increasingly turns from objects of knowledge to method, or the transcendental field of the relation between the faculties employed, to make "experience" into a "system." Ideally, every science has "its determinate position in the encyclopedia of the sciences" which must contain "*a priori* the principle of a complete division." But this total encyclopedia being so elusive, in the critiques Kant focuses instead on "all faculties of the mind that are determinable *a priori*," allowing him to make the Introduction to *CJ* both "propaedeutic" to judgment and retrospectively "encyclopedic" in placing it within a complete division of a "system in the mind."[50] By contrast, Hegel's goal is a system of the sciences themselves. The Jena drafts show him already working with the broad divisions of logic, nature, and mind constituting the *Encyclopedia* with its pansophical ambitions. From these drafts, through the Nürnberg *Propaedeutic* (1808–11), Hegel is interested in disciplines, providing what looks like a complete division in the *Encyclopedia*. But in the Berlin years, through the additional lecture-series on religion, history, art, and the history of philosophy, the system expands into polyhistory, granted that Hegel wants to reclaim the "rational" and noncontingent core of polyhistory for philosophy, by narrativizing these histories as a transition from necessity to freedom. This narrative, in which "the idea" departs from and "returns to itself from its otherness," is also that projected for the *Encyclopedia* itself as an envelope for all the separately developed modules of the system.[51]

Theoretically, Hegel adheres to Kant's notion of what constitutes a "philosophical" science and his view of the encyclopedia as an architectonic where each area has its a priori place. However, the narrative form makes Hegel's *Encyclopedia* not just a "chart" of disciplines[52] but a labour of the negative vulnerable to failure. For Hegel's work is more content-specific than Kant's, and his architectonic is more intricate. Hegel also applies Kant's theory of organisms back to the functioning of systems and makes the organism a subject of *PN* in ways that release its autoimmunity, as Kant's logic of the organism becomes a bio-logic. Echoing Kant, Hegel writes that a system must be an "organism," not an "aggregate," but *PN* is rather the story of nature's *attempt* to achieve the Kantian organism. Moreover, as we shall see, in personifying spirit in its struggle with a nature that is the "negative of the idea,"[53] Hegel often makes biology (including physiology) a proxy for psychology, which is why this text is an autobiography of the system. As Robert Smith suggests, in discussing Hegel and Derrida, autobiography exceeds "subjectivity," which can still be contained within "philosophical method." Autobiography is the "dehiscence of the literary into the philosophical," the damage that remains "long after the subjective has been taken up… into the universal," "throwing it into disarray."[54]

For present purposes, I focus on *PN*, because it is the most autobiographical of Hegel's texts: a "weak link" in the system that "produces things contrary to [the system's] norm," stranded as it is in nature as the "negative" of the Idea.[55] Kant's discussion of the organism provides Hegel with both *telos* and method. Kant conceived organisms as integrities whose parts support and produce each other in a self-organizing whole, a norm Hegel can evoke only negatively when he describes as "disease" what occurs when one of the organism's "systems" "establishes itself in isolation" and persists "against the activity of the whole."[56] The Kantian organism as *Naturzweck* (natural purpose) is both "end" and "means," both "cause and effect of itself," such that "the thing which is… an effect" is also "in ascent… a cause of the same thing of which it is the effect."[57] Hegel echoes much of this language in *PN*, where the animal is distinguished from the vegetable organism as both means and "end," both "product and also productive," and where nature further comprises a *"system of stages"* narrativized as developing toward this idea(l).[58] These graduated stages, or *Stufenfolge* in Schelling's term, realize purposiveness not "in the individual but in the whole" or genus-process, "through continuous deviations from a common ideal."[59] In Hegel's dialectical tightening of the paradigm, especially once we get to "Organics," each stage resolves a contradiction in its antecedent, or as Samuel Taylor Coleridge says, the *"Princip. Individui* in every Animal finds itself incomplete [or] incompletely finds itself," so that "parts are seen" whose purpose is "realized higher up in the scale."[60] As such, a higher stage is also "in ascent" the teleological cause of the earlier stage of which it is the effect. For Alison Stone, who sees Hegel as successfully executing this *Aufhebung*, *PN* is therefore a "strong a priori" reading of nature that combines philosophy and nature in increasingly close "constellations of concept/matter relations" as it moves up the chain of being.[61]

Both Hegel and Schelling admit that this "system of grades of which one arises necessarily from the other" is not a natural evolution but an "idea" of "reason" (in Kant's sense).[62] But it is an "Idea" Hegel struggles to realize. For as Coleridge says, in a highly apposite comment, "life" is not "mind." Mind is complete in itself as "a Subject possessing its object in itself," whereas life is "a Subject" with a "tendency to produce an Object, wherein and whereby to *find* itself," and is incomplete and lacking.[63] In *PN*, Hegel produces nature as an object in which "philosophy" struggles to recognize itself, an "alien existence, in which Spirit does not find itself" except through part-objects, in psychoanalytic terminology.[64] As the working through of these partial "shapes" of consciousness, *PN* has the form of a phenomenology, or rather what Gasché calls a phantasmatology. In the *Phenomenology*, as Paul Ricoeur says, "consciousness" is "directed toward another" that "is lacking to it," while "spirit," though "complete within itself," falls short of this completeness till the final moment. Until then the *Phenomenology* "keeps a moment of intentionality" involving "pain, separation,... or the distance of the self from itself." *PN* is likewise a phenomenology of "mind" or "spirit" "*in* the milieu of consciousness," and never reaches this vanishing moment, ending instead with the dissolution of the organism. Indeed, though Ricoeur sees the *Encyclopedia* as overcoming phenomenology through a "contraction of [phenomenology's] space" into just one section of its last part,[65] the entire encyclopedia project, as it ramifies through Hegel's lectures, remains a phenomenology.

For while *PN* is widely seen as positing a logical rather than natural evolution, what is not emphasized is that Hegel casts this evolution as a *Stufenfolge* of sciences. He thus makes the "history of nature" a "preface [to] the history of man" and its knowledge "a branch of self-knowledge," as Coleridge's collaborator J. H. Green puts it. This "physiogony" (Green's term in responding to Idealism's desire to move beyond the "misnomer" natural history, which is a mere aggregate, to something more purposive[66]) provides for Hegel the underpinning for the evolution of disciplines as an idea of Reason. The focus on disciplines is already evident in the *Phiosophical Propaedeutic*, a skeleton that names several sciences: geometry, geology, oryctognosy, and medicine. It becomes increasingly detailed in the *Encyclopedia*, where *PN* has three large divisions: Mechanics (initially, Mathematics), Physics, and Organics (with their further subdivisions). Developing his view of system as an organism, Hegel applies Kant's syllogism of the reciprocity of cause and effect in organisms to the very organization of systematic knowledge, such that each stage in *PN* is "the proximate truth of the stage from which it results," as "each sphere... complete[s] itself" and passes into a "higher one." The whole of "nature" then becomes one "circle" in the larger circle of philosophy, where each "member" also has "an antecedent and a successor,"[67] as we proceed to the *Philosophy of Mind*. The Kantian organic logic is what allows for the structure described by Petry, where disciplines that are "spheres" in themselves, containing "levels and hierarchies," are supposedly sublated into "more comprehensive spheres" where "they are simply levels arranged as hierarchies," thus providing the organizational principle Hegel calls "the Notion."[68]

However, the double-remove from nature itself into the disciplines by which mind organizes nature concedes the idealism, even solipsism, of Hegel's project. For contrary to received wisdom, Hegel does not cross Kant's regulative/constitutive boundary, since he deals with nature only as it appears to us in the shapes through which we approach it, some of which are not yet "sciences" yielding certain knowledge. But it would also be ingenuous to suggest that Hegel fully observes the Kantian precaution, since he does not hold the "Idea"—a word charged with affect—fully separate from nature, referring to "the inner idea lying at the base of nature."[69] Rather than positing the Idea transcendentally as an Idea *of* nature, *PN* makes it an Idea *in* nature, which becomes a scene of disappointment, as nature's "ever-increasing wealth of detail" proves "recalcitrant towards the unity of the Notion." Symptomatically, Hegel describes the sciences as "man's non-organic nature," something outside him which he must "make his own," or "devour," as he says more aggressively in the *Phenomenology*, but which remains inorganically inside him. Throughout *PN*, this struggle to "tak[e] possession" of sciences[70] in which the idea is the negative of itself is thematized in the difficulty of overcoming the persistence of the inorganic in nature itself, as we see in epistemic contact zones like geology and physiology.

As Hegel revised the schema of his *Encyclopedia* in his Tables of Contents, he increasingly emphasized "Organics." In the *Propaedeutic* and 1817 *Outline*, the first division is Mathematics, while Mechanics is under Physics. In 1827, Mechanics is demoted to being the first division, absorbing mathematics. The second division can then move more decisively away from any suspicion of a static, Newtonian physics to a more internally dynamic theory of matter—a goal already announced in *De Orbitis Planetarum* (1801).[71] Physics thus firmly leaves quantification behind. But the organic also becomes strongly separated from physics (and chemistry as a sphere within physics). For in 1817 the second and third divisions were called Physics of the Inorganic and Organic,[72] but in 1827 "Physics" disappears from the title of the third division, which is simply "Organics." As John Zammito comments, late eighteenth-century science shifted from mathematics to an "experimental physics" concerned with volatile forces and the problems "of 'organized form' or life."[73] Trying to regulate this "Proteus" nature, Hegel sought in Kant's theory of the organism as *Naturzweck* a *telos* that would bind the volatile forces unloosed by the new sciences within an ascension of life toward Mind. Hence, *PN* tries to proceed from the inorganic to the organic through entities like planets and plants to the animal organism. The animal as *telos* is, importantly, a body made up of interdependent "members" (*Glieder*) rather than separate "parts" (*Teile*). Where an organism composed of parts (like the plant) does not fully possess those parts, ideally in one composed of "members," as Stone puts it, the universal is revealed in the part(icular) so that the body is "intelligibly structured" throughout.[74]

In moving toward this ideal body, the 1827 *Encyclopedia* reschematizes Physics in dialectically progressive stages, as "Physics" of the "Universal," "Particular," and "Total Individuality." But it is not till the last subdivision of Organics that we arrive at the maximum of "individuation" and "integration," in Green's terms,[75] the animal organism as "*Selbstzweck*" or an "individuality" and "totality" that "internally develops into its differences." The emphasis on biology rather than physico-chemistry as the crowning science marks Hegel's decisive difference from British natural philosophy, which he dismisses for calling pumps and wood "philosophical instruments," but whose potential he also wants to activate in *PN* within an ascent of disciplines.[76] Hegel's argument with natural philosophy depends on the difference between major levels being "qualitative" rather than "quantitative," so that the animal (and then mind) is not just a higher intensity or potency of matter, as for Schelling. Instead, the stages of "Life" must be "qualitatively determined against each other." The higher stage must "posit," project, and abject the "lower" as "its non-organic nature, over against itself," lest these lower stages "destroy the organic."[77] In Organics, Hegel thus becomes increasingly anxious about chemistry, insisting that it "destroys the living organism" and deals "only with inanimate matter," though he also says that life is essentially chemical.[78] He struggles to protect what Georges Canguilhem calls the "originality" of the living being, but can do so only negatively, characterizing it as a "subject which preserves itself" by "negat[ing] the specific quality of the other,"[79] as biology must negate chemistry.[80]

But the problem with this "eliminative idealism"[81] is the doubling of levels and spheres in Hegel's encyclopedic system, which has troubling consequences given that nature is part of man's self-knowledge. Each sphere may be absorbed into a level in a hierarchy, but each level itself contains levels which are spheres in their own right, containing further actual and potential spheres at odds with this totalization. Thus, even as Hegel's macrosystems (of nature, art etc.) are panlogically compounded into larger unities, they are also particularized into specialized microsystems. The logic is that of Leibniz' *Monadology*, where the supreme Monad God (or absolute knowledge) guarantees the preestablished harmony of individual monads which, given this divine insurance, are subdivisible into further monads.[82] Or as Schelling puts it, similarly allowing *Naturphilosophie* to double as epistemology, even as nature is (de)limited into spheres, "within every sphere other spheres" are "formed, and in these spheres others."[83] Likewise in *PN*, where (going beyond Leibniz) this monadological deconstruction unfolds in an empirical and not just transcendental way, "Organics" is the final level in an ascending hierarchy. But as a sphere in its own right, it is subdivided into the "terrestrial," plant, and animal organisms, or, geology and geognosy, botany, and physiology. That Hegel studies the animal internally in terms of physiology, rather than externally and mechanically as anatomy, is already a problem, compounded by the fact that physiology contains pathology (and indeed is pathological throughout). Furthermore, though the levels of the organism form a hierarchy, there are rhizomatic connections between them that bring back earlier material, making the history of nature what Foucault calls a "counter-science"[84] that continuously aborts the philosophical subl(im)ation required by the Notion.

Thus, plant structures recur within us, in the ganglia or "sympathetic nerves," which Hegel approaches through his contemporary Xavier Bichat's discussion of a double life in the animal: waking and sleeping, animal and "organic" (meaning vegetative), and "connect[ed] with an other" versus "quiescent."[85] As Roberto Esposito says of Bichat, this duality deals a "violent blow" to "the nucleus of will and reason" in "the consciousness-based tradition of modern thought."[86] Throughout the module on animal physiology Hegel draws on a handbook by the Tübingen professor J. H. Autenrieth (who treated Hölderlin in his asylum), but psychosomatizes Autenrieth's physiology. Thus, in following the "sensibility which has withdrawn into itself," Hegel discovers a "somnambulistic state, where… self-consciousness is turned inwards" and "passes… into the brain of a dark independent self-consciousness."[87] Nor can this material be left behind, despite the transition into a higher sphere at the end of *PN*, because, importantly, the animal in *PN* includes the human. This double life of the human across two parts of the *Encyclopedia* overlaps the philosophies of nature and mind, allowing animal somatology to return in the convolutes of anthropology and psychology, and preventing them from becoming pure sciences of spirit

Likewise, "bones" are a "dead force" that recalls "the wood of the plant."[88] But through bones the animal organism is looped back even further to the "petrified wood" of the terrestrial organism. Hegel places the earth sciences under Organics but sees the earth as "inorganic and inanimate (*unbegeistet*)," comparing its calcified and "stillborn" structures to "bone-fibres" that were never "veins or nerves."[89] This quasi-anthropomorphic account of the earth-organism—and the puzzling desire even to see it as an organism[90]—is preceded by the passage on the sciences as a resistance to the organic, and shows how difficult it is to find a "stirring… rationality" in the epistemic trauma of a science like "geognosy."[91] Hegel repeatedly cites Schelling's early account of nature as "petrified intelligence" or as unconsciously intelligent. But Schelling describes a smooth emergence of mind from nature, and the words "frozen" and "petrified" are Hegel's addition, reflecting his resistant Fichtean dualism of the I and Not-I.[92] Petrified intelligence also resonates curiously with the petrified wood of geology as the site of an unconscious in (human) nature that is nonvital, yet again "quiescent," what Sartre calls the practico-inert or deadweight of the past that cannot be released from its psychic rigidity and made "fluid in the universal," as is Hegel's norm for the fully organic body.[93] And yet, in the fully organic body, bones differ from wood only in experiencing "pathological changes," a significant difference to be sure, since only the animal can fall ill and be "turned against its structure," while a "stone" is just "chemically decomposed" in "the negative of itself."[94]

To fit science into philosophy, Hegel imposes the Notion and the dialectic on deeply resistant material like bones, or, further on, digestion and excretion. In Hegel's translation of physiology into philosophy, "digestion" involves "mediation," and allegorizes the process whereby the subject "assimilates" the external "non-organic being."[95] Assimilation is part of a metaphorics also linked to knowledge (as in "food for thought" or encyclopedias as "digests"). At the same time, this metaphorics is surreally defaced by the literal—yet emotionally overdetermined—account of excretion, in one of the most bizarre sections of *PN*. Technically, excretion is necessary to the digestive cycle, a process Bichat describes in terms of the linked functions of "assimilation" (the animal digesting what nourishes it) and "exhalation [and] secretions" that eliminate "heterogeneous substances."[96] The "Notion of digestion," according to Hegel, is that finally the organism "triumphs over the food," "comprehend[s]" itself, and "return[s] into itself" through excretion, which "preserv[es]" it as "self-identical." But Hegel's vivid account of this process autobiographically backfires on the very apparatus of mediation and translation/ transition that it wants to naturalize at the animal level. On the one hand, the animal does "not need to ingest anything ...superfluous" and so excrement consists "mainly of digested matter" which "the organism itself has added to the ingested material." On the other hand, Hegel concedes that excrement contains "undecomposed" food, forcing the animal to "get rid of, what it has itself produced," much of which is "unchanged," meaning that if we "apply" this part to the whole of the *Encyclopedia*, the *Encyclopedia* contains "indigestible material."[97] Failing to digest its material fully, and to sublate the literal into the metaphorical, the granular account of how food is broken down in digestion also involves a resurgence of chemistry within animal physiology, of a lower stage that threatens the higher with a "second death." This section is also studded with philosophically indecorous affective terms, as the organism, in the "disjunctive activity" of digestion, is "disgusted with itself," "angrily oppos[es] itself to the outer world," is ashamed of its "lack of self-confidence," and "divided within itself."[98]

Indeed, we can apply the categories of the *Aesthetics* to Hegel's metaphysical conceit of catachrestically extorting spirit from nature. For *PN* never achieves an "adequate embodiment" of its "Idea," a "conformity of concept and reality" reflected in a classical clarity of style. It is closer to the Symbolic, which Hegel characterizes as a state of "restless fermentation," a digestive process he also describes in *PN*. The Symbolic is caught in the "labour" of "producing its content and making it clear to itself," and "stretch[es]" the Idea "unnaturally" to grotesquely fit it into a "determinate... shape."[99] The section on digestion is followed by *PN*'s final section on disease, which poignantly sutures physiology and ontology together, generating a zone of indistinction between body, psyche, and mind that profoundly threatens the self-identity of philosophy. Hegel begins this section by saying that the "individual organism" can "as well not conform to its genus as preserve itself in it." As in Schelling's account of freedom as the disease wherein the individual member asserts a life of its own, for Hegel disease occurs when one of the organism's "systems or organs" is "stimulated into conflict with the inorganic power" and "establishes itself in isolation," obstructing "the fluidity... of the whole." The organism then exists "in the opposed forms of *being* and *self*," as the "negative of itself"[100]—a suitable culmination to Hegel's traversal of a nature in which the very Idea is the negative of itself, and a complete derailment of the schema in which this final division of Organics was given the Kantian designation "Teleology."[101] To rid himself of what he has himself produced, Hegel ends with the apocalyptic image of the phoenix which rises from its ashes, figuring how spirit, which in the Romantic mode exceeds embodiment in material form, breaks through the "husk" of nature.[102]

As this chapter suggests, *PN* is a profoundly reflexive moment, a *mise en abime* of Hegel's system, which reads the Idea against the grain, as the negative of itself. What possibilities, then, does it open up for systems? Systems are a topic throughout *PN*, and are part of a *Stufenfolge* that proceeds toward the "*absolute* organism" through "continuous deviations from [the] ideal." Yet the idea of system is what

Schelling calls an "invasion of Nature...through freedom," which "compel[s]" nature "to act under... conditions which... exist only as modified by others." Nature can "reply" to this "experiment,"[103] and does so by confronting Hegel with multiple systems. A crystal is not "mechanically compounded" but organic, and is "articulated through and through," thus meeting Hegel's criterion of a whole/universal present in each part(icular); but it is "rigid" and its molecular structure makes the parts uniform rather than differentiated.[104] In the planetary system—a frequent model for systems—there are a "number of earths or planets which together form an organic unity," each with its own center, though even here Hegel must account for the "eccentric motion" of comets, which have no "nucleus," and for the fact that the "body of dissolution" rather than "rigidity" "behaves *aberrantly*." Moreover, despite the Pythagorean harmony of the planetary system, its parts remain a "plurality" and are external to each other.[105] Higher up the scale, the plant grows from within and "differentiates itself into distinct parts," but overabundantly "sprout[s] from bud to bud." Rather than being "a subjective unity of members," it is "only the basis (*Boden*)" for "a number of individuals" and does not "attain to a relationship between individuals."[106] These arrangements suggest different models for system, all differently deficient in ways we can use to think about Hegel's own multicomponent system. The difficulty is that if one system is superior to another, it falls below it in another respect. Thus planets (covered under both Mechanics and Physics) achieve an "arrangement... in space" associated with volition, because it is "the act of the planets themselves." But the plant, discussed at the higher level of Organics, is "impotent to hold its members in its power,"[107] raising questions about the organic.

Hegel's ideal for systems is the "organism" rather than aggregate, by which he means the *animal* organism as a "whole" architectonically "present in each member." But going beyond Kant's purely structural use of the animal body, Hegel repeatedly emphasizes that as "life," the animal contains "profound differences" that "preserve themselves" in a "more intense diremption," yet are "held in a single subject." *PN* does not include man as a separate category, and zoologically the human is a subset of the animal. But Hegel's language—subjectivity, self, being—suggests that the animal often *is* the human, but as a natural, affected, and afflicted subject. Thus, when we reach the animal organism, its idea too can be presented only negatively as a failure to conform to its genus in disease.[108] That *PN*'s exploration of the organism ends with pathology rather than normal physiology bears out Canguilhem's claim that the "biologically normal" is "revealed only through infractions of the norm": this is the "originality" of the biological phenomenon.[109] In disease, an individual "system" retreats into a "hypochondria" of the self; the organism then inhabits "the opposed forms of *being* and *self*," where the "*self* is precisely *that* for which the negative of itself *is*."[110] But at this point the very unity and integrity of the animal body, which the plant avoids, also means that all its systems—nervous, digestive, circulatory—"interpenetrat[e]." The "isolated activity" that occurs when a member withdraws from the whole is therefore still a "moment of the whole," as the "entire organism" is "deranged because one wheel *(Rad)* in it has made itself the centre."[111] Aesthetics or biology cannot just be subtracted from the whole that is philosophy. If illness is a state of dys-synthesis between the organism and its physiological or disciplinary systems, Hegel faces a choice between the Scylla and Charybdis of chronic and acute illness. Because chronic illness "remains in one organ" and only this "organ is irritated or depressed," it is "easier to cure." On the other hand, it hangs on obstructively, leading Hegel to prefer a crisis in which the whole organism is "morbidly affected" and can be "cure[d]" by being kathartically "released" back into its fluidity through fever. Yet this cure too cannot be definitive, since the "disparity between [the organism's] finitude and universality is its *original disease* and the inborn *germ of death*."[112]

That Hegel ends the long road traveled in *PN* by admitting that disease is endemic to organic systems returns us to the pathos of philosophy as autobiography. Moving beyond Derrida, Catherine Malabou in *The Future of Hegel*[113] takes up the notion of plasticity, actually introduced by Nancy, though she differs in later developing it through neuroscience and regenerative medicine rather than Nancy's linguistics of literariness. In relation to Hegel's famous statement that the "wounds of the Spirit heal and leave no scars behind,"[114] Malabou proposes three hermeneutic "paradigms": the phoenix, tissue, and salamander. The first "dialectical" paradigm of the bird reborn from its ashes is Hegel's own deus ex machina in *PN*, by which he somersaults from the wreckage of nature into spirit. But we might better describe the phoenix as an *apocalyptic* figure that fantasizes an *Aufhebung* without remainder. In the second "deconstructive" figure of tissue as both biological and textile, "there are only scars," and thus no possibility for the Hegelian text to "self-regenerate," to return other than as a "ghost." Finally the salamander/hydra allows Hegel's texts to "reconstitute themselves from their deconstruction," and allows deconstruction itself to "return," again with no remainder.[115] Like Malabou, I differ from Derrida in "The Pit and the Pyramid" and *Glas*[116] in seeing the auto-deconstruction of Hegel's text as more than just a "spoliation of reason."[117] To use the biological concept Malabou adapts in discussing Kant,[118] this spoliation allows for an epigenesis in the very concept of system. The same could be said of Hegel's work more broadly: the system's deficits and obstructions generate new ideas of art and the writing of philosophy.[119] Its failed translations of one discipline into another also open new ways of knowing; thus, the projection of philosophy onto physiology in *PN* produces a "*psychical physiology*"[120] that both verges on psychoanalysis and allows us to read Hegel's own philosophy as a symptomatic body.[121] But if Hegel returns, it is not with the painless autopoiesis of Malabou's plasticity. Because system unfolds as subject, there will always be scars and lacunae attending future potentials.

4 Schelling

Schelling never produced an encyclopedia, but suggested *OUS* could function as one.[122] Like Hegel's *Aesthetics*, Schelling's *Philosophy of Art* (1804/5) is a mixed transcendental-historical encyclopedia of aesthetic modes (schematic, symbolic, and allegorical) and specific art forms and works, while the late *Philosophy of Mythology and Revelation* (*PMR*) is also encyclopedic in its subject matter and historical span.[123] Schelling also used the word "system" repeatedly, by which he did not mean something definitive and architectonic but an experimental hypothesis for unifying material. For before withdrawing from print in 1809, he published numerous outlines, "ideas for," and systems—terms that seem interchangeable; *FO* alone contains three "possible" systems. The multiplication of published texts and the retreat from publication (while producing drafts and lectures) are inverse ways of putting anything definitive under erasure. In the construction of a system, as Hegel observes, Schelling continually "began again from the beginning" because he was not "satisf[ied]," even thematizing beginning in three extant versions of *The Ages of the World* (1811, 1813, 1815). Hegel complains that because Schelling, at least initially, "worked out his philosophy" in "public," his writings are "the history of his philosophic development" and do not yield a "final work."[124] In effect, Schelling's work is its own autobiography, something we could also say of Hegel.

In the Preface to the 1809 collection that included the *Freedom* essay, Schelling does hold out the ideal of a "complete, finished system," saying that hitherto he has only produced "facets" and "fragments" of this "whole."[125] Indeed, throughout his career Schelling worked across several areas (mythology, religion, transcendental, and natural philosophy), and although the early, middle, and late periods are different in tone and emphasis, his work cannot be neatly divided into progressive stages related to different subject matters, as Manfred Schröter does in his edition of Schelling.[126] Schelling does sometimes suggest that these areas are facets of a whole, for example that "appearing nature" is simply a temporal mode of what exists synchronically and "eternal[ly]" in "true Nature" (272), or that "transcendental philosophy" and "philosophy of nature" are "one science, differentiated only in the opposite orientation of their tasks."[127] But this synchronization is itself only one possible system, since even while working within a transcendental envelope in his 1800 *System*, Schelling was giving his *Naturphilosophie* a freedom and life for itself in *FO*, where it embraces an internal derangement that threatens the very concept of a "whole." This double transcendental-natural trajectory accords with Schelling's later recasting of the very nature of dialectic, in which synthesis itself becomes only a hypothesis. Thus, Schelling writes in *Ages* (1815) that the "third is incapable of continuance" because "each of the three has a right" to have "being": "unity" therefore cannot "elevate itself… outside the antithesis," because unity is itself the antithesis of antithesis and is just one system.[128]

In *OUS*, which we have touched on, Schelling does imagine a loose (rather than architectonic) unification in which "primordial knowledge" "flows" from the "central organs" of philosophy and mathematics "through various channels to the outermost parts." He conceives individual disciplines as modes of one substance in Spinozist terms, or branches of one tree (a frequent image in encyclopedias); he also synchronizes "real" and "ideal" sciences by arguing that the former are only the actuality of which the latter are the potentiality or potency.[129] *OUS* can sustain this view because it operates on a purely "ideal" plane. But two decades later, in "On the Nature of Philosophy as Science" ("NPS"), Schelling argues that the need for system arises because knowledge "does not exist in a system" but is an "[asystaton]," something "in inner conflict"; indeed, this *dissensus* is the very "fabric" of systems.

While Schelling's concern is the multiplicity of philosophical systems, we could extend the argument to the disciplines he takes up: philosophy, history, aesthetics, religion, and numerous sciences including medicine. In the *System*, these are bound into a single architectonic through relationships of foreshadowing, analogy and homology. But in "NPS," criticizing Kant's modeling of philosophy as "science" on mathematics, Schelling turns to the organic and the many systems that "doctors distinguish" in the body ("digestive, etc."). In "health," which "probably means... *whole*," one is "free" from their difference, from which Hegel suffers in the last section of *PN*. Schelling still wants a "system" that "establishes the unity of unity and opposition." But he also accuses Kant of ignoring that the "human body" hosts "germs of every possible illness," where illness, as for Hegel, results from one "system" becoming "particularly prominent."[130] Though illness might seem undesirable, the metaphor should be read alongside Schelling's famous comment that "the individual body part like the eye," though "only possible within the whole of an organism," has its "own freedom" and "life," evident in "the disease of which it is capable." Or as he says in *Ages*, "when the copula of the unity dissolves," life-forces "appear that previously lay concealed."[131]

In "NPS" Schelling argues that before constructing a system "the human spirit must already have searched in every possible direction," and it is that ongoing process, mobilized by a primordial "asystasy," that generates an "absolute subject" which, unlike the Cartesian subject, is "in everything and does not remain in anything." "Absolute" here means being *absolved* from or "leav[ing]" "all presuppositions," leaving "*everything...* even *God*." It means putting all "*definable* science[s]" under erasure since defining is confining,[132] whereas "every science that is *science* at all has its unconditioned," that original asystasy or outside of thought to which any necessary delimitation of a science must remain responsible. Consequently, "system" is not Kant's unity of manifold cognitions under one idea, as one system does not "become master over another": they "coexist, like the different systems of an organism,"[133] which is what allows for the unity of unity and opposition.

With such "absolute" knowledge in mind, a knowledge "without condition" rather than the onto-encyclopedic totalization Derrida attributes to Idealism,[134] I suggest we approach Schelling's corpus as what Deleuze calls a "great work which contains all the complicated series," and into which "divergent series," like the transcendental and natural, "lead out and back in" through relations of "complication-explication-implication."[135] But if the subject cannot "remain in anything" lest "life and evolution" be "inhibited," Schelling asks how we can "connect" divergent series. Hegel raises the same problem when he argues that in philosophy "nothing can be developed" without systematic interconnection and criticizes Schelling's *Freedom* essay as "isolated and independent," while praising it as "deeply speculative." Schelling's response to his own question is precisely that system is subject: just as one subject "lives in the different elements of an organism," so too one subject "proceeds through all the aspects of the system," yet without these elements allowing for a panlogical translation.[136]

Two texts evoke the notion of system as a speculative "coexistence" that includes asystasy. Rather than unifying manifold cognitions under one idea—even an immanently developing rather than preexisting idea—*FO* and the unpublished *Ages of the World* (1815) are archives of ideas, the second standing to the philosophy of spirit as the first stands to the *Naturphilosophie*. In discussing Gustave Flaubert, Foucault describes a text that exists "alongside" Flaubert's other texts, "suspended over his entire work": a text or archive Flaubert had "to silence gradually" to achieve "clarity," but whose "prodigious reserve" persists despite Flaubert's "conflagration" of this "primary discourse."[137] Schelling draws attention to *FO* as a text not submitted to secondary revision, in insisting that "the same demands" cannot "be made upon a treatise" written "as a guide for lectures" as on one "intended for the public at large."[138] Accordingly *FO* is not a linear argument, or even like *OUS* an array of chapters on specific topics or disciplines, but a chaos of undivided parts without a clear architecture. Rather than a book, it is an unbound conceptuality, a "text" in Roland Barthes' sense of not "clos[ing] upon a signified" but being a weave of possibilities produced and shifted within its writing.[139]

Yet Schelling published this (un)public text, which appeared with further notes and complications in his collected works. Extending the notion of a great work, Deleuze and Guattari describe a "burrow" or "rhizome" with "multiple entrances" that have different "rules of usage" and open different trajectories and "impasse[s]," defying attempts "to interpret" what is "only open to experimentation."[140] *FO* archives Schelling's work so far, and is a "Romantic Encyclopedia" in which nature and the topology it creates for thought are de- and recomposed through several sciences, including transcendental philosophy. Rather than being related in the subject-object form of the *System* that speculative realists critique as correlationism, in *FO* mind and nature are folds of each other. Mind takes new forms unfolded by the forms in which nature causes it to think, which are opened by the fields through which mind focalizes nature. These fields—not "philosophical sciences" determined by philosophy but ones that have philosophical consequences—run into and generate each other. For *FO*, unlike *OUS*, posits no "central organs" from which knowledge "flows" but is what Deleuze calls a "body without organs." Indeed, Schelling himself suggests that organs form epigenetically in relation to situations and needs rather than being preformed,[141] which we can extrapolate to sciences as organs of knowledge. An intensity or potency hypostatizes in an organ of knowledge, and the text moves to another organ, sometimes not explicitly identified (like geology), or without formal existence in the canon of sciences (like pedology, unnamed till 1862).

Deploying *OUS*'s image of fluidity less idealistically, *FO* evokes an "original fluidity" which is unconditioned (*unbedingt*) and then determined in "figures" that occur when actants (*Aktionen*) of thought matter are bound, only to be unbound by the pressure of other repressed actants.[142] In this theory of "dynamic atomism," adapted from the speculative physics of Leibniz, all products contain "an infinite multiplicity of unified tendencies." Sciences and fields are momentary bindings of these "productivities," figures deconstructed by nature's complexity. As "Nature organizes to infinity," the "sphere" or field which it delimits "again contain[s] an infinity," so that within it further and yet further spheres are formed.[143] These spheres include physics as the above theory of dynamic atomism that recasts thought as a finding of differences within differences and the earth sciences (geology, pedology) which open up processes of composition and decomposition in soils and other solids that have consequences for the materials of thought as absolutely "indecomposable" and yet capable of being "[re]inserted...into the universal circulation of matter through composition."[144] They also include chemistry, as a space of volatile exchanges which allows us to know only "effects instead of causes."[145] Chemistry as physiology or the body's chemistry is also physiology in a broader Romantic sense of *natura naturans* or the forces in nature,[146] which is to say that the individual and universal organisms are thought and rethought through each other.

The text thus functions as a great work whose various series complicate and implicate each other. These include scientific fields, theories of matter, and organization that Schelling puts in play (atomism, monads and actants, epigenesis), and the philosophical syntheses he (de)constructs as speculative invasions to which nature responds. Chief among the last is his own transcendental idealism, projected through the "graduated stages of nature" as not just "natural history" (in the sense of an enumeration of nature's products), but a "*history* of Nature" which "realizes the Ideal" through "continuous deviations from" it, not "in the individual, but in the whole."[147] Schelling develops this idea of the *Stufenfolge* straightforwardly in the *System*,[148] where it forms the basis for an evolution from nature to spirit that underpins much German Idealism across different fields, and which may derive from Herder's *Outlines of a Philosophy of the History of Man*. But in *FO* the *Stufenfolge* is no more than a hypothesis complicated by other fields: natural history as an aggregate rather than the history of nature as purposive development; comparative physiology as a site where the graduated series of existents and that of functions within organisms may not align; and most of all disease (since the curative discipline of medicine is not named). Disease is a "deviation" from "rule" or "proportion," and because the concept is relative—what is disease in one organism may be health in another—it provides the "perspective" of the "individual" against "*the whole of organic nature*." This relativity or bio-diversity calls into question the very notion of rule and proportion, unsettling the normativity of a history of nature where the "universal organism operates" by "assimilation," and "admits no production" into the whole "that does not fit" into its subsumption of manifold phenomena under one idea or goal.[149]

As an experimental field composed and recomposed in its reading, *FO* can be constructed along vertical and horizontal axes, the vertical being the *Stufenfolge* and the horizontal the fields that envelop and interrupt it. Hegel laments nature's resistance to the unity of the notion; but *FO* thus opens an ongoing dialogue between idealist paradigms and their (de)construction by *Naturphilosophie*. However, its transcendental materialism, though not the absolute idealism Hegel dismissed as a "night in which...all cows are black,"[150] is plenitudinous and lacks the auto- and onto-encyclopedic pathos of *PN*. If system is subject, the "general economy" of Schelling's system, in Georges Bataille's sense of a thought-environment, where nothing exists "as an isolatable system," must also include both a dialogue between Schelling's two major "archival" texts and the "restricted" systems[151] that lead into and out of them, as well as between these asystatic texts themselves. Moreover, as

Schelling writes, philosophizing depends on writing "the history of [one's] own life" and confronting "the abysses of that past which are still in one."[152] This auto-encyclopedic reflection begins in the *Freedom* essay, which imbues philosophy with the "personality" that marks Hegel's *Phenomenology* as a new departure but that Schelling, stung by Hegel's criticisms, now highlights as a concept.

The *Freedom* essay, contrary to Hegel's comment that it is profound but "isolated," is precisely an attempt at systematic and autobiographically situated interconnection. Schelling introduces it by saying he has hitherto "confined himself" to *Naturphilosophie*, and is only now addressing "the ideal part" of philosophy, a surprising statement given his earlier work. But in remembering and working through his past, and connecting his earlier concerns with religion, transcendental, and natural philosophy, Schelling must see his earlier *System* as the "denial and nonacknowledgment" of the negative he now criticizes.[153] In the *Freedom* essay, where God is the ground and also in this ground which he contains and which contains him, Schelling therefore reconceives the transcendental series through a feedback loop that holds the "ideal part" or "soul" of philosophy open to the dark ground of nature as the "realism" which is its "body."[154] He begins with the asystasy of multiple systems of pantheism that complicate the relation between nature and spirit, implicating God and nature in each other in ways that put the very notion of God under erasure. This segment is an intellectual equivalent to the rotary movement in *Ages* (1815), which stalls any beginning that "does not always begin again but persists" as the "ground" of a "steady progression." In struggling to wrest a history of freedom from the "history of nature"[155] (an idea Schelling revisits in his middle work from 1809–1815), the text eventually overcomes its asystasy, projecting a steady progression from "darkness" to "light" that absorbs evil into theodicy. But it does so through a decision, an *Entscheidung* that is a repression, as the even stronger synonym *Entschluss* suggests: "If in making a decision [*Entschluss*], somebody retains the right to reexamine his choice, he will never make a beginning at all."[156] As such, the *Freedom* essay is not a "finished system" but a hypothesis performatively produced under the pressure of overcoming the asystasy underlying knowledge.

To achieve "clarity," Foucault's Flaubert had to gradually "silence" an archive whose "black unmalleable coal" persisted despite its attempted "conflagration." *Ages* (1815) opens with this black coal, the "abysses of the past," what Schelling had called the "absolutely indecomposable" which is always also "*composable*," including through a decision for clarity.[157] The history of nature is at the core of the ideal part of philosophy that occupies Schelling after 1809, and the drafts of *Ages* from 1811 to 1815 all wrestle with it, though the *Weltalter* project vastly exceeds these texts. The *Freedom* essay and the first two *Ages* share a decisionary structure that "breaks out" of "the rotary motion of drives… into temporal succession,"[158] but performs the transition from past to present and nature to spirit quite differently. *Ages* (1811) is the most narrative of the texts, clearly mapping a "system of ages" onto a trinitarian model that it describes as a "system of spirit," and "repress[ing]" pantheism into the past, as a stage of cultural evolution rather than a site of urgent philosophical problems.[159] This repression is also how Schelling deals with nature in *PMR*, which develops in a direct line from the 1811 *Ages*, allowing some commentators to see a steady progression from the middle to late work that bypasses the more problematic 1815 *Ages*.[160]

But significantly *Ages* (1813), which is more condensed and apocalyptic than 1811, frames the decision itself linguistically. All three versions are seen as incomplete because they contain only one book called "The Past," but as Schelling says in 1811, the three times may be "concentric[ally]" "reunited in one time." While recollecting a past that is "preworldly," 1811 contains only a rational schema that includes a future "coming after the world."[161] However, 1813, is visionary in its leap through the unfolding of "archetypes" from past to future; and the "great decision" that initiates the "posit[ing]" of the "unconditioned," with which Schelling had been concerned from *FO* onward, occurs through a "unanimity of the expressing and the expressed," where the expressing is one, though the expressed and the expressible may be "two." In the expressing, that is, "one force posits itself as governing, as the common exponent of the whole."[162] This linguistic theme that raises the question of identity and difference within predication, and which is first introduced by Hegel,[163] is throughout Schelling's middle work[164] and goes back to *FO*'s dynamic theory of matter, in which every "action" is in truth "*highly composite*" and every product (or judgment or decision) represses a number of "bound" actants that compete for mastery, just as systems compete for mastery in "NPS."[165]

Then in 1815 Schelling opens up the "mollifying unity" of the decision reached in previous versions and allows that if the "copula of the unity dissolves," "forces appear" that were "previously concealed." In the 1815 section on mesmerism, which in 1813 paved the way to the future, Schelling further describes the dissolution of a "unity" that holds the "forces of the person" "together" and "expresses them (or is their exponent)."[166] The same could be said of the 1815 text itself. Schelling twice allowed *Ages* to be printed (1811, 1813) only to cancel the decision expressed in publication. Indeed, the discussion of the linguistics of decision in 1813 occurs at the point where the text shifts to proof-sheets and cancelled passages, as Schelling writes, according to his son, that "the text falls into utter falsehoods *from this point forward*."[167] The 1815 text, which was never published, then loosens the unity imposed by a decision that involves what deconstruction calls "the violence of position."[168] Abandoning Schelling's previous emphasis on development, 1815 resembles *FO* in having no "exponent" and no architecture, its subtitles being added by editors. Instead, it is an "archival" text that gathers together and disseminates many of the series and topics that occur in both the natural and the transcendental philosophy, thus creating and multiplying feedback loops and disseminative associations between these modes of philosophy.

One example is the pair evolution/involution in *FO*. Following his suggestion that we can "translate" or "construct" empirical propositions in "the idealist potency,"[169] Schelling repeats these terms in 1815, not to idealize them but to potentiate their philosophical significance, while reinvolving this translation of physics into metaphysics in a self-criticism of the ideal by the real. 1815 transfers into history *FO*'s (cosmological and embryological) idea that nature is "an infinite evolution from one original involution," arguing that all "evolution begins from involution" and that "contraction" is the "original" and "root force of all life."[170] The result of this transference is both an ontology that castigates idealism as the "nonacknowledgment" of a "negating primordial force" and a nascent psychoanalysis that sees this primordial scene as "contracted and concealed" within the "affirming principle." For psychoanalysis is the involution of which history is the evolution: there is no "consciousness" without "positing something as past"; hence, "consciousness" occurs on the ground of "something... excluded and contracted," "the unconscious," which can always "again c[o]me to the fore."[171]

Not only do earlier topics come to the fore differently in 1815. Passages are redistributed and acquire new resonances, becoming Schelling's equivalent to Hegel's words that contain different and opposite meanings. In 1811, the passage on involution is placed in the middle, thus leaving behind the primal scene that opens and closes in 1815, while in 1813 Schelling removes the passage almost entirely.[172] Likewise in 1811, Schelling discerns a "rotary movement" at the origin of the planets and "every individual life." This is quietened into a "constant" motion in "the revolving wheel of the planets" where the "concealed unity of the world," which initially seems an "unstructured whole," "first shows itself" before becoming a "higher unity." But in 1815, "each single, particular nature" (whether in "individuals" or "the world system") begins in a "state of inner revulsion" with "the rotation about its own axis," replacing Leibniz' preestablished harmony with a number of "rotary wholes" that (de)center cosmos and psyche in "anxiety," "terror," and "despair."[173] That this primal scene comes at the end of the text is because in 1815 all three times are simultaneously present, but in an explosive derangement. Comets are one figure Schelling uses to constellate this asynchronicity: comets are rotary wholes, (in)composable elements that are "living witnesses" of a "primordial time" which also "migrat[es] through later time," bearing both turbulence and potential.

This derangement of time and narrative is also present in the rotary movement earlier described, where all three moments have "a right" to "being," and there is no third, no synthesis or indifference, beyond "antithesis"[174]; instead, the third as future is within antithesis. As such the unpublished 1815 text possesses the "prodigious reserve"[175] of the archival text, into which more decisionary versions of the ideal part of philosophy, whether published and withdrawn or given as lectures, lead out and back in. Thus, the 1815 *Ages* (and *FO*) are like hypertexts avant la lettre, which allow multiple particular systems to coexist. Or they can be seen as what Hegel calls a "night-like mine or pit in which is stored a world of infinitely many images and representations," allowing Schelling to recast "system" as "the unity" or compossibility "of unity and opposition."[176]

Notes

1. Immanuel Kant, *Critique of Pure Reason*, trans. and ed. Paul Guyer and Allen Wood (Cambridge: Cambridge University Press, 1998), 691.
2. Mark Wigley, *The Architecture of Deconstruction: Derrida's Haunt* (Cambridge, Mass.: MIT Press, 1993), 21, 25.

3. G. W. F. Hegel, *Phenomenology of Spirit*, trans. A.V. Miller (Oxford: Oxford University Press, 1977), 1, 166.
4. F. W. J. Schelling, "On the Nature of Philosophy as Science," in *German Idealist Philosophy*, ed. Rüdiger Bubner (Harmondsworth: Penguin, 1997), 212. Hereafter "NPS."
5. Novalis, *Notes for a Romantic Encyclopedia: Das Allgemeine Brouillon*, trans. and ed. David Wood (Albany: SUNY Press, 2007), 86.
6. For instance, Philip Huneman (ed.), *Understanding Purpose: Kant and the Philosophy of Biology* (Rochester: University of Rochester Press, 2007); Maurizio Esposito, *Romantic Biology, 1890–1945* (London: Pickering and Chatto, 2013), 1–32.
7. Ludwig von Bertalanffy, *General System Theory: Foundations, Development, Applications* (New York; George Braziller, 1968), 6, 19, 32.
8. F. W. J. Schelling, *First Outline of a System of the Philosophy of Nature*, trans. Keith Peterson (Albany: SUNY Press, 2006), 6, 105, 160; hereafter *FO*.
9. Humberto Maturana and Francisco Varela, *Autopoiesis and Cognition: The Realization of the Living* (Dordrecht: D. Reidel, 1980).
10. Immanuel Kant, *Critique of the Power of Judgment*, trans. Paul Guyer and Eric Matthews (Cambridge: Cambridge University Press, 2000), 254; hereafter *CJ*.
11. Alexander Baumgarten, *Metaphysica*, 7th ed. (Halle: 1779), #533.
12. F. W. J. Schelling, *Philosophical Investigations into the Essence of Human Freedom*, trans. Jeff Love and Johannes Schmidt (Albany: SUNY Press, 2006), 18.
13. I distinguish deconstruction from post-structuralism in *Deconstruction and the Remainders of Phenomenology: Sartre, Derrida, Foucault, Baudrillard* (Stanford: Stanford University Press), xii–xvi, 1–54. Briefly, though post-structuralism unsettles stable notions of structure and system, its erasure of depth, consciousness, and the subject in a world of surfaces is often euphoric. More genealogically entangled with phenomenology, and mediated by the French Hegelians' focus on consciousness as distinct from spirit (10–14), deconstruction, even after the linguistic turn of the 1960s, still assumes what Foucault calls a "modern cogito": a cogito exposed to its unthought, to ontological concerns, and thus to a certain pathos (187–190).
14. G. W. F. Hegel, *Philosophy of Nature*, trans. A.V. Miller (Oxford: Clarendon, 1970), 6; hereafter *PN*. I use the Miller translation. "Organism" is Miller's translation of "Organisation"; M.J. Petry translates it as "organic whole" (*Philosophy of Nature*, 3 vols. [London: Allen and Unwin, 1970], 1.197).
15. Bruno Latour, *Politics of Nature: How to Bring the Sciences into Democracy*, trans. Catherine Porter (Cambridge: Harvard University Press, 2004), 20–22.
16. I borrow Arkady Plotnitsky's Deleuzian rethinking of Hegelian conceptuality in his brilliant "Curvatures: Hegel and the Baroque," in Rajan and Plotnitsky, ed., *Idealism without Absolutes: Philosophy and Romantic Culture* (Albany: SUNY Press, 2004), 121–125.
17. Slavoj Žižek, "The Abyss of Freedom," in Žižek and Schelling, *The Abyss of Freedom/Ages of the World* (Ann Arbor: University of Michigan Press, 1997), 11–12.
18. G. W. F. Hegel, *Encyclopaedia of the Philosophical Sciences in Outline* (1817), trans. Stephen A. Taubeneck, in *Encyclopedia of the Philosophical Sciences in Outline and Critical Writings*, ed. Ernst Behler (New York: Continuum, 1990), 53.
19. Jacques Derrida, *Points ... Interviews 1974–1994*, trans. Peggy Kamuf (Stanford: Stanford University Press, 1995), 212.
20. Jacques Derrida, *Who's Afraid of Philosophy: Right to Philosophy 1*, trans. Jan Plug (Stanford: Stanford University Press, 2002), 125, 60, 137, 101.
21. Ibid., 148.
22. Hegel, *Encyclopedia* (1817), 51; F. W. J. Schelling, *On University Studies,* trans. E. S. Morgan, ed. Norbert Gutterman (Athens: University of Ohio Press, 1966), 42; hereafter *OUS*.

23. G. W. F. Hegel/F. W. J. Schelling, "On the Relationship of the Philosophy of Nature to Philosophy in General," in *Between Kant and Hegel*, trans. And ed. George di Giovanni and H.S. Harris (Indianapolis: Hackett, 2000), 366. On the uncertain authorship, see Harris' introductory note (365).
24. Žižek, "Abyss," 11–12.
25. Hegel, *Phenomenology*, 18–19.
26. Immanuel Kant, *Vorlesungen über philosophische Enzyklopädie*, ed. Gerhard Lehmann (Berlin: Akademie Verlag, 1961), 32. Translations mine.
27. G. W. F. Hegel, *Philosophy of Mind*, trans. William Wallace (Oxford: Oxford University Press, 1971), 295. This is Part 3 of the 1830 *Encyclopedia* with additional *Zusätze* from the 1845 Boumann edition, trans. A.V. Miller. Schelling's *Philosophy of Art* (1804/5) is also a typology rather than a historical system of art, in which the Symbolic (equivalent to Hegel's Classicism) forms a midpoint between the opposite failures of the schematic and allegorical to achieve artistic synthesis (trans. Douglas Stott [Minneapolis: University of Minnesota Press, 1989], 46–48).
28. G. W. F. Hegel, *Aesthetics: Lectures on Fine Art*, trans. T.M. Knox (Oxford: Clarendon, 1975), 1.76–9, 81, 158, 181.
29. G. W. F. Hegel, *Lectures on the History of Philosophy*, trans. E. S. Haldane and Frances H. Simson (Lincoln: University of Nebraska Press, 1995), 3.555, 542. Unless otherwise noted, further references are to this edition. In one lecture series, Hegel rationalizes his placement of Schelling in claiming that all "preceding philosophies" find their "final idea" in him, but retains all his criticisms of Schelling *(Lectures on the History of Philosophy: The Lectures of 1825–1826*, ed. Robert F. Brown, trans Brown, J.M. Stewart and H.S. Harris [Berkeley: University of California Press, 1990], 1.204).
30. Hegel, *Phenomenology*, 17, 10, 13, 37, 39.
31. Ibid., 39, 37; Jean-Luc Nancy, *The Speculative Remark: (One of Hegel's Bons Mots)*, trans Céline Surprenant. (Stanford: Stanford University Press, 2001), 10–13, 61, 48.
32. The four parts of Arthur Schopenhauer's 1817 *The World as Will and Representation* (trans. E. F. J. Payne [New York: Dover, 1969], Vol. 1) stage a journey through Logic, Philosophy of Nature, Aesthetics, and Ethics, which is meant to deconstruct the Hegelian auto-encyclopedia. But the parts remain in agonistic contention.
33. Hegel, *Phenomenology*, 50.
34. Schelling, *OUS*, 79.
35. Jacques Derrida, "Theology of Translation," *Eyes of the University: Right to Philosophy 2*, trans. Jan Plug and others (Stanford: Stanford University Press, 2004), 67, 78–9.
36. Antoine Berman, *The Experience of the Foreign: Culture and Translation in Romantic Germany*, trans. S. Heyvaert (Albany: SUNY Press, 1984), 15, 82.
37. Novalis, *Romantic Encyclopedia*, 76.
38. Kant, *Vorlesungen*, 31.
39. Schelling, *OUS*, 33, 37, 76, 80–1.
40. Hegel, *Encyclopedia* (1817), 53. See Immanuel Kant, *Metaphysical Foundations of Natural Science*, ed. And trans. Michael Friedman (Cambridge: Cambridge University Press, 2004). 4; hereafter *MF*.
41. Immanuel Kant, *The Conflict of the Faculties*, trans. Mary J. Gregor (New York; Abaris Books, 1979), 45.
42. Kant, *MF*, 4.
43. Hegel, *Encyclopedia* (1817), 51–52.
44. Kant, *CJ*, 41–42.
45. Immanuel Kant, *Physical Geography*, trans. Olaf Reinhardt, in *Natural Science*, ed. Eric Watkins (Cambridge: Cambridge University Press, 2012), 445.
46. Ibid., 445–447.
47. Kant, *MF*, 4–7.
48. Kant, *Geography*, 447–453.

49. Schelling, *FO*, 44.
50. Kant, *CJ*, 17, 42, 285.
51. Hegel, *Encyclopedia* (1817), 53–4.
52. Immanuel Kant, *Logic*, trans. Robert S. Hartman and Wolfgang Schwarz (New York: Dover, 1974), 48.
53. Hegel, *PN*, 6, 19.
54. Robert Smith, *Derrida and Autobiography* (Cambridge: Cambridge University Press, 1995), 3–4.
55. Rodolphe Gasché, *Georges Bataille: Phenomenology and Phantasmatology* (Stanford: Stanford University Press, 2012), 3; Hegel, *PN*, 13.
56. Hegel, *PN*, 3, 428.
57. Kant, *CJ*, 243–4, 247.
58. Hegel, *PN*, 20, 279, 377.
59. Schelling, *FO*, 53.
60. Samuel Taylor Coleridge, "On the Passions," in *Shorter Works and Fragments*, ed. H. J. and J. R. de J. Jackson (Princeton: Princeton University Press, 1995), 2.1436; "Observations on the Scale of Life," in *Shorter Works*, 2.1194.
61. Alison Stone, *Petrified Intelligence: Nature in Hegel's Philosophy* (Albany: SUNY Press, 2005), xviii, 57–8.
62. Hegel, *PN*, 21; Schelling, *FO*, 49.
63. Coleridge, "Passions," 1426–7, 1436.
64. Hegel, *PN*, 3.
65. Paul Ricoeur, "Hegel and Husserl on Intersubjectivity," *From Text to Action: Essays in Hermeneutics II*, trans. Kathleen Blamey and John Thomson (Evanston: Northwestern University Press, 1991), 229–31.
66. Joseph Henry Green, *Vital Dynamics* (London: William Pickering, 1840), 99–102, 107.
67. Hegel, *PN*, 2, 20–1.
68. M. J. Petry, "Introduction," to Hegel, *Philosophy of Nature*, 1. 31–2.
69. G. W. F. Hegel, *The Philosophical Propaedeutic*, trans. A.V. Miller, ed. Michael George and Andrew Vincent (Oxford: Blackwell, 1986), 143n; cf. *PN*, 20.
70. Hegel, *PN*, 444, 276; *Phenomenology*, 16.
71. G. W. F. Hegel, *De Orbitis Planetarum*, trans. David Healan (Berlin and Yokohama, 2006), 13. http://hegel.net/en/v2123healan.htm.
72. In the *Propaedeutic*, Division 2 is called "Physics" and subdivided into "Mechanics" and "Physics of the Inorganic."
73. John Zammito, "Kant's Persistent Ambivalence Toward Epigenesis, 1764–90," in *Understanding Purpose: Kant and the Philosophy of Biology*, ed. Philippe Huneman (Rochester: University of Rochester Press, 2007), 52.
74. Stone, *Petrified Intelligence*, 46–50, 75; Hegel, *PN*, 277, 291.
75. Green, *Vital Dynamics*, 37. 39, 41, 105.
76. Hegel, *PN*, 6, 27; *Encyclopedia*, 49–50.
77. Hegel, *PN*, 22, 27.
78. Ibid., 269, 344.
79. Ibid., 394; Georges Canguilhem, *Knowledge of Life*, trans. Stefanos Geroulanos and Daniela Ginsburg (New York: Fordham University Press, 2008), 69–70.
80. Hegel does not use the word biology, but cites Treviranus' *Biologie* (*PN*, 365n), which coins the term.
81. Iain Hamilton Grant, *Philosophies of Nature After Schelling* (London: Continuum, 2006), 106, 202.
82. G. W. Leibniz, *Monadology*, in *Basic Writings*, trans. George Montgomery (La Salle: Open Court, 1968), 261, 266, 268. Hegel opposes Leibniz as a thinker who does not quite embrace difference to Spinoza as a thinker of substance, and attributes to Leibniz an ascent of monads

from "inorganic" to "organic" to "conscious" that seems more Hegelian than Leibnizian (*History of Philosophy*, 3.330, 337).
83. Schelling, *FO*, 44.
84. Foucault defines a counter-science, such as psychoanalysis, as one that "flow[s] in the opposite direction" from, and "unmake[s]" the sciences in which man creates his "positivity" (*The Order of Things: An Archeology of the Human Sciences* [New York: Vintage, 1970], 379).
85. Hegel, *PN*, 364, 373, 376.
86. Roberto Esposito, *Third Person: Politics of Life and Philosophy of the Impersonal*, trans. Zakiya Hanafi (Cambridge: Polity, 2012), 25–6.
87. Hegel, *PN*, 364.
88. Ibid., 361.
89. Ibid., 281, 284, 293.
90. Earth is also extensively covered under physics. Further entangling the levels, the vivification of the earth at the end of the section on the terrestrial organism, while allowing for a transition to plant nature, does so through a regression to physics and chemistry.
91. Hegel, *PN*, 276, 279.
92. Hegel, *PN*, 15; *History of Philosophy*, 3.517; Schelling, *System of Transcendental Idealism* (1800), trans. Peter Heath (Charlottesville: University Pres of Virginia, 1978), 6.
93. Hegel, *PN*, 284, 428.
94. Ibid., 361, 429.
95. Ibid., 395, 402–3.
96. Xavier Bichat, *Physiological Researches Upon Life and Death*, trans. Tobias Watkins (Philadelphia: Smith and Maxwell, 1809), 119.
97. Hegel, *PN*, 396, 404–5.
98. Ibid., 387, 397, 402–3, 405.
99. Hegel, *Aesthetics*, 1.76–7, 438–9.
100. Hegel, *PN*, 428–9.
101. Ibid., 275.
102. Ibid., 444.
103. Schelling, *FO*, 53; "Introduction to the Outline" in *FO*, 196–7.
104. Hegel, *PN*, 160; *Encyclopedia* (1817), 51.
105. Hegel, *PN*, 104, 80, 99, 77.
106. Ibid., 303, 343.
107. Ibid., 106, 276.
108. Ibid., 6, 278, 358, 428.
109. Canguilhem, *The Normal and the Pathological*, trans. Carolyn Fawcett (New York: Zone, 1991), 118; *Knowledge*, 69–70.
110. Hegel, *PN*, 438, 428–429.
111. Ibid., 372, 428, 433.
112. Ibid., 432–434, 441.
113. Catherine Malabou, *The Future of Hegel: Plasticity, Temporality, Dialectic*, trans. Lisabeth During (London: Routledge, 2005).
114. Hegel, *Phenomenology*, 407.
115. Catherine Malabou, "Again: 'The Wounds of the Spirit Heal and Leave No Scars Behind,'" *Mosaic* 40:2 (2007): 29–37.
116. Jacques Derrida, "The Pit and the Pyramid: Introduction to Hegel's Semiology," in *Margins of Philosophy*, trans. Alan Bass (Chicago: University of Chicago Press, 1982), 69–108; *Glas*, trans. John P. Leavey and Richard Rand (Lincoln: University of Nebraska Press, 1990).
117. Smith, *Derrida*, 3.
118. Catherine Malabou, *Before Tomorrow: Epigenesis and Rationality,* trans. Carolyn Shread (Cambridge: Polity, 2016).
119. See my articles "Towards a Cultural Idealism: Negativity and Freedom in Hegel and Kant," in *Idealism Without Absolutes: Philosophy and Romantic Culture*, ed. Tilottama Rajan and

Arkady Plotnitsky (Albany: SUNY Press, 2004), 51–71; "How (Not) To Speak Properly: Writing 'German' Philosophy in Hegel's *Aesthetics* and *History of Philosophy*," *Clio* 33:2 (2004), 119–142.
120. Hegel, *Philosophy of Mind*, 76.
121. See my articles "(In)Digestible Material: Illness and Dialectic in Hegel's *The Philosophy of Nature*," in *Cultures of Taste/Theories of Appetite: Eating Romanticism*, ed. Timothy Morton (Basingstoke: Palgrave, 2004), 217–36; "Hegel's Irritability," *European Romantic Review*, 32:5–6 (2021): 499–517.
122. Schelling, *OUS*, 41.
123. Schelling, *The Philosophy of Art*, trans. Douglas W. Stott (Minneapolis: University of Minnesota Press, 1989). PMR has not been fully translated, though the *Historical-Critical Introduction to the Philosophy of Mythology* (trans. Mason Richey and Markus Zisselsberger [Albany: SUNY Press, 2007]) provides the first ten lectures, and Klaus Ottmann has translated H. G. Paulus' unauthorized version of the *Philosophy of Revelation (1841–42)* (Putnam, CT: Spring, 2020).
124. Hegel, *History of Philosophy*, 3.515, 513.
125. Schelling, *Freedom*, 5.
126. Schröter's chronological division consists of Early Writings, *Naturphilosophie*, Identity Philosophy, Philosophy of Freedom, Historical Philosophy, and Religion (*Schelling's Werke*, 6 vols. and Supplements [Munich: Beck'sche Buchhandlung, 1965–1969]).
127. Schelling, *Ideas for a Philosophy of Nature*, trans. Errol E. Harris and Peter Heath (Cambridge: Cambridge University Press, 1988), 272; "Introduction to the Outline," in *FO*, 194.
128. F. W. J. Schelling, *Ages* (1815), trans. Jason Wirth (Albany: SUNY Press, 2000), 19, 36.
129. Schelling, *OUS*, 43, 9, 45.
130. Schelling, "NPS," 210–213.
131. Schelling, *Freedom*, 18; *The Ages of the World* (1815), 48.
132. Schelling, "NPS," 210, 216–217.
133. Schelling, *FO*, 13; "NPS," 213.
134. Derrida, "The University Without Condition." *Without Alibi*, ed. and trans. Peggy Kamuf (Stanford: Stanford University Press, 2002), 202–37.
135. Gilles Deleuze, *Difference and Repetition*, trans. Paul Patton (New York: Columbia University Press, 1994), 123–124.
136. Hegel, *History*, 3.514; Schelling, "NPS," 215.
137. Michel Foucault, "Fantasia of the Library," *Language, counter-memory, practice*, trans. Sherry and Donald F. Bouchard (Ithaca: Cornell University Press, 1977), 87–8.
138. Schelling, *FO*, 3.
139. Roland Barthes, "From Work to Text," *Image, Music, Text*, trans. Stephen Heath (New York: Hill and Wang, 1977), 155–8.
140. Deleuze and Felix Guattari, *Kafka: Toward a Minor Literature*, trans. Dana Polan (Minneapolis: University of Minnesota Press, 1986), 3.
141. Deleuze, *Francis Bacon: The Logic of Sensation*, trans. Daniel Smith (New York: Continuum, 2002), 47; Schelling, *FO*, 38n, 113.
142. Schelling, *FO*, 13–27.
143. Ibid., 21, 19, 43–44.
144. Ibid., 29–32.
145. Ibid., 110.
146. Green, *Vital Dynamics*, 101–102.
147. Schelling, *FO*, 53.
148. Schelling, *System*, 122–127.
149. Ibid., 158–159, 54.
150. Hegel, *Phenomenology*, 9.

151. Georges Bataille, *The Accursed Share: Volume One*, trans. Robert Hurley (New York: Zone Books, 1988), 19–22.
152. Schelling, *Ages* (1815), 3–4.
153. Schelling, *Freedom*, 4; *Ages* (1815), 6–7.
154. Schelling, *Freedom*, 4, 26.
155. Schelling, *Ages* (1815), 20, xxxvi, 65.
156. F. W. J. Schelling, *Ages of the World* (1813), trans. Judith Norman, in Žižek and Schelling, in *The Abyss of Freedom/Ages of the World*, 182. Schelling uses *Entscheidung* in the *Freedom* essay, but uses both words in 1813. See F. W. J. Schelling, *Die Weltalter Fragmente in den Urfassungen von 1811 und 1813*, ed. Manfred Schröter (München: Biederstein und Leibniz Verlag, 1946), 169–84.
157. Schelling, *Ages* (1815), 6; *FO*, 31.
158. Žižek, "Abyss," 31.
159. Schelling, *The Ages of the World (1811)*, trans. Joseph Lawrence (Albany: SUNY Press, 2019), 67, 128, 133,112.
160. *PMR*, which occupied Schelling for years, is seen as his final system, because it is his last and most monumental work. But it is itself arguably an archive that the Hegelian narrative of a *Stufenfolge* of worldviews inserted into it cannot silence.
161. Ibid., 42, 148, 167.
162. Schelling, *Ages* (1813), 176–178.
163. Hegel, *Phenomenology*, 12–13, 29, 37.
164. In addition to *Ages* (1813), see *Freedom*, 13–14; *Ages* (1811), 86–87, 124.
165. Schelling, *FO*, 23–24, 31; "NPS," 211–212.
166. Schelling, *Ages* (1815), 48, 68.
167. Schelling, *Ages* (1813), 182n. Schelling's actual comment, now lost, would have occurred on 167, just before the discussion of expression. See Schröter's explanation *(Weltalter Fragmente*, 169).
168. Paul de Man, "Shelley Disfigured," *The Rhetoric of Romanticism* (New York: Columbia University Press, 1984), 118
169. Schelling, *FO*, 77, 187–188, 192; F. W. J. Schelling, "On the True Concept of Philosophy of Nature and the Correct Way of Solving Its Problems," *The Schelling-Eschenmayer Controversy (1801), Nature and Identity*, ed. Benjamin Berger and Daniel Whistler (Edinburgh: Edinburgh University Press, 2020), 51, 47–48.
170. Schelling, *FO*, 77; *Ages* (1815), 83.
171. Ibid., 7, 64, 44, 61.
172. Schelling, *Ages* (1811), 83.
173. Ibid., 97, 242–243; *Ages* (1815), 91–92.
174. Ibid., 19.
175. Foucault, "Fantasia," 89.
176. Hegel, *Mind*, 204; Schelling, "NPS," 210.

Psychoanalysis

Gord Barentsen

1 The Speculative Unconscious: Hegel, Schelling, Deleuze, and Guattari

What we now know as the scientific domains of psychology only came into their own in the late nineteenth century, and as products of an epistemic shift from "soul" to "mind" in tandem with the rise of "rational psychology" (which attempted to hypostatize the soul into a thing to which categories of force and activity could be applied) and "empirical psychology" (which saw mind as an object for the observation and categorization of perceptions). Psychology for German Idealism in the late eighteenth and early nineteenth centuries, however, was a complex interdisciplinary amalgamation of biology, medicine, metaphysics, logic, aesthetics, morals, anthropology, and natural science; this fluidity, moreover, allowed for an undercurrent of ideas resistant to this epistemic shift, and thus open to the emergence of a proto-psychoanalysis through soul and mind's deterritorializations of each other. Thus Kant claims, for example, in his *Anthropology from a Pragmatic Point of View* (1798), that we are immense repositories of "*obscure* representations," "sensuous intuitions and sensations of which we are not conscious, even though we can undoubtedly conclude that we have them."[1] Indeed, "more often we ourselves are a play of obscure representations, and our understanding is unable to save itself from the absurdities into which they have placed it, even though it recognizes them as illusions."[2]

Hegel and Schelling—both typically seen as German Idealist thinkers—also countered empirical psychology with very different kinds of speculative thought. Hegel's *Encyclopedia of the Philosophical Sciences* (1830) is founded on

G. Barentsen (✉)
University of Western Ontario, London, ON, Canada
e-mail: gordbarentsen@LiquidFractal.org

dialectical sublation as the engine of a genuinely speculative philosophy capable of authentic knowledge, which is unavailable to an empirical psychology that takes both mind and its faculties as givens "without deriving these particularities from the concept of mind and so proving the necessity that in mind there are just these faculties and no others."[3] Schelling, too, critiques empirical-rational psychology in his *Naturphilosophie*, particularly his *First Outline of a System of the Philosophy of Nature* (1799), which is a speculative physics that sought to discern the dynamic forces and drives behind the objects that natural science takes for granted. Yet where Hegel attempts to make sublation the groundwork for a dialectical, discursive knowledge—a thinking that ultimately returns to itself—Schelling's *Naturphilosophie* bids to articulate the forces anterior to thought and which make thought possible (hence Hegel's harsh condemnation of Schelling's "charlatanism" in the opening pages of his own philosophy of nature[4]).

Through the lens of this resistance to empirical-rational psychology, Hegel and especially Schelling can be seen as foundational and pervasive influences on the emergence of psychoanalysis in its broadest sense. Freud's formulation of the unconscious as a repository of repressed wishes, and later the instinctual charges of id, ego, and superego and source of timeless unconscious processes; Jung's understanding of the unconscious as primordial Nature itself, denizened by archetypal forces and marked by humanity's connection with planet and cosmos; and Lacan's unconscious as the constituted third term in intersubjective discourse with the Other, neither primordial nor instinctual—their intellectual pedigrees can be traced back in various forms to the complex of ideas emerging from the differences between Hegel and Schelling. Indeed, reflecting on these two figures Eduard von Hartmann writes in his *Philosophy of the Unconscious* (1869) that the unconscious is "the necessary, if also hitherto for the most part only tacit *presupposition* of every objective or absolute *Idealism*."[5] And this proto-psychoanalytical potency in German Idealism is ultimately based on the *unconscious* nature of the Idea. In Hegel's *Encyclopedia* the Idea, as thinking "utterly identical with itself,"[6] must necessarily begin as unconscious, even as an optative tenor in the *Encyclopedia* promises a sort of fulfillment of thinking. Yet Hegel does not think the unconscious as such; it is encrypted in the murky depths of sensation and perception—particularly in the first two stages of soul-life in the *Philosophy of Mind*. Schelling, who is credited with the first properly psychological use of the term "unconscious" (*unbewußt*) in the *System of Transcendental Idealism* (1800), more willingly embraces the idea of an unconscious that mutates Kant's free play of the faculties into a non-ground or *Ungrund*, an alien domain where thought lacks the specifically Hegelian drive to return to itself. Ultimately, and for different reasons, both Hegel and Schelling articulate an unconscious that destabilizes the idealist impetus to systemic completion as a site of intensity.

With this in mind, while the broader history of the unconscious has been written elsewhere,[7] this chapter will narrate what I call the *speculative unconscious* as it is developed in the oeuvres of Hegel and Schelling and carried forward into post-structuralist thought. Hegel's speculative unconscious is an unconscious under erasure, subjected to sublation even while sublation becomes infected with Nature's indeterminacy—that is, Nature psychoanalyzes the violence intrinsic to sublation itself. In Schelling, the unconscious marks the absolute subject *of* speculative thought, a purposive organizational force to thinking that remains anterior to it. Hegel's unconscious marks what is unthought; Schelling's unconscious marks the un(pre)thinkable. Schelling's speculative unconscious is also an important precursor to the dissociationist model of the psyche (the idea that the psyche and its processes function in terms of autonomous clusters, or complexes, of affects and forces), which is carried forward, via Carl Jung's analytical psychology, to the post-structuralist thought of Deleuze and Guattari, whose *Anti-Oedipus* (1972) marks the "speculative turn" in Continental philosophy against the grain of the linguistic turn most strongly represented by Lacan. Indeed, this lineage strongly contests a reductive identification of post-structuralism with the linguistic turn, even as it thinks the idea of "language" otherwise in an intensive shift from discourse to a chthonic or cosmic poiesis.

This shift is precisely where Jung's significance is most clear: It is Jung's mature theory of the archetypes that articulates a theory of self that is based not in teleology, but a poiesis irreducible to intersubjective discourse. Indeed, while Jung profoundly influenced Deleuze (who takes up Jung's contemporary "questioning" unconscious), it is his metapsychological thinking of the archetype as intensity within a general economy traversing human and nonhuman (and organic and inorganic), and of the Self as centripetal organizing force, which articulates a far more radical post-structuralism avant la lettre than is possible with either Freud or Lacan. Jung's metapsychology also allows for a counter-deconstruction between Deleuze and Guattari's thinking and his metapsychology. In this counter-deconstruction, Deleuze and Guattari molecularize Jung's often more orthodox expressions of the archetype within a therapeutics of presence, just as Jungian metapsychology essentially deconstructs the schizoanalytic idea of meaning as one ironically enmired—and at least partially blinded—by its own Oedipalization, thereby further articulating the human subject position without compromising its post-structuralist intensity.[8] I begin with Franz Anton Mesmer (1734–1815) and animal magnetism, where the connection between Nature and abnormal modes of consciousness lays the groundwork, via the Marquis de Puységur's innovations, for a dynamic experience of the unconscious in German Idealism. Hegel and Schelling saw this acutely, and their radically contrasting engagements with magnetic sleep inform key differences in their understandings of the speculative unconscious.

2 Mesmer, Animal Magnetism, and Magnetic Sleep

Mesmer is known for the therapeutic method of animal magnetism he developed based on his experience treating patients in the late eighteenth century. Resisting the eighteenth-century soul–mind shift in psychology, animal magnetism was "the property of the animal body which brings it under the influence of the heavenly bodies, and the reciprocal action occurring among those who are surrounded by it."[9]

Thus, animal magnetism is fundamentally grounded in a deep relationship of mutual influence, or rapport, between Nature and the human organism—the belief that "NATURE AFFORDS A UNIVERSAL MEANS OF HEALING AND PRESERVING MEN" and that "the laws which govern the universe are the same as those which regulate the harmony of the animal."[10] The magnetizer could use this rapport to direct the flow of this universal fluid to cure various physical maladies such as convulsions, hemiplegia, colic, and ophthalmia.[11]

In a series of twenty-seven "Propositions" Mesmer defines animal magnetism as a means of directing an absolute force—a "universally distributed fluid… which surrounds all that exists."[12] The movement of this fluid is subject to a certain rhythm of "ebb and flow," alternating effects of "intensification and remission" that could be induced by the magnetizer.[13] This fluid relativized space and time; it could be controlled at a distance and could be exerted on organic and inorganic objects alike.[14] Moreover, all sickness and "aberration[s] in the animal body" could be ultimately cured (and could *only* be cured) through the inducement of magnetic *crisis*—an "intermediate" state "between wakefulness and perfect sleep"[15] brought about by stimulations of the universal fluid meant to overcome diseases that lead to "critical symptoms" (convulsions, fever, bodily evacuations, and other unpleasant feelings) as part of "the 'cure' of Nature," or the balancing of natural magnetic forces.[16] Patients in magnetic crisis could "foresee the future and bring the most remote past into the present," and extend their senses "to any distance and in all directions, without being checked by any obstacles," and could even diagnose and prognose diseases in themselves and others. "In short, it seems that all Nature is present to them."[17]

Despite their underlying metaphysics, however, Mesmer's innovations remained mechanistic and materialist in nature; his universal magnetic fluid was tangible, ultimately founded on matter itself, and Mesmer himself was confident that animal magnetism would ultimately be completely verifiable through empirical research.[18] Animal magnetism's specifically psychological dimensions, popular with Romantic thinkers, would come from French aristocrat Armand Marie Jacques de Chastenet, Marquis de Puységur (1751–1825), who developed magnetic somnambulism ("magnetic sleep") as a "sleep-waking kind of consciousness, a 'rapport' or special connection with the magnetizer, suggestibility, and amnesia in the waking state for events in the magnetized state," which often includes "a notable alteration in personality."[19]

Magnetic sleep marked a significant development in animal magnetism. Where Mesmer was preoccupied with curing physical maladies, magnetic sleep created a profound psychological connection between magnetizer and magnetized. Puységur argued that instead of violent, convulsive crises, the gentle, calming crises of magnetic sleep were the most beneficial,[20] guided by the magnetizer under an ethic of care that anticipated the analyst–analysand ethos. Most significantly, however, the rapport between magnetizer and magnetized gained new intersubjective significance: with Puységur rapport was "a profound and immediate communication" between magnetizer and magnetized and not between the magnetizer and other objects,[21] which meant that the magnetizer could suggest actions that the somnambulist would then perform. From this, Puységur concluded that the external existence of a magnetic fluid was irrelevant compared to the magnetizer's *will* to heal; this will can direct the vital principle of human beings, and "since will is beyond matter, there must be a *nonmaterial principle* operating at the heart of human action and therefore at the heart of magnetic healing."[22] This nonmaterial principle was also behind the possibility of "magnetization at a distance" (the magnetizer's ability to magnetize through walls and from different buildings) and a "sixth sense," the ability to perceive objects and situations not available to everyday consciousness.[23] Magnetic sleep not only marked the beginnings of the psychoanalytic concept of transference; it also interposed the psyche of the magnetized into the rapport between magnetizer and world, transforming a materialist relationship into a psychological dynamic with far-reaching implications for the concept of the unconscious in German Idealism. We now turn to Hegel, who associates magnetic somnambulism with a Nature that fundamentally troubles both the coherence of his *Encyclopedia* and the emergence of consciousness from the depths of soul life.

3 Hegel: The Unthought Unconscious

While Hegel credited animal magnetism with freeing the mind from the fetters of rational-empirical psychology, and while he grudgingly admits an affinity between the higher workings of philosophy and Mesmerism's "liberation of mind… from the limitations of space and time," he nevertheless saw animal magnetism as "a disease and a decline" in which the mind "surrenders its thinking."[24] In contrast, Hegel develops "absolute Idealism" as a speculative thinking promising a system of absolute knowledge in which knowledge ascends through the domains of Logic, Nature, and Mind, always returning to itself under the aegis of Reason in a process Hegel extends to life itself as the very essence of speculative thought.[25] This movement is powered by sublation, the transition of "finite determinations" into their opposites, negating these opposites and returning to themselves with the "*immanent connection and necessity*" of their Others in a movement that constitutes all scientific knowledge.[26]

But Nature causes fissures that unwork the *Encyclopedia*'s ascensionist teleology: thus Derrida describes Hegel's system as "more and other than the closure of its representation," producing a "remainder of writing" with an ambivalent relationship to Hegel's thought.[27] And while the *Philosophy of Nature* bids to sublate Mechanics into Physics and Physics into Organics (and inorganic matter into organic life) in its own circular whole, Tilottama Rajan points out that this project is plagued by each domain's existence as "a sphere in its own right, made up further levels that also insist on being understood on their own terms [in] an autonomy that at times threatens to derail the very project of encyclopaedic totalization."[28] And at the end of the *Logic* we do not find Logic's sublation by Nature; instead, the Idea "*resolves to release… itself as nature.*"[29] Contradiction without a proper dialectical relationship (an entity or organ remaining "for-itself") is precisely what disease is for Hegel, and at the beginning of the *Philosophy of Nature* he describes Nature as "the self-degradation of the idea"[30]—the "trash" of the system[31] which cannot be assimilated or sublated, "an alien existence in which Spirit does not find itself."[32] Nature is "impotent," hopelessly bound by organisms endlessly "entangled with other alien existences," yet this impotence *"sets limits to philosophy"* and renders Nature impenetrable to the Concept.[33] Indeed, the Concept's feebleness before Nature's immediacy is responsible for not only "alien" forces that continually subject animal life to danger and violence, but also "monstrosities" in the human organism.[34] And just as in disease the organism "separates itself into its separate moments,"[35] the Logic-Nature transition infects Hegel's system with fissures that persist in his account of Mind's evolution from soul-life.

The *Philosophy of Nature* ends with the death of the organism, and Rajan has noted how Hegel uses "transsubstantiative Christian rhetoric" to rescue the transition to Mind from the text's death drive.[36] Indeed, like the Idea in the *Logic*, Nature seems to release itself in death to Mind; this transition is awkwardly deferred to the Introduction to the *Philosophy of Mind*, where Hegel problematically posits an "absolutely first" Mind "in and for itself,"[37] different from the mind of the *Logic* (and indeed the *Encyclopedia* in general) in a preformationist bid troubled by the textual abruptions in the *Encyclopedia*'s three major "organs." Hegel's text reaffirms Nature's sheer contingency and externality before turning to Mind, which alone can overcome "the externality and finitude of its embodied reality" and *differentiate* itself from Nature in a movement that, however, is not sublation; Mind "does not emerge in a natural manner from nature."[38] Indeed Mind, in its ideality, must grasp Nature's "infinitely manifold material"—material that "is *at once poisoned* [vergiftet] *and transfigured* by the universality of the I [into] spiritual reality."[39] What ought to be sublation in a "circle of circles" is tainted as Mind is put under analysis by Nature to reveal the poison intrinsic to its sublative processes—a non-sublation within sublation, a fundamental violence which ruptures the work of the Concept.[40] Thus, sublation's violent textual displacement here dis-eases it into a *pharmakon* for Spirit—both a necessary cure for Nature's diseased contingency and a taint, a natural infection that ensures this contingency's claim upon Mind. Through this affliction of sublation's twofold speculative nature as both cancelling and preserving, Hegel's speculative unconscious emerges as a domain of the mind infected with the bad infinity of Nature's contingency—the "surrender of thinking" he associates with magnetic sleep.

This violence persists in the first subsection of Subjective Mind, "Anthropology," which focuses on the soul, or "natural mind," as the lowest tier of mind, "the truth, the ideality, of *everything material*, as the *entirely universal*."[41] Here soul is Nature; it exists before the particularizations and judgments that work on the soul's basic "stuff." Natural soul, as the primary process of the *Philosophy of Mind*, is attuned to "universal planetary life," or "the universal life of nature"; it is "the *substance*, the absolute foundation of all the particularizing and individualizing of mind, so that it is in the soul that *mind* finds all the stuff of its determination... [It is] *the unity of thinking and being*."[42] But while "universal planetary life" is ultimately insignificant as a mere milestone on the road to self-consciousness, it once again sets the stage not for Mind's sublation of Nature, but rather Mind's raising (*erheben*) itself above Nature and "subjecting [*unterwerfen*] the world to its thinking."[43] Hegel equates a state of unison with Nature with those suffering from illnesses, yet sublation's displacement here into *erheben* and *unterwerfen* infects Mind with the abruption of Nature's subaltern disease.

Feeling soul hovers between the unfree naturalness of mere Being as immediate, individualized sensation, and consciousness, as an "*objective totality*" of external objects in an ordered objective world.[44] While the feeling soul is not purely subsumed in Nature's contingency, it nevertheless remains "a *totality* of infinitely many distinct determinacies which in the soul unite into *one*, so that in them the soul remains, *in itself*, infinite *being-for-itself*" in a "timeless, undifferentiated interior of the soul."[45] Feeling soul's "simple inwardness" constitutes each individual as "an infinite wealth of sensation-determinations, representations, information, [and] thoughts" and it is only

> [s]ometimes, in sickness, [that] representations or information, supposed to have been forgotten years ago,… once more come to light. *They were not in our possession, nor perhaps by such reproduction as occurs in sickness do they for the future come into our possession; and yet they were in us and remain in us from now on.* Thus a person can never know how much information he really *has in him*, even if he has forgotten it. It belongs not to his actuality, not to his subjectivity as such, but only to his implicit being.[46]

These sensation-determinations and representations are uncannily present as a bad infinity of alien material connected to soul and Nature; seemingly impervious to sublation, they remain unaltered "amidst all the determinacy and mediation of consciousness that is later installed in it."[47] But this material only appears in sickness; indeed, the feeling soul's suspension between consciousness and immediate sensation is precisely what makes it diseased, for in this state "a contradiction between the freedom and unfreedom of the soul"[48] prevails without healthy sublative movement.

The beginning of subjectivity in soul-life manifests in the relationship between mother and child in a "being of feeling" that informs the child's character: predispositions, temperaments, and future relationships in the world.[49] Here, the potentiation of the speculative unconscious manifests as a Derridean écriture avant la lettre that Hegel aligns with magnetic sleep. As the determining "genius" of the child, the mother's ability to bestow temperament, talent, and the susceptibility to illness puts her squarely in the domain of indeterminate sensation, especially in her capacity to write her strong impressions and sensations on to the child.[50] Moreover, Hegel links the "magic relationship" of the mother's "writing" the child with monocotyledons,[51] clearly associating this "magic" with a dissociationist paradigm relegated to the plant kingdom as a lower, "feeble [and] infantile" level of development;[52] as such each plant's parts constitute "an infinite number of subjects" that the plant itself cannot control.[53] When detached from the parent stem, the bulbs of certain monocotyledons put forth their own roots and leaves, which for Hegel constitutes an impotent "aggregate of a group of individuals which form a single individual" bereft of unifying subjectivity.[54] And in the relationship between parents and children we find Hegel's only use of *unbewußt* in the *Philosophy of Mind*,[55] in a context again associated with childhood—the possibility of a "magical" relationship between separated parents and children, which entails an unconscious "mutual attraction" between two parties who do not know each other due to their separation—a situation clearly reminiscent of magnetic sleep's action at a distance.

Hence Hegel's dismissal of magnetic sleep in his discussion of the feeling soul. The "stage of dreaming and intimation" that marks the feeling soul in its immediacy is a "state of disease"[56] virtually identical to magnetic sleep, in which "the individual stands in *unmediated* relationship with the concrete content of its own self."[57] Disease occurs when the soul's abstractions of dreams and intimations seep into conscious rationality as a dissociationist recrudescence of the plant's bad infinity of subjects. Puységur's healing crises is for Hegel the subsumption, by feeling, of the individual who "is *at the mercy* of all its own *contingency* of feeling, of imagining, etc.," as well as the possibility of contagion by the magnetizer.[58] Hegel ultimately eschews the *unbewußt* power of the cure without offering another way to overcome the mere contradiction of mental disease and resume thought's proper work of knowledge. For an entirely different and more constructive engagement with magnetic sleep we must turn to Schelling's own philosophical psychology.

4 Schelling: The Un(pre)thinkable Unconscious

In his 1821 Erlangen lecture "On the Nature of Philosophy as Science" Schelling argues that systems of knowledge emerge from a state of *asystasy*, a differential economy of inner conflict that primordially (un)grounds all knowledge.[59] Knowledge and experience are organized not by the labor of the Concept but by the absolute subject—a purposive, individuating force which "*proceed*[s] *through everything and* [is not] *anything*,"[60] moving through the primordial fluidity of knowledge without being reduced to its predicates. As a fundamental critique of egoity, the absolute subject harks back to Schelling's *Naturphilosophie*, which casts this force as the mythical figure of Proteus who draws all the possible forms of Nature's free productivity into a paradoxically predetermined circle, thus emblematizing the paradoxical freedom and necessity inherent in the *Naturphilosophie*'s general economy of forces.[61] Indeed, Schelling later takes aim at precisely that point in Hegel's *Encyclopedia* where Nature becomes the trash of the system[62] to question the very necessity of movement at all in Hegel's Idea, and to gesture to what Fred Rush calls Hegel's "massive mistake of fundamental ontology… that is supposed to culminate immanently in establishing that 'the Concept' is coextensive with all that there is."[63] We must therefore begin with the *Naturphilosophie*, whose tensions become crucial to the proto-psychoanalytical emphasis of Schelling's later work.

The speculative physics of Schelling's *Naturphilosophie* attempts to "heave [Nature] out of the dead mechanism to which it seems predisposed, to quicken it with freedom and to set it into its own free development"[64]—a free development in a general economy of forces that expresses the productive power in matter itself. The *Naturphilosophie* forms the unconscious groundwork for what would later become the asystasy of Schelling's philosophical psychology. Where Hegel's *Philosophy of Nature* in effect psychoanalyzes the sublative violence in his philosophical psychology,[65] Schelling's *Naturphilosophie* connects with a fundamentally creative force unbeholden to an ascensionist teleology. *Naturphilosophie* is ultimately "doing philosophy in accordance with nature" as "a gateway into the originating experience of philosophizing" itself,[66] and thus to explore Nature is to explore one's *own* nature in something more than a strictly teleological framework.

In the *First Outline*, Nature is fundamentally a *"most primal fluid... receptive to every form."*[67] Schelling explains the existence of matter, and the natural products that emerge from this pre-individual fluidity, by positing the *actant* as a nonmolar, monadic force; actants are matter's "constituent factors... seed[s] around which Nature can begin to form itself."[68] In a dramatic struggle "between form and the formless,"[69] actants are "decombined" into free individuality just as they are simultaneously "combined" into new formations with other actants in a radical productivity that is inhibited into natural objects.[70] This productivity follows the trajectory of a *Stufenfolge*, a graduated scale of development with increasing complexity leading to the *"absolute product"* that "lives in all products, that always becomes and never is, and in which the absolute activity [of Nature] exhausts itself."[71]

This actantial drama of simultaneous freedom and compulsion is described in distinctly proto-psychoanalytical terms as their mutual derangement (*sich stören*): Each actant's "constant drive [*Trieb*] toward free transformation" is inhibited by the "compulsion" (*Zwang*) of its combination with other actants in what cannot be articulated by a Freudian or Lacanian unconscious. Rather, in this quasi-subjective site of forces constellated by the individuative force of the absolute subject we are closest here to Jung's unconscious, whose consubstantiality with Nature[72] always already connects the human psyche with the indeterminate forces of material production. Expressing an economy of forces remarkably similar to that of Schelling's *Naturphilosophie*, Jung writes of the unconscious:

> The unconscious depicts an extremely fluid state of affairs... [In the system of drives] [o]ne drive deranges and represses [*stört und verdrängt*] the others [and] their blind, compulsive character [*blinder Zwangscharakter*] frequently causes mutual disturbances. The differentiation of function from the inevitable compulsion of the drives... is vitally important with regard to the maintenance of life[, but] increases the possibility of collision and creates... those dissociations which time and again put into question the unity of consciousness.[73]

What for Hegel is unconscious soul-life's derangement and disease, which must be subject-ed to sublation's speculative movement, is for Jung vitally constitutive of psychic life. And the same holds true for Schelling's *Naturphilosophie* as a philosophical antecedent of analytical psychology; Nature's own productivity is a *pharmakon* from which it cannot escape. On the one hand, Schelling writes, Nature wants to deny its creation of individual products as *"misbegotten attempts"* to achieve the absolute product[74]—Nature wants to turn backward to its primordial fluidity. On the other hand, Nature needs this productivity in its forward drive to the absolute product and the final cessation of its activity, "for all natural activity aims toward an absolute product."[75] This ambitendency of Nature toward its own products, and the procreative force that creates them, makes Nature a fundamentally destabilizing force that troubles Schelling's efforts to unite mind and Nature in his own brief flirtation with an idealist system.

The *System of Transcendental Idealism* (1800) is Schelling's eccentric, abortive attempt to bond Idealism with the *Naturphilosophie*—to "[materialize] *the laws of mind into laws of nature*"[76] and thus into an internally complete system of knowledge. But there is a certain irony here: Schelling writes in the Foreword that while only the twin sciences of *Naturphilosophie* and transcendental philosophy can create such a system, "on that very account the two must forever be opposed to one another, and can never merge into one."[77] While this may seem to mirror the failure of Hegel's Idealism to assimilate the speculative unconscious that (un)grounds it, from this abortive parallelism emerges instead a productive unconscious that marks an alien materiality in the *System* that is ultimately taken up as intellectual intuition—the union of ideal and real that, far from being an imperfect starting point for selfhood, grounds its very existence. Like the *Naturphilosophie*, the *System* narrates the development of self-consciousness as a *Stufenfolge*, a graduated set of stages whereby the self raises itself to consciousness. Consciousness emerges in a "pure act" that is paradoxically (and problematically) indistinct from its concept.[78] Yet near the end of the *System*, the productive unconscious intrudes on the autoaffection of thought as "hidden necessity"[79] intervening in the *System*'s thought-project of conceptual freedom: "[Through freedom] something I do not intend is brought about unconsciously, i.e., without my consent; [consciousness] is to be confronted with an unconscious, whereby out of the most inhibited expression there arises unawares something wholly involuntary."[80]

This hidden necessity is fundamental to Schelling's formulation of intellectual intuition as the core of the *System*'s Idealist subject. The self *is* intellectual intuition, the convergence of ideal and real, mind and Being as "the organ of all transcendental thinking"[81] that powers the *System*'s path to a science of knowledge, "a knowing that has its object outside itself."[82] But this knowing, grounded in absolute identity (A=A) as the principle of transcendental Idealism that determines the *System*, is always already ungrounded by its alien other, an objectivity and materiality (A=B) that binds all logical statements to "something alien to the thought, and distinct from it."[83] Intellectual intuition is, in short, the unconscious aspect of consciousness, the latter's inescapable tie to Being. The *System*'s concluding section turns to the philosophy of art to cast knowledge as the aesthetic "odyssey of the spirit."[84] Here, echoing Kant, Schelling wants to transform intellectual intuition into "aesthetic intuition" that, through the production of the work of art, unites conscious and unconscious potencies in a "blessed" union that outstrips intellectual intuition's lower understanding of human identity.[85] In this way, the materiality of Schelling's productive unconscious is repressed as the unruly Nature that exists in uneasy tension with transcendental Idealism—but Schelling's later work resuscitates the indeterminacy of this unconscious[86] as he leaves transcendental Idealism behind in a "darkening" of his thinking inaugurated by his pathbreaking work on human freedom.

By the time he writes *Philosophical Investigations Into the Essence of Human Freedom* (1809), Schelling is no longer interested in a conventionally idealist system of thought. Here, the unconscious is no longer suppressed into a theological aesthetic but rather marks a darker, more Romantic intensity of Being as that which is anterior to thought and which recedes from conceptual or dialectical understanding. In this sense the *Freedom* essay and *The Ages of the World* (1815) are complementary texts that crystallize Schelling's speculative unconscious into a potentiated dynamic linking mind and Being that, as such, cannot be contained within the boundaries of either the Freudian or Lacanian unconscious (indeed, this dynamic will ultimately lead us to the fluxes and flows of schizoanalytic desiring-machines and the nomadic subject).

As Schelling's theory of personality, the *Freedom* essay returns to the *Naturphilosophie* as the only philosophy adequate to the task of articulating human freedom: "God himself is not a system, but rather a life"[87] that, like any other life, must individuate in time and history. But just as Schelling had to answer the question of how things come to be from Nature's fluidity, here he is faced with the question of how time and history emerge from a God that already encompasses all things. Schelling answers that they are ultimately grounded in "that which in God himself is not *He Himself*, that is, in that which is the ground of his existence"[88]—the not-God within God that is unknown to God and that, through a primordial scission in Being, always already involves God in Nature. God *must* have an unconscious, which Schelling calls the *Ungrund*, the non-ground of Being that lies in "the yearning the eternal One feels to give birth to itself"[89] and individuate through Nature's deranged materiality. And just as God is compelled to enter time and history in an unprethinkable moment of creation, so the individual personality is inaugurated in an unconscious act that "precedes consciousness just as it precedes essence, indeed, first *produces* it."[90] The *Freedom* essay thus reads the *Naturphilosophie*'s speculative unconscious into God and the human psyche in a final collapse of the death drive toward a conceptually closed self that was promoted by the 1800 *System*. Indeed, the *Freedom* essay deconstructs the *System*'s ontotheology to paradoxically awaken this self to a new, if more imperiled, life embroiled in evil's *pharmakon* energy.

This unprethinkable moment watermarks the theodicean dynamic of the *Freedom* essay. Paradoxically both free and necessary, this act also determines the individuation of human personality as the freedom to individuate *as one must*, and this individuation underpins the *Freedom* essay's concern with the problem of evil not as (Hegelian) negation, but rather as an *energic* force that generates a necessary, productive imbalance in Being. In other words, disease and evil are integral to the free necessity of personality, which necessarily recapitulates the tension of the *Naturphilosophie*'s actantial economy and emerges in "the connection between a self-determining being and a basis [*centrum*] independent of him,"[91] the *centrum* being the unconscious, the *Ungrund* as it exists in the person. Evil is a misrelation between the self-will of consciousness and its unconscious universality, compelling the psyche to ego-tistically appropriate the *centrum* for consciousness. This "involution" is necessary for the "evolution" of individuation,[92] and just as natural production is a *pharmakon* that both ensures Nature's progression to the absolute product and makes this endpoint impossible, so the *Freedom* essay's return to the

Naturphilosophie casts individuation as a connection with the *Ungrund*, which both ensures and forecloses its completion in the form of "evil" misrelation.[93] As the *Ungrund* of Being reflected in the *centrum* of the human personality, this speculative unconscious is the anthropocentrized écriture avant la lettre of the derangement of forces subject to such problematic and violent sublation in Hegel's *Encyclopedia*. Here, however, the unconscious is imbricated in an inscrutable rhythm of involution and evolution which remains unbound by the ascensionist teleology that watermarks the *Encyclopedia*—indeed, Schelling's later *Ages of the World* (1815) complicates this unconscious further while returning to the very idea of magnetic sleep Hegel rejects.

As what Jason Wirth calls a "self-composing cosmic poem,"[94] Schelling's *Ages of the World* takes up where the *Freedom* essay's theory of personality leaves off. Where the *Freedom* essay articulates a systolic–diastolic rhythm of the relationship between conscious self and unconscious *centrum*, *Ages* delves deeper into the dynamics of this individuation, particularly through articulating the doctrine of the potencies (*Potenzenlehre*)—a tripartite movement of potentiation by which time and history come into being. Moreover, by casting the mesmeric crisis as an intrapsychic and deeply autoimmune *Potenzenlehre* to allegorize the emergence of Being, Schelling sets the stage for a cosmologization of the *Freedom* essay's human drama into an analyst-analysand dynamic that connects with a potentiated speculative unconscious irreducible to intersubjective discourse, the excavation of personal history, or any ego psychology.[95] Indeed the *Potenzenlehre*, as "a metaphysics of God which is indissolubly linked to a metaphysics of Nature,"[96] provides a psychoanalysis of history "that may well make history impossible, in the Hegelian sense of a transition from nature to spirit and from spirit to freedom."[97]

Here, dissociationism is ontologically charged: the person is "the combinatory point of the cosmos"[98] involving forces unbeholden to consciousness or concept. To discover human knowledge as the self-development of primordial life, *Ages*' cosmic poetry begins with an anamnestic dialectic[99] between questioning and answering beings, a "secret circulation" in the psyche in which the supramundane is tied to a lower, "unknowing and dark" principle in which "rests the recollection of all things of their original relationships."[100] In this dialectic, the person possesses "that which must again be brought back to memory," which must be discerned by an unconscious Other that is "free from everything and is capable of thinking everything," but which cannot express itself without being *witnessed* by consciousness.[101] This "doubling of ourselves" is articulated by the *Potenzenlehre*, which begins with A^1 as the first potency of primordial negation, God's self-withdrawal and contraction. But A^1's "rotatory motion" in "loathing and anxiety"[102] compels it to inaugurate time and history via a dissociative act of conation in which it "dislocate[s] itself from itself in order to be... its own complete being."[103] Hence A^2, the second potency and "Being to the second power" with which A^1 forms a "primordial antithesis."[104] In a paradoxical uplifting through a "pulling downward" whereby "each subordinate potency attracts the potency immediately higher in it,"[105] each potency sees its future in its higher counterpart and attracts it through a "bewitching": A^2 is pulled down (bewitched) to A^1 and thereby A^3 emerges as the posited unity of A^1 and A^2, a counter-projection of the latter in which A^2 sees its completion.[106] A^3 is thus spirit in nature, an animating force representing the free relationship between A^2's affirmative force and the negating force of A^1.[107]

Where Hegel sees magnetic sleep as a perilous sinking into soul-life, Schelling sees the primordial entrance of yearning into eternal nature itself as a cosmic "crisis,"[108] casting magnetic sleep as an intrapsychic *Potenzenlehre* that allegorizes the inauguration of time and history.[109] Schelling describes this first in terms of the liberation and harmonization of "the freest play and circulation of forces" attempted by the hypnotist as he connects with the psychological dissociation and derangement of Schelling's speculative unconscious. This prepares the way for spirit's psychoanalysis of soul, in which soul is shown "things hidden in the soul's interior… (pertaining to what is future and eternal in the person)."[110] *Ages'* dialogue between questioning and answering beings, in which authentic knowledge must be witnessed by both,[111] unfolds in a dynamic that anticipates the psychoanalytic concept of countertransference—which Freud and Lacan staunchly opposed, but to which Jung was more open.[112] Yet this countertransferential opening of the subject to not only the human Other, but also to the forces of cosmos and Nature, leads us beyond Hegel's "agony of the Concept"[113] to the domain of fluxes and flows that mark Deleuze and Guattari's schizoanalysis.

5 Deleuze and Guattari: The Molecular Unconscious

"What is thought's relationship with the earth?"[114] The spirit of this question frames Deleuze and Guattari's collaborative engagement with the dissociative paradigm we have seen developed in Schelling while at the same time dynamizing Jung's more structural equation of psyche with Nature. Deleuze and Guattari, too, see no ultimate distinction between humanity and Nature; rather, they are united in a materialist psychiatry based on a desiring-production that traverses organic and inorganic domains. Thus, the schizoanalytic project of *Anti-Oedipus* (1972) is involved in "tirelessly taking apart egos and their presuppositions" in the name of liberating repressed "prepersonal singularities"—for "everyone is a little group and must live as such."[115] And although there is no explicit reference to Schelling in the collaborative work of Deleuze and Guattari,[116] their later work implicitly takes up a question the later Schelling puts to Hegel: "What if concepts can be shown which [Hegel's] system knows nothing about?"[117] As early as the *Encyclopedia Logic* Hegel had attempted to claim drive (*Trieb*) for the Concept and dialectical sublation,[118] but in *Anti-Oedipus*'s critique of Idealism there is scant reference to drives—rather, what Deleuze earlier describes as transcendental empiricism (which "undertakes the most insane creation of concepts ever seen or heard [and] treats the concept as object of an encounter, as a here-and-now"[119]) is impelled by the flows of desire itself.

The desire at the heart of *Anti-Oedipus* "does not take as its object persons or things, but the entire surroundings that it traverses, the vibrations and flows of every sort to which it is joined."[120] Under the rubric of this desire *Anti-Oedipus* reconceives libido neither as the work of a Concept nor as desire for the mother or the phallus, but as the specific transformative energy of production articulated by desiring-machines, organic and mechanical assemblages that connect desire with real material operations to exhibit desire's flows, breaks, and conjugations in terms of units of production.[121] Thus, desire is not lack; unbound by objects that Oedipalize a particular regime of production, the continuous flow of desire leaves objects in its wake in what can only be the production of a non-Lacanian Real unbarred from the Symbolic—indeed, the Real-Symbolic distinction does not exist in the first place.[122]

This productivity marks the speculative unconscious of schizoanalysis. In *Difference and Repetition* Deleuze adopts the idea of a "serial, problematic, and questioning" unconscious directly influenced by Jung,[123] which exists in a compensatory relation with consciousness that engages more with the demands of the present as opposed to the implications of childhood.[124] This contemporaneity is cast in *Anti-Oedipus* as a transcendental-empirical unconscious "defined by the immanence of its criteria,"[125] which rejects a Hegelian-dialectical subjectivity in favor of a "residual subject" that "sweeps the circle [of intensive states] and concludes a self from its oscillations."[126] Yet this schizoanalytic unconscious cannot be understood without first briefly explicating the dynamism of the three passive syntheses of connection, disjunction, and conjunction—ubiquitous and simultaneous virtual processes that constitute both the objects and experiences of the schizoanalytic unconscious. As constitutive of this post-structuralist speculative unconscious, the passive syntheses materialize, as the social work of desire, the epistemological gap between Schelling's primal fluid and the theoretical monadism of the actants; they also discern the flows of libidinal desire that remain encrypted in the structural tendencies of Jung's archetypal economy.

As the production *of* production, the *connective* synthesis unfolds in the continuous polymorphism of libidinally charged connections between partial objects and desiring-machines in a general economy of flows and connections ("and... and then... and then"): the infant's mouth and breast, eyes and the nape of the neck; the foot connects to the bicycle pedal, then connects to pavement, then to a tile floor. This productive energy is then transformed by the *disjunctive* ("recording") synthesis ("either... or... or"), the force of anti-production that inhibits (in ways remarkably similar to Schelling's Nature in the *First Outline*) and inscribes the desiring-machines' production as discrete networks of relations between connections—often defined by Oedipal lack, but that are nevertheless open-ended (the foot leaves the bicycle pedal connection to generate a cobblestone connection as it walks).[127] In this synthesis, the unconscious field is figured as the Body without Organs (BwO): a recording surface, an "amorphous, undifferentiated fluid" constituted by desiring-machines in an attraction-repulsion that both courts and resists the differentiation of life into organs and organisms, and libido into instincts and drives.[128] Deleuze and Guattari describe the BwO's repulsion of desiring-machines in anti-production as Freudian primary repression, which emerges as secondary repression in material practice as the *socius*, an "unengendered, nonproductive attitude," a field of non-production (the Earth, the tyrant, the State, or capital itself and its Oedipal triangulations) against or upon which forms of production emerge.[129]

The subject finally emerges as an epiphenomenon of the *conjunctive* synthesis, in which the tension between free production (connective synthesis) and restriction of the BwO (disjunctive synthesis) is "resolved" through the constitution of an "I" from the permutations of desire across the first two syntheses. Recorded on the surface of the BwO are the affects and experiences of a subject which, in its delusion of sovereignty, claims them as its own. Yet this is Deleuze and Guattari's *nomadic* subject, always dissociated, whose "schizoid" potential to perceive the seethe of desiring-machines can put it beside itself in ways reminiscent of Schelling's ecstasy, but which nevertheless organize knowledge as a constellation of affects and intensities while being "continually reborn" from state to state, never culminating in a fixed subject. Thus, what for Hegel is the speculative unconscious as the "abyss of all representations"[130] is rescued as desiring-production itself as the perpetual constitution of the subject. Moreover, the tripartite movement of Schelling's *Potenzenlehre* is molecularized: Here we do not talk about a drama of potentiation or Spirit's psychoanalysis of soul, but rather of a desire that moves *transversally* through and between these concepts. And there is a particularly interesting chiasmus here, a counter-deconstruction between Jung's analytical psychology and the work of schizoanalysis. On the one hand, the machine-connections of the schizoanalytic unconscious molecularize Jung's general archetypal economy of figures, symbols, and experiences into spatiotemporal perception and awareness: seen through this lens, the "baby's mouth-breast" machine connection is "archetypal"; the transition from "baby's mouth-breast connection" to "baby's mouth smiling at a toy connection" is "archetypal"; the transition from "shoe on bicycle pedal" to "shoe on cobblestone" to "shoe on tile floor" is "archetypal" (as is the parallel desire-production "boot in stirrup" to "boot on dirt road" to "boot on saloon floor"), and so forth. What Jung figures as the "linguistic matrices... derived from primordial images"[131] from which archetypes come, Deleuze and Guattari deconstruct as the confluence of flows and machine connections. On the other hand, Jung's nonteleological Self, as a purposive, centripetal force constellating archetypal images and experience,[132] offers a tenable framework for the nomadic production and organization of "meaning" beyond what Deleuze and Guattari criticize, somewhat myopically, as a *merely* Oedipalized meaning that forecloses on desire.[133] In this chiasmus, meaning is not transcendentally signified—it is corpuscular, consubstantial with the work of desire itself.

Hence the "nonfigurative and nonsymbolic unconscious" of schizoanalysis, "a figural dimension... apprehended below the minimum conditions of identity"[134] Deleuze and Guattari offer as antidote to the "neoidealism" of Oedipal psychoanalysis.[135] While Deleuze and Guattari credit Freud with the discovery of desiring-machines—the loci of disjunctions, flows, and endless connections between intensities,[136] they see Freud as compelled to inhibit these flows of desire into the Oedipal triangulations of psychoanalysis—the "daddy-mommy-me" dynamic that not only congeals the family unit, but also readies the subject for its capitalist permutations. In contrast, schizoanalysis reads desire away from despotic signifiers (God, the phallus, the organism) to jump-start, as it were, the analysand's desiring-machines apart from "meaningful" connections with imaginary objects in an economy of lack. Thus, the schizo experiences Nature as a productivity predicated on humanity and Nature as "one and the same essential reality, the producer-product"[137] as opposed to either the theatre of psychoanalysis or a Lacanian unconscious constituted by political intersubjectivity as an effect of the Symbolic.

Concluding rather speculatively, I want to turn to a question left in the wake of *Anti-Oedipus*' reconception of psychoanalysis: Is there a "beyond post-structuralism" where the unconscious is concerned?

6 Conclusion: Beyond (?) Post-structuralism

Shortly after its publication, *Anti-Oedipus* seems to have provoked a line of escape from within post-structuralism itself: Jean-François Lyotard's *Libidinal Economy* (1974) can be read as an expressionist resistance to precisely the theorizing represented by *Anti-Oedipus*. Setting out from the position that "the place of theory… must be vanquished,"[138] *Libidinal Economy* seeks to surpass the categories of critical thought through a Romantic-libidinal blend of ideal and real, a fluidity of style reflecting a "politics of flight" with no claim to theoretical consistency, serving instead the sheer poiesis of libidinal flow: "We do not interpret, we read, and we effect by writings."[139] To this end, the libidinal economist is tasked with feeling "the unrepeatable singularities of the passages of affect," experiencing the pagan intensities of the one-sided Moebius band of the libidinal as a "disorder of machines."[140] No "unconscious," but intensities in a work of immanence written in an ekphrastic, ecstatic mode that nevertheless shares many of *Anti-Oedipus*' themes. Lyotard's later disavowal of the work as an "evil book" of rhetorical immodesty[141] perhaps reflects its tenuous claims to have escaped post-structuralist critique.

If, as Deleuze writes, the speculative unconscious must be thought not as history but as geography,[142] perhaps we must do so by invoking history ironically. As part of the Speculative Realism/Object-Oriented Ontology (OOO) movements some claim to be "after" post-structuralism, Timothy Morton's *Hyperobjects* (2013) argues that post-structuralism has unfinished business insofar as it has remained in the fantasy of a metalanguage untainted by its object of inquiry.[143] Thus Morton's conception of the hyperobject, which can only be known inter-dynamically from its assemblages and effects, but is nevertheless an object in its own right with its own "undulating" space-time.[144] Hyperobjectivity is part of OOO's project of restoring a certain integrity to objects elided to some extent by the linguistic turn within post-structuralism and the correlationism it has, in part, brought about; indeed, the unconscious itself is a hyperobject, embodying the nonlocal, atemporal asymmetry between thought and Being as it imbricates with other hyperobjects (Earth, capital, ocean microplastics, climate) in a transdisciplinary poiesis that dissociatively writes the human psyche.[145] The unconscious, as a certain kind of in-itself, exists beyond and between the disciplines and discourses that can only measure its effects, which—beyond orthodox Freudianism, Lacanism, and Jungianism—are written within and through other hyperobjects.[146]

Psychoanalysis

The speculative unconscious is inescapably entwined with Nature—be it a subaltern Nature whose writing must be colonized through the violence of Hegelian sublation, a Schellingian general economy of forces that impel the individuation of both God and humanity through the productive necessity of evil, Jung's unconscious and its isomorphism with cosmos and material Nature, or Deleuze and Guattari's unconscious as intensive autoproduction of the Real. Moreover, in the so-called Anthropocene, the speculative unconscious as hyperobject forces us to come to terms with "the immanence of thinking to the physical"[147] in discomfortingly contemporary ways, and involves seeing the violence inherent in our species' unsuccessful and self-destructive attempts to sublate Nature. There is, of course, merit to hyperobjectivity's demand for a metalanguage without pretense to objectivity, a language capable of doing justice to its object as *part* of that object—but what would this language of engagement with the speculative unconscious look like? Perhaps an authentically post-structuralist engagement with the speculative unconscious could be brought about in a non-anthropomorphic "no-man's land" between scientific discipline and poiesis; with this we are ironically brought back to the desire in the "Oldest Program Toward a System in German Idealism" for a mythological science, a unity of philosophy and mythology that would finally bring about "the *equal* formation of *all* forces."[148] Would this take the form of a portmanteaulogy, an ontology of clashing word-senses that reveal, however fleetingly, the (sense of an) object=X? And would this poiesis not also involve its counterpart as a mythological *science*? Could such a language even resonate with a species that seems permanently bound on the Procrustean bed of its discourses and for whom, as Schelling once famously said, Nature seems not to exist?[149]

The idealist desire for this language has nevertheless persisted into the twentieth century at least, in the form of Jung and quantum physicist Wolfgang Pauli's unfinished collaboration on a "neutral language" meant to reflect "a simultaneous religious and scientific function of... archetypal symbols,"[150] an automorphic language that could straddle psychological (archetypal) and (quantum) physical discourses while remaining irreducible to either. As I write this, Vladimir Putin's Russia is subjecting Ukraine to a full-scale invasion—itself a hyperobject amidst the movement of other hyperobjects, intensities, potentiations, desiring-machines, and archetypal images. The discourse this hyperobject will inevitably spawn will just as inevitably cloud the possibilities for understanding the fog of meanings, affects, and images that emerge in its wake. Even if such a neutral language—irreducible to either political *Schwärmerei* or the cunning of Reason—remains transcendental, composed of twin forces that "must forever be opposed to one another, and can never merge into one," the need for such a language to glimpse and glean the rhizomatic complexity of the speculative unconscious suggests that the agonized engagements of German Idealism with both "Nature" and "the unconscious" resonate with us no less today.

Notes

1. Immanuel Kant, *Anthropology from a Pragmatic Point of View*, trans. Robert Louden (Cambridge: Cambridge University Press, 2006), 24.
2. Ibid., 25.
3. G. W. F. Hegel, *Philosophy of Mind*, trans. William Wallace, rev. Michael Inwood (Oxford: Oxford University Press, 2007), 5.
4. G. W. F. Hegel, *Philosophy of Nature*, trans. A.V. Miller (Oxford: Oxford University Press, 1970), 1.
5. Eduard von Hartmann, *Philosophy of the Unconscious*, vol. 1, trans. William Coupland (London: Routledge, Trench, Trubner & Co, 1931), 28. Tilottama Rajan also points out the importance of German Idealism to the genesis of psychoanalysis: "[T]he history of nature in German idealism is the site where concepts such as inhibition, drive, archetype, 'crisis,' the primal scene of trauma, and the (im)possibility of remembering and working through this trauma to enlightenment, receive their earliest expression" ("'The Abyss of the Past': Psychoanalysis in Schelling's *Ages of the World* (1815)," *Romantic Circles* (2008): https://romantic-circles.org/praxis/psychoanalysis/rajan/rajan.html).
6. G. W. F. Hegel, *Encyclopedia of the Philosophical Sciences in Basic Outline, Part I: Science of Logic*, trans. Klaus Brinkmann and Daniel Dahlstrom (Cambridge: Cambridge University Press, 2010), 46.
7. See, for example, Günter Gödde, "The Unconscious in the German Philosophy and Psychology of the Nineteenth Century," in *The Edinburgh Critical History of Nineteenth-Century Philosophy*, ed. Alison Stone (Edinburgh: Edinburgh University Press, 2011), and Angus Nicholls and Martin Liebscher, "Introduction," in *Thinking the Unconscious: Nineteenth-Century German Thought*, ed. Angus Nicholls and Martin Liebscher (Cambridge: Cambridge University Press, 2010), 4ff.
8. For these reasons, while I can only make brief references to psychoanalytic thinkers here I shall focus more on Jung, about whom much less has been written. For Jung's importance to Deleuze—who placed Jung firmly in the tradition of the "differential unconscious" (Deleuze, "Leibniz Seminar" (29 April 1980): https://www.webdeleuze.com/textes/54)—see Christian Kerslake, *Deleuze and the Unconscious* (London: Continuum, 2007); Gilbert Simondon also significantly develops Jung's idea of individuation and credits him with discovering "affectivo-emotive themes" in myths, whose "quantum nature" fundamentally organizes human beings as higher organisms (*Individuation in Light of Notions of Form and Information*, vol. 1, trans. Taylor Adkins [Minneapolis: University of Minnesota Press, 2020], 274). Jung could be seen as a "Romantic" thinker within a territory comprised of Romantic and Idealist thinking on the one hand, and on the other a psychology which culminates in Deleuze and Guattari's philosophical potentiation of non-Freudian psychoanalysis. That Deleuze and Guattari's critiques of Jung did not fully understand his metapsychology is beyond my scope here, but merits serious study. I explore the Schelling-Jung connection(s) in my *Romantic Metasubjectivity through Schelling and Jung: Rethinking the Romantic Subject* (London and New York: Routledge, 2020). By Jung's "therapeutics of presence" I mean his tendency to render archetypes as ontotheologically self-present entities (Shadow, Anima-Animus, Wise Old Woman, etc.) in the interests of helping his patients (ibid., 18).
9. F. A. Mesmer, *Mesmerism: A Translation of the Original Scientific and Medical Writings of F. A. Mesmer*, trans. George Bloch (Los Altos: William Kaufmann, 1980), 68.
10. Ibid., 44, 101.
11. Ibid., 56.
12. Ibid., 81.
13. Ibid., 46.
14. Ibid., 67ff.
15. Ibid., 124.
16. Ibid., 103–4.

17. Ibid., 112.
18. Adam Crabtree, *From Mesmer to Freud: Magnetic Sleep and the Roots of Psychological Healing* (New Haven and London: Yale University Press, 1993), 51.
19. Ibid., 39. For more detail see ibid., chap. 3.
20. Ibid., 47.
21. Ibid., 41.
22. Ibid., 50–1 (my italics).
23. Ibid., 44.
24. Hegel, *Philosophy of Mind*, 24.
25. Hegel, *Philosophy of Nature*, 274.
26. Hegel, *Science of Logic*, 129.
27. Jacques Derrida, *Positions*, trans. Alan Bass (Chicago: University of Chicago Press, 1981), 77.
28. Tilottama Rajan, "(In)digestible Material: Illness and Dialectic in Hegel's *Philosophy of Nature*," in *Cultures of Taste, Theories of Appetite: Eating Romanticism*, ed. Timothy Morton (New York: Palgrave Macmillan, 2004), 220.
29. Hegel, *Science of Logic*, 303.
30. Hegel, *Philosophy of Nature*, 17.
31. David Krell, *Contagion: Sexuality, Disease, and Death in German Idealism and Romanticism* (Bloomington and Indianapolis: Indiana University Press, 1998), 195 n. 2.
32. Hegel, *Philosophy of Nature*, 3 (trans. mod.).
33. Ibid., 23 (trans. mod.; my italics).
34. Ibid., 416.
35. Ibid., 433.
36. Rajan, "(In)digestible Material," 231.
37. Hegel, *Philosophy of Mind*, 9–10.
38. Ibid., 12, 15.
39. Ibid., 12 (my italics).
40. This is extended to Hegel's discussion of the European mind, whose "self-conscious reason" "invades everything [*alles antastet*] in order to become present to itself therein" in the interests of mastering the world (Hegel, *Philosophy of Mind*, 43). *Antasten* means to touch or contact but also to violate, offend, or impinge upon something. Petry, Wallace, and Miller sanitize this verb, but Inwood retains the word's invasive nature.
41. Hegel, *Philosophy of Mind*, 102.
42. Ibid., 35, 29–30 (my italics).
43. Ibid., 36.
44. Ibid., 84.
45. Ibid., 85.
46. Ibid., 88 (trans. mod.; my italics).
47. Ibid.
48. Ibid., 84.
49. Ibid., 90.
50. Ibid. This repressed writing, closely aligned with what comes to light through sickness, is analogous to what Jung articulates as the general economy of archetypal forces in the psyche. Despite his desire to construct an archetypal taxonomy of Shadow, Anima/Animus, etc., Jung ultimately admits there are "an indefinite number of archetypes representing situations" (C.G. Jung, *Two Essays on Analytical Psychology*, 2nd ed., trans. R.F.C. Hull [Princeton: Princeton University Press, 1966], 110; trans. mod.). "You will never be able to disentangle an archetype. It is always interwoven in a carpet of related ideas, which lead ever further toward other archetypal formations, which constantly overlap" (C.G. Jung, *Dream Interpretation Ancient and Modern: Notes from the Seminar Given in 1936–1941*, trans. Ernst Falzeder [Princeton: Princeton University Press, 2014], 237). Jung goes further, describing archetypes as paradoxically both producers and products of experience (Jung,

Two Essays, 95 n. 3), which lays the groundwork for a radically dissociationist, materialist psyche.
51. Hegel, *Philosophy of Mind*, 90.
52. Hegel, *Philosophy of Nature*, 304.
53. Ibid., 276.
54. Ibid., 314.
55. Hegel, *Philosophy of Mind*, 94. Almost without exception, in this text Hegel uses *bewußtlosigkeit* ("without consciousness," unconscious in the sense that one is knocked out or in a coma) to describe the unconscious in terms of a *lack* of consciousness. Conversely, *unbewußt* denotes what is both more primordial and inaccessible to conscious processes.
56. Ibid., 90.
57. Ibid., 95.
58. Ibid., 96.
59. F. W. J. Schelling, "On the Nature of Philosophy as Science," trans. Marcus Weigelt, in *German Idealist Philosophy*, ed. Rüdiger Bubner (London: Penguin, 1997), 210.
60. Ibid., 215.
61. F. W. J. Schelling, *First Outline of a System of the Philosophy of Nature*, trans. Keith Peterson (Albany: State University of New York Press, 2004), 28.
62. F. W. J. Schelling, *On the History of Modern Philosophy*, trans. Andrew Bowie (Cambridge: Cambridge University Press, 1994), 153ff.
63. Fred Rush, "Schelling's Critique of Hegel," in *Interpreting Schelling: Critical Essays*, ed. Lara Ostaric (Cambridge: Cambridge University Press, 2014), 224–5.
64. Schelling, *First Outline*, 14.
65. Just as *Naturphilosophie* is Schelling's philosophical unconscious that "challenges systems to reveal what they eliminate," the same is true for Hegel. See Iain Grant, *Philosophies of Nature After Schelling* (London: Continuum, 2006), 21.
66. Jason Wirth, *Schelling's Practice of the Wild: Time, Art, Imagination* (Albany: State University of New York Press, 2015), 17.
67. Schelling, *First Outline*, 6.
68. Ibid., 21n.
69. Ibid., 28.
70. Inhibition (*Hemmung*) is Schelling's term for Nature's self-limiting of its productivity and an expression of "[the] original diremption in Nature itself... that original antithesis in the heart of Nature, *which does not... itself appear.*" See Schelling, *First Outline*, 6, 205.
71. Ibid., 16, 43n.
72. For Jung, "*the unconscious is Nature, which never deceives*" (*Symbols of Transformation*, 2nd ed., trans. R.F.C. Hull [Princeton: Princeton University Press, 1967], 62).
73. C. G. Jung, *The Structure and Dynamics of the Psyche*, 2nd ed., trans. R.F.C. Hull (Princeton: Princeton University Press, 1969), 182 (trans. mod.).
74. Schelling, *First Outline*, 35.
75. Ibid., 24.
76. F. W. J. Schelling, *System of Transcendental Idealism (1800)*, trans. Peter Heath (Charlottesville: University Press of Virginia, 1978), 14.
77. Ibid., 2.
78. Ibid., 25–7.
79. Ibid., 204.
80. Ibid.
81. Ibid., 27.
82. Ibid.
83. Ibid., 22. This uneasy bond between identical and synthetic propositions, of course, recapitulates the tenuous connection between idealism and the *Naturphilosophie*.
84. Ibid., 232.
85. Ibid., 233.

86. Indeed, roughly twenty years later, in "On the Nature of Philosophy as Science" (1821), Schelling recasts the *System*'s intellectual intuition as *ecstasy*: a fundamentally dissociative experience of the absolute subject as the organizational principle of knowledge. In this ecstatic state, the ego "is placed *outside* itself... [It must] give up its place, it must be placed outside itself, *as something that no longer exists*" ("On the Nature," 228).
87. F. W. J. Schelling, *Philosophical Investigations into the Essence of Human Freedom*, trans. Jeff Love and Johannes Schmidt (Albany: State University of New York Press, 2006), 62.
88. Ibid., 28.
89. Ibid.
90. Ibid., 51.
91. Ibid., 59.
92. Schelling writes that "All evolution presupposes involution." F. W. J. Schelling, *The Ages of the World* (1815), trans. Jason Wirth (Albany: State University of New York Press, 2000), 83.
93. Against the dynamic of this tension, Peter Dews rightly criticizes Slavoj Žižek's Lacanian reading of Schelling in *The Indivisible Remainder* (1996), which interpolates an inescapable distance between an "impenetrable-inert" ground and an essentially separated subject. This reading misses the *Ungrund*'s role as a fundamentally unknowable substratum that allows for the reconciliatory horizon of the *Freedom* essay (and which Schelling explains elsewhere as copular logic). See Peter Dews, "The Eclipse of Coincidence: Lacan, Merleau-Ponty, and Žižek's Misreading of Schelling," in *After Poststructuralism: Writing the Intellectual History of Theory*, ed. Tilottama Rajan and Michael O'Driscoll (Toronto: University of Toronto Press, 2002), 186–8.
94. Schelling, *Ages*, x.
95. Unavailable to Freud and Lacan, this cosmologization is finely expressed by the Jungian unconscious. We have seen that Jung understands the unconscious as consubstantial with Nature, and his later (post-WWII) thinking about the archetype develops its specifically non-human material, or "psychoid" aspect. Using the analogy of a light spectrum, the archetype exists on both a physiological "psychic infra-red" pole (in which it recedes into the "chemical and physical conditions" of the organism) and a "psychic ultra-violet," or a pole that *manifests* psychically but cannot be designated with certainty *as* psychic (Jung, *Structure and Dynamics*, 215f.). Jung's analogy between the archetype's formation and "the axial system of a crystal, which, as it were, preforms the crystal formation in the mother liquid without having a material existence of its own" (C. G. Jung, *Archetypes of the Collective Unconscious*, trans. R. F. C. Hull [Princeton: Princeton University Press, 1968], 79) is particularly illuminating.
96. Sean McGrath, *The Dark Ground of Spirit: Schelling and the Unconscious* (London and New York: Routledge, 2012), 141.
97. Rajan, "'The Abyss of the Past'."
98. Schelling, *Ages*, 2, 71–2.
99. Schelling's dialectic is not Hegelian dialectic. Edward Beach distinguishes between *Aufhebungsdialektik* (Hegelian *sublation* as a logical progression of the Concept) and *Erzeugungsdialektik* (a Schellingian dialectic of production that explores the will underpinning rational thought, based on experience beyond abstract logic). See Edward Beach, *The Potencies of God(s): Schelling's Philosophy of Mythology* (Albany: State University of New York Press, 1994), 84–5.
100. Schelling, *Ages*, xxxvi.
101. Ibid.
102. Ibid., 32.
103. Ibid., 9.
104. Ibid., 34.
105. Ibid., 56.
106. Ibid., 59.
107. Ibid., 36.

108. Ibid., 28.
109. Ibid., 69f.
110. Ibid., 70.
111. Ibid., xxxvi.
112. Although Jung was ambivalent about countertransference and its possible outcomes, this dynamic is nevertheless integral to what Jung called the transcendent function, or the energic tension between analyst and analysand that creates new knowledge. See Jung, *Structure and Dynamics*, 90.
113. Schelling, *On the History*, 153.
114. Gilles Deleuze and Félix Guattari, *What is Philosophy?*, trans. Hugh Tomlinson and Graham Burchell (New York: Columbia University Press, 1994), 69.
115. Gilles Deleuze and Félix Guattari, *Anti-Oedipus: Capitalism and Schizophrenia*, trans. Robert Hurley, Mark Seem, and Helen Lane (Minneapolis: University of Minnesota Press, 1983), 362.
116. Deleuze, however, read and cited Schelling extensively in his own work; for example, in *Difference and Repetition*, contra Hegel, he credits Schelling with being a true thinker of powers—one who, with the *Potenzenlehre*, "brings difference out of the night of the Identical, and with finer, more varied and more terrifying flashes of lightning than those of contradiction: with *progressivity*" in the form of a "differential calculus adequate to the dialectic" (Gilles Deleuze, *Difference and Repetition*, trans. Paul Patton [New York: Columbia University Press, 1994]), 191.
117. Schelling, *On the History*, 144.
118. Hegel, *Science of Logic*, 139.
119. Deleuze, *Difference and Repetition*, xx.
120. Deleuze and Guattari, *Anti-Oedipus*, 292.
121. Here Deleuze and Guattari are much closer not only to Jungian libido as "neutral energy" but also to Jung's conception of a non-mechanistic, *energic* libido based on the dynamic relations *between* substances (Jung, *Structure and Dynamics*, 4). Yet where Jung designates libido as psychic energy and (problematically) resists its physicalization (ibid., 7), Deleuze and Guattari's desiring-machines traverse the organic and inorganic domains: "We are in fluxes, we are not people facing objects" ("Interview on *Anti-Oedipus* with Raymond Bellour," in Gilles Deleuze, *Letters and Other Texts*, trans. Ames Hodges [South Pasadena: Semiotext(e), 2020], 201).
122. Deleuze and Guattari, *Anti-Oedipus*, 26–7.
123. See Deleuze, *Difference and Repetition*, 108, 317 n. 17.
124. Jung, *Two Essays*, 128.
125. Deleuze and Guattari, *Anti-Oedipus*, 75.
126. Ibid., 88.
127. Ibid., 73.
128. Ibid., 345.
129. Ibid., 9, 11.
130. Hegel, *Philosophy of Mind*, 31.
131. Jung, *Archetypes of the Collective Unconscious*, 32–3.
132. "So far I have found no fixed or precisely determined center in the unconscious, and I do not believe such a thing exists... Like Nature, so man strives to express himself, and *the self fulfils this dream of wholeness*. It is therefore a purely ideal center" (C.G. Jung, "Talks with Miguel Serrano: 1959," in *C. G. Jung Speaking: Interviews and Encounters*, ed. William McGuire and R.F.C. Hull [Princeton: Princeton University Press, 1977], 394 [trans. mod.; my italics]).
133. Deleuze and Guattari, *Anti-Oedipus*, 109.
134. Ibid., 351.
135. Ibid., 308.
136. Ibid., 54.

137. Ibid., 5.
138. Jean-François Lyotard, *Libidinal Economy*, trans. Iain Grant (London: Continuum, 2004), 104.
139. Ibid., 19, 94.
140. Ibid., 18, 28.
141. Jean-François Lyotard, *Peregrinations* (New York: Columbia University Press, 1988), 13.
142. Gilles Deleuze and Claire Parnet, *Dialogues II*, rev. ed., trans. Hugh Tomlinson and Barbara Habberjam (New York: Columbia University Press, 2007), 102.
143. Timothy Morton, *Hyperobjects: Philosophy and Ecology After the End of the World* (Minneapolis: University of Minnesota Press, 2013), 2.
144. Ibid., 63.
145. Ibid., 22, 85.
146. "Is it not highly likely that [our minds are] to some extent, perhaps a large extent, influenced by hyperobjects?" (Ibid., 85). This said, it is nothing short of puzzling that Morton insists on positioning Freud—a consummately anthropocentric thinker—as a "humiliator of the human following Copernicus and Darwin" who "displaces the human from the very center of psychic activity" (ibid., 16).
147. Ibid., 2.
148. "The Oldest Program Toward a System in German Idealism," trans. David Krell, in *The Tragic Absolute: German Idealism and the Languishing of God* (Bloomington: Indiana University Press, 2005), 25–6.
149. See Schelling, *Philosophical Investigations*, 26 (trans. mod.).
150. C. Jung and W. Pauli, *Atom and Archetype: The Jung/Pauli Letters, 1932–1958*, ed. C.A. Meier (London and New York: Routledge, 2001), 87.

Art

Anna Ezekiel

1 Introduction: Romantic Women Writers, Post-structuralism, and Art

This chapter explores the importance of writings by early nineteenth-century women for post-structuralist engagements with the philosophy of art in German Idealism and Romanticism. During the period in question (and at other times), women, as the Other of the creative, active, rational, and linguistic male subject, were, by definition, excluded from artistic production and genius, as well as from philosophical discussion of these concepts. How did women respond to these exclusions, and how might their writings confirm, resist, or expand post-structuralist accounts of German Idealist philosophy of art?

There is currently only scant scholarship on women's contributions to early nineteenth-century philosophy of art, and this chapter aims to facilitate work to close this gap by suggesting a number of starting points for approaching this topic. The chapter focuses on work by two women writing in the German Romantic tradition—Karoline von Günderrode (1780–1806) and Bettina Brentano-von Arnim (1785–1859)—and brings their work into contact with post-structuralist analyses of various aspects of philosophy of art of this period, specifically the sublime, the fragment, the work of art, and the artist/genius.

Historically, attitudes to women's originality, rationality, and ability to use philosophical language have underpinned their exclusion as artists and philosophers of art. The chapter begins with some remarks on this exclusion, and its relationship to the emergence of specific forms of "women's writing" among German Romantic women. Attention to Romantic-era women's writing and thought on art reveals parallels with feminist post-structuralist calls for new forms of writing and thinking

A. Ezekiel (✉)
University of York, York, UK

that resist patriarchal structures, and alters how we understand the development of European aesthetics.

2 Women and Women's Writing in the Early Nineteenth Century

Various social institutions obstructed women in late eighteenth- and early nineteenth-century Europe from participating in philosophy, scientific exploration, certain forms of literature, and the most highly regarded forms of artistic production. However, many women, especially wealthy and upper-class women, circumvented these obstructions in various ways. Recently, scholarship has begun to rediscover these women's contributions to the development of European philosophy.[1] Partly in order to evade proscriptive norms about writing, women's philosophical thought at this time was rarely recorded in the form of obviously philosophical essays or monographs. Instead, it was usually communicated in letters or couched in literary forms: novels, epistolary novels, short stories, fairy tales, poems, or dramas. The rediscovery of women's philosophical thought from this period has therefore occasioned a reexamination of the nature and boundaries of philosophy and philosophical writing, and of the social conditions for the emergence of the discipline of philosophy in its modern form in the West.[2]

In addition to, and underlying, institutional obstruction, women at this time faced barriers to participation in both philosophy and art due to gendered discourses regarding thinking, creativity, and originality. It was common to conceptualize experience on dualistic lines, and dualisms such as rationality and emotion, mind and body, activity and passivity, form and material, and civilization and nature, were heavily gendered. In the context of Early German Romanticism, these gendered dualities took on a specific form: women, seen as closer to nature, religion, intuition, and poesie, fell, together with these things, outside language, or at least outside language as it is spoken in a patriarchal society.[3] In the work of Friedrich Schlegel and Novalis, the fragmented male subject, imagined as rational and active, recreates his connection to nature and the divine and becomes whole through reincorporating the lost "feminine" into himself.[4] To be fair, Schlegel and Novalis recognized and highlighted the patriarchal nature of their contemporary discourse and claimed that women must have a different relationship to a language that rendered them either silent or spoken-for.[5] However, as many scholars have argued, Novalis' and Schlegel's attempts to integrate women, nature, and other Others such as "the East" continued to instrumentalize them while reifying their construction as the Other to masculine language, reason, and agency.[6] As Christine Battersby phrases it, "[t]he 'feminine' principle idealized by the Romantics is not a feminist starting point, since it starts from the notion of a 'feminine' that is excessive to a self that is already gendered as male."[7]

Thus, Early German Romanticism ascribed to women a relatively significant but limited, gender-specific role. Women were granted an outsider status not just in relation to language, but also in relation to rationality—and therefore to philosophy and the ability to think independently at all—as well as to genius and artistic production. It is therefore not surprising that the originality and philosophical value of work by Romantic women has been neglected. Now that scholars are beginning to recognize that originality and value, a crucial question to bear in mind is: How did these women's constitution as outsiders to rationality, creativity, and genius shape their philosophical claims? To what extent did women within this tradition supply the missing feminine perspective, as imagined by male Romantics (as Dorothea Veit-Schlegel is sometimes said to have done in her novel *Florentin*)[8] and to what extent did they attempt to circumvent this discourse, ignore it, critique it, appropriate or subvert it?

This construction of women as having a different relationship to language than men has led to explorations of women's innovations in the use of language and writing at this time. Scholars have argued that a tradition of women's writing emerged in German-speaking lands in the early nineteenth century. This tradition is often aligned explicitly or implicitly with post-structuralist calls for the development of women's writing.[9] Among others,[10] Alan Corkhill and Kay Goodman argue that Brentano-von Arnim and Günderrode, as well as other women such as Rahel Varnhagen and Sophie Mereau, developed new techniques of writing to convey experiences that were excluded from male discourse and that women were not permitted to express. These include forms of silence (such as ellipses), imitations of patriarchal forms, new forms of syntax, inventive vocabulary, new genres, new literary styles, and new forms of self-awareness and self-construction. Goodman describes Varnhagen's writing as follows: "Her style, so admired by progressive writers of the 1830s, is rich in metaphor, neologism and unusual syntactics. If fairly erupts with misplaced relative pronouns; postplaced modifiers; awkward, unbalanced phrasing; asyndeton; faulty punctuation, spelling, diction; frequent intrusions of French... One suspects... that this disruption of rational discourse was a further intentional refusal to learn a 'dead order.'"[11] Goodman explicitly connects these writing practices to "French post-structural thought" and the work of Cixous in particular.[12] Similarly, Corkhill attributes the development of a *weibliches Sprachdenken* ("female spoken thought" or "female thinking speech") to Varnhagen, Mereau, and Brentano-von Arnim, writing that "this *weibliches Sprachdenken* is predicated on the need to overcome a dependency on the imitation, citation, and paraphrasing of phallocentric language constructs (*weibliche Sprachlosigkeit* [female speechlessness]), in order to discover an 'authentic' language that could adequately incorporate the range of women's experience."[13] He argues that Varnhagen "defends a language authenticated by experience... over and against one 'borrowed' or 'appropriated' from the symbolic order of patriarchy."[14]

These authors argue plausibly that women in the German Romantic tradition developed new ways of writing that expressed their experiences as outsiders to male forms of reason and language. This paper argues that Romantic women writers also developed ways of thinking about concepts in Idealist and Romantic aesthetics that subvert or circumvent the ways these concepts are structured and spoken about in the philosophy of art of their male contemporaries.

3 Women's Writing and Philosophy of Art

The two women whose work is considered in this chapter, Karoline von Günderrode and Bettina Brentano-von Arnim, were very conscious of their outsider status in relation to philosophy, creativity, and genius; however, their approaches towards masculinist constructs of philosophy were widely divergent. Günderrode wanted to be a poet and philosopher and to be accepted into the circle of (male) creative literary and philosophical geniuses.[15] She studied Fichte, Schelling, Herder, Hemsterhuis, Kant, Novalis, and Schlegel (among others), and, partly in response to these thinkers, developed original positions on metaphysics, the nature of the self and consciousness, ideal social relations, and death.[16] Her small oeuvre encompasses numerous genres: poems, plays, short stories, dialogues, letters, fictionalized epistolary exchanges, and actual letters, as well as notes and short essays on her philosophical and other studies. While generally considered a Romantic, Günderrode's work undermines the gendered dichotomies at the foundations of Early German Romanticism, and this difference has far-reaching implications for reimagining Romantic ideas about fragmentarity, personal identity, and the sublime.

In contrast to Günderrode, the writer and social activist Brentano-von Arnim vehemently rejected patriarchal—especially intellectual—norms. Brentano-von Arnim's epistolary novels *Günderode*, *Goethe's Correspondence with a Child*, and *A Spring Wreath for Clemens* were based on edited versions of her letters with, respectively, Günderrode, Goethe and his mother Katharina Elisabeth Goethe, and her brother, the writer Clemens Brentano. She also wrote fairy tales and political works couched in literary and dialogical forms. Brentano-von Arnim valorizes aspects of experience that, on the prevailing model, were constructed as feminine, including nature, physical experience, and emotion, although she does not particularly associate these with women. Within this context, Brentano-von Arnim develops a conception of female genius, threatening the patriarchal order and troubling the borders between the work of art and that which lies beyond it.

4 The Sublime

Christine Battersby has argued that Günderrode provides an alternative to Kantian and Romantic models of the sublime, in the form of an "immanent" sublime that rejects masculine models of transcendence. Battersby maintains that this "immanent sublime" implies a different relationship of self and other than is (a) presented in accounts of the sublime by male writers such as Kant and the Early German Romantics, and (b) recognized in accounts of the philosophy of this period by post-structuralist writers including Cixous, Derrida, Patricia Yaeger, and Irigaray (for whom Battersby describes Günderrode as a "foremother"[17]). Expanding on Battersby's account, I suggest that Günderrode's work contains resources for evading the tendency to delimitation described in post-structuralist analyses of the Kantian sublime, and for imagining a sublime that is "here and now."

On Kant's account, the feeling of the sublime emerges from the recognition of the capacity of human beings to transcend nature; that is, the recognition that we are more than just physical beings. In the experience of the mathematical sublime, an encounter with something massive provides, first, a feeling of displeasure at our failure to grasp that thing aesthetically and, second, a feeling of pleasure as we recognize our own striving to transcend this inadequacy. In the experience of the dynamic sublime, the pleasant thrill we may experience when considering something threatening and overwhelming reveals that our physical survival is not all-important, and thus that we are more than merely physical creatures. Both types of experience involve the elevation of the individual self, conceived as a non-physical, rational being, over nature and the self's own physical existence.

Like Battersby, Barbara Claire Freeman and Patricia Yaeger note the dynamics of domination, domestication, and exclusion that attend Kantian (and Romantic) models of the sublime. Freeman claims that the major (male) theorists of the sublime "conceptualize it as a struggle for mastery between opposing powers, as the self's attempt to appropriate and contain whatever would exceed, and thereby undermine, it. Within the tradition of romantic aesthetics that sees the sublime as the elevation of the self over an object or experience that threatens it, the sublime becomes a strategy of appropriation."[18] Similarly, Yaeger describes "the old-fashioned sublime of domination, the vertical sublime which insists on aggrandizing the masculine self over others."[19]

Although the Kantian sublime seemingly revolves around a genderless, rational self that transcends the physical body, Battersby, Freeman, and Yaeger point out the gendered implications of this model. The traditional association of femininity with matter[20] means that, as Battersby puts it, on this model "women are normatively trapped within immanence and debarred from transcendence."[21]

The association of women and physical matter or immanence underlies what Battersby calls "the problem facing women writers and artists who attempt the sublime"[22] (i.e., the sublime of Kant and other male writers). As properly contained within and bound to the physical world of nature, women were not supposed to transcend this sphere. In addition to the problematic implications of Kant's account of the sublime for women's moral development and humanity,[23] this posed a serious problem for the idea of women artists, as we will see below in the section on genius.

Battersby claims that Günderrode's work presents an alternative to Kantian and Romantic ideas of the sublime, including to "Kant's account of the mastery of nature through a transcendent or disembodied I."[24] As Battersby points out, Günderrode rejects the dualisms that underlie Kantian and Romantic metaphysics, together with their gendered implications; she also rethinks the self-other or self-nature relationship to avoid hard borders and an oppositional stance.[25] On this basis, Battersby claims, "Günderrode develops a female sublime, which refuses many of the oppositional categories of Kantian aesthetics that were so central to the Romantic sublime. In particular, she collapses the Kantian distinctions between mind and body; self and other; individual and infinity. She does not abandon all notion of self; but she wants an individuality that is in harmony with, and permeated by, the opposing forces that together constitute Nature and the All."[26]

In "Once I Lived Sweet Life" and "An Apocalyptic Fragment," Günderrode describes fluid, repeated movements between heaven and earth, and between an individual self and an expanded self that exceeds its own borders and experiences union with the universe. Instead of the Kantian experience of the sublime "in which ego is threatened and then recuperated," or other models of the sublime that involve "a move from body to transcendence, and then back to an (ennobled) self,"[27] Günderrode's work presents a gentle movement back and forth between self and world/other, in which there is no antagonism, struggle for dominance, mastery, or transcendence of an abandoned, inferior precipitate (the "slime" or "mud" of the physical world). Instead, Günderrode describes the permeation and penetration of individual and world, and body and spirit. "Once I Lived Sweet Life" ends with the following lines:

> [I]t seemed as if I had sprung
> from the deepest life of the mother,
> and had tumbled
> in the spaces of the ether,
> an errant child.
> I had to weep,
> flowing in tears
> I sank down to the
> womb of the mother.
> Colored calyxes
> of perfumed flowers
> caught the tears,
> and I penetrated them,
> all the calyxes,
> trickled downwards
> down through the flowers,
> deeper and deeper,
> down to the womb
> of the enclosed
> source of life.[28]

Battersby writes that "Günderrode fundamentally subverts models of the self and its relation to materiality in ways that undermine the masculinist model of the 'I' as separate from nature and of the sublime as involving a transcendence of materiality and the earth."[29] Selfhood, for Günderrode, does not involve negating or dominating the other; instead, the other is embraced as part of the self, as permeating and permeated by the self. This Günderrodean sublime resembles the forms of "feminine sublime" advocated by Freeman and Yaeger. For Freeman, this is a sublime that "does not attempt to master its objects of rapture"; that "involves taking up a position of respect in response to an incalculable otherness"; and that formulates "an alternative position with respect to excess and the possibilities of its figuration."[30]

For Yaeger, the various forms of the feminine sublime all reflect "a horizontal sublime that... expands towards others, spreads itself out into multiplicity."[31]

On this basis, Battersby draws a connection between Günderrode's model of the self-other relationship in the sublime and Irigaray's efforts to rethink subjectivity in a way that allows "identity [to] emerge through a non-agonistic link with the other, rather than through a defensive gesture of refusal."[32] However, according to Battersby, Irigaray did not realize she had predecessors in this work among Romantic women writers, and recognized only the male sublime as having been expressed in the history of Western philosophy. The excavation of Günderrode's alternative, "immanent" sublime is an opportunity to investigate the possibilities expressed by women writers in the Romantic and post-Kantian era for a female aesthetics of the sublime.

Battersby also draws attention to Derrida's description of the sublime as the "inadequation of presentation" or, more generally, as "that which is 'beyond' language."[33] "[T]he [Kantian] sublime," Derrida writes in *The Truth in Painting*, "exists only by overspilling: it exceeds cise and good measure, it is no longer proportioned according to man and his determinations."[34] He adds: "'Prodigious' things become sublime objects only if they remain foreign":[35] as excessive, they cannot be represented or reclaimed for conceptual thought. By contrast, for Günderrode the sublime is not foreign; her descriptions of the sublime involve intermingling with "the infinite [that] cannot be bordered"[36]—an intermingling that is pleasant (though intensely moving), familiar, welcoming, and peaceful. There is no sharp division between the experiences of the individual self and the expanded self that is unified with the rest of nature; there is also no sharp division between the physical body (whether the body of the individual or the physical material of nature) and the mind.[37] Günderrode's sublime resists the idea of a limit that can be exceeded (in the sublime) or contained (in beautiful art), which characterizes Derrida's analysis of the Kantian sublime. Instead, the Günderrodean sublime involves interpenetration of the human and the infinite.

Like Derrida, Lyotard characterizes the Kantian sublime (and other models of the sublime from the seventeenth and eighteenth centuries) in terms of the activity of delimitation or determination. In his 1984 essay "The Sublime and the Avant-Garde," Lyotard considers work by the abstract expressionist artist Barnett Baruch Newman, who in 1948 wrote an essay called "The Sublime is Now." Lyotard asks, "How is one to understand the sublime, or let us say provisionally, the object of a sublime experience, as a 'here and now'? Quite to the contrary, isn't it essential to this feeling that it alludes to something which can't be shown, or presented (as Kant said, *dargestellt*)?"[38] He adds: "What we do not manage to formulate is that something happens, *dass etwas geschieht*."

Lyotard explains the concept of the sublime as it emerged in the seventeenth and eighteenth centuries as a way of describing a complex human response to the possibility that "nothing happens." This possibility is frightening, but at the same time can involve a pleasurable feeling of suspense in the face of the unknown or indeterminate, and a joyful "intensification of being" when something does happen.[39] Lyotard does not focus on the violence and domination involved in the Kantian overcoming of that which overwhelms and escapes us (although he alludes to it[40]). Instead, he addresses the notion that the "fundamental task" of art is "that of bearing pictorial or otherwise expressive witness to the inexpressible." What is inexpressible, he says, is simply "that (something) happens."[41]

In contrast to the Kantian approach to art, which attempts to give form and limitation to what is essentially formless and infinite, Lyotard characterizes the avant-garde, and the sublime of the "here and now" as "[l]etting-go of all grasping intelligence and of its power."[42] This suggestion of a non-grasping, non-mastering experience of the indeterminate recalls the sublime that Battersby finds in Günderrode's work. The Günderrodean sublime involves a relinquishing of control and of firm conceptual boundaries, and even of the borders of the individual self, which is absorbed into an ocean, the heavens, or the earth. Her work depicts fluid, gentle movement between the individual and the infinite, and between the determinate, physical world and the indeterminate world of the heavens. There is no "agitation" of judgment[43] as the individual attempts to provide determination to what is other than the self; instead, she "sails easily" on the infinite ocean,[44] content to be immersed in what happens.

5 The Fragment

In "The Sublime and the Avant-Garde," Lyotard notes that, for Kant, judgment, including aesthetic judgment, "is only possible if something remains to be determined, something that hasn't yet been determined."[45] He continues: "One can strive to determine this something by setting up a system, a theory, a programme or a project—and indeed one has to, all the while anticipating that something. One can also inquire about the remainder, and allow the indeterminate to appear as a question mark." This inquiry about "the remainder," including the use of a program or project to anticipate this inquiry, is central to the Early German Romantic strategy of poetic production, creativity, or "Romanticization." In this section, I consider the ways that Günderrode's work, while in some respects close to that of the Early German Romantics, entails a different approach to fragmentarity, and especially to the possibilities for creating a self on the basis of fragmentary and transient experience.

To Friedrich Schlegel and Novalis, the fragment embodied the necessary incompleteness of knowledge and representation, as well as the advantage of forms of communication that draw attention to this incompleteness.[46] This incompleteness, which suggests an absent whole, is valuable as a stimulus to further thought. In *The Literary Absolute*, Philippe Lacoue-Labarthe and Jean-Luc Nancy argue that this impetus to more work, to more creative production, which they call "the fragmentary exigency," is the essential characteristic of the Romantic fragment and of Early German Romanticism itself. For the Romantics, they write, "every fragment is a project" (drawing on the sense of a projection or an initiation of a task).[47] They claim that, for the Romantics, "[r]uin and fragment conjoin the functions of the monument and of evocation; what is thereby both remembered as lost and presented in a sort of sketch (or blueprint) is always the living unity of a great individuality, author, or work."[48]

Importantly, Lacoue-Labarthe and Nancy connect the Romantic search for a lost whole to the attempt to reconstitute the self or the subject. This, they note, became necessary due to Kant's eradication of the subject as a substance that underlies one's experiences and to which one can have access through internal reflection. For Kant, the "transcendental unity of apperception" is a regulative ideal, not a substantive, whole self. Thus, after Kant, "all that remains of the subject is the 'I' as an 'empty form' (a pure logical necessity, said Kant...) that 'accompanies my representations.'"[49] Hence the need for Kant's successors, including the Early German Romantics, to find a way to constitute the subject without reference to a substantial substratum for experience: "From the moment the subject is emptied of all substance, the pure form it assumes is reduced to nothing more than a *function* of unity or synthesis. Transcendental imagination, *Einbildungskraft*, is the function that must form (*bilden*) this unity, and that must form it as a *Bild*, as a representation or picture."[50] Thus, "the fundamental question contained in the fragmentary exigency... is none other, as we now know, than that of auto-production. Or the question of the Subject itself."[51]

Günderrode's idea of the fragment, however, resists the fragmentary exigency—the allure of the absolute, or the stimulus to create a whole, including the whole of a unified self. Günderrode does not theorize the fragment as a literary form;[52] instead, her engagement with fragmentarity emerges in her account of the self, which has been called "momentary," "catastrophic," and "fragmentary."[53]

Günderrode follows Kant in rejecting the idea that there is an underlying substratum to experience, and the Romantics in recognizing this as a problem for the emergence of a stable self.[54] However, Günderrode goes further than either and denies the idea of an enduring self even as a regulatory ideal. She writes: "I believe my essence is uncertain, full of fleeting phenomena that come and go changeably and without enduring, inner warmth";[55] and "sometimes I have no opinion of myself at all, my self-observations are so fluctuating."[56] Instead, Günderrode imagines a self that is radically alterable from one moment to the next, with nothing connecting these moments. For instance, she writes to a friend: "[I]n general I never get further than understanding your moments a little. Of their connection and basic tone I know nothing at all."[57] And:

> [I]t seems to me, oddly, that I listen to how I speak and my own words seem almost stranger to me than those of strangers. Even the truest letters are, in my opinion, only corpses: they describe a life that inhabited them and, whether or not they are like the living, the moment of their life is already past. But for that reason, it seems to me (when I read what I wrote a while ago) as if I saw myself lying in my coffin and my two Is stare at each other in amazement ... Thus, if I understand you in one moment, I can't conclude anything from this about all the others."[58]

In a recent paper,[59] I argue that one respect in which Günderrode's work differs from that of Novalis and Schlegel is in the way she thinks we construct a self (or, rather, selves) on the basis of the isolated incidents and accidents of our experience.

For the Early German Romantics, the self constructs itself primarily through narrative, which is used to form a coherent whole.[60] Günderrode acknowledges that we often use narrative in this way;[61] however, she maintains that, prior to this, we obtain a sense of self through our relationships with others, not over time but in discrete moments. Karl Heinz Bohrer claims Günderrode's model of the self results in an alienated and isolated individual composed of a series of moments that cannot be shared or communicated.[62] By contrast, I argue that Günderrode develops a model of friendship based on interactions between individuals at specific moments, which involves others in co-creating these "momentary" selves.[63] Günderrode uses images of mirrors, echoes, and shared secret chambers to convey this idea of an interaction between individuals at specific times.[64] This immediate engagement is more important to Günderrode in constituting the self than are narratives that string together some of the moments of a life into a coherent story. For instance, she writes to a friend: "[I]f you continue to keep your pen idle, then I have nothing of you but a memory, which may not look at all like your so-called I (if I see it again) any more, for you are changeable."[65] Günderrode is concerned neither with salvaging a single self nor with maintaining the boundaries that separate the self from others and the world beyond it. Instead, the Günderrodean self emerges as a radically changeable set of experiences, always constituted and reconstituted each moment through connections with others and the rest of the world.

6 The Work of Art and the Artist/Genius

According to Lacoue-Labarthe and Nancy, for the Early German Romantics the fragment is a particularly productive form because of its incompletion, through which it points beyond itself to other fragments and the whole that escapes it—that is, to the *organon*, or work.[66] This "fragmentary exigency"—the invitation to further work—shifts the focus from the work itself to the productive force that creates the work: the artist, author, poet, or genius. As Lacoue-Labarthe and Nancy put it, "The poetic is not so much the work as that which works, not so much the organon as that which organizes."[67] Correspondingly, the Early German Romantics construe genius as the formative, aesthetic power itself, that is, as "the power of putting-into-form."[68] And, as Lacoue-Labarthe and Nancy note, the possibility of "putting-into-form" depends on the existence of something that is not yet formed: the formless chaos that exists prior to and beyond the work of the artist.[69]

While the Early German Romantics may have shifted the emphasis from the work of art to the productive work of the artist, the idea that the artist, or genius, was characterized by an ability to create form from formlessness, or finite presentations of the infinite, was not unique to Romanticism. Kant, for example, claimed that the distinctive characteristic of genius is its ability to display "aesthetic ideas"—that is, ideas for which no concept (or "determinate thought") can be found. As indeterminate, these ideas are inexpressible in language, and keep the imagination continually in play. However, they can be given "sensible expression" in poetry and art; to do so is the task of the artist.[70]

The above section on the sublime indicated the concern of eighteenth-century philosophy of art with the determination and presentation of that which escapes language and thought. Post-structuralists have also attended to the role of the artist in this process and, in particular, to situations where the domesticating effects of aesthetic representation fail or falter. In his 1975 article "Economimesis," Derrida explores the Kantian response to those things that resist the aesthetic framing conducted by the artist/genius—things that are caught between the work of art and its excessive other, and which cannot be controlled, assimilated, or domesticated.[71] For Kant, art can idealize and thereby assimilate almost everything, including things that are ugly, evil, false, or monstrous. The only thing that resists this domestication is the disgusting.[72] The disgusting, Derrida claims, "is unrepresentable" and, therefore, "in-sensible and un-intelligible, irrepresentable and unnamable"; it is "the absolute other of the system."[73] Derrida uses the analogy of vomit—of what sticks in the throat—to convey the status of the disgusting as unassimilable: "[W]hat this very work excludes, is what does not allow itself to be digested, or represented, or stated—does not allow itself to be transformed into auto-affection by exemplorality. It is an irreducible heterogeneity which cannot be eaten either sensibly or ideally and which—this is the tautology—by never letting itself be swallowed must therefore *cause itself to be vomited.*"[74]

Kristeva, too, associates vomit, disgust, and repulsion with the threat of encroachment from that which lies outside—or rather, has been excluded from—the symbolic order. The enduring presence of this excluded thing,[75] which Kristeva calls the "abject," threatens the boundaries that sustain this order. It cannot quite be ignored—in fact, it often fascinates—but its existence challenges an order that has no place for it. There is, Kristeva claims, "a threat that seems to emanate from an exorbitant outside or inside, ejected beyond the scope of the possible, the tolerable, the thinkable. It lies there, quite close, but it cannot be assimilated. It beseeches, worries, and fascinates desire, which, nevertheless, does not let itself be seduced. Apprehensive, desire turns aside; sickened, it rejects."[76]

Kristeva explicitly associates the abject with the feminine, especially the maternal. On her account, the abject is what is thrust out and repressed in the emergence of the subject and its world of objects from its "prenominal" and "preobjectal" state as an infant (where the child does not experience itself as an individual, separate from its mother).[77] Abjection is therefore integral to the emergence of the self within a logocentric order, and threats to that order are threats to the subject itself: "It is thus not lack of cleanliness or health that causes abjection but what disturbs identity, system, order. What does not respect borders, positions, rules. The in-between, the ambiguous, the composite."[78] Disgust is a response that protects the individual from "defilement" by those things outside the system—the things a subject "permanently thrust[s] aside in order to live": refuse, corpses, sewage, and "muck."[79] The threat of defilement is made present to us by things that hover on the threshold, reminding us of the permeability of the boundary between ourselves and the world outside us.[80]

In German Idealism and Romanticism, the association of genius with establishing a symbolic order—that is, with providing representations of that which exceeds or precedes language and thought—combined with the gendered dualisms of the time, contributed to the exclusion of women from artistic and other forms of genius. Women were associated with the excessive Other of patriarchal discourse and art—that which is beyond language and representation, "completely unassimilable and absolutely repressed"[81]—rather than with the civilizing, representing power of the artist. As Battersby writes, eighteenth-century models of genius "claimed females could not—or should not—create. To buttress the man/animal, civilized/savage division, the category of genius had to work by a process of exclusion."[82] Women, along with "animals, primitives, children," fell outside the category of "civilised European man" who could manifest genius. Those women who did not remain on their proper side of the boundary were seen as dangerous, threatening—even disgusting.

Bettina Brentano-von Arnim is one woman who troubled the constitutive boundaries of male logocentric culture. She scorned social norms regulating behavior[83] and in her writing rejected distinctions between mind and body, nature and culture, knowledge and feeling, adult and child. Her model of female genius and her own claims to genius undermined or disregarded distinctions that were important to the patriarchal order; one result is that she has herself been construed as a boundary figure, troubling and repellant.[84]

Brentano-von Arnim develops her account of female genius in her fictionalized epistolary exchanges *Günderode* and *Goethe's Correspondence with a Child*. The reception of her work on Goethe in particular has tended to be hostile: She has been seen as opportunistic and parasitic, aiming to achieve celebrity through presenting herself as closer and more important to the "German genius" than she really was. Correspondingly, her alteration of her letters to and from Goethe for the book has been presented as inauthentic or deceitful, and motivated by an urge for self-aggrandizement.[85] However, Brentano-von Arnim's modifications to her correspondence served to create original works that developed her political and philosophical ideas. As Margaretmary Daley writes, in *Correspondence with a Child* the subject is not really Goethe; rather, "Goethe serves as a topic enabling ... [Brentano-von] Arnim to display her own immense powers of expression and to discover her identity as an artist."[86] The central theme of this work is Brentano-von Arnim's creative development and her self-discovery as a writer. More broadly, the work presents her account of the development of genius, and the constitutive role of others in this development.

Brentano-von Arnim's notion of genius builds on Early German Romantic accounts of the development of the poet or artist and the mediating role of love in this development. However, her account differs in several ways, especially in her rejection of the Romantic view of gender as dichotomous and complementary.[87] Encounters with others, who serve as mediators for the development of one's creative potential, are important to Brentano-von Arnim as they are to Novalis and Schlegel, but for Brentano-von Arnim genius is a universal power that circulates between creative individuals of any gender and can be transmitted from one person to another—or, rather, developed in one person with the aid of another—through loving engagement. Thus, Ingrid Fry writes that in *Correspondence with a Child* Brentano-von Arnim "and her fictional character were able to 'blossom' as intellectuals and creative individuals through love. The importance of Goethe in the 'novel' is that he represents not only the inspiring instance of this love, but also an ideal of self-actualization and expression against whom the progress of her character is mirrored."[88] Importantly, this development is reciprocal, rather than unidirectional: "Bettine (the fictional character in the book) is obviously seeking Goethe's admiration and affection; she wants to be his muse, his prophetess, and she seeks a spiritual union with him, but at the same time, he becomes *her* muse."[89]

Lisa Roetzel, Renata Fuchs, and Edith Waldstein find that Brentano-von Arnim's account of the development of female genius is more successful in *Günderode* than in *Correspondence with a Child*, largely because the relationship there is more symmetrical: The text displays the development of both correspondents through close and loving engagement with each other.[90] Karoline, older and more educated, shapes, guides, and "tempers" Bettine's[91] wild, emotional, enthusiastic outpourings. Meanwhile, Karoline's mentorship of Bettine initiates self-reflection on her own poetic efforts,[92] and she both admires and is inspired by the younger woman's spirited "genius."[93] The outcome of their correspondence, as Roetzel puts it, is "a concept of feminine genius that oscillates between creativity and aesthetic control. Bettine, who 'acts out' in ways that challenge social mores, becomes the source of creative actions. These are then tempered by Karoline's careful attention to artistic and cultural history. The result is a subversive form of feminine genius that challenges conventional concepts of art and artistic practice."[94]

Roetzel argues that Brentano-von Arnim's repeated descriptions of her breaches of social conventions, especially those relating to women's behavior, are a means of resisting and questioning the patriarchal structures that relegate women to the outside of language: "Bettine takes up the free license of a spoiled child and violates concepts of propriety, manners, and bodily behaviour. However trivial and charming such actions might seem…, when taken as a whole, they add up to a serious confrontation with rules and mores, and pose questions of power and agency."[95] She describes Brentano-von Arnim's "'inappropriate' actions" as similar to contemporary feminist performance art, insofar as this activity "foregrounds the lack of power and voice allotted to both women and children in patriarchal cultures" and "mak[es] visible that which has been repressed by hegemonic cultures."[96] Roetzel thus situates Brentano-von Arnim's account of female genius as occupying the margins of, and expanding, male discourse on art.[97]

A central aspect of Brentano-von Arnim's account of creative genius is her resistance to logocentric forms of representing experience, that is, her rejection of intellectual and linguistic norms. As an alternative to what she sees as dry, deadening conceptual categorization, she seeks a more total and bodily engagement with the world through physical activity and immersion in nature:

> My coat swung on and out the window and all clutter left behind me, that's *my* way of thinking; I want to learn like drinking air.—To breathe in spirit, which I live on but breathe out again; not to swallow spiritual ballast that would choke me. But no-one will admit to me

that this kind of irrationality is natural. To be sure, in the end I'd know [*wissen*] nothing, which I gladly admit, but I would be aware [*Wissend*].[98]

It is important to Brentano-von Arnim to share this combined spiritual–physical engagement with others, and she seeks a language that allows her to do so.[99] She locates this language in nature, which, as Claire Baldwin writes, she claims "reveals a realm of creative sensual imagination, of knowledge greater than rational understanding."[100] In her depictions of the all-encompassing language of nature, Brentano-von Arnim merges speaking and kissing, and lips, eyes, thought, and feeling:

> [L]anguage is also kissing. Every word in a poem kisses us, but everything that isn't poeticized isn't spoken; it's only barked like dogs. Yes, what do you want from language other than to touch the soul, and what else does the kiss want? [...] I've learnt this from nature, she kisses me constantly—I may go or stay wherever I want; she kisses me, and I'm so used to it that I come to meet her with my eyes, for the eyes are the mouth that nature kisses. [...T]his kissing is speaking—I could say: nature, your kiss speaks to my soul.[101]

Brentano-von Arnim's use of language reflects her goals for absorbing and communicating experience. Words tumble across the page, with run-on sentences that sweep the reader along in a flood of feelings, descriptions of nature, episodes of synaesthesia, narration of mundane episodes, and reflections on concepts including love, spirit, poetry, God, religion, music, language, and time.[102] As Fuchs puts it, "In her search for new words, the author theorizes language as a universal system of expression able not only to organize but also to disorganize."[103] Brentano-von Arnim's hyperactive, inspired narrator troubles categories and distinctions—including those between thought and feeling, between language and its excess—that lie at the foundation of Kantian and Romantic discourse on creativity, the artist, and art. Her vibrant, enthusiastic female genius dances, leaps, and climbs on the threshold between civilization and nature, between words and feelings, refusing to respect the border between them.

7 Her Unintelligible Language

To the masculine, logocentric order, the possibility of a woman encroaching on the prerogatives of the genius is threatening: both unnatural and uncivilized. The fact that Brentano-von Arnim does so not just by claiming a man's place, but by overthrowing the categories by which the order is maintained, adds to her monstrosity. A striking reaction from within the patriarchal tradition to Brentano-von Arnim's advocacy of female genius is found in Milan Kundera's 1990 novel *Immortality*, which includes an account of Brentano-von Arnim's relationship with Goethe. Kundera presents the female genius as both an impossibility and a threat; she hovers at the borders of male creative activity, where she can be neither assimilated nor safely rejected.

Kundera's narrative begins with an argument between Brentano-von Arnim and Goethe's wife, Christiane, about art which, according to Kundera, neither of them knows much about: "Christiane does not understand art," Kundera writes, "but she remembers what Goethe said about the paintings and she can comfortably pass off his opinions as her own."[104] Brentano-von Arnim disagrees with these opinions, and: "The more excited Bettina gets, the more she uses words she has learned from young university graduates of her acquaintance."[105] The result, according to Kundera, is "unintelligible," at least to Christiane. However, much worse than Brentano-von Arnim's pretentious (and, Kundera implies, uncomprehending) aping of the educated language of her male friends is her presumption that she can herself become an artist. According to Kundera, Brentano-von Arnim "seemed dangerously ambitious and took it for granted (with an aplomb bordering on shamelessness) that she would be a writer."[106] Kundera depicts this ambition—Brentano-von Arnim's inappropriate aspiration to genius and to the "immortality" conferred by recognition as such—as both revolting in itself and threatening to the patriarchal order. Goethe, representing this order in general and the ordering male genius in particular, must contain and control Brentano-von Arnim: "He reminded himself of something he had known for a long time: Bettina was dangerous, and it was therefore better to keep her under benign surveillance";[107] "she was too dangerous; he preferred to keep her under constant, kind control."[108]

The story culminates in a visit from Brentano-von Arnim, during which Goethe drinks heavily and finally tries to usher her out, picking up a lamp to indicate that he will lead her to the door. In response, Brentano-von Arnim kneels in the threshold, blocking his passage, and says: "I want to see whether I am able to stop you and whether you are a spirit of good or a spirit of evil, like Faust's rat; I kiss and bless this threshold, which is crossed every day by the greatest of spirits and my greatest friend.'"[109] Goethe, according to Kundera, "carefully bypassed her kneeling body," saying "I will pass by you carefully, and I won't touch you, I won't embrace or kiss you."

Brentano-von Arnim's position in the threshold, where she is denied entry to, but also threatens, the male world of the genius, is indicative of the unstable and destabilizing position of women artists according to mainstream (male) German Idealist and Romantic aesthetics. As something that resists constraint or control by logocentric male activity, the female genius is an uncomfortable and unwelcome intrusion of that which escapes representation into the patriarchal order. It is something that cannot, or at least should not, be expressed. Kundera presents Goethe as rejecting Brentano-von Arnim's physical language of natural excess—her language that foregrounds the lips rather than the word. He will not touch her. Fascinated and repelled, when he cannot cast her out he edges past.

8 Concluding Remarks

In the space of this chapter, it has been possible to do little more than sketch a few points of contact between post-structuralist accounts of German Idealist and Romantic philosophy of art and the work of just two women writing within these traditions. Even within those limits, this chapter has focused only on the broadest shape of Günderrode's and Brentano-von Arnim's philosophical claims, and has not provided a close reading of their positions on art. We have not considered Günderrode's writing on beauty, the artist,[110] or music,[111] or Brentano-von Arnim's reflections on music, language, and poetry.[112] We only mentioned the work of Varnhagen and Mereau in passing; we might also consider work by Veit-Schlegel, Pauline Wiesel, Amalia Holst, and many other women writing around this time. Lastly, this paper selected only a few themes from a handful of works in the post-structuralist traditions of engagements with Idealist and Romantic aesthetics. The contributions of Romantic-era women to the history of the philosophy of art, as well as to broader post-structuralist concerns with language and subjectivity, are still awaiting our attention.

Notes

1. For example, Anna Ezekiel, "Women, Women Writers, and Early German Romanticism," in *The Palgrave Handbook of German Romantic Philosophy*, ed. Elizabeth Millán (Palgrave Macmillan, 2020), 475–509; Lorely French, "'Meine beiden Ichs': Confrontations with Language and Self in Letters by Early Nineteenth-Century Women," *Women in German Yearbook* 5 (1989): 73–89; Dalia Nassar, "The Human Vocation and the Question of the Earth: Karoline von Günderrode's Reading of Fichte," *Archiv für Geschichte der Philosophie* (2021).
2. For example, Catherine Villaneuva Gardner, *Rediscovering Women Philosophers: Philosophical Genre and the Boundaries of Philosophy* (Boulder, CO: Westview, 2000); Sarah Tyson, *Where Are the Women? Why Expanding the Archive Makes Philosophy Better* (New York: Columbia University Press, 2018).
3. Ezekiel, "Women, Women Writers," 488–489.
4. For example, Novalis, *Schriften*, ed. Paul Kluckhohn and Richard Samuel (Stuttgart: W. Kohlhammer, 1960–), 1.311–2; Friedrich Schlegel, *Kritische Ausgabe seiner Werke*, ed. Ernst Behler et al. (Paderborn et al.: Ferdinand Schöningh, 1958ff.; hereafter "KFSA"), 5.1–82.
5. *KFSA*, 8.41–62. See Martha B. Helfer, "The Male Muses of Romanticism: The Poetics of Gender in Novalis, E. T. A. Hoffmann, and Eichendorff," *The German Quarterly* 78.3 (2008): 300; Lisa C. Roetzel, "Feminizing Philosophy," in *Theory as Practice: A Critical Anthology of Early German Romantic Writings*, ed. Jochen Schulte-Sasse, Haynes Horne, and Andreas Michel (Minneapolis: University of Minnesota Press, 1997), 370.
6. Martha B. Helfer, "Gender Studies and Romanticism," in *The Literature of German Romanticism*, ed. Dennis Mahoney (Rochester: Camden House, 2004), 33; Elena Pnevmonidou, "Die Absage an das romantische Ich. Dorothea Schlegels *Florentin* als Umschrift von Friedrich Schlegels *Lucinde*," *German Life and Letters* 58.3 (2005): 273–275; Roetzel, "Feminizing Philosophy," 370.
7. Christine Battersby, *The Sublime, Terror and Human Difference* (New York: Routledge, 2007), 133.
8. Helfer, "Gender Studies and Romanticism," 142.
9. Alan Corkhill, "Female Language Theory in the Age of Goethe: Three Case Studies," *The Modern Language Review* 94.4 (1999): 1048; French, "Meine beiden Ichs," 74 n4; Kay Goodman, "Poesis and Praxis in Rahel Varnhagen's Letters," *New German Critique* 27 (1982): 132.

10. Corkhill, "Female Language Theory"; Goodman, "Poesis and Praxis." See also French, "Meine beiden Ichs"; Elke Frederiksen, "Die Frau als Autorin zur Zeit der Romantik. Anfänge einer weiblichen literarischen Tradition," *Gestaltet und Gestaltend. Frauen in der deutschen Literatur*, ed. Marianne Burkhard, *Amsterdamer Beiträge der Germanistik*, vol. 10 (Amsterdam: Rodopi, 1980), 83–108; Renata Fuchs, *"Dann ist und bleibt eine Korrespondenz lebendig": Romantic Dialogue in the Letters and Works of Rahel Levin Varnhagen, Bettina Brentano von Arnim, and Karoline von Günderrode* (Diss. 2015).
11. Goodman, "Poesis and Praxis," 132. See also Corkhill, "Female Language Theory," 1048.
12. Ibid., 133–134.
13. Corkhill, "Female Language Theory," 1042.
14. Ibid., 1048.
15. See, e.g., Günderrode, Letter to Clemens Brentano, 10 June 1804, in Günderrode, *Philosophical Fragments*, ed. and trans. Anna Ezekiel (New York: Oxford University Press, forthcoming).
16. See Anna Ezekiel, Introduction to "Piedro," "The Pilgrims," and "The Kiss in the Dream," in Günderrode, *Poetic Fragments* (Albany: SUNY Press, 2016), 87–105; Ezekiel, "Earth, Spirit, Humanity: Community and the Nonhuman in Karoline von Günderrode's 'Idea of the Earth,'" in *Romanticism and Political Ecology*, ed. Kir Kuiken (Romantic Circles Praxis: forthcoming).
17. Battersby, *Sublime, Terror and Human Difference*, 129.
18. Barbara Claire Freeman, *The Feminine Sublime: Gender and Excess in Women's Fiction* (Berkeley: University of California Press, 1995), 2–3.
19. Patricia Yaeger, "Toward a Female Sublime," in *Gender and Theory*, ed. Linda Kauffman (Blackwell, 1989), 191.
20. Battersby notes especially the association of the feminine with the "slime" or "mud" left behind by alchemical sublimation. She argues that eighteenth- and nineteenth-century conceptions of the sublime, including Kant's, were informed by alchemical concepts of "sublimation" and the escape of "vapours or spirits" from base matter (notwithstanding the different etymology of these concepts in German) (*Sublime, Terror and Human Difference*, 105–107, 110).
21. Battersby, *Sublime, Terror and Human Difference*, 110. See also Freeman, *The Feminine Sublime*, 3; see also Yaeger, "Toward a Feminine Sublime," 191, 198.
22. Ibid., 105.
23. See Battersby, "Stages on Kant's Way: Aesthetics, Morality, and the Gendered Sublime," in *Feminism and Tradition in Aesthetics*, ed. Peggy Zeglin Brand and Carolyn Korsmeyer (University Park: Pennsylvania State University Press, 1995), 96–97.
24. Battersby, *Sublime, Terror and Human Difference*, 113.
25. See also Ezekiel, "Metamorphosis, Personhood, and Power in Karoline von Günderrode," *European Romantic Review* 25.6 (2014): 773–791; Ezekiel, "Narrative and Fragment: The Social Self in Karoline von Günderrode," *Symphilosophie: International Journal of European Romanticism* 2 (2020).
26. Battersby, *Sublime, Terror and Human Difference*, 118–119.
27. Ibid., 119, 124.
28. Günderrode, *Philosophical Fragments*.
29. Battersby, *Sublime, Terror and Human Difference*, 127.
30. Freeman, *The Feminine Sublime*, 3, 11, 10.
31. Yaeger, "Toward a Feminine Sublime," 191.
32. Battersby, *Sublime, Terror and Human Difference*, 129.
33. Ibid., 130.
34. Jacques Derrida, *The Truth in Painting*, trans. Geoffrey Bennington and Ian McLeod (Chicago: University of Chicago Press, 1987), 122.
35. Ibid., 124.
36. Ibid., 128.

37. Günderrode's monism is underpinned by her metaphysics, in which individual beings emerge temporarily from changing constellations of eternal "elements" that constitute the universe. For details, see Ezekiel, "Earth, Spirit, Humanity"; Nassar, "The Human Vocation."
38. Jean-François, Lyotard, *The Inhuman*, trans. Geoffrey Bennington and Rachel Bowlby (Stanford: Stanford University Press, 1991), 89.
39. Ibid., 92.
40. "Thought works over what is received, it seeks to reflect on it and overcome it.... We know this process well, it is our daily bread. It is the bread of war" (ibid., 91).
41. Ibid., 92.
42. Ibid.
43. Ibid., 91.
44. Karoline von Günderrode, *Sämtliche Werke und ausgewählte Studien. Historisch-kritische Ausgabe*, ed. Walter Morgenthaler (Basel: Stroemfeld/Roter Stern, 1990–1991), 1.383.
45. Lyotard, "The Sublime and the Avant-Garde," 454.
46. See, e.g., *KFSA*, 2.159, nr 103; 2.182, nr 116; 2.200, nr 200; Novalis, *Schriften*, 2.672–673.
47. Philippe Lacoue-Labarthe and Jean-Luc Nancy, *The Literary Absolute: The Theory of Literature in German Romanticism*, trans. Philip Barnard and Cheryl Lester (Albany: SUNY Press, 1988), 43.
48. Ibid., 62; see also 12, 36–37, 62. See also *KFSA*, 2.183, nr 116.
49. Ibid., 30.
50. Ibid., 30.
51. Ibid., 62.
52. I can find only six references to fragments in Günderrode's writing, and in some cases her use of the term seems to be conventional, rather than reflecting philosophical commitments. For example, Günderrode reveals in a letter that she subtitled her play *Muhammad* "A Dramatic Fragment" in response to criticism from a friend, who wanted her to follow the fashion of pointing out the shortcomings of one's own work (Günderrode, Letter to Karl v. Savigny, June 1804, in *Sämtliche Werke*, vol. 3: 134).
53. Karl Heinz Bohrer, "Identität als Selbstverlust. Zum romantischen Subjektbegriff," *Merkur* 38.4 (1984): 367–379; Ezekiel, "Narrative and Fragment."
54. See Karl Heinz Bohrer, *Der romantische Brief. Die Entstehung ästhetischer Subjektivität* (Frankfurt: Suhrkamp, 1989), 78–79, 119–120; Ezekiel, "Narrative and Fragment."
55. Günderrode, Letter to Carl Friedrich von Savigny, 26 February 1804, in Günderrode, *Philosophical Fragments*.
56. Günderrode, Letter to Kunigunde Brentano, 11 August 1801, in Günderrode, *Philosophical Fragments*. See Ezekiel, "Writing with the Body."
57. Günderrode, Letter to Clemens Brentano, 19 May 1803, in Günderrode, *Philosophical Fragments*.
58. Günderrode, Letter to Clemens Brentano, 1803, in Günderrode, *Philosophical Fragments*.
59. Ezekiel, "Narrative and Fragment."
60. See, e.g., Novalis, *Schriften*, 2: 580 nr 242; KFSA 2: 182 nr 116; 185 nr 121; 200 nr 220; 205 nr 242; 236 nr 383.
61. Günderrode, Letter to Bettina Brentano, in Günderrode, *Philosophical Fragments*.
62. Bohrer, *Der romantische Brief*, 119.
63. Ezekiel, "Narrative and Fragment."
64. Günderrode, Letter to Kunigunde Brentano, 11 August 1801; Letter to Kunigunde Brentano, 4 September 1801; and Letter to Carl Friedrich von Savigny, 3 August 1804, in Günderrode, *Philosophical Fragments*.
65. Günderrode, Letter to Kunigunde Brentano, 4 September 1801, in Günderrode, *Philosophical Fragments*.
66. Lacoue-Labarthe and Nancy, *The Literary Absolute*, 46, 47.
67. Ibid., 48.
68. Ibid., 59; see also 35, 52.

69. Ibid., 48, 51.
70. Immanuel Kant, *Kritik der Urtheilskraft* (Berlin and New York: Georg Reimer, 1913; hereafter "KU, AA"), 5.314.
71. Jacques Derrida, "Economimesis," trans. R. Klein, *Diacritics* 11.2 (1981): 5.
72. Kant, *KU, AA* 5.312.
73. Derrida, "Economimesis," 22.
74. Ibid., 21; see also 22–25.
75. "A 'something' that I do not recognize as a thing" or "what is *abject*,... the jettisoned object" (Julia Kristeva, "Approaching Abjection," trans. Leon S. Roudiez, in *The Portable Kristeva*, ed. Kelly Oliver [New York: Columbia University Press, 1997], 230).
76. Ibid., 229.
77. Ibid., 239; see also 235–240; see also Kristeva, "From Filth to Defilement," trans. Leon S. Roudiez, in *The Portable Kristeva*, ed. Kelly Oliver (New York: Columbia University Press, 1997 [1980]), 255.
78. Ibid., 232.
79. Ibid., 231; see also 230.
80. See also Kristeva, "From Filth to Defilement," 252–254.
81. Derrida, "Economimesis," 25.
82. Christine Battersby, *Gender and Genius: Towards a Feminist Aesthetics* (Indiana University Press, 1990), 3.
83. Margaretmary Daley, "The Loving Self: Bettina von Arnim," in *Women of Letters: A Study of Self and Genre in the Personal Writing of Caroline Schlegel-Schelling, Rahel Levin Varnhagen, and Bettina von Arnim* (Columbia: Camden House, 1998), 82; Lisa C. Roetzel, "Acting Out: Bettine as Performer of Feminine Genius," *Women in German Yearbook: Feminist Studies in German Literature and Culture* 14.1 (1998): 113.
84. Among other things, Brentano-von Arnim had to abandon publication of her work on the living conditions of weavers in Silesia after she was linked with the 1844 Weaver's Revolt. There is not space here to consider Brentano-von Arnim and her work in relation to eighteenth- and early nineteenth-century concerns with the sublime, femininity, and revolution; for some general remarks on the latter topic see Paul Mattick, "Beautiful and Sublime: 'Gender Totemism' and the Constitution of Art," *The Journal of Aesthetics and Art Criticism* 48.4 (1990): 293–303.
85. Elke P. Frederiksen and Katherine R. Goodman, "Locating Bettina Brentano-von Arnim, A Nineteenth Century Woman Writer," in *Bettina Brentano-von Arnim: Gender and Politics*, ed. Elke P. Frederiksen and Katharine R. Goodman (Detroit: Wayne State University Press, 1995), 18; Milan Kundera, *Immortality*, trans. Peter Kussi (New York: HarperPerennial, 1991), 74.
86. Daley, "The Loving Self," 84.
87. See Frederiksen and Goodman, "Locating Bettina Brentano-von Arnim," 24; Ingrid E. Fry, "Elective Androgyny: Bettine Brentano-von Arnim and Margaret Fuller's Reception of Goethe," *Goethe Yearbook* 10 (2001): 247.
88. Fry, "Elective Androgyny," 255–256; see also Daley, "The Loving Self," 84.
89. Frederiksen and Goodman, "Locating Bettina Brentano-von Arnim," 18–19; see also Claire Baldwin, "Questioning the 'Jewish Question': Poetic Philosophy and Politics in *Conversations with Demons*," in *Bettina Brentano-von Arnim: Gender and Politics*, ed. Elke P. Frederiksen and Katharine R. Goodman (Wayne State University Press, 1995), 222.
90. Renata Fuchs, "'I Drink Love to Get Strong': Bettina Brentano von Arnim's Romantic Philosophy and Dialogue in *Die Günderode*," *Women in German Yearbook: Feminist Studies in German Literature and Culture* 32 (2016): 17; Edith Waldstein, "Goethe and Beyond: Bettine von Arnim's *Correspondence with a Child* and *Günderode*," in *In the Shadow of Olympus: German Women Writers Around 1800*, ed. Katherine R. Goodman and Edith Waldstein (Albany: SUNY Press, 1992), 96–97, 107.

91. The characters in *Günderode* use their first names; it is not clear to what extent they are intended to be literary characters as opposed to genuine representations of Günderrode and Brentano-von Arnim.
92. For example, Bettina Brentano-von Arnim, "Selections from *Günderode*," trans. Anna Ezekiel, in *Women Philosophers in the Long Nineteenth Century: The German Tradition*, ed. Dalia Nassar and Kristin Gjesdal (New York: Oxford University Press, 2021), 102, 103, 118–119, 121.
93. Ibid., 103; see also 101, 102.
94. Roetzel, "Acting Out," 109.
95. Ibid., 118; see also 113.
96. Ibid., 116.
97. Ibid., 120–121.
98. Bettina Brentano-von Arnim, "Die Günderode," in *Werke und Briefe*, vol. 1, ed. Walter Schmitz (Frankfurt: Deutscher Klassiker, 1986), 626–630. My translation. See also Brentano-von Arnim's invectives against philosophers (Brentano-von Arnim, "Selections from *Günderode*," 114–115).
99. See, e.g., Brentano-von Arnim, "Selections from *Günderode*," 95, 114–115.
100. Baldwin, "Questioning the 'Jewish Question,'" 224; see also Frederiksen and Goodman, "Locating Bettina Brentano-von Arnim," 28; Janson, "The Path Not (Yet) Taken," 14; Waldstein, "Goethe and Beyond," 102.
101. Brentano-von Arnim, "Selections from *Günderode*," 110. Cf. Luce Irigaray, "Quand nos lèvres se parlent," in *Ce sexe qui n'en est pas un* (Paris, Les Éditions de minuit, 1977), 203–217.
102. See, e.g., Brentano-von Arnim's description of music in ibid., 106–107.
103. Fuchs, "I Drink Love," 14.
104. Kundera, *Immortality*, 45.
105. Ibid., 46.
106. Ibid., 60.
107. Ibid., 68.
108. Ibid., 60.
109. Ibid., 69.
110. See esp. "Letters of Two Friends" and the poems "Love and Beauty," and "Tendency of the Artist."
111. See especially "The Realm of Tones," "Music," "Music for Me," "The Nightingale," "The Cathedral in Cologne."
112. Especially in *Günderode*.

Nature and Extinction

Thomas Moynihan

1 Introduction: Deep Time in German Idealism and Continental Philosophy

One thing that connects recent trajectories in continental philosophy, across the past handful of decades, with German Idealisms from two centuries ago is that both unfolded against a backdrop of subtle, but profound, alterations in humanity's understanding of the natural world. These alterations also both changed humanity's sense of its own placement—and destiny—within nature. Both, that is, unfolded and are unfolding in tandem with important inflection-points on the long laborious road to acknowledging the natural reality, range of persistence, and deep scope of consequence of species extinctions.

German Idealism took place during the period when prehistoric extinctions, and the deep time of the Earth system, were first widely accepted as natural realities. However, simply accepting the fact of extinction does not require accepting extinction's fuller consequences and range of impact. Ideas don't come fully formed. There was wild variance in interpretation, even confusion. Even after Darwinism fleshed out a fuller picture of life's history in the mid-1800s, the fuller ramifications of extinction—past, present, and future—have only very lately come into view at the close of the 1900s. So it is that the current moment in continental philosophy similarly finds itself developing during a turning point in understandings of nature: that period in which the true significance and severity of extinction—for lifeforms and the shape of life as a whole—is sinking in.

In this chapter, in a rhyme across time, the *initial discovery* of extinction—and its philosophical fallout—during the epoch of German Idealism will serve as parallel to put into further relief the recent discovery of extinction's *fuller significance*

T. Moynihan (✉)
Cambridge University, Cambridge, UK

© The Author(s), under exclusive license to Springer Nature Switzerland AG 2023
T. Rajan, D. Whistler (eds.), *The Palgrave Handbook of German Idealism and Poststructuralism*, Palgrave Handbooks in German Idealism,
https://doi.org/10.1007/978-3-031-27345-2_13

alongside its influence on the shape of contemporary continental philosophy. Though widely different, each respective moment is alike in that they mark heightening sensitivity to the contingency of the human and the philosophical ramifications thereof.

2 Extinction and Deep Time in Contemporary Theory

Starting with a trickle in post-'68 philosophy, and arriving at a position of clear prominence in the new millennium, themes of deep time and extinction have become progressively more important for continental theory of late. In the present moment, both themes are wedded within timely master-ideas such as the Sixth Mass Extinction or the Anthropocene.

Such musings on human terminus and non-human chronologies were perhaps once uncommon for continental theory. Foucault, indeed, intended his "death of man" in no literal, biophysical sense; and Derrida in the 1980s concluded that "there is not, there has never been, there will never be apocalypse," whilst collapsing the distinction between individual death and human extinction.[1] Perhaps deconstruction's stress on the interminability of signification stymies accommodation of the extermination of human significance. However, early signs of sincere interest in such topics can be found in Deleuze and Guattari's proposal of a "Geology of Morals"; or, elsewhere, in Jean-François Lyotard, who, in 1987's "Can Thought go on without a Body?", provocatively made the inevitable death of the sun and extinction of all terrestrial life, within "4.5 billion years," into a problem for phenomenology. (Note that contemporary forecasts predict an end to complex terrestrial life, due to increasing solar luminosity, in something like ~1 billion years.)[2] Taking up Lyotard's precedent, extinction becomes central to the philosophy of Ray Brassier. In his 2007 *Nihil Unbound*, he uses physical eschatology (the science of the future fate of the entire cosmos) to scale up the catchment area of inexorable future extinction beyond our Earth. Any far future diasporas from the Solar System will, he argues, only "postpone the day of reckoning":

> because sooner or later both life and mind will have to reckon with the disintegration of the ultimate horizon, when, roughly one trillion, trillion trillion (10^{1728}) years from now, the accelerating expansion of the universe will have disintegrated the fabric of matter itself, terminating the possibility of embodiment. Every star in the universe will have burnt out, plunging the cosmos into a state of absolute darkness and leaving behind nothing but spent husks of collapsed matter.[3]

Brassier sees the thought of extinction as culminating rationality's deracinating and alienating tendency: detaching itself from all arbitrary attachments and parochial horizons, in a depersonalizing drift from here and now, towards nowhere and nowhen.

Inverting Brassier's deep future, Quentin Meillassoux invokes the depths of the prehuman past in his 2006 *After Finitude*. He uses this to contest a reigning assumption of post-Kantian philosophy, stipulating that we cannot think of an objective world in independence of a subject cognizing it.

> Empirical science is today capable of producing statements about events anterior to the advent of life as well as consciousness. These statements consist in the dating of 'objects' that are sometimes older than any form of life on earth.[4]

Such "ancestral" realities and "arche-fossils," Meillassoux argues, point to a "great outdoors"—a roominess of reality—beyond the correlation of object and subject. Deep time is the cure to the agoraphobia of post-Kantian continental philosophy. As we shall see, ironically, empirical science was first arriving at such statements during the time of Kant, Fichte, and Schelling, when (ironically) philosophy was, seemingly, first constricting itself to the confines of mind iworld correlation.

Fusing both anterior and ulterior, deep time and contingent extinction, Iain Hamilton Grant connects the moment of Schelling with the present in his 2006 *Philosophies of Nature After Schelling*. Grant's book resuscitates Schelling's nature-philosophy (or, in German, *Naturphilosophie*), arguing that Schelling paves the way for a faithfully post-Kantian philosophy of nature that can at once accommodate both the reality of prehuman pasts and the prospects of human extinction. Indeed, he argues variously that Schellingianism sees no finality in *Homo sapiens*, citing a cryptic hint by Schelling that nature will eventually render "a new race equipped with new organs of thought."[5]

More widely, there is in contemporary theory a growing and sustained interest in the topic of the posthuman and the geological: prominent in the work of writers ranging from Claire Colebrook, to Rosi Braidotti, to Donna Harraway.[6] So, why all this interest in extinction and ancestrality? Why *now*? To truly understand, we have to recount the roots of these ideas, and that takes us straight to the epoch of Schelling and the *Naturphilosophen*.

3 Extinction: A Missing Concept?

We know *now* that species are unique ways of life each of which emerged only once in the past: propagating, from one common origin, outwards in space and forwards in time. We know *now* that lifeways never appear spontaneously: divorced from long lines of parentage, descending from earlier, more rudimentary, origins. Because of this we know now that if a species is lost here and now, it is safe to assume it is also gone, everywhere and forever. We know these things now, but people didn't always know these things clearly.

For most of human history, indeed, extinction was seemingly a missing idea. Full recognition that species can be annihilated, alongside acknowledgement of just how significant and permanent this is, represents a late addition to our collective understanding. Before fossil-hunting became a global endeavour, with results recorded and communicated across continents, it wasn't obvious that absent species wouldn't simply persist on other landmasses, or that they couldn't, once lost, appear again. Before Darwin, there was no understanding or consensus on how species originate, so there was no agreement about the fact that the same species couldn't commence more than once, in independent times and locations. Going back at least to Augustine, a prevalent theory held that species pre-exist their manifestation, as indestructible "seeds" or "germs," suspended latently throughout the ether. When conditions are right, it was thought these seeds simply mature into fully formed animals.

In the 1720s, the French naturalist used this theory to argue that, though it may appear that myriad animals have "vanished from Earth," it is nonetheless true that they "certainly survive"—invisibly—as "their seeds still occur in the air surrounding it and therefore could reappear again any day."[7] In the 1760s, Bonnet argued that *all life on Earth* is periodically wiped out, but it then returns because the "germs" of species remain and can simply grow anew.[8] Such belief was linked to an assumption prevalent in the Western tradition, the Principle of Plenitude.[9] This holds, in short, that nature is—at any given time—as full as it can be of all its possible forms, or, that it *tends* towards this state. In other words, all possibilities become actual eventually. Put differently, there's nothing that can permanently stop a possibility from becoming actual. In this way, all change is reversible and directionless: possibilities can come and go, being manifested here and there, but they are never permanently lost, because everything returns eventually.

Such conviction persisted well into the modern period, with writers like William Paley proclaiming, as late as 1802, that creation must have in-built mechanisms for "preventing the loss of certain species from the universe," because this "misfortune" simply *must* be "studiously guarded against" by nature. "Her species never fail," Paley preached.[10]

4 A Revolution in Earth History

But, starting in the first half of the 1700s, remains of megafauna—such as the mastodon and mammoth—started to be uncovered, especially in the Americas and Siberia, and documented by the European scientific community. These were very conspicuous animals, almost certainly no longer surviving anywhere except as petrified remains, evidentially from very long ago. It became harder to maintain that, should species disappear here and now, they will return elsewhere and at another time.

This was a revolution in world view: revealing, first, the depth of prehuman time; and, second, an irreversible direction to this past history; because it forced acknowledgement that certain forms had disappeared, *never to thereafter return*. This combined revolution in world view provided essential context to the emergence of *Naturphilosophie* at the end of the century.

In the 1760s, William Hunter first used comparative anatomical techniques to argue that the mastodon evidenced an organism no longer extant. By the end of the 1770s, Swiss geologist Jean-Andre De Luc was proposing a model of two separate epochs of creation, punctuated by a catastrophe, in order to explain such relics. Not long after, J. F. Blumenbach would also promulgate a similar binary theory, of two successive "creations." During the 1780s, no greater an authority than Georges Buffon—though he had vacillated on the extent and significance of extinction—accepted not only that species could go extinct, but that the evidence of extinction provides a *direction*, legible within the fossil record, that speaks of multiple "successive" (and faunally distinct) epochs of prehuman nature.[11] Buffon wrote of abundances of "species, now annihilated, whose existence preceded that of all present living… beings." We know this because we "do not find any analogous individuals to them in living nature." From this, we can surmise a "succession of existences that have preceded us."[12] Providing the first vague lineaments of the stages of this directional history, Buffon identified an era of marine life, succeeded by an era of terrestrial life, succeeded by the present era of "human dominion." Humanity was "created last," Buffon claimed.[13]

By the end of the 1780s, Petrus Camper also professed belief in the reality of extinctions and the evidence of successive epochs throughout geohistory anterior to the emergence of humanity. Read by Kant, Novalis, and other German philosophers, Camper wrote in 1788 that, due to the "very numerous examples of extinct animals" in his fossil collection, he had become convinced that creation can "terminate" species "as soon as they had satisfied a main object unknown to us": "Now I am also convinced that our planet has been exposed to different, terrible catastrophes, some centuries before the creation of mankind." Clearly extending and retrojecting this history far beyond the current human lifeworld, he noted, adroitly, that "I have never seen, in any collection, a real petrified or fossil human bone."[14] This made it explicit: the world not only pre-existed humanity—as a whole—by eons, but, during these other ages, it had exhibited its own form of sequential and variegated history, entirely independent of all human witness. This was no longer an argument that a species here and there were randomly lost, but that paleontology provides the thread through which we can read *direction* into Earth's epochal development.

In 1793, in a speech on "organic forces" that proved deeply influential on the course of *Naturphilosophie*, C. F. Kielmeyer readily accepted the prospect of extinction and intended "his theory to explain" it.[15] Poetically, Kielmeyer compared the delay, in the disappearance of the creature and our exhumation of its remains, to the way that we only learn about "annihilated stars" after many "years" (due to light's finite speed).[16] When we look at distant stars, we are looking into the deep past, because their ancient light only reaches us after eons have elapsed: indeed, some stars, as Kielmeyer notes, might have, in reality, ceased "living" epochs ago. So it is when we look upon the petrified remains of the creatures of the past. Like the sky, the ground itself had become a museum, or, perhaps better, a mausoleum.

A few years later, in 1796, the French paleontologist Georges Cuvier used comparative anatomy to conclusively prove that the unearthed remains of the mammoth and mastodon represented species distinct from the Indian and African elephant, thus providing undeniable evidence of prehistoric species extinction. Towards the close of the talk, he marvelled at the denizens of this "primitive earth," this "nature that was not subject to man's dominion," whilst asking "what revolution was able to wipe it out," leaving behind only "half-decomposed bones?"[17] Moreover, Cuvier had been an erstwhile student of Kielmeyer's whilst at the Karlschule in the 1780s. The two thereafter became friends and remained in contact, corresponding about post-Kantian developments and *Naturphilosophie* in 1807. Towards the end of his life in the early 1830s, Cuvier mentioned Schelling in one of his final lectures, whilst calling Kielmeyer "the father of *Naturphilosophie*."[18] Schelling, in turn, wrote shortly after Cuvier's death that his recent lectures betrayed the strong influence of "German ideas."[19]

Ultimately, thanks to Cuvier's groundbreaking 1796 paper, prehistoric extinction had become fact by the close of the eighteenth century. (Though, as explored below, the full scope of its biotic-historical significance was, as yet, incapable of being understood.) Together, the thinkers mentioned above were representative of a new school of thinking about geohistory, later called *catastrophism*. Cuvier spoke rapturously of "living organisms without number" destroyed throughout prehistory, entire species "finished forever," leaving only "debris" for us to decipher.[20] But this all pointed to a further, more troublesome, question: *what future catastrophes lay ahead?* and, *could humanity itself go extinct?*

Scientists had already started asking. Indeed, in the manuscript for his 1796 lecture, Cuvier added a few lines to the concluding section, speaking of how lost lifeforms have been replaced in the past by successive ones, whilst further pondering whether today's fauna "will perhaps one day find themselves likewise destroyed and replaced by another."[21] In his own influential talk a few years earlier, Cuvier's ex-teacher, Kielmeyer had himself alluded, elliptically, to the possibility of *Homo sapiens* being "replaced by another, newer species."[22] But the query was even older than that: as early as 1753, Buffon had already been asking the question. "[I]f the human species were annihilated," he had mused, "to which of the animals would the scepter of the Earth belong?"[23]

Such shifts, profound but subtle, would go on to provide an essential part of the matrix of influence that rendered *Naturphilosophie* by causing Schelling to see the question of the autonomy and precedence of nature, over and above everything human, as a central problem for thought.

5   A Revolution in Epistemology

However, whilst German and French naturalists were conducting this profound revolution in natural history, Immanuel Kant was precipitating his own revolution in views on the human mind. Part of Kant's pathbreaking innovation was to fold thought into insuperable self-relation. There is no objective representation without a question of what is represent*able* to the subject, such that all knowledge about the world necessarily proceeds in tacit-yet-tight negotiation with our cognitive framing upon it. Or, in other words, the world is always *correlated* to thinking about the world. That is, in speaking about an objective world, you are already presupposing a system of subjective concepts through which that world is categorized and apprehended. To say otherwise is like saying you could speak without first learning a language.

Part of this project was critical: to stop the long-held "dogmatic" habit of philosophizing which, uncritically, mistakes humanity's contingent desires and framings upon reality as indwelling features of independent reality. (One of the root causes of belief in the Principle of Plenitude, after all.)[24] Another part was constructive, because Kant wanted to save the possibility of a special type of uniquely philosophical knowledge (in an era when science first appreciably started encroaching on philosophical domains). This was the possibility of discovering novel knowledge not arising from experience of immediately available sensory objects. Agreeing with empiricists, Kant argued that, for finite minds, all knowledge is rooted in sensation, but he also argued that we can legitimately go beyond immediate experience, and we can do so by productively reflecting upon the *boundary conditions of possible experience*. That is, given that concepts give coherent structure to incoherent sensory impressions by *ruling* how they ought to be synthesized and categorizing, they thus carve up a plumbable space of all possible experiences, and thought's self-relation is therefore actually a type of productive *self-legislation*.

The problem of folding knowledge into self-relation is that humans evidently know, even if indirectly, about certain events and entities beyond *all* possible experience. Think of the ancestral and fossiliferous, as hinted by Meillassoux and Grant, or the posteriority of extinction, as contested by Lyotard and Brassier.

Of course, Kant's idea of "possible experience" was capacious enough to accommodate things that *haven't*, but *could*, be met with in experience. He wrote that "there could be inhabitants of the moon, even though no human beings have ever perceived them"; but "this means only that in the possible progress of experience we could encounter them." In other words, we can admit their reality insofar as it is possible that humans *could* observe them within the "progress of experience," and they thus stand in *potential* "empirical connection with… consciousness." In other words, the reality of selenites and lunarians cannot be denied, because it is at least possible for humans to one day experience them.[25]

But what of ancestral events that existed eons before the debut of human witness within the Solar System? What of realities unfolding after humans are extinct and their "laws of empirical progression" disappear? These were all possibilities that Cuvier was to bring, into view.

6 Post-Kantian Accommodations of Ancestral Reality

6.1 Kant

Knowledgeable regarding contemporary science, Kant recognized the paleontological revolution unfolding simultaneously to his epistemological one. Having briefly hinted at Earth's ancient revolutions in the third *Critique*, he returned to the topic in an essay intended to answer the question of whether the human species is progressing. Kant concluded progress probable, provided "a second epoch of natural revolution [*Naturrevolution*]" does not, "by some chance," extinguish humanity "to clear the stage for other creatures, like that which (according to Camper and Blumenbach) submerged [the] animal kingdoms before human beings ever existed."[26] Kant assumed humanity had not yet achieved all its potential, and commented that frustrating and truncating this historic vocation prematurely would "destroy all practical principles,"[27] commenting elsewhere that "without" humans, "the whole creation would be a mere waste [and] without final purpose."[28]

But does this mean he could truly countenance nature's persistence, and precedence, before or after all *possible* human experience? It appears not entirely.

In his final work, *Opus Postumum*, Kant returned to catastrophism, saying the Earth has previously called forth different species after "destruction" of prior "world-epochs [*Weltepochen*]." In this way, many extinct animals "preceded the existence of man," and we cannot tell how "many such revolutions" provided our prologue. So, too, can we not tell how many more "are still in prospect." So far so good. But, hereafter, Kant lapses into teleological assumption that vitiates all claim to accommodate a world without mind. For he simply assumes that humanity will be replaced with other humanoid beings of "a more perfect organization," who will appear "sequentially" in another "*Weltepochen*." (The "sequence" here is probably not to be interpreted as one of literal descent, but probably as new species brought forth, from scratch, through nature's inherent teleological progression.) Kant even speculates that this might be *why* humans exist: to prepare the ground for higher organizations.[29]

Are these posthumans to be included in the "laws of empirical progression"? If so, Kant has only accepted the possibility of a posthuman world by invading it with superhumans—hardly an accommodation of the prospective or precedential reality of radically non-human pasts or futurities.

Schelling's post-Kantian *Naturphilosophie* purports to be far more capacious in its views of nature, whilst not slipping into the dogmatism that Kant had prohibited. So, did it openly accommodate ancestrality and extinction?

6.2 Naturphilosophie

Schelling was intimately aware of geological breakthroughs. Starting with references to a "past-in-itself" in his early *System of Transcendental Idealism*, Schelling's writings sustain a recurrent preoccupation with the ancestral, stratigraphical, and paleontological.

In his 1798 *World Soul*, he postulates that the disjunction between human observation and geological time forbids us to conclude it impossible that one species transform into another simply because we haven't seen it.[30] Thereafter, in 1802, Schelling mentions Buffon and his explanations of mammoth fossils.[31] Mid-career, his *Ages of the World*, in its various drafts, explicitly deals with the Earth's oldest formations. In his final Berlin lectures, delivered in the 1840s, he mentions Cuvier multiple times: reflecting upon the "earliest states of the Earth," and referring to "monstrous lizards [and] pterodactyls," whilst marvelling at their "strange, fabulous [and] even ghostly character."[32]

The interest in conceptualizing nature's autonomous chronology (or, as Novalis often put it, "oryctognosy," or, the science of *"things dug up"*) was inherited by other *Naturphilosophen*, most obviously Heinrich Steffens, who wrote in 1801 of how one can read the historical succession of life by moving from the deepest, and oldest, strata up to the newest and shallowest. Having catalogued an admirable list of then-known fossil species, from mammoth to cave bear, Steffens summarizes:

> [I]n the oldest mountains we find the fossils of the lowest animal level, gradually in the younger mountains the remains of the higher ones appear, and only in the youngest do we find the remains of mammals. So, we see nature gradually going through the same stages of animalization that are now all here at once, from the very first point in the emergence of animalization in general, until man crowns and completes the work.[33]

Sometimes it is hard to discern whether authors of the time are talking of progression in a truly chronological manner, as successive stages in causal time, or in a relatively atemporal manner as the upbuilding subcomponents logically necessary to add up to some whole. But Steffens here certainly seems to be intending genuine, aeonic sequence.

S. T. Coleridge—probably England's only genuine post-Kantian philosopher during the early 1800s—admired Steffens greatly. He too identifies the deep philosophic importance of palaeontology, writing that we appear to have evidence of a genuine history:

> Stratum below stratum, each seems to have its own history distinct from that of the foregoing; all unite their suffrages against the conception of their having been formed in one <and the same> moment or epoch, and all alike declare in the most intelligible language that their formation has been successive.

"Whithersoever this may lead us," he continued, "and however long our journey may be, it must still stop infinitely short of an eternal time." In other words, this is a genuine history, wherein direction can be discerned, rather than the directionless meanderings of an eternity wherein everything possible has already come to pass and all things lost will later be regained. There is no sign of "a re-commencement of a cycle," Coleridge mused.[34]

6.3 *Interlude: English Empiricism's Escape from Extinction*

In referring to a "commencement" and "cycle," Coleridge was certainly thinking of the Anglophone and empiricist competitor to the German style in geology at the time: *uniformitarianism*. This theory rests on the Principle of Uniformity: that "the present is key to the past"; or, more properly, one should only conscript currently observable causes in one's explanations of prehistoric processes. Enforced to shave supernatural causes from the body of legitimate geological theorization, and to provide the maturing science a firm inductive-empirical basis, uniformitarianism was established by James Hutton in the 1780s and expanded by Charles Lyell in the 1830s. It thereafter triumphed over the catastrophism the sort proposed by Camper or Cuvier, installing itself as the reigning outlook well into the twentieth century.

As a methodological rule, the Principle of Uniformity operates as a norm of inquiry that is essential to modern geology, motivating the search for coherent laws and lawlike processes. However, Hutton and Lyell both mistook this methodological principle, and overapplied it, as a fundamentally ontological constraint and substantive fact of reality. This led British uniformitarian geology to have a stunted sense of what is specifically historical about geohistory, reducing what is historically possible to the confines of what is presently, observably, actually the case. In this way, the past and future cannot be markedly different from the present. Uniformitarians therefore stressed the balance and compensatory nature of the Earth system across time, wherein what might appear to be local loss or direction will actually be cancelled out by a compensatory gain or return in the depths of immeasurable time. Local directionality washes out into global directionlessness. This even led Lyell to go so far as to deny the reality of extinction in the 1830s, suggesting that, at some distant future date in the Earth system, dinosaurs would eventually return.[35] This is nothing but the Principle of Plenitude all over again: nature cannot permanently lose possibilities, it only temporarily or regionally loses them.

As William Whewell (a British philosopher of science who was also literate in Kantian philosophy) put it, in 1840, it is the expansion of the range of scientific explanation beyond the confines of the currently observable that upgrades merely "Descriptive Geology" into properly "Ætiological Geology."[36]

Contrary to their British counterparts, Schelling and the *Naturphilosophen* were no enemies of signs of *genuine change* within nature—of irreversible lasts and genuine firsts, of possibilities previously entirely unrealized, and previous existences persistently lost—and, unlike the uniformitarians, they did not attempt to explain these signs away as mere appearances or artefacts of our limited perspective on the extent of nature's compensatory meanderings.

Coleridge, abreast of both the Anglophone and Teutonic strains, noticed this distinction and invested in what he saw as the distinctly German, *naturphilosophische* side. He defended the inherently *historical* nature of geohistory over and above uniformitarianism. This was a specifically philosophical battle for him, and he deemed it the single most important debate since that "between the Realists and Nominalists" during the 1300s. Championing the "German… Hypothesis of a progressive Geogony, with its successive Epochs & their Catastrophes" (and even insisting upon the precedence of Germany over France and Cuvier in this innovation), Coleridge defended this German hypothesis against "Lyell" and "its English opponents," whose "hopeless" and "Cyclical" vision loses "all pretention to the name of *Geology*—not to speak of the yet higher Geogony—[and] is merely *Geography*."[37]

Coleridge's 'German hypothesis' would have alluded primarily to Steffen's system, who (in Coleridge's admiring assessment) had put together a "more dynamic… Schematism of the terrestrial and planetary phænomena" than any before.[38] (Coleridge himself speculated upon the process that first "formed the nuclearus of the Planet", whilst also complaining that most cosmographers "picture" planetary bodies as "bald solid globes, forget[ting] that such is an infinitely organised Body, in no part merely passive.")[39]

Hence, *Naturphilosophie* didn't just "accommodate" a prehuman, ancestral past: such a past was one of its *distinguishing features*. Reflecting on *Naturphilosophie*'s project to "rejoin philosophy with nature," Schelling couldn't have been more explicit. "Hardly were the first steps taken" before "the enormous age of the physical" had to be accommodated for.[40] He continued:

> If the world that lies before us has come down through so many intervening eras to finally become our own, how will we even be able to recognise the present era without a science of the past?[41]

6.4 Routes to Commodiousness

But if one is not going to limit the past to the empirical present, nor step beyond bald empiricism naively into dogmatic speculation, how does one critically philosophize about the "past-in-itself"?

One of Kant's breakthroughs consisted in demonstrating that there are certain concepts, utterly necessary for objective experience, that nonetheless do not themselves directly describe objects of experience. Such concepts are functionally required for describing objects, yet are not at all targets of objective description of what is, because they instead govern and regulate how descriptive judgements should or ought to be used. (In other words, not all concepts can straightforwardly describe a world, because at least some concepts must deal with discriminating apposite and inapposite instances of description.)

Such concepts therefore *precede* all objective experience because they are presupposed by it: though they are never met with within objective experience, they nonetheless underwrite its possibility. But so too do they thus also *exceed* experience: because, insofar as they legislate how descriptions *ought* to be, their content will never be exhausted by directly describing how objects *in fact are*. (That is, rules don't point to facts alone, but beyond them, to counter-to-fact cases, highlighting what holds *normatively* or across 'merely possible' instances as much as any actual cases.)

This is what Kant meant by *transcendental*: concepts that precede, and exceed, the entire empirical domain. One can read Kant as having intended this precedential and irreducible aspect of the transcendental, over the empirical, as purely methodological: as functional, formal, logical or semantic; rather than declarative, ontological, chronological, or substantive. But this minimalist reading of the transcendental-empirical bifurcation opens the way for a maximalist reading, one that takes the partition as itself an *ontological* aspect of independent nature. This was precisely Schelling's route towards a philosophy more capacious, putatively more open to the "great outdoors."

6.5 Maximalism of the Transcendental

Kant had identified the transcendental as a mysterious domain, preceding and exceeding everything tangible and immediate about everyday experience, whilst somehow at the same time facilitating the possibility of such experience—lying beneath it, before it, yet fomenting it. Schelling noticed these qualities and, taking a step begging to be taken, *identified the transcendental with natural history*. After all, geology had just recently established how nature definitively *precedes* everything empirical; palaeontology had recently indicated how this prehistorical domain contains forms in *excess* of everything currently available; taken together, both fields were providing the rudiments of an evolutionary picture seemingly telling the story of how prehuman nature provided the *conditions of possibility* for the arrival of mind itself. Elegantly, Schelling thus reformulated the transcendental–empirical bifurcation as nature's unconscious and primordial productivity over and above all its consciously and currently available products. The former productivity, allied with *natura naturans*, was mapped onto the depths of the past—from which all tangible products had emerged—whilst the latter was identified with the *natura naturata* of the produced present.

This worked well given that it could explain how nature could produce—and already had produced—forms in excess of the entirety of the empirical and humanly accessible throughout deep time; but so too could it at the same time profess to be post-critical, in that cognitively accessing this domain is not dogmatism, in that it doesn't go beyond relation to possible experience: and this latter was because, for Schelling, *nature's primordial powers just are the conditions of possibility for mind*.

Asking the question, "How does it come about that I have ideas?" Schelling concluded that spirit's "unfathomable" depths and "abysses" *just are* what is "oldest" in nature.[42] Or, nature is mind in embryonic and germinal form, such that its entire past is reconstituted as the necessary preconscious steps on the way to full self-consciousness. Thus, for Schellingianism, in sounding these depths, thought is not stepping beyond self-reflection, insofar as it is in fact inspecting its own conditions of possibility. The Romantic poet Percy Shelley once wrote that a "catalogue of all the thoughts of the mind [is] the cyclopædic history of the Universe."[43] Schelling agreed: "One who could write completely the history of their own life would also have, in small epitome, concurrently grasped the history of the cosmos."[44] What's past is prologue. Or, as Schelling characteristically put it, philosophy is "nothing other than a natural history of our mind" (IPN 30/SW II 39).

As the child is parent of the adult, necessarily so, so too, for *Naturphilosophie*, could nature not be mind "straight away" but had to assume the status, only through some mediating steps. As Steffens had it, each non-human species therefore represents an arrested "stage of development" within the "*true history of Earth*"—leading up to the human mind.[45] But, in this way, the human mind thus "contains" or "includes" the entire deep past as moments on nature's journey from unconsciousness inactivity to active consciousness, with other species representing stages and steps on this journey. This allowed for idealism's identity of nature and mind, but in a version that is mediated and dynamic rather than immediate and static.

6.6 Geophysical Voluntarism

Further, by identifying the transcendental with natural history in this way, Schelling was led to "hypostatize" freedom as a feature of primordial nature. As Kant allied the transcendental with the spontaneity by which the active mind *freely* synthesizes a world for itself, so too did Schelling identify primal nature with a basal freedom: the primeval and pluripotent power to be any which way whatsoever, to never be any one thing, to never be entirely exhausted by any one mode, an irreducible excess of productivity over its products.

Schelling, in this way, can be said to have reified "freedom" and "will" as essential qualities of nature. This is bodied forth in the "*Ungrund*" of the 1809 *Freedom* essay, which denotes an anarchic voluntarism in "the depths of the natural ground"; the "primal will" of "primal nature"; an "omnipotence of nature."[46] This power, to have been otherwise, means that, no matter how complete an account of existence—of mind or nature—that one gives, there will always be an irrecuperable and "indivisible remainder": the indeterminable and unconditioned power, to have been utterly different, that is presupposed by yet also exceeds all determined, conditioned existences. And this freedom and contingency implies erring and the capacity for errancy. It, indeed, is precisely how Schelling interpreted previous extinctions in his *Freedom* essay. "The sight of nature as a whole convinces us," he argued, that freedom is active throughout: the "irrational and contingent" is bodied forth in the signs of extinction and erratic development throughout the history of life. Schelling ventured this as an explanation for mass extinctions. Freedom after all is the capacity to not be monotonously one way, but it is also the ability to be mistaken and errant. Perhaps, therefore, nature, in its overflowingly fertile freedom, was compelled to have produced multiple errant and ultimately unworkable systems of life "prior to the present creation" could be completed and become "enduring":

> as the initial ground of nature was active alone perhaps for a long time and attempted a creation for itself with the divine powers it contains, a creation which, however, again and again… sank back into chaos (perhaps indicated by the series of species that perished and did not return prior to the present creation.)[47]

So strange to us now, Schelling's idiosyncratic yet enchanting exegesis of extinction is testament to how underdeveloped interpretations of extinction were at the time: They couldn't but be, because the web of wider evidences and further discoveries within which extinction becomes the idea we recognize today simply wasn't yet in place.

7 Extinction Accepted, but Not Yet Understood

Here, then, we come to the limitations of early nineteenth-century accounts of extinction. Indeed, with so little of the wider picture in place (i.e., in the absence of awareness of natural selection or the true severity of mass extinctions throughout the past), it is absolutely forgivable that there was high variance and idiosyncrasy in different interpretations of extinction's meaning. Kielmeyer worried whether a coherent picture of the diachronic succession of life Earth was even possible to piece together. For example, he expressed suspicion as to whether we could ever know for certain that the appearance of new organisms in the fossil record rests in Earthly causes or whether "they could [be] *alien* arrivals from another planet."[48] This seems outlandish now, perhaps, but such speculation was reasonable given the sparse knowledge at the time. Philosophers were even more speculative, with Schopenhauer (whether seriously or not) arguing that prehistoric extinctions prove that we live in *the worst of all possible worlds*: the prior worlds evidence creations that look even worse than ours, and were thus below the minimal threshold of goodness to provide an enduring and viable world, and so became iteratively less bad until ours was instantiated as sitting just above the threshold of "too bad to exist."[49]

Naturphilosophie, too, had its limitations. These were: (1) a remaining, though modified, sense of Plenitude—which led to a sense that complex life is everywhere and that it is constantly beginning again, anew, divorced of any backward descent and independently of any laborious and fragile historical process; and (2) a residual sense of teleology, which even if it no longer saw humanity as "final," stymied sensitivity to extinction's true severity by foregrounding both the inevitable emergence and inevitable superiority of any posterior forms. Or, as with Kant's posthumanities, there was a conviction something would necessarily replace humanity—assumedly "better"—and there was little awareness that a complete break or discontinuity in ecosystems would lead to persistent loss of biodiversity and complexity that had accumulated erratically and unrepeatably over many millions of years of continuous, unbroken descent and uninterrupted survival.

So, to take each in turn, how was Plenitude retained?

7.1 Not Full, Overflowing

Strong forms of Plenitude traditionally assumed that nature was, at any one time, or on average across time, as full of all its forms as possible. *Naturphilosophie*, as we have seen, certainly stepped beyond this, insofar as it "temporalized" the Great Chain of Being.[50] However, whilst Schelling's nature is not full in any static sense, and forms are changed and can even be lost, it is certainly *overflowing* with forms. So, nature is not full, but overflowing. "Nature organizes to infinity," he wrote.[51] Having identified nature as a superlative productivity overreaching all its products, the unchanging persistence of products even became a problem, such that Schelling had to search for ways to account for the stability of species and sexual reproduction's propagation of continuous morphologies across time.

Briefly, if life is overflowing, then lifeforms can be gained or lost, but no damage or loss can be inflicted upon life as a whole. If complexity and diversity is not something that owes its present existence to accumulation over long and fragile chains of succession in the past, but is continually emerging and beginning afresh, divorced of backward descent, then life changes interminably and infinitely, but its net complexity and diversity are never at risk.

Lorenz Oken presented a deeply progressivist view of natural history. But, for him, the new and better species emerged, each time, without backward descent. The lines of progression and direction are there in that each species must pass through the general ascent before it reaches its point of arrest and stability, but this makes directionality more of a logical affair (robust, and infinitely repeatable, because independent of origin) than a properly historical one (contingent, fragile, potentially unrepeatable, because dependent on its own past states). Oken wrote: "Every generation is a new creation."[52] Schelling, similarly, wrote in 1799 that "[n]ature must have begun all over again [with] each product that appears fixed to us."[53] Furthermore, Oken held that "higher organic forms" emerged, *de novo*, from "slime" in the "shallows of the sea."[54] Indeed, Nicolaas Rupke has shown how many *Naturphilosophen* believed in similar doctrines of the unrelenting spawning of complex animals without "parents." Elsewhere, as Rupke notes, Oken elaborated a theory that humanity itself had emerged spontaneously from the ocean mucus: gestating into small frogspawn-like embryos, floating free in the ocean's womb, until they washed up. Rupke glosses Oken:

> These had originated by the thousands, some thrown ashore prematurely and left to die, others crushed against rocks, yet others eaten by predatory fish. Enough would have been beached on soft sand at the right age, however, and the children broke out of their membranous enclosure to survive by starting to eat simple foods.[55]

Oken ventured this in 1819. Another German writer, J. G. J. Ballensted, went so far as to suggest that animal species are created from scratch so commonly that "organisms were spontaneously generated not just on land and in the sea, but also in the air, like hailstones [and] meteorites."[56] But similar ideas persisted well into the nineteenth century. Louis Agassiz, pioneer of continental glaciation and scientific racist, opined in 1848 that the signs of "connection" across the tree of life are "not the consequence of a direct lineage between the faunas of different ages":

> There is nothing like parental descent connecting them. The Fishes of the Palaeozoic age are in no respect the ancestors of the Reptiles of the Secondary Age, nor does Man descend from the Mammals which preceded him in the Tertiary age. The link by which they are connected is of a higher and immaterial nature.[57]

Each stage represents fresh creations, which may have been successive in actual time, but not in the *truly historical* sense we now recognize: where life's complexity and diversity has accumulated, contingently and gradually, through unbroken backward histories, and thus these laboriously wrought accruals are thus fragile and not robust or repeating under forward interruptions.

Simply, there was, as yet, no clear or obvious awareness that existence, for a species, is a capacity maintained by *unbroken* chains of succession, stretching back for vast stretches of time, such that there could be no obviousness to the most salient consequence of extinction: that, should an interruption take place, re-emergence would require a retracing of all those prior steps, or, that the loss of that way of life—*and, moreover, anything else that might have potentially proceeded from it in the future*—will be meaningfully persistent and irreversible. If complex life is constantly emerging afresh, accumulated complexity and lifeways cannot be persistently lost.

If complex species spontaneously emerge, without descent, then how could any sense of the forward interruption of extinction—as the future prospect of a complete break in succession—accrue any true weight or clarity?

7.2　The Approaching Humanity

Musing on the "higher and immaterial" connection between the animals, Agassiz (who had encountered Schelling and Oken at university) revealed that the connecting tissue he had in mind was the intention of "the Creator, whose aim, in forming the earth [and] in creating successively all the different... animals which have passed away, was to introduce Man upon the surface of our globe": "Man is the end towards which all the animal creation has tended, from the first appearance of the first Palaeozoic Fishes."[58] Coleridge previously had marvelled at the evolution of life as so many premonitions prophesying "the approaching humanity."[59] Citing Coleridge and Agassiz, one geologist in the 1850s classified fossils as "*Geological Prophecies*" for humanity.[60] Though nowhere near as triumphalist and anthropocentric, something similar lurks behind the hints of Kant and Schelling that humanity might not be final—not because rational beings are contingent in the cosmos—but instead precisely because *Homo* will necessarily be replaced by other rational beings.

Indeed, before a clear understanding that species are wrought by long, continuous, and cumulative histories—rather than atemporally "baked into" the cosmos somehow—there could also, as yet, be no clear understanding that the species of Earth are likely unique to our planet and unlikely to be found elsewhere. In this way, the Copernican Revolution of the seventeenth century—which encouraged belief in a vast multiplicity of exoplanets—actually, and somewhat counter-intuitively, initially made *true extinction* recede further from grasp. The idea of the planetary-specificity of species was not obvious, and only started to become so in the later 1800s and early 1900s, after Darwinism tied species to descent, and thus their place and time of birth.[61]

For example, the French naturalist Benoît de Maillet used his aforementioned theory of indestructible "seeds" to claim in the early 1700s that, whenever species are destroyed on one planet, they will re-emerge on another because their seeds circulate throughout space (agglomerating around planetary bodies like "filings of iron" around magnets).[62] In this way, all species are independent of any one particular planet, and are even shared between them. Indeed, all the way up to the close of the 1800s, the widespread assumption—led by plenitude—was that more or less all planets are populated, or, tend to be populated (otherwise, it would be a vast waste of space). This even led some, such as the pre-critical Kant, to argue that the destruction of a populated planet ought to be met with "complacency" or even "appreciation" ("*Wohlgefallen*").[63]

Hence, when H. C. Ørsted (also a student of *Naturphilosophie*) wrote in 1852 that "[t]he same fundamental idea of the globe and of man must be repeated in each [solar system]," he was, in essence, repeating Saint Bonaventure's thirteenth-century claim that "[the world] cannot exist without men, for in some sense all things exist for the sake of man."[64]

7.3 Schelling's Aliens

Nonetheless, all this shouldn't obscure the genuinely progressive features of *Naturphilosophie*. Schelling boldly, and consistently, sought the *historical* in nature even if the results are sometimes counter-intuitive and strange. In the 1840s, Schelling even took Cuvier to task for the paleontologist's backsliding equivocation that the signs of genuine faunal succession and extinction he had documented might just be due to the *circulation* of animal groups between continents, due to land-bridges, and subsequent erasure of the fossils of a continent's previous residents, due to inundations and other catastrophes. This would mean that there is thus no genuine history to life, and that Cuvier's theory did not necessarily demand any "creation" of "new" forms, but simply one original stock of different faunal groups that moves around the globe perpetually. Schelling rebuked this in his Berlin lectures, stating unequivocally that "[w]however believes in an actual, historical course of things must at least also accept actually successive creatures."[65]

Moreover, Schelling was amongst the first thinkers to *explicitly state* that it is unlikely that humanoids are found everywhere throughout the cosmos. In his final lectures, he returns to the topic more than once. In one lecture, Schelling exclaimed that

> as naïve as it was for an earlier age of man to believe and assume that the entire universe, that the innumerable lights so far from and independent of our little earth are still constructed for the good and benefit of man, it is no less naïve if a later time, to which a larger view of the cosmos is available [continues believing] that humanoid beings are found everywhere and are the ultimate end.[66]

Several decades earlier, Buffon had typified the biases of the time by recoiling from the prospect of the sheer scale of unoccupied space, should we "depopulate" the planets and turn them to "frightful masses of inanimate matter."[67] Schelling would later take such thoughts to task. Exploding anthropocentrism, he mused that, although it is true that the more things "approximate humanity, the more traces of divine wisdom and goodness we might think we recognize [in them]," it is also true that those "heroic creations"—that is, the deep expanses of sidereal space—"that know nothing of humanity [are] self-sufficient at their own scale." He concluded that it cannot "be assumed that [nature's] process always leads to the same goal, that human or humanoid beings must be distributed everywhere."[68]

To give some context: During the same decade, one bestselling English book on natural history was still arguing that it is probable that "inhabitants of all the other globes of space bear not only a general, but a particular resemblance to those of our own"; whilst leading anatomist Richard Owen, in 1849, remained confident that vertebrates would be repeated across all inhabited plants.[69]

8 Darwinism

With 1859's *Origin of Species*, and natural selection's stress on inheritance and thus lineal succession came much greater sensitivity to the idea that, for a species, not just present existence, but *all future potential to exist*, rests upon unbroken descent, retrospectively and prospectively, such that any break in the chain would enforce the *persistent* forward consequence of pushing the species irreversibly into a state *of extinction*. Darwin was clear:

> When a species has once disappeared from the face of the earth, we have reason to believe that the same identical form never reappears... for the link of generations has been broken.[70]

Complex lifeways aren't simply spawned but are forged and wrought by long histories, where the loss of an ancestor-species would have wiped out all forward progeny. Darwin argued that this lent dignity to life, by revealing its fragility but therefore also throwing the perseverance of extant forms into relief. When viewed "not as special creations, but as the lineal descendants of some few beings which lived before... the Silurian system," species "seem to me to become ennobled."[71] As already mentioned, this also anchors life to its place of birth, implying that Earth's lifeforms are probably unique to Earth, as island lifeforms are unique to islands. Illuminating the attachment of Earth's life to its birthplace in this way helped throw into relief the probably cosmic catchment and scope of the loss of lifeways.

However, Darwin inherited from his British uniformitarian forebears a fundamental assumption: that uniformity of rate across time. Because of this he argued that the evidence of mass extinctions—or what had recently been recognized by John Phillips as a handful of major 'dips' in fossil diversity across time—were simply artefacts of limited perspective and evidence. This led him to think extinctions are roughly always matched by speciations across time, such that life remains constantly diverse in the main, and the process moves gradually and steadily through deep time. In support of this, he thought that extinction wasn't caused by environmental events or catastrophes (which are unprecedented and rapid), but, instead, extinction is primarily caused by competition within or between groups. Further to this, although natural selection is deeply dysteleological in its theoretical core (in that, in changing environmental settings, 'fittest' and 'best'—or even 'more complex'—come apart), Darwin nonetheless often fell afoul of the progressivist proclivities of the age and interpreted his theory as invariably involving a steady 'weeding out' of the worse in continual promotion of the better. So, all in all, extinction was now accepted as 'forever,' but progressivism still lurked: a species would invariably go extinct by being *replaced* by its 'better' progeny, rather than it being wiped out contingently—leaving behind no successors, all of its further potential and opportunity forever frustrated—utterly devoid of assurances of there being any better replacements. Extinction couldn't permanently scar life's potentials, for further exploration, but in fact remained their facilitator, acting as an invisible hand pruning to the tune of 'bad genes' rather than 'bad luck' or lottery.

Indeed, Darwin awed at the fact that "succession by generation has never once been broken"—that "no cataclysm has desolated the whole world"—such that, in his mind, we could expect a future of similar length. His prediction for the arc of this future was as such: "And as natural selection works solely by and for the good of each being, all corporeal and mental endowments will tend to progress towards perfection."[72] Indeed, in a letter from the same year, Darwin professed to the convergent inevitability of something "intellectual," should evolution have to retrace its steps:

> If every Vertebrate were destroyed throughout the world except our now well-established Reptiles, millions of ages might elapse before Reptiles could become highly developed on a scale equal to mammals [&] possibly more intellectual![73]

9 A Romantic Strain in Modernist Nature-Philosophy

As the 1900s dawned, the reservoir of untapped power and past time in nature—stretching beyond human utility and memory—was vastly extended by the discovery of a new force: radioactivity. Acting like a natural clock, the decay rates of radioelements provided much more accurate measurements of the Earth's past. This expanded the comparatively paltry estimates of Victorian physicists, resting in the low tens of millions, as allocations of Earth's age swiftly swelled into hundreds of millions and billions.[74] By this time, a sense of the major epochs and outlines of life's evolutionary development, based on the establishment of a global geological timescale since the mid-1800s, had begun to firmly consolidate. Geologists and the physicists of the opening 1900s, had gained a solid sense of how, for the vastest majority of this time, nothing resembling humanity or its recent ancestors had existed. Humanity, many now readily accepted, was but a "late arrival." Where Buffon's era was talking about a prehuman past in the thousands of years, it was now spoken of in the *thousands of millions*.

Nature's past had massively grown again. But not only did radioactivity expand what's past: where Victorian physicists had assumed the world was essentially cooling down (and was nearer the end of its lifetime than its beginning, having spent the lion's share of its thermal budget), radioactivity revealed, to the great surprise of the scientific community, that, within the atoms of mundane matter, is corked up vast reservoirs of energy, on a scale previously entirely unappreciated. The world suddenly seemed virile, full of youthful energy. And so, radioactivity not only expanded the past, it also radically expanded the sense of headroom on available energy within the natural world. Similar to Romantic cogitations upon the sublime powers of nature a century prior, this gave a renewed sense of latent powers and unruly energies locked up throughout the natural world around us.

Quickly, there were suggestions that humanity may be able to artificially accelerate the decay of radioelements, unlocking and releasing vast internal energies. Almost immediately, in response, fears spread that such tampering might produce chain reactions spreading through all available matter and, in the words of physicist Ernest Rutherford in 1903, therefore "blast the entire world into thin air."[75] Thus, as radioactivity lengthened the alien prehuman past, it was already gesturing nascently towards tangible ways to usher in, seemingly prematurely, a posthuman posteriority.

For those still inspired by Schellingian *Naturphilosophie* this meant that the reservoir of nature's preconscious and unruly productivity had once again been expanded to dwarf the human realm of conscious, ordered experience. Just as the categories and contents of human experience are apparently but an island within a wider space of past and possible forms, so too was it possible to stipulate that our sense of the coherence of "the present" remains just an imposition of our minds upon a nature that never truly forgets what's past. Such a recognizance was dramatized, early in the century, by Alfred Döblin, in his 1924 novel *Mountains, Oceans, Giants*.

9.1 Döblin

Döblin was directly influenced by Schelling, sympathetic to Romantic science, and wrote his own sweeping and evolutionary treatises of latter-day *Naturphilosophie* and *Universalgeschichte* (*Das Ich über der Natur* of 1927 and *Unser Existenz* [1933]). His aforementioned 1924 novel—*Mountains, Oceans, Giants*—is a dramatization of such interests: a sprawling future history, narrating nature's revenge upon advanced technological civilization in 2700 AD. The novel imagines nature biting back in response to being displaced by ever-expanding civilization.

With Europe becoming overcrowded, a plan is made to create more living space by melting the entirety of the Greenland ice sheet, using a newly discovered energy source (clearly modelled on radioactivity) which is accumulated and stored in "tourmaline veils." The plan is successful, unleashing a vast explosion, the description of which uncannily resembles accounts of the Manhattan Project's A-bomb tests two decades later:

> Iceland torn apart, Earth's furnaces opened.... A wave of light stepped over the horizon... rose and rose and rose unchecked.... The light, the fire, higher and higher over the endless vault of the heavens.[76]

Peeling away underlying strata to Cretaceous bedrock, this vast disruption punctures a hole in the thin veneer of nature's equilibrium, stability, and order. Just as Schelling thought that the "*Ungrund*" and "abyssal freedom" of nature remain latent and buried, but can break out once again in unruly outbursts, when properly provoked, so too does Döblin imagine humanity's tampering unleashing nature's prodigal metamorphic powers and overflowing primordial productivity. Literalizing the *naturphilosophische* blurring of natural forms, this triggers a mutative cataclysm which—rebuking all lines between lithic, botanic, and organic—ripples outwards across the entire Northern hemisphere. Tumefying organic masses, made up of clumps of familiar and unknown creatures blurring into one another, spill outward, rippling from the blast-zone, through the oceans: "Greenland flung out endless living masses like a blossoming tree its sun-dust. They crashed onto Scandinavia, the first land they encountered."[77] And, as Schelling had said that "nothing prevents [an] earlier time from migrating through later time," Döblin imagines that this disruption of nature's veneer of orderliness applies not just to morphological boundaries but also established evolutionary linearity (i.e., the directionality of life in time, such that some species exist now and others no longer do): a revocation of linear time tales place, as long-extinct forms and paleontological relics re-emerge. The "ghostly" saurian forms Schelling had reflected upon become revenant, as the Schellingian "past-in-itself" regurgitates, from the disturbed ground, crashing into the present. Döblin's vigorous prose is worth quoting in full:

> On the islands of Greenland, rosily radiant, everything had changed since the great upheaval of the Earth. Strata and rock masses from earliest times were now laid bare. Animal remnants seeds plants, fragments of an age millions of years ago, were once again exposed to light [and] arose what just now had lain buried, dead.... A furious craving entered into things, made them bend and stretch. Plains lifted, everywhere strata became exposed, pushed high, overlay one another. More swift were mosses algae ferns grasses fishes snails worms lizards, large mammals... relics of the Cretaceous, bones plants fragments found like again.... Confusions of bone, shattered skeletons in the mud sucked in the glacial damp, pulled themselves together.... Earth clotted every residue and every relict into something living.... Ribs writhed like worms. The living Earth streamed together around a spine, hardened.... Saurians coiled street-long serpent bodies across rocks, plunged into water, beings pale at first, then streaked black-brown, with spines growing from a toothy skull.[78]

At length, the mega-malignance—this "jumble of emergent Life"—reaches Western Europe: strange beasts and growths wash ashore and begin invading. Huge networks of biomatter weave across the countryside. They unlock and unleash, within everything they touch, latent biotic capacities. Like fleshy-flowers, afflicted creatures grow heavy under their own weight: blossoming into mutated growths, their hearts become unable to support outsized appendages and new-bulbed organs. Döblin's delirious prose describes the chaos, across many pages. Closing out the novel, humanity eventually largely succumbs to this disaster of its own making.

Couched in the languages of a more contemporary science, this is Döblin's modernist reoccupation of a conceptual option initially set out by Schelling: the suggestion that, if empirical orderliness, both in terms of temporal order and morphological categorization, is just the veneer that we flimsily paste over a nature which otherwise overflows all categories, then there remains the possibility of the violent revocation of this veneer, in the form of the return of primordial disorder and overflow.

9.2 Jaspers

As the Atomic Age dawned in 1945, and humanmade disasters such as Döblin had imagined became reality, the deepening of the past produced other disturbing reflections. Deeply influenced by Schelling, Karl Jaspers, in his 1949 *Origin and Goal of History*, innovatively combined reflections on the depth of the past lately revealed by nuclear physics—both on our planet *and* beyond—with troubling questions regarding post-nuclear humanity's future and fate.

Reflecting on fears that atomic explosions could trigger a world-destroying chain reaction, igniting the oceans and Earth itself, Jaspers wrote that this was the culmination of the "Promethean idea":

> With the atom bomb, a piece of solar substance has been brought to the earth. The same thing happens to it on the surface of the earth which has hitherto happened only in the sun.

We cannot know, he implied, that this doesn't risk the "possibility of pulverising the globe in space," creating general "conflagration." "The whole globe would explode, whether intentionally or unintentionally. Then our solar system would be temporarily lit up, a *nova* would have appeared in space." From this, Jaspers formulated a fascinating question, based on the observed vastness of space and time in the revealed cosmos:

> Our history has lasted some six thousand years only. Why should this history occur just now, after the immeasurable ages of the universe and of the earth that have preceded it? Do not humans, or at all events, rational beings, exist anywhere else in the universe? Why have we not long since had news, through radiations, from the universe? Communications from rational beings infinitely further advanced in technology than ourselves? Can it be because all high technological development has so far led to the point at which the beings have brought about the destruction of their planet with the atomic bomb? Can some of the *novae* be end-effects of the activities of technological rational beings?[79]

Nova, or exploding stars, are—as Kielmeyer had intimated back in the late-1700s—like fossils. The remnants of ancient extinctions, only reaching us, via exhumation of earth or propagation of light, after the elapse of untold epochs. Jaspers is here theorizing that, due to the depth of past time, there must have been past civilizations in space, but since we do not see any sign of their ongoing rationality, perhaps we only see the "end-effects" [*Endeffekte*] terminating irrationalities. In other words, it may be inevitable for intelligent beings to unlock atoms, and burst their planets, creating the novae that we observe intermittently, and periodically, across the sky. When seeing other stars explode, we are merely witnessing part of a wider natural cycle of evolution.

Jaspers here is cogitating, in highly speculative mode, like a modern-day *Naturphilosoph*. In doing so, he conscripts the expanded range of deep time, and deep space, in order to speculatively affect a *naturalization* of not just the emergence of rational life but also its extinction (where here "naturalization" conveys the conversion of what is chancy, unique, and unprecedented into what is instead unremarkable, generalizable, and lawlike). Given his theory, extinction is something we see in the heavens, as much as we see in the Earth's past. Moreover, Jasper's theorization—which he, himself, readily admits is nothing but a "play of ideas"—seems to imply something about the stability of intelligence across time, or, perhaps better, its inherent instability. This resonates with the older tradition of *Naturphilosophie*, which variously cast self-consciousness as a merely regional contraction of external forces, a folding that generates interiority and reflexivity ("that establishes its sphere for itself," in Schelling's early words), but only as a transient and secondary effect of more fundamental and primary impersonal forces.[80]

Jaspers ends his conjecture by musing upon the following, one of the fundamental driving problems of Schelling's *Naturphilosophie*:

> The prodigious historic phenomenon of this thinking consciousness, and of the human in it and through it, is, in its entirety an evanescent event in the universe, entirely new, entirely of the present instant, just beginning in fact—and yet, for itself and seen from within, as old as if it comprehended the universe.[81]

9.3 Kojève

Jaspers had claimed that the exhaustive exploration of all human historical possibilities, achievable within the vastness of nature's deeper timescales, would lead to a "state of fulfilment," wherein humanity as a species survives, but which would usher in a "new sleep of spirit"—symmetrical to the one prior to the beginning of human history and dawn of self-conscious activity.[82] A fuller exploration of this interesting suggestion for the "end" of humanity comes from Alexandre Kojève: responsible for an influx of German Idealist concepts into French theory, via his 1933–1939 lectures on Hegel.

In the Twelfth Lecture, given in 1938–1939, Kojève offers an updated account of Hegel's idea of the "end of history." Here, he seems to assume that self-conscious activity is defined by a kind of *instability*: a fundamental disharmony, relative to external nature, fomented by the subject's recognition—incipient in all distinctions between subjective and objective—that the external world remains rebarbative to its practical wishes and recalcitrant to its theoretical beliefs. Given this, how do we interpret the projected answering of all questions, and completion of all projects, at the end of history? Kojève offers an explanation, attempting to fit Hegel's idealist conception of history into the—by now undeniable—scientific realist conception of natural history as exceeding and preceding all human history.

Admitting that "Nature is *independent* of Man," and "subsists before him and after him" insofar as "[i]t is in it that he is *born*," Kojève nonetheless holds that

"Time" proper (i.e., subjective time) is generated by the disharmony internal to the subject and her relation to the world. Because only insofar as there is disharmony (recalcitrance or rebarbativeness; error or injustice) can there be things to *overstep* and *overcome*, and thus a *direction* to history and time. In this way, Kojève seemingly demotes natural history relative to human history, disappointingly relating it to what is "eternal" and merely "spatial." Nonetheless, the problem remains: How, then, can humanity, from which all "Time" putatively issues, itself have an ending within time? Kojève's answer is that: the human "who *is* Time … *disappears* in spatial Nature," and thus "Nature *survives* Time." In a footnote, he clarifies what this might mean. He argues that "[t]he disappears of [humanity] at the end of History, therefore, is not a cosmic catastrophe" (insofar as the cosmos continues without humankind), and "it is not a biological catastrophe either" (insofar as the biotic human germline remains uninterrupted). What disappears, instead, is humanity "properly so-called": that is, "Error, or, in general, the Subject *opposed* to the Object."

In point of fact, the end of human Time or History—that is, the definitive annihilation of Man properly so-called or of the free and historical Individual—means quite simply the cessation of Action in the full sense of the term. Kojéve is quick to point out this is not just the "disappearance of wars and bloody revolutions," but also the extinction "of Philosophy": "all the rest can be preserved indefinitely; art, love, play, etc. etc.; in short, everything that makes Man happy." But would there be any lights on inside? In a footnote added to the second edition, Kojéve explains that this would make humanity an "animal again," all our "arts" and "play" must "become purely 'natural' again," in the sense of unreflecting and instinctual.

> Hence it would have to be admitted that after the end of History, men would construct their edifices and works of art as birds build their nests and spiders spin their webs, would perform musical concerts after the fashion of frogs and cicadas, would play like young animals, and would indulge in love like adult beasts.

The species *Homo sapiens* would remain the same biologically, but no longer be human philosophically. It would even still speak, but only in the following manner:

> Animals of the species *Homo sapiens* would react by conditioned reflexes to vocal signals or sign 'language', and thus their so-called 'discourses' would be like what is supposed to be the 'language' of bees. What would disappear, then then, is not only Philosophy or the search for discursive wisdom, but also that wisdom itself. For in these post-historical animals there would no longer be any [discursive] understanding of the World and of self.[83]

It may not be the removal of a biological morphology or lineage, or a catastrophe in an empirical sense, but it is a catastrophe in the transcendental sense of the collapse of all action-fomenting distinction between subjective and objective. Another speculative naturalization of extinction, similar to Jasper's offering: But here it is not the human organism or germline that is extinguished; rather, it is all the things that made the human think it was separate or dislocated from nature, such that—abraded of all transient "transcendence"—only all that is truly natural about the species *Homo sapiens* remains.

10 Neocatastrophism and Contemporary Theory

10.1 Extinction Still Misunderstood

In lectures influenced by Kojève's reflections on the relation between animality and humanity, Georges Bataille in 1955 reflected that "[i]t has become commonplace today to talk about the eventual extinction of human life," adding that it is ironic that, at the same time, archaeology and anthropology have only just started truly getting to grips with the genesis of humanity in the past. Across the tumults of the ensuing twentieth century, continental philosophy would every now and again return to the topic of extinction and human extinction. Whether in Lévi-Strauss's claim, issued the same year as Bataille's, that anthropology should be renamed "entropology," alongside his assertion that "[t]he world began without man and will end without him"; or whether in Sartre's 1960 musing upon the "possibility that a cooling of the sun might stop History."[84]

In the realm of scientific knowledge, the century was obviously cut in half by the Atomic Age's birth in 1945: which, indeed, was the context for Bataille's claim that talk about human extinction had "become commonplace." Nonetheless, in wider scientific beliefs about nature and life there was a broad continuity with Darwin's own interpretation of extinction (as a broadly progressive force, weeding out the 'worse' to make way for the 'better'). There was also continuity with his generation's views on the illegitimacy of sudden and mass extinctions throughout life's past. Uuniformitarianism still ruled the day: life may have been proven beyond doubt to be directional, but uniformity of rate, and steadiness of direction, remained orthodox. Speculation upon vast prehistoric cataclysms were stigmatized as backward and unscientific: partly contributing to the stereotyped image of the overly speculative Romantic "nature-philosopher" of the unempirical past.[85]

Moreover, prior to the triumph of the 'modern synthesis,' there were—aside from Darwin's natural selection—countless competing theories for the true mechanics of evolution and extinction. Most, however, held in common the lingering assumption that extinction befalls species because, somehow, they *deserve* it. Some scientists held that species, like individuals, have an allotted lifespan and so become inevitably "softened," and "senile," needing to be wiped away to make way for more vigorous and youthly creatures. Others believed that lineages disappear because they become "decadent": over-investing in luxuries like gigantic size, ornate antlers, or baroque spines.

As *Life Magazine* declared mid-century: "It is conventional to speak of any animal order that suffered extinction as an unsuccessful experiment of nature."[86] Allotting blame for prehistoric extinctions on the contingencies of external environmental, versus inherent personal flaws, one paleontologist in 1929 strongly concluded: "Death comes from within."[87]

Such prejudice applied with particular force to the dinosaurs, where it was often assumed that they died somehow because of laziness, lassitude, or lumbering stupidity. American humorist Will Cuppy summarized the sentiment: "The Age of

Reptiles ended because it had gone on long enough and it was all a mistake in the first place."[88] (One, possibly apocryphal, suggestion even held that the dinosaurs died out of sheer boredom, or, "*Paleoweltschmerz.*") This all led to overriding, and self-serving, assumption that a creature as evidently successful and dominant as humanity stood no chance of going extinct any time soon (from natural causes, at least).

On top of all this, throughout the century, there remained a popular suspicion that, should humanity ever wipe itself out, then something anthropoid would return: whether in James Elroy Flecker's 1908 *The Last Generation: A Story of the Future*, which imagines ruined cities after humanity's extinction populated by "repulsive little apes" and ends with the observation that "[o]ne of them was building a fire with sticks," or in 1968's *Planet of the Apes*, which relies on much the same idea.[89]

10.2 Neocatastrophism

But then, in the closing decades of the twentieth century, a revolution took place in evolutionary and Earth sciences. Catastrophism returned. In the 1960s and 1970s, a few sparse—but prominent—scientific voices started to pronounce renewed belief in catastrophe as the explanation for saltation in the fossil record. Otto Schindewolf and Iosif Shklovsky suggested supernovae had caused mass extinctions, extraterrestrial impactors were later hypothesized by Digby McLaren, Harold Urey, and Ernst Öpik, among others. Moreover, developments like satellite photography enforced a view that large craterlike structures on Earth were signs of external bombardment rather than endogenous volcanism. But the major inflection point came in 1980, when the father–son team of Louis and Walter Alvarez found convincing evidence of a violent dinosaur-killing bolide impactor event. This came in the form of discoveries of iridium strata at the Cretaceous-Paleogene boundary (indicating an extra-terrestrial source), alongside a crater, of similar age, beneath Mexico's Yucatán Peninsula. This would go on to overturn generations of uniformitarian orthodoxy. Where once cometary impacts and mass extinctions had been smirked at, as the romantic reveries of the melodramatic catastrophists and nature-philosophers of yore, they suddenly became all too real in 1994 when comet Shoemaker-Levy smashed into Jupiter, leaving visible scars. As one of the discoverers of the comet remarked, the "giggle factor disappeared."[90]

Debate raged throughout the 1980s about the true significance of mass extinctions, but the Alvarez paper can be compared to Cuvier's original 1796 paper on elephants and mammoths in the extent and depth with which it changed background views of nature. Some now even speak of "neocatastrophism" as the current paradigm in historical sciences. Spearheaded in the 1980s by paleobiologists such as Stephen Jay Gould and David M. Raup, a new view of life emerged: one that foregrounded *contingency*, or, the idea that species could die out, suddenly and abruptly, due to "bad luck" rather than "bad genes."[91]

Contingency was always at the core of Darwin's theory, but its true centrality had never before been made properly explicit. For if species can die out due to lottery rather than laziness or lassitude, then the entire history of life is pockmarked with the unfulfilled, and thereafter forever frustrated, potentials that these ancestors might have passed onto countless progeny, *but now never can or will*. This is genuine loss and irreducibly squandered opportunity (whereas in the 'bad luck' view, any further exploration of an extinct lineage's unexplored potential, would of course not *really* be a loss of life's potential). The implication then being: perhaps humanoid and intellectual life is the offshoot of one very contingent twig of the tree of life, such that if it had been removed, we—and nothing like us—would have ever emerged. So too, if we disappear, would nothing like us return. Extinction's fuller scope came to light.

Throughout the 1980s, myriad writers reflected on this. In a 1983 essay, "The World as Cataclysm," Stanisław Lem wrote the following, denying Darwin's speculative possibility of "intelligent saurians":

> The balance sheet looks like this. Man could not emerge from the differentiated biological legacy of the Mesozoic, because that mass represented capital invested in species incapable of anthropogenesis. The investment (as always in evolution) was irreversible; the capital was lost. New capital began to form from the surviving vestiges of life scatted over the Earth. It increased and multiplied until the rise of the hominids and anthropoids.... the limb of the evolutionary tree that created the mammals would not have branched and would not have given them primacy among the animals had there not been, sixty-five million years ago, between the Cretaceous and Tertiary, a catastrophe in the form of an enormous, 3.5-to-4-trillion-ton meteorite.

The universe, Lem concluded, is "an enormously profligate investor, squandering its initial capital on the roulette wheels that are galaxies," and we are the chance product of immeasurable "hecatombs and holocausts."[92]

History means not only that not all possible species can survive, but that abundances more *simply won't ever exist at all because of that*, because the death of an ancestor wipes out the "potential to exist" for countless downstream possible progenies, alongside all further exploration of whatever potentialities that lineage possessed. In 1989, Gould put all of this together, imagining what would happen if we "replayed the tape of life," and one of our ancestors is wiped out:

> One little twig on the mammalian branch, a lineage with interesting possibilities that were never realised, joins the vast majority of species in extinction. So what? Most possibilities are never realised, and who will ever know the difference? ... Arguments of this form lead me to the conclusion that biology's most profound insight int human nature, status, and potential lies in the simple phrase, the embodiment of contingency: Homo sapiens is an entity, not a tendency.[93]

This enforces a genuinely, deeply historical view of life: in that it is not just directional, but it is also explicit in *not* being unidirectional. Instead, natural history traces a path that could well have branched otherwise. Life's history becomes a pathway through of a wider space of possibility, much wider than everything actual, wherein the trajectory of the past canalizes the possibilities of the future, closing off or opening up some regions of possibility, whilst making others forever incapable of being returned to. Or, *extinction is forever*. But within this space, most possibilities—entirely viable ones—simply are never realized.

This is the final dismemberment of Plenitude: not only is Earth's evolutionary story not full, but neither is it overflowing. On the contrary, multitudes of its possibilities will never—can never—come to pass. Relatedly, there is no need for anything human to have emerged or to ever emerge again should we somehow leave the scene. Others had said similar things before, though very sparsely before the latter 1900s, and none before had put it so forcefully and persuasively.

Gould (who, alongside being a scientist, was also a masterful historian of science) knew the *Naturphilosophen*, discussing them in-depth in his first book. He will have appreciated the radicality of the "German hypothesis" of natural history when it was first suggested in the 1780s and 1790s. The *Naturphilosophen* were amongst the first to accept the fact of extinction and life's historical depth, and the first to attempt to delineate the philosophical meaning of this. Two centuries afterwards, with the piecing together of the Alvarez theory for dinosaur extinction in 1980, natural scientists finally arrived at a fuller picture of the meaning, and scope, of extinction.

10.3 Contemporary Theory

In 1984, Gould made the connection between this new contingent and discontinuous view of life and a certain cultural "*Zeitgeist*" being expressed in other fields and areas. Namely, Gould cited Michel Foucault's "punctuational theory of history," which cast intellectual history not as gradual and smooth growth but as a series of "wholly novel mutation[s] in the possibilities for human observation, thought, and action."[94] But this was convergence rather than cross-current: The Gouldian and neocatastrophist message, on the true contingency of *Homo*, would take a while to find root; it would be the next generation of philosophers who truly responded to it.

Whilst analytic-inspired philosophy has birthed its own response in the form of the study of "existential risk,"[95] which is currently a growing and diversifying field, so too has continental philosophy begun responding to the issue of extinction. Those cited above—Grant, Brassier, Meillassoux—are prime examples, in that all of their work is deeply invested in responding to the contingency of the human within nature. In the past couple of decades, post-structuralism has in many ways morphed into posthumanism in theory. What does it mean for philosophy that it is eminently plausible that humanity, and all its cognitive architecture, may be transient within the universe? What does it mean for philosophy that it appears that, should things in the past have gone slightly differently, nothing even equating to our human forms of cognition need have ever emerged in the first place?

Notably, both Grant and Brassier cite Gould's work. For Brassier, Gould's evisceration of the progressivist interpretation of evolution is a key weapon in his conceptual arsenal as he attempts to dismantle all vitalist attempts to deny the hard reality of death by sublimating it as a mere "moment" in life's indefatigable becomings (i.e., making death secondary to life, as the transition between forms and necessary step on the road to self-organizing telos, rather than accepting that life is merely a very rare—and seemingly non-necessary—form of otherwise dead matter).[96] For Grant's updated Schellingianism, a naturalism of the idea (rather than an idealism of nature) is pursued such that human witness and reason can be conceptualized as just one local (and therefore contingent) way in which nature-as-idea subjectivates itself. For Meillassoux's part, contingency is core: the aim of his project is to accommodate "not only statements about possible events occurring prior to the emergence of humans, but also statements about possible events that are *ulterior* to the extinction of the human species."[97] Rather than taking the contingency of human concepts as limiting the ability of thought to grasp a world independent of thought, Meillassoux absolutizes contingency itself—at the cost of denying the reality of causality and uniform laws of nature—in order to procure for thought one firm avenue for saying it knows a totally mind-independent truth. For Meillassoux, Schelling's hypostatization of freedom would presumably be classified as what he calls "subjectalism" (which is the attempt to arrogate that you are stepping beyond the thought–world correlation simply by quietly reifying some "trait" of subjectivity as an aspect of *all* reality—whether the trait be sensation, will, creativity, irritability, or freedom).[98] Nonetheless, it is ironic that Meillassoux's resultant world-without-laws ends up being strangely similar to Schelling's unruly time and Cuvier's catastrophist saltation (where, in the French scientist's words, epochal change is tantamount to discovering that nature is "found [each time] to be subject to new laws").[99]

Nonetheless, regardless of the minutiae and tensions between contemporary trajectories in continental thought, it is undeniable that two topics, perhaps previously ignored, are taking prominence: deep time and human extinction. The outdoors is back on the agenda. Indeed, how could continental theory and post-structuralist philosophy *not* start responding to extinction? During the Sixth Mass Extinction—in a time of anthropogenic climate calamity, marked by revenant fears of thermonuclear immolation, with pandemics arising from human activity—the reality of extinction is all too obvious. It is, in some ways, *the* philosophical question of the day. Meanwhile, two centuries ago, Schelling and the *Naturphilosophen* were the very first philosophers who responded, philosophically, to the question of extinction and the depths of time, prehuman and posthuman. They were the first to see that extinction poses a deeply conceptual problem *demanding a deeply philosophical answer*. In this, the limitations of their views must be forgiven, and their pioneering prescience remembered and celebrated.

Notes

1. Jacques Derrida, "Of an Apocalyptic Tone Recently Adopted in Philosophy," *Oxford Literary Review* 6, no. 2 (1984), 3–37.
2. Fernando de Sousa Mello and Amâncio César Santos Friaça, "Converging to an Estimate of Life Span of the Biosphere?," *International Journal of Astrobiology* 19, no. 1 (2020): 25–42.
3. Ray Brassier, *Nihil Unbound: Enlightenment and Extinction* (London: Palgrave Macmillan, 2007), 228.

4. Quentin Meillassoux, *After Finitude: An Essay on the Necessity of Contingency*, trans. Ray Brassier (London: Continuum, 2008), 9.
5. Iain Hamilton Grant, *Philosophies of Nature After Schelling* (London: Continuum, 2006), 13, 54, 205.
6. For example, Richard Grusin (ed.), *After Extinction* (Minneapolis: University of Minnesota Press, 2018).
7. Benoît de Maillet, *Telliamed*, trans. Albert Carozzi (Illinois: University of Illinois Press, 1968), 228–30.
8. Charles Bonnet, *La Palingenesie philosophique* (Geneva, 1769).
9. Arthur Lovejoy, *The Great Chain of Being: A Study in the History of an Idea* (Cambridge, MA: Harvard University Press, 1936).
10. William Paley, *Natural Theology* (London, 1802), 514–15.
11. For details, see M. J. S. Rudwick, *Bursting the Limits of Time: The Reconstruction of Geohistory in an Age of Revolution* (Chicago: University of Chicago Press, 2007); and J. C. Greene, *The Death of Adam: Evolution and its Impact on Western Thought* (Ames: Iowa State University Press, 1959).
12. Georges Buffon, *Histoire naturelle des minéraux*, vol. 4 (Paris, 1783–1788), 156–58.
13. Georges Buffon, *Les époques de la nature* (Paris, 1788), 222.
14. Petrus Camper, "Complementa varia," *Nova Acta Academiae Scientiarum Imperialis Petropolitanae*, 2 (1788), 250–64.
15. Lydia Azadpour, "The Path of the Great Machine: Kielmeyer's Economy of Extinction," in *Kielmeyer and the Organic World: Texts and Interpretations*, ed. Lydia Azadpour and Daniel Whistler (London: Bloomsbury, 2020), 123.
16. C. F. Kielmeyer, "On the Relations between Organic Forces," in *Kielmeyer and the Organic World*, 47.
17. Georges Cuvier, *Fossil Bones and Geological Catastrophes: New Translations and Interpretations*, trans. M. J. S. Rudwick (Chicago: University of Chicago Press, 1997), 24.
18. Robert Richards, *The Romantic Conception of Life: Science and Philosophy in the Age of Goethe* (Chicago: University of Chicago Press, 2002), 248.
19. F. W. J. Schelling, *Werke*, ed. K. F. A. Schelling (Stuttgart: Cotta), 9.397.
20. Cuvier, *Fossil Bones*, 190.
21. Ibid., 24.
22. Kielmeyer, "Relations between Organic Forces," 47.
23. Georges Buffon, *Histoire naturelle, générale et particulière*, vol. 6 (Paris, 1749–1789), 62.
24. Kant tackles this question at *Critique of Pure Reason*, trans. Paul Guyer and Allen W. Wood (Cambridge: Cambridge University Press, 2013), A230-A232/B282-B284.
25. Ibid., A493/B521.
26. Immanuel Kant, *Religion and Rational Theology*, ed. and trans. Allen W. Wood and George di Giovanni (Cambridge: Cambridge University Press, 1996), 7.89. (Page references are to the *Akademie* edition, as standard.)
27. Immanuel Kant, *Anthropology, History and Education*, ed. and trans. Robert B. Louden et al. (Cambridge: Cambridge University Press, 2013), 8.19.
28. Immanuel Kant, *Critique of the Power of Judgement*, ed. Paul Guyer and trans. Eric Matthews (Cambridge: Cambridge University Press, 2013), 5.442.
29. Immanuel Kant, *Opus Postumum*, ed. and trans. Eckart Förster and Michael Rosen (Cambridge: Cambridge University Press, 2012), 21.214–15.
30. Schelling, *Werke*, 2.348–49.
31. Ibid., 4.489.
32. Ibid., 11.495–500. My heartfelt thanks to Iain Hamilton Grant for sharing, and allowing me to use, his translation of this lecture.
33. Heinrich Steffens, *Beyträge zur innern Naturgeschichte der Erde*, vol. 1 (Freyberg, 1801), 87–88.

34. Samuel Taylor Coleridge, *Opus Maximum*, ed. Thomas McFarland (Princeton: Princeton University Press, 2002), 292.
35. Thomas Moynihan, *X-Risk: How Humanity Discovered its Own Extinction* (Falmouth: Urbanomic, 2020), 168–72.
36. William Whewell, *The Philosophy of the Inductive Sciences* (London, 1840).
37. Samuel Taylor Coleridge, *The Notebooks of Samuel Taylor Coleridge*, vol. 5 (Princeton: Princeton University Press, 1957–2002), 6713, 6597.
38. Samuel Taylor Coleridge, *Marginalia*, vol.1, ed. George Whalley and H. J. Jackson (Princeton: Princeton University Press, 1980–2001), 663.
39. Samuel Taylor Coleridge, *Marginalia*, vol. 5, 430.
40. F. W. J. Schelling, *The Ages of the World (1811)*, trans. J. P. Lawrence (Albany: SUNY Press, 2019), 63.
41. F. W. J. Schelling, 'Ages of the World (1813)', trans. Judith Norman, in *The Abyss of Freedom* (Ann Arbor: University of Michigan Press, 1997), 121.
42. Schelling, *Ages of the World (1811)*, 173.
43. Percy Shelley, *Prose Works*, vol. 2 (London: Chatto & Windus, 1912), 186.
44. F. W. J. Schelling, *Ages of the World (1815)*, trans. Jason Wirth (Ann Arbor: University of Michigan Press, 2000), 3.
45. Steffens, *Beyträge*, 96.
46. Schelling, *Ages of the World (1815)*, 3.
47. Schelling, *Werke*, 7.375–79.
48. C. F. Kielmeyer, "Ideas for a Developmental History of the Earth and its Organisations: Letter to Windschmann, 1804," in *Kielmeyer and the Organic World: Texts and Interpretations*, 65–67.
49. Arthur Schopenhauer, *World as Will and Representation*, trans. E. F. J. Payne, vol. 2 (New York: Dover, 1969), 380–81.
50. Alexander Gode-von Aesch, *Natural Science in German Romanticism* (Columbia: Columbia University Press, 1941).
51. Schelling, *Werke*, 3.108.
52. Lorenz Oken, *Lehrbuch der Naturphilosophie*, vol. 2 (Jena, 1809–1811), 18.
53. Schelling, *Werke*, 3.102.
54. Ibid., 16.
55. Nicolaas Rupke, "Neither Creation nor Evolution: The Third Way in Mid-Nineteenth-Century Thinking about the Origin of Species," *Annals of the History and Philosophy of Biology* vol. 10 (2005): 143–72.
56. Ibid.
57. Louis Aggasiz and Augustus Gould, *Principles of Zoölogy*, vol. 1 (Boston, 1848), 206.
58. Ibid.
59. Samuel Taylor Coleridge, *Aids to Reflection* (London, 1825), 112.
60. Hugh Miller, *The Testimony of the Rocks* (Edinburgh, 1857), 215.
61. Moynihan, *X-Risk*, 45–126.
62. Maillet, *Telliamed*, 225–26.
63. Immanuel Kant, *Allgemeine Naturgeschichte und Theorie des Himmels* (Leipzig, 1755), 122.
64. H. C. Ørsted, *The Soul in Nature*, trans. L. L. Horner and J. B. Homer (London, 1825), 53–74.
65. Schelling, *Werke*, 11.498–99.
66. Ibid., 10.312. Thanks again to Iain Hamilton Grant for his translation here.
67. Georges Buffon, *Histoire naturelle, générale et particuliére*, vol. 31, 527–28.
68. Schelling, *Werke*, 11.494.
69. Robert Chambers, *Vestiges of the Natural History of Creation* (London, 1844), 164; Robert Owen, *On the Nature of Limbs, A Discourse* (London, 1849), 83.
70. Charles Darwin, *On the Origin of Species* (London, 1859), 344.
71. Ibid., 489.
72. Ibid.

73. Charles Darwin, *The Correspondence of Charles Darwin*, ed. Frederick Burkhard, vol. 8 (1993), 379.
74. Stephen Brush, "The Age of the Earth in the Twentieth Century," *Earth Sciences History* 8 (1989): 170–82.
75. See Spencer R. Weart, *The Rise of Nuclear Fear* (Harvard: Harvard University Press, 2012).
76. Alfred Döblin, *Mountains, Oceans, Giants: A Novel of the 27th Century*, trans. C. D. Godwin (Cambridge: Galileo, 2021), 344–46.
77. Ibid., 380.
78. Ibid., 370–71.
79. Karl Jaspers, *The Origin and Goal of History*, trans. Michael Bullock (London: Routledge, 1953), 209.
80. F. W. J. Schelling, *Idealism and the Endgame of Theory: Three Essays by F.W.J. Schelling*, trans. Thomas Pfau (Albany: SUNY, 1994), 88.
81. Jaspers, *Origin and Goal*, 240.
82. Ibid., 211.
83. Alexandre Kojève, *Introduction to the Reading of Hegel: Lectures on the Phenomenology of Spirit*, trans. J. H. Nichols (Ithaca: Cornell University Press, 1969), 158–60.
84. Georges Bataille, *The Cradle of Humanity: Prehistoric Art and Culture*, trans. Michelle and Stuart Kendell (New York: Zone, 2005), 87; Claude Lévi-Strauss, *Tristes Tropiques*, trans. John and Doreen Weightman (New York: Atheneum, 1974), 472; Jean-Paul Sartre, *Critique of Dialectical Reason*, trans. Quintin Hoare, vol. 2 (London: Verso, 1991), 306.
85. See Henry H. Bauer, *Beyond Velikovsky: The History of a Public Controversy* (Chicago: University of Illinois Press, 1984).
86. Lincoln Barnett, 'The Pageant of Life', *Life Magazine* (7 September, 1953), 74.
87. John Hodgdon Bradley, 'The Tribes that Slumber', in *The Century*, 117 (1929), 55–58.
88. Will Cuppy, *How To Become Extinct* (New York: Dover, 1941), 93.
89. James Elroy Flecker, *The Last Generation: A Story of the Future* (London: New Age Press, 1908), 56.
90. Gordon Dillow, *Fire in the Sky: Cosmic Collisions, Killer Asteroids, and the Race to Defend Earth* (New York: Simon & Schuster, 2020), 129.
91. David M. Raup, *Extinction: Bad Genes or Bad Luck?* (New York: Norton, 1992).
92. Stanisław Lem, *One Human Minute*, trans. C. S. Leach (London: Mandarin, 1986), 92–96.
93. Stephen Jay Gould, *Wonderful Life: The Burgess Shale and the Nature of History* (London: Vintage, 2000), 320.
94. Stephen Jay Gould, "Toward the Vindication of Punctuational Change," in *Catastrophes and Earth History*, ed. W. A. Berggren and J. A. Van Couvering (Princeton: Princeton University Press, 1984).
95. Toby Ord, *The Precipice: Existential Risk and the Future of Humanity* (London: Bloomsbury, 2020).
96. Brassier, *Nihil Unbound*, 226–27.
97. Meillassoux, *After Finitude*, 112.
98. Quentin Meillassoux, 'Iteration, Reiteration, Repetition: A Speculative Analysis of the Sign Devoid of Meaning', in *Genealogies of Speculation: Materialism and Subjectivity Since Structuralism*, ed. Armen Avanessian and Suhail Malik (London: Bloomsbury, 2016).
99. Cuvier, *Fossil Bones*, 184.

Language

Oriane Petteni and Daniel Whistler

1 Introduction: Bright Lights and Bovine Nights

On 9th May 1992, *The Times* carried a letter signed by 14 philosophers in anticipation of a ballot at the University of Cambridge on the election of Jacques Derrida to an honorary fellowship. The letter accused Derrida of obscurantism in no uncertain terms:

> In the eyes of philosophers, and certainly among those working in leading departments of philosophy throughout the world, M. Derrida's work does not meet accepted standards of clarity and rigor. ... Above all—as every reader can very easily establish for himself (and for this purpose any page will do)—his works employ a written style that defies comprehension.[1]

These kinds of criticisms of "semi-intelligible" writing[2] are common within the annals of Derrida-reception: from Althusser's remark that Derrida's undergraduate dissertation was "too difficult, too obscure"[3] to Foucault's reported charge of "*obscurantisme terroriste*."[4] And Derrida is not alone among poststructuralists in receiving this kind of treatment—think also of Manfred Frank's vitriol at Deleuze's and Guattari's *Anti-Oedipus*.[5] Nevertheless, this treatment of Derrida, Deleuze and others pales in comparison to the long history of charges of obscurantism levelled at Immanuel Kant, J. G. Fichte, G. W. F. Hegel and F. W. J. Schelling. Both German Idealists and poststructuralists—readers are warned time and time again—write opaque texts: they block out the light of reason through their difficult writing. To take one example among legion: Schopenhauer speaks of the fateful moment at

O. Petteni (✉)
Laboratoire ETHICS EA-7446, Université Catholique de Lille, Lille, France

D. Whistler
Department of Philosophy, Royal Holloway, University of London, London, UK
e-mail: daniel.whistler@rhul.ac.uk

which "Kant's occasionally obscure language" became dominant in Germany, allowing philosophy "to take refuge" behind the opaque: "Fichte was the first to seize this new privilege and use it vigorously; Schelling at least equaled him... But the height of audacity, in serving up sheer nonsense, in stringing together senseless and extravagant mazes of words, such as had previously only been heard in madhouses, was finally reached in Hegel."[6] In other words, reactions to German Idealist texts—just like poststructuralist ones—are framed in terms of obscurity, opacity and a lack of transparency, that is, in terms of a rhetoric of light and darkness. The reception-history of both movements is written in what Derrida has called "photological" categories.

What is more, while traditionally being charged with obscurity, the German Idealists are equally interpreted—especially by those who might be labelled poststructuralists—as too wedded to an ideal of *absolute transparency*, a speculative fulfilment of philosophy in *too-much-light*. A dialectic of dark words and bright concepts emerges. In particular, the German Idealist insistence on pure intellectual light-without-shadow, invoked under the figure of "the absolute," is subject to constant interrogation by poststructuralist readers, who are often precisely concerned with reinserting an opaque remainder into German Idealist thinking. Jean-Luc Nancy's *The Speculative Remark* is exemplary of this tendency. It concertedly reads one passage from Hegel's *Logic* against the grain, as a site where "the construction of the concept slides and skids... carries us off course or... disturbs or forbids the grasping of meaning."[7] Nancy reads Hegel's texts despite themselves as an "abyss" teeming with "metaphorical chaos," with linguistic "surplus" and with "the driftings of figures."[8] Nancy's Hegel errs from his own ideal of self-transparency *because he writes*. Similarly, Michèle Le Doeuff—adjacent to the poststructuralist tradition as a post-Bachelardian ally of Deleuze and adversary to Derrida—reads Kant's invocation of a "land of truth... surrounded by a wide and stormy ocean, the native home of illusion"[9] as an instance of a "philosophical imaginary" that "sustain[s] something which the system cannot itself justify, but which is nevertheless needed for its proper working," that is, as an image that "works both for and against the system."[10] For Le Doeuff, this kind of imagery resists conceptual transparency at the same time as being a constitutive component of the philosophical project. For these readers, the German Idealists are somewhat deluded: they misrecognize the ineffaceable obscurity of their own texts.[11]

In an added complication, the category of obscurity (and so the entire photological dialectic of transparency and obscurity) is not foreign to German Idealist thinking itself. Kant, Fichte, Hegel, and Schelling tend to read each other's work precisely through a lens of anxiety over obscurity. This anxiety comes to the surface in Fichte's tellingly entitled reaction to absolute idealism, *A Sun-Clear Report to the Public*, or in Schelling's response to the *Phenomenology of Spirit* as "written in a completely incomprehensible language and abounding with barbarism."[12] In a more metaphysical vein, in 1802 Schelling will criticize the lesser "lights" of German Idealism for "seeing in the essence of the absolute nothing but empty night... the mere night of difference"[13]—a sentiment famously repeated in Hegel's 1809 reference (possibly targeted back at Schelling himself) to "the night in which all cows

Language   293

are black," that is, an absolute construction of everything as "the same."[14] The 1802 Schelling will equally betray this kind of anxiety by celebrating "the appearing light that is itself the day and knows no darkness" in which "there is nothing but transparency, pure light... no shadows of obscurity or confusion."[15] For Schelling in 1802, darkness is a philosophical vice; and, more generally, all the German Idealists appear worried about the appropriate levels of light in their texts.

The continual presence of these dialectics of light and dark is unsurprising: they are necessitated by the baggage of an entire Platonic-Christian inheritance—over 2000 years' worth of metaphysics of light. As Derrida noted, "The metaphor of darkness and light (of self-revelation and self-concealment) [is] the founding metaphor of Western philosophy as metaphysics," to such an extent that "the entire history of our philosophy is a photology."[16] But, at times in German Idealism, these photological categories also emerge out of a determinate research agenda into the workings of physical light itself, optical, material and naturephilosophical models for which seep into the movement's texts. And this is the point at issue in what follows: these textual dialectics of light and shadow call for a naturephilosophical and ultimately cybernetic approach, that is, an examination of the ways in which German Idealist and poststructuralist writings are informed by *natural* models for the production of light and shadow.[17] Ultimately, what is at stake in this chapter is an interrogation of the poststructuralist turn to the materiality of the signifier "in light of" German Idealist naturalist models of light and shadow. It takes the form of an essay in the photology of philosophy.

To put it another way: Prior to becoming a bit more pessimistic about the rapprochement between philosophy of nature and French theory in *Philosophies of Nature after Schelling*, Iain Hamilton Grant had made the optimistic claim in his earlier work that naturephilosophical strands of German Idealism are *alone* able to open up "a materialist current in French thought that has remained more or less beyond the range of Anglophone hearing."[18] In this chapter, we want to apply this idea to language, signs and linguistic processes in particular—that is, we intend to uncover some of the conjunctions and disjunctions between German Idealist philosophies of nature and poststructuralist philosophies of language *by way of staging a confrontation between matter and light*. This is an encounter, then, between poststructuralist materialisms of language, on the one hand, and German Idealist naturalisms of language, on the other hand—be it Derrida's and Jean-François Lyotard's criticisms of idealist semiology via Hegel's philosophy of nature or Gilles Deleuze's appropriation of Schellingian reflections on the opacity of the written text.

Following this introduction, the second part of the chapter considers the Derridean critique of Hegel as a problem of dematerialization: for Derrida's Hegel, to encounter language is to leave matter behind. Implicit here is a poststructuralist concern to reinsert matter into the linguistic domain—and this operation is further explored in the third part of the chapter that describes some of the "semantic materialisms" proposed in the early 1970s culminating in Julia Kristeva's 1974 *Revolution in Poetic Language*. What we want to suggest is that all of these materialisms betray an uneasy relation to the idea of nature—a relation that can be rendered visible, tested, and, in some sense, corrected by way of a naturephilosophical framework.

And this is what we set out to do in the final two parts of the chapter on Goethe and Schelling, respectively. These sections return to the problematic of light and dark to rethink writing practices naturephilosophically—hence, the Goethe section turns to his *Theory of Colors* to put into question his apparent commitment to visual and linguistic transparency by way of the opaque bodies with which light is necessarily in productive relation, whereas the Schelling section concentrates on the textual practices of the *Ages of the World* drafts, read—in line with Deleuze's invocation of these texts in *Cinema II*—to bring out their function in constituting a *book of light*.

2 The Dematerializing Word

Derrida's and Lyotard's early criticisms of idealism provide a helpful way-in: They reveal the naturephilosophical background to the poststructuralist turn to the materiality of the signifier and particularly how this turn is used to question the ideal of pure transparency present in some strands of German Idealism.

2.1 The Cybernetic "Center"

One of the founding gestures of poststructuralism—located most famously in Derrida's "Structure, Sign and Play in the Discourse of the Human Sciences"—is the dislocation of the center, dramatized through Derrida's reformulation of the history of metaphysics as the history of the various forms taken on by such a center in systematic architectonics. The center (whether linguistic, biological, or cosmological) guarantees the stability and conservation of the system; it has, above all, a *restricting function*. This is a theoretical gesture strongly influenced by the flourishing cybernetics and systems theory of the 1960s, which can help us read Derrida's early invocation of "the center" in terms of its "negative feedback" within the system it controls.[19] In systems theory, negative feedback maintains the system, feeding the system's output back into its input, so as to reduce this output and stabilize internal equilibrium. Likewise, Derrida reads the center as preventing the proliferation of differences, noises or mutations by balancing the interplay between negative and positive feedbacks. The dislocation of the center announced by poststructuralism is therefore, in part, a liberation from this kind of equilibrium without any guarantee against accelerating, out-of-control positive feedback.

Derrida's dislocation of the center occurs, of course, in dialogue with Hegel, for whom very explicitly "spirit... is that which has its center in itself."[20] And for our purposes what is crucial is that Hegel's defense of the centered system is closely linked to a fantasy of transparency. For example, spirit—characterized by self-centering, circularity and closure—is opposed to matter as extended, dispersed and opaque. That is, matter creates forms by differentiating itself from its environment qua undetermined matter (i.e., qua noise[21]), and such a process is inherently inferior, according to Hegel, to spiritual value-creation. And this is because matter is dependent on exchanges and negotiations with its outside (i.e., its environment), whereas absolute spirit is a "center of reference" in and for itself[22]: it is autarchic and exists in absolute freedom. The process of absolute spirit's self-becoming is a story of gaining precisely this kind of freedom, defined as withdrawal from relation with "exteriority"—that is, any medium alien to spirit itself. Hence, in the philosophy of nature, "exteriority" designates the terrestrial environment (and its specific spatiotemporal conditions) in which living beings evolve; in the philosophy of mind, it designates the external data collected by the senses organs (what Hegel calls "intuition's own content"[23]); in semiotics, it designates both the residual sensory data to which the sign refers and the materiality of the sign itself, in opposition to its—supposedly—purely idealistic meaning; and, in the last stage of the Hegelian system, spirit becomes absolute, that is, liberated from its incarceration in these successive media, at the conclusion of its journey toward self-transparency. To sum up, Hegelian spirit takes on increasing capacities of dematerialization—or even de-mediatization—eventually enabling spirit to come into itself in a transparently self-referential sphere. It is precisely this fantasy of self-transparency that Derrida interrogates in the name of the persistence of the opaque.

His "The Pit and the Pyramid: An Introduction to Hegel's Semiology" undertakes that task in exemplary fashion. For Derrida, this fantasy of transparency motivating Hegel's treatment of linguistic "exteriority" is inherited by orthodox structuralist linguistics in the Saussurean tradition; indeed, he intends to show that "structural linguistics itself unknowingly perpetuated the Hegelian inheritance."[24] In particular, Derrida points to the Hegelian articulation between the sensible and the intelligible as the problematic nexus upon which this whole tradition of linguistics from Hegel onwards is established, and, in so doing, he decisively singles out the philosophy of nature as the primary site where a rudimentary semiology appears. This is a non-trivial choice, we argue, since we will go on to suggest that the various competing philosophies of nature of the period provide a fruitful resource for very different semiological models.

2.2 *Reading as Dematerialization*

In "The Pit and the Pyramid," Derrida goes about excavating the hierarchical chain of nature described by Hegel, in which natural products are positioned on an ascending scale toward absolute freedom, insofar as they exhibit features that anticipate the emergence of ideality in nature:

> Since sensory matter is differentiated, it forms hierarchies of types and regions according to their power of ideality. Among other consequences, it follows from this that one may consider the concept of physical ideality as a kind of teleological anticipation, or inversely that one may recognize in the concept and value of ideality in general a "metaphor."[25]

The philosophy of nature is the battlefield on which the fight between materiality and ideality (or meaning) takes place. In *Discourse, Figure*, Lyotard will make a similar point concerning the idealist account of the sign as that which "inhabits the sensory," but also "comes from elsewhere to immobilize, preserve and remove [language] from the [sensory] fluctuation of the instant" and "determines [language] through repeated negations... of its spatial and temporal environment."[26] Likewise for Derrida's Hegel, the dialectic of language is modeled on the animal organism's tendency to detach itself from its initial terrestrial (and therefore contingent) spatiotemporal coordinates (space, time and gravity); the spiritual in language repeats, continues and evolve further this logic of dematerialization that starts in nature. Hence, Derrida makes clear in "The Pit and the Pyramid," the prevalence given to sound over light in the philosophy of nature (of the acoustic over visibility) repeats itself at the spiritual level in the prevalence given to the voice over writing and, at the semiological level, in the prevalence of the Latin alphabet over all other types of non-Western writings (Egyptian hieroglyphs, Chinese characters, etc.).[27]

The logic of Hegel's framework is motored by a negation of linguistic "naturalness." Egyptian hieroglyphs, for instance, appear too entangled in the sensory reality they designate because of their mimetic mode of reference. To use Lyotard's terms from *Discourse, Figure*, the defect of these superseded forms of language is the way they attract the reader's attention back to their materiality, their retention of the *graphic* dimension of the sign and so their resistance to a dematerialized and phonocentric approach to language. On the contrary, reading "dematerialized" signs may well still be a visual act, but it is one that, as Lyotard emphasizes, requires the intervention of a specific kind of vision—focal vision—performed by the zone located at the center of the retina (the fovea). And Lyotard will argue that this model of focal vision is a more disembodied—we can almost say "idealist"—form of reading. That is, focal vision is at the service of the reproduction of the idealist image of the world, erasing any event happening at the periphery of the retina, to secure the stability and efficiency of the visual system. Lyotard writes,

> Although it is true that the letters' "rhythm," "position," and "sequence" refer to a position occupied by the reader, which serves as reference-point, this calibration owes nothing to the body's aesthetic power... It is not the sensory body that finds itself implicated in this relationship [between text and reader]; on the contrary, the body suffers a complete cancellation in the latter... The letter's form, energy, thickness, size, "weight" do not have to make themselves felt by the reader's body... The letter is the support of a conventional, immaterial signification, identical in every respect to the presence of the phoneme.[28]

The above matches quite precisely Hegel's description of the sign as it operates in Western modes of writing. Compare, for example, Hegel's claim that

> In the sign as such, the intuition's own content and the content of which it is a sign, have nothing to do with each other. In signifying therefore intelligence displays a freer willfulness and mastery in the use of intuition than in symbolizing... The right place for the sign is the one indicated: intelligence—which in intuiting generates the form of time and of space, but appears as the recipient of the sensory content and as forming its representations out of this material—now gives its independent representations a determinate reality out of itself, uses the filled space and time, the intuition, as its own, deletes its immediate and peculiar content, and gives it another content as its meaning and soul.[29]

What this quotation makes clear above all is Hegel's conception of intelligence as the organizing principle that shapes material contents (namely, in the context of language, sense data) and eventually becomes independent from them. This has resonance precisely in terms of the cybernetic reading offered of Derrida above: Hegel's approach to semiology appears to exemplify what Hayles calls "a conception of information as a (disembodied) entity," that is, involving the systematic "erasure or downplaying of embodiment" equally present "in the cybernetic construction of the posthuman."[30]

2.3 The Posthuman Hegel

While "The Pit and the Pyramid" does not itself call Hegel posthuman, Derrida's "The Ends of Man" does indeed vehemently reject anthropocentric readings of Hegel (such as Wahl's or Kojève's). Derrida instead emphasizes, in line with a different kind of Hegel, that "one may imagine a consciousness without man."[31] This image of Hegel approaches what Hayles, in a Kittlerian vein, writes of the relation between the posthuman imaginary and contemporary writing technologies:

> The relation between striking a key and producing text with a computer is very different from the relation achieved with a typewriter. Display brightness is unrelated to keystroke pressure, and striking a single key can effect massive changes in the entire text. The computer restores and heightens the sense of word as image—an image drawn in a medium as fluid and changeable as water. Interacting with electronic images rather than with a materially resistant text, I absorb through my fingers as well as my mind a model of signification in which no simple one-to-one correspondence exists between signifier and signified. I know kinesthetically as well as conceptually that the text can be manipulated in ways that would be impossible if it existed as a material object rather than a visual display.[32]

There is—despite it all—a Hegelian resonance to this description of electronic media, where sense appears "as fluid and changeable as water," seemingly independent from any "materially resistant text." Of course, there are differences too: electronic media can give rise to a proliferation of signs *à la* Baudrillard, which lies in tension to the centering of Hegelian spirit. Nevertheless, the poststructuralists (as a loosely assembled group) are for the most part united in their intention to resist both of these modalities of semiotic dematerialization—be it through Derridean *espacement*, through Deleuzean pragmatics, through Lyotardian desire or, more generally, through the materiality of the signifier. They construct a materialist alternative to Hegelian-cybernetic semiology, and this alternative forms the subject matter of the next section. Moreover, it is worth emphasizing that this materialist alternative is constructed, as we have seen, in opposition equally to both the fantasy of transparency and the logic of dematerialization—two motifs that are fused together in the above reading of Hegelian semiology. That is, the case of Hegel naturally suggests that the transparent and the immaterial are two sides of the same coin in German Idealist treatments of language. On the contrary, what we want to show in the later sections of this chapter is that transparency and dematerialization are not necessarily intertwined, and that those philosophers of nature in competition with Hegel provide accounts of transparent language that are both naturalist and materialist—and thereby complicate the poststructuralist critique set out above.

3 "Revolutionary Semiotics"[33]

The above, then, forms the Derrido-Lyotardian diagnosis of "idealist" semiology as a closed, dematerializing system that conceals the materialist moment in meaning in the name of a fantasy of self-transparency. And the poststructuralist alternative broadly takes the form of an injunction to rematerialize language. This countertendency to "semantic materialism," as Philippe Sollers dubbed it,[34] is exemplified most radically in the early poststructuralisms of the late 1960s and early 1970s, prior to the partial occlusion of this materialist moment by successive theological and ethical turns within poststructuralism's anglophone reception. It is a selection of these materialisms of the word that are described in the present section: What we want to argue is that, despite being framed as means of resisting this "idealist" tendency to dematerialization, these materialisms are still complicit in an analogous *denaturalization* of language. That is, semantic materialisms have often been accompanied by a refusal to naturalize language and so have been constructed out of a *double gesture of materialization and denaturalization*. But this moment of denaturalization remains uncannily similar to the Hegelian negation of nature in language rehearsed above: it does not fully escape the Hegelian hierarchy of spirit. The one obvious exception, we will suggest, is Kristeva's early philosophy of language that lends itself to a very different naturephilosophical reading and so, we argue, offers a more radical, even more anti-"idealist" alternative: a materialization *and naturalization* of linguistic processes.

3.1 The Materialist Moment in "British Poststructuralism"

A relatively forgotten but illuminating episode in the history of poststructuralism was what Easthorpe has labelled the phenomenon of "British poststructuralism," in which, during the 1970s, the texts of Derrida and others found their home among British sociologists, rather than philosophers, theologians, or literary theorists, and were taken to supply the scientific foundations of an all-encompassing dialectical materialism.[35] For our purposes, Rosalind Coward's and John Ellis's 1977 *Language and Materialism* exemplifies this episode, for the book describes—via Derrida, Kristeva, and Lacan—"the revolution undergone by structuralist thought" since the late 1960s and the enriched Marxist theory that resulted.[36]

Coward and Ellis are palpably excited at the new poststructuralist moment emerging out of what they see as the ruins of structuralism. "Structuralism," they claim "failed to produce a genuinely materialist theory of language, and ultimately rested on idealist presuppositions."[37] And this is true not only of structuralism itself, but an entire "idealist" trajectory in Western thought, for which, as they put it, "the very notion of the sign is deeply implicated in the flight from materiality."[38] As this makes clear, the dichotomy between an idealism of language and a materialism of language structures Coward's and Ellis' book, and what distinguishes the two turns out to be whether or not the subject is exempted from wider semiotic processes. "Idealism," they write, "depends on notions of 'human essence' which somehow transcend... the social system" and results in a "conception of language as a transparent, neutral milieu." Hence, they too identify the fantasy of linguistic transparency with "idealism" and go on to claim that it is precisely this position that has been "shaken by the extension of a materialist analysis to language itself."[39] Whereas classical structuralism was "inhibited from developing any real materialist understanding of language and ideology" by its "complicity with idealism," Kristeva and Derrida, among others, have taken on the task "to rethink the foundations of structuralism."[40] Coward and Ellis therefore understand this "poststructuralist" moment as a struggle, in the name of an extended Marxist theory of language, against the "politically regressive elements of structuralism," that is, against those who "seek to reinstate idealism against materialism."[41] Or, to put it another way, dialectical materialism should become poststructuralism, for only poststructuralism can absolutize dialectical materialism to include a materialist theory of signification.

This materialist turn has three relevant features. First, in a gesture that resonates with German Idealist philosophies of nature, it is articulated—following Kristeva (see below)—in terms of a shift from product (the sign as given) to productivity (the sign as one moment in a process). According to Coward and Ellis, structuralism, at its worst, had "removed any emphasis from productivity, stressing instead a pregiven meaning" and so neglected what they take to be a Marxist axiom: "Everything that exists consists... in the process of transformation."[42] Second, Coward and Ellis also follow Kristeva (and thus take a very different tack from Derrida's early treatment of Hegel described above) in taking Hegelian dialectic as their major reference point for this turn to productivity: They argue for a materialist transformation of the Hegelian process of "division, movement and process" into a series of "movements of rupture, of renovation, of revolution" by a material substrate.[43] Indeed, they even claim that Kristeva's interpretation of Hegel in *Revolution in Poetic Language* marks "the real beginning of a materialist theory of language," in which language is reduced to the material forces out of which it is produced.[44] Third, Coward and Ellis follow Roland Barthes in particular[45] in an insistence that this materialization of language occurs in opposition to any naturalization of the linguistic process. Materialisms of language refuse to ascribe any "naturalness" to the sign. Ultimately, nature is sacrificed in this kind of account for a generic concept of matter. And this polemic against the natural is undertaken along traditional dialectical materialist lines: to naturalize the sign is seen to involve fetishizing one, single moment in the linguistic process, to reduce it to a permanent given rather than a transient snapshot in the unending movement of material rupture. Recourse to nature is uncritical; and so the concept of nature is consigned to "idealism."

This distrust of the *nature of language* is frequent in contemporary theory, far beyond the confines of Coward's and Ellis' "British poststructuralism." For example, Alain Badiou opens *The Logic of Worlds* contrasting two possible modes of materialist dialectic—one in which "there are only bodies and languages... the axiom of contemporary conviction" and Badiou's own variant according to which "there are only bodies and languages, except that there are truths."[46] The idea that languages might themselves be natural bodies (i.e., a naturalism of words) cannot be countenanced; the assumption that words are non-natural is axiomatic. The most visible example of this refusal of the nature of language occurs in an entirely different theoretical tradition, even if it is still in some sense a materialist one—Paul de Man's development of Yale deconstruction in conversation with idealist accounts of language. What Derrida calls the textual "materialism"[47] present in de Man's late readings of the German Idealists (Kant, Schiller, Hegel) is always accompanied by a distaste for naturalist descriptions of the signifying process. De Man thus offers a paradigmatic version of a *materialism without nature*. For example, his concept of ideology is informed by this rejection of the naturalization of language: "What we call ideology is precisely the confusion of linguistic with natural reality, of reference with phenomenalism";[48] it, he continues, falsifies the non-natural "essence of language."[49] His reading of Friedrich Hölderlin's couplet, "Nun aber nennt er sein Liebstes, / Nun, nun müssen dafür Worte, wie Blumen, entstehn (But now he names his most loved, / Now, for this reason, words, like flowers, must arise),"[50] in "Intentional Structure of the Romantic Image" provides a helpful summary of this position: ideological perversions result from the "priority" accorded to "natural substances" in accounts of language. Thus, when Hölderlin describes the genesis of words on the model of flowers (i.e., the organism), he exemplifies the ideological trap of transferring "the intrinsic ontological primacy of the natural object" into the linguistic domain. The word comes to be understood as a natural object—and this, for de Man, is a failure to understand language correctly.[51] De Man's materialism of the signifier comes at the expense of the *nature* of the signifier. Like so many others in contemporary theory, he keeps nature out of language at the same time as bringing matter in, resulting in an oddly *denaturalized conception of linguistic matter*.

3.2 Matter and Nature in the Early Kristeva

While Coward and Ellis might celebrate Kristeva's early philosophy as "the real beginning of a materialist theory of language," her own work goes far beyond their reconstruction of it in its embrace of *the natural in language*. It thus stands as an exception to the double operation of materialization-denaturalization described above. Indeed, her creation of a Freudianized Hegel allows for a psychobiological model of the genesis of the sign grounded in an account of the movement of not denaturalized matter in general, but bodily matter in particular. Kristeva verges on philosophy of nature (e.g., when she understands language on the model of geological "strata" effected by "energy discharge" from "a chemical reaction"[52]).

The early Kristeva does indeed (like Coward and Ellis after her) begin from the premise that "Marxist-Leninist theory [is] the only revolutionary theory of our times" and that the task of the theorist is "to carry the social revolution to its real accomplishment in the order of its languages."[53] And this is, in turn, likewise interpreted as an encounter between "the materiality of writing" and idealist sciences of language.[54] As a result, Kristeva is always looking to catalogue "the 'material' within the 'logical'" or "the semiotic" within "the symbolic,"[55] that is, the ways in which an occluded "materialist foundation" of language constantly erupts forth to destabilize, exceed and interrogate the classical sign.[56] Her philosophy takes the form of a polemic "against the sign": "The sign implies an idealism,"[57] a denaturalization of words that neglects the subterranean, energetic processes that circulate beneath them, creating and destroying them in turn.

This polemic is, once again, premised on a genetic turn in the treatment of language—what Lewis calls (in words that unintentionally cite Schelling), Kristeva's "new theory of production-prior-to-the-product."[58] Just like the German philosophers of nature before her, she is interested in bearing witness to a subterranean process and charting "the production of meaning prior to meaning."[59] Moreover, just like the German philosophers of nature, this is a resolutely *natural* process—a collision of bodily energies in a "physiological process" modeled on corporeal expulsion, in which signs are merely points of inhibition or "blockages of the process."[60] In short, it is by means of a quasi-Freudian theory of expulsion[61] that matter becomes linguistic; it names "the path from object to sign, this passage to the sign occurring when the object is detached from the body and isolated as a real object."[62]

Moreover (and despite the Schellingian resonances), this is a Freud read rigorously *through Hegel*. As Lewis warned on introducing her philosophy to an anglophone audience, "Kristeva is bound to incur many attacks for what will be called her Hegelianism. Hegel is extraordinarily prominent in *La Révolution du langage poétique*, and whereas [Husserl] is an object of attack, the Hegelian concept of negativity undergoes elucidation and appropriation."[63] In Kristeva's own words, "a materialist reading of Hegel allows a thinking of negativity as the trans-subjective and trans-semiotic moment of the separation of matter which is constitutive of the conditions of symbolicity."[64] According to this Hegel of the natural body, pulsional energies become signs by way of what Kristeva explicitly calls a "*Aufhebung*";[65] a dialectical negativity identified with "a corporeal, physiological and signifiable excitation within the symbolizing structure."[66] Kristeva situates her Hegelianism "at the crossroads of sign and rhythm, of representation and light, of the symbolic and the semiotic"[67] and, in doing so, first brought the body—"the flesh of writing"[68]—into poststructuralist theory.

3.3 Semantic Materialisms with and without Nature

Kristeva's trajectory is anomalous. Most poststructuralist materialists identify the concept of "nature" with "idealism." But the early Kristeva returns to a richer, quasi-naturephilosophical conception of linguistic genesis that begins with the pulsional body. To put it another way: Kristeva's early philosophy implicitly stands in judgment over the operations of denaturalization that otherwise motivate poststructuralist accounts of language, and so, in contrast to them, it can fruitfully be put into dialogue with naturephilosophical models that also reinsert the question of nature into materialism.

As mentioned at the beginning of this chapter, such a confrontation between poststructuralism and philosophy of nature takes place in Iain Hamilton Grant's shadow. Grant has repeatedly attempted to counter the tendency "to eliminate the concept, even the existence of nature" in French theory by supplementing it with the resources provided by German philosophies of nature.[69] The result, he claims in his early work, is "an alternative version of postmodernity"[70] that uncovers "the energetics beneath representation" and "the dynamic core of nature" as part of "an uninterrupted physicalism leading from the real to the ideal."[71] That is, the early Grant argues for "the naturalization of ideality" in an eclectic synthesis of philosophy of nature and poststructuralist theory.[72] And yet, while Grant's project hopefully resonates with some of the above, he situates himself as part of an anti-linguistic or post-linguistic turn (attacking, e.g., "the linguistic idealism" of the philosophical tradition[73]). Hence, what is at stake in this chapter (language) constitutes an extension of the Grantian project against the grain: a thinking through of a naturalism *of language* by bringing together the resources of poststructuralism (described above) and philosophies of nature (set out below).

This extension could have been undertaken in a variety of ways; for example, one might directly confront de Man's anti-naturalism with a reactivated version of Hölderlin's invocation of "words like flowers," using this couplet as the clue to an ontology of meaning that embeds signs within a process of natural genesis.[74] Our tack in the second half of this chapter is different. We want to read naturephilosophical texts naturephilosophically,[75] and, in particular, to return to the problematic of light and shadow with which this chapter began as an example of the operation of naturalizing language. At stake are the ways in which German Idealist ideals of light emerge out of very specific textual practices that depend on particular naturephilosophical models. German Idealist texts generate light according to very distinctive processes borrowed from the physical realm. Take, for example, Hölderlin's last (i.e., post-1806) poems, which deliberately move away from understanding "words like flowers" (as above) to understanding them *as translucent*.[76] The last Hölderlin writes in bright lights, creating a world without shadows and speaking in a voice "beyond all exertion."[77] His poems from this period suggest an underlying physics of light in which (according to the poem, *Der Sommer*[78]) transparency-without-shadow does not result from the beams of the summer sun as a transcendent (Platonic) source, but from a this-worldly atmosphere of radiance—Constantine helpfully describes it as "the visible vehicle of an immanent joy."[79] The light-writing of the last Hölderlin is non-dialectical, non-reflective, and non-refractive, unmuddied by negativity; its translucence is synonymous with a cheerful affirmation of the simple plenitude of what is.

Our conjecture is that distinctive textual practices of light-writing are correlated to different naturephilosophical models, and we provide two case studies of this correlation so as to take seriously some of the ways in which language is modelled naturalistically in German Idealism.

4 Goethe and the Philosophical Production of Light

The first case study centers on models of vision (as they relate to light and shadow) in J. W. Goethe's scientific writings. In particular, Goethe reconfigures the traditional hierarchical relationship between types of vision—a gesture later repeated by Lyotard—and attends to the innumerable effects resulting from the ineluctable encounter between light and opaque bodies. In so doing, Goethe's work exemplifies the kind of naturalization process, and consequently the kinds of textual practice, at stake in this chapter.

4.1 Goethean Transparency

On the face of it, Goethe might be considered a relatively unproductive dialogue-partner for our discussion of the ways in which photology and language are entwined in the age of German Idealism. And this is because two images of Goethe have come to dominate his philosophical reception: "the phenomenological Goethe" and the "neoplatonic Goethe." Both of them render him a traditional proponent of a fantasy of self-transparency, one which is so radical as to refuse any kind of signification or linguistic mediation whatsoever. Light, according to these interpretations of Goethe, is the enemy of the word.

Hence, Goethe is often cited as a hero of phenomenology—for example, by Dominique Janicaud in the closing words of *Le Tournant phenomenologique* as a means to resist the theological perversions of phenomenology of Jean-Luc Marion and others.[80] And this is because, in line with the Heideggerian definition of phenomenological method as "bringing to the light of day, putting in the light,"[81] Goethe is read as advocating an unproblematic "perception of the universal shining in the particular."[82] Meanings ("the universal") *light up* the intuitive gaze of the Goethean phenomenologist; no hermeneutic effort or other form of mediation is required to *bring them to light*, since they are already present to the gaze bathed in the full glow of epistemic transparency. Similar implications follow from a neoplatonic image of Goethe that takes seriously his 1782 Plotinian turn—the moment at which "all at once neoplatonic philosophy and especially Plotinus touched me emotionally in a quite extraordinary way as if inspiration had struck."[83] Notably, it is vision, once again, that orients Goethe's reception of neoplatonism: His 1805 translations of the *Enneads* describe the way in which light makes knowledge possible, that is, "Were the eye not of the sun, / How could we behold the light?".[84] As Goethe himself glosses in the opening to his *Theory of Colors*, "The eye is formed by the light and for the light so that the inner light may emerge to meet the outer light."[85] A "latent form of light"[86] is present within the self—and its metaphysical affinity with external light is what makes meaning, knowledge and theory all possible. All the theorist need do is unlock an inner seeing in order to see everything else transparently.

Key to our argument in this chapter is the implications of the above for language. And ultimately, for both these images of Goethe, words get in the way: "Words transform living things into dead ones,"[87] he states, because they impede immediate perception. Goethe is understood as a proponent of "the prison-house of language,"[88] for whom—as poet and scientist—words are the problem to be transcended and cast off. As he puts it in *Faust*, "the name's merely smoke and noise—what does it do / But cloud the heavenly radiance?"[89]—or, as he insists in his essay "Symbolism," "Intuitive perception… cannot take place in language."[90] The problem for both the phenomenological and neoplatonic Goethe is "words as surrogates,"[91] the way linguistic mediation draws attention away from what is "present before our physical eyes."[92] To put it bluntly, Goethe—on these readings—is to be placed in a tradition of an apophatics of immanence: language must negate itself and fall silent before the lighting-up of the thing itself. And so, critics speak of Goethe's "rhetoric of paradox,"[93] his commitment to "language's self-effacement,"[94] and his productive employment of negation and silences.[95]

There is no denying the power of these interpretations of Goethe; however, they have their limitations. We want to suggest that there are far more interesting relations between light and sense-making in the Goethean oeuvre than those suggested above. Take, for example, the neoplatonic image of Goethe. As well as affirming a Plotinian idea of a dazzling light-source that the subject must access internally, Goethe also puts this very idea into question: after including his Plotinus-translations in *Wilhelm Meisters Wanderjahre*, Goethe adds critically, "A spiritual form is by no means diminished by emerging into appearance… What is begotten is not inferior to the begetter, and indeed, the advantage of live begetting is that what is begotten can be superior to that which begets it."[96] In other words, Goethe rejects the broadly neoplatonic idea that the further one gets from the primordial light, the obscurer things become, that transparency is only to be found at the origin. And, in so doing, Goethe here rejects the idea that mediation necessarily obscures the light of phenomena (or even the subject's own "inner light"). Intermediaries, "surrogates," and substitutes (like words) can beget even more light and increase how much the subject sees. This is a very different conception of the word.

Another way of flagging up the limitations of the above images is to contrast them with another powerful image of Goethe—"the structuralist Goethe" of Lévi-Strauss and others,[97] the Goethe of morphological rationality whose concept of structural transformation has been so influential on "the theoretical genealogy of structuralism."[98] For this Goethe, transformations in structural and systematic form must always be understood naturalistically, that is, as part of a wider ecology of organic development. This is far from a Goethe of the immediate percept; it is a Goethe of conceptual modeling, of systems-theory, and of naturephilosophical speculation. And it is precisely this intersection of naturalism and structuralism—or even *post*-structuralism—that interests us: to put it crudely, Goethe thinks the material play of the signifier by way of specific natural models, including the dialectic of light and darkness.

The example of Goethe's meteorological reflections helps. As always in his scientific writings, Goethe is interested in the laws of transformation that hold within nature as a self-regulated structure. But when it comes to an intelligible syntax for the series of transformations out of which cloud-formations are constituted, things are not that easy. The "fundamental law of weather" only makes sense by "paying close attention to endless physical, geological, and topographical differences, so that we can understand deviations in the phenomena as far as possible."[99] This is more than cataloguing a set of rules for structural transformation; it is cataloguing a set of anomalies and disequilibria, that is, Goethean meteorology *also* grapples with the atmospheric disturbances that trouble any reduction of the weather to structural laws. In sum, this natural space is a troubled one, a space of "atmospheric haze" where everything is slightly distorted and concealed.[100] The light of the sun is subject to disturbances by atmospheric phenomena: mists, hazes, fogs and clouds do not negate this light, but distort it. The phenomena are still lit up, but across various forms of diaphanous mediation. Structural laws encounter natural opacity—and Goethean science is born from this encounter. This results in the key Goethean profession of faith that motivates his entire *Theory of Colors*:

> I am confronting light with obscurity; there would be, once and for all, no relation between them if matter did not come to interpose itself; and whether it is opaque, transparent or even animate, it is [by means of matter] that the clear and the dark are manifest and that colour is born with its thousands of modalities… [And out of this] the meteorological process thus determines, in its thousand variations, but also according to the most rigorous laws, the element in which and from which we live.[101]

4.2   *Figural Space: Goethe and Lyotard*

Goethe's *Theory of Colors* is a key text in the history of the disruption of what Lyotard calls the rationalized, hegemonic spaces of early modern thinking. His work—particularly his revalorization of shadow in the production of color—obscures the traditional universal space of meaning, in which a geometry of the line dominates, in the name of a metamorphic, opaque space determined by fleeting shadows and visual disturbances. Goethe is clear: "The eye sees no form, inasmuch as light, shade, and color together constitute that which… distinguishes object from object."[102] Instead of the formalism of an optics of lines and shapes, Goethe lets back in curves, the lateral, peripheries and the phantasmagorical. And he does so by turning to vision's physiological, psycho-physical and even sociological aspects, by explicitly reclaiming premodern ideas of light (such as Plotinus's) and by thereby constructing a conception of sight that disrupts some of the foundational assumptions of what he sees as Newton's abstract, geometrical, optical investigations. This is ultimately a naturalization—or, better, corporealization—of color and of vision, refusing the abstract and empty space of the Newtonian tradition of geometrical optics to attend to the particular distortions that occur in an environment endlessly open to disturbance.

Goethe's gesture is one that Lyotard will later repeat in *Discourse, Figure*. As mentioned above, Lyotard reconceptualizes the relationship between the discursive space of an easily readable external image seen through the focal zone of the retina, and the figural space glimpsed by peripheral vision, whose visual grid is looser than the focal one and therefore more open to the eruption of the new, the irregular and that which resists the rationalized geometry of discursive space. Lyotard creates space for those figural events that disrupts the visual syntax of discursive space, associated systematically with linear perspective.[103] Moreover, the stakes of this polemic against discursive space do not solely concern vision, but—as its name implies—linguistic discourse too (a space which corresponds broadly to Derrida's "space of the system"[104]), for Lyotard's ultimate target will be Saussure, who had "allow[ed] the linguistic sign to escape the attraction of motivation," creating a semiotic cut between discourse and nature. Lyotard resists this cut in both its visual and linguistic variants by looking at modernist poetry and painting, in which signs can be motivated such that "the configuration of the signifier is not separated from the situation in which the sign is produced."[105] The result of this alternative is "an expression itself deprived of stability," that refuses "constant signification." And Lyotard's use of painting is particularly pertinent, since it parallels the Goethean impulse to reevaluate the primacy of linear perspective. Lyotard insists, for instance, on how van Gogh's or Klee's uses of colors and peripheral vision reinject thickness, material heaviness, and dynamism into the pictorial space, in order to let us see the genesis of object-vision prior to the constitution of any stable object.[106]

To be clear, what Lyotard and Goethe share is, first, a tendency to resist an ideal of geometrical optics, which grounds linear perspective as well as the ideal discursive space, and which requires an empty space where light (or meaning) can circulate freely, that is, without friction from any encounter with matter. They emancipate vision from the hegemony of the line, contour and form. In this vein, Goethe argues that all transparent spaces are actually—at least, *a minima*—turbid: there is no such thing as pure transparency in nature ("All mediums called transparent are in some degree dim"[107]). Moreover, secondly and more precisely, they share an opposition to the *restricted visual economy* of the retina presupposed by those conceptions of vision that privilege geometrical optics and linear perspective. That is, like Lyotard, Goethe reasserts the rights of the *general economy of the retina*, where peripheral vision plays an equal—if not more important—role to focal vision. Since peripheral vision is responsible for nocturnal vision and focal vision for diurnal vision, Goethe is equally reevaluating precisely how light and darkness are intertwined in the production of the visible world, and—crucially for our purposes—this also implies, from a linguistic point of view, a reevaluation of how shadows, figures and imaginaries generally (in Le Doeuff's sense above) are always at play in the process of signification and cannot be sublated into some final transparent language. To put it another way: Goethe liberates the retina, defining it in terms of its "vitality" and its "lively mobility," its "desire to modify its own state continually and, in the simplest instance, to pass from the clear to the obscure and back again."[108]

4.3 The Constitutive Function of the Opaque Body

The fame of Goethe's *Theory of Colors* rests on its attack on Newton's theory of light, which had claimed to demonstrate that, when passing through a prism, clear white light decomposes into seven different colors. Goethe vehemently opposes this model of the birth of color, in which a single transparent entity (white light) is posited as naturally and even metaphysically prior to the diversity of empirically perceived colors. The Goethean alternative understands light (as well as all other natural phenomena) as generated out of a continual interplay between opposed polar forces. The primal scene of Goethe's rejection of Newtonianism is described as follows:

> Along with the rest of the world I was convinced that all the colors are contained in the light; no one had ever told me anything different... But how I was astonished, as I looked at a white wall through the prism, that it stayed white! Only where it came upon some darkened area, it showed some color, then at last, around the windowsill all the colors shone... It didn't take long before I knew here was something significant about color to be brought forth, and I spoke as through an instinct out loud, that the Newtonian teachings were false.[109]

Against Newton, Goethe presents an alternative *experimentum crucis*, where color only appears *when light encounters its other*, namely, darkness or corporeal opacity. He continues, "the theory we set up against this begins with colorless light;" nevertheless, it "does not arrogate to itself developing colors from the light, but rather seeks to prove by numberless cases that color is produced by light as well as by what stands against it."[110] The stakes of Goethe's alternative to Newton are clear in this passage: They involve a gesture towards the opaque body—as a dense, even thick medium—which is to play a constitutive role in the production of the visible world. Mere light is invisible; it requires bodily matter to become visible and to express itself in infinite, colorful ways, according to the type of material medium it encounters. Particularly relevant is Goethe's description of what he calls "objective colors" through the conjunction of light and an opaque body.[111] These are colors that seem to be produced outside of us, before being reflected back into our eyes—they function as the natural analogue to the metaphysical reappropriation of spirit through nature. But whereas Hegel forever understands this process as a dematerializing one that moves toward absolute transparency, Goethe resists this teleology. Indeed, his insistence in the *Theory of Colors* that there is no such thing as pure, transparent, self-identical light (at least, on earth) is accompanied by an extension of this claim into the domain of meaning: There is no such thing as transparent meaning—no "pure" meaning that could be detached from the sign that expresses it. As soon as light appears, it is forever subject to disturbances, distortions, diffractions and reflections—and these effects are dependent on the nature of the opaque matter it encounters. Nowhere can light be manifest "pure" or free itself from material contamination. For example, Goethe enumerates the various ways in which the encounter of light and opaque body can generate "catoptrical" effects ("when [light] flashes back from the surface of a medium"), "paroptical" effects ("when [light] passes by the edge of a medium"), "dioptrical" effects ("when [light] passes through either a light-transmitting or an actually transparent body") or "epoptical" effects (when "phenomena exhibit themselves on the colorless surface of bodies under various conditions").[112] To put it another way: increase of darkness entails increase of color and this is a function of supposedly transparent light.

Earlier in the *Theory of Colors* (in the initial section on "physiological colors"), Goethe had made the same point with respect to vision. Indeed, this opening section stands as an epochal effort to re-embody vision in opposition to a whole tradition of geometrical optics that sustained many epistemological, pictorial and linguistic "idealisms" in early modern philosophy. Goethe's initial gesture is a normalization of "optical illusions," such that they become customary manifestations of an embodied eye encountering its environment. Goethe writes that what has "hitherto been looked upon as extrinsic and casual, as illusion and infirmity" must become "the foundation of the whole doctrine," for these phenomena "belong altogether, or in a great degree, to the *subject*—to the eye itself." They must be recovered from the margins of theory where "they were banished into the region of phantoms," so as to become normative of "the eye in a healthy state" as "necessary conditions of vision."[113] In addition, Goethe goes on to equally revalorize the role played by the entirety of retinal topology in the visual process, including peripheral vision, in opposition to any privileging of focal vision alone. Take, for example, Goethe's observations in §54:

> On the 19th June, 1799, late in the evening, when the twilight was deepening into a clear night, as I was walking up and down the garden with a friend, we very distinctly observed a flame-like appearance near the oriental poppy,... We approached the place and looked attentively at the flowers, but could perceive nothing further, till at last, by passing and repassing repeatedly, while we looked sideways on them, we succeeded in renewing the appearance as often as we pleased... In looking directly at a flower the image is not produced, but it appears immediately as the direction of the eye is altered. Again, by looking sideways on the object, a double image is seen for a moment, for the spectrum then appears near and on the real object.[114]

In this passage, focal (and therefore discursive) vision appears merely as one particular instance of vision among others. In fact, the whole chapter on physiological colors charts an endless flow of continuously moving images, with diverse rhythms (flashes or slow-motion) and according to different types of transitions or "montage" between stable objects. For example, Goethe attends to those remnant images that leave a trace on the retina for a moment after the phenomenon that caused them disappears, such that new images might imprint themselves on top of the old ones. Here, the main difference between Goethe's *Theory of Colors* and Hegel's *Phenomenology of Spirit*—where the posthuman eye of Spirit dives into phenomenal opacity, but in search of itself—is that Goethe posits no all-seeing eye that transforms everything that is seeable (such as these various moving images) into the sayable.

At first glance, Hegel seems to follow Goethe in his construction of color in the *Philosophy of Nature*. For Hegel, light is matter in its "pure elementary state," namely, qua "pure identity not inwardly, but as existing, that is, the relation to itself determined as independent in contrast to the other determinations of totality," and, as such, light only becomes concrete in its encounter with dense matter.[115] Yet, as we have seen, Hegel goes on to fantasize absolute Spirit accessing a dematerialized sphere, transparent and self-identical, just like the pure light, which, for Goethe, never exists in the natural world. The closest that Goethe comes to Hegel's all-seeing eye is his construction of a chromatic circle that looks like a synthesis of all structural relations between different colors.[116] And it is quite probably for this reason Hegel is so enthusiastic about it—it is "so admirably suited to our purpose," Hegel writes, of "leading the Absolute fully out into the light of day."[117] However, Goethe insists that the structure is never complete, that the chromatic circle cannot in the end encompass every transformation. He is adamant: "Nature perhaps exhibits no general phenomenon."[118] Goethe's attention to the specific diversity of colors, opaque bodies, and structural transformations leads theory away from the pure transparent light of the Hegelian absolute; he immerses meaning in many colors and many darknesses, and so ultimately obscures the discursive space of signs. That is, signifying processes are also built on a turbid space, full of shadow and lingering traces that are never exhausted or "led fully into the light of day."

To put it another way, Goethe's critique of idealized discursive space is, as we have seen, always a critique of both a certain kind of vision *and a certain kind of sign*. Hence, Goethe's alternative theory of vision likewise implies an *alternative writing practice*. And it is an alternative that becomes explicit in the note on "On Language and Terminology" that concludes the *Theory of Colors*. As Goethe summarizes this note elsewhere, in the Newtonian tradition, "phenomena were placed in an uneasy position of subordination" to "a general theoretical precept or a quick explanation without taking the trouble to study them in detail."[119] In Nygaard's gloss, Newtonians "were essentially reductive": the words they used "static and fixed and hence inadequate to deal with dynamic, nature processes."[120] Newton and his followers abstracted, whereas Goethe wants to make use of words to return to variety, nuance, and shade. This is not a negation of signification, but an appropriation of it for the delicate, for the diaphanous, and for the precise. Language does not need to get in the way, if it itself participates in natural distortion-effects and itself renders the light of meaning hazy, misty, foggy and cloudy, thereby enhancing its power to beget the "delicate" particular.

5 Schelling and the Philosophical Production of Light

Our second case study centers on models of light in F. W. J. Schelling's philosophical texts and particularly how his serialization of light-images—later appropriated in a poststructuralist context by Gilles Deleuze—exemplifies the naturalization of textual practice at stake in this chapter.

5.1 Shadows and Riddles in the Middle Schelling

There is a tempting, if ultimately inadequate reading of Schelling's trajectory that charts his development from the pure transparency-without-shadows of the identity philosophy (c. 1801–1806) to the obscure, shadowy and riddling depths of his middle period (c. 1809–1815). There is, indeed, a change of emphasis over this period that roughly takes the form of a genetic turn (with parallels to Kristeva)—that is, a turn to charting the genesis of the word out of obscure depths. Nevertheless, this is not a qualitative shift. Already in 1799, Schelling had anticipated this turn in his *First Outline*,[121] and then, in 1802, concerned himself with what "falls outside the thing as light," that is, the "ground of existence—primordial night, the mother of all things."[122] The conclusion to his 1806 *Treatise on the Relationship of the Real and the Ideal in Nature or... the Principles of Gravity and Light*, for instance, calls on the philosopher to attend to "a deeply hidden fire" within inorganic nature that testifies to the "storming forth out of an unfathomable depth."[123] This fire operates as a flash of light through which the initiated observer may hope to glimpse the dark recesses of groundless essence. And this call for the philosopher to bring light to the depths and chart the production of light out of darkness is an imperative central to Schelling's entire philosophical project—a project that renders the genesis of light and transparency a central meta-philosophical commitment. What is relatively new in the middle Schelling, however, is the rearticulation of this productivity (via the *Logosmystik* tradition) as the birth of the Word, that is, as a fundamentally semiotic process. It is for this reason that the middle Schelling has repeatedly been read as a philosopher of language—from Hogrebe's *Urtext, Prädikation und Genesis*, to those who follow in his wake like Bowie or Žižek.[124] For all of them, Schelling's philosophical project from 1809 to 1815 describes the production of words out of opaque, pre-linguistic strata.

The model implied here of the geological depths that bring forth the word tends to motivate Schelling's more explicit discussions of language—be it in his 1803 pronouncement that the geological excavation of minerals "is a real philological problem"[125] or in his converse 1811 claim that "there are... homologous language formations like there are mountain formations" and that one must "cognize the physical in language, and pursue... language in connection or at least in analogy to the geological."[126] Linguistic analysis is modeled on the excavation of rocks. That is, before the gaze of the philosopher of language stands a "physical abyss," a lost realm of immeasurable productivity to be sifted through to unearth the beginnings of linguistic desire. The late Schelling's lecture course on the *Historical-Critical Introduction to the Philosophy of Mythology* pursues this project still further by postulating that the crises and floods of the earth's history are repeated in the formation of language, that is, physical disturbances erupt in poetry. "The crisis through which the world of the gods unfolds," Schelling writes, "is not external to the poets. It takes place in the poets themselves, forms their poems."[127] To put it another way, the late Schelling is interested in obscure and riddling mythological language because it reveals traces of a "pre-historical time... of the cision or crisis of the people."[128] In Schelling's own words, "In the formation of the oldest languages a wealth of philosophy can be discovered."[129] His 1815 *Deities of Samothrace* exemplifies this running-together of language and geological depth—making use of etymological analysis to reveal "a primordial system older than all written documents," according to which "the world is an eternal living fire, which at intervals... flares up and is extinguished."[130] The catastrophic unruliness of nature etymologically contained in the names of the Samothracean gods mirrors the workings of nature itself. As Schelling will write elsewhere, language is a subject "which push[es] us back into the abyss of human nature."[131]

The abyssal nature of language is most palpable in the *Freiheitsschrift*, particularly the transition that Schelling here traces from opaque grounds to transparent Word—from *der Worträtsel* to *das Wort*. This process consists of two beginnings: "the first beginning of creation" is identified with a "longing" for language "or the will of the depths," whereas the second is the moment at which "the Word is pronounced in nature."[132] Significantly—and just like Kristeva—Schelling does not render the depths silent, but rather identifies a quasi-"logos" ("the logic of that longing") to this pre-linguistic depth, which is identified with "das Wort des Räthsels" ("a Logos in Logogriphs").[133] What Guttman translates here as "logogriph" denotes a riddling and playful form of speech that the philosopher is tasked with deciphering—"a dark, prophetic (still incompletely spoken) Word."[134]

The antecedent-consequent relation between opaque riddles and the transparent Word is to be understood as part of an overarching account of the emergence of natural structures. A natural process subtends the opaque-transcendent dichotomy. And it is thus unsurprising that Žižek, for example, will return to the middle Schelling as a resource for rethinking that very psychobiological model of the cission of the pulsional body into the sign with which Kristeva inaugurated poststructuralist linguistics. For Žižek's Schelling, the symbolic is born out of pre-linguistic drives—a process equally present in the early Kristeva's rereading of Hegelian negativity as a bodily movement that generates signs.

5.2 The Ages of the World *as a Book of Light*

Schelling is a philosopher of refraction. That is, when nature does come to light in the articulated word, this light operates according to a model that distinguishes it from Goethean optical distortions, from Hegelian reflection and from Hölderlinian translucence. Crucially, on the model of refraction, Schelling will always think "lights" in the plural: many kinds of light disperse from the prism of his philosophy.

At stake here is the close relation between the problematic of light and the problem of difference (already alluded to in the Introduction above): might not the particular individual be lost in the pure light of the absolute? This is seemingly Hegel's charge against the Schelling of the identity philosophy, although inverted into the language of obscurity, such that monochromatic light becomes indistinguishable from sheer darkness. The unadulterated transparency of the absolute is ultimately no more than "a night in which all cows are black."[135] This is, nevertheless, to miss the point of Schelling's refractive model for light: The pure light of the absolute passes through a differentiating prism and, by means of this moment of dispersion or refraction, generates various shades of light. Even in the middle period, his writings are bathed in a dazzling array of lights; they are among the most colorful of German Idealist texts.

Ultimately, this concerns a series of writing practices derived from Schelling's naturephilosophical account of the phenomenon of light. Whereas reflection accounts for the behavior of light from the standpoint of the ideal (i.e., from the dematerialized perspective of "the second potency"), refraction is a superior model for explaining the workings of light from the absolute perspective of "the third potency."[136] It provides the proper philosophical description of how light "becomes empirical and sensible."[137] Hence, Schelling will affirm the value of refraction as an all-encompassing naturephilosophical model (its "symbolic meaning occupies the highest position") and even as a heuristic for creation.[138] Tilliette and Maesschalck both speak of Schellingian reality constituted by "a refraction of identity" in which "identity unfolds into an efflorescence of forms, a streaming forth and profusion," spreading out "across degrees of being… like a diamond with a thousand faces."[139] Our point is, moreover, that *refraction is a textual model* as well as a metaphysical one. Schelling's writing *refracts into a series of images*. These images are not explanations, deductions, demonstrations, syllogisms or descriptions; indeed, Schelling will in turn critique all of these philosophical methods as failing to hold together the particular word with the universal concept.[140] What his texts do instead is *exhibit light*: they construct a series of icons that bring forth the depths in all different shades of light. This is what the Schelling of the identity philosophy means by an "idea"—the way in which light refracts into an "absolute profusion" of shining particulars, each of which "is for itself absolute."[141]

Such is Schelling's understanding of the functioning of philosophical discourse—one that is, of course, very different from Hegel's (for instance). Whereas Hegel broadly understands discourse as *mediation motored by negativity*, Schellingian discourse consists in *serialization produced by refraction*. The Ages of the World drafts provide an illuminating example, for here the Schellingian text most obviously takes the form of a series of dazzling images and a profusion of ideas that appeal to the eye and call for a special kind of seeing. The three drafts of the text (1811, 1813, 1815) are kaleidoscopic: they catalogue different kinds of light and darkness and their various mixtures. For example, the following list gives some sense of the various lights at stake in these drafts:

(a) "The original light of divinity," "an utterly pure fire" of primal lucidity that should be opposed to "a shadow of shadows";[142]
(b) "Night the fertile mother of things," which in its "darkness and concealment" characterizes "the primordial age" (i.e., the indifference of the first light has now become negative)[143]; it is not just a privation of light, but "a dynamic hiding-away, an active striving backward into the depths, into concealment";[144]

(c) The dialectical opposite of this negating darkness—an "inaccessible light that no one can express,"[145] which constitutes the point at which the divinity "ascends in the inaccessible glare of its purity" (i.e., the original light posited without negation or determination)[146];
(d) The mixing of the dark No and the inaccessibly bright Yes in "the clarity of essence" that comes "out of the night" and, through it, "a milder being of light emerges that differs from the unbearable brilliance of primal lucid purity insofar as it has been modified by the principle opposed to it";[147]
(e) A later eruption of "searing radiance," which indicates the "combustion" and "flash" of emergent freedom within "the clarity of essence."[148]

In sum, *The Ages of the World* tells (and performs) the story of the emergence of "the light of philosophy... from darkness"[149]; however, this is no simple opposition of obscurity and transparency, but a series of multiform lights and darknesses, which mix, collide with, and react to each other to generate yet more shades of light and dark.[150] The story of the ages of the world is a story of many lights.

And these various shades of light and dark in turn demand a particular modality of seeing from the reader (in a way that returns us to Goethe's and Lyotard's commentaries on idealist dematerialization). Indeed, the question of *how best to see the past* is a pressing one in *The Ages of the World*—Schelling is very concerned with the "sharp-sightedness"[151] required to gaze into the abyss: just as early modernity has enhanced scientific vision so that "with the help of the right instrument, what a normal eye perceives as an indefinite glow of floating nebula in the night sky can be seen as a cluster of individual stars,"[152] analogous instruments need to be wrought for philosophical vision. The philosopher must be armed with the prostheses and tools necessary to see better. Hence, while the introduction to *The Ages of the World* drafts insists that "the goal is not attained in pure vision," the task is still one of *seeing the past* through textual imagery: the philosopher must discern "a gleam of eternal light" or "a lightning flash."[153] As Schelling writes more fully, the geologist-philosopher requires "an eye somewhat practised in free consideration" to discern, "in and around" visible objects, "the full sparkle and shine of life... an overflow, as it were, playing and streaming around them."[154] These are "individual sparks of light... glimmering in the darkness of matter" which unearth forms of the past.[155] To give but one linguistic example of this method: the Old Testament should be read, according to Schelling, in a way that does justice to its "singular lightning flashes that strike from the clouds [and] illuminate the darkness of primordial times."[156]

5.3 Schelling, Deleuze, and the Series

Deleuze was one of poststructuralism's most concerted readers of Schelling. And one of his most sustained, if entirely implicit engagements with him can be found among his playful invocations of the "ages of the world" in *Cinema II*. Even if Deleuze never tells the reader so directly, he makes use of Schellingian concepts to construct various "time-images," iconic signs that directly capture eras beyond the present.[157] The task here is geological, just as in *The Ages of the World*: the subject must dig up "the depths of time" and its "innumerable strata" and bring to light a dazzling effusion of shades. Both Schelling and Deleuze are interested in making their texts "open directly onto time" and "affirm a pure power of time which overflows all memory, an already-past which exceeds all recollections."[158] This is what Schelling demands when he invokes a "science of the past" that should "disclose entirely the abysses of the ages."[159]

Hence, in *Cinema II*, Deleuze will write of the need, as philosophical readers, to "place ourselves with a leap into the past in general, into those purely virtual images which have been constantly preserved through time." In an exact parallel to the middle Schelling, the task is "to extract non-chronological time," "a universe of prehistory"—and Schelling finds his cinematic analogue, according to Deleuze, in a director like Alain Resnais, who plunges the viewer "into a memory which overflows the conditions of psychology… memory-world, memory-ages of the world."[160] Deleuze identifies in Resnais' films "the ages of… the world," understood as "images of a past *in general* which move past at dizzying speed."[161] At its climax this Resnaisian-Deleuzean procession of images of the past become "a burst of series" described in particularly Schellingian language: "The before and after are no longer successive determinations of the course of time, but the two sides of the power, or the passage of the power to a higher power. The direct time-image does not here appear in an order of coexistences or simultaneities, but in a becoming as potentialisation, as series of powers."[162] There is an intimation here by Deleuze concerning the cinematic nature of the middle Schelling's textual practice—his texts take the form of a screen upon which images constantly appear and make manifest strata of the past.

This emphasis on serialization is key to *The Ages of the World*. The drafts both describe and perform series of flashes, gleams, and sparks: this is no "mere" indifferentiated transparency, but a panoply of multiple lights. However, this is not to say that *The Ages of the World* exists without any teleological tendency towards an absolute kind of light; it is merely to insist that there is for the middle Schelling no one transparent image that might mark the eschatological completion of time. Rather, the fullness of time is itself transposed into a series—a series of different shades of lights that, together, cumulatively express absolute light. That is, on the one hand, Žižek, for example, might describe *The Ages of the World* in terms of a narrative of failure (the failure of the word to articulate its inexpressible beginnings), such that as soon as reality is expressed, it is always ineluctably alienated.[163] But, on the other hand, Schelling himself insists that "nature" (reality as articulated) is "brought into unity with eternal being" by means of his philosophy[164]: No single image might itself achieve this "unity" (i.e., might approximate to "that absolute I of divinity as it was before the activation"[165]); nevertheless, the "unity" does still occur *"as a succession of times"*[166]— *as a series*. Schelling labels his method of serialization "narrative." Such is the masterconcept for his textual practice of coordinating the stream of images that run through his texts (to render them as potent as possible). *The Ages of the World* drafts form a narrative series in which one shade of light follows another.

6 Conclusion: Light-Writing

The above analyses and case studies are evidently incomplete; the "photological text" in German Idealism and poststructuralism—along with its metaphorics of obscure and transparent meanings—is too diverse and diffuse to be surveyed in one chapter. However, what we have hopefully managed to identify are two dialectics. The first—arising from poststructuralist critique—pits the fantasy of transparency against the materiality of the signifier, so as to side with matter (in some form) against light. In so doing, this critique necessarily ties together the desire for transparency with the tendency toward dematerialization in some German Idealist writing. However, we have also attempted to trace a second dialectic that corresponds to a possible naturephilosophical response to this poststructuralist critique. Here, the abstract and denaturalized materialities of "semantic materialism" are to be interrogated from the perspective of specific natural models, including various naturephilosophical accounts of light. The result pulls the idea of transparency apart from the tendency to dematerialization; they are not necessarily coupled. Far from it: there are models of light and of color that are grounded in material bodies and forces. This naturephilosophical response therefore sides with a (naturalized) light against abstract matter, and we have developed such a response in the two case studies above. Goethe and Schelling both radicalize and pluralize the photological tradition to the point of fracture. In their writing, there is—despite appearances—no fantasy of a monolithic transparency, but rather a diversity of lights, of colors, of shadows. Goethe's and Schelling's texts testify to photological writing—light-writing—at its kaleidoscopic best.

Notes

1. Barry Smith et al., "Letter to the Editor," *The Times* (London), Saturday 9 May 1992.
2. Ibid.
3. Jacques Derrida, *Negotiations: Interventions and Interviews, 1971–2001*, trans. Elizabeth G. Rottenberg (Stanford: Stanford University Press, 2002), 148.
4. Reported by John Searle in Steven Postrel and Edward Feser, "Reality Principles: An Interview with John R. Searle," *Reason Magazine* (February 2000), https://reason.com/2000/02/01/reality-principles-an-intervie/ (last accessed: 28/03/22).
5. Manfred Frank, *What is Neostructuralism?* (Minneapolis: University of Minnesota Press, 1989), 332–45.
6. Arthur Schopenhauer, *The World as Will and Representation*, vol. 2, trans. R. B. Haldane and J. Kemp (London: Trubner, 1883), 22.
7. Jean-Luc Nancy, *The Speculative Remark (One of Hegel's Bon Mots)*, trans. Céline Surprenant (Stanford: Stanford University Press, 2002), 46.
8. Ibid., 94, 115, 121.
9. Immanuel Kant, *Critique of Pure Reason*, trans. Norman Kemp Smith (London: Palgrave, 1922), B295.
10. Michèle Le Doeuff, *The Philosophical Imaginary*, trans. Colin Gordon (London: Continuum, 1989), 6.

11. Of course, poststructuralist readers are not the only ones to read German Idealists in this way—see, for example, Theodor Adorno, *Three Studies*, trans. S. W. Nicholsen (Boston: MIT Press, 1993), 100.
12. F. W. J. Schelling, *Clara or, On Nature's Connection to the Spirit World*, trans. Fiona Steinkamp (Albany: SUNY Press, 2002), 63.
13. F. W. J. Schelling, *Werke*, ed. K. F. A. Schelling (Stuttgart: Cotta, 1856–61), 4.403–4.
14. G. W. F. Hegel, *Phenomenology of Spirit*, trans. A. V. Miller (Oxford: Oxford University Press, 1977), 9.
15. F. W. J. Schelling, *Bruno, or On the Natural and Divine Principle of Things*, ed. and trans. Michael G. Vater (Albany: SUNY Press, 1984), 139.
16. Jacques Derrida, *Writing and Difference*, trans. Alan Bass (London: Routledge, 2001), 31.
17. For cybernetic readings of German Idealism more generally, see, e.g., Oriane Petteni, "Entre conservation, destruction et extinction. Une relecture écocritique de la *Naturphilosophie* en temps de crise," *L'art du comprendre* vol. 26 (2022).
18. Iain Hamilton Grant, "Schellingianism and Postmodernity: Towards a Materialist *Naturphilosophie*" (1998). Available at: www.bu.edu/wcp/papers/cult/cultgran.htm; last accessed: 01/04/2010. Compare with Grant's criticisms of Deleuze and Badiou at the opening to *Philosophies of Nature after Schelling* a few years later ([London: Continuum, 2014], x-xii).
19. See further Christopher Johnson, *System and Writing in the Philosophy of Jacques Derrida* (Cambridge: Cambridge University Press, 1993); Ingo Berensmeyer, "Reframing Deconstruction in Systems Theory: Niklas Luhmann, Jacques Derrida and the Culture of Writing," *Studies in English Literary and Cultural History*, vol. 61 (2014): 75–93.
20. G. W. F Hegel, *Introduction to the Philosophy of History*, trans. Leo Rauch (Indianapolis: Hackett, 1998), 20.
21. See Oriane Petteni, "Breaking Free from Material Terrestrial Contingency: The Path of the Hegelian Spirit towards Absolute Freedom," *Cosmos and History*, vol. 17, no. 2 (2021): 224–49.
22. In Georges Canguilhem's phrase—see, e.g., his *Knowledge of Life*, ed. Paola Marrati and Todd Meyers (New York: Fordham University Press, 2008), 114.
23. G. W. F. Hegel, *Philosophy of Mind*, ed. Michael Inwood and trans. W. Wallace and A. V. Miller (Oxford: Oxford University Press, 2007), 194.
24. Richard Macksey and Eugenio Donato, "Introduction," to *The Structuralist Controversy: The Languages of Criticism and the Science of Man*, ed. R. Macksey and E. Donato (Baltimore: Johns Hopkins University Press, 2007), xvi.
25. Jacques Derrida, *Margins of Philosophy*, trans. Alan Bass (Chicago: University of Chicago Press, 1982), 91.
26. Jean-François Lyotard, *Discourse, Figure*, trans. Antony Hudek and Mary Lydon (Minneapolis: University of Minnesota Press, 2020), 39.
27. For example, Derrida, *Margins*, 101–5.
28. Lyotard, *Discourse, Figure*, 206.
29. Hegel, *Philosophy of Mind*, 194.
30. N. Katherine Hayles, *How We Became Posthuman: Virtual Bodies in Cybernetics, Literature and Informatics* (Chicago: University of Chicago Press, 1999), 2, 4.
31. Derrida, *Margins*, 118.
32. Hayles, *How We Became Posthuman*, 26.
33. See Philip E. Lewis, "Revolutionary Semiotics," *Diacritics* vol. 4, no. 3 (1974): 28–32.
34. Philippe Sollers, *L'Ecriture et l'expérience des limites* (Paris: Seuil, 1968), 6. Implicit here and in the rest of this section is a question whether such "semantic materialism" is intended as an extension, confirmation, supplement or replacement of dialectical materialism.
35. Anthony Easthorpe, *British Post-Structuralism since 1968* (London: Routledge, 1988). See also David Silverman, *The Material Word* (London: Routledge, 1980).

36. Rosalind Coward and John Ellis, *Language and Materialism: Developments in Semiology and the Theory of the Subject* (London: Routledge, 1977), 153.
37. Ibid., 2.
38. Ibid., 123.
39. Ibid., 2.
40. Ibid., 2–3.
41. Ibid., 4.
42. Ibid.
43. Ibid., 86, 146.
44. Ibid., 152.
45. For example, ibid., 31.
46. Alain Badiou, *The Logics of Worlds*, trans. Alberto Toscano (London: Continuum, 2010), 2–4.
47. See Jacques Derrida, *Memoires for Paul de Man*, trans. Cecile Lindsay et al. (New York: Columbia University Press, 1989), 67.
48. Paul de Man, *The Resistance to Theory*, ed. Wlad Godzich (Minneapolis: University of Minnesota Press, 1986), 7. For further discussion of the antipathy between de Man and philosophy of nature, see Daniel Whistler, "Naturalism and Symbolism," *Angelaki* vol. 21, no. 4 (2016): 91–109.
49. Paul de Man, *The Rhetoric of Romanticism* (New York: Columbia University Press, 1984), 6.
50. Friedrich Hölderlin, *Sämtliche Werke: Großer Stuttgarter Ausgabe*, ed. Friedrich Beissner (Stuttgart: Kohlhammer, 1985), 2.90–5, ll. 89–90.
51. De Man, *Rhetoric of Romanticism*, 196.
52. Julia Kristeva, *Revolution in Poetic Language*, trans. Margaret Waller (New York: Columbia University Press), 145. The following naturephilosophical reading of Kristeva is anticipated most obviously by Alison Stone, who has repeatedly pointed to the partial affinities between philosophy of nature and French feminism. In her words, "There is one key idea that I take from Schelling and Hegel and that runs through my work in feminist philosophy, and this is the idea that both nature and mind consist of a multiplicity of levels of development… This connects up with feminism, and especially feminism of sexual difference: our thoughts are always going to arise from and bear the traces of our bodies; take, for instance, Julia Kristeva's distinction between the semiotic and the symbolic." Luca Corti et al., "Hegelian Interviews: Alison Stone," *HPD* (December 2019), http://www.hegelpd.it/hegel/hpd-hegelian-interviews-alison-stone/ (last accessed: 30/03/22); see further, more generally, Alison Stone, "The Incomplete Materialism of French Materialist Feminism," *Radical Philosophy* no. 145 (2007): 20–7.
53. Jean-Louis Baudry et al. [including Julia Kristeva], "La Révolution ici maintenant. Paris, mai 1968," *Tel Quel* vol. 34 (1968), 3–4.
54. Julia Kristeva, *Polylogue* (Paris: Seuil, 1977), 31.
55. Julia Kristeva, "The Subject in Process," in *The Tel Quel Reader*, ed. and trans. Patrick Ffrench and Roland-François Lack (London: Routledge, 1998), 172.
56. Kristeva, *Revolution*, 15.
57. Julia Kristeva, "L'Expansion de la sémiotique," in *Essais de sémiotique*, ed. Julia Kristeva et al. (Paris: Moulan, 1971), 34.
58. Lewis, "Revolutionary Semiotics," 30. Kristeva is not the only figure at this time to undertake a genetic turn in her treatment of language—Hélène Cixous is another obvious candidate (see Oriane Petteni, "L'Amour de l'orange aussi est politique. Genèse, vision et assimilation dans les œuvres d'Hélène Cixous et de Clarice Lispector," in *Écriture des origines, origines de l'écriture. Hélène Cixous*, ed. K. Gyssels and C. Stevens [Leiden: Brill, 2019], 141–58). But we focus on Kristeva's work because she undertakes this turn in sustained dialogue with Hegel.
59. Kristeva, *Revolution*, 40.
60. Kristeva, "Subject in Process," 167, 172.
61. Ibid., 145.

62. Ibid.
63. Lewis, "Revolutionary Semiotics," 29.
64. Kristeva, "Subject in Process," 139.
65. Kristeva, *Revolution*, 51.
66. Ibid., 180.
67. Kristeva, *Polylogue*, 414.
68. Kelly Oliver, *Reading Kristeva: Unravelling the Double Bind* (Bloomington: Indiana University Press, 1993), 34.
69. Grant, *Philosophies of Nature*, x.
70. Grant, "Schellingianism and Postmodernity."
71. Iain Hamilton Grant, "'Philosophy Become Genetic': The Physics of the World Soul," in *The New Schelling*, ed. Judith Norman and Alistair Welchman (London: Continuum, 2004), 133; *Philosophies of Nature*, 11.
72. Grant, *Philosophies of Nature*, 173.
73. Ibid., 15.
74. For this strategy, see Whistler, "Naturalism and Symbolism," as well as Daniel Whistler, "Language After Philosophy of Nature: Schelling's Geology of Divine Names,' in *After the Postmodern and the Postsecular*, ed. Anthony Paul Smith and Daniel Whistler (Newcastle: Cambridge Scholars Press, 2010): 335–59; Daniel Whistler, "Improper Names for God: Religious Language and the 'Spinoza Effect'," *Speculations* vol. 3 (2012): 99–134; Joshua Ramey and Daniel Whistler, "The Physics of Sense: Bruno, Schelling, Deleuze," in *Gilles Deleuze and Metaphysics*, ed. Edward Kazarian et al. (Lexington: Lexington Books, 2014), 87–109; Daniel Whistler, "Living and Dead Forms: The Factuality of Meaning in Schelling and Other Naturalists," in *Living Ideas: Dynamic Philosophies of Life and Matter, 1650–1850*, ed. Peter Cheyne (forthcoming).
75. An important model for our work in this regard is Gabriel Trop's "The Aesthetics of Schelling's *Naturphilosophie*," *Symposium* vol. 19, no. 1 (2015): 140–153.
76. See further Daniel Whistler, "The Production of Transparency: Hölderlinian Practices," *Studies in Romanticism* vol. 23, no. 2 (2016): 155–74.
77. Anselm Haverkamp, *Leaves of Mourning: Hölderlin's Late Work*, trans. Vernon Chadwick (Albany: SUNY Press, 1996), 6.
78. Friedrich Hölderlin, *Sämtliche Werke: Frankfurter Ausgabe*, ed. D. E. Sattler (Frankfurt am Main: Stroemfeld Verlag, 1999), 9.175.
79. David Constantine, *Hölderlin* (Oxford: Clarendon Press, 1998), 310.
80. Dominique Janicaud, *Le Tournant théologique de la phénoménologie française* (Paris: Eclat, 2001), 243.
81. Martin Heidegger, *Being and Time*, trans. J. Macquarrie and E. S. Robinson (Oxford: Blackwell, 1962), 51.
82. Henri Bortoft, *The Wholeness of Nature: Goethe's Way of Science* (Edinburgh: Floris, 1996), 79.
83. J. W. Goethe, *Werke: Weimarer Ausgabe*, ed. S. von Sachsen et al. (Weimar: Böhlau, 1887–1919), I/27.382. See, e.g., Werner Keller, "Variationen zum Thema: 'Wär' nicht das Auge sonnenhaft…'," in Peter-André Alt et al. (eds), *Prägnanter Moment* (Würzburg: Königshausen und Neumann, 2002), 439–57.
84. J. W. Goethe, *Theory of Colors*, trans. C. L. Eastlake (Cambridge, MA: MIT Press, 1982), xxxix; translation modified in accordance with J. W. Goethe, *Scientific Studies*, ed. and trans. Douglas Miller (New York: Suhrkamp, 1988), 164.
85. Ibid.
86. Ibid.
87. Ibid., §752.
88. Maurice Marache, *Le Symbole dans la pensée et l'oeuvre de Goethe* (Paris: Nizat, 1960), 218.
89. J. W. Goethe, *Faust: Part One*, trans. David Luke (Oxford: Oxford University Press, 1987), ll. 3451–7.

90. Goethe, *Scientific Studies*, 26–7.
91. Goethe, *Maxims and Reflection*, ed. Peter Hutchinson, trans. Elisabeth Stopp (London: Penguin, 1998), §675.
92. Goethe, *Theory of Colors*, §242.
93. R. L. Stephenson, *Goethe's Conception of Knowledge and Science* (Edinburgh: Edinburgh University Press, 1995), 63; Andrew O. Jaszi, "Symbolism and the Linguistic Paradox: Reflections on Goethe's World View," in Helmut Rehder (ed.), *Literary Symbolism: A Symposium* (Austin: University of Texas Press, 1965), 82.
94. Marache, *Le Symbole*, 218.
95. Marianne Henn, "'*Individuum est ineffabile*': Goethe and the Tradition of Silence," in M. Henn and C. Lorey (eds), *Analogon Rationis* (Edmonton: University of Alberta Press, 1994), 252.
96. J. W. Goethe, *Wilhelm Meister's Journeyman Years, or the Renunciants*, ed. Jane K. Brown and trans. Krishna Winston (New York: Suhrkamp, 1989), 420.
97. See, e.g., Claude Lévi-Strauss and Didier Eribon, *De Près et de Loin* (Paris, Odile Jacob, 1988), 158–9; Jean Petitot, "La généalogie morphologique du structuralisme," *Critique*, no. 620–1 (1999), 97–122; Thomas Vercruysse, *De Goethe à Piaget: le versant biologique du structuralisme* (Madrid: Estudos Semanticos, 2017).
98. Petitot, "La généalogie morphologique," 97–8. See Oriane Petteni, "The Contemporary Legacy of Goethean Morphology: From *Anschauende Urteilskraft* to Algorithmic Pattern Recognition, Generation and Exploration," *Goethe Yearbook* no. 29 (2022).
99. Goethe, *Scientific Studies*, 149.
100. Goethe, *Theory of Colors*, §158.
101. J. W. Goethe, *Schriften zur Naturwissenschaft*, ed. D. Kuhn et al. (Weimar: Böhlaus, 1970), 11.266.
102. Goethe, *Theory of Colors*, xxxix; translation modified in accordance with Goethe, *Scientific Studies*, 164.
103. On the role of linear perspective, see Hubert Damisch, *L'origine de la perspective* (Paris: Flammarion, 1987).
104. Lyotard, *Discourse, Figure*, 87.
105. Ibid., 83–4.
106. On this topic, see—as well as Lyotard—Jonathan Crary, *Suspension of Perception: Attention, Spectacle and Modern Culture* (Cambridge, MA: MIT Press, 2000).
107. Goethe, *Theory of Colors*, §868 (see also §178).
108. Ibid., §§33, 38.
109. Goethe, *Werke*, II/4.295–6.
110. J. W. Goethe, *Briefe*, ed. K. R. Mandelkow (Hamburg: Wegner, 1968), 2.528.
111. Goethe, *Theory of Colors*, §123ss.
112. Ibid., §140.
113. Ibid., §§1, 3.
114. Ibid., §54.
115. G. W. F. Hegel, *Philosophy of Nature*, ed. and trans. Michael J. Petry (London: Routledge, 1970), §220.
116. See, e.g., Goethe, *Theory of Colors*, §810.
117. G. W. F. Hegel, *The Letters*, ed. and trans. Clark Buttler and Christian Seiler (Bloomington, IN: Indiana University Press, 1984), 701.
118. Goethe, *Theory of Colors*, §815.
119. Ibid., xxxviii; translation modified in accordance with Goethe, *Scientific Studies*, 163–4.
120. Loisa Nygaard, "'*Bild*' and '*Sinnbild*': The Problem of the Symbol in Goethe's *Wahlverwandtschaften*," *Germanic Review* vol. 63, no. 2 (1988), 63–4.
121. See F. W. J. Schelling, *First Outline of a System of the Philosophy of Nature*, trans. Keith R. Peterson (Albany: SUNY Press, 2004), 13–14.
122. Schelling, *Bruno*, 176.

123. Schelling, *Werke*, 2.378.
124. Wolfram Hogrebe, *Prädikation und Genesis: Metaphysik als Fundamentalheuristik im Ausgang von Schellings "Die Weltalter"* (Frankfurt am Main: Suhrkamp, 1989). See also Andrew Bowie, *Schelling and Modern European Philosophy: An Introduction* (London: Routledge, 1993), 91–126; Slavoj Žižek, *The Indivisible Remainder: On Schelling and Related Matters* (London: Verso, 2006).
125. F. W. J. Schelling, *On University Studies*, ed. Norbert Guterman, trans. E.S. Morgan (Athens: Ohio University Press, 1966), 40.
126. Schelling, *Werke*, 8.453.
127. F. W. J. Schelling, *Historical-Critical Introduction to the Philosophy of Mythology*, trans. Mason Richey and Marcus Zisselsberger (Albany: SUNY Press, 2008), 18.
128. Ibid., 162.
129. Ibid., 39.
130. F. W. J. Schelling, *The Deities of Samothrace*, ed. and trans. Robert F. Brown (Missoula: Scholars Press, 1977), 34, 37.
131. Schelling, *Werke*, 8.454.
132. F. W. J. Schelling, *Philosophical Inquiries into the Nature of Human Freedom*, trans. James Gutmann (La Salle: Open Court, 1936), 74.
133. Ibid., 36.
134. Ibid., 92.
135. G. W. F. Hegel, *Phenomenology of Spirit*, trans. A. V. Miller (Oxford: Oxford University Press, 1977), 9.
136. Schelling, *Werke*, 6.362–3.
137. Ibid., 6.429.
138. Ibid., 7.172, 6.441.
139. Xavier Tilliette *Schelling: Biographie* (Paris: Calmann-Lévy, 1999), 147; Marc Maesschalck, *Philosophie et révélation dans l'itinéraire de Schelling* (Louvain: Peeters, 1989), 83.
140. See, e.g., Schelling, *Werke*, 4.336–58.
141. Ibid., 4.405.
142. F. W. J. Schelling, *The Ages of the World (1811 version)*, trans. Joseph P. Lawrence (Albany: SUNY Press, 2019), 111, 198.
143. Ibid., 83.
144. F. W. J. Schelling and Slavoj Žižek, *Abyss of Freedom/Ages of the World (1813 version)* (Ann Arbor: University of Michigan Press, 1997), 143.
145. Schelling, *Ages (1811)*, 201.
146. Schelling, *Ages (1813)*, 170.
147. Schelling, *Ages (1811)*, 91.
148. Ibid., 100–1.
149. Ibid., 174.
150. On this mixture, see further F. W. J. Schelling, *The Ages of the World (1815 version)*, trans. Jason M. Wirth (Albany: SUNY Press, 2000), 18.
151. Schelling, *Ages (1811)*, 203.
152. Ibid., 192.
153. Schelling, *Ages (1815)*, 71, 77.
154. Schelling, *Ages (1813)*, 151.
155. Ibid.
156. Schelling, *Ages (1815)*, 51.
157. Gilles Deleuze, *Cinema II: The Time-Image*, trans. Hugh Tomlinson and Roberto Galeta (London: Bloomsbury, 2013), 18. The language of a "book of light" we have been using in this section is itself, in part, an adaptation and application of Deleuze's claim that Spinoza's *Ethics*, Part V, is "an aerial book of light." ("Spinoza and the Three 'Ethics'," in W. Montag and T. Stolze (eds), *The New Spinoza* [Minneapolis: University of Minnesota Press, 1997], 30)
158. Ibid., 50.

159. Schelling, *Ages (1811)*, 70.
160. Deleuze, *Cinema II*, 121, 124.
161. Ibid., 129, 57.
162. Ibid., 282.
163. Schelling does certainly write in this way—e.g., "In the very moment when the Highest is supposed to express itself, it becomes the inexpressible." (*Ages [1813]*, 170). According to Žižek, Schelling here articulates "a primordial, radical, and irreducible alienation… a constitutive 'out-of-jointedness'." (*Abyss of Freedom*, 41)
164. Schelling, *Ages (1813)*, 177.
165. Ibid., 170.
166. Ibid., 178.

Difference

Arkady Plotnitsky

1 Introduction: Thinking Difference

This chapter considers the question of difference and its implications in the context of the relationships between German Idealism and contemporary philosophy—a context important and even indispensable for our understanding of this question and its implications. Indeed, one might argue that what is at stake in this conjunction and what still defines our own thinking concerning difference and our philosophical thinking in general is enormous, as Jacques Derrida said referring specifically to G. W. F. Hegel and Derrida's own rethinking of the question of difference: "What is at stake here is enormous [*L'enjeu est ici énorme*]."[1] The signifier *jeu* [play] in French is worth registering: the concept of play is important for Derrida and is, like it is in Hegel ("the play [*Spiel*] of forces"), a concept of difference.[2] Derrida here expressly juxtaposes his most famous concept or, as he saw it, neither a term nor a concept, that of *différance*, to Hegel's concept of *Aufhebung* (an operation combining a negation, conservation, and sublation of a given concept in a new concept). Specifically, Derrida sees *différance* as "the limit, the interruption, the destruction of the Hegelian [*Aufhebung*] *wherever* it operates."[3] Derrida qualifies: "I emphasize the Hegelian *Aufhebung*, such as it is interpreted by a certain Hegelian discourse, for it goes without saying that the double [technically, triple] meaning of *Aufhebung* could be written otherwise."[4] It follows that at stake in the question of *différance* is also a reading of Hegel, and hence Immanuel Kant and German Idealism, where, at least in its dominant reception-history, the confrontation between Kant and Hegel occupies center stage.

A. Plotnitsky (✉)
Purdue University, West Lafayette, IN, USA
e-mail: plotnits@purdue.edu

2 The Real Beyond Thinking, the Concept of Concept, and Two Concepts of Difference

The designation "difference" in a philosophical discourse usually implies a concept, ideally a *philosophical* concept, which I will define below following Gilles Deleuze and Félix Guattari. Even, however, when one considers one or another form of difference in its everyday sense, as a difference between something, A, and something else, B, doing so implies a concept of some sort, insofar as this difference is defined by a relation between A and B, a relation represented by this concept—for example, "A is larger than B." Such a relation may also involve, usually in philosophy or mathematics and science, something, known or unknown, or possibly unknowable or even inconceivable, that precedes this relation, or A and B themselves, and makes them and the difference between them possible as its effects. The ultimate concept of "difference" that I shall introduce in this chapter is this "real-beyond-thinking" (hereafter "RBT"), which, while responsible for such effects, is beyond the possibility of being represented in terms of these effects, or is beyond any possible representation or even conception. It follows that the terms, or at least concepts, of "beyond," "difference," or "real" cannot ultimately apply to this real either, although they can apply to the effects of this real. I qualify because "real" or "RBT" can function as a term that, akin to a mathematical symbol, has no concept associated with it, and so is, as it were, a concept without concept (which is, as I shall explain, different from Derrida's "neither terms nor concepts," because it is still a term, a name). An RBT is literally un-thinkable, ultimately unthinkable even as unthinkable, because the unthinkable is still an instance of human thinking. An RBT is, therefore, also a real-beyond-Being, insofar as Being is something that is still, in principle, thinkable, as it is, for example, for Martin Heidegger, the subtlety of his argument concerning thinking Being (vs. other forms of thinking) notwithstanding. Heidegger's Being is still a real-within (the reach of)-thinking (hereafter designated as RWT vs. RBT), just like any real that is an effect of an RBT. I use "real" in this phrase "real-beyond-thinking" to emphasize that this real is assumed to exist, as something material or mental, even though no concept designated "real" ultimately applies to it, thus, giving this "concept without concept" an affinity with Jacques Lacan's concept of the Real. Indeed, I would argue that it is possible to read Lacan's Real, just as it is Derrida's *différance* and a few other concepts mentioned below, as an RBT-*type* concept, which need not mean that they are strictly the same as the concept of RBT adopted here.

The concept of RBT is grounded in more general concepts of reality and existence, assumed here to be primitive concepts and not given analytical definitions. By "reality" I refer to that which is assumed to exist, without making any claims concerning the *character* of this existence, for these are claims that define various concepts of reality-within-thinking, RWT, often associated with terms like realism or ontology. By contrast, the absence of such claims allows one to place this character beyond representation or even conception, making the corresponding reality an "RBT." I understand existence as a capacity to have effects on the world. By "the world" I understand, following Ludwig Wittgenstein, "everything that is the case."[5] Thus, matter is commonly (including in this chapter) assumed to exist independently, which also means that it is assumed to have existed before we existed and that it will continue to exist when we no longer exist. On the other hand, any mental reality, assumed to be an effect of (living) matter, is only assumed here to exist while we exist, and to exist only as an effect of an individual human body, specifically an individual brain. There are exceptions to the view of the independent existence of matter (such as those of Plato, George Berkeley, or William Blake) that deny the existence of matter or nature, or anything apart from thought, altogether. Such views are useful in suggesting that any conception of how anything exists, or even that it exists, including when it is assumed to be independent of human thought (as ideal reality is assumed to be in some forms of Platonism, even if not arguably by Plato himself), is a creation of thought. This is the view adopted here. It need not follow, however, that what such concepts relate to, representationally or by placing it beyond representation or even conception, does not exist, bearing in mind that this existence is still an assumption or inference that belongs to thought.

As understood here, RBT, like Lacan's Real or Derrida's *différance*, refers to the ultimate character of the overall reality considered by a given (RBT-type) theory. Other strata of this reality, in particular those defined by the effects of this RBT, are conceivable and hence are of RWT-type. These strata are knowable or representable, necessarily so for this RBT to be a rigorous theoretical inference from these effects, rather than being merely postulated uncritically or metaphysically. The ultimate character of the reality could also be conceivable, thinkable, or representable, and thus of an RWT-type, even if different in character from its effects, the reality of which is of an RWT-type as well. This is the case, for example, in Kant (the difference between things-in-themselves, which are only thinkable, and phenomena, which are representable), in Hegel (the difference between the history of *Geist* and human history), in Heidegger (the difference between Being, which is only thinkable, and beings, which are representable), and in most philosophical thinking from the pre-Socratics and Plato onwards.

I shall now consider the concept of concept, particularly of the philosophical concept. The centrality of concepts in philosophy was emphasized by the post-Kantians, such as Friedrich Schlegel and especially Hegel, and, in mathematics, by Bernhard Riemann, whom I bring up because he was a major influence in this regard on Gilles Deleuze and Félix Guattari's concept of concept in *What is Philosophy?*, which I shall adopt here (Deleuze and Guattari 1994).[6] It builds on Deleuze's earlier concept of the idea in *Difference and Repetition*.[7]

This concept of concept (technically, of the philosophical concept) is grounded, along with philosophy itself, in the concept "thought" [*la pensée*], essentially that of creative thought, as against more common uses of the term thought (mostly synonymous with thinking) as referring, for example, to mental states and processes. (The term "thought" will be used in Deleuze and Guattari's sense henceforth; otherwise, thinking will be used.) They understand thought as a confrontation between thinking, or the brain, and chaos. On the surface, this view is hardly surprising: Much of our thinking, even our daily thinking, is this type of confrontation, because our existence requires bringing one or another form of order to our interactions with the world. Deleuze and Guattari, however, define thought as a special form of the confrontation between thinking, or the brain, and chaos and, hence, the real (in their terms, virtual), a form manifested especially in philosophy, art, and mathematics and science.

They define chaos itself as follows: "Chaos is defined not so much by its disorder but by the infinite speed with which every form taking shape in it vanishes. It is a void that is not a nothingness but a *virtual*, containing all possible *particles* and drawing out all possible forms, which spring up only to disappear immediately, without consistency or reference, without consequence."[8] This concept of chaos is unusual. It appears to be derived from quantum field theory, which contains the concept of virtual particle formation—the birth and disappearance of particles from the so-called false vacuum, a kind of sea of particles transforming into each other. Thus defined, the virtual is a form of the real that always ultimately escapes thought and thus never becomes actual: it is real without being actual. While this relation itself is parallel to that between the RBT-type real and its effects, Deleuze and Guattari's sense of the real is not the same, and it may be argued to be of the RWT-type. Their concept of chaos could, however, be supplemented, as it is in quantum field theory[9] and as it will be here, by both that of chaos as disorder, defined by chance (as Deleuze and Guattari's "not so much" above suggests) and, perhaps against their own grain, by that of chaos as the unthinkable, chaos as an RBT. Deleuze and Guattari's (virtual) real, still being a form of RWT would therefore be underpinned by the real as RBT, while retaining their understanding of thought.

Although thought extracts more stable forms of order from speedily disappearing forms of order inhabiting chaos, it cannot avoid new invasions of chaos into orders we create, thus forcing us to pose new problems amidst solutions to old problems and bringing in new possibilities for creative thought. A concept in Deleuze and Guattari's sense is always a problem, a posing of a problem. They appear to take advantage of the fact, observed in many theoretical domains, that our solutions to what may be seen as "technical" problems, especially difficult ones, tend to create new, equally or more difficult problems, some of which are in turn concept-problems, thereby ensuring the original concepts-problems persist in both these technical solutions and new concepts-problems. This fact makes concepts, in Deleuze and Guattati's sense, "always new" or at least never old, insofar they persist within this process, which need not be seen in terms of Hegel's *Aufhebung*.[10]

Thus, while unremittingly at war with chaos, creative thought also works together with chaos, instead of protecting us against chaos, as certain other forms of thinking, such as opinion, do. Deleuze and Guattari see opinion as an enemy of thought:

> [The] struggle against chaos does not take place without an affinity with the enemy, because another struggle develops and takes on more importance—the struggle against opinion, which claims to protect us from chaos. ... [T]he struggle with chaos is only the instrument in a more profound struggle against opinion, for the misfortune of people comes from opinion. ... But art, science, and philosophy require more: they cast planes [of thought] over chaos. These three disciplines are not like religions that invoke dynasties of gods, or the epiphany of a single god, in order to paint the firmament on the umbrella, like the figures of

an Urdoxa from which opinion stem. Philosophy, science, and art want us to tear open the firmament and plunge into chaos.[11]

Philosophy, science, and art are different, if sometimes interrelated, primary modes of this creative confrontation, that is, by creating new concepts in philosophy, new propositional structures in mathematics and science, and new compositions in art. More accurately, philosophy, science, and art, manifest the capacities, inherent in human thinking, for creating concepts, propositional structures, and compositional arrangements. Thus, chaos is not only an enemy but also a friend of thought and its best ally in a yet greater struggle—the struggle against opinion, which is solely an enemy.[12] The dogmatism of opinion is, in the first place, a dogmatism to which Hegel (Deleuze and Guattari's precursor and one of their sources here) also opposes creative thought. "*Dogmatism*," he says in the Preface to *The Phenomenology of Spirit*, "of the way of thinking, in both knowing or in the study of philosophy, is nothing but the opinion that truth consists in a proposition which is a fixed result or else in a proposition which is immediately known [*der unmittelbar gewußt*]."[13]

According to Deleuze and Guattari, a concept is not merely a generalization from particulars (as in the common definition of concepts) or a general or abstract idea, although a concept may contain such generalizations or ideas; it is, instead, a multicomponent entity defined by the *organization* of its components (some of which components may in turn be concepts). What is crucial is how these components relate to each other in the structure of the concept. A concept in Deleuze and Guattari's sense allows one to include, as its part, that which is beyond conceptualization or thinking, including thought—making this concept an RWT-type concept. Such a concept is defined by the combination of representational elements or (sub)concepts, on the one hand, and, on the other hand, the ultimate RBT-type real responsible for representational entities, as effects. Simple, single-component concepts are rare; as Deleuze and Guattari say: "There are no simple concepts. Every concept has components and is defined by them. It therefore has a combination [*shiffre*]. It is a multiplicity... There is no concept with only one component... The [philosophical] concept of a bird is not found in its genus or species but in the composition of its postures, colors, and songs: something indiscernible that is not so much synesthetic as syneidetic. A concept is a heterogenesis."[14] Each concept is a multi-component conglomeration of concepts (in their conventional senses), figures, and so forth, which, however, have a heterogeneous, if interactive, architecture rather than form a unity.

In practice, there is always a cut-off in delineating a concept, which results from assuming some of the components of this concept to be primitive entities whose structure is not specified. These primitive concepts could, however, be specified by an alternative delineation, which would lead to a new overall concept, containing a new set of primitive (unspecified) components. The history of a given concept—and every concept, however innovative, has a history—is a history of such successive specifications and changes in previous specifications. Concepts are never created out of nothing, as, proverbially, Athena was from the head of Zeus, fully grown and armed. They are constructed from elements borrowed from earlier concepts, sometimes used in very different lines of development or even different fields. Subsequently, new concepts become used, either in their original form or by being modified, and thus acquire their history.

Across the spectrum of concepts of difference, two types of such concepts are especially important in terms of their history. The first, sometimes advanced under the rubrics of "alterity," "exteriority," or "otherness," is a form of difference central to RBT-type thinking—RBT functioning as the limit of this concept. It is based on the discontinuous relations separating two entities, that is, one or another form of the real (it need not be RBT) from a representation or conception of it. I shall call this difference "Difference A" (A for alterity). This difference is sometimes thought of in spatial terms, but it need not be. Emmanuel Levinas's concept of infinity (vs. totality) as a radical otherness [*Autrui*] is a concept of this type.[15] It is not spatial, because, along with the ethical other, which is a more "spatial" concept (although Levinas resist this view), it also refers to a radical form of temporality, as the past that has never been present.

The second concept, often associated with the term "becoming," is that of a difference defined by transformations from one entity or one state of an entity to another, transformations that may be either continuous or discontinuous. I shall call this difference "Difference B" (B for becoming). This concept is often associated with temporality, especially, but not always, with continuous temporality, but, again, it need not be, because not all becoming is temporal. This concept forms part of RBT-type concepts, because these concepts always involve and, as noted above, are derived (inferred) from effects of the RBT-type real. These effects are essentially discontinuous but are governed by this second difference, which is enriched by RBT thinking, and thus by a radical RBT-form of "Difference A."

Kant's and Hegel's thought, *at least in certain readings*, could be seen as *oriented more toward* (which is not to say fully defined by) "Difference A" and "Difference B," respectively. One can also similarly position Plato and Aristotle, or Parmenides and Heraclitus. However, Heraclitus's thinking, to the degree we can *think* it given the sparsity of the available texts, is equally based on both forms of difference, as ultimately is Hegel's thinking, or that of Heidegger, who saw Hegel and Friedrich Hölderlin as Heracliteans, and as precursors of his own thinking as Heraclitean. Along the scale of "Difference A" (the gradient established by Kant), it is possible to position Hölderlin, Heinrich von Kleist, Percy Bysshe Shelley, John Keats, and then Friedrich Nietzsche, Georges Bataille, Maurice Blanchot, Lacan, Levinas, Derrida, Paul de Man, and Alain Badiou, and some modernist literary figures, such as Franz Kafka, Robert Musil, or Samuel Beckett. Along the scale of "Difference B," one can, by contrast, position, in alignment with Hegel, Gottfried Leibniz and Baruch Spinoza (major influences on Deleuze, who is, however, closer to Hegel than he claims), and then Henri Bergson, Alfred North Whitehead, and Deleuze himself (also in his work with Guattari). J. G. Fichte and Schlegel are clearly, and unfairly, omitted here, in part, because, as stated from the outset, the confrontation and *difference* between Kant and Hegel has dominated the reception-history of the concept of difference.

As just mentioned in connection to Kant and Hegel, it is not a matter of associating their thought strictly with either type of difference but of a relative balance or a relative emphasis. In some cases, it is difficult to give any priority to either. My main concern is, however, an orientation in their thinking toward the RBT-type, which involves both types of difference, insofar as "Difference A," in its RBT form, becomes the efficacity of effects conforming to "Difference B."

3 "I Can *Think* Whatever I Like": From Kant's Noumena to the Real Beyond Thinking

My main argument in this section and, in several key respects, in this chapter in general builds on Kant's remarkable elaboration in the first *Critique*. This elaboration brings subtle complexities to his philosophical system, which distinguishes between "noumena" or "objects," as things-in-themselves, as they exist independently, and "phenomena," as appearances or representations in our thinking, including those that we assume represent "objects" of nature or mind. While one can, more immediately, think of Kant's things-in-themselves as referring to nature as matter, they may also be mental, and thus pertain to human nature (to which the term nature equally refers in Kant). Henry Lebesgue, one of the founders of modern integration theory, observed (in commenting on the paradoxes of set theory) that the fact that we cannot imagine or mathematically define objects, "sets," that are neither finite nor infinite, does not mean that such objects do not exist.[16] Lebesgue did not say in what type of reality, material or mental (likely the latter, given that we are dealing with mathematics), such entities might exist. The statement is, however, a profound reflection of the limits of our thought of the nature of reality possibly existing beyond thought, a reflection rarely, if ever, commented on. An RBT-type reality, defined along the lines suggested by Lebesgue, can be mental, too; for example, following the view of the unconscious in Sigmund Freud, whose thinking was, arguably, short of RBT thinking, and Lacan, whose thinking was closer to it. While Kant positions objects beyond *knowledge*, he nevertheless allows, at least through a practical justification, that one can *think*, form a conception of, objects, rather than (on the RBT view) placing them beyond thought altogether. As he says:

> [E]ven if we cannot *cognize* these same objects as things in themselves, we at least must be able to *think* them as things in themselves... To *cognize* an object, it is required that I be able to prove its possibility (whether by the testimony of experience from its actuality or *a priori* through reason). But I can *think* whatever I like, as long as I do not contradict myself, i.e., as long as my concept is a possible thought, even if I cannot give any assurance whether or not there is a corresponding object somewhere within the sum total of all possibilities. But in order to ascribe objective validity to such a concept (for the first sort of possibility [that of conceiving of it] was merely logical) something more is required. This "more," however, need not be thought in the theoretical sources of cognition; it may also lie in practical ones.[17]

A justification by way of "theoretical sources of cognition" refers to a justification by a concept that is assumed to be *objectively true* concerning the object it represents and a justification by way of "the practical sources of cognition" to a concept that works in practice and is *objectively accepted* (has "objective validity"), even if it cannot be rigorously proven to correspond to the object in question. For simplicity, I shall speak of a theoretical versus a practical justification. It might be noted that Kant's statement "I can *think* whatever I like" is also an expression of creative nature and freedom of thinking and thought in Deleuze and Guattari's sense (including when it comes to concepts), which enables us to approach reality either with a theoretical or practical justification.

Both forms of justification are *objective* in the sense of being unambiguously definable and communicable, at least to some extent, and, for Kant, ideally, universally, although he could not have expected this to be the case in practice. As its etymology indicates, the origin of the term "objective" is linked to the concept of an *object* (as something existing independently of us). This allows our claims concerning it, as opposed to those concerning phenomena, to be more general and, in principle, even universal, a view assumed by Kant, again, as only in principle possible to become universal. Whether, according to Kant, such a proof is ever possible in dealing with things-in-themselves is a complex question, which (along with other accompanying complexities in Kant's philosophical system) will be put aside here. In RBT-type situations, such a proof is strictly impossible, either as things stand now or ever, even with a practical justification. In RBT-type thinking, it is not any given representation or conception of the ultimate nature of reality responsible for quantum phenomena, but the *inapplicability* of any such representation or conception that is practically justified, either as things stand now, even if such a conception is in principle ever possible. This makes RBT thinking more radical than Kant's thinking. If such a conception eventually becomes possible, even if only as practically justified, then a representation based on this conception also becomes possible, at least as practically justified, thus agrees with Kant's view. Such a conception may, however, not become possible, thus leaving this real an RBT.

If, however, such a real is beyond representation or knowledge, or even is unthinkable, that is, is ultimately unthinkable even as unthinkable (a thought of the unthinkable is still a human thought), can one speak of it at all? Thus, according to Derrida, in considering *différance* (a concept of an RBT type):

> What am I to do in order to speak about the *a* of *différance*? It goes without saying that it cannot be *exposed*. One can expose only that which at a certain moment can become *present*, manifest, that which can be shown, presented as something present, a being present in its truth, in the truth of a present or the presence of the present. Now if [while?] *différance* [is] (and I also cross out [is]) what makes possible the presentation of the being-present, it is never presented as such. It is never offered to the present. Or to anyone. Reserving itself, not exposing itself, in regular fashion it exceeds the order of truth at a certain precise point, but without disseminating itself as something, as mysterious being, in the occult of a non-knowledge or in a hole with indeterminable borders (for example, in a topology of castration). In every exposition it would be exposed to disappearing as disappearance. It would risk appearing: disappearing.[18]

One cannot miss the gestures here against negative theology, Heidegger, and Lacan's Symbolic. Derrida's readings of Lacan tend to bypass the Real, which might be read as proximate to what Derrida outlines here. On such a reading, the Symbolic (roughly, as the play of primarily linguistic signifiers governed by the Oedipal economy of desire) is defined as an effect of the Real and, as such, as something that can be disrupted by the Real. The Real can, for example, shift our thinking to the Imaginary (roughly, as the free or freer representational play, associated more closely with images), keeping in mind that both, indeed all three, registers exist in complex interactions. For the moment, it is clear that, while the *a* in *différance* is a figure of this difficulty and ultimately impossibility even of *writing différance*—even if one gives writing Derrida's sense, that is, that of an *effect* or a manifold of effects of *différance* and its satellites, such as dissemination, trace, supplement, and so forth. This efficacious relationship is a crucial point, to which I return below. One might say that when this real is an RBT, it functions as a *term* without a concept, akin to a mathematical symbol. This in part explains Lacan's interest in such symbols or signifiers, such as, and in particular, "*i*," the imaginary number $\sqrt{-1}$—mathematical entities that do not represent anything outside mathematics, although they can have nonrepresentational relations to the Real. Given that it may be impossible to fully dissociate a term from a concept, "real" may even be understood as a term without a term, which compels Derrida to speak about entities like *différance* as neither terms nor concepts. Among others figures who consider this type of "radical alterity" (Derrida's term), on or close to RBT lines, are (in addition to Lacan) Nietzsche, Bataille, Levinas, Blanchot, or de Man, and several literary figures, Romantic or modernist.

Do Kant and Hegel, or other philosophical figures associated with Idealism or critical philosophy, do so as well? This would depend on one's reading of them, as with the figures mentioned above. My short answer in the case of Kant and Hegel is: yes when it comes to their engagement with the *possibility* of such a real, RBT, but not necessarily when it comes to seeing this real as a necessary and positive condition of thinking. As suggested earlier, I am inclined to read Kant's and Hegel's works as ultimately not reaching an RBT-type view of the real. On the other hand, I am inclined to see Romantic authors as closer to reaching this limit, for example, and in particular Hölderlin in his thinking the unthinkable, the *Undenkbare*, via caesura.[19] While this subject is for the most part beyond the scope of this chapter, it is nevertheless worth pointing out, in affinity with Derrida's strong dissociation of his thinking *différance* from mystical or negative theology, one aspect of Hölderlin's thinking of the unthinkable.[20] As RBT thinking, Hölderlin's thinking cannot be theological, although it took Nietzsche to expressly announce this impossibility; it is true that, at the moment of caesura, in a tragic representation, the God is, according to Hölderlin, "nothing but time," and it is for that reason that the God forgets himself at this moment—which may suggest that the God, "the Father of Time," is the efficacity of time.[21] But, then, this efficacity would not be unthinkable: the divine, the God, is still thinkable, thinkable as God, even if, as in negative or mystical theology, none of God's actual attributes is thinkable. It is the unthinkable (and hence, again, un-divine) efficacity that ultimately creates "the conditions of [pure or empty forms] of time and space," which are exposed at the moment of a caesura, unlike the unthinkable itself, which cannot be exposed.[22] This move toward the unthinkable appears to be characteristic of Sophocles, who, unlike other Greek tragic writers, knows how to portray human thought as "wandering beneath the Unthinkable [*unter Undenkbarem wandelnd*]"[23])—the unthinkable above the divine. If this is the God's withdrawal, one could read it as the unthinkable un-divine efficacity of the divine, announcing at least a figure of the death of God. The same orientation is found in Shelley and Keats—for example, in Keats's *The Fall of Hyperion* read as an allegory of the fall from the divine, at least from the thinkable of the divine, and the thinkable itself.

One the other hand, it is perfectly possible to think, represent, or speak, the *workings* of this real, because, while one cannot speak or even think of it, one can still speak of its thinkable or representable effects, building on Freud's, arguably, less radical view of the unconscious, and giving it an RBT sense. For Freud, in accord with Kant to whom he refers in this connection, the unconscious is still at least thinkable and indeed, ultimately, psychoanalytically accessible and knowable.[24] As stated from the outset, it is through, and only through, such effects and particular configurations of them—defying the possibility of representing or thinking of their emergence as effects—that an RBT can be inferred, thus also making this inference analytically unavoidable. One might say that such effects of the RBT-type real, defined by our thought interaction with it, may even be assumed to be *theoretically* justified in Kant's sense. This assumption, however, still only holds as things stand now and is subject to interpretation, which ultimately amounts to a practical justification after all. The effects in question, as with any phenomena, involve assumptions and concepts shaping their formulations and communication, and may, as a result, be subject to interpretive qualifications and disagreements. It is even more difficult to assume a theoretical justification for a theoretical scheme of either an RBT or RWT type, when dealing with such effects. Theories can become obsolete, and the same effects can be theorized otherwise, which would, however, also mean these effects can no longer be rigorously considered the same either.

RBT thinking thus implies a new type of epistemology of the real, an epistemology without an ultimate ontology, apart from an ontology of the effects of the real—an epistemology of the knowable (i.e., the effects) and of the unthinkable (i.e., the efficacity of these effects in the absence of causality). Our predictions of these effects, when possible, are unavoidable probabilistic, and the calculus of such probabilities may, in principle, be interminable and only terminated by a decision. Both Lacan and Derrida (differently) understand this calculus in a similar way.[25] But probability is not reality, and our symbolic (in Lacan's sense) or allegorical (in de Man's sense) expectation can always be defeated by the real, as Lacan, Derrida, and de Man expressly argue. To cite de Man's famous statement of the lesson of Shelley's *The Triumph of Life*: "[*The Triumph of Life*] warns us that, nothing, whether deed, word, thought or text, ever happens in relation, positive or negative, to anything that preceded, follows, or exists elsewhere, but only as a random event whose power, like the power of death, is due to the randomness of its occurrence."[26] For de Man, allegory always masks and unmasks this a-causality beyond any apparent order, or even apparent randomness or chance. One still needs to consider (perhaps, against de Man) the question of probability, which is not the same as randomness, but instead reflects the interplay of randomness or order. This is an important difference because, as discussed in the next section, at stake in RBT thinking is ultimately the nature of order rather than only randomness. De Man does consider how certain forms of order, such as those of uncritical aesthetic or historical ideology, come about, and suggests that *The Triumph of Life* may teach us to think different forms or figures of order, arising from RBT-type "disfiguration," but he does not elaborate on the nature of this order as the interplay of chance and necessity.

4 Causality, Chance, and Probability: The RBT View

As I am arguing here, the philosophical and practical, including political, stakes in the difference between RWT- and RBT-thinking of contingency and the real are enormous. It is a matter of a confrontation between two fundamentally different views of the world, based on two ontological hypotheses. The first assumes the ultimate, and specifically, causal order underlaying chance, and the second in principle precludes this assumption, at the ultimate level of the real, making it an RBT-type.

Suppose something has happened: How did it come about? Something must have caused it, or so it would appear and so it is generally assumed, especially if the event belongs to an ordered configuration or arises according to some law. Kant calls this assumption the principle of causality, a principle found already in Plato or even the pre-Socratics. Kant defines that which causes an event as its cause (which may be multiple) and the event itself as an effect of this cause.[27] Causality proceeds from causes to effects, while the principle of causality proceeds, by inference, from effects to causes. The principle of causality implies that reality has a causal character. The question becomes whether one can conceive of this character, define it, describe it, and so forth; in short, whether this character allows for a realist treatment. This is the problem of causality, astutely analyzed by David Hume. It is, Hume contended, beyond our reach ever to ascertain actual causal connections between events, even if they existed; we can at most surmise probable connections between events, although in certain cases such connections appear to be nearly certain. Nevertheless, one might still reason as follows. While such ultimate causal connections between events and the architecture of the underlying reality responsible for these connections may be *unknowable* for us, they—contra the strong form of the RBT view assumed here—may still be *thinkable*, conceivable, even if without certainty as to whether such conceptions are correct. At the very least, one can assume, as both Kant and Hume did, that there is an order, natural or divine, defining the ultimate nature of the real, thus in agreement with RWT thinking. This view has a spectrum of instantiations, not all of which are causal, although most are and there is some debate concerning Hume's position in this regard.

By contrast, the reality-beyond-thinking (RBT) ontological hypothesis, while it assumes that the world exists, is *real*, rejects the applicability of the principle of causality and, again, more fundamentally, the assumption that one could represent or even conceive of the ultimate constitution of the real. The situation becomes especially enigmatic, even mysterious, because the RBT-type real may have ordered effects as well and may be productive of order, even if only probabilistic order. The deepest mystery of RBT is the possibility of order arising from chaos. An underlying hidden causal order would provide a reason. Such an order is, however, not compatible with the ordered effects found in those situations that lead to RBT-type thinking. The answer, based on RBT-type thinking, is that we do not or, more radically, cannot know or even conceive how this order comes about, any more than randomness or chance (which would, in RBT-type theories, be an effect of the RBT-type real as well). They are effects of that which is neither ordered nor random, or any combination of both. There is no story to be told and no concept to be formed concerning the processes that lead to this order or this randomness. Fortunately, however, we still have probability—probability without causality—by means of which we can deal with these effects.

To understand this better, one needs to consider the difference, not always sufficiently appreciated, between randomness or chance and probability. Randomness and chance can be defined as different from each other as well, but they are close to each other in most definitions, and can be treated as roughly interchangeable for the purposes of this chapter. For convenience, I shall primarily speak of chance. Chance is a manifestation of the unpredictable, in terms of either future events or events that have already happened but were unexpected, even though both types of events might have hidden causes and thus are in fact not random. By its unpredictability, chance brings an element of chaos into our interactions with the world. By contrast, the use of probability, which has to do with estimates, which are sometimes numerical, concerning the likelihood of events, allows us to restore a degree of order in dealing with situations in which chance plays a shaping role. Probability is, therefore, related to the interplay of chaos and order. It is chaosmic, in James Joyce's famous coinage (favored by Deleuze and Guattari), possibly influenced by quantum theory, where the term may be more fitting than in classical physics, particularly chaos theory, in describing which it has been used sometimes.[28]

By contrast when this interplay is found in RWT-type thinking, this interplay is assumed to be ultimately underwritten by an order defined by causality. A causal order connects all events considered by a law or set of laws and makes chance and probability merely a practical, epistemological matter, due to our inability to access this order. In dealing with simpler (nonchaotic) causal systems, like those considered in classical mechanics, chance could be avoided altogether, at least ideally, and our predictions concerning behaviors could be ideally exact, deterministic. By determinism, I refer, epistemologically, to the possibility, at least ideally, of such exact predictions, in contrast to causality, which refers, ontologically, to the behavior of physical objects. While both classical statistical physics and chaos theory are ontologically causal, they are not epistemologically deterministic, because the mechanical complexity of the systems they consider makes the recourse to

Difference

probability unavoidable in predicting their behavior. Thus, the "chaosmos" of classical physics, even chaos theory, is merely a practical, epistemological matter, and hardly merits the name. In recent history, these theories, especially chaos theory, often served as models for the human or social sciences, and for readings (sometimes justified) of some of the figures considered here, in particular Deleuze and Guattari when dealing with "Difference B."

The case is fundamentally different in RBT thinking, defined by the impossibility of *assuming* any underlying causal order, rather than the difficulties or impossibility of accessing this order. Because this concept only assumes the concept of the real, defined as something that is assumed to exist, while placing the *character* of this existence beyond representation or knowledge, or even conception, it automatically excludes causality, as based on the assumption of such a conception. RBT thinking should not, however, be seen as assuming, on Parmenidean or Platonist lines, a form of undifferentiated Oneness, however beyond knowledge this Oneness may be. Being One (or Being or One separately) is already a concept of the real.[29] The RBT-type real is each time different, even as it is each time inconceivable, a difference that is manifested in its different effects, which follow "Difference B," although, since it is probabilistic, this difference takes a discrete form (each effect is discrete in relation to any other). Probability is always the probability of estimating the likelihood of events on the basis of other events, always discrete in relation to each other. Any assumption of the underlying continuity, connecting them, causal or not, implies an RWT-type ontology, an ontology that, one might argue, is found in Deleuze's and Deleuze and Guattari's thinking, as a continuous ontology ultimately underlying chance or probabilistic, effects. In RBT thinking, which is closer to Bataille, Derrida, and de Man, there is no underlying continuity any more than any underlying discreteness, or randomness, defining the efficacity of the effects considered. The scope of this chapter does not allow me to address the question of probability in Romantic thought, which has not been given due attention: Rüdiger Campe's study of Kleist is a rare exception;[30] however, it still bypasses more radical, RBT dimensions of Romantic thought (including in Kleist himself) by reading probability as supported by a hidden causality.[31]

Since it is beyond thought, the ultimate nature of the real at stake in RBT-thinking cannot be assumed to be random either, any more than it can be assumed to be causal. Nor can it be assumed to be defined by any combination of chance and causality, or order and chaos, unless one uses the term "chaos," as I do here, to refer to that which is beyond all comprehension. RBT-type theories are chaosmic because of the chaosmic nature of the effects of the real. The same type of situation is found in quantum theory.[32] Murray Gell-Mann famously borrowed the term "quark" from *Finnegans Wake*: Joyce's novel, was, however, itself influenced by quantum theory and perhaps even the discovery of antimatter. As Joyce writes in *Finnegans Wake*, clearly referring to the novel itself, "I am working out a quantum theory about it for it is really most tantumising state of affairs."[33] In the novel, words transform into each other just as particles do in high-energy quantum physics. The word "chaosmos" is an example of such a transformation.

I close this section by returning to Hegel, and the conclusion of the *Phenomenology*.[34] Although I cannot offer a proper reading of the two final paragraphs of the book, which would be necessary to properly support my suggestion here, I shall, nevertheless, risk a wager on the following hypothesis. In juxtaposing Absolute Knowledge (essentially a form of thought in Deleuze and Guattari's sense) to science [*Wissenschaft*], as a still-incomplete form of thought and the development of *Geist*, Hegel considers the relation and synthesis of two sides of this becoming of *Geist*: its free chance-like event or happening [*Zufälligkeit*], as nature in space, and "spirit coming-to-be, *history* [*Geschichte*] [as] *knowing self-mediating coming-to-be of the spirit relinquished into time,...* [as] likewise the relinquishing of itself."[35] My hypothesis (possibly against the grain of Hegel's own thinking) is that *Geist*, Hegel's *Real*, is only to be defined by probability, but not by randomness and chance, even if nature is defined by them. *Geist* only gives rise to one possible wager on the future, as Hegel bet in the *Phenomenology*—and it proved to be a very good bet. It is not unlike Derrida's wager on "democracy-to-come" in *Specters of Marx*, which are also the ghosts and "*Geists*" of Hegel.[36] It remains an open question whether this bet, or any other bet concerning the future of *Geist*, is defined by a causal and thus RWT-type real or an RBT-type real, as in Nietzsche, who famously spoke of his love for "the uncertainty of the future, [*amor fati*],"[37] or Bataille, Lacan, or Derrida, who also read Hegel against the grain, betting on Hegel against Hegel. On the other hand, none of them speak of *Geist* as the *spirit* of betting on the future—something that is perhaps more true of Hölderlin, the thinker of the caesura of the unthinkable [*Undenkbare*][38], than Hegel, "the last philosopher of the book and the first thinker of writing" (in Derrida's sense of writing).[39]

5 Difference Against Presence, and Against Difference

The emergence of radical forms of thinking difference, especially of the RBT-type or even more radical forms of the RWT-type, tends to be *irruptive* and often singular in nature, and is resisted and often defeated by a persistent work of containment. The reasons for this containment range from psychological, and possibly neurological, to social, cultural, and political, including institutional ones. The early Derrida elaborates this problematic in broad terms when writing of both writing itself and temporality:

> What always threatens this [precarious] balance [of the representation of the *Anthropos* linked to the manual visual scripts of audio-phonetic writing] is confused with the very thing that broaches the *linearity* of the symbol. We have seen that the traditional concepts of time, the entire organization of the world and of language, was bound up with it. Writing in the narrow [rather than Derrida's] sense—and phonetic writing above all—is rooted in the past of nonlinear [Derrida's] *writing* [that] had to be defeated, and here one can speak, if one wishes of technical success; it assured a greater security and greater possibilities of capitalization in a dangerous and anguishing world. But that was not done *one single time*. A war was declared, and the suppression of all that tested linearization was installed.[40]

De Man would in a similar vein link such ruptures of the continuity of the symbol, with the radical *discontinuity* of allegory or, still more radically, irony, a discontinuity beyond discontinuity. These figures belong, in de Man's phrase, to the rhetoric of temporality, a connection shared with Derrida who refers to the linearity of the symbol.[41] It is also worth mentioning in passing Foucault's "power," which may be read as his name for something like radical difference, manifested only through its effects[42], akin to the way Derrida's *différance* is understood. For Foucault, we can only try to estimate these effects of power, but we cannot know the Power itself—and this makes such estimates unavoidably probabilistic. Derrida's appeal to a war reflects the long history of emergences and uses of radical concepts and practices of difference, on the one hand, and, on the other hand, their containment, which tends to be more successful. And yet, the final outcome of this "war," which is to say, the next stage of it (the only "final" outcome possible here), remains unclear and depends on the specific space of thinking and reading, for we are actually dealing with a plurality of local wars, rather than a single one.

"Presence" is a concept-problem, too, which includes certain RWT-type forms of difference, multiplicity, or alterity. Heidegger offers arguably the culminating conception of such difference as multiple in his late work *The Question of Being*: "The [multiple] meaningfulness [*Mehrdeutigkeit*] is based on a play [*Spiel*] which, the more richly it unfolds, the more strictly it is held... by a hidden rule [*Regel*]... This is why what is said remains bound into the highest law [*Gesetz*]."[43] To assume this play to be so "held" and "bound" is to remain within RWT limits. Hence, Derrida responds to Heidegger's position via Nietzsche, if not without an allusion to Hegelianism and Platonism ("all dialectic"):

> There will be no unique name, even if were the names of Being [or even *différance*, which is not a name, however]. And we must think this without *nostalgia*, that is, outside the myth of a purely maternal or paternal language, a lost native country of thought. On the contrary, we must *affirm* this, in the sense in which Nietzsche puts affirmation into play, in a certain laughter and a certain step of the dance. From the vantage of this laughter and this dance, from the laugher of this affirmation foreign to all dialectic, the other side of nostalgia, what I will call Heideggerian *hope*, comes into question. I am not unaware how shocking this word might seem here. Nevertheless I am venturing it, without excluding any of its implication, and I relate it to what still seems to me the metaphysics [in the sense of the metaphysics of presence] part of "The Anaximander Fragment": the quest for the proper word and the unique name. Speaking of the first word of Being (*das frühe Wort des Seias: to khreon*), Heidegger writes: "the relation to what is present that rule in the essence of presencing itself is a unique one (*ist eine einzige*), altogether incomparable to any other relation. It belongs to the uniqueness of Being itself (*Sie gehört zur Enzigkeit des Seins selbst*). Therefore, in order to name the essential nature of Being (*das wesende Seins*), language would have to find a single word, the unique word (*eing einziges, das einzige Wort*). From this we can gather how daring every thoughtful word (*denkende Wort*) addressed to Being is (*das dem Sein zugersprochen wird*). Nevertheless such daring is not impossible, since Being speaks always and everywhere throughout language" (p. 25). Such is the question: the alliance of speech [accordingly, not writing in Derrida's sense] and Being in the unique word, in the finally proper name. And such is the question inscribed [now *written*] in the simulate affirmation of *différance*. It bears (on) each member of this sentence: "Being/speaks/always and everywhere/throughout language."[44]

A parallel argument is found in Derrida's critique, again via Nietzsche, of Claude Levi-Straus, and structuralism, and the concept of play (*jeu*) as a (controlled or centered) play of difference in "Structure, Sign and Play in the Discourse of the Human Science."[45] These two references to Derrida's work return us to a question brought up earlier, but now with a new, perhaps counter-Derridean slant: how are we, then, to think *différance*, which is to say, to think the unnamable or even the unthinkable or, if this unthinkable is rigorously beyond thought, unthinkable even as unthinkable? As Derrida says in the conclusion to "Structure, Sign and Play":

> Here there is a kind of question, let us still call it historical, whose conception, formation, gestation, and labor we are only catching a glimpse of today. I employ these words, I admit, with a glance toward the operations of childbearing—but also with a glance toward those who, in a society from which I do not exclude myself, turn their eyes away when faced by the yet *unnamable* which is proclaiming itself and which can do so, as is necessary whenever a birth is in the offing, only under the species of the nonspecies, in the formless, mute, infant, and terrifying form of monstrosity.[46]

As discussed above, in *"Différance,"* the "as yet unnamable" becomes that for which there can be no name, not even the name Being, not even the name *différance*, "which is not a pure nominal unity, and unceasingly dislocates itself in a chain of differing and deferring substitutions."[47] Perhaps, however, at stake here is not only the unnamable but also the unthinkable, invoked but then dropped by Derrida when referring to "a structure lacking any center" representing "the unthinkable [*l'impensable*] itself."[48] As suggested earlier, one could give this unthinkable a "name" insofar as no conception could be associated to it, and if the unthinkable is a name, it implies that what it names is unthinkable even as unthinkable. But is it a name, then? Derrida speaks of *différance* as "neither a word nor a concept."[49] Is Derrida's unnamable also unthinkable? It may or may not be, but as his thought and the thought of the modern sciences tell us, the thought of this unthinkable, the thought of that which is beyond thought, is possible.

In thinking the unthinkable, RBT-thinking in the work of earlier figures, such as Nietzsche, Freud, Heidegger, or Bataille, and even Niels Bohr, is important too. Like every other concept, any RBT concept has its history and depends on it: Derrida understands *différence* as a juncture (not a summation) of the thought of Nietzsche (the play of difference and forces), Freud (the unconscious), Levinas (the radical alterity of the past that has never been present), Heidegger (the difference between beings and Being), and Bataille (restricted vs. general economy)—and finally, at the moment of "the very enigma of *différance*" (via Bataille), Hegel, "the last philosopher of the book and the first thinker of writing."[50] Much of the writing on difference in all these figures may be seen as rewritings of Hegel's work, from the *Phenomenology* on, however radical this rewriting may be, because we are still dealing with both infinitesimal, "almost absolute", proximity and radical difference from Hegel.[51] According to Derrida, then, building on Freud's argument in *Beyond the Pleasure Principle*,

> Here we are touching upon the point of greatest obscurity, on the very enigma of *différance*, on precisely that which divides its very concepts by means of a strange cleavage. We must not hasten to decide. How are we to think *simultaneously*, on the one hand, *différance* as the

economic detour which, in the elements of the same, always aims at coming back to the pleasure or the presence that have been deferred by (conscious or unconscious) calculation, and, on the other hand, *différance* as the relation to an impossible presence, as expenditure without reserve, as the irreparable loss of presence, the irreversible usage of energy, that is, the death [drive], and as the entirely other relationships that apparently interrupt every economy? It is evident—and this is the evidence itself—that the economical and the non-economical, the same and the entirely other, etc., cannot be *thought* together. If *différance* is unthinkable in this way, perhaps we should not hasten to make evident, in the philosophical element of evidentiality which would make short work of dissipating the mirage and illogicality of *différance* and would do so with the infallibility of calculations that we are well acquainted with, having precisely recognized their place, necessity, and function in the structure of *différance*. Elsewhere, in the reading of Bataille[52], I have attempted to indicate what might come of a rigorous and, in a new sense, "scientific" *relating* of the "restricted economy" that takes no part in expenditure without reserve, death, opening itself to non-meaning, etc., to a general economy that *takes into account* the nonreserve, that keeps in reserve the nonreserve, if it can be put thus. I am speaking of a relationship between a *différance* that can make a profit on its investment and a *différance* that misses its profit, the *investiture* of a presence that is pure and without loss here being confused with absolute loss, with death. Through such a relating of a restricted and a general economy the very project of philosophy, under the privileged heading of Hegelianism, is displaced and reinscribed. The *Aufhebung—la relève*—is constrained into writing itself otherwise. Or perhaps simply into writing itself [in Derrida's sense]. Or, better, into taking account of the consumption of writing.[53]

Elsewhere Derrida further elaborates on this crucial point in the composition of *différance*:

> Since it is still a question of elucidating the relationships to Hegel—a difficult labor, which for the most part remains before us, and which in a certain way is interminable, at least if one wishes to execute it rigorously and minutely—I have attempted to distinguish *différance* ... from Hegelian difference, and have done so precisely at the point at which Hegel, in the greater *Logic*, determines difference as contradiction, only in order to resolve it, to interiorize it, to lift up (according to the syllogistic process of speculative dialectics) into the self-presence of an onto-theological or onto-teleological synthesis. *Différance* (at a point of almost absolute proximity to Hegel...) must sign the point at which one breaks with the system of the *Aughebung* and with speculative dialectics.[54]

Hegel—against Hegelianism, including Hegel's own Hegelianism—often appears to invade philosophical "economies" of the RWT- or RBT-type alike. But then, if Hegel is present, can Kant be far behind? We remain inside the great philosophical "Bermuda triangle" of Kant, Hegel, and Nietzsche, the names of difference and difference beyond difference. We are still subjects to their winds and storms. Is not "weather," too, a figure of difference, one of its archetypal, primordial figures, a figure naming the difference that we cannot predict even probabilistically outside of very restrictive limits, as chaos theory tell us? This is not to leave Descartes, Leibniz, or Spinoza, out of the picture (especially given Deleuze's place within such a picture), and, as I stated at the outset, Plato and Aristotle too are part of this history, as is Heraclitus and his *diapherein*.

I close on a literary *note* (also in the musical sense of "note"), and literary version of Derrida's thought of a "democracy-to-come," as one of Shelley's dreams, or one of the great closing (and yet also opening) questions of Shelley's poetry—perhaps (perhaps!) not as dark as "What is Life?"—closing or unclosing *The Triumph of*

Life, even if it may not be as optimistic as it has been read. Or perhaps, it is best read as a bet, manifested in the final question of the poem, Shelley's great "in-between" question; "If Winter comes, can Spring be far behind?" Nietzsche, also in Italy (in Genoa rather than in Florence, where Shelley wrote his poem), speaks of his *Die fröliche Wissenschaft* in the language of Shelley's "Ode" (which he may have known). He says: "It seems to be written in the language of the wind that thaws ice and snow; high spirits, unrest, contradiction, and April weather are present in it, and one is instantly reminded no less of the proximity of winter than of the triumph over winter that is coming, must come, and perhaps has already come."[55] Rather than referring to seasonal change alone, Shelley's question might also be read as relating to a local moment in time, a moment between moments, even time between time (*zwischen den Zeiten*), either in the Autumn or in the Spring, as in Nietzsche's April. At such a moment, the wind and the weather can move in either direction, toward winter or toward spring. It can be further argued that the ultimate power, Shelley's West Wind, can be given a Foucauldian sense, or the sense of the ultimate efficacy of the movement of the wind, beyond all knowledge or thought itself. We can only bet on where it will move, without any guarantee our bet will succeed. Shelley's poetic physics could be read as closer to quantum theory and its RBT nature than to chaos theory, the part of classical physics that predicts the weather probabilistically, but only due to the practical, epistemological impossibility of accessing the ultimately causal ontology of the corresponding RWT-type real. As such, Shelley's physics is closer to the RBT-type thinking of the real and the interplay of chance and order. This interplay still allows for probability, which cannot, however, be calculated by means of a calculus of causality, still defining chaos theory.

Either way, "If Winter comes, can Spring be far behind?" is a question and not an anticipatory celebration of Spring. Nietzsche does not forget his "perhaps" in April either. Can Spring be far behind, if Winter comes? Yes, it can, sometimes in April, for even then Winter can still hold its power or return. But it does not have to be far behind either. It just may or may not be, although it will inevitably come at some point. But then, Spring is not always a happy time either, while Autumn and even Winter are sometimes. This process is still governed by Shelley's darker question, "What is Life?". Over life, that is, over death, never too far ahead, we cannot triumph. Death is the difference that always triumphs over us. But, just like the autumn (vs. the spring) in Keats's "To Autumn," death has its "music too"—and this is Keats's way of asking "What is Life?" It is still the question of difference.

Notes

1. Jacques Derrida, *Positions*, trans. A. Bass (Chicago, IL: University of Chicago Press, 1981), 41; *Positions* (Paris: Les Éditions de Minuit,1972), 55.
2. See Jacques Derrida, *Of Grammatology*, trans. G. C. Spivak (Baltimore, MD: Johns Hopkins University Press, 1977), 51; *Writing and Difference*, trans. A. Bass (Chicago, IL: University of Chicago Press, 1978), 292; *Margins of Philosophy*, trans. A. Bass (Chicago, IL: University of Chicago Press, 1982), 7.

3. Derrida, *Positions*, 40–1.
4. Ibid., 41.
5. Ludwig Wittgenstein, *Tractatus Logico-Philosophicus*, trans. C. K. Ogden (London: Routledge, 1985), 1.
6. Gilles Deleuze and Félix Guattari, *What is Philosophy?* trans. H. Tomlinson and G. Burchell (New York, NY: Columbia University Press,1994).
7. Gilles Deleuze, *Difference and Repetition*, trans. P. Patton (New York, NY: Columbia University Press, 1995).
8. Deleuze and Guattari, *What is Philosophy?*, 118.
9. Arkady Plotnitsky, *The Principles of Quantum Theory, from Planck's Quanta to the Higgs Boson: The Nature of Quantum Reality and the Spirit of Copenhagen* (New York, NY: Springer), 207–46.
10. Ibid., 5.
11. Ibid., 203, 206, 202.
12. Ibid., 203.
13. G. W. F. Hegel, *Phenomenology of Spirit*, trans. T. Pinkard (Cambridge: Cambridge University Press, 2019), 31.
14. Deleuze and Guattari, *What is Philosophy?*, 16, 20.
15. Emmanuel Levinas, *Totality and Infinity: An Essay on Exteriority*, trans. A. Lingis (Pittsburg, PA; Duquesne University Press, 1969).
16. See J. F. Dauben, *Georg Cantor: His Mathematics and Philosophy of the Infinite* (Princeton, NJ: Princeton University Press, 1990), 258.
17. Immanuel Kant, *Critique of Pure Reason*, trans. P. Guyer and A. W. Wood (Cambridge: Cambridge University Press, 1997), 115.
18. Derrida, *Margins of Philosophy*, 5–6.
19. See Arkady Plotnitsky, "The Calculable Law of Tragic Representation and the Unthinkable: Rhythm, Time, and Thought from Hölderlin to Deleuze," in *At the Edges of Thought: Gilles Deleuze and Post-Kantian Thought*, ed. C. Lundy and D. Voss (Edinburgh: Edinburgh University Press, 2015), 123–45; and "The Paradoxical Interplay of Exactitude and Indefiniteness: Reality, Temporality, and Probability, from Hölderlin to Heisenberg to Musil," in *Physics and Literature*, ed. A. Heydenreich and K. Mecke (Berlin: de Gruyter, 2021), 202.
20. Following Plotnitsky, "The Paradoxical Interplay," 212.
21. Friedrich Hölderlin, *Essays and Letters* (New York, NY: Penguin, 2009), 323.
22. Ibid.
23. Ibid., 326 (translation modified).
24. Sigmund Freud, *General Psychological Theory: Papers on Metapsychology* (New York, NY: Touchstone, 2008), 121.
25. For example, Derrida, *Margins of Philosophy*, 7.
26. Paul de Man, *The Rhetoric of Romanticism* (New York, NY: Columbia University Press, 1984), 122.
27. Kant, *Critique of Pure Reason*, 305, 308.
28. James Joyce, *Finnegans Wake* (Oxford: Oxford University Press), 118.
29. A prominent recent critique of the concept of the (Platonist/Parmenidean) One was offered by Alain Badiou via the mathematics of set and category theories ("the multiple-without-One"). There are, it should be noted, concepts of the One that are not Platonist/Parmenidean, such as that of François Laruelle within his framework of non-philosophy.
30. Rüdiger Campe, *The Game of Probability: Literature and Calculation from Pascal to Kleist*, trans. E. Wiggins (Palo Alto, CA: Stanford University Press, 2013).
31. Plotnitsky, "The Paradoxical Interplay", 208.
32. See Plotnitsky, *The Principles of Quantum Theory*; and "The Paradoxical Interplay".
33. Joyce, *Finnegan's Wake*, 149.
34. Hegel, *Phenomenology of Spirit*, 413–4.
35. Ibid., 413.

36. Jacques Derrida, *Specters of Marx: The State of the Debt, the Work of Mourning and the New International*, trans. P. Kamuf (New York, NY: Routledge, 1993).
37. Friedrich Nietzsche, *The Gay Science*, trans. W. Kaufmann (New York, NY: Vintage, 1974), 223.
38. See Plotnitsky, "The Calculable Law"; and "The Paradoxical Interplay."
39. Derrida, *Of Grammatology*, 26.
40. Ibid., 85 (my emphasis).
41. Paul de Man, *Blindness and Insight: Essays in the Rhetoric of Contemporary Criticism* (Minneapolis, MN: University of Minnesota Press, 1983), 187–228.
42. See Michel Foucault, *The History of Sexuality, Volume I: An Introduction*, trans. R. Hurley (New York, NY: Vintage, 1990).
43. Martin Heidegger, *The Question of Being*, trans. J. T. Wilde and W. Kluback (Woodbridge, CT: Twayne, 1958), 104–5.
44. Derrida, *Margins of Philosophy*, 27.
45. Derrida, *Writing and Difference*, 292–3.
46. Ibid., 293 (my emphasis).
47. Derrida, *Margins of Philosophy*, 26.
48. Derrida, *Writing and Difference*, 279.
49. Derrida, *Margins of Philosophy*, 3.
50. Derrida, *Of Grammatology*, 26.
51. Derrida, *Positions*, 44.
52. See Derrida, *Writing and Difference*, 251–77.
53. Derrida, *Margins of Philosophy*, 19.
54. Derrida, *Positions*, 43–4.
55. Nietzsche, *Gay Science*, 32.

Nothing

Andrew W. Hass

1 Introduction: Nothing's Situation

The question of nothing, as Nothing, has agitated Western philosophy and theology since at least Parmenides. The paragon of that question might take the form first intimated by John Scotus Eriugena in the ninth century, and later articulated by Leibniz and Heidegger in the familiar words: Why is there something rather than nothing? And there is no doubt that when German Idealism began to wrestle with the reconciliation of opposites in the late eighteenth century, that between something and nothing was foremost among them. There is much more doubt, however, about the return of nothing in the latter half of the twentieth century. For when nothing was reintroduced into the theoretical, philosophical, and theological discourse of poststructuralism or postmodernism, reconciliation seemed a distant, if not irrelevant, motivation. What then revived late interest in nothing? Was it the nihilisms that had pervaded since the earlier *fin de siècle*? Was it the existential concerns that Heidegger had brought to bear from phenomenology, and that the likes of Sartre had made, at least for some parts of European sensibility, fashionable? By the end of the twentieth century, as a certain apocalyptic fear gripped a West turning over its clocks to a new millennium, the presiding question seemed to be an inverted form: Why might there be nothing rather than something? But the question of nothing since Bataille reintroduced it, via Kojève, into European thought was not, I want to argue, chiefly in response either to nihilism's unflinching march through two world wars, nor in response to existentialism's drive through post-war Europe, even if these factors cannot in any way be excluded from Europe's conceptual map. It was in fact a return to German Idealism itself, and to the matters of something and nothing that there remained, fundamentally, unreconciled.

A. W. Hass (✉)
University of Stirling, Stirling, Scotland
e-mail: andrew.hass@stir.ac.uk

© The Author(s), under exclusive license to Springer Nature Switzerland AG 2023
T. Rajan, D. Whistler (eds.), *The Palgrave Handbook of German Idealism and Poststructuralism*, Palgrave Handbooks in German Idealism,
https://doi.org/10.1007/978-3-031-27345-2_16

There is a temptation, to which many scholars have too easily succumbed, to see the concerns of German Idealism with nothing and negativity culminating in Hegel's notion of a "negation of negation." For here nothing is overcome, even if by its own powers, so that the question of something—its derivation and its persistence—is answered by affirming existence over that which threatens it. The powers of negation, dialectically, may be necessary and unavoidable, but always toward the "honor" of the positive, in the nuanced sense that Gadamer drew out through the strangely coded practice of a duel, whereby the restoration and confirmation of the person offended must be valorized in "the full reciprocity of the life and death conflict."[1] Pistols at dawn might lead to one's negation, but honor emerges victorious. The same for "something": existence in idealism, having come to confront its nemesis in non-existence, and in a way that realism could never countenance, nevertheless walks away honorably triumphant, and in Hegel, absolutely triumphant.

But were this reading of post-Kantian negation to remain definitive, we'd have little grounds on which to build a late twentieth century re-appropriation of nothing as negation. For, "positive" results were hardly the guiding light that drew the sustained critiques of the postmodern condition. Nihilism and existentialism, whatever else their role, made sure of this. We might say the opposite was true, that any critical enterprise marked by the prefix "post-," starting, one could argue, with "post-Holocaust," was in fact a counter-reaction to a positive negation of negation. This counter-reaction was already inherent in the Left Hegelians (Feuerbach and Marx most renownedly), who complained that Hegelianism's dialectical third term, the *Aufhebung* of two opposing forces, had been co-opted as an inexorably "positive" Absolute, speculative and ideal in nature, and deployed in the service of the "negation" of finitude, or of materiality, or of the proletariat, toward hegemonic ends. And what goes under the banner of postmodernism has often been construed along the lines of this Leftist tradition, by which the systems of reason, logocentricity, colonial power and patriarchy, all operating, in their way, as Absolutes, are "deconstructed"—a term that becomes synonymous (misleadingly) with negation. And this prevailing argument, elaborated from many disciplinary angles, is not without its merits. But it is hardly the entire story, and, in terms of nothing, may not even be the dominant story. What I want to suggest is that poststructuralist concerns with nothing, even in the form of negation (and let's be clear that nothing and negation are far from identical), return us to the wranglings of German Idealism, not merely to negate the negation of negation, but to readdress the *possibilities* that nothing presented to the fertile German mind of the late eighteenth and early nineteenth centuries.

2 Negative Power from Kant to Hegel

The picture changes radically if we see these possibilities in the general form of a constituting power. If German Idealism was twin-born with early German Romanticism (*Frühromantik*), or better, if they emerged joined at the hip, it was the conception of nothing as an active and generating force that typified their fusion. Here we might characterize the labor that gave birth to this conception as the attempt to overcome the defining limit that Kant had set out for the operation of pure reason, as he stated it in the Antinomy of Pure Reason in his First Critique: that reason can never cross the boundary to the unconditioned.[2] To endeavor such a crossing quickly leads to what Kant calls the antithetic of reason, contradictions that are inherent to the endeavor, and which, because they are "natural" contradictions, might be understood as reason's own self-denial, or more strikingly, "the *euthanasia* of pure reason."[3] That reason should internally harbor such negation was both the incentive and the means for finding a way to overcome the critical limits between the conditioned and the unconditioned.

We could say that, broadly speaking, three features emerging from Kant's project would determine the nature and employment of nothing as it was then understood by Kant's successors. The first is the centrality of self-consciousness. What is possible for reason is only possible by way of an Ego that functions in the unity and totality of a self-consciousness, as Kant had worked out in detail within his Transcendental Deduction. What is pivotal is not merely that self-consciousness unifies subjective intuitions with objective appearances, but that it is aware precisely of this operation *and its limits*, especially as it makes its own consciousness its object. It is the full recognition of the limits of self-recognition that will become crucial for notions of nothing. The second follows from the first: freedom. In order for the self-conscious Ego to transcend, and thereby unify, the manifold of representations it produces, it must remain free from the necessities of nature that would dictate, through the empirical conditions of cause and effect, just how self-consciousness must be conscious of its objects, including its own self. To maintain a fundamental freedom, however, opens consciousness to the possibilities of its own non-existence, to its "not-I," insofar as freedom frees existence from necessity. The third follows from the productive or creative nature of this free self-conscious mind: its capacity, in effect, to self-generate, or to create consciousness for its own consciousness. Within any concept of creation comes the question of the non-existence that is presumed before the act of creation took place. When this act is turned on one's own self, when self-begetting thought must think its own self-begetting, as it begets its own thinking, the specter of nothing looms always in the shadow of the self that is produced.

We could trace out these three interconnected features through numerous iterations of German Idealism after Kant, but we see them in relation to nothing most prominently in Fichte, in Schelling, and in Hegel, each in their way. The first two features, self-consciousness and freedom, became the hallmarks of post-Enlightenment philosophy, and are carried through modernity as axioms. The third, self-creation, was picked up and refashioned by Nietzsche, and to some extent Heidegger in his 1940s lectures on Nietzsche, but it was not fully understood in any determining way until the second half of the twentieth century, when the question of what becomes created—by whom, and with what agenda—receives unstinting critical interrogation.

One way we might characterize all three of these features is that they reached the last decades of the twentieth century as a *burden*, and in a manner much more comprehensive than incidental. This may seem a strange evolution for what modernity had come to see as foundational to being human. But the burden was already there in German Idealism. In the conclusion to his analysis of Kant, Jacobi, and Fichte in *Faith and Knowledge*, the young Hegel points out the repercussions of what these three philosophies entailed in understanding the freedom of idealist thinking in terms of infinity, and the pure concept of infinity in terms of an absolute principle. To remain in the Absolute, the infinity of the thinking Ego must uphold indifference, and to do so, it must eternally nullify the objectivity of finitude (or difference) that is outside it. Thus, Hegel can infer that "the inner character of infinity is negation"; it becomes "the abyss of nothingness in which all being is engulfed." And this abyss leads to an "infinite grief," which manifests itself not only in the feeling that "God Himself is dead," but that the free thinking and transcendental Ego, in its infinitude, is bound to a negativity inherent within its very existence.[4] To rescue itself from outright self-nullification, it must come to terms with this burden. As Hegel famously writes, "Thereby it must re-establish for philosophy the Idea of absolute freedom and along with it the absolute Passion, the speculative Good Friday in place of the historic Good Friday. Good Friday must be speculatively re-established in the whole truth and harshness of its God-forsakenness."[5] This Passion is repeated in the final sentences of the *Phenomenology of Spirit*, when Hegel speaks of a "Calvary of absolute Spirit."[6]

If the young Hegel had sensed this burden, the mature Hegel did not fully recant it, despite what many have argued. At best, he tempered it. In his 1820 Preface to the *Elements of the Philosophy of Right*, Hegel speaks of "reason as the rose in the cross of the present," as if reason now has a mollifying effect for the burdens we must carry. This becomes a reason that is not "content with that cold despair which confesses that, in this temporal world, things are bad or at best indifferent, but that nothing better can be expected here, so that for this reason alone we should live at peace with actuality. The peace which cognition establishes with the actual world has more warmth in it than this."[7] Hegel does not state the nature of this warmth, but of course, many would interpret the reference to "actuality" as a reference to the systems of the State in which one finds oneself, as the rest of the *Philosophy of Right* seems to establish unequivocally. And many would interpret the "peace" as individual acquiescence to that State. That is, to give ourselves over to reason is to give ourselves over to the reasonable State. But a close reading of the Introduction shows a consistency with the earlier understanding of the Ego developed in view of Hegel's immediate predecessors, where the self-determination of the "I" is possible only by means of the "I" positing itself as the negation of itself. Hegel is explicit about this: "'I' determines itself in so far as it is the self-reference of negativity."[8] The interpretation of this self-reference was generally colored by what was to follow in the argument of the *Philosophy of Right*, in which the self appeared lost to the structures of right, of morality and of the ethical life set up within the text's political framing. Most readers did not read the self-reference *of negativity*; instead, they read self-reference *as negated*. Self-reference became self-reference of the

State, or the "interest of the universal," to which the individual must recognize its full subordination, must "knowingly and willingly acknowledge this universal interest even as their own *substantial spirit*, and *actively pursue it* as their *ultimate end.*"[9] We can be sympathetic to any who might construe these words as the will of the State over the will of the individual, and it can be argued that the later Hegel did far too little to counter this reading. But it is a reading predicated on a misreading of the self-reference. It is not that self-reference transfers from the "I" to the State, a State that appropriates all reference to itself in universal interest. The self-reference is *of negativity*, which means that in all the State's appropriations and determinations of itself, it must remain bound to self-related negativity. This is not to say that it relinquishes its sovereignty, but that its sovereignty is infected with the negative, is possible only by means of the negative, or, as Derrida will later say, is forever calling itself into question through the logic of the negative.[10] Self-referencing becomes an activity weighted with its own self-questioning, and threatened always by its own self-erasure. The mature Hegel continued to see this burden in the very heart of self-consciousness, when he describes the infinity of self-consciousness "as self-referring negativity, *this ultimate source of all activity, life and consciousness*."[11]

Critical reception of Hegel following his death in 1831 did not accept this ultimate source, and instead focused the problem—the problem of any negativity—on the System. From Kierkegaard and Marx through to the twentieth century, culminating in the systematic atrocities of the Shoah and in the Cold War that followed, the question of System became burdened with the charge that, rather than incubating the warmth of peace, the State and its structures froze individual freedoms, blanketed out individual consciousness, and conditioned the masses to a cold despair. This became a typical anti-Hegelian refrain; but it also found later expression in the twentieth century by those who, in prying open the fault lines of structuralism, drew both directly and indirectly upon Hegel to develop a poststructuralist critique. By that point, however, it was not simply that System, whether of a political, philosophical, theological, economic, or social nature, was infected with internecine forces of the kind that oppressed the freedom of consciousness, or worse, deracinated certain elements in the name of systemic purification. It was that the freedom of self-consciousness and self-determination was itself burdened with a loss at its center. That Hegel helped to inform this later critique suggests that the nub of the problem lay not in System exclusively, and not even principally, but in the very structures of the modern self, a problem which Hegel helped both to expose and to redress, by showing how system and self are referential to each other, that they are self-references, but self-references of negativity.

3 A Burden unto Death

The burden of the self for poststructuralist thinkers is of course mediated by a long tradition of existentialist concern, through which the dilemmas of negativity and nothing bequeathed by German Idealism were to be inexorably drawn.[12] Though

Kierkegaard railed against the System with special vituperation, this did not mean he saw that System, like others did, as the sole source of burden. He was astute enough to see the burden both in self-consciousness and in freedom, and not just as a Hegelian by-product but as constituent in the very experience of existing, as the individual negotiates between infinitude and finitude. His reaction against any system, as System, was that it held back the passion of existence, but it was by no means his belief that passion would relieve us from the heaviness of existing. Passion is at root suffering. The point of Kierkegaardian pathos is that, if system and existence cannot co-exist ("because in order to think existence, systematic thought must think it as annulled and consequently not as existing"[13]), existence is nevertheless burdened with its own despair, a sickness unto death, which can only be overcome by placing oneself before God as if sailing out over 70,000 fathoms.

Dostoyevsky brought his burden to bear upon the freedom of self, as most famously described by the Grand Inquisitor in Ivan Karamazov's poem. There the freedom offered by the Christ of the Gospels is too much for any to bear, and so must be mediated—or in effect eradicated—by the Church, whose genius lies in its ability to preserve the sense that people remain absolutely free. But there is little in Ivan's poem to suggest this abrogation of freedom amounts to a loss of self. Dostoyevsky's "Ridiculous Man" is much more indicative in this regard. The protagonist of this short story (1877) is ridiculous on account of a hyper-self-consciousness that is self-fulfilling: so aware is he of his own absurdity, that it is that very self-awareness that makes him all the more absurd. Caught in this *circulus vitiosus*, he comes to the conviction that *nothing in the world matters*: "I suddenly felt that it made *no* difference to me whether the world existed or whether nothing existed anywhere at all. I began to be acutely conscious that *nothing existed in my own lifetime*."[14] This profound nihilism, and the suicidal intention that results, set the stage for his dream to come, in which he is taken to a parallel universe in which the same earth exists, but exists as if the Fall had never taken place, and all inhabitants remain morally pristine. Over time, our ridiculous, hyper-self-conscious man corrupts this world and the entirety of its inhabitants. It is only upon waking from this nightmare that he finds a renewed sense of the value of living, of striving for paradise. This value, however, is placed over against his own consciousness. "The consciousness of life is higher than life… that is what we have to fight against!"[15]

Nietzsche's response to this problem of self's burden was for many what properly triggered the crisis of modernism, and the twentieth century built upon it: that the very notion of Kantian self-consciousness was already infected with System, an infection great enough not only to annul God as a metaphysical *Summum Bonum*, but to annul the autonomy of self and its lifeblood, self-consciousness. Nietzsche's critique drew out most emphatically the burden of self-creation or self-generation. It was the only recourse for humans, if they were to thrive beyond good and evil, or beyond the inherited value systems they themselves had rendered moribund, and yet its path ran through *self-overcoming*: "whoever must be a creator in good and evil—truly, he must first be an annihilator and break values," beginning with those within one's own self.[16]

This all-too brief and sketchy profiling of existentialism's founding figures simply marks out what became crucial for late twentieth century thought: the burden rested not so much on nothing as the possible reality of our own annihilations, but on nothing as the possible reality of our own *creations*. Self-consciousness, freedom, self-begetting—*these* are what have carried us into our own abysses, and these now need some form of reckoning with our late modern realities. Let us then see how late modern thinkers returned to German Idealism as the grounds for this reckoning, even as the existential burdens accompanied their every step like boots lined with lead.

4 Recreating Negativity in the Twentieth Century

Our entry point here must go back to the first half of the twentieth century, and to Bataille. Certainly Alexandre Kojève, on whom Bataille so relied, had spoken clearly of negativity and nothingness in relation to self-consciousness, freedom, and self-constitution (through creative action) in his influential lectures on Hegel during the 1930s.[17] But it was Bataille who translated this negation for a new generation of French philosophical thinkers. And he translated it by re-constituting Heidegger's question about why there is being and not nothing. Bataille writes, in his section on Hegel in *Inner Experience,* "why must there be *what I know*?"[18] Here Bataille draws together a fundamental ontology, as was being worked out by Heidegger, with a fundamental epistemology, as inherited from Kant, just as Hegel had done in his response to the Kantian enterprise. Heidegger's ontological question, which Bataille references immediately thereafter, is now recast: it is no longer a question merely of a gap in ontological meaning, a black hole that sits at the center of existence, and of why this black hole has not consumed everything around it; it is now a question of an abyss whose perimeter is knowledge itself. It is not a movement from the unknown to the known, providing the answer to the question of nothing, but from the known to the unknown, approaching an all-important limit to experience.

What Bataille stresses from Kojève is precisely this movement as *action*. Bataille repeatedly speaks of negativity as a principle of action, and in his later essay of 1955 on Hegel, death, and sacrifice, he quotes Kojève: "the central and final idea of Hegelian philosophy" is "the idea that the foundation and the source of human objective reality [*Wirklichkeit*] and empirical existence [*Dasein*] are the Nothingness which manifests itself as negative and creative Action, free and self-conscious."[19] Here, in eliciting our three features of modernity, Bataille sees life in terms of death, of "death living a human life," a nothingness that nevertheless enacts, through negativity, the creation of the world (particularly the historical world, the world of human endeavor). This creation is indivisible from knowledge, but it is not knowledge culminating in its own self-fulfillment; it is rather a knowledge that ultimately understands its own blind spots, and in that understanding gives over to nonknowledge. "Final possibility: that nonknowledge still be knowledge. I will explore the night!"[20]

Bataille's exploration of this night, through such things as death, sacrifice, laughter, poetry, ecstasy, and eroticism, is a journey both shared and informed by his compatriot and close friend, Maurice Blanchot. But in Blanchot, the nothingness of night is taken to a new level. Whereas Bataille, following Kojève, seeks a negativity that, in its employment, in its ceaseless, restless activity, in its "circular agitation,"[21] brings us to the limit of knowledge as nonknowledge, beyond Hegel's system of absolute knowledge, and toward a new mystical theology, Blanchot seeks a negativity that is a pure nothingness, that is, a nothingness in the paradox of its full presence.

To help us understand what Blanchot could mean by a full presence of nothing, and how this undermines the modern notions of subjectivity, we need to consider more closely the variegations of nothingness and negativity, which we have already indicated should not be seen merely as an expanded family of strict synonyms. The abiding problem with nothingness as utter void or as pure abyss is that it cannot be grasped as absence in the sense of some "being" that is then taken away. To assume that nothing is displaced being or privation predisposes the nothing to presence: something was at one point present but is now rendered absent. But pure nothing, as Nothing, has no object outside of it to displace or render nihilated. Nothing in its purity is—*wholly nothing*, which means it cannot even lend itself to the grammatical construction of a subject and predicate. There is no *it is* to nothing. But to suggest there is no verb operating in nothing is what worried Hegel with the early Schelling's *Indifferenz*, which he famously called "the night in which all cows are black,"[22] a night in which no action is possible, or an Absolute that is wholly inoperative, unable to issue forth anything, not even itself. It is for this reason that Hegel introduces negation through becoming: a circular agitation, in Bataille's words, by which beginning is always, through negation, beginning anew, and by which the Absolute gains a potency, even if only through an absolute negation. If there is a night in Hegel, it is a night forever giving birth to the day—not an owl flying at dusk, but a blackbird singing to bring in the dawn. It is therefore not *nothing* that drives Hegelian thought, and certainly not the indifference of Schelling's nothing, as was later expressed in his *Ungrund*, but *negation*, the active power that, as Heidegger later describes it, *nothings*,[23] which is to say, that incites action as a verb, even if it is the action of its own doing as negation.

Blanchot, ever conscious of Hegel in all his work, and employing negation accordingly, is interested in a night that is made real, not by a Hegelian system of becoming toward a teleological third term, and least of all by a knowledge that becomes absolute in the totality of that process, but by a nothing that is so pure that it "can no longer be negated. It affirms, keeps on affirming and it states nothingness as being, the inertia of being."[24] This inertia is not the inertia of Schelling's indifference or *Ungrund*, nor of Bataille's "unemployed negativity."[25] It is the inertia of *being*; what Blanchot seeks, *pace* Hegel, is a pure nothingness that, in its being, has nothing outside itself, which is to say, a nothing completely self-contained with no remainder and, at the same time, a nothing that is *all* outside. And this nothing he glimpses in the midnight of Mallarmé's short work *Igitur*.

In this unclassifiable text, the French poet seeks, according to Blanchot, the abyssal creative act at the heart of the poetic task. In the story, the singular character, Igitur, moves at midnight toward an empty chamber in which, with Socratic purpose, he will drink a vial of poison ("the drop of nothingness") as the self-enactment of his own death. The movement begins at midnight, which is to say, with the night that is already the prefiguration of nothing, as "that pure presence where nothing but the subsistence of nothing subsists."[26] But how does one enact the paradox of a nothing that subsists in the purity of its own presence? The question for Blanchot is predicated upon death, but not on the *experience* of death, which always eludes both the living and the dying. To explicate this Blanchot draws upon the image of balancing scales, where on either side of perfect equilibrium lies either death that is too early (the past) or death that is too late (the future). Language can capture the one, as living (one can see that death is coming, and speak of oneself, in advance, as having died), and language can capture the other, as dead (one can see that one will have died, and speak of this inevitability[27]), but language cannot capture the instant of one's death, that moment when the scales of death are "level upon a single plane."[28] This equilibrium, as night and pure nothingness, or what Blanchot elsewhere calls the impossibility of death, is what Igitur on the one hand pursues, but on the other hand forfeits—and forfeits precisely by reflecting on his move from midnight to the tomb. The movement for Blanchot is crucial, for moving between beginning and end, between past and future, between midnight and the empty chamber, is an oscillation or rhythm of disappearance, the disappearance of the present, the instant of one's death never experienced, so that "the pulsating death which is the heart of each of us, must become life itself, the sure heart of life," which is the very heart of the poetic enunciation that is the work. Here we get a glimpse of how being is bestowed upon nothingness, for the rhythm *around* the presence of death becomes the heart *by which* death beats, and were we to strip back the language, as the enunciation of the work, we'd find a rhythm, as Blanchot says in *The Writing of the Disaster*, "whereby, being in play or in operation within measure, it is not measured thereby."[29]

In the density of his writing, Blanchot is trying to work out negation as the motive force that drives the process by which the work might come to life and be measured, only to be measured for disappearing back into the inert nothingness from which it came. In the final essay that ends *The Work of Fire*, "Literature and the Right to Death," an essay at whose center Hegel is ever-present, Blanchot speaks of the oscillating movement between a work's emergence and disappearance: in writing, a writer "has put himself to the test as a nothingness at work, and after having written, he puts his work to the test as something in the act of disappearing. The work disappears, but the fact of disappearing remains and appears as the essential thing, the movement which allows the work to be realized as it enters the stream of history, to be realized as it disappears." This paradox of being realized in disappearance Blanchot calls the truth of the work, "where the individual who writes—a force of creative negation—seems to join with the work in motion through which this force of negation and surpassing asserts itself."[30] Unlike in the existential nihilism of his mid-century compatriots, nothingness here is not the foil, however unavoidable, over against which we assert the plenitude of our conscious being, even in the consciousness of its mortal condition. Nothing is rather that creative power which, following the concerns of German Idealism, and Hegel above all, motivates the negating movement in the very heart of consciousness. In *The Infinite Conversation* Blanchot writes of the same phenomenon in relation to conceptual language, again drawing directly upon Hegel: "the force of the concept does not reside in refusing the negation that is proper to death, but on the contrary in having introduced it into thought so that, through negation, every fixed form of thought should disappear and always become other than itself."[31] This negating movement is what Blanchot sees in *Igitur*: Hegel haunts the narrative as the protagonist becomes, by the end, other than himself, other than subjectivity, just as, Blanchot insists, Hegel haunts Mallarmé.[32] For in the circular movement of negation that brings one from Midnight to "the drop of nothingness," Hegel's words of the Preface to the *Phenomenology of Spirit* are realized: "But the life of the Spirit is not the life that shrinks from death and keeps itself untouched by devastation, but rather the life that endures it and maintains itself in it."[33]

Both Foucault and Derrida saw this negation at work in Blanchot with particular perspicacity. If the instance of death cannot be experienced, and yet, death lives with us as the very nothingness that accompanies our every step—"death living a human life," as Bataille says, or death as the "sure heart of life," as Blanchot follows—then the "not" of death marks experience at the very point of the instant where pure presence would reside, where the compression of time brings the present into its full immediacy, where there is the impossibility of escaping into the past or toward the future. Foucault and Derrida understood this each in their way, Foucault as the question of the neutral Outside (*Dehor*) of language, Derrida as the question of the deconstructive inside of language, or *différance*.

When Foucault writes in his short but dense piece "Maurice Blanchot: The Thought from Outside" that "the being of language only appears for itself with the disappearance of the subject," we gain a sense of how self's burden is carried through the poststructuralist waters.[34] For unlike modernist poetics, the being of language is not commensurate with the being of self. The *being* of language, like the *being* of nothingness, disappears in what is other than itself, through a dispersal outside subjectivity, which takes us to the space of the void, while the being of self wants pure consciousness to ground itself in its inviolable interiority. The two form a chiasmic relation: the more the self disappears, the more the being of language, as void, can find its own voice; the more that void finds its own voice, in nothingness, the more the self realizes, as it were, its own fiction, its own outside (*dehors*). For Foucault, Blanchot is the very embodiment of this inverse relation, this negating force, as manifested in his own work. The thought of the *dehors* is what becomes unthinkable because, like the instant present (or the instant moment of death), it eludes the "I think" of the autonomous self, and Blanchot's writings—his essays and his fictions—bring us to the abyss of this thought: "So far has he [Blanchot] withdrawn into the manifestation of his work, so completely is he, not hidden in his texts, but absent from their existence and absent by virtue of the marvelous force of their existence, that for us he is that thought itself—its real, absolutely distant, shimmering, invisible presence, its inevitable law, its calm, infinite, measured strength."[35] Measured, we might say, by virtue of that which lays outside measurement.

Derrida's sense of *différance* falls into this play within measure that is not thereby measured, into the presence of nothing that cannot be properly experienced or that, as he says in speaking about not speaking, "calls for another syntax ... written completely otherwise."[36] We can see this in two key texts that are in direct response to

Blanchot: "Pas" (1986) and *Demeure: Fiction et témoignage* (1998).[37] *Pas* in French can be translated either as the nouns "step" or "pace," or as the negative adverb "not"; *demeure* translates as "abode" or "residence." Between these two texts, we can say what is "not" is always on the move, and yet, it also abides in the fictions we create, and in the testimonies of those fictions we offer. Nothing, then, resides within us, but only as a step beyond—or *Le Pas Au-dela*, the title of one of Blanchot's fragmentary texts (*The Step Beyond* but also *The Not Beyond*), in which he writes: "Only the *nomadic* affirmation *remains*."[38] Derrida intuits this Hegelian rhythm between moving and abiding where the "pas" is forever situated in movement. But because Hegel is a rhythm that operates *beyond* the text, a measure not thereby measured, Hegel only enters Derrida's two texts as if he is standing apart from them.

In "Pas," Derrida refers to Blanchot's 1953 *récit* entitled *Celui qui ne m'accompagnait pas* (*The One Who Was Standing Apart from Me*) as a text "apparently still very Hegelian" and yet at the same time still "self-evidently far from a certain Hegel." Why does this text simultaneously remain and depart from Hegel? Because, in an apparent quote from Blanchot: "Speaking man exercises at once the negation of the existent of which he speaks and of his own existence, and this negation is exercised *starting from* his power to *distance himself from self*, to be other than his being."[39] Here the negating power to step beyond oneself is the power that brings language into being, for as the word distances itself from its referent, so the one speaking distances herself from her being, just as Hegel would say that language as word-signification involves a concrete negativity in which what is outward, as intuition, is made inward through intelligence.[40] But this starting point of negation is also *not* the traditional Hegel insofar as what lingers in language, and the language of literature especially, is not substance turned into subject, but rather the very death that infects the initiating power, so that subjectivity as intelligence or mind can never absolutize itself (in knowledge, in presence, in *Geist*), but is forever passing itself by, distancing itself, effacing itself, making a *faux pas*.[41] And yet this stepping between the Hegel that is and the Hegel that is not is precisely an abiding with Hegel who has always encouraged this movement, this faltering step, which Blanchot describes as the very *initiation* of the dialectic (not its culmination or sublation), or, as he immediately qualifies, "the experience which none experiences, the experience of death."[42]

In *Demeure*, Derrida points out what might seem merely an incidental reference to Hegel in Blanchot's *The Instant of My Death*. The Château before which the young man in the story had awaited his execution was spared the fate of all the other farmhouses in the vicinity, for when the Nazi army lieutenant returned and noticed the date 1807 inscribed on the front, suggesting a certain nobility, he did not commit the Château to flames. But what was in that date? Blanchot tells us: this was the year when Napoleon, riding through Jena, passed beneath the windows of Hegel's *demeure*, inspiring the philosopher to remark that there in the figure of the great French Emperor went the "spirit of the world." This remark may seem disingenuous, given that Hegel's house was later ransacked and pillaged by French soldiers, except that "Hegel knew how to distinguish the empirical and the essential."[43] Now Derrida cannot resist this remark—both Blanchot's and Hegel's, or each as the imprint of the other. "This Château becomes a palimpsest for the entire history of Europe."[44] 1807 becomes, that is, a trace, and the *demeure* a text on which the trace of all of Europe shimmers, a trace not merely of the *Geist* embodied in the figure of Napoleon, and his European campaigns, but of a Hegel who can only see that *Geist* in passing, before it despoils his own *demeure*, just as Nazism will later do to the soul of Europe. Within the comment made in passing, Hegel both emerges and disappears, a "spectral shadow," Derrida tells us earlier, "who will not be long in passing."[45] At the place of abiding, then, is a stepping beyond. Derrida wishes he could abide with Hegel here, and in fact admits that, if there were time—if he could hold time open to the immediate present—he "would insert here, in a big book, an immense chapter on Hegel and Blanchot via Mallarmé."[46] (A book for which *Igitur* would therefore be the trace.). But in reality the plan amounts to nothing, except as a testimonial to the haunting nature of Hegel's negation that, through Mallarmé, through Blanchot, reverberates in the passing or vacillating "pas" of the text (Derrida's *Demeure*, which remains; Derrida's book on Hegel and Blanchot, which does not).[47] Instead, we are left with Blanchot's text, the autobiography that is both fiction and testimony, but which, ultimately, as far as Blanchot the author is concerned, "confesses *nothing*—in short, gives nothing, nothing to be known except his death, his inexistence, addressing himself to another in whom he trusts the instant that he confides *everything as nothing* to him."[48]

We should note that this "everything as nothing," which we might see as a reconciliation of opposites in the classic sense with which early German Idealism was obsessed, now takes place only at the instant of confiding with the other that (or who) is never fully present, be it Hegel or death or language or God or Nothing itself, but that (or who) one also cannot avoid speaking about, as if it is always present. This simultaneous abiding/passing is at work in Derrida's most explicit discussion on nothing, the 1987 essay "Comment ne pas parler: Dénégations," published in translation as "How to Avoid Speaking: Denials," but which could just as well be translated "How not to Speak," so as to better capture the dual nature of keeping silent and of speaking in the right way (or not in the wrong way).[49] Here too Hegel remains largely unspoken, as Derrida tries to place the haunting question of nothing in language through such figures as Plato, Pseudo-Dionysus, Meister Eckhart and Heidegger, not by focusing on nothing as Nothing, and even less by focusing on a Hegelian "negation of negation,"[50] but by focusing on apophasis, that is, on how one might speak about, or avoid speaking about, or avoid speaking improperly about, nothing. The "place" becomes of crucial importance in his *dénégations* or denials— the place of the denial in one's speaking, but also, taking us forward to 1998's *Demeure*, the denial of Hegel as the place at which Hegel and his negation abides in their most potent state, as passing. In the Postscript to the essay, Derrida alludes to Heidegger's comment (made to students) that if he were to write a theology (something we know the young Heidegger had contemplated) he would not allow the word *being* to enter it, that there would be no place for *being*, even *Being*. But the conditional tense ("Heidegger's pass, impasse, or dodge"[51]) suggests to Derrida a *pas d'écriture*, a step of writing that is also not writing, and we might suggest this *pas d'écriture* is in operation as well for the later Derrida in *Demeure*, who states that, if time were not a factor, he would write an immense book on Hegel and Blanchot, a book that remains unwritten, a step beyond.

The step of writing, of speaking, of philosophizing that is also *not* writing or speaking or philosophizing is the *pas* that accompanies all of Derrida's reflections on Hegel and nothing. This is even the case for the much earlier texts devoted directly to Hegel: "From Restricted to General Economy: A Hegelianism without Reserve" (1967), "The Pit and the Pyramid" (1971), and *Glas* (1974).[52] In the latter text's left-hand column devoted to Hegel, Derrida writes, "Yet death does not resolve the contradiction [inherent within the self proper]. To say 'on the contrary' would be too simple and one-sided. One must again speak of relief: the *Aufhebung* is indeed the contradiction of the contradiction and of the noncontradiction, the unity as well of this contradiction. Here, strictly, unity and contradiction are the same."[53] Tolling the bell of Fichte, the young Schelling and the young Hegel, and yet pushing Hegel's *Aufhebung* to its logical self-inflicted conclusion, Derrida's thoughts here both are emblematic of *Glas*'s very structure (Hegel the philosopher standing apart from, or in contra*diction* to, the artist Genet), and return us to the "everything as nothing," whereby everything that is the text making up *Glas* is organized around an absent middle, the blank margin that separates the two columns, philosopher and artist, entailing a rhythm that oscillates between the two sides.[54]

What we can see emerge here is how self-conscious being (subjectivity, autonomous self, transcendental "I," etc.) reveals its creative powers only through its internal negation, and its internal negation only through its creative powers. This is why literature and the literary become so central to Blanchot's entire *oeuvre* and to Derrida's philosophical engagement (with Blanchot, with Hegel, but also with every other thinker in whom he entangles himself). Both writers operate as *literary thinkers*, which is to say, both see the experience of self-conscious thinking as a fundamentally rhythmic and tonal play between creative freedom and self-abandoning thought. And the measurement of this play—its very measurability—belongs not to placing nor positioning nor founding but to the intensity of negativity as it plays itself across and between and into the gap of the two sides. In Jean-Luc Nancy's words, "nothing that is nothing 'at bottom' and that is only the nothing of a leap into nothing, is the negativity that is not a resource, but the affirmation of ek-sistent tension: its intensity, the intensity or the surprising *tone* of existence."[55]

5 Toward the Present: Nancy's Restless Thought

Nancy worked out the intense rhythmic, trembling nature of this Hegelian tone in his text *Hegel: L'inquietudé du négatif* (1997; translated as *Hegel: The Restlessness of the Negative* [2002]), and it is in this text on the negating of Hegel that the problem of modernity we have been tracing out, that of self-consciousness, freedom and self-begetting, culminates, and culminates absolutely in negativity (even as a kind of absolution).[56] Nancy, as a close interlocutor with Blanchot and Derrida, only ever sees negativity as activity, as an act, yet an act that involves taking our foundational acts of consciousness, freedom, and self-creation outside of themselves. We might say it is the act of the act as non-act, except we can't *say* this without spurring the non-act—or death—into action.

Here Nancy employs Hegel's reconciliatory power toward the language of separation and relation. If the self begets itself by means of separating itself out from the rest of the world, by separating the outside from the inside, the separation, as an act of distancing, is already operative within, so that the self necessitates a separating of itself from itself. How then does it reconcile itself as both the actor and the one being acted upon, as the separator and the separated? How does it renew relation with itself? The self has to negate its separation. There is nothing not Hegelian here, even read in the most conventional sense. But to penetrate this act of negation, one needs to go further than standard readings of dialectic. Here Nancy returns us to language, along the distinct paths of Blanchot and Derrida. "To penetrate negativity demands 'another language' than the language of representation."[57] Representational language involves a language of separation, where concepts and propositions are made distinct from their predicates through the process of signification. To move to another language is, for Nancy, not now a move to the "Outside," or the "Night," or even *différance*, but a move to "thought"—a move seemingly very Hegelian, insofar as it is "not to speak a mysterious extra language" nor "to enter the ineffable," yet it is a move that subjects Hegel's ideal mind to its own negating power. "Thought is not language: it is beyond it, beyond the exteriority of the relation between word and thing." It nevertheless *functions* like a language, inasmuch "as it articulates things in the play of their differences."[58] What is this functioning that, at the same time, is not the normal functioning of language, because it is "the exhaustion of determined signification"?[59] It is the manifesting of the play itself, of the restlessness, which restores relation, a relation that—and we've seen this now in several iterations—is a relation between relation and separation, or a negation of their separation, which Nancy calls manifestation, so that the negative activity "manifests manifestation"—"But it manifests it as other than itself."[60]

The thinking self, then, or the self of thought, is the self becoming self-conscious of going outside itself to maintain a relation to its own separation. "The subject is the experience of the power of division, of ex-position or abandonment of self."[61] And this, Nancy will say, is the basis of self's freedom—not a freedom to make decisions in the authenticity of the self before nothing, nor a freedom based on rights and liberties, but a freedom to liberate self from itself. "One cannot say that the self is free, for such a *being* is in itself the negation of freedom. Freedom, to the contrary, is the negation of this negation, or negativity for itself."[62] This constitutes absolute liberation.

We use Nancy by way of conclusion because in Nancy we see a clear through line from Bataille to Blanchot to Derrida, but a line that gains its coordinates invariably and constituitively from Hegel and his active negation, and carries it forward. "We must begin, then," wrote Nancy in his first published text devoted fully to Hegel, "by moving around Hegel's text," and this "around" becomes across, through, in, out of, and by means of Hegel's restless negativity, or in both separation and relation to Hegel's negation.[63] If the absolute subject of metaphysics requires separation, it is negation that, ironically, restores relation, by offering an end to the self's separation of itself from the world, by drawing community back into the self's fold. In *The Inoperative Community* Nancy will draw directly upon Bataille to point out the rupture needed here, a rupture at the heart of Bataille's reformulation of "Why is there something rather than nothing?" as, "why must there be *what I know?*," an extreme rupture "so deep that only the silence of ecstasy answers it." This rupture, Nancy says, "defines a *relation* to the absolute," where the absolute, etymologically, separates us, just as the ecstasy places us outside, so that negativity ruptures both the self-contained Self as much as the totality of (Hegel's) Being.[64] It is toward this sense that Blanchot, in responding directly to Nancy's "la communauté désoeuvrée," will conclude that the community, as much as it unworks its own sufficiency, by being open to its possibilities beyond itself, is also *inavouable*, or unavowable. It cannot say what it needs to say. So Blanchot concludes his response to Nancy by re-invoking Wittgenstein:

> Wittgenstein's all too famous and all too often repeated precept, "Whereof one cannot speak, there one must be silent"—given that by enunciating it he has not been able to impose silence upon himself—does indicate that in the final analysis one has to talk in order to remain silent. But with what kind of words?[65]

Blanchot will here anticipate Derrida's essay on how to avoid speaking, written three or so years later. But Nancy will have his answer too: words made manifest in the restless movement of the negative, Hegel's movement, but also, taking us to Bataille's limit, a "knowing of restlessness" that "absolutely negates the independence and consistency of all self-certainty," and brings us to an absolute knowing of "we."[66] This "we" Nancy describes, avowedly, with Hegel's own words: "the absolute ... from the beginning, is and wants to be in itself and for itself *near to us*."[67] This reconciliation of separation and relation becomes "concrete negativity."[68] But its concretion is never fixed, never at rest. It is forever in movement, Hegel's immanent rhythm, like the rhythm between meter and accent, which Hegel tells us "results from the floating center and the unification of the two."[69] Nancy, right from the beginning, as an understanding of beginning as nothing, beginning *qua nihilo*, calls this rhythm a "meter without poetry... discourse without accent."[70] In the rhythm of this floating center, we lose ourselves, in order that we might begin to create ourselves anew, together.

Notes

1. Hans-Georg Gadamer, *Hegel's Dialectic: Five Hermeneutical Studies*, trans. Christopher Smith (New Haven: Yale University Press, 1976), 65.
2. Immanuel Kant, *Critique of Pure Reason*, trans. Norman Kemp Smith (London: Macmillan, 1933), 451.
3. Ibid., 385.
4. G. W. F. Hegel, *Faith and Knowledge*, trans. Walter Cerf and H.S. Harris (Albany: State University of New York Press, 1977), 190.
5. Ibid., 191.

6. G. W. F. Hegel, *Phenomenology of Spirit*, trans. A.V. Miller (Oxford: Oxford University Press, 1977), 493.
7. G. W. F. Hegel, *Elements of the Philosophy of Right*, trans. Allen W. Wood (Cambridge: Cambridge University Press, 1991), 22–23.
8. Ibid., 41.
9. Ibid., 282.
10. See, for example, Jacques Derrida's two "political" essays in *Rogues: Two Essays on Reason*, trans. Pascale-Anne Brault and Michael Naas (Stanford: Stanford University Press, 2003). On the one hand, Derrida writes, "As soon as there is sovereignty, there is abuse of power and a rogue state. Abuse is the law of use; it is the law itself, the 'logic' of a sovereignty that can reign only by not sharing" (102). On the other hand, Derrida concludes the second essay: "it would be imprudent and hasty, in truth hardly *reasonable*, to oppose unconditionally, that is head-on, a sovereignty that is itself unconditional and indivisible. One cannot combat, *head-on*, *all* sovereignty, sovereignty *in general*, without threatening at the same time beyond the nation-state figure of sovereignty, the classical principles of freedom and self-determination" (158).
11. Hegel, *Elements of the Philosophy of Right*, 41–42 (italics added).
12. The close relationship between German Idealism and Existentialism is fully explored in what might be seen as a companion to this volume: *The Palgrave Handbook of German Idealism and Existentialism*, ed. Jon Stewart (Basingstoke: Palgrave Macmillan, 2020).
13. Søren Kierkegaard, *Concluding Unscientific Postscript to* Philosophical Fragments, *Vol. 1*, trans. Howard V. Hong and Edna H. Hong (Princeton: Princeton University Press, 1992), 118.
14. Fyodor Dostoevsky, "The Dream of the Ridiculous Man," in *The Very Best Short Stories of Fyodor Dostoevsky*, trans. David Magarshak (New York: Modern Library, 2001), 265.
15. Ibid., 285.
16. Friedrich Nietzsche, *Thus Spoke Zarathustra*, trans. Adrian Del Caro and Robert Pippin (Cambridge: Cambridge University Press, 2006), Second Part, "On Self-Overcoming," 90.
17. See especially "The Dialectic of the Real and the Phenomenological Method in Hegel: Complete Text of the Sixth through Ninth Lectures of the Academic Year 1934–1935," in *Introduction to the Reading of Hegel*, trans. James H. Nichols, Jr., ed. Allan Bloom (Ithaca: Cornell University Press, 1969), esp. 199ff.
18. Georges Bataille, *Inner Experience*, trans. Stuart Kendall (Albany: State University of New York, 2014), 111.
19. In *The Bataille Reader*, ed. Fred Botting and Scott Wilson (Oxford: Blackwell, 1997), 280. The original essay "Hegel, Death and Sacrifice" appeared in *Deucalion*, 5 (1955), and was translated by Jonathan Strauss, *Yale French Studies*, 78 (1990), 9–28.
20. Bataille, *Inner Experience*, 113.
21. Bataille, *Inner Experience*, 112.
22. Hegel, *Phenomenology of Spirit*, 9.
23. "*Das Nichts selbst nichtet*," or "Nothing itself nothings," Heidegger wrote in his 1929 essay "Was ist Metaphysik?," or "What is Metaphysics?" (in *Pathmarks*, ed. William McNeill, trans. David Farrell Krell [Cambridge: Cambridge University Press, 1998], 90).
24. Maurice Blanchot, *The Space of Literature*, trans. Ann Smock (Lincoln: University of Nebraska Press, 1982), 110.
25. See Bataille's "Letter to X, Lecturer on Hegel," in *The Bataille Reader*, 296–299.
26. Blanchot, *The Space of Literature*, 112.
27. In *The Instant of My Death* (trans. Elizabeth Rottenberg [Stanford: Stanford University Press, 2000], 5, 9), Blanchot describes the family who, about to witness the young man of the house before the firing squad, are asked to move back inside, and who in their retreat are "silent, as if everything had already been done." For the young man himself, spared of his execution, there was a feeling that "changed what there remained for him of existence. As if the death outside of him could only henceforth collide with the death in him. 'I am alive. No, you are dead.'"

28. Blanchot, *The Space of Literature*, 117.
29. Maurice Blanchot, *Writing of the Disaster*, trans. Ann Smock (Lincoln: University of Nebraska Press, 1986, 1995), 112–113. Blanchot continues: "The enigma of rhythm—dialectical-nondialectical, no more than the other is other… That we should speak in order to make sense of rhythm—which is not sensible—perceptible and meaningful: such is the mystery which traverses us" (113).
30. Maurice Blanchot, *The Work of Fire*, trans. Charlotte Mandell (Stanford: Stanford University Press, 1995), 307–308. In the very next line of the new paragraph, we read, "This new motion, which Hegel calls the Thing Itself, plays a vital role in the literary undertaking" (308). Kevin Hart describes literature for Blanchot this way: "Released from the concept's grip, literature shakes itself free of death as a shaping force and in that movement renders negativity unemployed. Literature will have no work to do—or, if you prefer, its work will *be* this nothing." *The Dark Gaze: Maurice Blanchot and the Sacred* (Chicago: University of Chicago Press, 2004), 86.
31. Maurice Blanchot, *The Infinite Conversation*, trans. Susan Hanson (Minneapolis: University of Minnesota Press, 1993), 35.
32. Blanchot, *Space of Literature*, 109.
33. Hegel, *Phenomenology of Spirit*, 19.
34. Michel Foucault, "Maurice Blanchot: The Thought from Outside," in *Foucault/Blanchot*, trans. Jeffry Mehlman and Brian Massumi (New York: Zone Books, 1987), 15.
35. Ibid., 19.
36. Jacques Derrida, "How to Avoid Speaking: Denials," trans. Ken Frieden, in *Languages of the Unsayable*, eds. Sanford Budick and Wolfgang Iser (Stanford: Stanford University Press, 1987), 4.
37. Jacques Derrida, "Pas," translated "Pa*ce Not*(s)," in *Parages*, trans. and ed. John Leavy (Stanford: Stanford University Press, 2011); *Demeure: Fiction and Testimony*, trans. Elizabeth Rottenberg (Stanford: Stanford University Press, 1998).
38. Maurice Blanchot, *The Step Not Beyond*, trans. Lycette Nelson (Albany: State University of New York, 1993), 33.
39. Derrida, "Pa*ce Not*(s)," 85. In a note, the translator admits he cannot find this exact quote in Blanchot, even though it is found in altered form within the essay most imbued with Hegel, "Literature and the Right to Death." See "Pa*ce Not*(s)," 255, fn. 37; and *The Works of Fire*, 324, in a paragraph which culminates in the following: "Negation is tied to language. When I first begin, I do not speak in order to say something; rather, a nothing demands to speak, nothing speaks, nothing finds its being in speech, and the being of speech is nothing."
40. As in the *Zusatz* of §462, in *Philosophy of Mind*, trans. A.V. Miller (Oxford: Oxford University Press, 1971), 220–221. Derrida treats Hegel's "semiology" directly in his essay "The Pit and the Pyramid" (1971) published in *Margins of Philosophy*, trans. Alan Bass (Chicago: Chicago University Press, 1982).
41. Derrida, "Pa*ce Not*(s)," 85. Derrida would also add here, being exposed to *différance*.
42. Derrida, "Pa*ce Not*(s)," 85; Blanchot, *The Writing of the Disaster*, 68.
43. Blanchot, *Instant of My Death*, 7. The historical date, Derrida points out in a footnote (112–113, fn. 16), was actually 1806, the autumn of which Hegel was finalizing and sending off his manuscript of the *Phenomenology of Spirit*.
44. Derrida, *Demeure*, 82.
45. Ibid., 63.
46. Ibid., 83–84.
47. In a footnote, Derrida alludes to a letter Hegel wrote to his friend Niethammer while at Jena, worried that the manuscript of *Phenomenology of Spirit* he had just completed and had just sent off to his publisher—two copies—would get lost in transit. "My loss would indeed be too great" (*Demeure*, 112–113, fn. 16). Here the essential is all too reliant upon the empirical, and Hegel cannot bear to see his Spirit fall to nothing.
48. Ibid., 44.

49. Derrida, "How to Avoid Speaking," 3–70. Derrida's "Comment ne pas parler: Dénégations" first appeared in his *Psyché: Inventions de l'autre* (Paris: Galilée, 1987), 535–595.
50. Derrida, "How to Avoid Speaking," 30: "Despite appearances, here we are involved in a thinking that is essentially alien to dialectic… even if it is difficult to read Hegel without taking account of an apophatic tradition that was not foreign to him (at least by the mediation of Bruno, hence Nicholas of Cusa and of Meister Eckhart, etc.).''
51. Ibid., 60.
52. "From Restricted to General Economy: A Hegelianism without Reserve," in *Writing and Difference*, trans. Alan Bass (London: Routledge, 1978); for "The Pit and the Pyramid," see fn. 40 above; *Glas*, trans. John Leavy and Richard Rand (Lincoln: University of Nebraska Press, 1986).
53. Derrida, *Glas*, 139.
54. For more on *Glas's* relation to Hegel's negation, see my *Hegel and the Art of Negation* (London: I.B. Tauris, 2014), Chapter 5, esp. 101–112.
55. Jean-Luc Nancy, "The Surprise of the Event," in *Hegel after Derrida*, ed. Stuart Barnett (London: Routledge, 1998), 102; *Being Singular Plural*, trans. Robert D. Richardson and Anne E. O'Byrne (Stanford: Stanford University Press, 2000), 173–174 (translation slightly modified).
56. Jean-Luc Nancy, *Hegel: The Restlessness of the Negative*, trans. Jason Smith and Steven Miller (Minneapolis: Minnesota University Press, 2002), 28.
57. Ibid., 34.
58. Ibid., 35.
59. Ibid.
60. Ibid.: "only language, exposing itself of itself as infinite relation and separation, also exposes this being-of-itself-outside-itself-in-the-other that is manifestation." Here, in this extension of Hegel, we get close to the making present or the being of the nothing that was Blanchot's concern, though now much more "positively" Hegelian.
61. Ibid., 43.
62. Ibid., 70.
63. Jean-Luc Nancy, *The Speculative Remark (One of Hegel's Bon Mots)*, trans. Céline Surprenant (Stanford: Stanford University Press, 2001), 23. Cf. Hass, *Hegel and the Art of Negation*, 119–127.
64. Jean-Luc Nancy, *The Inoperative Community*, ed. Peter Connor, trans. Peter Connor et al. (Minneapolis: Minnesota University Press, 1991), 5–6; Bataille, *Inner Experience*, 111.
65. Maurice Blanchot, *The Unavowable Community*, trans. Pierre Joris (Barrytown, NY: Station Hill, 1988), 56.
66. Nancy, *Hegel: The Restlessness of the Negative*, 75.
67. Ibid., 78; Hegel, *Phenomenology of Spirit*, 47, trans. Modified by Nancy. Italics added.
68. Nancy, *Hegel: The Restlessness of the Negative*, 56.
69. Hegel, *Phenomenology of Spirit*, 38. Hegel continues: "So, too, in the philosophical proposition the identification of Subject and Predicate is not meant to destroy the difference between them, which the form of the proposition expresses; their unity, rather, is meant to emerge as a harmony" (ibid.).
70. Nancy, *The Speculative Remark*, 101. See also Andrew W. Hass, "Creatio qua Nihil: Negation from the Generative to the Performative," in *The Meaning and Power of Negativity*, eds. Ingolf U. Dalferth and Trevor W. Kimball (Tübingen: Mohr Siebeck, 2021).

Apocalypse

Agata Bielik-Robson

1 Introduction: The Harnessed Lightning—Tarrying with the Apocalypse in Hegel and Derrida

How to connect the topic of religion in poststructuralist thought with German Idealism? There are so many ways in which the religious thought of Kant, Hegel and Schelling influenced Derrida, Deleuze, and Lacan that it is simply impossible to cover them all in one essay. I will thus focus on the specific legacy which links religion, dialectics, and deconstruction—or, more precisely, the thread that begins in Hegel's sublation of religion into philosophy, weaves through his dialectical "tarrying with the negative," and then, after more than a century of critical evolution, metamorphoses into Derrida's deconstructive method. Religion plays a crucial role in this process: just as for Hegel, the dialectical "tarrying with the negative" is a philosophical synonym of "tarrying with the apocalypse," for Derrida too, deconstruction is a "delayed destruction" which defers the apocalyptic Last Judgment.

Yet, with the passage from Hegel to Derrida, religion also multiplies into religions: while for the former the only religious horizon to deal with was Reformed Christianity, for the latter it is Christianity *and* Judaism or a certain form of a Marrano Judeo-Christianity where the Christian desire for the apocalyptic *parousia* is 'held in check' by the Jewish doctrine of restraint/*retrait* that defers the eschatological finale. Derrida's concept of *différance*, which inaugurates the poststructuralist turn, can thus also be conceived in the postsecular perspective as a Jewish form of tarrying with the Christian desire for the apocalypse. For, unlike in the Christian tradition, where the apocalyptic finale brings more hope than fear and is avidly awaited as a positive renewal of creation, Jewish thought is more cautious in its

---

A. Bielik-Robson (✉)
University of Nottingham, Nottingham, UK
e-mail: agata.bielik-robson@nottingham.ac.uk

approach to the messianic end, perceived as primarily a catastrophic event. Talmud often stresses the connection between the fall of mankind and the painful "birth pangs of the Messiah" who will come to judge the world and find it irreparably wanting. The apocalyptic end, therefore, will indeed be the end of the world as we know it and it may be good news only to those who, in this world, have nothing to lose—or, as Marx put it, deeply informed by this antinomian messianic logic, nothing to lose but their chains.[1] For the rest, however, it is a cataclysmic prospect of an annihilating Judgment which will have repeated the Flood or any other divine *khurban* that, in the past, threatened to put an end to *experimentum mundi*, only this time with full success. Hence the characteristic reserve of the Talmudic sage who accepts the inevitability of the messianic advent, but would like to delay it: "May he come, but I do not want to see him."[2] This *but*—the reservation which expresses a desire to defer the apocalyptic end/judgment without negating its inevitability—constitutes a natural bedrock of dialectical thinking, operative long before Hegel. It will be my aim to show that this dialectical deferment of the apocalypse, started by the talmudic rabbis, can also be glimpsed in Hegel himself. A short detour through Franz Rosenzweig, Derrida's important precursor, will confirm this conjecture, by demonstrating that a form of the restraint/postponement involved in the concept of Jewish revelation can also be found in Hegel's master-slave dialectic.

This reserve, however, should not be confused with Carl Schmitt's concept of the *katechon* as the "restrainer of the apocalypse." Although the religious motif of tarrying with the apocalypse creates a political theology of its own, it is polemical toward Schmitt's enterprise, advocating a *simple*, non-dialectical postponement of the apocalyptic event, which can be paraphrased in the statement: "May he not come *and* I don't want to see him."[3] The role of the earthly *katechon* is to delay the apocalypse as a potentially catastrophic event (here Schmitt shows more affinity with the Jewish understanding of the messianic end than with the Christian, more hopeful, one), but also negate its relevance for worldly politics in the manner of a Grand Inquisitor who, even when faced with Christ's Second Coming, would still choose not to see him. The alternative notion, which Rosenzweig and Derrida propose explicitly and which can also be found in Hegel in hindsight, is restraint as *tsimtsum*: originally a contraction of God, due to which the divine limits its power in relation with the world.[4] Here, the restraint of the infinite creative-destructive force comes not from without, but from within—and, precisely as such, constitutes the defining feature of the divine power. When conceived under the aegis of *tsimtsum*—God's self-contraction, self-limitation, self-retraction, even self-negation—monotheistic religion appears as the opposite of the theological doctrine of absolute potency, the nominalist *potentia absoluta et inordinata*: it redefines the notion of power which now proves itself precisely in the capability of self-limitation. The self-limitation, dismissed by William Ockham as a secondary form of lesser power, *potentia ordinata*, would thus determine the specific difference of the monotheistic faith out of the sources of Judaism.[5] While the so-called pagan pre-monotheistic gods may be worshiped as absolutes, full of unscathed vitality and power, the proper Mosaic distinction lies in what Derrida calls a *restraint, le trait de re-trait*, a characteristic feature of God in withdrawal. This God restrains his wrath so that the world can evolve and eventually stand on its feet as an autonomous entity (as in Isaiah), contracts his presence to make it endurable for humans (as in the Arc of Covenant, described in the rabbinic midrashes), or diminishes his lights in order not to overshadow the last sphere of emanation which is the material world (as in the kabbalistic thinkers). The restraint within the *tsimtsum* paradigm is thus originally and paradigmatically a *self-restraint*: a divine gesture itself which—as in Dickinson's great phrasing—"eases" the blinding light of the revelation to the "children of the world" and which the talmudic tradition associates with God's 'lenience.'[6]

The *tsimtsum* paradigm is thus the very opposite of the notion of restraint which emerges in Schmitt, who is wholly indebted to the nominalist theology of sovereignty as *potentia absoluta*. Although arguing with Hans Blumenberg on the issue of Trinity, Schmitt must nonetheless agree with the latter when he quotes Goethe's famous sentence—"*Nemo contra deum nisi deus ipse...*] Goethe believes that ,'A god can only be balanced by another god'"—and then concludes, "That power should restrict itself is absurd. It is only restricted, in turn, by another power."[7] The Schmittian "restrainer of the apocalypse"—the eschatological event in which God will reveal his absolute power to destroy what he created—can thus only "hold back the end of the world" from without or even *against* the divine intervention, which then creates an antithetical relation between God and the world, conceived as counter-principles (*Gegenprinzipen*) in the state of rivalry: precisely as in the Cappadocian concept of Trinity as a *stasis*—eternal conflict—where God the Father, representing the infinite divine power, is opposed by the Son, the God incarnate, representing the interests of the created world. As we shall yet see, the *tsimtsum* paradigm, which Derrida evokes in "Faith and Knowledge," while talking about "the religious trait or retreat,"[8] is not completely free from antagonistic moments, which are inevitable in the uneven relation between God and the world, but it never allows for a *stasis*. that is, a dualistic eternal conflict of the counter-principles that can only be reconciled by the third supervening agency of the Holy Spirit. Once the restraint gets inscribed into the operations of the divine power itself, the relation between God and the world becomes less the matter of a rigid antithesis and more of a gradual difference—just as in the *tsimtsum* metaphor of "dimming of the lights" where the original *Or Ein Sof* (the Light of the Infinite) obfuscates and attenuates itself as "Lightning to the Children eased / With explanation kind." The revelation, therefore, "must dazzle gradually." I will thus argue that this *reductio lucis*—the diminution of the light—is best visible in Derrida's concept of *différance* as, at once, the differentiation, deferral and diffusion of the blinding origin/center which itself de-centers and withdraws from presence.

The alternative idea of the restraint as a gradual *attenuation* or *easing* results in a very different understanding of faith, which radically departs from the power-oriented notion of religious submission to the divine *potestas*—from Hegel to Derrida, the political and philosophical practice that derives from what I call here the *tsimtsum* paradigm. This paradigm consists in maintaining a distance/difference between God and the world, that is, between the all-mighty and sovereign power which can create and destroy, and the weaker pole of this relation, the created world as dependent on creative force but, at the same time, striving for as much independence as it can get. This metaphysical struggle for independence, which applies the strategy of distancing/differentiation, involves something more than just a defense against the infinite power: it also reclaims the messianic expectation, which Schmitt excluded from his concept of the *katechon*. Yet, it does not reclaim it in the manner of the messianic apocalyptics who, similarly to Jacob Taubes, avidly await God's ultimate revelation and hasten the end of the world. The messianic political theology, based on the notion of restraint/*tsimtsum*, not merely defers but also feeds on the apocalyptic force of divine revelation, even if it can take it only in a pharmakonic small dose. Neither simply restraining it, nor simply hastening it, this new formula takes a third dialectical position between the *katechon* and the *apocalyptic*, which consists in "easing the lightning to the children": the world as God's child—weak, fragile, and potentially exposed to the infinite force of creation and destruction, even if it withdraws and self-diminishes—must nonetheless find a way to use the revelatory power of the *eschaton* for immanent purposes. This use, however, does not exhaust itself in the maneuver which Eric Voegelin famously criticized as the "immanentisation of the *eschaton*": a hubristic attempt of modernity to domesticate the powers of transcendence and make them serve the materialistic utopias of a "paradise on earth."[9] It has a different goal: while it does not negate transcendence, it nonetheless wants to make immanence stronger—as strong as possible within the uneven relation with God.

Hegel, Rosenzweig, and Derrida are the true masters of such carefully mediated messianic political theology: while they offer different solutions, deriving from their disparate philosophical and religious traditions, their common denominator is the variation on the theme of the *utilization of the apocalypse*. In Hegel, the philosophical sublation of the apocalyptic eschatology—the message of the redemptive/annihilating end of the world—plays a major role in his philosophy of history, particularly in *Phenomenology of Spirit*, where the apocalyptic *Furie der Zerstörung*, "fury of destruction," pressing toward the end of all things—and to be witnessed in its full terrifying glory during the French Revolution—becomes an engine of the dialectical transformation of worldly reality: while it undergoes a philosophical sublation, it gets tamed and disciplined to serve the process of historical work as a "delayed destruction." The Hegelian idea of the work is thus a compromise between the passive affirmation of the worldly *status quo*, which accepts the world as it is, on the one hand, and the violent negation of the world *as such*, which leads to the apocalyptic annihilation of all being, on the other. A century later, Franz Rosenzweig—both a great Hegel scholar and a brilliant philosopher of Judaism—will prove that this dialectical neutralization of the apocalypse in the concept of work is not Hegel's original invention. According to the author of *The Star of Redemption*, it goes back to the very origin of the apocalyptic genre, which sprang up among the messianic Jewish sects of the Hellenistic era, and was already then used by Rabbinic Judaism as a defense against the powers pressing toward the grand finale: the works of the Law play exactly the same dialectical role as "work" in Hegel's *Phenomenology*. And finally, a similar mechanism will appear in the Derridean method of deconstruction which—only prima facie anti-Hegelian—continues Hegel's strategy of utilizing the 'tremendous power of the negative' in the poststructuralist decentered mode of thinking. Derrida's notion of the "apocalypse without apocalypse," which emerges in the essay "On the Apocalyptic Tone Recently Adopted in Philosophy"—apocalypse deferred and diffused—chimes perfectly with Hegel's dialectical attenuation of the energy of the negative, which now can be directed not toward the end/destruction of the world, but toward the historical working-through of its substance.

What unites these three thinkers—Hegel, Rosenzweig, and Derrida—is the conviction that without the apocalyptic genre there would be no concept of history at all: no sense of a grand messianic narrative, which stakes itself on the historical work/task and patiently transforms worldly reality, by fostering its struggle for metaphysical independence. Their messianic political theology, therefore, tarries with the common negative: the apocalyptic *nearness of God* or the danger of coming too close to the naked divine power (*korban*), which threatens to destroy the precarious worldly existence. Yet—and this is the very gist of the messianic dialectics which they put in motion—this danger is not to be simply averted: it is also to be transformed into an energy that fuels the historical process of the world's emancipation. This dialectic is possible only within the paradigm of restraint/*tsimtsum*, operative in both realms, creation and destruction: just as the world can enter the path of emancipation only because God's original withdrawal "liberated creation," the world can also enter the path of justice only because God "withdrew his anger" and contracted his powers of destruction.

2 Tarrying with the Apocalypse: Hegel

The subtitle derives from a painting by Paul Klee, *Gebannter Blitz*, which can be found in the Albertina Gallery in Vienna. This little tribute to Utopian Socialism fleshes out the secret dream of modern mankind: to harness the lightning, bring it down to earth through a complex grounding device and, instead of letting it destroy the world, make it work for the sake of material reality. But the "harnessed lightening" has also a clear religious connotation: the lightning being a traditional allegory for revelation, it represents the absolute clash between the infinite transcendent power and the finite, fragile, and weak, existence. *Apocalypsis* is, therefore, simultaneously a revelation—coming to the fore of the hidden God—and a destruction, for "no one can see God face to face and live."

But to harness the lightning means precisely to go beyond the destructive antithetical nature of this clash: it is to outwit transcendence and, in the Promethean gesture of stealing the fire, intercept its energy for worldly purposes and thus ascertain that the revelation no longer kills the world, but makes it stronger instead. Hence, Klee's painting can also be seen as belonging to the long series of pictorial allegories of the Tower of Babel, together with works by Peter Breughel: the lightning rod which harnesses the flash is a Babelian construction heading toward the sky to challenge its divine inhabitant. It thus offers the best pictorial representation of Hegelian dialectics: the secular heir of the Promethean myth of stealing the fire, the Babelian myth of challenging God, and the myth of *Apocalypsis* as the violent end of the world.

For Hegel, to tarry with the negative is most of all to tarry with the apocalyptic: with forces of fury and destruction that can either end the world or, when cunningly harnessed, make the world stronger. Hegel, therefore, might have thought about himself as a good Lutheran till the end of his life,[10] but, unlike so many other Protestant thinkers—from Kierkegaard to Karl Barth—he never wished to side with God's power against the world's weakness and then revel in the apocalyptic imagery of the latter's just and total destruction, according to the rule advocated by Kant: *pereat mundus, sed fiat iustitia*. The release of pure negativity, no longer harnessed by the dialectical *List der Vernunft* [cunning of reason]—whether in the case of the sectarian Beautiful Soul dreaming about the triumph of righteousness over the sinful material realm, or in the case of the revolutionary unleashing of an unlimited *Furie der Zerstörung* [fury of destruction]—is, for Hegel, always a sign of evil: of a failure to protect the weak element of the worldly against the creative/ destructive omnipotence of the otherworldly, incarnating itself in these two perverted figures of the subjective spirit—the Beautiful Soul and the Revolutionary, both ready to punish the extant precarious reality with the furious *ungebannter Blitz*. Hegel sides firmly with the weakness of the world: its imperfection, moral lapsarianism, death-anxious finitude, and care for the precarity of always endangered life. This strong spiritual investment in the world's initial weakness—its ontological difference in regard to God—is the very essence of both his religious commitment and political theology.[11]

Yet, as already indicated, Hegel's solution has nothing to do it with the katechonic gesture of avoidance, which simply restrains, evades and keeps at bay the apocalyptic fire of revelation/destruction. Hegel's is not the Pauline *katechon*, "the restrainer of the apocalypse," as described by Carl Schmitt, who would like to postpone the lightning and the thunder forever. Hegel's invention of dialectics is precisely intended to cut into the dualism of the restrainers and the hasteners of the apocalyptic finale. In order to protect the weaker pole of the relation between transcendence and immanence, he wants to *use* the apocalyptic fire in order to make the world stronger: to solidify its precarious *Dasein*, immunize it against the punitive furies of the divine Spirit which, within Protestant nominalist theology, is given the sovereign right to destroy what it created, as and when he wishes, obedient to nothing but his own lordly desire that needs no justification apart from *quia voluit*: "because He wanted it that way." The world, occupying the position of the slave in this metaphysical extrapolation of the master/slave dialectic, begins as absolutely weak and dependent, but eventually outwits the master, by exposing his inherent weakness. Yet, this strategy of emancipation does not consist in imitating the master, which Hegel ultimately rejects as a wrong ideal of *theosis*: man/world becoming God, and, thanks to that, as strong as God. The human-worldly strategy retains its distance, difference, and separation, by relying on the utilization of God's nihilistic and destructive attitude toward beings in a wholly different manner. This other way Hegel calls *work*, as opposed to the master's annihilating *desire*:

> Desire has reserved to itself the pure negating of the object and thereby its unalloyed feeling of self. But that is the reason why this satisfaction is itself only a fleeting one, for it lacks the side of objectivity and permanence. Work, on the other hand, is desire held in check, fleetingness staved off; in other words, work forms and shapes the thing. The negative relation to the object becomes its form and something permanent, because it is precisely for the worker that the object has independence.[12]

According to Hegel's distinction, desire—for which the apocalyptic desire for the world's annihilation serves as the paradigmatic case, just as God constitutes the paradigm of the simple "unalloyed self"—negates its object purely and disregards its independent existence, aiming at its immediate consumption as something weak and destined only to enhance the lordly power. Work, on the other hand, as desire mitigated, "held in check," subdued and cooled down, delays the destruction of its object and due to this postponement gives it shape and form, in this manner bestowing on it objectivity and permanence. Instead of destroying the world altogether, work, still utilizing the negative energy of desire, manages to destroy it methodically and partially—that is, to transform it. Work, therefore, is also a force of negativity (for pure positivity would merely issue in a passive contemplation of the world's beauty), but "held in check" and deferred, and because of that played out in the ongoing process of transformation that constitutes a dialectical compromise between simple affirmation and equally simple destruction of its object. In other words, also Hegelian, it is the *negation of negation*, which has a creative-transformative effect: the immediate destruction, resulting from the desire, becomes negated in its immediacy and thus "staved off" in its gratification. In consequence, the object is challenged in its current weak form and given a new more stable one with a specific purpose. Hegel then extrapolates this model of creative destruction to the whole world as still not fully formed and lacking purpose; from this moment on, Spirit in all its avatars—subjective, objective, and becoming-absolute—will "form and shape" the material realm with a redemptive *telos* in mind. The *eschaton*—the end of the world—will no longer threaten the world as a verdict/judgment hovering about it, but will be drawn into the very dynamic of the historical process. Instead of rushing toward apocalyptic destruction, the world will thus *develop* toward its grand finale, when it reaches "objectivity and permanence."[13]

Work as the transformation of the worldly *status quo,* therefore, changes being without destroying it: it is an absolute power, derived from the lightning of revelation/apocalypse, yet in a state of *tsimtsum*—self-contraction and self-limitation—which defers the moment of fulfillment. It works through the material world in the process of purposeful *Durcharbeiten*, the goal of which is the final affirmation of secular reality as pervaded by "objectivity and permanence," so far attributable only to the divine Absolute and its "unalloyed feeling of the self." No longer just a Pauline "passing figure of the world"—a realm of pitiful transience and ontological weakness—the material realm will have thus become as real and metaphysically strong as the Spirit which created it, and, because of that, immune to its destructive apocalyptic interventions. This is what modern theology calls the principle of the univocity of being (*univocatio entis*), here driven to its ultimate conclusion: Duns Scotus's promise that the existence of the world will one day be as strong as the existence of God, and because of that, no longer dependent on *creatio continua*, it realizes itself fully in Hegel's dialectical notion of work. At the same time, however, although containing an element of rivalry—the Lutheran *Anfechtung Gottes* clearly persists in Hegel—work does not belong to the strategies of *theosis*, the aim of which is to imitate God and become *sicut Dei*. According to Hans Blumenberg, who, similarly to Hegel, criticized the motif of "man-becoming-God" as the false *telos* of history, work is the means of human self-assertion in a world always already endangered by the uneven relationship with its Creator: its goal is not self-deification, but independence from God and assuredness of one's separate existence.[14] It is only work, therefore, which is capable of creating a safe distance between God and the world and securing the latter the desired emancipation: by harnessing the apocalyptic *Blitz*, work *incarnates* the energy of the Spirit into the texture of material reality and, in this manner, assists its struggle for recognition. Thus, while Hegel begins the history of the spirit with a *kenosis in creation*—a Christian-kabbalistic variant of *tsimtsum* taking the form of the original *Entäusserung*/ exteriorization/ self-voiding of God into the world—he also postulates a parallel *kenosis in destruction*: an attenuating diminution of the apocalyptic finale which, harnessed and disciplined, metamorphoses into the historical work.[15] While the creative *kenosis* makes the whole world the arena of divine incarnation as "the Golgotha of the Absolute Spirit"—the destructive *kenosis* allows it to incarnate the ideal of truth and justice, by transforming the immediate desire for apocalypse into a mediated process of the work which defers and diffuses the moment of self-destructive satisfaction. When tracing the lines of influence between German Idealism and poststructuralism, one cannot fail to notice that the same scheme will later return in Lacan's theory of the drives, where the system of pleasure, chained to the reality principle, defers and diffuses the advent of *jouissance*. Unlike Hegel, however, Lacan openly protests against such "diminution" and neutralizing dispersal: his slogan is a modified version of the old dictum, *pereat mundus, sed fiat jouissance*. Hegel, on the other hand, makes his pro-cosmic position absolutely clear, stating in *Philosophy of Right*: "*Fiat justitia* ought not to have *pereat mundus* as a consequence."[16]

Schiller's line, often quoted by Hegel[17]—*Die Weltgeschichte ist die Weltgericht*, "the history of the world *is* the judgment over the world"—should thus be read literally: the history of the world *is* indeed the judgment over the world, *but* delayed, deferred, and suspended. While Schiller's aphorism wholly belongs to nominalist Protestant theology, which praises the ultimate manifestation of God's infinite power in the apocalyptic execution of the Last Judgment over worldly reality, Hegel changes its meaning, by introducing a motif of deferral, attenuation, and gradual diminishment, which derives from the alternative theological paradigm of *tsimtsum* as the divine self-contraction, here taking the form of generalized *kenosis*—Spirit making itself small—operative at all levels of divine revelation, both creative and destructive. The apocalyptic judgment, therefore, no longer *hovers* over the world as a threat, but, cunningly intercepted, *works* through worldly reality as "the infinite in the finite." The world, therefore, will eventually reach its end—but it won't be a blow of divine punishment ending the *stasis* of hopeless fallenness, weakness, and mere transience, as Schiller's sentence originally suggests. It will rather be a long "staved off" fulfillment in which the world will have achieved an "objectivity and permanence" that even the most nominalist God, immersed in his infinite "unalloyed desire," would be forced to recognize.

3 The Law as the Lightning Rod: Rosenzweig

As I have already suggested, the cunning use of the "diminished" apocalypse is not exactly Hegel's original invention. It has its antecedent in the non-philosophical language of the late-Hellenistic rabbis who tarried with the apocalyptic negative in a fully developed dialectical manner avant la lettre: this is where the *tsimtsum* paradigm arises for the first time and creates a new theology of power, no longer defined by absolute infinite will, but by a faculty of self-limitation. According to Franz Rosenzweig, it is precisely the Rabbinic concept of the Law/Torah which offers the dialectical possibility of "working" as a functional transformation of the creaturely realm over against the direct revelation which always threatens to annihilate the world: the Law works as a necessary defense mechanism or a mediator of the "endurable portion" of the original violent flame of revelation, precisely as in Dickinson, "eased to the children." Torah, therefore, is a *Weltgericht*, but in the state of contraction/reduction: the works of the Law consist in the delayed destruction of the world, which results in its patient transformation, but always on the side of the world as the weaker pole to be defended in the asymmetrical relation with God. And it is precisely this delay and partial neutralization that allows the apocalyptic energy, contained within the Law as the Last Judgment deferred and differed, to be more precise in the act of targeting its object; instead of exploding the whole of creaturely reality, deemed to be fallen in its entirety and unworthy of, in Taubes's words, any "spiritual investment," it provides a more subtle missile which destroys only those aspects of worldliness which hinder its process of achieving "objectivity and permanence": transience, inertia and indifference, which the Jewish tradition associates with the amorphous sub-existence of *tohu va-vohu*, the pre-creational undifferentiated waters of chaos before they were formed by God into a manifold of separate creatures. Just as in Hegel, therefore, work continues the act of creation by different means; if God has the power of *creatio ex nihilo*, human being must resort to *continuous creative destruction*. Yet, whether these are the works of the Slave or the works of the Law, the mechanism is the same: they destroy the world in its current "passing figure" and transfigure it, by giving it a new—ethical—form which also bestows on the world "permanence and objectivity." The Law, therefore, is a dialectical bridge that connects transcendence with immanence, by simultaneously preserving the contrast between them and attenuating the destructive effect of this contrast. Rosenzweig conceives it as the tension between the world as it is and the world as redeemed (*olam ha-ba*):

The fact that the world, this world, is created and yet is in need of the future Redemption, the disquietude of this twofold thought, is *quieted in the unity of the Law*. The Law... therefore, in its diversity and power that puts everything in order, the entire "outside," namely all this-worldly life, everything that can draw up some worldly law or other, makes this world and the world to come indistinguishable. According to rabbinic legend, God himself "learns" in the Law. *In the Law, everything that can be grasped in it is this-worldly*, all created existence is already immediately endowed with life and soul for becoming content of the world to come.[18]

The Law is "this-worldly," "no longer in heaven" (*lo bashamayim hi*) and God himself "learns in it": while the Law is studied and developed here on earth by the Rabbinic hermeneutic community, God learns how to limit his power or even enjoy defeat in confrontation with his "learned children." The Law thus evolves from the codex originally revealed in the act of *matan Torah* (giving of the Law), when it serves as a means of easing the flash of transcendence to the children of immanence, into a complex system of grasping all the aspects of worldly existence, which lifts it up to the level of the world redeemed—perfect "objectivity and permanence"—able to challenge God himself and, in a typically Hegelian manner, demand recognition.[19]

Gershom Scholem—the great historian of Judaism, but also a speculative thinker with his own philosophical-messianic agenda—felt no sympathy for Rosenzweig's project, which he saw as too mellow in its wish to be "quieted in the unity of the Law," but it was nonetheless he who spotted the crucial role of the Rosenzweigian concept of the Law as a defense mechanism producing the effect of distance and delay: time and space as the proper place of the world, *olam*—and thus functioning as a sort of stopping device designed to interrupt, arrest and ease the apocalyptic fire to prevent both the subject and the world from instantaneous annihilation. In order to explain the functioning of this defense, Scholem introduces two useful metaphors. One, the traditional metaphor of lightning, symbolizes the vertiginous moment of revelation as an antagonistic clash of the transcendent in the immanent: an infectious fire that, when unstopped, burns down the soul and the world to ashes. When God reveals himself fully, there is no longer a *place*—space and time, distance and delay—for the world. The second metaphor, of his own making, is that of a "lightning rod": the device that both uses and tames the divine energy of absolute justice, by directing it toward the ground of the creaturely condition, thus making it separate, "no longer in heaven" and thanks to that operative in the creaturely realm. Between revelation itself and the ethical works of the Law functioning as the "lightning rod," there appears a moment of non-identity as the Derridean différance avant la lettre, in terms of both difference/spacing and deferral/timing, which allow the world to come to the fore and then work on its "permanence and objectivity." The following fragment from Scholem's essay refers critically to Rosenzweig, but it could just as well be targeting Hegel:

> Here, in a mode of thought deeply concerned for order, it (the anarchic element) underwent metamorphosis. The power of redemption seems to be built into the clockwork of life lived in the light of revelation, though more as restlessness than as potential destructiveness. For a thinker of Rosenzweig's rank could never remain oblivious to the truth that *redemption possesses not only a liberating but also a destructive force*—a truth which only too many Jewish theologians are loath to consider and which a whole literature takes pains to avoid.

Rosenzweig sought at least to neutralize it in a higher order of truth. If it be true that the lightning of redemption directs the universe of Judaism, then in Rosenzweig's work *the life of the Jew must be seen as the lightning rod whose task it is to render harmless its destructive power.*[20]

We could easily paraphrase Scholem's words as critical of Hegel's reformist timidity (and thus chiming well with Lacan, Comay and Žižek): If it be true that the lightning of apocalypse directs the universe of modernity, then in Hegel's work the life of the modern man must be seen as the lightning rod whose task it is to render harmless its destructive power. Scholem himself, personally more prone to apocalyptic solutions, objects to Rosenzweig's cautious ways; he reproaches him for his general intention to appease and quiet "the anarchic element." This assessment, however, is neither completely true nor fair: the lightning rod of the work and the Law does not serve to render the destructive power of apocalypse-revelation completely 'harmless' (as is indeed the case with the Schmittian *katechon*), but to make it operative and effective *in* the world and *for* the world as the dialectical bridge between the world-as-it-is and the redemptive world-to-come (*olam ha-ba*).[21] In Rosenzweig's post-Hegelian rendering, Rabbinic political theology does not simply neutralize the revelatory energy: rather, precisely as with the lightening rod, it directs this energy toward the ground, so that it can truly acquire transformative power and, as Levinas has aptly put it, "jolt the Real." *Meaningful movement jolts the Real*: the Torah as the *gebannter Blitz* works through the very structure of the world in order to make it less determined by natural laws, which condemn it to the indeterminate and all-leveling cycle of transience, and more enlightened by the laws of ethics, which respect 'the object's independence' and work toward its "permanence and objectivity" (PS 118).[22]

4 *Eucalypse, Now*: Derrida[23]

The thinker who managed to synthesize both Hegel's concept of work and Rosenzweig's emphasis on the ethical transformation of the world, by enhancing the dialectical thrust of the work as simultaneously using and taming apocalyptic energy, is the father of the poststructuralist turn himself: Jacques Derrida. In the light of what I have already said about Hegel's and Rosenzweig's tarrying with the apocalyptic/negative, Derridean deconstruction emerges as a method ideally fitting the Hegelian description of the work as *destruction deferred*: while it wards off the apocalypse, it also utilizes its destructive energy to subvert the *status quo* of worldly reality in order to keep us in constant ethical vigilance. In his essay on the "apocalyptic tone recently adopted in philosophy"—which directly refers to Kant's famous prototype but indirectly to all the contemporary Helpers/Hasteners of the Apocalypse (Derrida mentions here Heidegger, Blanchot, and Lacan)—Derrida defends deconstruction as a form of enlightenment which uses light against light or, in terms of the *tsimtsum* paradigm, forces light to self-contract and diminish. While it may be true that, in Heraclitus's words, "the lightning steers all," this flash of light must also be steered: harnessed and made to work for the sake of the world, not against it.[24] The apocalyptic frenzy, therefore, has to be partially *covered*: if it is to bring light and *not* destruction, it must be, in the Hegelian manner, "held in check." Derrida's name for this partial covering—the reduction of the light according to the *tsimtsum* paradigm—is the term antithetical to *apokalyptos*, "fully revealed": it is *eukalyptos*, "well covered."

On Derrida's account, enlightenment is not a simple secular formation, but a form of an emphatically *procosmic* religious commitment which maintains a complex relation with the apocalyptic lightning of revelation:

> It is difficult to separate the concept of secularization from the concept of *Lumières*, *Illuminisimo*, Enlightenment, or *Aufklärung*, and from the link between the Enlightenment [*Lumières*] of reason (according to Kant, for example) and the light, which is the very element in which revelation, revelations, and above all Judeo-Christian revelation have been announced and advanced. This connection between the light [*la lumière*] and Enlightenment [*les Lumières*] is already the site of secularization [*sécularisation*]. This is already the analogy that permits *the passage between religion and the world* [le siècle], *between revelation and the world*.[25]

Secularization, therefore, does not announce the age of atheism, but a more gradual passage from the traditional acosmic religion centered around the transcendent God to the modern procosmic "religion of new times" (Hegelian "*Religion der neuen Zeiten*") which de-centers the Absolute and focuses on the world as the arena of eschatological scenarios. As belonging to Enlightenment, deconstruction is always on the side of justice—as Derrida famously claims, "deconstruction is justice"—but this is not the otherworldly absolute justice which wishes the world to vanish according to the rule *pereat mundus, sed fiat iustitia*, enthusiastically affirmed by Kant[26]: it belongs to the *saeculum* or the world (*le siècle*). Voegelin would thus say that deconstruction indeed "immanentizes the *eschaton*" of absolute justice in order to turn it into a mundane justice, working in and through our every ethical and political decision, but, pace Voegelin, Derrida does not perceive this immanentization as a distortion or error. Justice is "no longer in heaven," *lo bashamayim*, which means that it must offer a mediation between the transcendent ideal and the immanent real—without giving in to too much of a betrayal. Betray we must, says Derrida, but the enlightenment gives precisely the right amount of light to vigilantly watch over the process of mediation. The slogan of Derrida's political theology could thus be a paraphrase of Beckett's famous line on failure: *betray, betray again, betray better*.

The first stage of this process is the dismantling of the apocalyptic discourse of the absolute light as *blindly* following the never questioned desire to reach naked truth and see it in all its beaming glory, *sonnenklar* and crystal-clear. In his critique of this enlightenment *Lichtzwang*, light-compulsion, Derrida continues Nietzsche's precursorial project of "gay science," which first criticized "the unconditional will to truth"—but also Hegel who restrains the apocalyptic "fury of destruction" and forces it to work within creaturely reality, not against it. Deconstruction's relation to the apocalypse is thus analogical to the relation between Hegel's working dialectics and the "rapturous enthusiasm which, like a shot from a pistol, begins straight away with absolute knowledge, and makes short work of other standpoints by declaring that it takes no notice of them" (PS 16). Instead of this violent rapture Hegel proposes a different type of *jener nüchhterner Rausch*: "the revel in which no member is not drunk" (PS 27), but which, when regarded as "the whole movement of the *life of truth*" and contrasted with the "rapturous enthusiasm," appears almost as a "state of *repose*": the True, no longer "regarded as something on the other side, positive and dead" (PS 16)—the verdict of the apocalyptic Last Judgment hovering over the world—begins to permeate the realm of appearances and, with this act of incarnation/diminution, acquires life. The strange double negative attribution—*no member not drunk*—hovers in between total abandon and sobriety: the whole point of the living and life-affirming revel is to have a sip from the intoxicating fountain of the Last Judgment/Verdict/ Ultimate Truth, but no more than that, just a *pharmakonic* amount. While rupture explodes with the immediacy of the "pistol shot" and indeed kills and poisons everything around, the revel eases the revelation of Truth, so that it can be received by the fragile vessels of this-worldly appearances and then chained to the works that would foster and sustain the immanent *life* of truth. When revelation/*apocalypsis* remains outside the world, it is not only dead but also *deadly;* but when it is *fused* with the course of the world, it begins to live. All this applies *a fortiori* to Derrida: the deconstructive *revel* is the methodical use of *revelation* only slowly and gradually "secreted" from the unconditional will to truth held in check: the desire to tear all the veils in "the imminence of the end, theophany, *parousia*, the last judgment," which cannot—but also should not—be totally repressed but rather diminished, eased, and attenuated, so that it can be of use in this world.[27]

There are many differences between Hegel and Derrida, especially in regard to the historical *telos*, which the latter firmly rejects, but the dialectical mechanism mediating between the procosmic affirmation and the acosmic negation remains similar in both.[28] In Derrida, the *tsimtsum* paradigm fleshes itself out in the concepts of *différance*, a destruction "held-in-check" and apocalyptic desire "staved off," partly covered and repressed in order to turn into methodical works of deconstruction. Deconstruction is a destruction delayed in the process of encryption: it carries within itself the crypt full of eschatological energy as the counter-worldly apocalyptic element of both, destruction and revelation, but allows only for its controlled "secretion"/ expression. In that sense, Derrida may indeed be seen as an heir not only to Adorno's negative dialectics as Hegelianism without teleology, but also his "inverse theology" which insists on turning the lamps of the Last Judgment on the world here and now: not in order to destroy it, but to see it critically as still lacking truth and justice, yet not to be totally condemned because of that deficiency.

The Light of Lights, therefore, must be *well hidden* [*eukalyptos*] in order to be of use to us, the worldly creatures who "betray" revelation in its blinding purity for the mundane practice of enlightenment in the impure, always contaminated and messy, world. Hence, against Kant's denunciations of cryptophilia as "a cryptopoetics" and "a poetic perversion of philosophy" (APO 14) which should be replaced by the enlightenment pursuit of clarity and purity, Derrida explicitly chooses a *cryptophilic* and *eucalyptic* solution.[29] On Derrida's account, cryptophilia emerges as a necessary condition of all discourse on truth, which must draw on the same energy as the "overlordly" apocalyptic tone of the Hegelian master, but in a tamed manner. Yet, this "taming," *Bannung* or "steering" is more challenging that it appears prima facie. The apocalyptic desire is full of ruses which press toward its instantaneous gratification and which deconstruction must patiently demystify. Just as in Hegel, the master's desire aims at the total annihilation of its object, in Derrida's analysis too, the seemingly positive desire for revelation hides a destructive death-wish directed against the fallen world:

> Such a demystification must give in [se plier] to *the finest diversity of apocalyptic ruses.* The interest or the calculus of these ruses can be so dissembled under the desire for light, *well hidden* (*eukalyptus,* as is said of the tree whose calycine limb remains closed after flowering), *well hidden under the avowed desire for revelation.* (APO 23; emphasis added)

Derrida, however, does not simply opt for the total restraint of apocalyptic desire: *eucalypsis,* the art of "hiding well," although opposed to *apocalypsis,* does not just push it away. In the eucalyptic strategy, which Derrida recommends, the crypt, where the "well-hidden" truth lies buried, should be neither fully veiled nor fully unveiled: it should rather "secret" an "enigmatic desire" which, when used as a *pharmakon*—in smaller weaker doses—does, in fact, a good job: instead of unleashing death and destruction, it fuels a deconstructive vigilance and its inner-worldly works of justice. The ideal of justice, which fulfills itself in the apocalyptic judgment over the world (*Weltgericht*), must thus be laid in the eucalyptic, well-hidden crypt, if it is not to destroy the world immediately. But it must also gradually "secrete" its message, if the world is to be an ethical place at all.

The crypt, therefore, must be *eukalyptos,* not only well hidden, but also hidden *well,* in a proper manner. For Derrida, the finest of the ruses, which he can list on the side of his eucalyptic strategy, consists in turning apocalyptic desire on itself, so that it begins to question the very desire for revelation: now it rather wishes to reveal the source from which all wishes to reveal—the unconditional will to truth—come. The apocalyptic desire turned on itself and reflexively "checking itself," submits to self-limitation in the act of *tsimtsum*: it goes partly into hiding, and reveals itself no longer as the annihilating negation, but as the desire deferred and diffused—*no apocalypse, not now.* This *trait de retrait*—the *tsimtsum* motif operative on all levels of Derridean thinking—manifests itself already at the earliest stage of the poststructuralist turn, when Derrida coins the concept of the *différance.* Seen in a postsecular perspective, *différance* appears as first and foremost the deferment of the apocalypse which spells the end of this world and the advent of the Kingdom:

> Not only is there no kingdom of *différance*, but *différance* instigates the subversion of every kingdom. Which makes it obviously threatening and infallibly dreaded by everything within us that desires a kingdom, the past or future presence of a kingdom.[30]

But, as we already know from Derrida's later analysis of the apocalyptic tone, the will to kingdom—"let Thy Kingdom come"—can also be a threat: the absolute *parousia* of the apocalyptic fulfillment ends the world based on the play of *différance* which, on its part, is supported by a counter-desire to subvert every kingdom. The calculus of *conatus,* with its interest and investment in the world, also "well hidden under the avowed desire for revelation/destruction," launches thus a defense which guards the divine inhabitant of the crypt—the ideal of absolute justice and truth—in his entombment, not completely dead but also not fully alive, just latent and spectral: *tsimtsem,* withdrawn and "held in check."

Yet, just as in the case of Hegel and then Rosenzweig, this defense is not merely katechonic, because some of the "enigmatic desire" wishing "the light of lights," becomes nonetheless manifest, yet deferred and inhibited in respect to its ultimate goal. It is then used in the deconstructive critique of the *status quo*, which, to paraphrase Taubes, invests spiritually in the world, yet not it the world *as it is*. It does not say to the world as such—*let it go down*—yet, at the same time, does not affirm it in its given "figure." The figures of the world may and should pass, but not the world itself. This is what Derrida, in the Blanchotian manner, calls an *apocalypse without apocalypse*: a dialectical fold or self-subversion of the apocalyptic discourse, which negates the catastrophe announced by the apocalypse (the end of the world) without, at the same time, negating the destructive energy which—delayed, transformed, harnessed, fused—can now serve the "*works* of the negative" within worldly reality, with the emphasis on *works*:

> *There is the apocalypse without apocalypse.* The word *sans*, without, I pronounce here in the so necessary syntax of Blanchot, who often says X without X. The 'without' marks an internal and external catastrophe of the apocalypse, an overturning of sense that does not merge with the catastrophe announced or described in the apocalyptic writings without however being foreign to them. Here the catastrophe would perhaps be of the apocalypse itself, its fold and its end, a closure without end, an *end without end*. (APO 35; my emphasis)

The Blanchotian *X sans X* substitutes here for the *tsimtsum* paradigm: God without God, religion without religion, light without light, apocalypse without apocalypse—all these phrases point to the self-negating moment of limitation inscribed into theological concepts which, in this manner, undergo *deabsolutization*. A deconstructor, therefore, may not be an *Aufhalter*/restrainer of the apocalyptic revealment, but he is also not an "accelerationist" who would rush to tell all the truth, where the "truth itself is the end, the destination... the end and the instance of the last judgment" (APO 23): "The end is soon, it is imminent, signifies the tone. I see it, I know it, I tell You, now you know, come. We're all going to die, we're going to disappear. And this death sentence [*cet arrêt de mort*] cannot fail to judge us" (APO 25). The structure of the truth as such is indeed apocalyptic. One cannot see Truth face to face and live—and yet, we cannot completely give up on truth either; we must apply it in pharmokonic small doses, in the *tsimtsum*/kenotic diminution of the absolutes "making themselves small and humble." Thus, as Derrida states in one of his early essays, "Force and Significance": "it will be necessary [for the Truth] *to descend, to work, to bend*,"[31] if it is to be *livable*, that is, to metamorphose from otherworldly sheer "force" into inner-worldly "significance," capable of guiding and enlightening our inner-worldly ethical works of deconstruction.

To find this *pharmakon* or the right "easy" dose of light constitutes the very gist of Derrida's eucalyptic strategy: if one wants to survive the brush with the Light of Lights—the ideal of Truth and Justice—one must avoid the face-to-face confrontation and, following Emily Dickinson, the great poet of mediated revelation, "tell all the truth, but tell it slant." Yes—says Derrida—we are weak, fallible, and we all are going to die; yes, the end is always near, *but* ... "being here is a lot,"[32] and this *a lot* cannot be simply eliminated by the abiding death sentence [*cet arrêt de mort*], the "dead already" of the Heideggerian *Sein-zum-Tode*, based on the principle that "the essence of life is nothing but death" (*Aber die Essenz des Lebens ist zugleich Tod*).[33]

Always affirm survival—Derrida's famous last words uttering a version of the Biblical imperative of *ubaharta bahayim*, "choose to live!"[34]—trump the higher knowledge of the "philosophical sect'" (APO 25), by moving the whole debate onto a different plane, where it becomes a matter not of knowledge but of choice and faith. I—continues Derrida—may know that I am going to die, but I still *choose* life; the world may appear weak when compared to theological and philosophical Absolutes, but I still side with its precarious existence. Hence the new command: *eucalypse, now*—meaning: let's hide well our desire to know and become *fröhlich* for a while, in the manner recommended by Nietzsche, when he, in *Gay Science*, tempts us to give up on the unconditional will to truth.

> This unconditional will to truth—what is it? Is it the will not to let oneself be deceived? Is it the will not to deceive?... But why not deceive? But why not allow oneself to be deceived?...[35]

To allow oneself to be a little deceived would mean precisely to "ease" the blinding light of truth in its absolute *parousia*/revelation and then "tell it slant." Once the will to truth becomes *conditional*—that is, self-restricted with respect to survival—the truth does not disappear completely, but now it can be pursued within the context of life as a *livable* goal and not as "the truth [that] kills."[36]

"Are not my few days almost over? Turn away from me, so I can have a moment of joy," says Job to God (Job, 10: 20). So says also Derrida to the Truth in its threatening apocalyptic glory. The *vere-diction*, "telling the truth," is always and inescapably a *verdict*, a death sentence or the Blanchotian *arrêt de mort*; so, in order to practice *sur-vie* instead of *melete thanatou*, the "exercise of death," one needs to resort to the cunning of unreason—and *choose* or *decide* instead of knowing. This is also where Derrida departs from Hegel who still wants to have his share in the Absolute Knowledge at the very end of history, when the Kingdom of God and the Kingdom of the World will have finally coincided in peaceful reconciliation. While, in his deconstructionist method, Derrida will always use the Hegelian-dialectical scheme of "delayed destruction" which, as *différance* allows the apocalyptic desire for absolute truth and justice to work in and through the mundane condition, he does not want the process of deferral to ever end. Ultimately, therefore, enlightenment *is* revelation/apocalypse, but (hopefully) forever differed and deferred: a revelation cum *différance*. We could thus sum up Derrida's tarrying with Hegel by the ironic inversion of his own phrasing from the early essay on Bataille: *Hegelianism with Reserve*—even more reserved, restricted and cautious in its wary ways of "amortizing" the light of lights than Hegel himself.[37]

5 Conclusion

If Derrida is the paradigmatic thinker of the poststructuralist turn, who introduced its two most important concepts—of the decentered structure and of *différance* as the play of differentials, deferring the moment of identity—are we then justified in claiming that poststructuralism is not as alien to religion and metaphysics, as it is often claimed, and that it champions its own political theology? My answer is, yes. In his theory of deconstruction, Derrida borrows heavily from two precursors: Hegel and Rosenzweig. From the former, Derrida takes the dialectical scheme of "tarrying with the apocalypse"; from the latter, the conviction that this dialectical model is older than Hegel and that it can be traced back to the Judaic paradigm of *tsimtsum*, which they both endorse in its procosmic choice of life and world over against the powerful divine Absolute. Whether in dialectics or in deconstruction, this mighty force of creation and destruction is not simply warded off, but utilized for the sake of the world: the tremendous power of the negative can be compared to Paul Klee's *gebannter Blitz*, a lightning "eased to the children" and harnessed to do the mundane work. What Derrida calls an "awakening of the Judaic tradition"[38] is precisely the conceptual heritage of the decentered form of theism which posits God as self-limiting and self-withdrawing for the sake of the world and its metaphysical autonomy.

The ultimate stake of Derrida's "Hegelian-Rabbinic" intervention, therefore, is to safeguard the transcendental possibility of the critique of the world as positioning itself between negation and affirmation. From Hegel on, *secularized chronic apocalypticism*—the fury of destruction which wandered into the profane to live with it on critical basis—forms such a transcendental condition: the dialectics of critical works that aim not at the destruction, but at the trans-formation of the worldly—secular—reality. In his attack on the "philosophical sect," Derrida reminds us that what today passes for a "critical theory" is often not a critique, but an exercise of simple negation—a virtual destruction of the world from the apocalyptic vantage point of the Last Judgment. The proper critique, on the other hand, maintains itself in a difficult, deconstructive-vigilant, position which firmly believes that, in Rilke's words, *even the destructive might transform into the world.*

Notes

1. "The proletarians have nothing to lose but their chains. They have a world to win": Karl Marx, Frederick Engels, *Manifesto of the Communist Party*, trans. Samuel Moore (Peking: People's Publishing House, 1965), 76.
2. *Sanhedrin 98a*. See also *Midrash Tehilim*: "Israel speaks to God: When will You redeem us? He answers: When you have sunk to the lowest level, at that time I will redeem you." On which Scholem succinctly comments: "the redemption, then, cannot be realized without dread and ruin... There can be no preparation for the Messiah. He comes suddenly, unannounced, and precisely when he is least expected or when hope has long been abandoned." Gershom Scholem, *The Messianic Idea in Judaism* (New York: Schocken, 1995), 13, 11. On the concept of *khurbn/korban*, see Leviticus 26:31: "I will give your cities over to destruction (*charbah*) and I will destroy (*vehashimotyi*) your Temples."
3. The *katechon* (in Luther's translation *der Aufhalter*, "the restrainer") derives from Paul's Second Letter to the Thessalonians (2:3–2:8): "And you know what is now restraining him, so that he may be revealed when his time comes. For the mystery of lawlessness is already at work, but only until the one who now restrains it is removed": (*The New Oxford Annotated Bible*, eds., Bernhard W. Anderson, Bruce Manning Metzger and Roland Edmund Murphy [Oxford/ New York: Oxford University Press: 1991]). In *Nomos of the Earth*, Carl Schmitt

creates an entire new political theology based on the concept of the *katechon* as the one who withholds the advent of the Antichrist representing the forces of lawlessness and disorder and as such is a true fulfillment of Christian religion; see most of all the chapter "The Christian Empire as a Restrainer of the Antichrist (*Katechon*)" in *The Nomos of the Earth in the International Law of the Jus Publicum Europaeum*, trans. G. L. Ulmen (New York: Telos Press Publishing, 1999), where Schmitt says: "I do not believe that any historical concept other than *katechon* would have been possible for the original Christian faith" (61). The claim that Paul, unable to wait for the Second Coming any longer, suffered a failure of the messianic nerve and because of that turned toward the figure of the *katechon*, derives from Jacob Taubes, *The Political Theology of Paul*, trans. Dana Hollander (Stanford: Stanford University Press, 2003), 103. While Schmitt represents the katechonic wisdom of anti-messianic and anti-apocalyptic politics, Taubes constitutes the ideal type of the opposite: a messianic theopolitics that stakes itself on the apocalyptic revelation of God as putting an end to the failed experiment of the world. Hence his famous declaration: "I can imagine as an apocalyptic: let it go down. I have no spiritual investment in the world as it is" (ibid.).

4. Compare the classical definition of *tsimtsum* offered by Gershom Scholem: "Creation out of nothing, from the void, could be nothing other than creation of the void, that is, of the possibility of thinking of anything that was not God. Without such an act of self-limitation, after all, there would be only God—and obviously nothing else. A being that is not God could only become possible and originate by virtue of such a contraction, such a paradoxical retreat of God into himself. By positing a negative factor in Himself, God liberates creation." Gershom Scholem, *On Jews and Judaism in Crisis. Selected Essays*, ed. Werner Dannhauser (New York: Schocken Books, 1976), 283; emphasis added.

5. The paradigm of *tsimtsum* as the germ-cell of an alternative theological tradition deriving out of the sources of Judaism is well explained by Joseph B. Soloveitchik, one of the best twentieth-century Jewish theologians, for whom it means that "infinity contracts itself; eternity concentrates itself in the fleeting and transient, the Divine Presence in dimensions and the glory of God in measurements. It is Judaism that has given the world the secret of *tsimtsum*, of 'contraction,' contraction of the infinite within the finite, the transcendent within the immanent." Joseph B. Soloveitchik, *The Halakhic Man* (New York: Jewish Publication Society of America, 1983), 48. In that sense, the *tsimtsum* paradigm would precede the Christian doctrine of the divine incarnation, but also make it broader, as is indeed the case with Hegel, for whom the incarnation of Spirit/Subject into the Substance/World leads to the dialectical intertwinement of "the infinite in the finite": a "diminished" presence of the divine within worldly reality.

6. The first version of *tsimtsum*, in which God "takes in his breath" and restricts his glory for the sake of something else to emerge, derives from Isaiah, as described by Elliot Wolfson in his interpretation of one of the bahiric texts: "The notion of withdrawal, itself withdrawn and thus not stated overtly, is a secret exegetically derived from the verse *lema'an shemi a'arikh appi u-tehillati ehetam lakh le-vilti hakhritekha*, 'For the sake of my name I will postpone my wrath and my glory, *I will hold in for you so that I will not destroy you*' (Isa 48:9)… One may surmise that at some point in ancient Israel the notion of a vengeful god yielded its opposite, the compassionate god who holds in his fury." Elliott Wolfson, *Alef, Mem, Tau. Kabbalistic Musings on Time, Truth, and Death* (Berkeley: University of California Press, 2006), 132–3. It is worth quoting the relevant passage of the Dickinson poem at length since it will inform much of my analysis in what follows:

Tell all the truth but tell it slant—
Success in Circuit lies
Too bright for our infirm Delight
The Truth's superb surprise
As Lightning to the Children eased
With explanation kind
The Truth must dazzle gradually
Or every man be blind.

7. Hans Blumenberg and Carl Schmitt, *Briefwechsel 1971–1978* (Frankfurt: Suhrkamp, 2007), 41.
8. Jacques Derrida, *Acts of Religion*, ed. Gil Anidjar (London and New York: Routledge, 2002), 55. For Derrida, the retreat which keeps the distance between transcendence and immanence is also a form of restraint: "Scruple, hesitation, indecision, reticence (hence modesty, *pudeur*, respect, restraint before that which should remain sacred, holy or safe: unscathed, immune)—this too is what is meant by *religio*" (ibid., 68).
9. See Eric Voegelin, *Modernity Without Restraint. The Political Religions, The New Science of Politics, and Science, Politics, and Gnosticism, Collected Works of Eric Voegelin*, vol. 5 (Kansas City: University of Missouri Press, 1999), 184–6.
10. On Hegel's relation to Martin Luther and the Reformed Theology, see most of all Ulrich Asendorf, *Luther und Hegel: Untersuchung zur Grundlegung einer Neuen Systematischen Theologie* (Wiesbaden: Franz Steiner Verlag, 1982).
11. By endorsing this position, I want to engage in a gentle polemic with the latest turn in Hegelian scholarship which revises the idea of Hegel the dialectical reformer of the world and attempts to reclaim his praise of revolution, championed mostly by Slavoj Žižek. While Žižek rejects the "common perception" according to which "Hegel condemns French Revolution as the immediate assertion of an abstract-universal Freedom" and insists on the repetition of the revolutionary *apocalypse now!* in the manner of an unstoppable *Wiederholungszwang* (repetition compulsion) pressing toward the catastrophe, I would like to emphasize the dialectical resumption of the apocalyptic fire in the Hegelian concept of the *work* as "delayed destruction," mediating forward between the apocalyptic "fury of destruction" and the passive conservation of the *status quo*. Slavoj Žižek, *Less than Nothing. Hegel and the Shadow of Dialectical Materialism* (London: Verso, 2012), 69.
12. G. W. F. Hegel, *Phenomenology of Spirit*, trans. A. V. Miller (Oxford: Oxford University Press, 1977), 118. Henceforth cited in-text as PS.
13. The metaphor of the master/slave dialectic as the best way to approach the evolution of Western metaphysical thought appears very strongly in Adorno's series of lectures devoted to metaphysics, where he presents Aristotle as the precursor of Hegel, the first thinker to emancipate worldly beings from the service to Platonic Ideas and to give them "permanence and objectivity": "Aristotle... makes a very strong and legitimate case, based on the argument that all the attributes of the Ideas are derived from the empirical world, on which they live, rather as the rulers lived on the work of their servants or slaves." Theodor W. Adorno, *Metaphysics: Concepts and Problems*, trans. Edmund Jephcott (London: Polity Press, 2001), 20.
14. Compare Hans Blumenberg, *Work on Myth*, trans. R. M. Wallace (Cambridge, MA: MIT Press, 1985), 545: "It is just this [the rivalry] that Luther... translated into monotheistic terms: He who wanted to be God and it was naturally self-evident for him that man had to want this could only want to be it in place of the one God. Where no equivalence is possible, thinking has to take the form of the desire to annihilate"—which, following Hegel, would be the desire to annihilate the master: this is precisely what the slave is *not* supposed to do.
15. On the influence of the heterodox religious motives deriving from the so-called Christian kabbalistic milieu on Hegel, see my "God of Luria, Hegel, Schelling: The Divine Contraction and the Modern Metaphysics of Finitude," in *Mystical Theology and Continental Philosophy*, ed. David Lewin, Simon Podmore, and Duane Williams (London and New York: Routledge, 2017), 32–50.
16. G. W. F. Hegel, *Philosophy of Right*, trans. S. W. Dyde (Kitchener, Ontario: Batoche Books, 2001), 130.
17. Hegel quotes Schiller's poem *Resignation* in section 340 of the *Philosophy of Right*: "The history of the world is the world's court of judgment." Hegel, *Philosophy of Right*, 266.
18. Franz Rosenzweig, *The Star of Redemption*, trans. Barbara Galli (Madison: University of Wisconsin Press, 2005), 429; emphasis added. Henceforth cited in-text as SR.

19. The rabbinic rule of "no longer in heaven," which places the Torah-Law on earth in the safe distance from God's miraculous interventions, derives from the talmudic story, told in the tractate *Baba Metsia 59b*. For the full description of this motif, see Gershom Scholem, *The Messianic Idea in Judaism. And Other Essays on Jewish Spirituality* (New York: Schocken Books, 1991), 130–31.
20. Scholem, *The Messianic Idea*, 323.
21. Rosenzweig is very well aware of the pitfalls of the total neutralization of the apocalyptic fire, which he calls "Jewish dangers" (SR 429): one of them consists in "squeezing it into the cozy domestic space between the Law and its, the Law's, people" (SR 430). Thus, while the Christians are endangered by an excessive expansion, which may contaminate their messianic work of the transformation of the worldly reality and make it forget its roots—the Jews are endangered by an excessive contraction of the divine "heat" which they overly domesticate and then, indeed, render useless for the actual world: "Christianity, by radiating outwards, is in danger of evaporating into isolated rays far away from the divine core of truth. Judaism, by glowing inwards, is in danger of gathering its heat into its own bosom far distant from the pagan world reality" (SR 430). The right concept of the Law, as the dialectical bridge between the transcendent heat/fire and the immanent worldly reality, is thus to counteract both, Jewish and Christian, dangers.
22. See Levinas' description of the Torah as the trace of the transcendent justice from without, which challenges the ontological order here and now: "Being receives a challenge from the Torah, which jeopardizes its pretention of keeping itself above or beyond good and evil. In challenging the absurd 'that's the way it is' claimed by the Power of the powerful, the man of the Torah transforms being into human history. Meaningful movement jolts the Real." Emmanuel Lévinas, *Nine Talmudic Readings*, trans. Annette Aronowicz (Bloomington: Indiana University Press, 1990), 39.
23. The title of this section alludes in reverse to Derrida's essay on nuclear danger: "No Apocalypse, Not Now (Full Speed Ahead, Seven Missiles, Seven Missives)," trans. Catherine Porter and Philip Lewis, *Diacritics*, Vol. 14, No. 2 (Summer, 1984), 20–31.
24. In Hermann Diels' *Fragmente der Vorsokratiker*, this is fragment nr 64: translation slightly altered after Martin Heidegger and Eugen Fink, *Heraclitus Seminar*, trans. Charles Seibert (Evanston: Northwestern University Press, 1993), 4–11, where this aphorism is thoroughly discussed.
25. Jacques Derrida, "Christianity and Secularization," trans. David Newheiser, *Critical Inquiry* 47 (Autumn 2020), 139; emphasis added.
26. While commenting on Kant's ethics, Michael Rosen does not hide his fear of the apocalyptic terror which it openly endorses: "The austere slogan of retributivism was always: let justice be done although the world perishes (*fiat justitia, pereat mundus*). Kant's position seems even harsher—let justice be done even if we have to create a hell for it to be done in": Michael Rosen, "Die Weltgeschichte ist das Weltgericht," in *Internationales Jahrbuch des deutschen Idealismus*, ed. F. Rush (Berlin: De Gruyter, 2014), 13.
27. Jacques Derrida, "Of an Apocalyptic Tone Recently Adopted in Philosophy," trans. John P. Leavey, Jr., *Oxford Literary Review*, vol. 6, no. 2 (1984), 22. Henceforth cited as APO.
28. Derrida was always critical of Hegel, perhaps to the point of being "unfair to Hegel"—especially in the 60's when he wished to inscribe the poststructuralist turn into the anti-dialectical rebellion of the students of Alexandre Kojève, most of all Georges Bataille, but also later, when he fell under the influence of Emmanuel Levinas, who saw in Hegel the destroyer of the transcendence and the main source of the historicist error in twentieth-century philosophy. Yet, already Derrida's concept of *différance* is a paradigmatic example of poststructuralist "dialectics beyond dialectics" which constantly tarries with the Hegelian legacy under the auspices of the Bataillean dictum that opens Derrida's essay on "Hegelianism without reserve": "Hegel did not know to what extent he was right." Jacques Derrida, *Writing and Difference*, trans. Alan Bass (London: Routledge and Kegal Paul, 1978), 317. In what prima facie appears as a sympathetic reported speech, Derrida laughs with Bataille at Hegel's thrifty ways of economizing every bit of negativity in the process of work and creating the "slavish" world of mean-

ing: "The notion of *Aufhebung*... is laughable in that it signifies the busying of a discourse losing its breath as it reappropriates all negativity for itself, as it works the 'putting at stake' into an *investment*, as it *amortizes* absolute expenditure" that aims at "the absolute sacrifice of meaning: a sacrifice without return and without reserves" (ibid., 324). Yet, the more he matures, Derrida is no longer willing (if he really ever was) to subscribe to the Kojèvian apology of the master and his unbound self-expenditure/*jouissance* at the expense of the slave's choice of life and survival, which invests in the "permanence and objectivity" of this world and, in order to do so, must "amortize"—diminish and harness—the apocalyptic powers of the masterly desire. Ultimately, therefore, Derrida ends up in the position that, for Bataille, would indeed appear "laughable": a certain unavowed "Hegelianism *with* reserve" where the negative becomes restricted by the higher imperative of the world's survival. On the poststructuralist reckoning with Hegel, see Małgorzata Kowalska, *Dialectics Beyond Dialectics. Essay on Totality and Difference*, trans. Cain Elliott and Jan Burzyński (Lausanne: Peter Lang, 2015).

29. See also Derrida on Kant in the 1998 text, "The History of the Lie": "Everything must be sacrificed to this sacredness of the commandment. Kant writes, 'To be truthful [*wahrhaft*; loyal, sincere, honest, in good faith: *ehrlich*] in all declarations is, therefore, a sacred [*heiliges*] and unconditional [*unbedingt gebietendes*] commanding law of reason [*Vernunftgebot*] that admits of no expediency whatsoever.'" Jacques Derrida, *Without Alibi*, ed. and trans. Peggy Kamuf (Stanford: Stanford University Press, 2002), 45.
30. Jacques Derrida, *Margins of Philosophy*, trans. Alan Bass (Chicago: The University of Chicago Press, 1982), 22.
31. Jacques Derrida, *Writing and Difference*, trans. Alan Bass (London: Routledge and Kegan Paul, 1978), 35; emphasis added.
32. Rainer Maria Rilke, *The 9th Duino Elegy*: "But because being here is a lot: because everything here/ Seems to need us, this fleeting world, which in some strange way/ Concerns us."
33. Martin Heidegger, *Introduction to Metaphysics*, trans. Gregory Fried and Richard Polt (New Haven: Yale University Press, 2000), 100.
34. The last words of Derrida, which he scribbled right before his death, were: "Always prefer life and constantly affirm survival": Jacques Derrida, "Final Words," trans. Gila Walker, in *The Late Derrida*, eds. W. J. T. Mitchell and Arnold I. Davidson (Chicago: The University of Chicago Press, 2007), 244.
35. Friedrich Nietzsche, *Gay Science*, trans. Josefine Nauckhoff (Cambridge: Cambridge University Press, 2001), 201.
36. *Wahrheit tötet*: Friedrich Nietzsche, *Unpublished Writings from the Period of Unfashionable Observations*, trans. Richard T. Gray (Stanford: Stanford University Press, 1995), 190. See Derrida's comment on Nietzsche's statement, deriving from his 1973 seminar: "the truth is suicide in its structure": Jacques Derrida, *Life Death*, trans. Pascale-Anne Brault and Michael Naas (Chicago: The University of Chicago Press, 2020), 153.
37. The rejection of Absolute Knowledge as modelled on the advent/restitution of *parousia*—the Light of Lights as the absolute presence—is the fundamental difference which sets apart Derrida from Hegel who ultimately cannot resist the allure of the main Christian symbol of the Second Coming. In "The Pit and the Pyramid," the essay from the *Margins* devoted to the Hegelian semiology, Derrida criticizes Hegel's conception of the sign as the "time of referral" in transition between the original and the final presence, whereas he wants to transform it into a *time of deferral* which suspends and "subverts every kingdom": "The time of the sign, then, is the time of referral. It signifies self-presence, refers presence to itself, organizes the circulation of its provisionality. Always, from the outset, the movement of lost presence already will have set in motion the process of its reappropriation." Derrida, *Margins*, 71–72.
38. Derrida, *Acts of Religion*, 289.

The University

Lenka Vráblíková

1   Introduction: Reading Kant against the Grain

Over a period of nearly thirty years, Jacques Derrida addressed the question of the university—concerning particularly the concept of the university, its relation to the conditions of its institutional possibility, and to the research and teaching in philosophy and the humanities more broadly—on several occasions and for various purposes. This rich and diverse body of work comprises lectures delivered in universities in France and the United States, reports, and interviews,[1] and, especially since the mid-1990s, it has been increasingly acknowledged as an indispensable part of Derrida's oeuvre as well as critical debates on the university and education.[2] In addition to mobilizing an approach that has been inextricably associated with Derrida's work—deconstruction—his engagement with the question of the university is marked by two prominent features. The first is Derrida's institutional involvements and activism concerning philosophical research and teaching in France from the 1970s onward. In 1974 and in response to a recommendation to remove philosophy from the high school curriculum, Derrida co-founded *Greph*, a Research Group on the Teaching of Philosophy. The work of *Greph* and of other initiatives culminated in a two-day Estates General of Philosophy in 1979, where over 1200 participants, including teachers, scholars, and non-academics gathered to defend the teaching of philosophy in French educational institutions. Another outcome of these efforts was the establishment of a state-funded institutional space that would enable philosophical research not accepted or marginalized in existing academic institutions, the International College of Philosophy (*Ciph*), founded in 1983 with Derrida as its first elected director.[3] The second prominent feature of Derrida's engagement with the

L. Vráblíková (✉)
Goldsmiths, University of London, London, UK
e-mail: l.vrablikova@gold.ac.uk

question of the university is his choice of philosophical texts upon which he draws on. Although working with various and diverse philosophers such as Martin Heidegger, René Descartes, F. W. J. Schelling and G. W. F. Hegel, it is Immanuel Kant, and particularly one of his last works, *The Conflict of the Faculties*, which occupies the most prominent position in Derrida's writings on the university.[4]

This persistent concern with and investment in this late, minor work of Kant's is not insignificant. *The Conflict of the Faculties* was subject to criticism by a younger generation of German thinkers, including Johann Erich Biester, the editor of the famous pro-enlightenment journal *Berlinische Monatschrift*, who in a letter to Kant from 1794 claims that Kant's argumentation regarding the university is a sign of his withdrawal from the struggle for enlightenment, leaving it to others to "continue to work on the great philosophical and theological enlightenment that… Kant [had] so happily begun."[5] In a different vein, Schelling, disagreed with Kant's conceptualization of the structural layout of the university: according to Schelling, Kant "treated the question from a very one-sided point of view," and so—in contrast to Kant who, as I will discuss further in the following section, ascribes a singular place for the faculty of philosophy within the university—Schelling maintains that "there is no such faculty, nor can there be, for that which is all things cannot for the very reason be anything in particular."[6] Finally, although Wilhelm von Humboldt modeled the University of Berlin, opened in 1810, on Kant's university—a model replicated in universities all over the world, and especially in the United States—Kant's *The Conflict of the Faculties* remains relatively neglected, as "a work unknown even to many specialists in Kant studies."[7]

The aim of this chapter is to show how Derrida's particular interest in *The Conflict of the Faculties* triggers not only a profound shift in the interpretation of this text but the work of Kant in general. More specifically, it demonstrates that Derrida's reading of Kant's discourse on the university represents an example of the kind of engagement called for by Howard Caygill in the introduction to *A Kant Dictionary*—an engagement which goes beyond "the impression of a monolithic corpus, a body of writings severed from the circumstances of their original publication and inhabiting a philosophical Valhalla" given to us by "the editors of the monumental Berlin Academy of Sciences edition of Kant's writings" and "the narrow focus of much Kant scholarship." I argue, following Caygill, that Derrida's deliberations instead bring "a complex appreciation of the internal diversity of Kant's work… and allow us to situate his authorship within the changing structures of intellectual life that characterized the German Enlightenment."[8] My second argument is that Derrida's work on Kant's university also inaugurates a shift in how we understand the *legacy* of Kant's work in the context of the current world and opens a way to articulate the possibility of its transformation, positioning the question of the university at the very heart of such efforts.

In what follows I especially draw on those works where *The Conflict of the Faculties* occupies a central place, namely "Mochlos, or The Conflict of the Faculties" (originally delivered as a lecture at Columbia University on the occasion of the celebration of the centennial of Columbia's Graduate School in 1980), "The Principle of Reason: The University in the Eyes of its Pupils" (first delivered as

Derrida's inaugural lecture as Andrew D. White Professor-at-Large at Cornell University in 1983), "Vacant Chair: Censorship, Mastery, Magisteriality," (a part of a lecture series titled "Transfer *Ex Cathedra*: language and institutions of philosophy" first delivered at the University of Toronto in 1985), and "The future of the profession or the university without condition (thanks to the "Humanities," what *could take place* tomorrow)," which Derrida first delivered as his Presidential Lecture at Stanford University in 1999.[9] The first section opens by outlining how Derrida reads Kant's *The Conflict of the Faculties*, with particular regard for the implications of this theorization for the institutional politics of the university. The second section further develops Derrida's reading of Kant's work through an examination of the former's engagement with performative speech acts. The chapter concludes by outlining how Derrida's work on the university, building upon Kant's *Conflict of the Faculties*, provides a useful tool for identifying concerns that have defined the institutional politics of the university at present and situates it as a site that is vital for struggles for a more just world.

2 Kant's University in Deconstruction

How does Derrida read Kant's *The Conflict of the Faculties*? And how does Kant conceptualize the university and envisions its institutional structure? For Derrida, Kant's deliberations on freedom of thinking are inexorably bound to the institution of the faculty of philosophy in the modern university and, simultaneously, inaugurate this bond. This is because the situation from which Kant theorizes the university is unprecedented—Kant is a "Dozent," someone who teaches disciples and whose qualifications are recognized by the State. He has a new status which inaugurates a "Kantian moment," a moment of "becoming-institution, more exactly, a becoming-state-institution of reason, a becoming-faculty of reason."[10] Kant thus represents one of the first philosophers to address the question of free thinking as a *teaching* philosopher from within the modern university, as "a professor and civil servant in a State university."[11] Derrida thus reads the discourse presented in *The Conflict of the Faculties* as a foundational discourse of the modern university and, as indicated above, instead of treating the work as a text severed from the circumstances of its original publication, he reads it against the events that defined the political and intellectual climate of its emergence.

As Kant famously argued in "The Answer to the Question: What is Enlightenment?" published in 1784, his age was not an enlightened age but "an age of enlightenment," since there was still "a long way to go before men as a whole can be in a position (or can even be put into a position) of using their own understanding confidently and well in religious matters, without outside guidance." According to Kant, the way was nonetheless being cleared to proceed in this direction mainly because Frederick the Great, the king of Prussia, was "himself enlightened" and "consider[ed] it his duty, in religious matters, not to prescribe anything to his people, but to allow them complete freedom."[12] However, two years after the publication of this famous article, Frederick the Great was replaced by his nephew Frederick William II, who, unlike his predecessor, was not favorable to enlightenment but "rigorously orthodox and mystically inclined."[13] Under his rule, the power of the church rose significantly, resulting in the reinforcement of censorship from the state authorities. These changes also affected Kant and his work. In 1792, the censorship commission prohibited the publication of his *Religion within the Limits of Reason Alone*. Kant protested this decision and managed to publish the book the following year, its publication was nonetheless followed by further censorship. An order was issued to the University of Konigsberg forbidding any professor to lecture on Kant's philosophy of religion, another order was issued to Kant, reprimanding him for the "misuse of philosophy" and demanding that, in the future, he should "be guilty of no such fault."[14] Kant published this decree, together with his response to it, in the Preface to *The Conflict of the Faculties* whose publication also did not escape the same repressive measures and so could be published only after Friedrich William II's death in 1797.[15]

Recalling the socio-political and institutional circumstances under which Kant formulated his discourse on the university, alongside his own institutional circumstances, is crucial for Derrida's texts. In his view, one's own positionality is not extraneous to philosophy but the two are intrinsically intertwined. *The Conflict of the Faculties* is thus to be understood as a singular philosophical response to the complex structural geo-political, socio-cultural and intellectual changes from within the modern university *and* an event which inaugurates and thus constitutes university practices and changes philosophical thought itself. For Derrida, Kant's *The Conflict of the Faculties* is both an inauguration and a response.

As Derrida reads it, *The Conflict of the Faculties* continues and further develops Kant's response to the reprimand which, as already mentioned above, features in the book's Preface. In the book, Kant asks the state to withdraw the university from its power and censorship and to guarantee, within this academic institutional space, freedom of thought and expression. The justification from this proposition stems from Kant's understanding of reason as an absolute and a priori human faculty that is inextricably aligned with freedom,[16] and consists in both legitimizing and delimiting state censorship. As already mentioned, in "What is Enlightenment?" Kant had argued that the King is himself "enlightened," that is, inspired by reason.[17] On the one hand, this implies that state censorship is, like every human moral action, also motivated by a priori reason. It is not an exercise of brute force, but a use of force *with* reason. On the other hand, reason is a human faculty that is inexorably bind with freedom of thought and expression. Securing a space where reason can be freely represented and developed is thus—because the state itself acts in accordance with and in the name of reason—in the interest of the state itself. Kant further supports the second part of his argument by stressing that the university—and the free thinking in the name of reason that takes place in it—does not represent any danger for the state. The freedom granted to the university is limited; the university's sole occupation is reason, it has no interest and no legitimate authority to influence and interfere with any outside affairs, including the affairs of the state.

According to this schema, the state and the university are both grounded in reason and are therefore in harmony. The argument for the division of the rights and the authorities between the two domains, and the justification for the foundation and existence of the university as a space of freedom of thinking and expression, is articulated through a conceptual distinction between reason with power and reason that is heteronomous to power. This limit however does not circumvent the university but passes right through it. In Kant's plan for the university, it consists of two classes of faculties—the higher faculties which include theology, law and medicine, and the lower faculty, which is the faculty of philosophy. The higher faculties are subjected to the authority of the state which they also represent. Theology, law, and medicine fall under state's regulation and censorship. However, they can also, in the state's name, regulate and censor. On the contrary, the lower faculty, the faculty of philosophy, is withdrawn from state power. In the lower faculty, the state cannot exercise its power and censor but nor can this faculty and its staff, teaching philosophers, interfere with any affairs outside of their competence, such as those of the higher faculties and, by proxy, those of the state.

This limitation is crucial for Kant's discourse on the university. He repeatedly insists that the faculty of philosophy does not have any executive power, that the teaching philosophers are not able to give orders or to censor, and that it is the faculty of philosophy which, within the structure of the university, is *the* place where reason, which is heteronomous to power, resides. Simultaneously, this argumentation has serious implications for freedom of thinking and expression both inside and outside the university. Firstly, because Kant legitimizes and justifies the state censorship of free thinking and expression anywhere but the university, his discourse on the university contradicts "the enlightenment proper," that is, Kant's previous attempts to theorize and thus establish freedom of thinking "for all," as he attempts to do, for instance, in the essay "What is Enlightenment?". This is the reason why Kant's early readers—such as Biester—and their followers[18] have considered *The Conflict of the Faculties* a withdrawal from the project of the enlightenment or, as John Mowitt puts it, as an "ill-conceived Faustian pact."[19] The second problem is that the argumentation Kant designed to justify and secure freedom of thinking and expression in the university has never been effective. As Derrida puts it, it exposes the university's vulnerability and

> the fragility of its defences against all the powers that command it, besiege it, and attempt to appropriate it. Because it is a stranger to power, because it is heterogeneous to power… the university is also without any power of its own.[20]

Yet, simultaneously, Derrida's reading suggests that Kant's discourse on the university may not solely be read as a failed project, let alone a retreat from the ideals of enlightenment, but also as opening up a path toward another kind of enlightenment and another kind of university, respectively.

As outlined above, Kant's plan for the university presupposes the establishment of a border, of a pure and decidable limit which withdraws the university from state power and its censorship. Deconstructing this dualism, Derrida shows how this limit between the state and the university, which, for Kant, also defines the relationship between the higher and the lower faculties, is impossible to maintain. Furthermore, Derrida argues that this impossibility is already present in Kant's text itself.[21] According to Derrida, Kant does not only establish a border between the state and the university but also its crossing, and this is made possible by the paradoxical nature of Kant's university schema grounded in the idea of absolute a priori reason. As argued, although a priori reason motivates every human moral action, including the actions of the state, it is also assigned a singular, unique place—the faculty of philosophy. The effect of this paradoxical layout is twofold. As Kant puts it, firstly, it would "finally prepare the way for the government to remove all restrictions that its choice has put on freedom of public judgment" and, secondly,

> the last would… be first (the lower faculty would be the higher)… counselling the authority (the government). For the government may find the freedom of the philosophy faculty, and the increased insight gained from this freedom, a better means for achieving its ends than its own absolute authority.[22]

In other words, this line of argumentation enables a reversal of forces within the university. It enables the "powerless" lower faculty to gain the upper hand over the higher faculties. The faculty of philosophy and its staff would gain a position of panoptical ubiquity from which they could comprehend and observe the entire field of knowledge, thus also the affairs of other university faculties and the affairs of the state.[23] According to this layout, the faculty of philosophy and the teaching philosophers would therefore not be "powerless" but would have a certain kind of power (or powers) and could therefore give orders and censor. On Derrida's reading, Kant's discourse on the university thus consists in a contradictory double gesture of the setting-up of a limit and the crossing of this limit. As I interpret it, this is one of the reasons why Derrida, in his deliberations on how we can theorize the university and its institutional possibility, again and again returns to *The Conflict of the Faculties*, why he re-thinks and re-articulates Kant's effort to conceptualize and negotiate a space where freedom of thinking would have been possible.

3 Envisioning the Enlightened University to Come

To develop his reading of Kant's *The Conflict of the Faculties* as an opening to another enlightenment, Derrida mobilizes J. L. Austin's theory of speech acts. In *How to Do Things with Words* Austin famously proposes that not all utterances are constative, that is, "state and describe something."[24] Performatives are utterances "in which to say something is to do something; or in which by saying something we are doing something."[25] Deconstructing Austin's distinction between constative and performative speech acts was long an essential feature of Derrida's work (e.g., "Signature Event Context," "Limited Inc," etc.).[26] Here, through themes such as the gift, forgiveness, hospitality, justice, friendship, and human-animal relations, Derrida re-elaborates his critique and further complicates the logic of the performative to propose a new conceptualization of ethico-political relations. This represents a way to theorize a possibility of transformation, which Derrida poses as a question of a future that would be absolutely different from the past and present and which, particularly in his later writings, is indexed with a phrase "to come" [à-venir], such as "the democracy to come" or, indeed, "a university to come."[27]

Throughout his work, Derrida repeatedly shows how European thinking has been founded upon a metaphysical determination of language which holds that language operates separately either as an action or as a verifiable description. In this respect, theorizations of institutions that rest upon the idea of a clear separation between the socio-political and institutional inside and outside—such as the one proposed by Kant in his discourse on the university—is but one example. As Derrida argues:

> In a way, Kant speaks only of language in *The Conflict of the Faculties*, and it is between two languages, between one of truth and one of action, between one of theoretical statements and one of performatives (mostly commands) that he wishes to trace the line of demarcation....] And yet he continually effaces something in language that scrambles the limits which a criticist critique claims to assign to the faculties, to the interior of the faculties, and... between the university's inside and its outside. Kant's effort... tries to limit the effects of confusion, simulacrum, parasiting, equivocality and undecidability produced by language.[28]

In the essay "Vacant Chair," where Derrida examines Kant's university in relation to censorship, the deconstruction of the border between the outside and the inside of the university, the domain of reason with power (performative language) and reason heteronomous to power (constative language), leads Derrida to argue that "one cannot construct a concept of the institution without inscribing in it the censoring function" because "the censoring delimitation remains unavoidable in a finite and necessarily agonistic field." The university, he thus argues, is "always censured *and* censoring."[29] The recognition that censorship is unavoidable when it comes to the university is, however, not meant to discourage the striving for freedom of thinking and expression. It does not it imply that we should not try to demarcate locations where freedom of thought can be pursued and that institutions, grounded in such an idea, are impossible. Derrida believes that "[t]he university should... be the place in which nothing is beyond question"[30] and, as he repeatedly claims, he is "absolutely in favor of a new university Enlightenment [*Aufklärung*]."[31] He therefore does not turn against Kant's idea of autonomy and emancipation, yet, nor does he pursue a fantasy of a place fully free of external pressures. He affirms independence and autonomy, while, simultaneously, putting these concepts and institutions into question.[32]

This generative aspect distinguishes Derrida's approach from much of the other theorization of the university in the Humanities in the West and/or the Global North. In these traditions, the prevailing approach has been defined by an uncritical adoption of a rhetoric of crisis. On the one hand, this scholarship thus presumes that there had been, in the past of the university, a time of a non-crisis, and, on the other, tends to various predictions of the end of the university.[33] Derrida avoids these nostalgic and apocalyptic teleologies. For Derrida, the university has always been an unsuitable formation, always inappropriate to the circumstances and locations of its time. We could say that "crisis" is integrated into the university as a condition of its possibility which, simultaneously, is the condition of the a priori impossibility of the university ever achieving a state of "non-crisis." The university therefore is not—and has never been—a self-contained entity but is rather an inexorably contingent formation fundamentally attached to the enabling limits of its (re)emergence.

Taking the university as a contingent formation orients Derrida toward the relationship between the university and its outside and becomes a way of proposing a new way of forming and sustaining ethico-political relationships, and thus also a way of theorizing the possibility of the university's transformation—a possibility that does not rely on subjectivity understood as a self-identical I. The reworking of the performative is fundamental to this line of argumentation. In "Mochlos," Derrida reminds us that "[t]he performative is not *one*: there are various performatives and there are antagonistic or parasitical attempts to interpret the performative power of language, to police it and use it, to invest it performatively."[34] Furthermore, he claims that, "it is too often said that the performative produces the event of which it speaks."[35] Derrida's work with *The Conflict of the Faculties* can indeed be read as one of the places where he critiques any understanding of the performative as a guaranteed path to transformative empowerment. He argues that "in a certain way, theories of the performative are always at the service of powers of legitimation, of legitimized or legitimizing powers," of pre-existing rules and conventions, such as the mastery of a self-identical conscious I that utters the speech act.[36] The performative thus, paradoxically, prevents the possibility of transformative empowerment, that is, the possibility of a future which would not be determined by the very powers that enable performative speech acts in the first place:

> As long as I can produce and determine an event by a performative act guaranteed... then to be sure I will not say that nothing happens or comes about, but what takes place, arrives, happens, or happens *to me* remains still controllable and programmable within a horizon of anticipation or precomprehension, within a horizon period. It is of the order of the masterable possible, it is the unfolding of what is already possible.[37]

To enable the possibility of a radical future, Derrida thus seeks to dissociate the performative from the powers of legitimation. One of the strategies he implements to achieve this is by incorporating reciprocity into the structure of the performative. In this sense, "my" performative utterance would not be mine but would always be that of the other. This re-elaboration is then reflected in the way Derrida conceptualizes the university and its institutional politics. As argued earlier, Derrida takes Kant's discourse on the university as a singular response to complex structural geopolitical, socio-cultural and intellectual changes within the society of his time *and* as an inauguration which constitutes the modern university. For Derrida, a response and inauguration—together with a profession of faith, a commitment, or a declaration of a promise, which are central to his last text on the university, "The Future of the Profession," where he envisions a new humanities—are examples of speech acts that say a performative "yes" to a performative demand made from outside. This "'yes' of the *affirmation*" he explains, "is not reducible to the positivity of a *position*. But it does, in fact, *resemble* a performative speech act. It neither describes nor states anything; it engages by responding."[38] Following this re-elaboration, the university can therefore be understood as an effect of perpetual negotiation, an event constituted through a reciprocal and continuously transforming performative relationship.

Such a conceptualization has several implications. Firstly, it enables Derrida to propose a new way of theorizing and inhabiting the university without the necessity of setting this effort in opposition to previous attempts. It allows him to "keep the memory and keep the chance" as he puts it.[39] It is in this sense that Derrida positions himself, and the academic community he addresses, as the inheritors of Kant's discourse on the university, that is, as inheritors of the task to respond and negotiate an institutional place where freedom of thought would be possible. Like Kant, Derrida is concerned with the question whether "the university can (and if so, how?) affirm an unconditional independence" and wants to "oppose the university to a great number of powers."[40] The way he approaches and proceeds with this task is nonetheless different from Kant. Secondly, it implies that the demand to respond and negotiate does not solely define instances where the question of the university is addressed directly or explicitly but it permeates all university discourses and practices. In other words, questions such as "[W]ho are we in the university?" or "*What* do we represent?"[41] are embedded in all practical decisions through which the university "practices its hierarchies, legitimations and canonizations in its teaching and research," such as those concerning the content of the curricula, pedagogic practices, student admission and assessment, offerings of study program and hiring of the faculty, the structuring and the accessibility of research funding, and the politics of citation and publishing.[42] Finally, it implies that setting up a finite and decidable limit that would regulate the antagonistic field of the university, as Kant attempted in *The Conflict of the Faculties*, is not possible. There is no one, final answer to how to constitute and sustain a university. Nor can be any of the questions concerning its teaching and research, such as those listed above, be settled once and for all. Derrida warns against any inclination toward the certitudes of a clear conscience, and repeatedly stresses that, because the university is a continuously transformed and transforming formation with a structure of a double bind, these questions cannot be traversed or overcome but demand constant reconsiderations and readjustments. In "The Principle of Reason," this imperative is framed as a problem of "strategic rhythm" or "cadence" in how the university "sets its sights and adjusts its views" which Derrida links to the specific topology of the campus of Cornell University.[43] In "Mochlos," he works upon the question of the university as a question of a "strategic lever." *Mochlos*, as he explains, is a Greek word for lever, wedge, or wooden beam, it is "something to lean on for forcing and displacing." In this sense, Kant's *The Conflict of the Faculties* can also be understood as a kind of "lever," a point of departure for envisioning "a foundation of a new university law."[44]

The focus on the significance of "strategic calculation" is another aspect that distinguishes Derrida's work from most of the scholarship on the university generated in the West and/or Global North.[45] Here it has predominantly taken the form of the critique of "instrumentalization," grounded in the concept of "instrumental reason," and following in the footsteps of Adorno, Horkheimer and particularly Habermas, that has been invoked to criticize various aspects of the so-called neoliberalization of knowledge or the "corporatization of the university."[46] According to Derrida, such an approach, which nowadays is most commonly deployed to "defend the humanities" or some of its disciplines, replicates the debate on the purpose of the university and the utility of knowledge through oppositions such as theoretical versus applied research, hard versus soft sciences, or sciences versus humanities. In "The Principle of Reason," he therefore warns that:

> Desiring to remove the university from "useful" programs and from professional ends, one may always, willingly or not, find oneself serving unrecognized ends, reconstituting powers of caste, class, or corporation. We are in an implacable political topography: one step further in view of greater profundity or radicalization… one step further toward a sort of original an-archy risks producing or reproducing the hierarchy.[47]

Simultaneously however, the emphasis on the role of instrumentality in relation to the university and, in this respect also the problematization of the performative, does not imply that Derrida promotes some kind of pragmatic empiricism.[48] On the contrary, the insight that the university is defined by an irresolvable dilemma, that is, has a structure of a double bind, not only implies the necessity of incessant strategic calculation but also itself functions as a "lever" which enables a leap in the direction of a radical future, the "to come" of the university. This focus on futurity is however not an expression of a utopian vision (e.g., one day there will be a new university enlightenment); what opens a future for the university, or leaves its future open, is the "here and now" of a singular engagement that is informed by the recognition that the university has a structure of an irreducible double bind.

For Derrida, the question of the university and its possibility is therefore above all an ethico-political problem. Drawing on Kant, who, as Derrida argues, was also "responding, and was responding in terms of responsibility,"[49] he articulates it as a call to a new university responsibility. Following the logic briefly described above, this responsibility has a structure of a reciprocal performative responding to the call from the other.[50] It is, Derrida argues, "infinite or it is not, excessive or null, forever disturbed or denied"[51] and, as already suggested, can be "invoked only by sounding a call to practice it"[52]—as for instance Derrida performs it in the opening of his essay "Mochlos":

> If we could say we (but have I not already said it), we might perhaps ask ourselves: where are we? And who are we in the university where apparently we are? *What* do we represent? *Whom* do we represent? Are we responsible? For what and to whom? If there is a university responsibility, it at least begins with the moment when a need to hear these questions, to take them upon oneself and respond, is imposed. This imperative for responding is the initial form and minimal requirement of responsibility.[53]

A new university responsibility thus implies a rigorous self-reflexive interrogation that aims to make explicit the political and institutional stakes of university discourses and practices in which we are involved, including the interrogation of the "we" itself. Today, Derrida argues, "we cannot not speak of such things"[54] and identifies "the taking of a position, in work itself, toward the politicoinstitutional structures that constitute and regulate our practice, our competences and our performances" as a minimal requirement and a defining feature of deconstruction.[55]

In "The Future of the Profession" where he envisions a new humanities, Derrida further elaborates that the examination conducted within the humanities should focus on the history of the concept of man and what determines it, such as the opposition human/animal and the question of the woman, that is, the question of sexual difference. The list of the themes that should be at the center of its research further includes the historical and contemporary conceptualizations of democracy and sovereignty (in relation to nation-states, globalization and virtualization); work, profession and professionalization both inside and outside the university; the distinction between the performative and constative speech acts; and questions concerning authorship, art, literature, and singular performative works which Derrida calls *oeuvres*.[56]

Assuming a new university responsibility should, however, not only determine the content of the interrogation but also its form. "These studies and analyses," Derrida argues, "would not be purely theoretical and neutral... [but] they would lead toward practical and performative transformations." This is a matter not only of assuming reciprocal performative relationships, such as the "taking into account the performative value of 'profession,'" that is, as a profession of faith, but also of accepting "that a professor produces '*oeuvres*' and not just knowledge."[57] *Oeuvres*, as he explains, are attached to "the modality of the 'as if,'" and their best-known examples are "*oeuvres d'art* [works of art]," such as "a painting, a concerto, a poem, or a novel." Within the conceptualization of the university that we have inherited from Kant, they have been objects of study but the treatment of works of art, and academic work in general, has depended "on *a knowledge that itself does not consist in oeuvres.*" To produce performative transformations, and thus help the university to protect itself from appropriative powers, Derrida suggests extending this modality also to "the work proper to the university and especially in the Humanities."[58]

Derrida suggests incorporating *oeuvres* within academic work precisely because of the position works of art have occupied in European modernity. For Derrida, literature, or art in general, is not an expression of one's "private life" but "a public institution" which "within a certain European history, is profoundly connected with a revolution in law and politics: the principled authorization that anything can be said publicly."[59] Because literature or art in general embodies "the right to say anything publicly, or keep it secret," it is inseparable from the institution of the university, and both (the university and art) are intrinsically tied to the institution of democracy.[60] By linking the university to *oeuvres*, Derrida thus introduces another way in which the university relates to its outside, a new way in which "the university is in the world that it is attempting to think."[61] He thus provides an answer to the question that we have inherited from Kant's *The Conflict of the Faculties*—the question of how to negotiate an institutional space where freedom of thought and expression would be possible. What is more, he simultaneously, situates the question of the university at the center of a striving to make possible a more just world. As Peggy Kamuf argues, Derrida seeks "to renew the belief that the university must have a future for there to be a future of the world."[62]

4 Conclusion: Mis-using the Enlightenment for the University to Come

Showing how Derrida's particular interest in *The Conflict of the Faculties* triggers a shift in the interpretation of Kant's work, this chapter has argued that the work of this key figure of German Idealism may provide a useful tool for identifying concerns that have defined the institutional politics of the university at present. As suggested in the Introduction, such reading primarily requires that we avoid treating Kant's work as a "monolithic corpus… severed from the circumstances of their original publication"[63] and, instead, focus our attention to the internal diversity of Kant's work and read it against the intellectual, socio-political and institutional conditions of its emergence. In relation to *The Conflict of the Faculties* specifically, I have also showed how Derrida's treatment of this text differs from interpretations that have dominated Kant-scholarship, in which Kant's theorization of the university has drawn relatively little attention. Furthermore, because *The Conflict of the Faculties* has often been understood as standing in contradiction with Kant's earlier theorizations of intellectual and political freedom, his university discourse has even been considered a failure, indicating, at its most extreme, Kant's withdrawal from the project of the enlightenment altogether. Derrida, on the other hand, proposes an entirely different reading, one that understands *The Conflict of the Faculties* as opening a path toward another kind of enlightenment and another kind of university.

Following Derrida, Kant's effort to conceptualize and negotiate an institutional space where free thinking would be possible can, therefore, be understood as providing a "lever" for those seeking to theorize and inhabit the university in a way which would not affirm the unjust configurations of powers that have defined the current university and the world more broadly.[64] Such productive use of Kant's theorization of the university nevertheless requires a particular protocol of reading. On the one hand, it requires close attention to the way in which Kant theorizes the institutional demarcation of the university as an inexorably antagonistic formation. Importantly, for Kant, the university is not only in conflict with its outside, namely the interests and the censorial power of the state but is also in conflict with itself. On Derrida's reading, this line of argumentation results in the university having a structure of a double bind and leads to a conceptualization of the university as a formation that is constituted through reciprocal and continuously transforming performative relationships. On the other hand, what follows from the above is a requirement to read Kant's work against itself. Gayatri Chakravorty Spivak makes a similar point in her deliberations on the university in terms of gendered postcoloniality. In a lecture first delivered at the University of Cape Town in 1994, she reminds us that we have inherited institutional structures—such as the university—from the enlightenment and stresses that she does not propose to turn our backs on this inheritance but to assume a relationship that would result in its "productive undoing." "The post-colonial academy," Spivak argues, "must learn to use the Enlightenment from below; strictly speaking ab-use it."[65] Sara Ahmed labels this kind of project of "productive undoing" a "queer use," and she concludes her own work on the institutional politics of the university by describing this kind of "mis-use" through an image of an out-of-use postbox occupied by nesting birds:

> This image of a postbox is a queer teacher. It teaches us that it is possible for those deemed strangers or foreigners to take up residence in spaces that have been assumed as belonging to others, as being for others to use. The postbox could have remained in use: the nest destroyed before it was completed, the birds displaced. A history of use is a history of such displacements, many violent—displacements that are often unrecognized because of how things remain occupied. It is because of this occupation, this settling of history, this weight, that queering use requires bringing things down. This is why it is not enough to affirm the queerness of use. To bring out the queerness of use requires more than an act of affirmation: it requires a world dismantling effort. In order for queer use to be possible, in order to recover a potential that has not simply been lost but stolen, there is work to do. To queer use is work: it is hard and painstaking work; it is collective and creative work; it is diversity work.
> Queer use is the work we have to do to queer use.
> This image has something else to teach us. Creating a shelter and disrupting usage can refer to the same action:
> A doorway becomes a meeting place.
> A kitchen table becomes a publishing house.
> A postbox becomes a nest.[66]

Notes

1. Most of these texts are collected in Jacques Derrida, *Du Droit à La Philosophie*, Galilée (Paris, 1990), translated into English as *Who's Afraid of Philosophy?: Right to Philosophy 1*, trans. Jan Plug (Stanford, CA: Stanford University Press, 2002) and *Eyes of the University: Right to Philosophy 2*, trans. Jan Plug (Stanford, CA: Stanford University Press, 2004).
2. See Simon Wortham, *Counter-Institutions: Jacques Derrida and the Question of the University* (New York: Fordham University Press, 2006); Michael A. Peters and Gert Biesta, *Derrida, Deconstruction, and the Politics of Pedagogy* (New York: Peter Lang Publishing, 2009); Peter Pericles Trifonas and Michael A. Peters (eds.), *Derrida, Deconstruction and Education: Ethics of Pedagogy and Research* (Oxford: Wiley, 2004); Richard Rand (ed.), *Logomachia: The Conflict of the Faculties* (Lincoln, NA: University of Nebraska Press, 1992).
3. See Wortham, *Counter-Institutions*, 1-24; Benoît Peeters, "In Support of Philosophy," in *Derrida: A Biography*, trans. Andrew Brown (Malden, MA and Cambridge: Polity Press, 2013), 267–87.
4. Immanuel Kant, *The Conflict of the Faculties/ Der Streit Der Fakultäten*, trans. Mary J. Gregor (Lincoln and London: University of Nebraska Press, 1979).
5. Immanuel Kant, "From J. E. Biester, December 17. 1794," in *Philosophical Correspondence, 1759-1799* (Chicago: University of Chicago Press, 1967), 220.
6. Friedrich Wilhelm Joseph von Schelling, *On University Studies*, trans. E. S. Morgan (Athens: Ohio University Press, 1966), 79; see also Jacques Derrida, "Vacant Chair: Censorship, Mastery, Magisteriality," in *Eyes of the University: Right to Philosophy 2*, ed. Werner Hamacher and David E. Wellbery (Stanford, CA: Stanford University Press, 2004), 63.
7. Richard Rand, ed., "Preface," in *Logomachia: The Conflict of the Faculties* (Lincoln and London: University of Nebraska Press, 1992), vii.
8. Howard Caygill, "Kant and the 'Age of Criticism,'" in *A Kant Dictionary* (Oxford: Blackwell Publishers Ltd, 1995), 7–8.

9. In addition to these works, Derrida mentions *The Conflict of the Faculties* in Jacques Derrida, "Theology of Translation," in *Eyes of the University: Right to Philosophy 2*, ed. Werner Hamacher and David E. Wellbery (Stanford, CA: Stanford University Press, 2004), 64–80; Jacques Derrida, "Titles (for the Collège International de Philosophie) (1882)," in *Eyes of the University: Right to Philosophy 2*, ed. Werner Hamacher and David E. Wellbery (Stanford, CA: Stanford University Press, 2004), 195–215; Jacques Derrida, "Privilege: Justificatory Title and Introductory Remarks," in *Who's Afraid of Philosophy: Right to Philosophy 1*, trans. Jan Plug (Stanford, CA: Stanford University Press, 2002), 1–66. See also Jacques Derrida and Richard Rand, "Canons and Metonymies: An Interview Jacques Derrida," in *Logomachia: The Conflict of the Faculties*, ed. Richard Rand (Lincoln and London: University of Nebraska Press, 1992), 195–218; Jacques Derrida, "The 'World' Of the Enlightenment to Come (Exception, Calculation, Sovereignty)," trans. Pascale-Anne Brault and Michael Naas, *Research in Phenomenology* 33 (2003): 9–52; Jacques Derrida, *The Other Heading: Reflections on Today's Europe* (Indiana University Press, 1992).
10. Derrida, "Vacant Chair: Censorship, Mastery, Magisteriality," 55.
11. Derrida, 43.
12. Immanuel Kant, "An Answer to the Question: 'What Is Enlightenment?,'" in *Kant: Political Writings*, ed. Hans Reiss, 2nd ed. (Cambridge: Cambridge University Press, 1991), Immanuel Kant, "An Answer to the Question: 'What Is Enlightenment?,'" in *Kant: Political Writings*, ed. Hans Reiss, 2nd ed. (Cambridge (NY): Cambridge University Press, 1991), 58.
13. Mary J. Gregor, "Translator's Introduction," in *The Conflict of the Faculties/ Der Streit Der Fakultäten* (Lincoln and London: University of Nebraska Press, 1979), ix.
14. Kant, *The Conflict of the Faculties/ Der Streit Der Fakultäten*, 11.
15. See Gregor, "Translator's Introduction"; Caygill, "Kant and the 'Age of Criticism'"; Derrida, "Vacant Chair: Censorship, Mastery, Magisteriality," 44.
16. Howard Caygill, *A Kant Dictionary* (Oxford: Blackwell Publishers Ltd, 1995), 346–50.
17. Kant, "An Answer to the Question: 'What Is Enlightenment?'" 58.
18. For instance, Howard Caygill agrees with Biester's evaluation and considers the argumentation Kant developed in his late work to be 'self-destructive.' Caygill, "Kant and the 'Age of Criticism,'" 8–11.
19. John Mowitt, "The Humanities and the University in Ruin," *Lateral*, no. 1 (2012), https://doi.org/10.25158/L1.1.13.
20. Jacques Derrida, "The Future of the Professor or University without Condition (Thanks to the 'Humanities,' What Could Take Place Tomorrow)," in *Jacques Derrida and the Humanities*, ed. Tom Cohen (Cambridge: Cambridge University Press, 2001), 27.
21. In my interpretation, this, however, does not imply that "there is no need to deconstruct Kant" as for instance Peter Gilgen argues in Peter Gilgen, "Structures, But in Ruins Only: On Kant's History of Reason and the University," *CR: The New Centennial Review* 9, no. 2 (2009): 190.
22. Kant, *The Conflict of the Faculties/ Der Streit Der Fakultäten*, 59.
23. Jacques Derrida, "The Principle of Reason: The University in the Eyes of Its Pupils," trans. Catherine Porter and Edward P. Morris, *Diacritics* 13, no. 3 (1983): 18, https://doi.org/10.2307/464997.
24. J. L. Austin, *How to Do Things with Words: Second Edition - John Langshaw Austin, J. L. Austin - Google Books*, 2nd ed. (Cambridge (MA), 1975), 13.
25. Austin, 94.
26. See J. Hillis Miller, "Performativity as Performance Performativity as Speech Act: Derrida's Special Theory of Performativity," *South Atlantic Quarterly* 106, no. 2 (April 1, 2007): 219–35, https://doi.org/10.1215/00382876-2006-022.
27. See Derrida, *The Other Heading*; Jacques Derrida, *The Politics of Friendship* (Verso, 2005); Derrida, "The Future of the Professor or University without Condition (Thanks to the 'Humanities,' What Could Take Place Tomorrow)."
28. Jacques Derrida, "Mochlos, or The Conflict of the Faculties," in *Logomachia: The Conflict of the Faculties*, ed. Richard Rand (Lincoln and London: University of Nebraska Press, 1992), 11.

29. Derrida, "Vacant Chair: Censorship, Mastery, Magisteriality," 46–47.
30. Derrida, "The Future of the Professor or University without Condition (Thanks to the 'Humanities,' What Could Take Place Tomorrow)," 26.
31. Derrida, "The Principle of Reason," 5.
32. I closely examine Derrida's text "Vacant Chair," where I show how Kant's paradoxical layout of the university is grounded upon and animated by phallogocentrism in Lenka Vráblíková, "Reading the Sexual Economy of Academic Freedom with Sarah Kofman and Jacques Derrida: A Feminist Deconstruction of Kant's Concept of the University," *Australian Feminist Studies* 35, no. 103 (2020): 54–69, https://doi.org/10.1080/08164649.2019.1698285.
33. For a more detailed critique of the rhetoric of crisis that has dominated the scholarship on the university, see Samuel Weber, "Ambivalence, the Humanities and the Study of Literature," *Diacritics* 15, no. 2 (1985): 11–25; Samuel Weber, "The Limits of Professionalism," *Oxford Literary Review* 5, no. 1/2 (1982): 59–79; Dominick LaCapra, "The University in Ruins?," *Critical Inquiry* 25, no. 1 (1998): 32–55; Adam Sitze, "Response to 'The Humanities and the University in Ruin,'" *Lateral*, 2012.
34. Derrida, "Mochlos, or The Conflict of the Faculties," 12.
35. Derrida, "The Future of the Professor or University without Condition (Thanks to the 'Humanities,' What Could Take Place Tomorrow)," 54.
36. Jacques Derrida, "Performative Powerlessness: A Response to Simon Critchley," *Constellations* 7, no. 4 (2000): 467.
37. Derrida, "The Future of the Professor or University without Condition (Thanks to the 'Humanities,' What Could Take Place Tomorrow)," 53.
38. Jacques Derrida, *Without Alibi*, ed. Peggy Kamuf (Stanford University Press, 2002), 301.
39. Derrida, "The Principle of Reason," 20.
40. Derrida, "Mochlos, or The Conflict of the Faculties," 26–28.
41. Ibid., 1.
42. Derrida and Rand, "Canons and Metonymies: An Interview Jacques Derrida," 198.
43. Derrida, "The Principle of Reason," 5.
44. Derrida, "Mochlos, or The Conflict of the Faculties," 30–31.
45. For a more detailed critique of this prevailing approach, see John Mowitt, "On the One Hand, and the Other," *College Literature* 42, no. 2 (2015): 311–36, https://doi.org/10.1353/lit.2015.0023; Robert Young, "The Idea of a Chrestomathic University," in *Logomachia: The Conflict of the Faculties*, ed. Richard Rand (Lincoln and London: University of Nebraska Press, 1992), 97–126.
46. Mowitt, "On the One Hand, and the Other," 311–12.
47. Derrida, "The Principle of Reason," 18.
48. Jacques Derrida, "Remarks on Pragmatism and Deconstruction," in *Deconstruction and Pragmatism*, ed. Simon Critchley and Chantal Mouffe (Routledge, 1996), 79–90.
49. Derrida, "Mochlos, or The Conflict of the Faculties," 3.
50. See for example Jacques Derrida, *The Gift of Death* (University of Chicago Press, 1996); Jacques Derrida, *Of Spirit: Heidegger and the Question* (University of Chicago Press, 1989); Derrida, *The Other Heading*.
51. Derrida and Rand, "Canons and Metonymies: An Interview Jacques Derrida," 204.
52. Derrida, "The Principle of Reason," 16.
53. Derrida, "Mochlos, or The Conflict of the Faculties," 1. I closely examine this opening passage of Derrida's essay in relation to feminist ethics in Lenka Vráblíková, "From Performativity to Aporia: Taking 'Tremendous Responsibility' toward Feminism and the University," *Gender and Education* 28, no. 3 (2016): 359–71, https://doi.org/10.1080/09540253.2016.1169250.
54. Derrida, "The Principle of Reason," 3.
55. Derrida, "Mochlos, or The Conflict of the Faculties," 22–23.
56. Derrida, "The Future of the Professor or University without Condition (Thanks to the 'Humanities,' What Could Take Place Tomorrow)," 50–52.
57. Ibid., 50.

58. Ibid., 38.
59. Derrida, "Remarks on Pragmatism and Deconstruction," 82.
60. Derrida, "The Future of the Professor or University without Condition (Thanks to the 'Humanities,' What Could Take Place Tomorrow)," 27. For a more detailed discussion of the relationship between Derrida's conceptualization of literature, democracy and the university, see J. Hillis Miller, "A Profession of Faith," in *For Derrida* (New York: Fordham University Press, 2009).
61. Derrida, *Without Alibi*, 236.
62. Peggy Kamuf, "The University in the World It Is Attempting To Think," *Culture Machine*, no. 6 (2004).
63. Caygill, "Kant and the 'Age of Criticism,'" 7–8.
64. I am thus in agreement with those who have already mobilized this body of work in their examinations of university's potential to help contest the effects of racial capitalism, cis-heteropatriarchy, ableism and what has become to be known as the Anthropocene. See for example Tuija Pulkkinen, "Identity and Intervention: Disciplinarity as Transdisciplinarity in Gender Studies," *Theory, Culture & Society* 32, no. 5–6 (September 1, 2015): 183–205; Ewa Płonowska Ziarek, "Reframing the Law: Derrida, Women's Studies, Intersectionality," *PhiloSOPHIA* 7, no. 1 (2017): 79–89; Rauna Kuokkanen, *Reshaping the University: Responsibility, Indigenous Epistemes, and the Logic of the Gift* (UBC Press, 2011); Premesh Lalu, "Apartheid's University: Notes on the Renewal of the Enlightenment," *Journal of Higher Education in Africa / Revue de l'enseignement Supérieur En Afrique* 5, no. 1 (2007): 45–60; Premesh Lalu, "What Is the University For?," *Critical Times* 2, no. 1 (April 1, 2019): 39–58; Alan Hodkinson, "The Unseeing Eye: Disability and the Hauntology of Derrida's Ghost—An Analysis in Three Parts"; Gayatri Chakravorty Spivak, *Thinking Academic Freedom in Gendered Post-Coloniality* (Cape Town: University of Cape Town, 1992),; Sara Ahmed, *On Being Included: Racism and Diversity in Institutional Life* (Durham: Duke University Press Books, 2012); Sara Ahmed, *What's the Use?: On the Uses of Use* (Durham: Duke University Press, 2019).
65. As Spivak explains, focusing on the word ab-use, which she gives with a hyphen and parenthesis, the Latin prefix 'ab' means 'below' but it also indicates a 'motion a way', 'agency, point of origin', 'supporting', as well as 'the duties of slaves.' Gayatri Chakravorty Spivak, *An Aesthetic Education in the Era of Globalization* (Harvard University Press, 2013), 3–4.
66. Ahmed, *What's the Use?*, 228–29.

Enlightenment and Revolution

Kyla Bruff

1 Introduction: The Role of Kant in Foucault's Remarks on Revolution

In his analyses of the French Revolution in the 1790s, Kant draws a crucial distinction, which allows him to ascribe a positive, philosophical significance to the Revolution, while at the same time condemning its isolated acts of terror, especially the execution of the King.[1] This distinction, which Foucault takes up in his 1983 lecture, "What is Revolution?," is between the French Revolution as an event which functions as a "historical sign [*Geschichtszeichen*]" on the one hand, and the morally unjustifiable acts that make up the Revolution on the other.[2] While he appreciates the enthusiasm of the spectators of the French Revolution and interprets the Revolution as a sign of the progress of humanity, Kant rejects the right to resist state authority, the right to revolt, and thereby the right to revolution.[3] In this way, Kant lays the foundation for the late Foucault's criticisms of revolutionary ideals and attempts to pursue them through means of terror and violence *and* his suggestion that the excitement for revolution can show something positive regarding the drive of human beings toward freedom.

By effectuating what appears to be a poststructuralist move in dividing the signifier (the Revolution itself) from the openness of the signified (the Revolution's potential meaning, which exceeds it and which is not completely fulfilled in the present, but rather extends into the future), Kant provides the grounds for Foucault to explore the philosophical significance of the enthusiasm of the spectators who live through revolutions, without therefore providing a justification, even retrospectively, of the right to revolution. That being said, from a poststructuralist point of

K. Bruff (✉)
Carleton University, Ottawa, ON, Canada
e-mail: kyla.bruff@carleton.ca

view, Kant perhaps gives too much shape to the signified by associating the meaning of the Revolution with the progress of humanity toward a more free, peaceful condition. Foucault remains cautious on such matters. Although he agrees with Kant that there *is* a will to revolution, or an enthusiasm for it, which is detectable in revolutions throughout history, the "work of freedom" and the form of its future manifestations are left "undefined."[4] In this way, both Kant and Foucault address crucial questions regarding revolutionary activity, equally important to the German Idealists and Romantics as to twentieth-century French Intellectuals,[5] without falling firmly on either side of the "pro-" or "anti-" revolutionary binary; these are questions such as whether terror and violence can be legitimized in the name of social progress, and whether enthusiasm for revolutionary movements is warranted or amounts simply to *Schwärmerei*. While Kant and Foucault generally answer the first question with a no, the second question is trickier, for their appreciation for revolutionary enthusiasm is primarily a retrospective one.

Foucault's statements on revolution are not unified throughout his writings. Indeed, the very concept of revolution presents an apparent tension in Foucault's work. This tension can be identified in his reading of Kant on the Enlightenment and the French Revolution, as presented in three lectures near the end of his life: "What is Critique?" (1978), "What is Revolution?" (1983), "What is Enlightenment?" (1983, published in 1984).[6] After referencing Kant both critically and appreciatively in various works throughout the 1960s and 1970s, Foucault turns to Kant anew in these lectures.[7] Kant's "What is Enlightenment?" essay is an important resource for Foucault's articulation of the Enlightenment-based *critical* attitude he sees himself as espousing, first toward modes of governance and their effect on subjectification, and then toward the ever-changing present out of which the thinker thinks and the shifting scope of possibilities for the self. The self is always caught between relations of power, truth, and subjectivity and should find ways to resist and transgress the limits which constrain it. This brings Foucault to revolution, the enthusiasm for which, as presented in Kant's *The Conflict of the Faculties*, can reveal aspects of the mentality and historical conditions of the pursuit of freedom in a given place and time. Foucault's interest in revolutions, therefore, is related to his attempts to critically understand the present and his late concern with finding localized instances of human freedom within historical conditions and networks of relations of power and knowledge.

To summarize his position on revolution in relation to Kant, on the one hand, Foucault shares with Kant a positive view of the exercise of a "will to revolution," which can be understood as a will to freedom, through history. This will was first detected by Kant in the French Revolution (and can be identified in prior "great revolutions") and persists within human beings today.[8] In his late lectures on Kant, Foucault proposes that the human drive to pursue freedom via the transgression of limits in the present time can be productively considered in terms of this will, also described as "enthusiasm."[9] The will to revolution, for Foucault, is a will to freedom, an enthusiasm for a future with more possibilities.

On the other hand, Foucault shares Kant's critical perspective of planned attempts to achieve a better political future through revolutionary activity. The late Foucault goes so far as to consider himself as a kind of disciple of Kant, linking his work on subjectivity and truth to Kant. Kant initiated the critical attitude through which Foucault proposes that one examine oneself and one's embeddedness in one's surroundings, as a speaker, thinker, and actor.[10] This post-Enlightenment approach to self-understanding and the present Foucault calls a "historical ontology of ourselves."[11] However, despite this shared perspective, Foucault and Kant differ on the questions of progress and freedom. Foucault rejects any notion of teleology or progress in history. For Foucault, freedom is not about the autonomous use reason, but is a more open concept, concerned with one's shifting sphere of possible speech and activity in relation to critique and transgression. As Johanna Oksala puts it, despite the fact that "Foucault's thought—and post-structuralist thinking as a whole—is often read as a rejection of the subject" as an "agent of social or epistemic changes," it is possible to "rethink freedom" with Foucault.[12] Despite their differences, as I will show, there is some overlap in Foucault's and Kant's identifications of historical conditions necessary, especially in relation to authority, to be able to exercise one's freedom, which Kant particularly investigates in reference to public reason in the "What is Enlightenment?" essay.[13]

In his late work, freedom is a positive concept for Foucault, rather a naïve, evasive one, which disappears under the new and hidden forms of domination produced by the Enlightenment.[14] Kant's notion of the Enlightenment, picked up on by Foucault, is not about "personal, private freedom," but is present "when the universal, the free, and the public uses of reason are superimposed on one another."[15] Of course, Foucault will not defend the universal use of reason, nor will he agree with Kant on the need to obey authority "in conformity with universal reason."[16] But Kant and the Enlightenment importantly open the questions of *historical* use of reason. This is the question of "knowing how the use of reason can take the public form that it requires, how the audacity to know can be exercised in broad daylight, while individuals are obeying."[17]

2 Foucault on Revolution and Transgression: A Constellation Between Kant, Nietzsche, and the Ancients

Foucault is not simply an anti-revolutionary. Despite many appearances of arguments against revolution in Foucault's work, there is evidence in favor of reading Foucault as a supporter of revolution in his repeated call for resistance to power. This advocacy for resistance amounts to Foucault's conditional support for "revolutionary action" in the struggle against the normative workings of power through institutions in the early 1970s.[18] Generally speaking, Foucault focuses on the way individuals challenge and transgress the limits to (what they identify as) their realm of possible experience. He advocates for resistance to the mechanisms of control in a society in which relations of domination and subjugation, perpetuated by the circulation of power through norms and institutions, are ubiquitous.[19] In the context of his positive endorsement of the will to revolution and his support for transformative change, despite his criticisms of the pursuit of revolution, the concept of revolution also seems to take on a positive, and even normative, significance in Foucault's work. Individuals are instructed to pursue freedom through transgressive activity.

In consideration of Foucault's ambiguous stance on revolution, it is important to note that Foucault visits Iran twice in 1978, penning thirteen essays, giving numerous interviews, and providing written responses, all on the topic of the Iranian Revolution.[20] On numerous occasions, he expresses support for this Revolution. He writes with great respect for the "dreams" of an Islamic Government in Iran, in which religious structures would be used "not only as centers of resistance, but also as sources for political creation."[21] In these texts, Foucault appreciates the readiness of people in "uprisings" to "risk their lives in the face of a power that they believe to be unjust."[22]

The journalistic medium in which Foucault expresses these opinions is not unimportant. His concern with his own relation to the present, especially in reference to the ongoing Iranian Revolution, finds a parallel in Kant's engagement with the present through the period of the French Revolution. Kant similarly expresses his views on the Revolution in the form of magazine articles, often in the *Berlinische Monatsschrift*—the magazine in which "What is Enlightenment?" was first published.[23] In this way, both Foucault and Kant take on the role of public philosophers of their own respective presents. However, Foucault takes this role a step further than Kant by his going to Iran as a public journalist, but at the same time as a private person, who was not representing the academy. As a private person, Foucault retained a public function to report back to newspapers and the media (especially to the Italian newspaper *Corriere della Sera*, as well as *Le Monde* and *Le Nouvel Observateur*). A trip with such a mission would be unacceptable for Kant. On Kant's account, the philosopher may go to Iran in his "private" role, but in his "public" role, he must only *reason* about revolution, not implicate himself in it. Of course, in Kant's example, the private individual is the one who is conservatively governed by the state and is performing his state-assigned function, while the public person claims the limited freedom of the lower faculty of philosophy.[24] Foucault thus blends the public and the private in his travels to Iran, expressing his own private partiality to the revolution in a public voice (for countermeasure, Foucault condemns the use of terror and violence by groups seeking to overthrow existing government in *Le Nouvel Observateur* and *Tribune socialiste* in 1977). One could never imagine Kant coming so close to revolutionary participation.[25] Nevertheless, by turning to Kant on the concept of revolution, Foucault allows his relationship to political activism to be mediated through the practice of a constant critical attitude, which promotes a cautious approach to revolutionary programs and involvement through self-oriented critique. Through critique and his analyses of power, Foucault acknowledges his own limitations and possible oversights as a historically situated thinker of his present.

On that point, despite his occasional expressions of appreciation for revolutionary activity, Foucault is skeptical of whether human beings can ever possibly envisage—let alone bring about through revolution—the conditions of a better, more just society. Foucault's assessment of the formative, conditioning role of power relations in all human life seems to undercut the possible value of any attempt to draw the contours of a society free of oppression, let alone the justification of the pursuit of such a society through revolutionary means. Foucault states, "I admit to not being able to define, nor for even stronger reasons to propose, an ideal social model for the functioning of our scientific or technological society."[26] He repeatedly denounces universalist political programs. Moreover, there is no reason to assume that any oppressed group that emerges victorious in a revolution would be immune from exercising and abusing their newly acquired power to oppress others, regardless of their intentions.

I argue that these apparently conflictual statements on revolution are compatible if we read them together as an endorsement of the will to revolution and "revolutionary," transgressive activity *without the encouragement to undertake specific, planned political revolutions*. Foucault encourages individuals to exercise and expand their capacities to speak and to act, a practice that originates in the critique of the historically contingent limitations of the scope of possible activity and experience. This critical work should lead to localized acts of transgression. The critique of such contingent limits, which are mistakenly taken to be absolute, whether in the form of theoretical or socio-political universals, should bring one to transgress these limits, change them, and experiment at the thresholds of the possible. This pursuit can lead individuals to "escape" or break through some of what appears to be necessary in history.

Foucault directly criticizes revolutionary political programs that are utopic or timeless. Preferable to planning or joining a revolution is the careful, rigorous, constant assessment of our present conditions and ways of thinking within our own specific moment in history. Once we identify restrictions on our field of possible speech and action, which is constantly being narrowed through practices, norms, and institutions that dominate and subjectify us, we can resist and transgress them. From here, we can engage in contextualized self-examination, participate boldly in public discourse, discover our capabilities, and, in this way, pursue freedom.

To develop this complex position on transgression, revolution, critique, and self-examination, Foucault requires more interlocutors than Kant alone. For Foucault, Kant's call for the courageous use of reason in public, while simultaneously recognizing that reason *itself* is has limits, must be supplemented by the resources Nietzsche provides to acknowledge the precarity of the subject, the roles of drive and power in human activity, and the non-linearity of history. Foucault also invokes the Ancient Greeks and Romans, particularly the Epicureans, Cynics and Stoics, on the concept of *parrēsia*, or speaking freely and openly, to show what it means to execute the critical attitude of the Enlightenment. In this section I will construct a "constellation," in which I read Foucault in dialogue with these thinkers to arrive at his final view of the transgressive activity and the self and of his position on revolution.

Foucault establishes an early pattern of turning to Nietzsche to counterbalance the universalist tendency in Kant, particularly the establishment of universal structures of knowledge. Foucault is convinced that Kant's critical project in fact leaves a space for historical, empirical, and cultural accounts of subjectivity and the creative production of knowledge, for which he invokes Nietzsche. As early as his secondary doctoral thesis on Kant's *Anthropology from a Pragmatic Point of View* (1959–1960), Foucault shows appreciation for Kant's critique of the limits of knowledge and the importance of an empirical and historical approach to human existence, while also turning to Nietzsche.[27] Empiricity, Foucault notes, cannot provide its own (theoretical) ground; its principles are revealed through the concepts and structures of the three *Critiques* (structures which Foucault, of course, will not accept, on his own account, as absolute).[28] Important for Foucault is that Kant identifies that we can only approach finitude as always already organized through the set of conditions under which we know it.[29] Finite being is always already conditioned by a set of forms that critical thought attempts to reveal.[30] This search for the hidden structures underlying conditions of finitude and subjectivity is a theme that recurs in Foucault's thought, even if his own critical attitude is *not* transcendental, but rather "genealogical in its design and archaeological in its method."[31]

For Foucault, there is no "natural access" to the foundational structures or "essence" of the human being.[32] Nothing we identify about the transcendental subject is natural or true in an unshakable, foundational sense. Foucault thus concludes that we ought to turn our attention to the *critique* of the self-grounding, epistemological subject, which is always enmeshed in a series of relations and conditions that it can never exhaustively identify. Anything deemed to be natural in the human being should be subject to constant critique, through which we uncover and scrutinize *who we are in the present*.[33] Concepts like "meaning," "structure," and "genesis," which "circulate indiscriminately throughout the human sciences," are insufficient to justify what we think an who we are.[34] What is needed is a "*critique* of the anthropological illusion*" of the self-grounding of finitude as a basis from which one can seek truth.[35] This is precisely what Foucault thinks Nietzsche can provide.

The "trajectory" of Kant's crucial question, "What is the human being [*Was ist der Mensch*]?" comes to "its end in the response which both challenges and disarms it: *der Übermensch* [the overman]."[36] Nietzsche, even for the young Foucault, holds a disruptive and liberatory function, especially though the concept of the overman. Nietzsche is a motivating force in Foucault's radical critique of, and thereby a way out from, existing illusions about the nature of the human being and of the infinite.[37] Nietzsche's "double murderous" gesture of critiquing the pre-established concept of "man in his finitude" while simultaneously critiquing (killing) God, for Foucault, is "as liberating with regard to man" as it is "with regard to the infinite."[38] From here, we can embark upon a liberatory "desubjectification" process.[39] This endorsement of Nietzsche foreshadows the radical depth of how far the late Foucault thinks we should take Kant's Enlightenment "ethos" of critique.

In Foucault's work more generally, especially *The Order of Things*, Nietzsche's critiques of the "last man," herd mentality, collective complacency, and idealistic thinking come together with Kant's identification of the constitutive role of the subject in her representations.[40] This hybrid critical attitude is at the root of Foucault's interpretation of revolution and utopia in relation to the Enlightenment. For example, Foucault recalls that one of the characteristics of the "arrangement of knowledge" in the second half of the Enlightenment critically addressed by Nietzsche is "the fulfillment of an end to History."[41] Any given population's vision of the ideal end of history that ought to be pursued through revolutionary means is itself historically conditioned, and therefore is not stable and immemorial. For example, Foucault explains that the utopias of development between the Classical and Enlightenment ages differed in a fundamental way, which he links back to the Copernican—in turn, Kantian—revolution regarding the center of representation and meaning.

In the Classical period, on Foucault's account, utopia is concerned with origins and what could unfold from them. "Utopia functioned rather as a fantasy of origins."[42] This view is connected with the one-to-one connection representations had with the presence of objects at that time.[43] By contrast, utopia in the nineteenth century was associated with deceleration, decline, and a slowing down—"the final decline of time rather than with its morning."[44] This, Foucault is clear, is linked to a paradigm shift in the nature of knowledge and the role of the finite, human being's place within it—a shift in which Kant holds an important historical role. Knowledge itself is now understood to be in movement, for, the connections that we make as situated human beings are part of its constitution. In consideration of this epistemic dynamicity, the last age of history, from the late-Enlightenment point of view, will be marked by either a "slow erosion or violent eruption," which will cause a breakthrough of the immobile secret, "man's anthropological truth."[45] This final expression of the truth of the human being at the end of history is accordingly linked to the reconceptualization of finitude and time. Any truth that is established within finitude is truth within time. In line with the Copernican Revolution in thought, whose consequences were brought to the fore by Kant, history and its events are specific to the human being. As a result, time is considered to be neither metaphysical nor cyclic. Historical events, such as revolutions, are *our* historical events, void of permanence, but with expressive potential. Finitude and the construction of history occur in time, and thus the "great dream of an end to History" is a utopia that is specific to "causal systems of thought," which have the finite human being as their self-confessed origin.[46] Enlightenment utopia is therefore concerned with the winding down of time and the development of knowledge, as relative to the finite human being, whose true essence exceeds her finitude and will be revealed at the end of history. But as a historically contingent utopia, it does not have the last word.

Nietzsche, particularly through his concept of the eternal return, dares to reconceptualize the possible relationship of human finitude to time. This is crucial for how we think about the role of the human being in history in relationship to ideal societies and utopian political programs. Foucault links Nietzsche's rethinking of this relationship to his proclamation of the death of God (which, it is to be noted, is *enabled* by the Enlightenment thesis on the end of time) and the "odyssey of the last man."[47] The human being ought to seize the opportunity of the end of time to find her own truth and values through the "prodigious leap" of the overman.[48] Moreover, the eternal return offers the individual an opportunity to relate to the concept of infinity *through finitude*, precisely by leveraging the power of one's finite existence in a way that matters uniquely to the single individual. Nietzsche encourages us to give significance to everything we do in the *context* of the infinite and the eternal, without thereby violating Kant's critique of reason, that is, without initiating a return to a metaphysics of absolute truths or to the old dogmas of the relationship of representation (and thus thought) to objects. The stability of the "archeological framework" of nineteenth-century Enlightenment and post-Enlightenment thinking was accordingly, to speak in a Foucauldian key, set ablaze by Nietzsche, who cleared a path for a rethinking of the "promises" of this period.[49]

Nietzsche problematizes the course of history as understood in (especially nineteenth-century) theories of utopia and revolution and the relationship of human action to different paradigms and structures (e.g., tragedy).[50] In general, he criticizes common understandings of Enlightenment ideals in relation to their historical context. As James Schmidt emphasizes, Nietzsche seeks to disentangle Enlightenment individualism from political revolutions.[51] The "egalitarian dreams" of the French Revolution, particularly as represented by Rousseau, for example, are in fact prohibitive to the individual's pursuit of "the work of the Enlightenment," especially insofar as the latter would signify free, independent thinking.[52]

Let us now turn our attention to how Foucault supplements Kant's defense of public reason and the courage it requires with the ability to speak freely in the ancient sense of *parrēsia*. *Parrēsia* refers to a way of speaking frankly and truthfully, and requires "the opening the heart."[53] As noted above, Kant makes a case for reason to be "free in its public use" and encourages people to debate rationally in public.[54] Everyone should be able to speak freely and participate in public debates regarding matters of common concern. On Foucault's account, this is the opposite of what is "ordinarily" called "freedom of conscience," which rather calls for one to think freely in private but obey in public. The capacity and courage to express oneself freely—the capacity for *parrēsia*—is necessary for carrying out the ethos of the Enlightenment and for developing one's self-relation, or for "caring for oneself."[55] It also involves a type of risk-taking familiar to us from Nietzsche—frankness, boldness, courage in speaking and acting. It is in moments of intense *risk* in the resistance and rejection of regimes and laws that freedom and the "subjectivity (not that of great men, but that of anyone)" is strongest for Foucault.[56]

Moreover, Foucault directly links Kant's "critique of the Enlightenment" with *parrēsia* in his lectures on *The Hermeneutics of the Subject* in 1982:

> Kant's text on the *Aufklärung* is a certain way for philosophy, through the critique of the *Aufklärung*, to become aware of problems which were traditionally problems of *parrēsia* in antiquity, which will re-emerge in the sixteenth and seventeenth centuries, and which became aware of themselves in the *Aufklärung*, and particularly in Kant's text.[57]

The ancients, just as Kant and the moderns, identify impediments to speaking freely and question power and processes of subjectification in view of the construction of truth. This can only be done in dialogue with others and must be tested through concrete action. One develops one's independence as a subject through speaking courageously and truthfully, which involves risk, as we often speak to those "who cannot accept [our] truth."[58] *Parrēsia* thus helps us, claims Foucault in reference to

Seneca, to "manage" the soul. We live its consequences.[59] When we speak freely, the "effectiveness and usefulness of the speech heard" must be put into action so we can assess the effectivity of what has been said.[60] Thus, the words I speak have a *function* that extends beyond them.[61]

The critical project, as initiated by Kant, requires an interrogation of the present, which begins from understanding *what* we are, as historically conditioned beings. The prominent role of *parrēsia* in Foucault's work in the early 1980s can thus be seen as an extension of Foucault's interest in Kant's critical attitude in reference to one's own speech and positions, both in theoretical and practical domains.[62] Self-awareness and freedom should be pursued through the exercise of the critical, *parrēsiatic* attitude. *Parrēsia*, as a type of free speech, concerns freedom. It is "bound up with the choice, decision, and attitude of the person speaking'" to such an extent that, Foucault notes, it was translated into "*libertas*" in Latin. "The telling of all *parrēsia* was rendered by *libertas*: the freedom of the person speaking."[63] *Parrēsia* is therefore bound up with the moral attitude that one adopts publicly, which engenders self-examination and self-liberation. For this reason, Foucault describes *parrēsia* as an ethical attitude.

While Foucault and Kant share an "Idealist" concern for freedom, their positions ultimately differ. For Foucault, practical freedom does not depend on "*transcendental freedom*," or "independence from everything empirical," as in Kant's *Critique of Practical Reason*.[64] Freedom is practical all the way down. It breaks open new possibilities for creative subjectivity through transgression. Through freedom, we can discover, in practice, new ways of speech, action, and self-relation, which we co-constitute in the historical spaces in which we operate through courageous, honest activity. The path one takes to resisting and transgressing limits, thus exercising one's freedom, cannot be determined through the universalization of maxims or an appeal to universal principles.[65] Additionally, we have no "innate right" to freedom, as in Kant.[66] These differences notwithstanding, Kant's definition of freedom in the "What is Enlightenment?" essay, "to make *public use* of one's reason in all matters," presents an opportunity for a possible overlap with the freedom exercised through the pursuit of *parrēsiatic* activity, and the courage and risk involved.

3 Foucault on the Will to Revolution as a Will to Freedom

Foucault's interest in revolutions is not about the future that could be, or even the injustice of the past. It is rather in the significance of the widespread experience and perception of major revolutions by the larger population—in his terms, the role of the revolution as a "spectacle"—that has value for the philosophical critique of the *present*, a task which Foucault appropriates from Kant. By critically reflecting on the present, Kant practices this "ethos" of the Enlightenment, which is an attitude of permanently critiquing the present from within. Kant simultaneously recognizes himself as a thinker of the Enlightenment and yet vehemently critiques the "immaturity" of his present moment from within, presenting a path, through the use of public reason, to transgress the external sources and structures of authority and control. Foucault attempts to uphold this attitude.

The importance of revolutions as collective experiences *and* as historical signs, which are overdetermined with philosophical significance for Foucault, does not amount to an endorsement of revolutionary political programs that aim to bring about a better society. Rather, Foucault focuses on the reflection of the philosopher on herself and the present and the exercise of the *will* to revolution (which is also the will to freedom). The critical approach that the philosopher takes to the present should, through its revelatory and destabilizing functions, present challenges and possibilities to transgress existing paradigms and universals, which not only constitute knowledge and truth but can be seen as limiting what is possible.

The *will* or *enthusiasm* for revolution is distinguished from the revolutionary event. The detachment of this "will" from the event is possible because the event, as is exposed through the poststructuralist tradition, is irreducible to a single occurrence that took place on certain dates. The effects of the event "French Revolution" are beyond the Revolution itself and yet to be fully comprehended. Accordingly, the will to revolution, shared by the *spectators* of the revolution, can hold back from mobilizing itself into rapid action and from a total unification with the development of reality.

This will, initially proposed by Kant in *The Conflict of the Faculties*, is first and foremost present in each individual, as the drive and enthusiasm, which, to borrow from one of Foucault's essays on Iran, motivates the type of "uprooting that interrupts the unfolding of history" as people "rise up."[67] It is a will, but also an *enthusiasm*, found not only in those who take part in a revolutionary uprising but also in those who experience the revolution as a moment in history. As Kant describes it, the will to revolution displays itself in a group of individuals as a risky "partiality" for one side, a "universal yet disinterested sympathy." It is detectable in the "mode of thinking of the spectators which reveals itself publicly in this game of great revolutions."[68] In a major revolution, it is found in the "hearts of all spectators," who share a "wishful participation."[69] One can appeal to it when inciting political change.[70]

Foucault claims that this will persists throughout history. His remarks suggest that there could be an ahistorical element to the human being—a source of freedom—that motivates her to resist her own domination and to will freedom in the face of power. On my reading, the will to revolution is the condition of the freedom of an individual to resist and transgress, which in turn prevents the individual's total dissolution into power relations or into the sum-total of the conditions of her own subjectification. To will her own freedom, the individual human being must exceed her social and historical conditions. Although it is internal to us, the will to revolution is *recognizable* as the enthusiasm that accompanies the collective experience of major political upheavals all throughout history. In rare moments, it can coalesce, as Foucault thinks was the case in Iran, into a fleeting, coordinated expression of a collective will.[71]

At a minimum, there is a great deal of openness as to how we interpret the will to revolution in Foucault, especially as a will to freedom from, for example, oppressive rule.[72] In 1978, after having steered clear of the will for many years, Foucault sees that it is "necessary to pose the problem of will" in both collective and individual senses.[73] Foucault himself says that he "tried to avoid" the "question of the human will," but in relation to revolution and the critique of governing practices, it became an "unavoidable" topic for him.[74] In relation to the "decision-making will not to be governed," the late Foucault, while expressing skepticism on the topic, will not totally rule out the possible existence of "an originary freedom, absolutely and wholeheartedly resistant to any governmentalization."[75] This contentious claim could support a case for a free will at the root of transgression.

Despite what has been said, Foucault himself is not intensely concerned with describing and testifying to the will to revolution, but rather with the more precise question of "what must be done" with it, "with this *enthusiasm* for the Revolution, which is something other than the revolutionary enterprise itself"?[76] The question of the presence and direction of this will—its historical manifestations and what to do with it—is linked, for Foucault, to how "give new impetus, as far and wide as possible, to the undefined work of freedom."[77] Freedom for Foucault on its own is an "empty dream"; it *requires* an "experimental," "historico-critical attitude," the work of which is done at the "limits of ourselves."[78] What is thus required is the critical work of a "historical investigation" of the present, specifically into our contingent conditions that appear to be necessary. Critique allows us to identify the "possibility of no longer being, doing, or thinking what we are, do, or think."[79] It can help us to discover how things could be different, for ourselves and for the society in which we live. Through such critical reflection, we can engage in a "patient labor giving form to our impatience for liberty."[80]

According to Foucault, Kant is the first proponent of this desirable philosophical attitude or "ethos." Kant engages in this critical, reflective "practice of liberty that simultaneously respects [the reality of modernity] and violates it."[81] He does so firstly by asking *persistent questions about who we are in the here and now*; in his writings on Enlightenment and the French Revolution, Kant carries out, in his own time, the "permanent critique of ourselves" and the critical analysis of "limits," both of which are part of the Enlightenment "ethos."[82]

However, Kant identifies an aim for the will to revolution that Foucault would not endorse.[83] Specifically, for Kant, the expression of this will is a sign of the teleological progress of history rooted in a shared moral disposition of humanity. He claims that the experience of the French Revolution in particular "points to the disposition and capacity of the human being to be the cause of its own advance towards the better."[84] The will or enthusiasm for revolution, like all "genuine enthusiasm," claims Kant, "moves only towards what is ideal and, indeed, what is purely moral, such as the concept of right, and it cannot be grafted onto self-interest."[85] It teleologically drives us on, whether or not we know it, toward a moral and political condition, which will culminate in a fair constitution and the freedom of all.[86] That being said, for Kant, this teleology remains an "idea of reason" that can only have regulative status. It is therefore not an ontological concept. Foucault, however, would never accord teleology even such regulative status.

Foucault's refusal to provide an assessment or judgment about this outcome of the will to revolution poses an interpretive challenge. Certainly, he would not commit to Kant's decision to place human beings, by virtue of their natural disposition, at the basis of any narrative of the inevitable progress of history. Even setting the concrete production of a people's constitution as the goal of the will to revolution would be too specific for Foucault. But this does not result in a problem, for Foucault's focus is on precisely *how* interpretations of revolutions as historically significant spectacles contribute to different interpretations of the present. Kant initiates an important move for Foucault, directing our attention to "what happens in the heads of those who do not participate in [the Revolution] or, in any case, are not its principal actors." He shifts our focus to their enthusiasm and "the relationship they themselves have to this Revolution of which they are not the active agents."[87] Kant impressively does this from within a tradition in which signs of progress were sought not in the collective experiences of revolution, but in the "reversal of empires," the disappearance of old states, and the "reversal of fortunes."[88] In the "What is Enlightenment?" essay, Kant alternatively encourages us to look to the "less grandiose," "less perceptible" events to identify the sign of progress.[89] It is noteworthy that although the French Revolution is indeed grandiose, Kant here anonymizes it as yet another revolution of a "gifted people."[90]

Foucault and Kant focus on the change that revolutionary events instigate within those who "watch" these events and have "sympathy" for them.[91] The change in the mentality of people who experience the exciting and turbulent times of political revolutions is more important than whether or not a given revolution is a success or failure. For example, in Kant's time, the events of the Revolution prompted people to reflect and understand that they *should* have their own constitutions, rights, and a state of peace and that they *should* use their own reason.

This approach to revolution requires a "recodifying" of values surrounding the signs of social change. We no longer seek to evaluate the outcomes of major political events, but rather look to their significance for how people understand and analyze their own present. Such a "recodification process" enables "us to express the important meaning and value we are seeking" (in this case, the past, present, and future value of the event of the revolution as signifier which "apparently, is without meaning and value," which for Kant proves that progress has a cause outside of time).[92]

While Kant's conclusions about the value of the French Revolution amount to problematic claims regarding the existence of progress and human nature, we can turn the analysis around and view Kant himself as a contextualized subject of history who *was looking for a cause of progress* to explain a theory he espoused in his own time. This allows for a Foucauldian reading of Kant against Kant, seeing the latter as seeking an *event* as the cause (and thus as evidence of, a sign of) "progress" in his changing time. Despite its significance for Kant, once again, the French Revolution is not to be evaluated in terms of its objective results for France or for Europe: the "content" of the Revolution, according to Kant, is "*unimportant*," because "its existence attests to a permanent virtuality."[93] This virtuality concerns the changing mentality of people, as individuals able to challenge external authority and who participate in the historical application of reason.[94]

On the topic of the will to revolution, Foucault once again merges the influences of Kant Nietzsche, this time without naming the latter. The proximity between Foucault's will to revolution and Nietzsche's will to power has been noted by scholars, such as Jürgen Habermas and Maurizio Passerin d'Entrèves.[95] D'Entrèves notes that any comparison between the two is complex and open to numerous interpretations. Habermas, however, narrowly aligns the will to revolution with the "will to knowledge."[96] While Habermas justly recognizes the importance of the will to revolution, his interpretation of Foucault's use of this concept is not without its own motive. Habermas' identification of this will with the "will to knowledge" allows him to claim that Foucault is contradicting himself through his late return to Kant (to whose philosophy, Habermas notes, Foucault sees himself as heir). "Up to now," writes Habermas, "Foucault traced this will to knowledge in modern power-formations only to denounce it. Now, however, he presents it in a completely different light, as the critical impulse worthy of preservation and in need of renewal."[97] Habermas concludes that Foucault's genealogical critique of power always needed "normative yardsticks," Foucault simply never admitted it. Thus, Habermas suggests, Foucault's late return to Kant could be his "re-entrance" into the "discourse of modernity" in which normative commitments undergird the analysis of human activity in history.[98]

However, the presence of normativity in Foucault's work is nothing new. Resisting illegitimate forms of governmental rule requires minimum normative commitments, and questions of *which* institutional practices to resist and *how* questions were already addressed by Foucault in reference to his genealogical analyses of power in the 1970s (discussed below).

I agree with d'Entrèves' proposal that a productive alternative to the Habermasian identification of the will to revolution with the will to knowledge is to identify it with the "will to freedom," which "would transgress the limits of the given and provide a space for the refashioning of subjectivity."[99] But this will to freedom need not be seen as "prosaic," "non-Nietzschean," and divorced from the "will to power," as d'Entrèves proposes. An interpretation of the will to power as the will to freedom (and thus the will to self-overcoming in the process of transgressing limits) is not antithetical to Nietzsche's own presentation of the will to power in *Beyond Good and Evil*. The "will to power" here describes "life itself,"[100] and philosophy is "the most spiritual will to power" which aims at the "creation of the world."[101] Philosophers are not just guided by the "will to truth," nor are they guided by a will to explicitly dominate others. Rather, they aim at a form of world-creation in the image of their own philosophical *decisions*. The will to power in this context is engaged in free creation, even though this drive is also admittedly described by Nietzsche as "tyrannical."[102] The creative aspect of the will to revolution, understood as a will to freedom in relation to becoming oneself while participating in the alteration of one's conditions, through transgression and creation, can thus be productively linked with Nietzsche's will to power.

4 The Distinction Between the Revolutionary Enterprise and the Revolution as a Spectacle

Foucault is interested not in revolution as a goal or "model" for a future society, but more specifically in the revolutionary will as a drive, an enthusiasm, and an "impatience for liberty."[103] "The question for philosophy," explains Foucault, is "not to determine which is the part of the Revolution that it would be most fitting to preserve and uphold as a model."[104] Kant's interest in the French Revolution is also *not* in the "revolutionary enterprise" itself as a vision for social change and its outcome. Rather, Kant explores the will to revolution and the broader *experience* of the revolution as a *spectacle* in European society in his time. Foucault picks up on this distinction between the revolutionary enterprise and the philosophical value of the revolution as a spectacle and develops it to refine his position on revolution insofar as it concerns an analysis of the present.

The critique of the "enterprise of revolution" or revolution as a "model" is linked to Foucault's criticisms of large-scale revolutionary activity, which he developed in the 1970s. While he encourages localized, revolutionary resistance to institutional practices, for example in schools and prisons,[105] he describes his own intellectual project as modest and not radical. From here stems his critique of revolutionary action, which he articulates in a debate with a number of French historians in 1978:

> I don't feel myself capable of effecting the 'subversion of all codes,' 'dislocation of all orders of knowledge,' 'revolutionary affirmation of violence,' 'overturning of all contemporary culture,' these hopes and prospectuses which currently underpin all those brilliant intellectual ventures which I admire… To give some assistance in wearing away certain self-evidences and commonplaces about madness, normality, illness, crime and punishment; to bring it about… that certain phrases can no longer be spoken so lightly, certain acts… no longer so unhesitatingly performed; to contribute to changing certain things in people's ways of perceiving and doing things; to participate in this difficult displacement of forms of sensibility and thresholds of tolerance—I hardly feel capable of attempting much more than that.[106]

In this passage, Foucault makes explicit that major revolutions and "overturnings" are not part of his thought. He repeats his opposition to the violence motivated by revolutionary goals of any class or political group, as he had articulated in an interview the year before.[107] But more importantly, he reminds us of the important, transgressive imperatives within his critical project: to challenge and change the status quo through productive, critical analysis, and to disrupt the limits of our possible experiences through the confrontation of "thresholds of tolerance."

A political revolution, even if successful on its own terms, would likely result in a redistribution of power that would simply bring about new configurations of the same relations of domination. The workings of power in history are more formative for human relations than our ideals about justice or utopia. Foucault, like Nietzsche, suggests our theories of utopia are deeply beholden to history. They are theories of our time. It is even "possible that the rough outline of a future society is supplied by drugs, sex, communes, other forms of consciousness, and other forms of individuality."[108]

Justice—and also human nature as something to be "fulfilled"—should be understood as a set of historically contingent concepts that cannot serve as stable revolutionary goals.[109] Absolute justice as an utopia to pursue through revolution is an equally pernicious ideal, for what we consider to be justice can serve as an "instrument of power."[110] In general, Foucault is skeptical of any appeal to ideal or perfect justice; even the proletarian struggle is a fight for power.[111] "If justice is at stake in a struggle, then it is an instrument of power."[112] Ideal or pure justice cannot transcend history, as contingent historical, social, and political factors are fundamental to it. For example, we often recast the question of what justice is in relation to a specific social or political struggle, in which we are involved. It is most frequently a specific type of political or social justice that we are after, one which is narrowly defined and fits our context, not the "hope that finally one day, in this or another society, people will be rewarded according to their merits, or punished according to their faults."[113]

Foucault does not trust the proletariat, or any oppressed group that rises up, to rule without domination: "When the proletariat takes power, it may be quite possible that the proletariat will exert towards the classes over which it has just triumphed, a violent, dictatorial, and even bloody power."[114] No ideals or revolutions can eliminate power relations. Referring to Spinoza, Foucault claims:

> the proletariat doesn't wage war against the ruling class because it considers such a war to be just. The proletariat makes war with the ruling class because, for the first time in history, it wants to take power. And because it will overthrow the power of the ruling class, it considers such a war to be just... one makes war to win, not because it is just.[115]

The power of the proletariat would "itself be an unjust power."[116] Foucault reiterates this view about the fundamental role of power relations in relation to socio-political confrontations in a conversation with Deleuze in 1971. In a post-Marxist vein, he adds that the proletariat is not the only one group or place from which one can "enter into a revolutionary process" against "particularized power."[117] However, as a possible path to solidarity, one can identify an overlap of the "controls and constraints," which serve the system of power that "maintain[s] capitalist exploitation."[118]

We must therefore exercise skepticism toward any ahistorical concepts of utopic societies, human nature, and justice when used to justify or motivate revolution.[119]

> These notions of human nature, of justice, of the realization of the essence of human beings, are all notions and concepts which have been formed within our civilization, within our type of knowledge and our form of philosophy, and that as a result form part of our class system; and one can't, however regrettable it may be, put forward these notions to describe or justify a fight which should—and shall in principle—overthrow the very fundaments of our society.[120]

For these reasons, the revolutionary enterprise and its goals in general are problematic for Foucault. But if a revolution happens, its value to the present, for Foucault and Kant alike, lies not in its concrete outcomes or even in the program that motivated it, but in its significance as a spectacle, which is itself an overdetermined sign:

overdetermined because it does not have one single meaning that is not relative to those who interpret it.[121]

Kant shares Foucault's skepticism regarding those who would come out victorious in a revolution, especially if the revolution is violent. In the overthrow of the head of state, for example, an inversion between this head and the people takes place.[122] "Violence" is raised above right.[123] This leads Kant to make the claim that such an act of revolutionary terror is akin to the state's own suicide.[124] Kant and Foucault are thus equally concerned about the *inversion* of relations of power within the state achieved through revolutionary violence.[125] For Kant, this inversion is a result of an overthrow based on a self-oriented maxim that is "hostile" to the law.[126] On Foucault's account, an inverted condition does nothing to dismantle the complex structures of power and knowledge that enable oppression.

The actual events and outcome of the revolution are consequently of little significance.[127] Rather, "for future history," the Revolution for Kant is a "*guarantee* of this continuity of an approach to progress," not necessarily a concrete, indestructible step to social progress itself.[128] Kant claims that if the revolution's aims and constitution failed and if everything were to fall backward, the "philosophical prophecy would lose nothing of its force."[129] And while a given revolution may mean something different to us now in the light of our own theoretical frameworks—take Foucault's digression from Kant on the progress of humanity, for example[130]—the will and enthusiasm for the revolution can always reveal something to us about our present.

Thus, on Kant's account, the significance of the revolution is *not* that it "topples things over," and reverses relations.[131] Its meaning as a sign does not come from "the revolutionary drama itself," but rather from "the way in which it is received all around by spectators who do not participate in it," but watch and "let themselves be dragged along by it."[132] Therefore, it matters little if the French Revolution "succeeds or fails," whether "it accumulates misery and atrocity," or whether, in view of its cost, it should ever be repeated.[133] Indeed, if we could foretell what the consequences of the French Revolution would be, we would not see it as an indisputable sign of progress. The historically specific inversion of ruling classes or groups caused by "revolutionary upheaval," combined with the fact that revolutions can never completely do away with the structures through which power circulates, means a revolution's outcome can never reliably be used as a basis for judgment.[134] Its significance also ought not to be derived from its viability as a model for future revolutions and political action.

However, the revolution as a spectacle, regardless of its results, is able to *signify* meaning. It functions as a "repository" or site of investment for "those who watch it."[135] On Kant's account, it is a sign that reminds us of or commemorates our moral predisposition.[136] It shows "things have always been like this (the rememorative sign)," that "these things are also presently happening (the demonstrative sign)" and that "things will always happen like this (the prognostic sign)."[137] Insofar as he identified a will to revolution in the French Revolution as a sign or spectacle, Kant could use it to encourage people to move beyond the condition of "immaturity" and use their reason. The manifestations of the will to revolution, in this case, help Kant to "encourage others" to be part of the change toward an "enlightened society," in which all would be equally free.[138] This is because the will—which is also a desire and enthusiasm—for revolution is also a will toward collective freedom and autonomy.

Foucault seems to agree with Kant that we have a tendency to will our own freedom, especially in our acts of resistance and disruption against power. However, unsurprisingly, he does not express agreement that a revolution can signify a timeless disposition of a humanity whose historical telos will be fulfilled. As seen above, Foucault is critical of the idea that politics can progress on the basis of a nature or permanent predisposition of the human being that will come to its full maturity or development.[139] Every will-for-revolution exercised in a "present" moment is precisely a historical expression of freedom *in that specific context*. It does not fulfill anything teleological. Kant's suggestion that revolution can be seen as "a value, as a sign of a predisposition that operates in history and in the progress of the human species"[140] is just one possible, contextualized interpretation of many at a given time. Rather than serving as proof of a predetermined telos, a revolution as an experienced spectacle or a sign rather presents the opportunity for a theoretical decision to be made in one's analysis of the present moment. It "allow[s] us to decide if there is progress," to make our decisions about meaning and value in the critical analysis of our time.[141]

5 Normativity and Critique

So, was Habermas right? In order to uphold his late philosophical views, informed by Kant, on revolution and the Enlightenment, does Foucault need to make normative claims at odds with his earlier work, especially his genealogical analyses of power? I have suggested "no," that normativity was always present in Foucault's work.

The imperative to actively resist constricting institutional practices, especially in schools, prisons, and in the context of psychiatry, is clear in Foucault's middle period. There is also no doubt that we should expose "the relationships of political power which actually control the social body and oppress or repress it."[142] But which normative measures or "yardsticks" does Foucault need to ascertain precisely *what* practices and *which* institutions are to be opposed? On precisely this point, Nancy Fraser and Charles Taylor perceive a contradiction in Foucault. Foucault invokes liberal values espoused by Kant, particularly freedom and autonomy, in order to judge certain disciplinary practices as wrong and worthy of opposition. This would not present a problem if Foucault had not, on Fraser's account, so heavily criticized these liberal, Enlightenment values in the past.[143] But no value ought to be immune from historical critique; Foucault, in continuation with the Enlightenment tradition on his own account, is constantly criticizing the values and norms of his present. He can therefore coherently refrain from taking a single, definitive position on freedom, yet still retain the concept when describing the engagement of individuals in transgressive activity, and even the uprising of individuals in revolutionary activity, directed against institutional practices and the limits placed on their knowledge and experience. James Schmidt and Thomas Wartenberg, Amy Allen, and Christina Hendricks have all defended the compatibility of Foucault's positions on freedom and autonomy with his analyses of power.[144]

Freedom, for Foucault, begins in the "critical attitude." Through critique—motivated by the will to revolution as a will to freedom—we attempt to "desubjugate" ourselves in the domains of the "politics of truth," which is, despite the expression, never absolute.[145] This desubjugation process could also be read as a process of liberation from the contingent, normative constraints placed on the self. This requires resisting certain oppressive governmental and institutional practices. Critique therefore also involves confronting "the arts of governing" through "defiance, as a challenge, as a way of limiting these arts of governing and sizing them up, transforming them, of finding a way to escape from them, or in any case, a way to displace them, with a basic distrust."[146]

Critique, especially insofar as it is directed toward methods of government control and illegitimate ruling practices, is political. It is, Foucault asserts, "the art" of "being governed" *less*.[147] On this point, one can identify the normative role of the concept of freedom, in relation to the will to revolution and resistance, in Foucault's project of critique. The history of critique is the history of identifying and "refusing, challenging, limiting" alternatives to unsuitable arts of governance in a given moment in history.[148] Critique means challenging the sources of authority in governance that lead to the domination and control human beings, thereby exercising the will to freedom. "Critique" will thus "be the art of voluntary insubordination, that of reflected intractability."[149] It occurs in the intersection of subjectivity, power, and truth.[150]

Despite Foucault's critique of ideal justice, he directly links this definition of critique to the resistance to "unjust" laws. Recall that concepts of justice are always situation-specific. If laws are "unjust," not because of their failure to measure up to some ideal notion of justice, but due to their "illegitimacy" based on "antiquity" or because a sovereign has invested them with power, they should be opposed.[151] Foucault, on this point, takes a surprising turn in the direction of Kant and universal rights. If historically specific critiques of forms of governance mean challenging unjust laws, Foucault notes, "critique means putting forth universal and indefeasible rights to which every government, whatever it may be… will have to submit."[152] Such an endorsement of universal rights is surprising for Foucault. If all concepts of justice are historical, we could surmise that all rights are, too. However, although the specific human rights we take to be universal and their scope of extension are constantly changing, they remain a viable way to limit, and even destabilize, the authority and power of governments as exemplified through their ruling practices.

Foucault returns to Kant's definition of the Enlightenment through the terminology of *limits* and the critique of authority. Governance always has limits and these limits must be challenged and transgressed.[153] Moreover, nothing should be accepted as true on the basis of authority alone.[154] Here, the critical enterprise and the "call for courage" to the people of the Enlightenment to free themselves from external sources of authority through self-directed understanding intersect.[155] Both Kant's critique of reason and the courageous pursuit of freedom in the Enlightenment describe a "critical attitude which appears as a specific attitude in the Western world starting with what was historically... the great process of society's governmentalization."[156] To dare to be beholden only to one's own exercise of reason and be thereby responsible for one's own decisions necessitates courage. According to Foucault, in Kant's "What is Enlightenment?" one finds a courageous uprising of the subject against historicized forms of authoritative rule. Foucault extends Kant's Enlightenment motto, "Have the courage to make use of your own intellect!," to the courage to first critically examine one's own capacities and limits as a subject enmeshed in relationships of power and truth in one's own time, and then transgress these limits.[157] Kant demonstrates that one ought to have the courage to identify the illegitimate origins of one's "minority condition," especially in "religion, law and knowledge," and to attempt to transgress them through one's own intellect.[158]

Critique, suggests Foucault, is a particular type of *virtue* with the normative aim to transgress. Foucault claims critique seems to be "supported by some kind of more general imperative... than that of eradicating errors. There is something in critique akin to virtue."[159] As Kant demonstrated, precisely through the identification of the limit of the scope of one's knowledge and the responsible and appropriate use of reason, "the principle of autonomy can be discovered."[160] In this endeavor, "our liberty is at stake."[161] In Kant, this autonomy is present in the regulative use of the "ideas" of reason in the First Critique (as opposed to their constitutive use), as well as in the applied us of practical reason. As a result of ascertaining the limits, together with the possibilities, of reason, "instead of letting someone else say 'obey'" and having to listen to another, "the *obey* will be founded on autonomy itself," as one will obey reason.[162] From this point, for Kant, *we* become the authors of the laws we obey. Expanding the link of his work to Kant's critique of reason, Foucault claims that we ought to "transform" Kant's critical project, insofar as it concerns "necessary limitation[s]," into "a practical critique that takes the form of a possible transgression."[163]

However, it is also important to highlight the discordance between Kant's and Foucault's critical projects, which Foucault identifies himself. To "obey" reason, he reminds us, is still to "obey" universal structures and is certainly "not at all opposed to obeying the sovereign."[164] In the face of the power of the state and the "supreme authority" that passes its laws, in Kant's account, citizens emerge rather powerless: "The power of the state which makes the law effective is also *irresistible*, and there is no lawfully constituted commonwealth without such power to put down all internal resistance."[165] Kant explains that laws should be passed by the head of state – who, as the "source of the laws, cannot do wrong."[166] These laws should be on the basis of right and are thus "irreprehensible." They are backed by the "authority to coerce" and "the prohibition" of any resistance against the "will of the legislators."[167]

The need to obey, for Kant, applies regardless of who governs. Even if a revolution is, in principle, never justifiable, Kant urges us to accept its results, and in particular its constitution. He writes, "when a revolution has succeeded and a new constitution is established, the unlawfulness of its beginning and implementation cannot release the subjects from the obligation to submit to the new order of things as good citizens."[168] Ironically, the results of the unjustifiable revolution can still positively contribute to human progress in history. The "new order of things" and replacement authority, states Kant, must be obeyed.[169] Although undesirable for citizens, the only pushback permitted is from the former head of state, whose "right" to their former "office remains, since the revolt that took it from him was unjust."[170] The question remains unsettled for Kant regarding whether former heads of state, with external aid, may attempt to reinstate the pre-revolutionary constitution after the revolution has already occurred.[171]

Constitutions can be reformed, claims Kant, but only by the sovereign—"not by the people, by means of revolution."[172] The conclusion is clear: "all resistance against the supreme legislating authority... all revolt that leads into rebellion, is the highest and most punishable offence."[173] Foucault does not agree that an individual's conduct should always be in accordance with state laws and that state authority should always to be respected to avoid civil unrest and the destruction of the state's foundations. Additionally, Kant specifically argues for social cohesion through a respect for the limits of reason in one's civic duty (he therefore restricts the use of "private reason").[174] Foucault endorses no such "acceptable" restraints on the subject's activity, whether in private or public. The acceptance of such restrictions by private citizens, especially as imposed from above, is always open to misuse to increase the social control of those in power. This discordance between Kant and Foucault on social unity is also highlighted by Habermas who suggests that Kant's theory of a final cosmopolitan state of freedom, along with his concerns for world-citizenship and proposed steps toward perpetual peace, would likely be criticized by Foucault.[175]

These objections notwithstanding, by linking the Enlightenment and his critical philosophy so closely, Kant, according to Foucault, motivates us to question the structures and use of reason itself in reference to the historical exercise of power.[176] From this critique, we can engage in a process of "desubjectification" within our present context. In this process, we have a responsibility to "know knowledge" or to know our present and how it subjugates us as thinkers *of* the present. This is the condition of the possibility of following the "ethos" of the Enlightenment, which calls us to identify and transgress limits as part of the "ontology of ourselves."

Foucault distinguishes between "two great traditions" *founded by Kant*, "which divide modern philosophy": the analytic of truth and the ontology of ourselves.[177] The first is rooted in Kant's critical enterprise, and concerns "the conditions under which true knowledge is possible."[178] The second is the "critical questioning" inaugurated by Kant's "What is Enlightenment?" and *The Conflict of the Faculties*, through which we ask about the present and what is *possible* in the present.[179] This ontology of ourselves is the type of philosophical inquiry that Foucault sees himself, together with Hegel, Nietzsche, Max Weber, Max Horkheimer, Habermas (and the "Frankfurt School" in general), as pursuing.[180] In one way or another, all of these thinkers pose the question "What is the Enlightenment?" out of their respective presents.

The "ontology of ourselves" (which is also an "ontology of actuality"[181]), first requires that we, as historically situated subjects, identify the limits of the conditions we take to be universal and true and expose their contingency. Then we ought to challenge and transgress these limits to widen "the present field of possible experiences."[182] In other words, we must (a) carry out a "permanent critique of our historical era,"[183] and (b) engage in the task of "producing" or re-inventing ourselves" as "autonomous subjects," as far as that is possible.[184] The goal is to constantly transgress the limits of what one takes to be permanent in the given and in our self-understanding, thereby initiating new configurations of our environments and our ourselves.

The ontology of ourselves is also an inquiry into *who we are* as successors of the Enlightenment who cannot deny this fact. What are the conditioning factors of who we are and how are they limiting what we can do and experience? The ontology of ourselves responds through a "permanent critique of ourselves" through our "reflective relation to the present."[185] This permanent critique must concern the possibility of our freedom, as we ask: in which institutionalized and social practices is reason used to play "strategic games of liberties" whose ends are not our freedom at all?[186] How can we liberate ourselves, even partially, from the disciplinary hold of power effected through structures, institutions, and norms that appear to be absolute?

Foucault's criticisms of revolutionary political programs are linked to the universalizing tendency he critiques through the ontology of ourselves. Any "projects" which have universal or "radical" aims, Foucault claims, are not part of the critical ontology of ourselves.[187] In fact, the heavily programmatic and universalist nature of revolutionary programs exposes not only a dangerous level hubris, but it demands critique. Revolutionary programs often promote a self-defeating form of escapism from our current conditions, instead of challenging us to carry out the difficult, necessary critical work on our present and ourselves. Foucault writes, "We know from experience that the claim to escape from the system of contemporary reality so as to produce the overall programs of another society, another way of thinking, another culture, another vision of the world, has led only to the return of the most dangerous traditions."[188]

Foucault proposes an approach to the present that is critical and contextual rather than revolutionary. "The historical ontology of ourselves," he explains, "must turn away from all projects that claim to be global or radical."[189] To analyze our own present—to construct an ontology of ourselves—in a way that is transgressive, we must instead look to "specific transformations" in "areas that concern our ways of being and thinking."[190] Once we provisionally outline the limits of what we are in our context, we can then challenge these limits specific to us and transform them.

Kant was working on such an ontology of the present when he conducted his analysis of the French Revolution. He examines his present from within, as someone who also experienced the spectacle of the Revolution. Kant's immanent critique of his time and incitement of transgressive activity is clear through his theory of public and private reason in relation to autonomy. Kant's call to use one's own reason in a liberatory fashion was highly relevant for social change and self-understanding in his time. Foucault thus saw Kant as a relevant public philosopher, emphasizing that Kant's "What is Enlightenment?" was published as "a newspaper article."[191] Similarly, as noted above, Foucault published in many newspapers and gave numerous interviews, especially on the topic of Iran at the time if the Iranian Revolution. Visiting the site of revolution as a journalist may have allowed Foucault, at least in his intentions, to get as close possible to present events as a true ontologist of the actual.[192]

In his investigation of the meaning of the French Revolution as a sign, Kant came to very different speculative conclusions about the will to revolution with regards to progress than Foucault. But this is to be expected, as both lived in very different presents, which they approached with their own independent sets of concerns and intellectual heritage. Despite their diverging views on the meaning of the will to revolution in history, Foucault successfully shows that Kant is not merely a thinker of ahistorical universalism, but also a relevant philosopher of historical change and self-examination—a real philosopher of the present. Kant, in turn, through his concept of the will to revolution that persists throughout history, his endorsement of the values of freedom and autonomy, and defense of universal rights, offers Foucault certain normative commitments, which prevent his transgressive, resisting individual from completely dissolving into the contingent development of history and the workings of power.[193]

Notes

1. Immanuel Kant, "Metaphysics of Morals, Doctrine of Right, §43–§62," in *Toward Perpetual Peace and Other Writings on Politics, Peace, and History*, trans. David L. Colclasure (New Haven and London: Yale University Press, 2006), 119–21. Kant claims that the "formal *execution*" of a monarch, such as "Charles I or Louis XVI," is "regarded as a crime that remains eternally and can never be expiated" (ibid., 120n).
2. Immanuel Kant, *The Conflict of the Faculties*, trans. Mary J. Gregor (New York: Abaris Books, 1979), 151–53. The Revolution is an "event," which "consists neither in momentous deeds nor crimes committed by men," but is simply "the mode of thinking of the spectators" (ibid., 153).
3. Immanuel Kant, "On the Common Saying: This May Be True in Theory, but It Does Not Hold in Practice, Parts 2 and 3," in *Toward Perpetual Peace*, 53–57. For Kant, the law, as formulated in a constitution, is more foundational than any right to revolution. Rebelling against a sovereign or the laws of the state produces a contradiction regarding how to legitimize the alternative. Therefore, Kant explains, in the constitution, there cannot be a right to rebel (Kant, "On the Common Saying," 52).
4. Foucault, "What is Enlightenment?," in *The Politics of Truth*, trans. Catherine Porter, ed. Sylvère Lotringer and Lysa Hochroth (New York: Semiotext(e), 1997), 127.
5. Regarding the debates on revolution and violence in German thought in the 1790s, see Frederick C. Beiser, *Enlightenment, Revolution, and Romanticism* (Cambridge, MA: Harvard University Press, 1992). On the German debate concerning the right to resistance in response to Kant's position on the French Revolution, see Reidar Maliks, "Revolutionary Epigones: Kant and His Radical Followers," *History of Political Thought* vol. 33, no. 4 (2012): 647–71. For an example of the conservative, anti-revolutionary turn in German Romanticism, see Friedrich von Schlegel, "Lecture XVII," in *The Philosophy of History: In a Course of Lectures, Delivered at Vienna*, trans. James Burton Robertson, 2nd ed (London: Henry

G. Bohn, 1846). For examples of the appearance of these questions in twentieth-century French thought, see Maurice Merleau-Ponty, *Humanism and Terror: An Essay on the Communist Problem*, trans. John O'Neil (Boston: Beacon Press, 1969) and Jacques Derrida, "Force of Law: The Mystical Foundation of Authority," in *Acts of Religion*, trans. Mary Quaintance, ed. Gil Anidjar (New York: Routledge, 2002), 228–98.

6. All three lectures are translated and published in the volume *The Politics of Truth*. "What is Critique?" was delivered to the French Philosophy Society in 1978. "What is Revolution?" is the first hour of Foucault's inaugural lecture of his 1983 course at the Collège de France. It was first published in 1984 as "Un cours inédit," *Magazine littéraire*, May 1984; the text was subsequently translated under different titles, including "Kant on Enlightenment and Revolution," trans. Colin Gordon, *Economy and Society* vol. 15, no. 1 (February 1986) and "The Art of Telling the Truth," in *Critique and Power: Recasting the Foucault/Habermas Debate*, trans. Alan Sheridan, ed. Michael Kelly (Cambridge: MIT Press, 1994). Finally, the text of "What Is Enlightenment?" is loosely based on the *second* hour of the aforementioned inaugural lecture. It was subsequently delivered in the spring of 1983 at Berkeley. A revised version of this lecture was published for the first time in *The Foucault Reader*, ed. Paul Rabinow (New York: Pantheon Books, 1984). On the history of these texts and their relationship to one another, see James Schmidt, "Misunderstanding the Question: 'What Is Enlightenment?': Venturi, Habermas, and Foucault," *History of European Ideas* vol. 37, no. 1 (March 1, 2011): 48; and Frédéric Gros, "Course Context, " in Michel Foucault, *The Government of Self and Others: Lectures at the College de France, 1982–1983*, trans. Graham Burchell, ed. François Ewald, Alessandro Fontana (London: Palgrave Macmillan, 2010). Gros explains that the 1978 lecture differs from the other two, for it is "situated in the perspective of a 'critical attitude'" in relation to how *not* to be governed (the question of "'desubjectification' in the framework of a 'politics of truth'") (Gros, "Course Context," 378). Contrastingly, "in 1983 the question of Enlightenment will be thought of as the reinvestment of a requirement of truth-telling, of a courageous speaking of truth that appeared in the Greeks," thus leading Foucault to explore the type of "government of self" that "should be posited as both the foundation and limit of the government of others" (ibid., 379). I discuss Foucault's return to the ancients in relation to Kant below. The first lecture concerns the breakdown of processes of subjectification, whereas the next two focus more on our active capacity to both critique and fashion ourselves in the present—how we can speak the truth a context, in which we play a constitutive part. It is noteworthy that as Foucault was preparing his material on Kant and the Enlightenment in 1983, he invited Habermas to a "private conference" with Paul Rabinow, Richard Rorty and Charles Taylor to discuss Kant's "What is Enlightenment?" essay—a conference which Foucault would not live long enough to see. See Jürgen Habermas, "Foucault's Lecture on Kant," trans. Sigrid Brauner and Robert Brown, *Thesis Eleven* vol. 14, no. 1 (1986), 4.

7. I discuss Foucault's earlier engagement with Kant in more detail below. For an overview of Foucault's reception of Kant and an argument in favor of the compatibility his early and late remarks, see Amy Allen, "Foucault and Enlightenment: A Critical Reappraisal," *Constellations* vol.10, no. 2 (2003), 180–98.

8. Michel Foucault, "What Is Revolution?" in *The Politics of Truth*, trans. Lysa Hochroth, Kant, *The Conflict of the Faculties*, 153.

9. Foucault, "What is Revolution?" 99, 94–95; Compare the discussion of liberty, autonomy and courage in Michel Foucault, "What is Critique?," in *The Politics of Truth*, trans. Lysa Hochroth, 35.

10. Foucault, "What is Critique?," 24. On subjectivity and truth as informative for Foucault's work in the 1980s, see Michel Foucault, *The Hermeneutics of the Subject. Lectures at the Collège de France, 1981–1982*, trans. Graham Burchell, ed. Arnold I. Davidson (New York and Basingstoke: Palgrave Macmillan, 2005) pp. 2–3 and Fréderic Gros, "Course Context," 377–378.

11. See Kant, "What is Enlightenment," 124, 126.

12. Johanna Oksala, *Foucault on Freedom* (Cambridge: Cambridge University Press, 2005), 1–2.
13. See Immanuel Kant, "An Answer to the Question: What Is Enlightenment?," in *Perpetual Peace*, 18–21.
14. For a summary of how Enlightenment "successes" have produced new forms of domination in the realms of the prison system, sexuality, and medicine, see James Schmidt and Thomas E. Wartenberg, "Foucault's Enlightenment: Critique, Revolution, and the Fashioning of the Self,' in *Critique and Power*, 284.
15. Foucault, "What is Enlightenment?," 109.
16. Ibid., 110.
17. Ibid.
18. Brent L. Pickett highlights that in the 1970s, Foucault supports local, contextualized resistance against the systems of practices of schools, prisons, and the judicial system. See Brent L. Pickett, "Foucault and the Politics of Resistance," *Polity* vol. 28, no. 4 (June 1996): 451–57. Compare Michel Foucault, "Revolutionary Action: 'Until Now'," in *Language, Counter-Memory, Practice*, ed. Donald F. Bouchard, trans. Donald F. Bouchard and Sherry Simon(Ithaca: Cornell University Press, 1977), 223, 228–9; and "Intellectuals and Power," in *Language, Counter-Memory, Practice*, 209.
19. Foucault's interest in emancipation and the scope of possible experience and actions is linked to his interest in politics and approach to the concept of society, the latter of which includes the range of what we can and cannot *do*. Foucault claims that politics, defined as "the society in which we live, the economic relations within which it functions, and the *system of power which defines the regular forms and the regular permissions and prohibitions of our conduct*," is "probably the most crucial subject to our existence." In Noam Chomsky and Michel Foucault, *The Chomsky-Foucault Debate: On Human Nature* (London: The New Press, 2006), 36–7; emphasis is mine.
20. Michel Foucault, "Appendix: Foucault and His Critics, an Annotated Translation," in *Foucault and the Iranian Revolution: Gender and the Seductions of Islamism*, trans. Karen de Bruin et al., ed. Janet Afary and Kevin B. Anderson (Chicago: The University of Chicago Press, 2005), 179–277.
21. Foucault, "What Are the Iranians Dreaming About?" in *Foucault and the Iranian Revolution*, 207.
22. Foucault, "Is It Useless to Revolt?," in *Foucault and the Iranian Revolution*, 263.
23. Kant published extremely regularly in the *Berlinische Monatsschrift*, producing 15 articles between 1784 and 1796. In the first of these pieces, the "Idea for a Universal History with a Cosmopolitan Aim" (also from 1784), Kant presents his view of the progress of humanity toward an Enlightened, cosmopolitan community, which is crucial for understanding his will to revolution. It is also important to note that the 1793 *Berlinische Monatsschrift* piece, "On the Common Saying'" is where we find Kant's early argument against revolutionary violence and uprisings against state authority.
24. Philosophy, as a lower faculty, must be kept at a "distance" from the "higher faculties" of theology, law, and medicine. But this "lower faculty" has the "duty… to see to it that everything put forward in public as a principle is true" (Kant, *The Conflict of the Faculties*, 35, 27, 53).
25. I am grateful to Tilottama Rajan for drawing my attention to the importance of this difference.
26. Foucault, *The Chomsky-Foucault Debate*, 40.For more on Foucault's long-term revolutionary pessimism, see Pickett, "Foucault and the Politics of Resistance," 448.
27. See Michel Foucault, *Introduction to Kant's Anthropology*, ed. Roberto Nigro, trans. Roberto Nigro and Kate Briggs (Los Angeles: Semiotext[e], 2008), 108–24.
28. See Ibid., 118–19.
29. Ibid., 119.
30. Ibid.
31. Foucault, "What is Enlightenment?," 125.
32. Foucault, *Kant's Anthropology*, 121.

33. Ibid., 122.
34. Ibid., 124.
35. Ibid.
36. Foucault, *Kant's Anthropology*, 124.
37. Ibid.
38. Ibid.
39. It is important to note that the question of "who we are, what our present is... today" is not only Kant's question, according to Foucault—it is "Nietzsche's question," too (Foucault, "What Our Present is," *The Politics of Truth*, 148).
40. Foucault praises Kant for initiating a great turn in the history of philosophy through an interrogation of the source of representation and its relationship to knowledge. Nevertheless, he is critical of Kant's handling of the genesis of the subject through transcendental subjectivity (Michel Foucault, *The Order of Things*, trans. Alan Sheridan [London and New York: Routledge, 1989]). In his argument for the discontinuity between Foucault's early and late approach to Kant, Habermas emphasizes Foucault's critique of Kant's "anthropocentric mode of knowledge," which supports the "dangerous façade of universally valid knowledge" (Habermas, "Foucault's Lecture on Kant," 8). For a detailed analysis of Habermas' juxtaposition of the two positions, see Schmidt and Wartenberg, "Foucault's Enlightenment."
41. Foucault, *The Order of Things*, 285.
42. Ibid.
43. Ibid., 286.
44. Ibid.
45. Ibid.
46. Ibid.
47. Ibid.
48. Ibid.
49. Ibid.
50. Foucault, *Folie et déraison* (Paris: Librarie Plon, 1961), quoted in Schmidt, "Introduction," 26.
51. James Schmidt, "Introduction: What Is Enlightenment? A Question, Its Context, and Some Consequences," in *What Is Enlightenment? Eighteenth-Century Answers and Twentieth-Century Questions* (Berkeley: University of California Press, 1996), 25.
52. Schmidt, "Introduction," 25; see also Friedrich Nietzsche, *Human, All Too Human*, trans. R.J. Hollingdale (Cambridge: Cambridge University Press, 1986), 25–26, 367; Friedrich Nietzsche, *The Gay Science*, trans. Walter Kaufmann (New York: Vintage Books, 1974), 293, as quoted in Schmidt.
53. Foucault, *The Hermeneutics of the Subject*, 137, 164.
54. Foucault, "What is Enlightenment?," 108.
55. Caring for the self involves an examination of "the historically situated 'techniques' by which a subject constructs a definite relationship to self, gives form to his or her own existence, and establishes a well ordered relationship to the world and to others" (Gros, "Course Context," 378).
56. Foucault, "Is it Useless to Revolt?," 266. "It is a fact that people rise up, and it is through this that a subjectivity (not that of great men, but that of anyone) introduces itself into history and gives it its life. A delinquent puts his life on the line against abusive punishment, a madman cannot stand anymore being closed in and pushed down, or a people rejects a regime that oppresses it."
57. Foucault, *The Government of Self and Others*, 350. See Andreas Folkers, "Daring the Truth: Foucault, Parrhesia and the Genealogy of Critique," *Theory, Culture & Society* 33, no. 1 (2016).
58. Michel Foucault, *Fearless Speech*, ed. Joseph Pearson (Los Angeles: Semiotext(e), 2001), 19.
59. Foucault, *The Hermeneutics of the Subject*, 403.
60. Ibid., 404.
61. Ibid.

62. See Gros, "Course Context," 379.
63. Ibid., 372.
64. Immanuel Kant, *Critique of Practical Reason*, ed. and trans. Mary Gregor (Cambridge: Cambridge University Press, 2015), 79. Kant here adds that transcendental freedom "alone is practical a priori," and without it, "no moral law is possible and no imputation in accordance with it" (79).
65. Foucault, "Is It Useless to Revolt?," 263.
66. Kant, "On the Common Saying," 47.
67. Ibid., 263-4.
68. Kant, *The Conflict of the Faculties*, 153.
69. Ibid.
70. On this point, see Hendricks, "Foucault's Kantian Critique," *Philosophy and Social Criticism* vol. 34, no. 4 (2008), 364.
71. See Foucault, "Iran: The Spirit of a World without Spirit," in *Foucault and the Iranian Revolution*, 253.
72. For different paths of navigation through this ambiguous space of the will and freedom in relation to Foucault's return to Kant, see Judith Butler, "What is Critique? An Essay on Foucault's Virtue," *The Judith Butler Reader*, ed. Sara Salih (Malden: Blackwell, 2004), 302-22; Charles Taylor, "Foucault on Freedom and Truth," *Political Theory* vol. 12, no. 2 (1984): 173-4; Carlos Palacios, "Freedom Can Also Be Productive: The Historical Inversions of 'the Conduct of Conduct,'" *Journal of Political Power* vol. 11, no. 2 (2018): 254-6.
73. Foucault, "What is Critique?," 74.
74. Ibid., 75.
75. Ibid., 73.
76. Foucault, "What Is Revolution?," 99.
77. Foucault, "What Is Enlightenment?," 126.
78. Ibid.
79. Ibid., 125.
80. Ibid., 133.
81. Ibid., 117, 124.
82. Ibid., 121.
83. For Foucault's summary of the function of the Revolution as a sign for Kant, see Foucault, "What is Revolution?," 94-96.
84. Kant, *Conflict of the Faculties*, 151.
85. Ibid., 155.
86. The will to revolution, for Kant, is "the sign" of "humanity's moral predisposition" which is "perpetually manifested in two ways: first, in the right of all people to provide themselves with the political constitution that suits them." Secondly, this constitution should conform "to the law" and morality "such that it avoids, by virtue of its very principles, any offensive war." Foucault, "What Is Revolution?," 95.
87. Ibid., 94.
88. Ibid., 92.
89. Ibid.
90. Kant, *The Conflict of the Faculties*, 153.
91. Foucault, "What Is Revolution?," 93-4.
92. Ibid., 92-3.
93. Foucault, "What is Critique?," 90.
94. Foucault, "What Is Revolution?," 98.
95. See Maurizio Passerin d'Entrèves, "Between Nietzsche and Kant: Michel Foucault's Reading of 'What Is Enlightenment?,'" *History of Political Thought* vol. 20, no. 2 (1999), 337-56, especially 347; Jürgen Habermas, "Foucault's Lecture On Kant," 7.
96. See D'Entrèves, "Between Nietzsche and Kant," 347; Habermas, "Foucault's Lecture on Kant," 7.

Enlightenment and Revolution

97. Habermas, "Foucault's Lecture on Kant," 8.
98. Ibid.
99. D'Entrèves, "Between Nietzsche and Kant," 347.
100. Friedrich Nietzsche, *Beyond Good and Evil*, ed. Rolf-Peter Horstmann and Judith Norman, trans. Judith Norman (Cambridge: Cambridge University Press, 2002), 15.
101. Ibid., 11.
102. Ibid.
103. Ibid., 99.
104. Ibid.
105. Foucault, "Revolutionary Action: 'Until Now'," 223, 228.
106. Foucault, "Questions of Method," in *Studies in Governmentality*, trans. Colin Gordon, ed. Graham Burchell, Colin Gordon, and Peter Miller (Chicago: The University of Chicago Press, 1991), 82–3.
107. In this interview, Foucault challenges movements of "terrorism where one says, in the name of the class, in the name of a political group, in the name of a vanguard, in the name of a fringe group: 'I'm getting up, planting a bomb and threatening to kill someone in order to gain this or that.'" Foucault, "La securité et l'État," *Tribune socialiste* (24–30 November 1977), 3.
108. Foucault, "Revolutionary Action: 'Until Now,'" 231.
109. Foucault, *The Chomsky-Foucault Debate*, 43.
110. Ibid., 50.
111. "The idea of justice ... has been invented and put to work in different types of societies as an instrument of a certain political and economic power or as a weapon against that power" (Ibid., 40).
112. Ibid., 50.
113. Ibid.
114. Ibid., 52.
115. Ibid., 50–1.
116. Foucault, *The Chomsky-Foucault Debate*, 53.
117. Foucault, "Intellectuals and Power," 217.
118. Ibid.
119. Ibid., 44.
120. Ibid., 58.
121. Foucault, "What Is Revolution?" 90–1.
122. Kant, "Metaphysics of Morals," 120n.
123. Ibid.
124. Immanuel Kant, "Metaphysics of Morals," 121n. For a critical analysis of this point, see Lewis W. Beck, "Kant and the Right of Revolution," *Journal of the History of Ideas* 32, no. 3 (1971), 416–17.
125. For Foucault's rejection of the use of terror and violence in revolutionary movements of a class or political group, see Foucault, "Va-t-on extruder Klaus Croissant?," *Le Nouvel Observateur*, 679 (14 November 1977), 62–63, and Foucault, "La securité et l'État,"3–4.
126. Ibid., 120n.
127. Ibid., 97.
128. Ibid., emphasis mine.
129. Kant, *Conflict of the Faculties*, 159; Foucault, "What Is Revolution?," 96.
130. On Foucault's critique of progress, see Amy Allen, "Adorno, Foucault, and the End of Progress: Critical Theory in Postcolonial Times," in *Critical Theory in Critical Times*, ed. Penelope Deutscher and Cristina Lafont (Columbia: Columbia University Press, 2017), 183–206.
131. Foucault, "What Is Revolution?," 92–3. See also Kant, "Metaphysics of Morals," 121n, where Kant explains that the act of executing a monarch "is based on a principle that would make even the reestablishment of the toppled state impossible."

132. Ibid., 93.
133. Ibid.
134. Ibid.
135. Foucault, "What is Revolution?," 95.
136. Ibid.
137. Ibid., 91; Kant, *The Conflict of the Faculties*, 151.
138. Hendricks, "Foucault's Kantian Critique," 363. For Kant's view on the final free, universal human community, see Immanuel Kant, "Idea for a Universal History from a Cosmopolitan Perspective," in *Perpetual Peace*, 3–16.
139. See, Foucault, *The Chomsky-Foucault Debate*, 42–3.
140. Foucault, "What Is Revolution?," 99.
141. Ibid., 91.
142. Foucault, *The Chomsky-Foucault Debate*, 40. This analysis and exposure must involve not only scrutinizing governmental and administrative institutions, but other institutions which mediate the transmission of power more insidiously (Foucault's examples include the family, as well as institutions in educational systems that serve to transmit knowledge, medical systems, and psychiatry).
143. Nancy Fraser, "Foucault on Modern Power: Empirical Insights and Normative Confusions," in Nancy Fraser, *Unruly Practices: Power, Discourse and Gender in Contemporary Social Theory* (Minneapolis: University of Minnesota Press, 1989), 30. Compare Taylor, "Foucault on Freedom and Truth."
144. See Schmidt and Wartenberg, "Foucault's Enlightenment"; Amy Allen, "Foucault and Enlightenment: A Critical Reappraisal"; Hendricks, "Foucault's Kantian Critique."
145. Foucault, "What is Critique?, " 32.
146. Ibid., 28.
147. Ibid., 29.
148. Ibid.
149. Ibid., 32.
150. Ibid.
151. Ibid., 30.
152. Ibid.
153. Ibid., 31.
154. Ibid.
155. Ibid., 32.
156. Ibid., 34.
157. Compare Foucault, "What is Critique?," 32.
158. Ibid.
159. Ibid., 25.
160. Ibid., 35.
161. Ibid.
162. Ibid.
163. Foucault, "What Is Enlightenment?," 125.
164. Foucault, "What is Critique?," 36.
165. Kant, "On the Common Saying," 53.
166. Immanuel Kant, "Metaphysics of Morals," 119n.
167. Kant, "On the Common Saying," 53.
168. Kant, "Metaphysics of Morals," 121.
169. Ibid.
170. Ibid.
171. Ibid.
172. Kant, "Metaphysics of Morals," 120.
173. Kant, "On the Common Saying," 53.

174. Immanuel Kant, "What Is Enlightenment?," 19. With regard to the restriction of private reason (reason used "in a civil post or office") and obedience and passivity in society, Kant states that in certain matters of concern to the whole, "some members of the commonwealth must play only a passive role, so that they can be led by the government in the pursuit of public ends by means of an artificial unanimity, or at least be kept from undermining those ends. In these cases, of course, one may not argue, but rather must obey" (ibid.).
175. Habermas, "Foucault's Lecture on Kant," 7.
176. Foucault, "What is Critique?, " 37–8.
177. Ibid., 98.
178. Foucault, "What Is Revolution?," 99.
179. Ibid.
180. Ibid., 32; Foucault, "What Is Revolution?," 100.
181. Ibid., 100.
182. Ibid.
183. Foucault, "What Is Enlightenment?," 121.
184. Ibid., 120–1.
185. Foucault, "What Is Enlightenment?," 121.
186. Ibid., 133.
187. Ibid., 126.
188. Ibid.
189. Ibid.
190. Ibid.
191. Foucault, "What is Critique?," 33.
192. Foucault claims in 1978, the year he went to Iran, that "there is much work to be done on the relationship between philosophy and journalism from the end of the 18th century"; we ought to observe how "philosophers intervene in newspapers in order to say something that is for them philosophically interesting and which, nevertheless, is inscribed in a certain relationship to the public which they intend to mobilize" (What is Critique?," 33–4). Cem Kömürcü emphasizes Foucault's dual role as a journalist *and* a "modern" philosopher in his travels to Iran, claiming "The Iranian Revolution was a challenge for Foucault to show how modern and therefore actual he was" (Cem Kömürcü, "Enlightenment and Revolution—Michel Foucault's Way to Iran," in *Aftershocks of an Event*, ed. Carlos Ramírez and Michael Schulz [Heidelberg: Winter Verlag, 2020], 182). For a rare appreciative analysis of Foucault's interest in the possible viability of a spiritual revolution in Iran, see Behrooz Ghamari-Tabrizi, *Foucault in Iran: Islamic Revolution after the Enlightenment* (Minneapolis: University of Minnesota Press, 2016).
193. I would like to thank the volume editors, Tilottama Rajan and Daniel Whistler, for their helpful comments on an earlier draft of this paper.

Sovereignty and Community

Ian James

1 Introduction: The Ends of Hegel

Writing in 1982 in his essay "Sign and Symbol in Hegel's 'Aesthetics'" Paul de Man notes that, "Whether we know it, or like it, or not, most of us are Hegelians, and quite orthodox ones at that."[1] This may seem like a hyperbolic claim. Yet de Man is alluding to the way in which a philosophical thinking, seemingly held within the impenetrability of a most inaccessible discourse, can nevertheless have a legacy which spills over into the wider sphere of history and culture and which can do so in the most diffuse ways that exceed the strict determinations of intellectual history and the discernible causal interplay between texts and their contemporaneous or subsequent contexts. In this case, de Man is referring to aesthetic prejudices that were almost certainly still widely held at the time in which he was writing whether the individuals that held them had actually read Hegel or not. These, he suggests, might include the tendency to think of literary history in Eurocentric terms as an articulation of Hellenic and Christian cultures, to think of literature itself as a system of relationships between forms and genres, of periodization as a development of collective consciousness, or, finally, to think of beauty as "the externalization of an ideal content."[2] In this respect his claim is indicative of the way in which, for so much twentieth-century French thought, and within poststructuralism or deconstruction in particular, Hegel, more than any other philosopher of German Idealism, came to represent the decisive figure whose thinking exemplifies the complex interplay between philosophy and historical, cultural, and most importantly, political becoming.

I. James (✉)
University of Cambridge, Cambridge, UK
e-mail: irj20@cam.ac.uk

© The Author(s), under exclusive license to Springer Nature
Switzerland AG 2023
T. Rajan, D. Whistler (eds.), *The Palgrave Handbook of German Idealism and Poststructuralism*, Palgrave Handbooks in German Idealism,
https://doi.org/10.1007/978-3-031-27345-2_20

To speak of the "ends of Hegel," as this chapter does, is not therefore simply or solely to pose the question of teleology, of the telos or final destination of the Hegelian system as it might be understood on its own terms and within the greater or lesser closure of the system (upon) itself. It is also to interrogate the outcomes of Hegelian thinking within the French reception of Hegel and how these outcomes are marked by, but not entirely reducible to, distinct historical moments. The wider intellectual context here is that of phenomenological and post-phenomenological philosophy in France in the twentieth century. The more specific trajectory that will be explored is one that runs from the thought of Emmanuel Levinas, Georges Bataille, and Jean-Paul Sartre through to a particular strand of poststructuralist and (post)deconstructive discourse that can be identified in the work of Jacques Derrida and Jean-Luc Nancy. The core concern that emerges within this strand of thought is not just the relation of philosophy to its historical and political contexts or legacies but is also that of a more fundamental mutual imbrication of the *philosophical* and the *political* as such. In this context the questions of philosophical subjectivity and of political subjectivity and their foundation or ground can be shown to be profoundly intertwined. What follows will discern an intellectual trajectory in which Hegelian synthesis, subjectivity, and the figures of philosophical totality or absolute knowledge find themselves mapped onto the political form of totalitarianism.

Within this trajectory of thought, "sovereignty," understood as the absolutely autonomous or non-dependent self-production of subjectivity (both philosophical and political) emerges as the desired, yet entirely impossible, end of the Hegelian system. "Community," concomitantly, emerges as its necessary and ineluctable outcome or point of issue: it is the necessity for all existence to be in relation, or to be produced *as* relation (that of one singular existence to another) that renders the production of the subject as sovereign impossible. Sovereignty and community emerge here as the twin ends of Hegel, impossible and ineluctable respectively. They also emerge as instances which, for Europeans and the European diaspora most commonly and loosely referred to as "the West," have been decisive conditions of our shared history and politics (and arguably still remain so). In this way, whether we know it, or like it, or not, Hegel may still be with us, and this most inaccessible of philosophies continues to spill over into, or permeate, our historical present.

2 A Totalitarian Philosophy—Philosophy as Totalitarian

The story of Hegel's reception in France in the twentieth century is a long and complex one which cannot be told in the space of a short chapter such as this. In *French Hegel: From Surrealism to Postmodernism* Bruce Baugh gives a compelling account of this reception which begins in the interwar years with anthropological readings of Hegel and the work of figures such as Jean Wahl, Jean Hyppolite, Alexandre Koyré, André Breton, Henri Lefebvre, Alexandre Kojève, and Georges Bataille. Many of these earlier thinkers leave their lasting mark on the post-war generation of

French philosophers for whom Hegel continues, in one way or another, to be a key point of reference. Baugh follows this thread of influence through from the work of Jean-Paul Sartre and Jacques Derrida, to what he dubs the new empiricism, transcendental and historical respectively, of Gilles Deleuze and Michael Foucault.[3]

The story Baugh tells is one in which Hegel is read in France as the philosopher of "unhappy consciousness" taking a cue from Jean Wahl's seminal 1929 text *Le Malheur de la conscience dans la philosophie de Hegel*.[4] His reading sets to one side what was the dominant story of the French reception of Hegel that took as its central theme the dialectic of master and slave (or lord and bondsman) as elaborated in Alexandre Kojève's hugely influential commentary lectures on the *Phenomenology of Spirit* in the 1930s.[5] So, rather than interpreting the core of the *Phenomenology* as a dialectic of desire and recognition in which consciousness is locked in a struggle with its other, and where this dialectic is then mapped onto wider intersubjective, historical, and political consciousness, the French reception of Hegel has in fact, Baugh argues, been more fundamentally preoccupied with the division of consciousness and of being from itself, its internal conflicts, and with the negativity which constitutes it as an always internally riven instance of becoming. Hegel himself describes the unhappy consciousness in the *Phenomenology* as "the consciousness of self as a dual natured merely contradictory being" and as life and activity that exists "as an agonizing over this existence" and therefore as "consciousness only of its own nothingness."[6] Readers of Sartre will immediately discern the profound resonance of this description of the unhappy consciousness with the Sartrean account of *being-for-itself* and its angst-ridden self-negation in *Being and Nothingness*. Baugh more generally assimilates the negativity and self-division of Hegelian Spirit with what will become the core concerns of poststructuralist thought in France after World War II: the privileging scission over synthesis, difference over sameness or identity, and abyssal groundlessness and fragmentation over foundational, totalizing, or absolute philosophical knowledge.

Baugh's compelling account of the French reception of Hegel and its focus on unhappy consciousness rather than on the dialectic of lord and bondsman certainly gives a deeper and fuller picture of the French philosophical preoccupation, throughout the twentieth century, with negativity, division, and difference. Yet it underplays to a certain degree the extent to which, and in the post-war years in particular, this emphasis on the negative or on the differential, was in a decisive way a reading of one version of Hegel against another. It is here that the interplay between the philosophical and the historical, and between the philosophical and the political, comes to the fore. Already in the 1930s Kojève's account of Hegel's dialectic of lord and bondsman and the question of the end of history was being interpreted in a Marxian (albeit not orthodoxly Marxist) fashion and in the light of the Bolshevik revolution and of the Soviet experiment.[7] In the wake of the Second World War the experience of totalitarianism, of Stalin's terror, and of Hitler's genocidal Nazi regime, casts a long shadow over the reception and understanding in France of the Hegelian system and, indeed, of the very nature of philosophical knowledge itself.

The career of Emmanuel Levinas is exemplary in this regard. In a coda to the English edition of his 1963 work, *Difficult Freedom: Essays on Judaism*, Levinas offers a "disparate inventory" that forms his biography, his intellectual formation, and subsequent career, from his Lithuanian origins, his education under the tutelage of those who were young during the Dreyfus affair, his mentoring by Jean Wahl, and all the way through to his appointment at the Sorbonne in 1973. It is a biography, he remarks, that is "dominated by the presentiment and the memory of the Nazi horror."[8] This dominant memory of the Nazi regime and of the subsequent genocide of European Jewry can be discerned in Levinas' work from the 1940s onwards and in particular in his understanding of the Western European philosophical tradition in texts such as *Totality and Infinity: An Essay on Exteriority* (1961). Here philosophical totality is characterized in a manner which resonates closely with both the philosophical structure of Hegel's system and the political structure of totalitarianism. In the preface to *Totality and Infinity*, just sixteen years after the end of World War II, Levinas assimilates both the structure of war and conflict and what he calls the philosophical "visage of being" to the same "concept of totality which dominates Western philosophy":

> Individuals are reduced to being bearers of forces that command them unbeknown to themselves. The meaning of individuals (invisible outside of this totality) is derived from the totality. The unicity of each present is incessantly sacrificed to a future appealed to bring forth its objective meaning. For the ultimate meaning alone counts.[9]

In the case of both the Hegelian and totalitarian systems, this line of thought runs, the particular is always suppressed and absorbed into the general, alterity is subsumed into sameness, and the individual sacrificed to the greater unity and totality of the whole, that of Spirit/Geist or of the State respectively. This resonance between Hegelian philosophy, the Western tradition of thinking being more generally, and the structure of totalitarianism, is implicit throughout *Totality and Infinity* and is made entirely explicit in Alphonso Lingis' introductory commentary to the English edition in which he notes: "Totalitarian thinking… aims to gain an all-inclusive, panoramic view of all things, including the other, in a neutral impersonal light, like the Hegelian Geist, or the Heideggerian Being."[10]

In this Levinasian understanding of philosophical totality, Hegel's system and its pretension to absolute knowledge have been retroactively tainted by the events of the 1930s and 1940s and by the historical experience of totalitarianism, fascism, and genocide. This understanding is by no means restricted to Levinas alone and, I would argue, forms what might be called the post-war "Hegelian paradigm" against which the poststructuralist privileging of difference, non-identity, and ontological groundlessness can be understood. Already this paradigm is nascent in works of the 1940s such as Georges Bataille's *Inner Experience* and Jean-Paul Sartre's *Being and Nothingness*, both written under German occupation and published by Gallimard in 1943 and 1947 respectively.

In a reading of Hegel that will become decisive for Jean-Luc Nancy, the Bataille of *Inner Experience* characterizes the journey of Spirit as the thought of a self that can "only make itself absolute by becoming everything," and describes the circular nature of Hegelian dialectical negation and synthesis as a grasping that "an unknown thing is the same as another known thing."[11] In *Inner Experience* Bataille privileges radical non-knowledge over absolute knowledge, nothingness over subjectivity, and void over substance. This reflects his desire for an end other than totality within the Hegelian system. Bataille's contention is that, in its circular movement and aspiration to "become everything," the self produced by the system must also necessarily *include* its own limitless negativity and thereby ultimately "invert itself at the summit and return to the unknown."[12] This affirmation of "the end of Hegel" as a non-knowledge that ultimately dissolves any possibility of consciousness becoming absolute knowledge, substance, Spirit, or "everything" emerges during the Nazi occupation of France but does so very much as the endpoint of Bataille's longstanding engagement with Hegel that dates back to the early 1930s. This is an engagement largely inspired by Kojève's lectures on the *Phenomenology* and deeply informs Bataille's complex and ambivalent understanding of fascism as articulated in essays such as "The Psychological Structure of Fascism" published in the review *Critique Sociale* in 1933 and 1934.[13] As early as the 1930s, then, the problematic of Hegelian dialectics and the totalitarian form of fascism are brought and thought together as being somehow fundamentally co-implicated each with the other.

Bataille's invocation of Hegelian totality as being formed in a circular movement that returns the unknown to the known and that produces the self in a "becoming everything" prefigures Levinas' later formulations relating to totality and is roughly contemporaneous with the reading of Hegel given by his rival Sartre in *Being and Nothingness*. Here Sartre understands Hegel's *Phenomenology* and its dialectic as a process in which "individual consciousnesses are moments in the whole" viewed in a philosophically panoramic perspective according to which Hegel "*is* the Whole," and synthesis or absolute knowledge is possible only as a result of "the totalitarian point of view he has adopted."[14] This allows Sartre to repeatedly ascribe to Hegel this "totalitarian point of view" or posture.[15] So, despite the Sartrean characterization of the *being-for-itself* of consciousness in terms that are barely distinguishable from Hegel's "unhappy consciousness," Sartre's understanding of the Hegelian system, and of the position of the philosopher himself in relation to that system, unequivocally assimilates the philosophical form of total or absolute knowledge with the political form of totalitarianism.

From the 1930s and 1940s onwards, then, Levinas, Bataille, and Sartre help to shape a Hegelian paradigm that will inform the poststructuralist understanding of Hegel and also, crucially, its understanding of the interrelation between the philosophical and the political. This is perhaps no more clearly exemplified in Derrida's seminal series of essays collected in *Writing and Difference* and originally published in French in 1967.[16] Containing essays on, amongst others, Foucault, Levinas, and Bataille, *Writing and Difference* marks one of the key turning points from French structuralism to poststructuralism.[17] In his discussion of Levinas Derrida carries over the understanding of Hegel as a "totalitarian" thinker that informed the perspective of *Totality and Infinity* discussed earlier.

In "Violence and Metaphysics," this perspective is repeated and Derrida criticizes the Levinasian text only to the extent that he thinks that it might not go far enough in its deconstructive strategies and therefore risks falling back into the violence of thinking being that it ostensibly challenges. Derrida explicitly uses the term "totalitarian," speaking of the "thought of being as totalitarian" and, pace Levinas, writing that, "the entire philosophical tradition would make common cause with oppression and with the totalitarianism of the same."[18] The negotiation with Levinas here involves a complex discussion of Lithuanian-French philosopher's own reading of Hegel in which the possibility of any escape from the "totalitarian" thinking of being is rendered problematic if not seemingly impossible. In these negotiations Derrida's discerns a risk which is run in any critical or deconstructive reading of Hegel, namely that "as soon as he speaks against Hegel, Levinas can only confirm Hegel, has confirmed him already."[19] This is a risk, Derrida, argues, that is also run in the context of Bataille's challenge to Hegelian totality and the Bataillian affirmation of non-knowledge against the absolute knowledge of speculative reason. Bataille's challenge "risks agreeing to the reasonableness of reason, of philosophy, of Hegel, who is always right, as soon as one opens one's mouth in order to articulate meaning."[20] For, "in speaking against Hegel," in denying totality, one may be engaging in an act of negation which both suppresses *and* conserves that which is negated. Going against Hegel might just confirm the very movement and structure (of *Aufhebung*) that Hegel himself describes.[21] In this way totality, and the violence of philosophical totalitarianism, may always ineluctably be re-inscribed in the very gesture that seeks to overturn them.

Derrida's suggestion that Hegel might always be proved right "as soon as one opens one's mouth to articulate meaning" implies also that this problem of the ineluctable re-inscription of totality could be much more than just a risk attendant on the deconstructive reading of Hegel. Hegel's account of conceptual determination and the genesis of symbolic or linguistic meaning are at play here. In this context the negative movement of Hegelian consciousness and its ultimate affirmation of totality is already at work in meaning-making as such and in the way that, for Hegel, semantic or conceptual determination is always a dialectical process of negation and conservation. If I say, "rose," the concept or signified of the flower in question exists as a universal for all roses in the absence (or negation) of any given rose. Accordingly, the enunciation of determinate meaning always involves the suppression of alterity (of the differential multiplicity and singularity of the given) and a resulting synthesis of identity (of "roseness"). The wider implication is that the production of stable, fixed, or determinate meaning as such involves an irreducible economy of violence and is therefore complicit with, or a condition for, a violence that lies both at the heart of our philosophical tradition in its search for metaphysical foundations *and* at the heart of the totalitarian political form that seeks to subsume all individual existence into the life and whole of the State.

The argument that the articulation of meaning per se always proves Hegel's philosophical totalizing system to be right and is therefore somehow implicated in Hegel's "totalitarianism" may, on the face of it, appear to be both hyperbolic and in itself very totalizing. Yet perhaps what is being worked out here philosophically in the wake of the early to mid-twentieth century experience in Europe and elsewhere is the acknowledgement that the *violence* of political forms and ideologies (whatever their nature) is an affair of everyday worldly meaning and of a desire for wholeness which is brought to its apotheosis in the totalitarian form. It is a question of the way in which everyday sense becomes a totalizing meaning and this is then presented in both philosophical texts and in political ideologies as the ultimate foundation and accomplishment of what it means *to be*. It is then *also* a question of the way this sense of being is desired as the accomplishment or effectuation of a political project or structure of State power. What is clear, in any case, is that for the Derrida of *Writing and Difference* the "thought of being as totalitarian" overspills the domain of philosophy to include all those domains that seek to fix or systematize meaning in enclosed wholes or totalities.

This is evident in his unequivocal assimilation of the philosophical logic of totality to the project of structuralism and its desire to give systematic descriptions of symbolic systems (linguistic, anthropological, cultural-historical, and psychical) understood as relational wholes. In his essay on the Cartesian *cogito*, "Foucault, and the *History of Madness*," Derrida explicitly speaks of "'totalitarian' in the structuralist sense of the word" and of "Structuralist totalitarianism," stopping just short of calling Foucault's book itself totalitarian.[22] Insofar as it seeks the systematization of the structures of meaning, structuralism and the traditions of knowledge that gave birth to it are, for Derrida, caught up within a mode of thought that presupposes the existence of "totalitarian structures that are endowed with unity of internal meaning."[23] This understanding, arguably, is what gives the key impetus to Derridean deconstruction's desire to highlight or affirm the decentering, the non-self-identity and therefore non-unity and ontological ungroundedness of all of the symbolic structures in which the genesis of meaning can be said to occur.[24]

More broadly speaking, this Derridean understanding of meaning, identity, and of the totalitarian, can, when understood in the context of the "Hegelian paradigm" elaborated here, explain or at least contextualize other seemingly hyperbolic claims relating to the "fascism" of language and identity made by prominent figures of poststructuralism and deconstruction. So, for instance, Roland Barthes speaking in 1977 during his inaugural lecture at the Collège de France affirms that "language— the performance of a language system—is neither reactionary nor progressive; it is quite simply fascist; for fascism does not simply prevent speech, it compels speech."[25] In a shift away from the (post-)structuralist preoccupation with language understood as system, Jean-Luc Nancy and Philippe Lacoue-Labarthe, write much later in "The Nazi Myth" (1990) that

> the ideology of the Total State is to be conceived as the Subject State... such that in the last instance it is in modern philosophy, in the fully realized metaphysics of the Subject, that ideology finds its full guarantee:... the logic or idea of the subject fulfilling itself in this way... is fascism. The *ideology of the subject* (which is perhaps no more than a pleonasm) is fascism[26]

So, whether it is a question of the abstract or everyday determination and enunciation of meaning or of the philosophical and political production of the "Subject," the Hegelian paradigm affirms a profound co-belonging of the philosophical and the political in the totalitarian form and even, in its most radical articulations, allows for an identification of all these instances with fascism. This is a co-belonging that, as has been argued, informs the way in which French thinkers in the wake of World

War II understood the Hegelian system to be unavoidably and retroactively tainted by the recent historical experience of the 1930s and 1940s. Hegel, as the thinker of system and of absolute knowledge, has become the exemplary figure who marks the possibility of a totalitarian philosophy or of philosophy itself and as such already being totalitarian. He also comes to represent the impossibility of untangling the historical event and dynamic of totalitarian regimes from the way we use language and the way in which, both individually, collectively, and above all ideologically, we are produced as subjects.

3 Sovereignty Undone: Hegel Deconstructed

It might appear from this characterization of the "Hegelian paradigm" of post-World War II French thought, and its manifestation in Derrida's writing in particular, that there is simply no way out from Hegelian totality. The violence of the totalizing system that Hegel elaborates appears always to be reaffirmed in the ineluctable closure of the system upon itself. Yet, as Baugh's account of the "French Hegel" argued, philosophers in France in the twentieth century sought to affirm the negativity described in the instance of the "unhappy consciousness." The key argument here is that they do so *against* the backdrop of this paradigm of seemingly inevitable synthesis, sameness, and totality. In the context of Derridean deconstruction and what might be called Nancy's post-deconstructive philosophy, this interplay between scission and synthesis informs the readings that are given of the Hegelian text itself and, in particular, of the Hegelian treatment of sovereignty.

It has been said that deconstruction has "always been the autocritique of sovereignty in all its given forms and analogues."[27] Certainly Derrida's more restricted negotiation with political sovereignty as a specific concept has been well documented.[28] Taken in its most common dictionary definition the political meaning of sovereignty can be understood first and foremost, of course, as the quality of being sovereign and as the wielding of supreme power or authority in a government, state, or community. The sovereign therefore stands at the very top or summit of the social and political pyramid or hierarchy in order to command all that lies beneath it. Yet the notion of independence is also key the concept of sovereignty. Sovereign is the power that has no relation of dependency upon another higher power and that cannot be subjected to any power or end other than itself. In an important sense, then, the sovereign, in general and as such is *withdrawn* from dependent relationality and perhaps even, by extension, from relationality as such. As Nancy says of the sovereign in his essay "*Ex nihilo summum*: Of Sovereignty": "Its withdrawal gathers it into itself by subtracting it from the dependency of all things that are pressed against each other, entangled in each other's reactions. The sovereign is set apart from this dependency and from the endless exchange of means and ends."[29] The sovereign, therefore, is its own end, an end in itself. Thus, the sovereign subject produces itself in an autotelic manner without regard to the ends of other subjects or things. It

Sovereignty and Community 437

stands at the summit; but is not in a relation of dependency to a higher power above or to that which sits below.

In this context, it could be argued that the Hegelian system, which would have as its endpoint the production of the subject of absolute knowledge, is always intimately bound up with the question of sovereignty. An "absolute" is that which, like the sovereign, is not dependent upon external conditions for its existence. The subject of absolute knowledge would be one which is no longer caught in a dialectic of self and other but which would be a self that, as Bataille insisted, has "become everything" and is therefore no longer in a relationship of possible dependency with any other instance. This proximity of the absolute and the sovereign indicates a fundamental interrelation of the philosophical and the political insofar as the subjects of absolute knowledge and of political sovereignty share a similar structure, that of non-dependence and non-relationality.

These stakes are borne out in two texts authored by Derrida and Nancy respectively. The first is a paper given by Derrida in New York in October 1968 and published in 1972 in *Margins of Philosophy*. The second is Nancy's first full-length single authored work *The Speculative Remark (one of Hegel's bon mots)* published in 1973.[30] Taken together these texts clearly present the two possible outcomes that deconstruction ascribes to the Hegelian system and the works in which it is elaborated: totalizing fulfilment on the one hand and irreducible self-division on the other.[31] In "The Ends of Man" Derrida discusses of the figure of the human and its relation to philosophical discourse and metaphysics or ontology. He takes pains to underline that, contrary to certain readings, Hegel's system and *The Phenomenology of Spirit* in particular, is not an anthropology; it is not a science of "man" but a science of consciousness (thus setting himself against the earlier French reception of Hegel described by Baugh). Nevertheless, Derrida argues, the figure of the human is everywhere at stake in the dialectical movement of Hegelian consciousness and of system as a whole:

> Consciousness is the *Aufhebung* of the soul of man, phenomenology is the *relève* of anthropology. It is *no longer*, but it is *still* a science of man. In this sense, all the structures described by the phenomenology of spirit... are structures of that which has *relevé* man. In them man remains in relief. His essence rests in *Phenomenology*.[32]

In this way, Hegel, the philosophical narrator of the journey of consciousness through its various stages towards its final accomplishment, becomes the bearer of a unity and totality that articulates all of the human and all of being in one and the same overarching perspective (thus recalling the "totalitarian point of view" ascribed to him by Sartre in *Being and Nothingness* and by Lingis in his introduction to *Totality and Infinity*). Derrida discerns this totalizing perspective in Hegel's use of the first-person plural pronoun as the focal point of the narration of consciousness's journey: "The *we* [in the *Phenomenology of Spirit*] is the unity of absolute knowledge and anthropology, of God and man, of onto-theo-teleology and humanism."[33]

This means that, ultimately, all aspects or instances of existence that can go by various names of man, consciousness, soul, spirit, God, and so on find themselves dialectically sublated and raised into a metaphysical totality which is the ultimate end or issue of the Hegelian system, a system which has incorporated each instance along its way and synthesized it into a final whole which leaves no remainder. Echoing Levinas and the Hegelian paradigm that has been elaborated here, Derrida concludes with regard to the philosophy of being, or ontology (explicitly referencing Heidegger): "the end of man is the thinking of Being, man is the end of the thinking of Being, the end of man is the end of the thinking of Being."[34] This tortuous formulation points to the way in which the circular movement of the Hegelian system and its closure upon itself may be repeated in one way or another by all ontology: if a total figure of Being is produced as an articulation of *all that is*, then the human that is able to produce, think, and therefore incorporate this ontological totality within its thought is both the *end* and the *means* of this accomplishment. There is also no higher accomplishment since this thought of Being includes everything without remainder. In ontology, the human is figured as a *sovereign* philosophical subjectivity. In thinking all being it stands at the summit of being and includes everything, knows no end other than itself, and in this enacts its autotelic self-production.

In "The Ends of Man," it seems, Hegel once again emerges (alongside Heidegger) as exemplary of the philosopher of being grasped as a totality. The relentless dialectical movement of negation always also conserves and raises anything and everything that is negated into a higher synthesis. And so, one might think once again that, as Derrida feared in *Writing and Difference*, Hegel is always right. And yet here, as elsewhere,[35] Derrida's more fundamental concern is to discern the possibility of an interruption of Hegel and of a deconstructive strategy of thinking and writing which would affirm such a disruption without succumbing to dialectical recuperation and to the closure of the system upon itself. "A radical trembling" Derrida writes, "can only come from the outside."[36] The question therefore becomes how the philosophical text of Hegel, and therefore the entirety of the system, are somehow exposed to an outside or exteriority which would resist recuperation into totality and thereby cause a trembling or interruption of the whole. Building on the Derridean engagement with Hegel, Nancy's *The Speculative Remark* argues that the movement of dialectical negation and conservation in Hegel is not, after all, fatally destined to absorb everything in its path or to recuperate every vestige of being into itself.[37] The hypothesis here is that the Hegelian dialectic and the system as a whole may always already be exposed to the "outside" and the synthetic movement of *Aufhebung* may always already have failed whether Hegel likes it, or knows it, or not.

At the very beginning of *The Speculative Remark* Nancy gives an indication of those French readings of Hegel which are to be taken as givens for his own reading. These include works by Alexandre Koyré and Jean Hyppolite and, crucially also, Derrida's "From Restricted to General Economy: a Hegelianism without Reserve" and "The Pit and the Pyramid: Introduction to Hegel's Semiology."[38] Where Derrida reflected in the former on Bataille's struggle to challenge Hegelian reason and on the possibility that Hegel "is always right," in "The Pit and the Pyramid" he asks, "What might be a negative that could not be relevé? And which, in sum, as negative, but without appearing as such, without *presenting itself*, without working in the service of meaning, would work... as pure loss?"[39] The question here is one of a negativity that the Hegelian text and system cannot always put to work in the service of totality (this being precisely the possibility of impossibility that Bataille sought in his earlier quest for non-knowledge in *Inner Experience*). This, for Derrida, would be, "Quite simply, a machine, perhaps and one which would function. A machine defined in its pure functioning, and not in its final utility, its meaning, its result, its work." What Hegel is incapable of doing, Derrida contends, is to think such a machine. If Hegel's philosophy is only able to grasp that which can be put in service of the system and its end or finality, then it will necessarily and fatefully fail to grasp any negativity that cannot be put to work. From this perspective that which at one instance appears all powerful (the Hegelian system) can now appear as impotent: "this entire logic, this syntax, these propositions, these concepts, these names, this language of Hegel's—and, up to a point, this very language—are engaged in the *system of this unpower*, this structural incapacity."[40] Derrida's gambit here is that the very language or system of signs that would prove Hegel to be always right is in fact always somehow marked by a negativity that cannot be mastered. Nancy takes this up as the starting point of his own argument in *The Speculative Remark*.

Here he focuses on the operation of the *relève* or of *Aufhebung* in Hegel and specifically on the question of its presentation or, in German, its *Darstellung*. In a close reading that will prefigure Nancy's subsequent interpretations in the 1970s of both Descartes and Kant, he focuses on the question of the discursive presentation of the concepts and dialectical movement of the Hegelian text itself.[41] In so doing, he finds that *Aufhebung* is everywhere presupposed and called upon by the system in its progress towards the assumption of absolute knowledge but it is in reality nowhere present or presented *as such*. This absence of, or resistance to, presentation is decisive for Nancy. The logical development that informs the dialectical method everywhere in Hegel's thought cannot just mention or invoke the operation of negation and conservation, of suppression and synthesis. It needs to enact or effectuate this operation, that is, to effectively present it in the very movement of its actualization or accomplishment. Nancy puts this as follows: "*Darstellung* is not, as we know, the accessory instrumental event of a performance or a publication… it is itself the actuality [*effectivité*] of the presence and of the present of the speculative."[42] Any failure of effective presentation with regard to the operation of *Aufhebung* in the Hegelian text is also and at the very same time a failure of the effectivity of speculative reason itself.

In arguing that *Aufhebung* is not presented as such in the Hegelian text, Nancy is also arguing that, ultimately, it is in reality a non-concept because it evades the very conceptual determination by the operations of negation and conservation that it itself seeks to describe. It "has to pass or to take place beside the play of determinations."[43] This means that the whole textual fabric of Hegel's discourse, its syntax, and the shape or form of the speculative propositions that constitute it as such, also ultimately evade or resist the proposed logic of dialectical reason. If the whole system relies on *Aufhebung* and *Aufhebung* itself is never present, presented, and therefore effective as such, then none of the tortuous linguistic or syntactical articulations of Hegel's prose accomplish the conceptual determinations and dialectical progression and synthesis that the system proposes: "There is, strictly speaking, no *aufheben* of grammar, nor, strictly speaking, in grammar."[44] This leads Nancy to conclude in terms that evoke the "machine" spoken of by Derrida above: "Between grammar and memory, language, in its very form, resolves itself into mechanism. Mechanism resists *aufheben*—and vice versa."[45] This is a mechanism that functions but not in order to produce the ideality or conceptual universality of meaning and logic or to effect their progress towards totality. In the end, the Hegelian text remains a contingent text, embedded in the spatio-temporal materiality of its unfolding as text, and therefore always exposed to the vagaries of grammar, to the indeterminacies and obscurities of its possible meaning, and necessarily falling short of the ideality and systematicity of the absolute knowledge to which it aspires.

This early reading of Hegel by Nancy leaves its mark on his later work. The question of *Darstellung*, or presentation, is also central to the 1990 reading of Hegel, "The Jurisdiction of the Hegelian Monarch."[46] Here the focus is on the place of the monarch in Hegel's account of the state and, in particular, on the way in which the sovereignty of the sovereign is made manifest in the person of the monarch. What is at stake is the monarch's power of decision that *presents* the law of the state in its effectuation or accomplishment and the way that this confirms or enacts the unity and cohesion of the state as such. The monarch's power of decision as an effectuation of the law and therefore of the unity of the state exactly parallels the problematic of *Darstellung* worked out in *The Speculative Remark*. In this context Nancy explicitly alludes to, but claims he will not dwell upon, "the general scheme... which characterizes Hegel's *Philosophy of Right* as the thought of the totalitarian State itself,... the thought of the social totality... as the organic character of the life of the Subject, which... is the culmination... of the 'self-consciousness of the world mind.'"[47] The Hegelian paradigm that has been elaborated throughout this discussion is therefore once again at play insofar as, in the person of the monarch, "the State is the final truth of the total system of subjectivity."[48]

In fact, the mutual imbrication of philosophical and political subjectivity and their co-implication in the totalitarian form is here more clearly and explicitly brought out than ever before. Nancy writes:

> the positing of the singular State is to be understood above all as the totalization in the Subject of subjects and of their union. By this account, whether monarch, Party, or Anführer... it is all the same: the essence of the totalitarian state is in subjectivity, and the organicity that makes its structure and its process.[49]

And yet what he will show is that the person of the monarch holds an at best equivocal position in relation to the union of subjects in the state form and their totalization as (State-)Subject. Everything hangs on the question that Nancy poses with regard to the way in which the juridical and the political are articulated in the *effective presentation* of the law of the state, that is, in the decision of the monarch which makes actual or effectuates the law as such.[50] This, ultimately, is the decision of the sovereign subject, who, in the manifestation of their person as such, would be the manifestation of the Subject-State *as such*, or, as Nancy himself puts it, "The monarch... is less the supreme individual in the State than the superior individual *of* the State, or the State itself as individuality."[51]

Yet it is in this that the monarch, as sovereign and as the wielder of sovereign decision making, comes to occupy an irreducibly equivocal, or indeed impossible, position. For as the "synthesis of the State... its organicity existing *for itself*" the monarch is both distinct or set apart from the people and from legislative and governmental powers as well as being, at the very same time, the fulfilment of the State as subject or as organic totality.[52] The personal unity of the sovereign accomplishes that of the State, but *as sovereign*, the monarch is not in any relation of dependency to the whole they come to embody and exists as a singularity outside of that whole. The sovereign both sits at the summit of the pyramidal hierarchy of the state edifice but is also in a certain crucial way detached from it. Nancy returns here to the central paradox of sovereignty: to be sovereign is to hold absolute authority without any relation of subordination to another instance, but this sovereignty is therefore at the same time constituted in a withdrawal of, or from, relation which sets it apart from the whole over which it is supposed to wield such authority. Nancy writes, "Between the totality of the subjectivity and the individuality of the monarch, there is as much dialectical linkage as absolute rupture," and what this means is that: "Strictly speaking, we should say that in the organic totalization of the Hegelian State the monarch is *lacking*: either he is not an individual, or else he is one, and then he is excepted from the totality, he exceeds it or he remains withdrawn from it."[53] Not being an individual the monarch would not be in a position to decide, would not be in a position to present or effectuate the law of and for the community of the State. Being an individual *as* sovereign, the monarch is excepted from or exceeds the totality of the community of the State and, in this withdrawal, interrupts the possibility of totalization. This would be an interruption of the accomplishment of the Subject-State, of its synthesis and organicity, and therefore of the union of subjects in the state form and as social totality.

The outcome of this equivocal position of the monarch, as sovereign individual, is therefore the failure of the dialectic, the failure of "the culmination... of the 'self-consciousness of the world mind'" in the form of the Subject-State.[54] The impossibility at play here would also mark the inevitable failure of any possible fulfilment of sovereignty as such and of the totalitarian form in both their philosophical and political manifestations. If the presentation of the law of the state in the decision of the monarch was supposed to articulate the relation of the whole to itself, its union as social totality, then what we are left with as the outcome of this impossibility and this interruption of totality is "the incompleteness of relation as such" and a necessity that "the incompleteness of the relation *is* the relation itself."[55] In this way Nancy's reading of Hegel and of the problem of presentation marks a passage from sovereignty understood as the (impossible) assumption of totality, to community understood as the (ineluctable) incompleteness of relation in excess of totality. Being should have found its accomplishment in the production of sovereign subjectivity and the culmination of this in the subjectivity of the sovereign placed at and as the summit of Being. Rather than presenting, at the summit, the unity of the pyramidal edifice of the State to itself, the failure of sovereign subjectivity also undoes any full accomplishment of the social edifice as State-Subject. In terms of actual existence and what is possible all that would subsist are singular existences in a relation of incompleteness, without identity or fulfilled subjectivity, and distributed on a horizontal plane of relation where, ontologically at least, there is no hierarchy and all are equal.

4 Community Without Identity

Such abstract considerations and the seemingly rarified minutiae of close reading which give rise to them might seem far removed from real or historical manifestations of political power and sovereignty or from the horrors of totalitarian states, as they were experienced in the twentieth century. Yet arguably, Nancy's reading of Hegel demonstrates exactly why political projects that orientate themselves to some pure form of sovereignty and to the production of a pure sovereign subject *in and as* a political community or totalizing state-form are always destined to very real historical failure. It might also indicate why this failure will also always come at the price of violence of one kind or another, up to and including that of mass killing or genocide. The Hegelian paradigm and its deconstruction show that the "end" of sovereignty, or sovereignty as an end, is not, and cannot be, accomplished subjectivity understood as totality, social union, or as the Subject-State. It cannot be an autonomous, independent subjectivity that would "become everything" and wield authority without the limitations that are imposed by relationality. If, as Nancy says, the sovereign is withdrawn from relation by dint of its very sovereignty, then it is set apart and is sovereign over nothing, and sovereign as *nothing*. If it *is* and nevertheless remains still in relation, that is to say, in "the dependency of all things that are pressed against each other, entangled in each other's reactions," then it is not sovereign.[56] And if it is embedded in relation(s), the subject that aspires to be sovereign, whether an individual or state, will be compelled to the more or less violent negation of those relations and of other existences in order to pursue that aspiration.

Nancy's reading of Hegel and of sovereignty explicitly develops Georges Bataille's thinking and the Bataillian affirmation that "sovereignty is NOTHING."[57] In "*Ex nihilo summum*," Nancy elaborates on the "nothing" of sovereignty as thought by Bataille in terms which closely echo the argument of "The Jurisdiction of the Hegelian Monarch." Here once again the sovereign is "a detached summit, without any contact with the outside of the whole structure built upon the base."[58] A sovereign existence is that which "depends on nothing," and: "Depending on nothing, it is entirely returned to itself," such that "the very same condition that gives the sovereign its concept takes away the possibility of being exercised as such."[59] What this means is that where the sovereign whole should or could be (the subject of absolute knowledge, of total social union, or *as* Subject-State), there remains only a nothing or void of substance since there is no final assumption of any sovereign subject that can be fulfilled or accomplished into order to bind the whole together in a substantive unity or self-identical totality. In this way, a certain thinking of community without identity, totality, or hierarchy emerges as the endpoint of Nancy's reading of Hegel and one which can be clearly discerned in his works of the 1990s.

In the essay "War, Right, Sovereignty—Technē" collected in *Being Singular Plural* (1996), Nancy speaks of the "empty place of sovereignty" in terms of the spacing of the finitude of the world as such: "This spacing of the world *is the empty place of sovereignty*. That is, it is the empty place of the end, the empty place of the common good, and the empty place of the common as a good."[60] Hegel is not mentioned here but, as should by now be clear, he is everywhere present where sovereignty and subjectivity are at stake in Nancy's thinking. These terms are taken up in his second and last full-length work dedicated to the German philosopher, *Hegel: The Restlessness of the Negative* (1997). This work comprehensively and explicitly breaks with the Hegelian paradigm that, in the wake of World War II, led French philosophers to view Hegel as a thinker of totality and as complicit with the totalitarian form. The end of Hegel, here, like the end of sovereignty elsewhere in Nancy's writing, is rather emptiness, absence, and the dissolution of substance. Thus, Hegel is "the opposite of a 'totalitarian' thinker."[61] What Nancy now sees in Hegel is not a thinker of totality and of a system in need of deconstruction, but one whose thinking of the negative and its relentless movement was always, *and knowingly*, a thinking of the empty place of sovereignty. And so, the Hegelian subject is now for Nancy not a subjectivity that synthesizes but "is essentially what (or the one who) dissolves all substance."[62] This dissolution of substance is also the dissolution of all ends or finality and with this the dislocation of any and every possibility of a sovereign subject, of the self-certainty and self-identity of subjectivity as such. What is left then is nothing but the spacing of relations in and as a nothing of substance and as a "we" that is without identity. What is left are singularities, always in relation, in common, and exposed as a nothing or void of substance, which will and never be sublated into a sovereign subject, social union, or the (hierarchical) whole of a political identity or form.[63] The end of Hegel is community but only on the condition that that community be thought as radically open and equal in its profusion of singular existences, without identity and without totality.

It may well be that the Hegelian paradigm was always something of a straw doll in relation to the actual text of Hegel itself and to a thinker who may have been very aware of the internal tension between scission and synthesis within the "system" of speculative rationality. Hegel, the philosopher of and apologist for the Prussian State, was also a thinker born in the wake, or out of, the shared historical experience of schism, revolution, and conflict (the Protestant Reformation, the French Revolution, and subsequent Napoleonic wars), and one who may have well understood the implications of the untameable, limitless, and limitlessly corrosive negativity that he had cloaked or hidden beneath the obscurity and esoteric form of his writing.[64] The enduring lesson of the poststructuralist and (post-deconstructive) reading of (impossible) sovereignty in Hegel remains however: namely that the "end of history" will never be a perfected, sovereign subject or identity, accomplished and made present in a political community, structure, or organization. Any project taking sovereignty as its aim or outcome effectively remains an illusory and harmful political theodicy destined both to the violent destruction of relation(s) and to ultimate failure. The lesson is that all we have is the possibility of a politics that, more or less pragmatically pursued in the absence of any sovereign end, embraces the incompletion and equality of ontological relation, the finitude of our co-belonging. This would necessarily be a politics of community but one in which community, without any end or goal other than that of its finite spacing as such, would be without identity and exposed just as much to its internal plurality as to its own ungraspable outside.

Notes

1. Paul de Man, "Sign and Symbol in Hegel's 'Aesthetics'," *Critical Inquiry* 8, no. 2 (1982), 761–775, 763.
2. Ibid., 771.
3. See Bruce Baugh, *French Hegel: From Surrealism to Postmodernism* (London: Routledge, 2003) and "Hegel in Modern French Philosophy: The Unhappy Consciousness," *Laval théologique et philosophique* 49, no. 3 (1993), 423–438. For other useful overviews of French philosophy in the twentieth century see Gary Gutting, *French Philosophy in the Twentieth Century* (Cambridge: Cambridge University Press, 2001); Alan Schrift, *Twentieth-Century French Philosophy: Key Themes and Thinkers* (Oxford: Blackwell, 2006); Vincent Descombes, *Modern French Philosophy* (Cambridge: Cambridge University Press, 1980). See also Michael Kelly, *Hegel in France* (Birmingham: Birmingham Modern Languages Publications, 1992) and Stuart Barnett (ed.), *Hegel After Derrida* (London: Routledge, 1998).
4. Jean Wahl, *Le Malheur de la conscience dans la Philosophie de Hegel* (Paris: Rieder, 1929).
5. Alexandre Kojève, *Introduction à la lecture de Hegel*, ed. Raymond Queneau (Paris: Gallimard, 1947).
6. G. W. F. Hegel, *Phenomenology of Spirit*, trans. A.V. Miller (Oxford: Oxford University Press, 1977), 126, 127.
7. See Dominique Auffret, *Alexandre Kojève: La Philosophie, l'état, la fin de l'histoire* (Paris: Éditions Grasset et Fasquelle, 1990), 242–52.
8. Emmanuel Levinas, *Difficult Freedom: Essays on Judaism*, trans. Sean Hand (Baltimore: Johns Hopkins University Press, 1990), 291.
9. Emmanuel Levinas, *Totality and Infinity: An Essay on Exteriority*, trans. Alphonso Lingis (Dordrecht: Kluwer, 1991), 21–22.
10. Ibid., 15.
11. Georges Bataille, *Inner Experience*, trans. Stuart Kendall (Albany: State University of New York Press, 2014), 110.
12. Ibid., 112.
13. Georges Bataille, "The Psychological Structure of Fascism," *Critique sociale*, no 10 (1933), 159–165 and no. 11 (1934), 205–211.
14. Jean-Paul Sartre, *Being and Nothingness*, trans. Hazel E. Barnes (New York: Washington Square Press, 1956), 328.
15. Ibid., 330, 339.
16. Jacques Derrida, *Writing and Difference*, trans. Alan Bass (London: Routledge, 2001).
17. Within France, however, the tendency has been not to distinguish between structuralism and poststructuralism, the latter having been understood as a development within the former so that one speaks only of structuralism. See for instance, Francois Dosse, *History of Structuralism*, trans. Deborah Glassman, 2 vols. (Minneapolis: University of Minnesota Press, 1998).
18. Derrida, *Writing and Difference*, 175, 113.

19. Ibid., 149.
20. Ibid., 332.
21. The German term *Aufhebung*, describing the movement of dialectical negativity, conservation, and synthesis has presented translated translators with great difficulties. Its senses in English, all implied in Hegel's use of the term include: *to sublate, annul* or *cancel, to save* or *preserve*, and *to raise* or *lift up*. In French, the term verb *relever*, or the noun *relève* is often used. Kojève uses the terms *négation* and *suppression conservatrice*.
22. Ibid., 69.
23. Ibid., 201.
24. In *Writing and Difference* this is most clearly exemplified in the essay "Structure, Sign, and Play in the Discourse of the Human Sciences," ibid., 351–70.
25. Roland Barthes, "Lecture in Inauguration of the Chair in Literary Semiology, Collège de France, January 7, 1977," trans. Richard Howard, *October* 8 (1979), 3–16.
26. Jean-Luc Nancy and Philippe Lacoue-Labarthe, "The Nazi Myth," trans. Briam Holmes, *Critical Inquiry* 16, no. 7 (1990), 291–312, 294.
27. Peter Gratton, "Sovereign/Sovereignty" in *The Nancy Dictionary*, eds. Peter Gratton and Marie-Eve Morin (Edinburgh: Edinburgh University Press, 2015).
28. See Paul Patton, "Deconstruction and the Problem of Sovereignty," *Derrida Today* 10, no. 1 (2017), 1–20.
29. Jean-Luc Nancy, *The Creation of the World, Or, Globalization*, trans. François Raffoul and David Pettigrew (Albany: State University of New York Press, 2007), 81 (translation modified).
30. Jacques Derrida, *Margins of Philosophy*, trans. Alan Bass (Chicago: University of Chicago Press, 1982); Jean-Luc Nancy, *The Speculative Remark*, trans. Céline Surprenant (Stanford: Stanford University Press, 2001).
31. It is not the aim here to give an exhaustive account of Derrida's writing on Hegel. His most famous text *Glas* sets two simultaneous commentaries, one on Hegel's philosophy, one on Jean Genet's fiction side by side staging the relation between systematic thought and writing that is at stake here also; see Jacques Derrida, *Glas*, trans. John P. Leavey & Richard Rand (Lincoln: University of Nebraska Press, 1986).
32. Derrida, *Margins of Philosophy*, 121.
33. Ibid., 121.
34. Ibid., 134.
35. See note 32.
36. Ibid., 134.
37. Nancy, *The Speculative Remark*, 8.
38. See Derrida, *Writing and Difference*, 317–50 and *Margins of Philosophy*, 69–108.
39. Derrida, *Margins of Philosophy*, 107.
40. Ibid., 107.
41. See Jean-Luc Nancy, *Ego Sum*, trans. Marie-Eve Morin (New York: Fordham University Press, 2016) and *The Discourse of the Syncope: Logodaedalus*, trans. Saul Anton (Stanford: Stanford University Press, 2008). For commentaries on these and their place in the evolution of Nancy's thought see, Ian James, *The Fragmentary Demand* (Stanford: Stanford University Press, 2006), 26–63.
42. Nancy, *The Speculative Remark*, 14; translation modified.
43. Ibid., 40.
44. Ibid., 93.
45. Ibid., 98.
46. Jean-Luc Nancy, "The Jurisdiction of the Hegelian Monarch," trans. May Ann and Peter Caws, *Social Research* 49, no. 2, 481–516.
47. Ibid., 482.
48. Ibid., 483.
49. Ibid., 513.

50. Ibid., 481.
51. Ibid., 487.
52. Ibid., 487.
53. Ibid., 513.
54. Ibid., 482.
55. Ibid., 514.
56. Nancy, *The Creation of the World*, 81 (translation modified).
57. Cited in ibid., 102.
58. Ibid.
59. Ibid., 104 (translation modified).
60. Jean-Luc Nancy, "War, Right, Sovereignty—Technē" in *Being Singular Plural*, trans. Robert D. Richardson and Anne E. O'Byrne (Stanford: Stanford University Press, 2000), 101–44, 137.
61. Jean-Luc Nancy. *Hegel: The Restlessness of the Negative*, trans. Jason Smith and Steven Miller (Minneapolis: University of Minnesota Press), 8.
62. Ibid., 5.
63. Ibid., 76–80.
64. On this see Horst Althaus, *Hegel: An Intellectual Biography*, trans. Michael Tarsh (Cambridge: Polity, 2000); see, in particular, 263–65.

Part III
Contemporary Stakes

Felix Culpa, Dialectic and Becoming-Imperceptible

Claire Colebrook

1 Introduction: Hegelian Immanence

One way to think about twentieth-century French thought and its supposed overturning of Hegel would be through the question of alterity.[1] Until Hegel, philosophy had borne a relation to something other than itself, but with Hegel what appears as reason's other or what appears as an ungraspable "in itself" is really the result of an absolute that becomes other to itself, recognizes itself, *and* recognizes the history of philosophy as a necessary journey toward closure.[2] In its political form, this reduction of otherness and the closure of history would take the form of liberalism and the "end of ideology."[3] History appears as a series of competing notions of the good, but, with liberalism, "we" recognize that there is no foundation for the polity other than that which forms itself, and does so by recognizing the self-forming capacity of others. Overturning Hegel amounts to finding a relation to the outside, breaking the circle of German Idealism; rather than reason closing in upon itself, liberalism will find self-recognition in an open relation to all others, with each polity forming its own relation to the world. This, in turn, generates a complex overturning of Platonism. There is no longer a transcendent Idea or Good toward which reason is oriented, and yet this overturning of Platonic transcendence remains in accord with a Platonic sense of philosophy as transcendental: reason must no longer see the world as given, but must intuit the genesis of the given. The twentieth-century French, and especially Deleuzean, relationship to Hegel is intertwined with a relationship to Plato and the notion of the beginning of philosophy. Plato is both preserver and destroyer of difference. "Plato" stands for the attempt to go beyond the merely given to the Ideas from which the given is generated, the invention of a "higher world" that would complete the truth of the experienced world. For Hegel,

C. Colebrook (✉)
Penn State University, State College, PA, USA

philosophy is the absolute appearing to itself—with Plato's positing of Ideas being but one (early) mode of the absolute's coming into appearance. The world is the Absolute appearing as object, for a reasoning subject who will ultimately recognize and close the gap between being and appearance, being and becoming.

Deleuze, in *Difference and Repetition*, will make a great deal of overcoming a representation that has been rendered infinite by both Hegel and Leibniz. If, for Plato, there are Ideas that are the truth of the experienced world—with a gap between what appears and the concepts that make sense of appearance—for Hegel and Leibniz the world itself is conceptual; the world represents itself. In Hegel and Leibniz, there is nothing outside representation. For Hegel, what might appear as negation—one being opposed to another—is life becoming different in order to arrive at its own truth. Just as a plant blossoms forth, so we should see the history of philosophy *less* as a field of contingent differences and more as a fruitful self-appearing.[4] Just as an animal's consumption of plant and animal life destroys, preserves and transforms the world (while individuating the animal as a distinctly world-negating being), so philosophy's task should be to recognize this negation, arriving at the point where difference is not external to but essential to being, and the coming into appearance of being:

> The distinguishing marks of animals, for example, are taken from their claws and teeth. Indeed, not only does cognition distinguish one animal from another by this means, but it is also by these means that the animal itself separates itself off from others. It is through these weapons that it preserves itself for itself and keeps itself detached from the universal. In contrast, the plant never gets as far as being-for-itself; instead, it only makes contact with the limit of individuality. It is at this limit where plants show the semblance of dividing themselves in two into sexes, and for that reason, it is at this very limit that plants have been surveyed and distinguished from each other. However, what stands at an even lower level cannot itself any longer differentiate itself from an other; instead, it dwindles away as it comes into opposition. The motionless being and the being in relationships come into conflict with each other, and the thing in the latter is something different from the thing in the former, since, in contrast, the individual is what preserves itself in relations with others.[5]

Truth *is* for Hegel this experience of being *as* the recognition of life's self-appearing. Nothing is more immanent than this moment in Hegel. Rather than a subject who is the condition of appearing, one might say that, "there is appearing" *or*, more accurately, "appearing appears as what is." The philosophical recognition of this truth is the fulfillment *and reason* of all that is. This amounts both to a hyper-rationalism and to narcissism. Even the smallest things are instances of a general negativity that recognizes itself in philosophy. Life is nothing more than a trajectory arriving at the philosophy of speculative idealism: *all* life is negation. A plant's response to light that will enable it to flourish is a transformation of being. When the philosopher grasps this event, they at once fulfill (by recognizing) the plant's life, while *also* overcoming the necessary and constitutive illusions of philosophy, including the idea that there is something like "a" subject for whom philosophy is a practice or discipline. Philosophy is not, or should not be, something some humans happen to do as an adornment to the world; nor is it a way for intelligent humans to reach their potential and provide guidance to those who operate in other (lesser) disciplines. Philosophy is the process by which life recognizes itself. *Ideally*, the philosopher would disappear, becoming nothing more than the means through which what *is* negates itself—appearing to be other, different, distinct—only to recognize itself as this process of negation, and return. With Hegelian philosophy, all forms of transcendence have been overcome. Why, then, do philosophers of immanence seek to overcome Hegel?

2 After Hegel

The question after Hegel for thinkers like Deleuze (and Deleuze and Guattari) was, in part, whether philosophy or thought and life more generally might achieve an immanence that would not be an immanence *to* something like reason, subjectivity, or being:

> This at least persuades us that the problem of immanence is not abstract or merely theoretical. It is not immediately clear why immanence is so dangerous, but it is. It engulfs sages and gods. What singles out the philosopher is the part played by immanence or fire. Immanence is immanent only to itself and consequently captures everything, absorbs All-One, and leaves nothing remaining to which it could be immanent. In any case, whenever immanence is interpreted as immanent to Something, we can be sure that this Something reintroduces the transcendent.[6]

Rather than an absolute that differs from itself in order to be recognized, there is difference from which events of recognition or identification might emanate, only to be exceeded, disrupted and ungrounded by a ceaseless repetition of difference. For Deleuze there was a dual imperative to release thought from the self-enclosure of recognition while also taking difference beyond thought and beyond negation. This led to an apparent tension between immanence and alterity. On the one hand, if philosophy is to be genuinely philosophical, responsible, and not yet another affirmation of opinion, it must untether itself from already given images of thought. In his early *Difference and Repetition* (1968) Deleuze argues for "thought without image,"[7] and then repeats this imperative later, with Guattari, in *What is Philosophy?* (1991). Rather than a proper image of thought, thought becomes nothing more than free movement. Philosophy may appear to have a Greek beginning in friendship, rival opinions, and a dialectic that extracts some truth from opposed opinions; but philosophy comes into its own when what was promised in this Greek origin is liberated from all doxa, from all competing opinions, and becomes *thought as such, as pure movement*:

> The plane of immanence is not a concept that is or can be thought but rather the image of thought, the image thought gives itself of what it means to think, to make use of thought, to find one's bearings in thought. It is not a method, since every method is concerned with concepts and presupposes such an image. Neither is it a state of knowledge on the brain and its functioning, since thought here is not related to the slow brain as to the scientifically determinable state of affairs in which, whatever its use and orientation, thought is only brought about. Nor is it opinions held about thought, about its forms, ends, and means, at a particular moment. The image of thought implies a strict division between fact and right: what pertains to thought as such must be distinguished from contingent features of the brain

or historical opinions. *Quid juris?*-can, for example, losing one's memory or being mad belong to thought as such, or are they only contingent features of the brain that should be considered as simple facts? Are contemplating, reflecting, or communicating anything more than opinions held about thought at a particular time and in a particular civilization? The image of thought retains only what thought can claim by right. Thought demands "only" movement that can be carried to infinity. What thought claims by right, what it selects, is infinite movement or the movement of the infinite.[8]

For Deleuze and Guattari, their own positing of a plane of immanence is the fulfillment of philosophy's potentiality. What distinguishes philosophy from banality is a movement beyond competing opinions, beyond communication, and beyond identification. It is in this sense that phenomenology (both Hegelian and Husserlian) can be understood as self-declared fulfillments of philosophy: by attending to that which appears, and then grasping the movement through which appearance takes place, philosophy no longer remains within the rigidity of the given but grasps givenness in its real possibility. This is how Hegel understands his own position in the history of philosophy: not one more move in a game or set of arguments, but the bringing of all arguments to the recognition of their possibility. There can only be the history of philosophy and competing systems because being is both subject and object, both idealism and empiricism, appearing both as finite and as infinite. In Husserl's terms phenomenology gives an account of the transcendent *from* the immanent, tantamount to explaining the origin of the world:

> ... the transcending of the world which takes place in performing the phenomenological reduction does not lead outside of or away from the world to an origin which is separate from the world (and to which the world is connected only by some relation) as if leading to some *other* world; the phenomenological transcending of the world, as the disclosure of transcendental subjectivity, is at the same time the *retention of the world* within the universe of absolute 'being' that has been exposed. The world remains *immanent* to the absolute and is discovered as lying within it.[9]

At an abstract level, philosophy becomes a pure formalism: rather than begin with any being—nature, life, matter, or perhaps even difference—philosophy gives an account of that which appears as being. How is it that life appears as that which requires explanation; how is it that life yields metaphysical distance, including both doubt and its overcoming? Philosophy must account for itself: there is not only this world and all that appears, but various ontological claims about the world's appearing. One could dismiss these as so many errors or accidents, *or* one could ask, what is life/existence/being such that it appears, and appears as a history of rival philosophies? One could dismiss the history of philosophy as opinion, *or* think of the plane from which opinions and their grasp might be thought. Philosophies are ways in which being appears, not theories imposed upon the world but the outcome of being's unfolding. What are "we" such that being appears as so much calculable matter? What have "we" lost such that we can only see being as *things*? For Deleuze the answer lies in the history of philosophy and the Platonic moment when difference was subjected to the demands of representation. Against the demands of identity and the model of truth as agreement, Deleuze posits difference as a plane of singularities that generates questions and problems: "Being is also non-being, *but non-being is not the being of the negative*; rather, it is the being of the problematic, the being of problem and question."[10] What exists has a force of its own, seemingly requiring neither the labor of philosophy nor the recognition of concepts.

This would leave two ontological paths: one that begins with where we are, such that philosophy opens with the question of being (and regards that question as inescapable given that one is faced with existence), and another path that would seek to step outside this parochialism. From Kant's insistence that the Cartesian question of how we know the world already presupposes a transcendental form of space and time, to Derrida's insistence that any attempted thought of the outside of metaphysics must take place from within concepts that one can solicit but not erase, there is an assumption that ontology is implicit in the being of the world. For Derrida, once one is discussing concepts one is out of the domain of common sense and vagueness, and necessarily obliged to seek clear and distinct definitions. Concepts are *not* experience but the tending of experience toward finer and more rigorous distinction:

> What philosopher ever since there were philosophers, what logician ever since there were logicians, what theoretician ever renounced this axiom: in the order of concepts (for we are speaking of concepts and not of the colors of clouds or the taste of certain chewing gums), when a distinction cannot be rigorous or precise, it is not a distinction at all.[11]

To experience the world is to have a sense of what is; one is already and inescapably ontological. The other path would insist that such an assumption may be true for "us," (either "we" humans or the "we" of European humanity) but that it is possible and desirable to abandon this parochialism. Post-Deleuzian work in anthropology, such as the work of Eduardo Viveiros de Castro, has insisted that the enclosure of the world within "the human" can be overcome by way of a radical perspectivism that acknowledges the plurality of worlds and natures.[12] The imperative to think of being *as such* would be but one metaphysics among others.

One way of reading Deleuze would be to locate his philosophy as an anti-Hegelian riposte to the insistence on identity, relations, recognition and the inescapability of philosophy. If the conditions for the possibility of experience already anticipate metaphysics—insofar as experience is made possible by forms of time and space, and categories that make logic possible—then philosophy would be the articulation of an already present transcendental ground. This emphasis on the transcendental as a condition animates the critical tradition that runs from Kant to Derrida.[13] If, however, one focuses on *real conditions* and not conditions of possibility, one is taken beyond logic, concepts and forms to the force of difference, of what makes a difference. Much has already been written about Deleuze beginning from the transcendental field as generative and differential[14]; before there is philosophy and its possibilities, one might think of life in general *not* as negation but production. It would then follow that one does not begin with concepts and their inability to capture the singularity of what is (the in itself), but instead one would begin with singularities and then look to the production of relations and concepts. Further, and more importantly, it would follow that philosophy is *not* the completion or fulfillment of what is lacking in life. For Hegel, if a concept misses the specificity of what it grasps this will generate negation and philosophical reflection, leading ultimately to philosophy recognizing itself as the journey of negation and difference, with the gap between concept and reality generating the path of reason. There is a simple and apparent opposition, between a Hegelianism driven by concepts and reason, and Deleuze's insistence on concepts being but one way in which the forces of difference express themselves. Yet there is also a convergence between Deleuze and Hegel, concerning both the genesis and the history of philosophy.

3 Deleuze's Hegel

Life itself, for Deleuze, bears all the qualities of expression that will also take the form of philosophy's concepts. Rather than see language and signification as radical breaks with the "in itself," Deleuze will locate signification *in life*: "phenomena flash their meaning like signs."[15] Referring to Leibniz and Hegel, Deleuze writes of an "orgiastic representation" that "makes things themselves so many expressions."[16] This expression is life in its expansive and fruitful emanation and not (as in Kantianism and deconstruction) a radically different and distanced series of relations that precludes any knowledge of life itself. What takes place in plant life as a form of perception that enables the formation of lived qualities is what ultimately appears as philosophy—the intuition of the forces of life that creates a contemplating self:

> What we call wheat is a contraction of the earth and humidity, and this contraction is both a contemplation and the auto-satisfaction of that contemplation. By its existence alone, the lily of the field sings the glory of the heavens, the goddesses and gods—in other words, the elements that it contemplates in contracting. What organism is not made of elements and cases of repetition, of contemplated and contracted water, nitrogen, carbon, chlorides and sulphates, thereby intertwining all the habits of which it is composed? Organisms awake to the sublime words of the third *Ennead*: all is contemplation![17]

There are, as histories of Hegelianism demonstrate, humanist and inhuman potentials in the journey of reason. It is humanist Hegelianism—where one thinks of the journey of history and philosophy as subjective, political, and linguistic—that Deleuze overturns. It is the vegetal Hegel that Deleuze affirms—the Hegel who begins the journey of reason from plant life. For the humanist Hegelians, the end of history is the end of ideology. Rather than thinking of the polity as having some transcendent foundation, politics reaches maturity when it is explicitly self-forming and anti-foundational. Rather than working toward some transcendent idea of the true or good, politics is the process of reflective self-constitution. Habermas describes this as post-metaphysical (where consensus becomes a regulatory ideal and not an end).[18] Habermas is not alone in melding the Marxist-Hegelian notion of political maturity to the liberal ideal of a reflective state no longer wedded to a specific good or ideology. What might seem to be a stark opposition between the liberal individualist notion of each subject determining their relation to the whole[19] (being regulated by the *ideal* of universality), versus a communitarian conception where being a subject *already* requires constitutive relations that enable one's sense of self, is better thought of as a dialectic in the tradition of immanence. What is significant is an intimate relation between closure and openness: philosophy arrives at a form of ungrounding, where there is no norm other than that of self-formation. The difference between Deleuze and Hegel might appear to be a difference between becoming and being, where immanence either embraces eternal becoming (with difference recurring) or where immanence closes in on reason as self-recognition.

I have already suggested that the opposition between a Hegelian closure of recognition and a Deleuzean politics of becoming is not as stark as it appears. Political recognition is not a dead end, where we finally arrive at who we are, but is a dynamic and relational achievement of relative stability. In both the Hegelian and Deleuzean accounts of history and politics, it is transcendence and a failure to account for temporality that must be overcome by way of an affirmative genealogy, with philosophy ultimately appearing to itself as a recognition of time. History—as the sequence of events—gives way to *time*, or the unfolding and expression of life. For Hegel this requires seeing the course of history and various forms of alienation as moments through which life takes on objective and external form, followed by a recognition of that externality as the appearance of political life. History is necessary, as is the path through which reason and philosophy travel, in order to recognize time and difference as productive. It is only through the history of philosophy that reason might appear as that which *must* become objective and alienated in order to arrive at the final moment in which being just *is* this becoming. The truth of plant and animal life is not some external fact that might be grasped in an objective manner but rather signals, expresses, and intimates the movement of life as reason in general. Life appears to itself, contemplates itself, and becomes aware of this contemplation. What later appears as history, the state, the subject, or reason is—for Deleuze and Guattari—ways in which difference and intensity are occluded.

Just as the political philosophy that Deleuze forges with Guattari begins with an intense germinal influx that produces the relations that allow States to come into being (with states being the "warding off" of free flows),[20] so in Deleuze's history of philosophy there is a clear genealogy of difference that always haunts the demands of representation. The long history of states and stable forms is made possible by differences that threaten its borders. Difference as intensity acts as the narrative drive in Deleuze's history of philosophy, and Deleuze and Guattari's history of capitalism. The Plato who forged the theory of Ideas also described a cave of simulations. Difference hovers at the border of relatively stable forms, both in philosophy and in history. From the point of view of capitalism, one can look back and recognize the flows of exchange that would eventually be released from territories and form the capitalist state. Deleuze's overcoming of history as a mere sequence—of political forms or philosophical concepts—relies upon an intuition of the more radical force that the history of states at once expresses and occludes. The state, like the organism, is both expression and containment of a life that can be intuited only through becoming and time. It is not just that Hegel will also intuit the force of becoming that unfolds in being, but that Hegel will also chart a narrative of alienation and redemption. For Hegel history is also an unfolding, with distinct and stable philosophies making sense only as moments in a trajectory of recognition. The history of philosophy is a journey, with the philosopher being the medium through which the absolute recognizes itself.

If the world appears as so many distinct things for a separate subject who must somehow come to grasp a world of discrete objects, this is because the forces that make such differences possible *disguise themselves*. For Deleuze, life occurs as simulation—everything that is appears, over and over again, as simulation without ground. For Hegel, life occurs as negation, but—as Deleuze notes—negation can be thought positively as an ongoing and ungrounding movement of questioning that continually transforms the world: the world does not go through change, but is change, and philosophy does not observe this change but is itself an aspect of that dynamic temporality. The philosophy that recognizes this journey of simulation or misrecognition not only takes up this dynamism that brings things into being, but understands itself as made possible by the journey of misrecognition.

Rather than philosophy as a form of analysis or interpretation, philosophy *is* the change of the world. Rather than being the agent of change, by providing a more accurate understanding, philosophy is creative of new modes of existence. Put more concretely, for Deleuze and Guattari the task of overcoming capitalism requires the practice of schizo-analysis, which demonstrates that the bounded psyche has a political history—a history in which the very concept of repression plays its role in producing who "we" as subjects are. The very idea of repression is itself productive or constitutive of a relation of desire; the subject relates to the world as so much prohibited content.

Concepts are the creation of relations, not simply forms of knowledge (though seeing concepts this way is itself a mode of existence). If one can understand "the subject" as itself an event of life, and one of the ways in which capitalism deterritorializes relations, then a genealogy of capitalism would be a reconfiguration of desiring relations, or desiring machines. The point of view from which one philosophizes is made possible by a critical and productive relation to history; without that relation and point of view, *life cannot free itself from its own tendencies toward capture*. For both Deleuze and Hegel it is from the point of view of the present that the forces that make philosophy possible might be intuited; this intuition would enable *both* an account of the history of misrecognition *and* a beatitude of the present that is liberated from transcendence. Only with the "fall" into exteriority—seeing the world as so much alien, objective being—can life be refound, regained, or intuited at a higher level as that which brought alienation and its overcoming into being. The reflexive awareness of philosophy's point of view—how is it that life generates such a thing as philosophy?—unites both Deleuze and Hegel in an affirmation of philosophy's felicity. One might think of this structure by way of Romanticism and its articulation of *felix culpa*: the power to account for the sense of paradise lost is itself a form of paradise, an "absolute deterritorialization" (or *Aufhebung*!): "deterritorialization is *absolute* when the earth passes into the pure plane of immanence of a Being-thought, of a Nature-thought of infinite diagrammatic movements. Thinking consists in stretching out a plane of immanence that absorbs the earth (or rather, 'adsorbs' it)."[21]

4 Felix Culpa

The trajectory of *felix culpa* not only unites both Hegel and Deleuze, but also bears a specific poignancy when one thinks about the geopolitics of philosophy. Knowing what we know now about Western philosophy, and after so many attempts to escape, overcome, destroy, or exit metaphysics, one might ask *why* we keep reading and working through the canon. Why does Western thought include its own exit or overcoming, but *not* its own erasure? We exit metaphysics, but allow it to haunt the present, or we remain within metaphysics and solicit its terms from within. In Hegel, it is quite clear that the European philosopher's grasp of other cultures enables an Anthropo-scenic point of view, in which various forms of difference are not just tolerated but affirmed as expressions of humanity's eventual immanent recognition, having no essence or being other than that of reason appearing to itself.[22] In the case of Deleuze and Guattari there is a far more intense articulation of fall and redemption, and one that is anticipated in Deleuze's history of philosophy in *Difference and Repetition*. At some "propitious moment," the cruelty of difference is tamed, subjected to the demands of concepts. To encounter difference in itself would be an intensity that the good will of philosophy could not bear. It is easy to see the Nietzschean resonance in this genealogy: from an intensive, non-moral, and generative force of difference, philosophy falls into a form of moral adjudication. If Nietzsche sees this moment as the origin of slave morality, and if Deleuze—following Nietzsche—will argue that consciousness per se is the consciousness of the slave,[23] it is nevertheless Hegel *rather than Nietzsche* who grants this event an inhuman and *propitious* force. Deleuze writes of *un heureux moment*—"l'heureux moment grec—où la différence est comme réconciliée avec le concept."

> La différence doit sortir de sa caverne, et cesser d'être un monstre; ou du moins ne doit subsister comme monstre que ce qui se dérobe à l'heureux moment, ce qui constitue seulement une mauvaise rencontre, une mauvaise occasion. Ici, l'expression « faire la différence » change donc de sens.[24]
>
> It is therefore a question of determining a propitious moment—the Greek propitious moment—at which difference is, as it were, reconciled with the concept. Difference must leave its cave and cease to be a monster; or at least only that which escapes at the propitious moment must persist as a monster, that which constitutes only a bad encounter, a bad occasion.... At this point the expression 'make the difference' changes its meaning.[25]

Difference and Repetition may use a Nietzschean language of a moment of "cruelty" prior to the subjection of the force of difference to concepts, but the continued reference to the propitious, happy, or *heureux* moment refers to a point when difference becomes moralized, while also generating an arc of redemption. If it is Aristotelian philosophy that will negotiate difference in relation to genus, species, contraries and relations, there is another philosophy made possible by this moment. By referring to a moment of difference dwelling in a cave, where what is perceived are simulations as such, Deleuze suggests that philosophy harbors and is haunted by a sense of a difference that expresses itself *not* as variations between kinds, but in a variability without model or ground. The Greek moment would be propitious (*heureux*) not only in its subjection of difference to a moralism of the orderly and the monstrous, but also as an event. It is the interrogation of this moment that generates Deleuze's philosophy, which will not simply be a narration of errors but an account of the struggle to form a *philosophy* of difference when it is philosophy (as a conceptual enterprise) that is responsible for the taming of difference:

> ... is difference really an evil in itself? Must the question have been posed in these moral terms? Must difference have been 'mediated' in order to render it both livable and thinkable? Must the selection have—consisted in that particular test? Must the test have been conceived in that manner and with that aim? But we can answer these questions only once we have more precisely determined the supposed nature of the propitious moment.[26]

Such questions—of how we fell into moralism—would not need to be answered had philosophy not given difference this new sense (as a difference between or among kinds), and one might then conclude that this moment is propitious or "heureux" only from the point of view of *overcoming* a philosophy of judgment that cannot deal with difference in itself. The event is felicitous only if regaining a difference of cruelty takes on a higher form. If one tracks where Deleuze takes "difference in itself" in *Difference and Repetition* it is Hegel and Leibniz who liberate difference from its Aristotelian mode (where one judges in terms of concepts and their distinctions). Both Hegel and Leibniz discern a difference that is generative. The supposed "propitious" moment that would mark the beginning of philosophy as a form of intellectual rigor and judgment needs to be set within a broader history where a difference is intuited beyond the bounds of good sense:

> When representation discovers the infinite within itself, it no longer appears as organic representation but as orgiastic representation: it discovers within itself the limits of the organised; tumult, restlessness and passion underneath apparent calm. It rediscovers monstrosity. Henceforth it is no longer a question of a propitious moment which marks determination's entrance into and exit from the concept in general, the relative maximum and minimum, the punctum proximum and the punctum remotem. On the contrary, a short-sighted and a long-sighted eye are required in order for the concept to take upon itself all moments: the concept is now the Whole, either in the sense that it extends its benediction to all parts or in the sense that the division between the parts and their misery are reflected back on the Whole, granting them a kind of absolution.[27]

At this Hegelian and Leibnizian moment, it is not, as Kant had argued, the task of philosophy to stay within the bounds of critical reason, capable of thinking but not knowing the depths of the soul that are the ground from which judgment arises. Instead, it is this ungrounding difference that becomes philosophy's task. The propitious moment, the event of philosophy, might not have been the birth of judgment and logos, but the trajectory that would allow difference to be returned to the cave: from organic representation, where differences are parsed by a judging subject, Hegel and Leibniz will affirm an orgiastic difference, a difference that is both infinite—not occurring between kinds—*and* ungrounding, insofar as it is the movement from which representable differences will emerge. For Deleuze, the initial difference between Hegel and Leibniz is less important than their capacity to take difference to the infinite: what appears as an opposition between terms will, for Hegel, eventually allow for a movement of negation so that a seeming binary or contradiction comes to appear as the movement of difference itself: "Such is the movement of contradiction as it constitutes the true pulsation of the infinite, the movement of exteriority or real objectivation."[28] What appears as a difference between two particulars will for Leibniz be more correctly grasped as each seemingly small difference bearing its own distinct relation to the infinite: "We know that each one of these completed notions (monads) expresses the totality of the world: but it expresses it precisely under a certain differential relation and around certain distinctive points which correspond to this relation."[29] At this propitious moment in the history of philosophy, difference is no longer submitted to the light of clear judgment, but becomes a force to take reason beyond itself.

Deleuze's often-cited counter-Hegelianism is sometimes explained as his affinity for Leibniz over Hegel, as a preference for intuiting the evermore acute differences that pulverize any seeming identity, rather than the negation of a concept's limits that will ascend to a grasp of the totality.[30] Leibniz will open the infinite from the smallest of events rather than thinking of the infinite as a movement of ongoing negation that will finally move to a grasp of the whole. Here, Deleuze argues, there is something theological about this Hegelian movement and its incapacity to allow for indifference: "Even though it is said of opposition or of finite determination, this Hegelian infinite remains the infinitely large of theology, of the *Ens quo nihil majus*."[31]

What might it mean, then, to think difference as orgiastic, but *not* in terms of the infinitely large of theology? The answer to this question, for Deleuze, is by way of a different theological arc—that of *felix culpa*. This would be different from the theology that posits an infinite being beyond which nothing is greater, but it is another theology (and theodicy) that is already at work in Hegel. Hegel will object to a "bad infinite" that is simply one thing after another, always expanding, and always being surpassed.[32] Against this, there would be an infinite that is utterly theological. Being that appears to and recognizes itself surpasses a being that simply is, without relation. If there is a form of philosophy that would seek to grasp what *is*, as such, without any interference or mediation, this would amount to an impoverished positivism. Hegel will begin his history of empiricism from the attempt to grasp what is as such, followed by the fall into despair and doubt when one can only grasp the object as mediated, and then the recognition that being just *is* this journey of appearance and recognition. This is a specific form of the theology of *Ens quo nihil majus*: this is a God who flows forth from Himself into the freedom of creation so that the world might express, pray, and freely reflect the glory of all that is. It is a departure, distance and return that ensures that being is not simply in-itself, but in-itself and for-itself, taking up a relation of difference and distance and then affirming that relation as immanent.

This theology of *felix culpa* also marks Deleuze and Guattari's philosophy in its Marxist-historical mode, and the sense of philosophy articulated in *What is Philosophy*? Assume that we take Deleuze, and Deleuze and Guattari, at their word and that the history of the Western bourgeois Oedipal subject occurs as an increasing contraction, privatization and repression of desire, *and* that philosophy may also have begun with a sense of simulation and difference without ground that was contained by representation, *and* that the history of art, cinema and music also take their time to free themselves from transcendence. Immanence, in Deleuze as much as Hegel, takes its time to be achieved. Deleuze will not be as flagrant as Hegel in attributing this journey to the West, and yet the final moment of recognition in *What is Philosophy?* is European high modernism. There are moments in *Anti-Oedipus* where non-European moments are hailed, but these fragments of wisdom are placed within a broader symptomatology so that the question of how it is that desire has taken the form of the miserable repressed individual requires placing collectivist and "primitive" social forms in a negative universal history. Only *after* the history of capitalism is it possible recognize the forces that bring the primitive socius into being.

Hegel will argue that knowledge strives to grasp the thing itself, then realizes that it can only know the thing *as* perceived. The end of history is not the end of relationality, but the recognition that knowledge just is this time required of coming into relation. Absolute knowledge includes, rather than overcomes, the relation that makes knowledge possible. Without distance, difference, and time there might be being, but not being that is known *and* known in its coming into being (phenomenology). This same structure, which Deleuze identifies as theological, arrives at a totality beyond which there is nothing greater, but does so while anticipating the truth of the whole in the minutest of particulars. The plant that absorbs light, and the animal who eats the plant, do so as events of negation and relation; to recognize the history of knowledge and desire as a relation that comes to know and affirm itself is both to close the circle, but also to affirm the becoming that brings being to self-appearance. The fall away from immediacy will appear as loss and distance until philosophy reaches immanence.

5 Immanence Regained

In both *Difference and Repetition* and *Anti-Oedipus*, history is at once the loss of immanence and intensity, and a journey toward an immanence that achieves a higher universality or "higher deterritorialization," to use the language of *A Thousand Plateaus*. In *Difference and Repetition* Deleuze will present a history of philosophy in which difference in itself is repeatedly managed, reduced to a relation among concepts, never granted the generative force that it will achieve in his own work. Far from the history of philosophy prior to *Difference and Repetition* being an error or inadequate posing of the problem, Deleuze describes difference as constantly menacing philosophy's good will. This is not a history of good and evil, where Spinoza and Nietzsche triumph over Kant and Hegel; it is the menace of difference which generates the ongoing labor of its philosophical containment. Those who appear to be heroes of this narrative at first glance—Duns Scotus, Spinoza, Nietzsche—never quite arrive at a moment of a truly immanent philosophy that would allow the ungrounding movement of difference to be intuited in itself. Those who appear as seeming villains nevertheless have a powerful sense of the force of difference that will then require the containment of representation. This history of struggle, between a philosophy of mastery and a "cruel" difference that would be beyond good and evil, not only places Deleuze at the moment of immanence, but also at the moment when immanence recognizes its intrinsic difficulty. Philosophy is the art of thinking, but what it is *to think* has been contained by an "image of thought."

Philosophy arrives at maturity when it becomes aware of its creative and constitutive role, entering into relation with the arts and sciences but providing its own plane of concepts. In the case of philosophy's relation to art, *What is Philosophy?* will argue that art's creation of affects and percepts allow qualities to stand alone, such that what is given to be perceived becomes the force from which the composed world is actualized. Philosophy's concepts of art—"affect" and "percept"—allow philosophy to intuit the forces of the cosmos that enter into relation to produce the world. It is through the relation to art and science that philosophy arrives at immanence and relative autonomy. Rather than providing an image or norm of good sense and communicative reason, philosophy is an ongoing creation and transformation of a plane of immanence—a relation among forces that enables the production of concepts. Philosophy becomes aware of itself as composition in relation to a dynamic whole. Universal history can only be written *ex post facto*. After the history of philosophy, it is possible to realize its productive (rather than reflecting or representative) power; after the history of various social formations, it is possible to recognize desire in general—not as a ground but as a power to unground or differ. In *Anti-Oedipus*, it is only from the cramped position of bourgeois interiority, cut off from the intensive differences of life, that one might be able to look back to a time of collective investments, chart their subjection to forms of despotism, and then recognize the despotism of subjectivity, and of the bourgeois man of reason. For the oedipalized subject what is beyond the bounds of the symbolic order appears as the chaos of the undifferentiated, the psychotic night in which all cows are black. However, it is because of this contraction that a more expansive historical sense becomes possible. If one were to undertake a genealogy of this subject, one arrives at an understanding of difference and intensity that is *only fully discernable* after its loss. What capitalism (and the philosophy of identity) both bring to the fore, and contain, are the free flows of forces from which points of stability and identity emerge. It is only after capitalism that one can see that the primitive socius was the outcome of the production of relations that bring bodies and territory into being; it is only after capitalism that one can understand despotism as a containment of the free flows of exchange that would decenter and (potentially) reterritorialize relations onto the axioms of capital. Only with late capitalism—and perhaps even neoliberalism, where subjects become nothing more than their selected and managed qualities—can one look back and see history as the ongoing "warding off" of capitalism; capitalism both exposes and contains relations among forces that are effectively ungrounding, affirmative and inhuman: "At capitalism's limit the deterritorialized socius gives way to the body without organs, and the decoded flows throw themselves into desiring-production. Hence it is correct to retrospectively understand all history in the light of capitalism, provided that the rules formulated by Marx are followed exactly."[33] Where a glib reading might find a simple contrast between Hegel and Deleuze, between everything coming to a close with recognition versus an ongoing affirmation of disruptive difference, two structural similarities bely this very (un-Deleuzian and un-Hegelian) opposition. The time taken to intuit the forces of difference that appear as simple identities is a necessary time, the time taken for difference to affirm itself as constitutive rather than relative is not accidental, but immanent. The differences between (or among) philosophers are ways in which the problem or force of difference appears.

This is how both Hegel and Deleuze read the history of philosophy; what looks like error or dispute is ultimately the way the force of difference comes into appearance. One might think of this as a differential phenomenology. Deleuze will object to Husserlian phenomenology's claim that what appears as presence is haunted by its past and future. For Deleuze, any supposed "now" bears within itself a complexity and difference that is *more than* the sense it bears within a representational whole. The present is replete with a sense that opens to time in general, or eternity. Just as every painting in the history of painting bears a transformative relation to the whole, so every concept in the history of philosophy bears a dynamic relation to the whole. This, too, is true for Hegel: reading a philosopher in the history of philosophy is not a question of oppositions—such as Kant versus Descartes—but seeing all philosophical positions as affirmations, or expressions of a being/life that recognizes itself through coming into philosophical appearance. Philosophy proceeds by refusing the limited, finite, or incomplete nature of its precursor texts, finally arriving at the awareness that this recognition of limits, or refusal of the finite, is philosophy itself arriving at maturity as the power of recognizing. What Deleuze objects to as the "Hegelian imprint" on twentieth-century phenomenology—the emptiness of the now—is ultimately Husserlian and Derridean rather than Hegelian:

> The imprint of the Hegelian dialectic on the beginnings of *Phenomenology* has often been noted: the here and the now are posited as empty identities, as abstract universalities which claim to draw difference along with them, when in fact difference does not by any means follow and remains attached in the depths of its own space, in the here-now of a differential reality always made up of singularities.[34]

The aftermath of Hegel, according to Deleuze, is to see the now (or what is) as haunted by the past and present; against this Deleuze will insist on the force of singularities, the force of making a difference. Deleuze's objection to Hegel does indeed mark a distinction between Deleuze and later phenomenology (and deconstruction). From Husserl's insistence on protention and retention at the heart of the living present, to Derrida's and Stiegler's claim that *techne* tears into the heart of the lived, one way of philosophizing in the aftermath of Hegel is to abandon the presence of the present.[35] The condition for possibility of presence is difference: the here and now is marked off, inscribed, or articulated by some form of grammatization. For Deleuze, however, rather than a difference of loss and dispersal, there are pre-individual and individuating singularities; difference affirms and diverges. The aim of philosophy is the creative (rather than identifying) formation of concepts, each time reconfiguring the entire plane of philosophy. For both Deleuze and Hegel philosophy is an intensification (if not a closure) of a differential movement of life. For both, a historical account of philosophy's genesis allows philosophy to assume its proper mode: rather than a critical project of considering the conditions of knowing or experience philosophy is the creation of life in its most affirmative mode.

The notion that philosophy creates concepts and that each concept reorients the plane of composition liberates philosophy from notions of truth as reference, and situates Deleuze and Guattari's own work as philosophy's moment of self-recognition. Transcendence had always tethered thought to something other than itself, such as right reason or communication; philosophy's realization that it operates on its own plane of composition liberates thought from the actual world and the lived—no longer mirroring what happens to be the case—and allows thought to appear as movement.

Notes

1. Vincent Descombes, *Modern French Philosophy*, trans. L. Scott-Fox and J.M. Harding (Cambridge: Cambridge University Press, 1979).
2. Alexandre Kojève, *Introduction to the Reading of Hegel: Lectures on the Phenomenology of Spirit*, ed. Allan Bloom, trans. James H. Nichols Jr. (Ithaca: Cornell University Press, 1969), 122.
3. Francis Fukuyama, *The End of History and the Last Man* (New York: Macmillan, 1992).
4. G. W. F. Hegel, *Phenomenology of Spirit*, trans. A. V. Miller. (Oxford: Oxford University Press, 1977), 4.
5. Ibid., 146.
6. Gilles Deleuze and Felix Guattari, *What is Philosophy?*, trans. Hugh Tomlinson and Graham Burchell (New York: Columbia University Press, 1994), 45.
7. Gilles Deleuze, *Difference and Repetition*, trans. Paul Patton (London: Athlone Press, 1994), 276.
8. Deleuze and Guattari, *What is Philosophy?* 37.
9. Eugen Fink, "The Phenomenological Philosophy of Edmund Husserl and Contemporary Criticism," in *The Phenomenology of Husserl: Selected Critical Readings*, ed. R.O. Elveton (Chicago: Quandrangle Books, 1970), 99.
10. Deleuze, *Difference and Repetition*, 64.
11. Jacques Derrida, *Limited Inc.* (Evanston: Northwestern University Press, 1988), 123.
12. Eduardo Viveiros de Castro, *Cannibal Metaphysics*, trans. Peter Skafish (Minnesota: Univocal Press, 2014).
13. Irene E. Harvey, *Derrida and the Economy of Difference.* (Bloomington: Indiana University Press, 1986).
14. Henry Somers-Hall, *Hegel, Deleuze, and the Critique of Representation: Dialectics of Negation and Difference.* (Albany: State University of New York Press, 2012).
15. Deleuze, *Difference and Repetition*, 57.
16. Ibid., 43.
17. Ibid., 75.
18. Jürgen Habermas, *Postmetaphysical Thinking*, trans. William Mark Hohengarten. (Cambridge: MIT Press, 1994).
19. John Rawls *Theory of Justice* (Oxford: Oxford University Press, 1970).
20. Gilles Deleuze and Felix Guattari, *Anti-Oedipus: Capitalism and Schizophrenia*, trans. Robert Hurley, Mark Seem, and Helen R. Lane (Minneapolis: University of Minnesota Press, 1983), 184.
21. Deleuze and Guattari, *What is Philosophy?*, 89.

22. Ronald Kuykendall, "Hegel and Africa: An Evaluation of the Treatment of Africa in *The Philosophy of History*." *Journal of Black Studies* 23.4 (1993), 571–81.
23. Gilles Deleuze, *Nietzsche and Philosophy*, trans. Hugh Tomlinson (London: Athlone Press, 1983).
24. Gilles Deleuze, *Différence et répétition* (Paris: Presses Universitaires de France, 1968), 45.
25. Deleuze, *Difference and Repetition*, 42.
26. Ibid., 30.
27. Ibid., 42.
28. Ibid., 45.
29. Ibid., 47.
30. Simon Duffy, "The Differential Point of View of the Infinitesimal Calculus in Spinoza, Leibniz and Deleuze," *Journal of the British Society for Phenomenology*, 37.3 (2006), 286–307.
31. Deleuze, *Difference and Repetition*, 49.
32. G. W. F. Hegel, *Hegel's Science of Logic*, trans. A.V. Miller (New York, Humanities Press, 1969), 137.
33. Deleuze and Guattari, *Anti-Oedipus*, 139.
34. Deleuze, *Difference and Repetition*, 51–52.
35. Ben Roberts, "Stiegler Reading Derrida: The Prosthesis of Deconstruction in Technics," *Postmodern Culture* 16.1 (2005).

Monism and Mistakes

Adrian Johnston

1 The Error of Immanence: Where Do Incorrect Ideas Come from?

Antonio Gramsci, at one point in his *Prison Notebooks*, alights upon a serious problem for any sort of radical monism or immanentism. Given Gramsci's combined theoretical and practical concerns as a Marxist thinker and activist, he addresses this problem insofar as it affects certain variants of historical materialism. He has in view apropos this difficulty the reductive economism of such late nineteenth- and early twentieth-century orientations as the Second International, German Social Democracy, and the more mechanistic strains of Bolshevism.

Gramsci alleges that all agents in a given socio-economic system would be, for a pseudo-Marxist economistic monism, so immanent to this system as to be direct instantiations of this system's groups. These groups would be, first and foremost, the classes composing a class-divided society. From the perspective of the economistic reductivism problematized by Gramsci, individual actors would be nothing but embodiments of the interests of the classes to which they belong. They would behave unerringly in accordance with these interests.

Yet, the past and present are littered with examples of individual actors erring in relation to their class, failing to act in accordance with what would be objectively in the material interests of the group to which they belong. Sadly, many of the examples that most readily spring to mind are of exploited and oppressed segments of societies deviating from and undermining their own interests through conducting themselves in conformity with the diametrically opposed interests of their

A. Johnston (✉)
University of New Mexico, Albuquerque, NM, USA
e-mail: aojohns@unm.edu

© The Author(s), under exclusive license to Springer Nature Switzerland AG 2023
T. Rajan, D. Whistler (eds.), *The Palgrave Handbook of German Idealism and Poststructuralism*, Palgrave Handbooks in German Idealism,
https://doi.org/10.1007/978-3-031-27345-2_22

exploiters and oppressors. In this vein, Gramsci, focusing instead on mistakes made by members of ruling classes, remarks:

> [A] particular political act may have been an error of calculation on the part of the leaders of the dominant classes, an error that historical development corrects and moves beyond through the governmental parliamentary 'crises' of the ruling classes. Mechanical historical materialism does not take the possibility of error into account; it assumes that every political act is determined directly by the structure and is therefore the reflection of a real and permanent (in the sense of secured) modification of the structure. The principle of 'error' is complex: it could consist in an individual impulse stemming from a mistaken calculation, or it could also be the manifestation of the attempts (which may fail) of specific groups or cliques to attain hegemony within the leading group.[1]

Gramsci's phrase "mechanical historical materialism" refers to reductive economism. As he points out, if, according to such a monism/immanentism, persons within a society are simply immediate expressions of this society's (infra)structure (i.e., its economic base), then their thinking and acting cannot ever involve making "mistakes" *vis-à-vis* their economic agendas, identities, and positions. The iron chains of causal determination by a given mode of production, with its classed relations of production, would keep each and every singular subject unwaveringly in line with these subjects' class positions and accompanying interests.

Thus, as Gramsci insightfully observes, the reductive economism of vulgarized historical materialism cannot account for errors as instances in which there are discrepancies between, on the one hand, subjective thinking and/or acting and, on the other hand, objective class status. Such flattening economistic monism leaves no space for the gaps of such discrepancies to arise. This leaves it with no explanation for the types of mistakes alluded to in the above quotation from the *Prison Notebooks*. One of Mao Tse-Tung's essays famously asks, "Where do correct ideas come from?"[2] Gramsci's question here amounts to wondering: Where do incorrect ideas come from?

In the present chapter, I will not be sorting out the issues raised specifically for Marxist historical materialism by Gramsci's invocation of mistakes, miscalculations, and the like. Instead, I bring up this moment in his *Prison Notebooks* with an eye to how the Gramscian problem of error theoretically undermines any and all extreme monisms or immanentisms. In particular, I see this Gramsci as reflecting on a challenge already confronting post-Kantian German idealism. Of the German idealists, this challenge is perhaps most troubling for F. W. J. Schelling, especially in connection with Schelling's more Spinozist leanings as manifest in, for instance, his early identity-philosophy (but also on display across the full arc of his intellectual itinerary).

An 1806 text critiquing J. G. Fichte contains a moment in which Schelling formulates his own version of the problem of error (or error itself as a major philosophical problem). Therein, he states:

> We recognize it to be the greatest puzzle (*die größte Ungereimtheit*), that knowledge (*Wissen*) is subsequent to being (*Sein*) or seeks after it as something later (*nach ihm zu fragen als einen hinzukommenden*), as if there could be a being that is not self-revelation

(*Selbstoffenbarung*), or as if living being (*das lebendige Sein*) could be something other than self-affirmation (*Selbstbejahung*).[3]

Schelling soon goes on to describe this as the "puzzle of all puzzles" (*Ungereimtheit aller Ungereimtheiten*).[4] This same text later identifies "the great question" (*die große Frage*) as being raised by the truth "*that splitting (Zerspaltungen) and division (Trennungen) in fact occur in reality (Wirklichkeit).*"[5]

The surfacing of this greatest puzzle of puzzles in the context of an anti-Fichtean polemic is arguably no accident. Schelling's embrace of Baruch Spinoza is strongest when his holding of Fichte at arm's length is at its most vehement. That is to say, Schelling tends to emphasize and reinforce his break with Fichte (as an anti-naturalist transcendental idealist) in part by doubling-down on his Spinozism (as naturalistic monism). This is evident starting with Schelling's public declaration of his rupture with his former mentor, namely, 1801's "Presentation of My System of Philosophy" (a treatise whose *more geometrico* form as well as its conceptual content deliberately echoes Spinoza's *Ethics*).[6]

Schelling's philosophy of nature and, even more so, his identity-philosophy—both take shape in the late 1790s and early 1800s—face the topic of error as a fundamental metaphysical problem. They do so precisely because of their affirmations of a radical monism in which everything is immanent to a unique One-All. The influence of Spinoza here intermingles with Eleatic and Neo-Platonic sources too.[7] Schelling utilizes a range of names for this One-All, including: Nature, God, Substance, Absolute, Identity, Indifference, and Infinity.

But, as soon as one adopts such a monism, a disturbing enigma promptly arises, an enigma described in the above quotation from Schelling's *Statement on the True Relationship of the Philosophy of Nature to the Revised Fichtean Doctrine* (1806). This kind of monist, if he/she is a rigorous and consequent philosopher, must come to wonder why errors ever occur in the first place. By contrast, for a dualist subscribing to a picture of existence in which subjective mind is partitioned from objective world, the human capacity for truth, rather than for falsity, is "the greatest puzzle" (with modern epistemological thinking from René Descartes to Edmund Gettier and beyond testifying to the intimate bond between dualistic worldviews and the metaphysical prioritization of true knowledge as one of philosophy's key problems, if not the Problem of all philosophical problems).[8] For a standard modern epistemologist, the big question is: How does the mind connect with the world so as to really know the latter? Or, asked differently, how does the subject bridge the divide between itself and the object in order to become truly acquainted and familiar with the object as it actually is in and of itself?

However, as some of Schelling's work reveals, the big metaphysical-epistemological line of questioning for a committed, consistent monist is the opposite of that for any dualist. On the one hand, the dualist is left wondering how, if at all, the gap between minded subjectivity and worldly objectivity is ever successfully crossed. On the other hand, the monist is forced to consider how this very same division, and the possibilities for error as subjective mind erring from objective world it generates, emerges in the first place out of a presumably undivided being grounding of and common to both mind and world, both subjects and objects (i.e., a being such as the Schellingian Absolute[9] or Indifference[10]). A dualist ontology leads to a preoccupation with truth as an epistemological difficulty. A monist ontology leads to a confrontation with error as an ontological as well as epistemological mystery.

Frederick Beiser is correct to emphasize that, for Schelling, metaphysics (as ontology) enjoys priority over epistemology.[11] And, the epistemology conditioned by Schelling's (nature-philosophical) ontology would have to be not only, as Beiser adds, a "*naturalistic epistemology*,"[12] but one for which the false, instead of the true, is the ultimate riddle for a theory of (non-)knowledge. Similarly, Wolfram Hogrebe claims that Schelling effectively recasts epistemology as cosmology.[13] If so, if knowledge is a matter of the universe coming to perceive and conceptualize itself, then the real conundrum has to do with those instances in which the cosmos fails to grasp itself, in which it becomes estranged from and opaque to itself.

Monism demands: How can an ontology insisting upon the exhaustive and inescapable immanence of all beings to a sole Being-with-a-capital-B license a corresponding epistemology allowing falsehoods as discrepancies with or distortions of this Being to transpire (in the guises of mistakes, misapprehensions, misunderstandings, etc.)? If there ultimately is only the pure, lone One-All, why would it not dwell in undiluted Truth, in the undimmed light of error-free "self-revelation" (*Selbstoffenbarung*) and "self-affirmation" (*Selbstbejahung*)? If the singular Being of extreme monism/immanentism even bothers to self-relate to begin with—this itself is a quandary sometimes prompting Schelling to criticize Spinoza for neither confronting nor resolving it—why would this Being not automatically and invariably enjoy full transparency to itself? Since, in its absolute infinitude, it has no Other, what possibly could interfere with and cloud over its self-reflection, rendering the latter inaccurate, false, or incoherent? Apropos Spinoza's metaphysics (and Schelling when he periodically embraces it very tightly), even if one grants that the dualism of the attributes of thinking and extension and the plurality of these attributes' modes are merely apparent *qua* illusory in relation to the underlying ontological oneness of substance as *Deus sive natura*, it still must be queried why and/or how such appearances and illusions ever arise at all.[14] In more theosophical terms, how can an outside external to and free from (Spinoza's) God ever come to be to begin with?[15]

The older Schelling brushes up against this same set of queries. In 1830, he portrays the creation of the world, with its finite determinate beings, as God putting Himself into doubt, as the divine becoming obscure to and uncertain of itself.[16] This should immediately prompt questions about why and/or how the deity ever would bother to muddy its own waters, to introduce truth-eclipsing and knowledge-thwarting distortions, illusions, mirages, and the like within itself. In 1841–1842, Schelling himself wonders aloud, "If reason (*die Vernunft*) is all Being in everything that has Being (*jedem Sein alles Sein ist*), then where does unreason (*die Unvernunft*), which is admixed with all Being (*die allem Sein beigemischt*), come from (*herzuschaffen*)?"[17]

In the 1811 first draft of the unfinished *Weltalter* project, Schelling once again alludes to the topic of error. Specifically, he there, albeit in passing, associates human freedom with being "exposed to error" (*der Verirrung ausgesetztes Wesen*).[18] The reasoning behind this association is based on the idea that the autonomy and self-determination of singular subjects is ontologically made possible by these subjects individuating themselves through emerging out of and partially detaching from pre-/non-subjective substance(s) as nature with its physical, chemical, and organic strata. For Schelling, such subject-creating individuation essentially involves the genesis of a self-relating point of contraction striving to sever its links to and dependence upon the rest of interconnected, trans-subjective Being. This contractive striving, through its willful turning inward and away from anything outer, renders its own ontological origins and surroundings opaque to itself. It comes to see what is outward through a subjective glass darkly.

This depiction of humanity's liberty provides Schelling with justification for a theoretical-epistemological explanation of error as well as a practical-ethical explanation of evil. Indeed, Schelling's related accounts of both error and evil are rooted in core features of his fundamental ontology. In 1804, and anticipating the ground-existence distinction of 1809's *Freiheitsschrift*, he stipulates, "*No individual entity contains the ground for its existence in itself* [*Kein Einzelnes hat den Grund seines Daseyns in sich selbst*]."[19] According to this ontological stipulation, a trans-individual Being (which goes by many names throughout Schelling's texts over the years) makes possible and gives rise to individuated beings, with the latter including singular human subjects.[20] While such beings and subjects depend on this Being, the latter does not depend on the former.

Then, in 1806's *Aphorisms to Introduce the Philosophy of Nature*, Schelling declares that "the sole and authentic sin is existence itself [*die einzige und eigentliche Sünde eben die Existenz selbst ist*]."[21] The unique proper sin is, as it were, the primordial lapse into the proper itself. That is to say, this *Ur*-fault is nothing other than the collapse of the trans-individual ground of the substance of Being into the individual existence of the being of the subject. In Schelling's speculative philosophical recasting of the Biblical narrative of the Fall of original sin, individuation is a (in fact, the) necessary evil. And, in line with this religious narrative, the finite subject's estrangement from infinite substance as its progenitor (i.e., God-as-Nature or Nature-as-God *à la* Schelling's version of Spinozism[22]), one, opens up the space of human freedom as enabling the possibilities for good and evil alike, and, two, is requisite for any eventual reconciliation and redemption between the creature and its creator (with this suggesting that the future highest good is made possible by a past primal evil).

One already can discern here the convergence, within Schelling's ontology of individuation, of theoretical-metaphysical and practical-ethical dimensions. The ontological becoming-finite of the infinite, as the becoming-subject of substance, involves "erring" at the level of both of these dimensions. At the theoretical-metaphysical level, ontological individuation leads to thinking's epistemological errors, its going astray as regards being. At the practical-ethical level, the contraction-into-ipseity enables acting's moral errors, in which the subject selfishly conducts itself as though it owed nothing to the inter- and trans-subjective relations actually engendering and sustaining it.

All of this is confirmed by and developed in Schelling's celebrated 1809 *Freiheitsschrift*, with its account of evil as a positive ontological reality unto itself.[23] Therein, Schelling associates evil, including that of the original sin of the ontologically fundamental primordial fall into individuation itself, with ravenous selfishness.[24] Driven by its essential and characteristic blind hunger, evil seeks perversely to invert the relation between ground (*Grund*) and existence (*Existenz*) by affirming the primacy of the latter over the former. Evil is agency run amok, deliberately trying (albeit in vain) to gain control over the ontological conditions of agency itself (with these conditions being forever refractory to any such control).[25]

As Schelling puts this in his roughly contemporaneous *Clara* dialogue, evil is, at root, always a matter of an attempt to turn the conditioned/conditional (as finite, created, produced, subject, existence, etc.) into the unconditioned/unconditional (as infinite, creating, producing, substance, ground, etc.), to stand things on their head and make the tail wag the dog.[26] And, in another text from the same period, 1810's "Stuttgart Seminars," he observes, "It could indeed be argued that evil itself proves perhaps the most spiritual [phenomenon] (*das reinste Geistige*) yet, for it wages the most vehement war against all *Being* (*es führt den heftigsten Krieg gegen alles Seyn*); indeed, it wishes to destroy the very ground of all creation (*es möchte den Grund der Schöpfung aufheben*)."[27] He soon adds, "[E]vil… is in its own way something pure."[28] Insofar as evil is epitomized by human subjectivity trying to break away from and assert its supreme sovereignty over the substance of natural being from which it arises in the first place, this rebellion against the ground of impure materiality indicates a striving toward pure spirituality inherent to the very essence of evil as the middle-period Schelling conceives it.

The *Freiheitsschrift* also has recourse to the metaphor of disease in its treatment of the topic of evil.[29] This metaphor, one G. W. F. Hegel also utilizes in manners similar to Schelling, reinforces the convergence of Schelling's accounts of evil as practical-ethical erring and error as theoretical-epistemological erring. These twin accounts both are grounded in his underlying metaphysics of the individuation of many beings out of one Being and the anthropogenesis of human transcendental subjectivity out of the immanence of natural substance. The Schelling of 1809 says of illness:

> Even particular disease (*die Partikularkrankheit*) emerges only because that which has its freedom or life only so that it may remain in the whole strives to be for itself (*es im Ganzen bleibe, für sich zu sein strebt*). As disease is admittedly nothing having inherent being [*nichts Wesenhaftes*], really only an apparent picture of life (*ein Scheinbild des Lebens*) and merely a meteoric appearance (*bloß meteorische Erscheinung*) of it—an oscillation (*ein Schwanken*) between Being and non-Being—yet announces itself nevertheless as something very real (*sehr Reelles*) to feeling (*Gefühl*), so it is with evil.[30]

As will become clear and significant below, Schelling wavers between positive and privative depictions of sickness, between illness as a reality unto itself and as a mere lack of health respectively (and this despite the focus of the *Freiheitsschrift* on developing a positive, rather than privative, conception of evil). This wavering attests to the lingering attraction for Schelling—this attraction profoundly and openly influences his earlier philosophy of nature and identity-philosophy—of a radical monism inspired by a combination of Eleatic, Neo-Platonic, and Spinozist sensibilities. This is precisely the sort of monism that makes error into, as Schelling himself admits in 1806, the "puzzle of all puzzles." Whether Schelling has a solution to this riddle remains to be seen.

That said, the rendition of illness in the preceding quotation audibly resonates with Schelling's fundamental ontology of individuation. For Schelling, a disease is an instance in which an organ rebelliously frees itself from its subordinate position within an organism so as improperly to attempt to impose itself as the governing center of the entire organism. This is a mereological revolt in which a part strives to usurp the whole.

The tumors of cancerous organs would be paradigmatic of sickness generally in Schelling's eyes. Moreover, the identification of the essence of illness, of erring from health, as based in a part's (capacity for) self-freeing *vis-à-vis* the whole to which it belongs permits Schelling to associate illness with practical-ethical autonomy and self-determination. It also permits me further to associate illness *à la* Schelling with theoretical-epistemological error too. In 1821, the later Schelling makes this further association himself, establishing a chain of equivalence between error (*Irrthum*), evil (*Böse*), and illness (*Krankheit*).[31] In the 1841–1842 Berlin lectures on the *Philosophy of Revelation*, he likewise pairs error and sickness as both privations that nonetheless are not nothing.[32]

In cancer-like diseases, excessive egotistical willfulness, and mistaken notions about reality alike, a mere moment somehow detaches itself from its foundational and encompassing ontological/metaphysical basis and introduces a topsy-turvy disorder by thrusting itself forward as the ruling principle of all. Both freedom, as freedom for evil as well as good, and falsehood, as ideational deviation from what is the case, are, from a Schellingian perspective, cancers on being. The human subjectivity central to both practical and theoretical philosophy is the cancer of creation. Moreover, if Schelling's practical philosophy could be described as an "evil-first ethics" (with the fall into contractive self-determinacy as the primordial sin uniquely enabling eventual reconciliation and redemption), his theoretical philosophy likewise could be branded an "error-first ontology" (with the *Ur*-erring of individuation bringing with it the risk of errors as symptoms of discrepancies between ground and existence, substance and subject).[33]

In addition to Schelling's above-discussed remarks about error in his *Statement on the True Relationship of the Philosophy of Nature to the Revised Fichtean Doctrine* and *Aphorisms to Introduce the Philosophy of Nature*, both from 1806, this topic also receives important treatment in his 1821 *On the Nature of Philosophy as a Science* (i.e., the Erlangen Lectures). Therein, Schelling explicitly confirms my exegetical hunches spelled out above in connection with his 1806 reflections on error and immediately subsequent related speculations in the *Freiheitsschrift*, "Stuttgart Seminars," and *Clara* dialogue. To begin with, *On the Nature of Philosophy as a Science* blames subjects falling into error on their inherent autonomous volition, on a "sheer will to know" (*das bloße wissen Wollen*).[34] The original underlying epistemic ill is nothing other than the will. Human freedom is not only being free for evil as well as good—it also likewise is being free for the false as well as the true. If freedom is a positive reality, then error as a symptom of it (like evil too) is not the pure negative of a mere absence of knowledge (or, with evil, a simple privation of or distance from goodness). Similarly, as S. J. McGrath nicely words this from a Schellingian perspective, "[T]he real problem for philosophy is not the absolute as such but the freedom which has deprived us of it."[35]

In this same 1821 context, the primary mistake which subjects are free willfully to commit, a foul frequently called out by Schelling throughout his corpus, is the modern philosophical sin of dualism (*Dualismus*). More precisely, Schelling faults the separation (*die Scheidung*) of the natural (*das Natürliche*) from the supernatural (*das Uebernatürliche*) for opening up the space for a proliferation of human-all-too-human falsehoods, fantasies, fictions, illusions, mistakes, and the like.[36] This *Ur*-dualism is the primordial form for all vertical dualistic distinctions between the low and the high, the immanent and the transcendent, the this-worldly and the other-worldly, and so on. Although monism must confront itself with the challenge of self-consistently accounting for error, dualism (as anti-monism) is itself already erroneous without knowing itself to be so. Anti-monism would be one of the errors, if not the Error of errors, for monism itself to explain.[37]

The later Schelling's Erlangen Lectures add a crucial ingredient to his (attempted) monistic explanation of error. Therein, Schelling points to the "struggle" (*Kampf*) of an original "inner conflict" (*innere Streit*) between "spiritual forces" (*geistigen Kräfte*).[38] This turmoil within the mind of the individual subject is itself said by Schelling to be an outgrowth of deeper pre-individual strife.[39] Although not entirely clear at this moment, somehow such strife engenders the errors to which humans are prone.

As I will go on to argue, this just-highlighted ingredient added to the Schellingian account of mistakes in 1821 retroactively brings to light a fundamental fault line of tension perturbing Schelling's thinking from the late 1790s onward. Schelling frequently, throughout his career, leans into a more Eleatic, Neo-Platonic, and/or Spinozist *hen-kai-pan* monism emphasizing identity, oneness, unity, and so on. But, he sometimes favors, starting in 1797's *Ideas for a Philosophy of Nature*, instead a very different sort of monism, one that fairly could be labeled a "conflict ontology."

Although still monistic, this ontology of conflict stresses antagonism, contradiction, discord, opposition, and the like (as opposed to privileging identity, etc.). Indeed, I would claim that Schelling's periodic endorsements of a conflict ontology testify, however inadvertently or not, to the fact that the problem of error is irresolvable within the parameters of any *hen-kai-pan* monism (including Schelling's own identity-philosophy as well as certain permutations of his philosophy of nature). The making of mistakes is not only the greatest puzzle of all puzzles for a metaphysics of a fundamental, ultimate One-All. It is simply unsolvable for such a metaphysics.

2 The Same Mistake Concerning the Mistaken Same: Schelling's Identitarian Lapses

I would contend that the affirmation of a conflict ontology and parallel rejection of a *hen-kai-pan* ontology in 1815's third draft of the *Weltalter*[40] offer Schelling his only means of doing justice to phenomena of the erroneous and the false, to the problem of mistakes that Schelling himself acknowledges is pressing for any monism or immanentism. His continual placements of an undivided Absolute (as pure, indeterminate Identity, Indifference, etc.) at the basis of the entirety of existence both before and after this passing 1815 moment render him unable to meet the challenge facing a monist of getting to grips with error and the like—and this despite Schelling enjoying the merit of glimpsing and admitting to this very challenge.

Schelling's own criticisms of Spinoza and Spinozism indicate why a radical monism of the absolute Unity of a unique One-All, such as Schelling himself repeatedly lapses into, creates the problem of error. Schelling's identity-philosophy and its multiple permutations throughout his corpus epitomize this monistic extremism of the *hen kai pan*. And, such monism cannot solve the problem of error it generates for itself. As Hegel would put it, this monism thereby does violence to itself at its own hands.

This is because too uncompromising an immanentism is incapable of explaining both why and how pure Identity (as Absolute, God, Infinite, Substance, etc.) generates the Differences constitutive of the realm of finite phenomenal appearances as the realm in which all subjects, speculative philosophers included, are embedded. This familiar domain of existence includes those appearances responsible for what come to be judged as errors, falsehoods, mistakes, and so on. In fact, were the original basis of all reality to be the One of a homogeneous total Being beyond, behind, or beneath beings, it seems likely that there would be no Many of beings *qua* the plurality of entities and events presenting themselves in the guise of the dappled existence humans continually both experience and, as it were, mis-experience. Why and how would an undivided Absolute disrupt itself so as to splinter into a multitude of non-Absolute appearances? Why and how would such an Absolute become obscure to itself, not only reflecting on itself, but doing so in a self-distorting fashion?

Even if (mis)experienced reality as a whole is illusory, is nothing more than a tissue of deceptive epiphenomenal seemings, a systematic absolute monism would be inescapably under an obligation to explain why and how the illusory arises. Yet, as Schelling himself concedes from time to time, the reasons for and mechanisms of any transition here—this would be a movement from, first, the Absolute, Identity, Indifference, Infinite, One, and so on to, second, the non-Absolute, non-Identity, Difference, Finitude, Many, and the like—cannot be satisfactorily supplied. Both Spinoza and the Schelling who follows him fail to deliver any such set of reasons and mechanisms.

Addressing these sorts of concerns, McGrath admits that Schelling's Absolute must have been breached for there to be the reality familiar to subjective experience.[41] That is to say, an inner interruption by an immanent split must afflict the primordial Unity for it to pour itself out into Diversity. Along these same lines, McGrath similarly avers, "Lack must first be introduced into being."[42]

However, for the more Spinozist Schelling favorably inclined toward a *hen-kai-pan* ontology, there is no Elsewhere, Other, or Outside in relation to the Absolute as infinite One-All. There is no Alterity that could inject division or deprivation into the pure positive plenum of something like the Identity of Identity. Schelling, at his more radically monistic, categorically excludes any foreignness, and whatever absences and antagonisms it might bring with it, from his fundamental Being of beings. Hence, he forbids himself recourse to what he needs in order to account for both non-absolute existence and the errors, illusions, and mistakes this existence integrally involves. Thus, Schelling's supposedly self-commencing *hen kai pan*, as Xavier Tilliette describes this Absolute,[43] cannot ever actually commence.

Of course, even before the coming into its own of the identity-philosophy starting in 1801, Spinoza exerts an influence on Schelling's philosophy of nature during the latter half of the 1790s. When Schelling is focused specifically on the philosophy of nature and is prone to equating the Absolute with Nature, Spinoza's *natura naturans* plays the role of the *Ur*-power of φύσις as primal productivity, the underlying creative ground of the existence of all thus-created things as its products. And, texts such as *Ideas for a Philosophy of Nature* (1797), *On the World Soul* (1798), and *First Outline of a System of the Philosophy of Nature* (1799) propose that Nature-as-Absolute is riven at its very foundations by an original division of clashing forces.

This split Absolute of the early philosophy of nature arguably reappears as the God at war with Himself of the third draft of *The Ages of the World*. In this 1815 draft, the nascent conflict ontology that begins to be articulated in Schelling's philosophy of nature of the 1790s gets translated out of terminology borrowed from the natural sciences and into the imagistic, evocative language of theology. This suggests that Schelling reads the *"sive"* (or) in Spinoza's *"Deus sive natura"* as an inclusive, rather than exclusive, disjunction.[44]

Moreover, the *natura* of Schelling's early philosophy of nature already is both spiritualized and deified as a cosmic creative agency. A *natura* as *Deus* lies at the very basis of existence even for the ostensibly more naturalistically minded Schelling. Hence, the purported "turn" to theology, religion, and mythology of the middle and late periods of Schelling's career is not really a turn so much as a making more explicit of the vitalistic, hylozoistic spiritualism inherent to his thinking from the mid-1790s onward.

In what follows, I will argue for the philosophical attractiveness today of an immanent-critical sublation of the Schelling of both the late 1790s philosophy of nature and 1815 draft of *The Ages of the World*. This *Aufhebung* perhaps best can be presented through a recasting of Spinoza's and Schelling's *"Deus sive natura"* involving three interlinked aspects. First, the *"sive"* here will be treated as an exclusive, instead of inclusive, disjunction—with this treatment blocking the problematic Schellingian slippage back-and-forth between Nature and God as synonymous and interchangeable. Second, a firm decision will be taken in favor of *"natura"* to the exclusion of "*Deus.*" That is to say, a choice will be made for a Godless material-natural Real. And, third, "*natura*" will not be understood as the immaterial *élan vital* of *natura naturans* envisioned as a mega-organism or even divine subjectivity. Nature, in line with recognizably scientific sensibilities justifiably eschewing such global supernaturalist outlooks as panpsychism and vitalism, will be construed instead as including ontological regions consisting of irreducibly unspiritual, non-anthropomorphic *natura naturata* as the empirically investigable material beings of such fields as physics and chemistry.

Combined with Schelling's emphases on the negativity of antagonism, strife, and tension in both the late 1790s philosophy of nature and the 1815 *Weltalter* apparatus, this atheistic re-reading of "*Deus sive natura*" pushes off from Schelling so as to arrive at a truly materialist, naturalist, and realist conflict ontology able to articulate from within its own framework an account of the sort of subjectivity also central to transcendental idealism. Although not to the letter of Schelling's quickly abandoned 1800 *System of Transcendental Idealism*, in which he provides a sketch of a synthesis of the philosophy of nature (as a theory of objectivity) with transcendental idealism (as a theory of subjectivity), my labors in this current vein carry forward the spirit of this text. To be more precise, I see a secularized ontology of nature as a not-Whole multiplicity convulsed by discrepancies and clashes as providing the basis for properly explaining the genesis and metaphysical status of the subject at the nucleus of transcendental philosophies. Importantly, my approach promises to meet the twin challenges Schelling intermittently registers as fatally undermining any *hen-kai-pan* fundamental ontology, namely, the non-transition from the One (as Absolute, Identity, Infinity, etc.) to the Many (as non-Absolute, Difference, finitude, etc.) and the enigma of error and the like for extreme monism/immanentism.

What could be characterized as a certain "return to Schelling" forms part of ongoing conversations about renewed varieties of realism, materialism, and naturalism in contemporary metaphysics. Admittedly, Schelling's reliance on such figures as Spinoza and Friedrich Hölderlin for ontological inspiration feeds into his neither-materialist-nor-naturalist *hen-kai-pan* tendencies (involving a shifting mixture of hylozoism, mythologization, panpsychism, pantheism, religiosity, spiritualism, and vitalism). Nonetheless, despite such downsides, these same sources of inspiration, specifically insofar as they play major roles in Schelling's break with the subjectivism of transcendental idealism (especially Fichte's subject-centrism), push him toward embracing a robust realism.[45]

As Beiser accurately observes, a realist philosophy of nature is a non-negotiable core component of both Schelling's and Hegel's philosophical endeavors.[46] Beiser likewise rightly underscores that recent and contemporary scholarship on German idealism has continued to neglect the Schellingian and Hegelian philosophies of nature—with this neglect being symptomatic of still-prevailing anti-realist, anti-materialist, and anti-naturalist inclinations among the majority of scholars of late eighteenth- and early nineteenth-century German philosophy.[47] Andrew Bowie also notes that the importance of nature and philosophy of nature for Schelling is precisely what has led to him in particular being downplayed or sidelined in recent and contemporary engagements with the German idealists.[48] On several occasions, I have reached the same conclusions as Beiser and Bowie when looking at Schelling's and Hegel's philosophies of nature and their receptions (or lack thereof).[49]

Schelling's anti-subjectivist departure from Immanuel Kant and Fichte, encouraged by Spinoza's and Hölderlin's influences (among others), is the negation corresponding to his affirmation of a realist philosophy of nature.[50] The latter reflects an interconnected ensemble of contentions about the subjectivity of Kantian and Fichtean transcendental idealism. This ensemble is crucial for absolute idealism as advanced by both Schelling and Hegel. According to these contentions: The transcendental subject is not an *unhintergehbar* ultimacy, an always-already-there enclosure whose origins are epistemologically out of bounds; This subject cannot ground itself, owing its genesis, existence, experiences, and structure to something (or things) other than itself. Both scientific evidence and philosophical speculation testify that the objective world gives rise to the subjective mind (and not vice versa), that natural history is much lengthier than and well precedes human history. In terms of *Natur* and *Geist* with respect to each other, the latter is conditioned by the former, with the former as itself the unconditioned.[51] Along the lines of this last contention in particular, Judith Schlanger helpfully characterizes the Schellingian subjectivity conditioned by nature, as per the philosophy of nature, as unstable, precarious, and continually in danger of being destroyed and dissipated by the natural ground making it possible in the first place.[52]

Schelling's realist naturalism is an important and much-needed corrective to the sorts of anti-realist subjectivism associated with transcendental idealism and its long shadow extending up through today. Yet, despite the fact that Schelling's 1801 break with Fichte involves making transcendental idealism secondary with respect to both philosophy of nature and the identity-philosophy, Schelling never seeks to reduce away or eliminate altogether the subjectivity at the center of such idealism. Instead, he wishes to account for the immanent genesis of the transcendental subject out of the Absolute (whether as Nature and/or Identity). But, I would maintain, this account requires such an Absolute to be non-self-identical *qua* fundamentally divided and agitated by collisions and (self-)estrangements.

Obviously, an essential feature of transcendental subjectivity *à la* both Kant and Fichte is its autonomy, its capacity for spontaneous self-determination. Human freedom is awarded pride of place in Kant's and Fichte's philosophical edifices. From Schelling's perspective too, preserving this freedom, while nonetheless re-situating the subject of transcendentalism within the non-subjective ontological/metaphysical framework of absolute idealism, remains a priority.

For instance, the 1796 fragment given the title "The Earliest System-Program of German Idealism," written in Hegel's handwriting but often attributed by scholars to Schelling as its author, lays out in hyper-condensed fashion much of what becomes agenda-setting for the whole rest of Schelling's lengthy intellectual itinerary.[53] (As I have argued on other occasions, and regardless of who originally is responsible for authoring the "The Earliest System-Program of German Idealism," this 1796 text lays down a number of what subsequently serve as red threads woven through the entire arc of Hegel's philosophical corpus as well.[54]) As multiple commentators assert, this 1796 programmatic statement's announced intention to pursue

Monism and Mistakes 477

the construction of a compatibilist metaphysics, one bringing together natural objectivity as per philosophy of nature (associated with Spinoza) and spontaneous subjectivity as per transcendental idealism (associated with Kant and Fichte), guides Schelling across the full span of his philosophical career. The compatibilism of Schelling's "Spinozism of freedom" aims to reimagine, in Rudolf Brandner's words, "the physical-cosmic world itself as the place of human freedom."[55]

Bowie nicely encapsulates the core challenge confronting anything like the Schellingian compatibilist Spinozism of freedom. He remarks, "The real question is what does a nature in which freedom plays an ineliminable role look like, if one does not rely on appeals to something ultimately mysterious 'in nature' that escapes the clutches of universal determinism?"[56] As I allege here and elsewhere,[57] Schelling's reliance on Spinoza (as well as on the Eleatics, the Neo-Platonists, and Hölderlin) often leads him to espouse a *hen-kai-pan* ontology in which it seems difficult, if not impossible, for him to meet this challenge and still hold onto an individuated autonomous subject partly independent of a pre-/non-subjective, anonymous, trans-individual Absolute. Schelling, at his more radically monist, frequently appears to be in danger of deserving Hegel's quip about the night in which all cows are black, with the free subject vanishing into the unfree void of the monochromatic abyss of the Identity of Identity, the divine One-All, and/or *natura naturans*.

As Schelling knows, Spinoza himself, consistent with his rigorous, uncompromising monism, is a thoroughgoing determinist (something made much of by F. H. Jacobi in the *Pantheismusstreit* he starts whipping up in 1785). Within the parameters of the substance ontology of 1677's *Ethics*, there are no individuated subjects independent of the infinitude of *Deus sive natura*, no loci within this infinitude of reflexive self-determination. Human mindedness, regardless of however it might fancy itself, is neither autonomous nor spontaneous. In Spinoza's view, the strength of the finite mind's belief in its freedom (i.e., its autonomy and spontaneity) is correlative to the depth of its ignorance regarding the true nature of being (as expressed by the metaphysics of the *Ethics*).[58] For him, everything that finite humans think and do is thoroughly determined, with all mental thinking and bodily doing as mere modes of attributes enchained within causal concatenations of other modes. God/Nature determines and encompasses all attributes and modes, including those constitutive of finite human (pseudo-)subjects.[59] Relatedly, with heteronomy as a matter of determination by external factors, only *Deus sive natura* enjoys autonomy in Spinoza's system, since this unique substance alone, in its singular absolute infinitude, has nothing outside itself to act upon it externally.[60] God/Nature hence is free *qua* self-determining at least by default, since it has no Other to determine it. In its loneliness, *Deus sive natura* is left to determine itself.

Schelling, throughout his lengthy speculative odyssey, wildly swings between certain moments when he vehemently embraces Spinoza and other moments when he holds the author of the *Ethics* at arm's length. As an instance of the latter, he intermittently criticizes Spinozism for rendering the Absolute in terms of objectivity (i.e., static, noun-like substantiality) but not also subjectivity (with the Schelling who voices this complaint preferring to characterize the Absolute as a subject-object unifying these seemingly discrepant dimensions). However, this line of criticism looks to be disingenuous on Schelling's part. His own sustained heavy reliance on Spinozist *natura* as *natura naturans* (i.e., "nature naturing" as a subject-like kinetic productive agency or creative power) bears witness to this disingenuousness.[61] In 1797's *Ideas for a Philosophy of Nature*, Schelling even admits with respect to Spinoza that "[t]he view of his philosophy as a mere theory of objectivity did not allow the true absolute to be perceived in it… he recognized subject-objectivity as the necessary and eternal character of absoluteness."[62]

So, how, if at all, can Schelling appropriate Spinoza's *natura naturans* as foundational for his own philosophical efforts while simultaneously avoiding the hard-nosed determinism Spinoza himself infers as inseparably bound up with the *Deus sive natura* of the *Ethics*? On a reconstruction of Schelling I carry out elsewhere,[63] he ends up, particularly in 1809's *Freiheitsschrift*, trying to depict human freedom as tantamount to the resurgence, within the constituted existence (*Existenz*) of *natura naturata*, of the ground (*Grund*) of this existence as *natura naturans*. But, why would a filtering of Spinozist *natura naturans* through apparently individuated beings (i.e., minded and like-minded human thinkers and actors) launder this God-like Nature's deterministic authority? Asked differently, why or how would subjects taken as channels or conduits for a divinized φύσις not still be heteronomous *vis-à-vis* this φύσις, mere vessels or vehicles for the lone Will of *Deus sive natura*? In yet other words, does not this Schelling fail to offer his promised post-Spinozist rendition of specifically human freedom (*menschliche Freiheit*), reducing this freedom instead to that of a Spinozist God/Nature, to a divine freedom (*göttliche Freiheit*) already espoused by Spinoza himself?

Similarly, the compatibilism of Schelling's "Spinozism of freedom" relies on a Spinozist spiritualization of nature (I also have critically examined this side of Schelling in a companion piece to the present essay[64]). This maneuver of identifying an intangible organism- and mind-like energetic *élan vital* as the underlying creator of everything under the sun indicates that Schelling falls short of meeting the challenge inevitably confronting the compatibilist Spinozism of freedom. To employ Bowie's above-quoted words again, how does Schelling's hylozoist and/or panpsychist dematerialization of natural matter "not rely on appeals to something ultimately mysterious 'in nature' that escapes the clutches of universal determinism?" Is not the *natura naturans* of *Deus sive natura*, at least from a naturalistic standpoint informed by modern natural science and correspondingly uncomfortable with anything resembling pre-modern animism, precisely this sort of enigmatic "x" placed in nature *qua natura naturata*? And, does not the Schellingian spiritualization and divinization of nature amount to a theosophical conjuring away of determinism? In what manner, if any, is this a true and proper compatibilism wrangling with the real difficulties of explaining how humans can be free while nevertheless immanently situated within a much wider non-human nature?

In the same companion piece to the present essay I referred to a moment ago,[65] I highlight an irony affecting the Schelling presently under consideration. Despite Schelling's repeated complaints about modern philosophers trafficking in contentiously rigid and debatably clear-cut either/or dualisms, he himself surreptitiously trades on a family of dualisms residing at the core of philosophical modernity. To be more precise, binary oppositions between subject(ivity) and object(ivity) as well as *Geist* and *Natur* undergird essential aspects of Schelling's Spinozism of freedom.

From the inception of the early philosophy of nature onward, Schelling latches onto aspects of nature—specifically its energies and forces as conceived in terms of electricity, galvanism, gravitation, magnetism, optics, and the like—that seem more active and immaterial by comparison with the dense inert bodies of a Newtonian worldview grounded in mechanical physics. In combination with this, Schelling implicitly endorses a dualism of subjective Spirit and objective Nature. He does so by assuming that whatever does not conform to a certain picture of what it is to be a natural object (with objectivity here exemplified by the static tangible entities of *natura naturata*) must be a spiritual subject (with Schelling identifying nature's kinetic intangible energies and forces as indicative of there being, at the basis of all *natura naturata*, a dynamic agency of productivity as *natura naturans*).

What Schelling, still partly in thrall to the modern philosophical dualisms he loudly and regularly denounces, does not contemplate is the possibility that nature does not (uniformly) conform to the Laplacean demon image of it (one composed out of the atomistic, mechanistic, and deterministic sensibilities of Newtonian physics) without, for all that, being a cosmic macro-organism and spiritual mega-subject. Admittedly, this possibility becomes more visible in and through scientific developments in fields such as thermodynamics, quantum mechanics, and even trans-finite set theory coming after Schelling dies in 1854. Schelling's dematerialization of matter and spiritualization of nature are of a piece with him remaining trapped in the binary terms of a false forced choice: Nature is either mindless matter (as per a one-sided absolutization of objectivity *à la* Enlightenment-era physics) or matterless mind (as per an equally one-sided absolutization of subjectivity *à la* the life sciences and the *Geisteswissenschaften*).[66] In relation to Schelling's program of pursuing a Spinozism of freedom, he is convinced that the only alternative to a materialism of mindless matter seeing nothing but efficient-causal determination in nature is a spiritualism (as hylozoism, panpsychism, pantheism, and/or vitalism) of matterless mind re-envisioning nature itself as self-determining intelligence (with human self-determination as a manifestation of nature's self-determination).[67]

This Schellingian either/or looks to be a false dilemma once one entertains the idea that nature can involve indetermination and under-determination without, for all that, being at root either deterministic or self-determining. I readily would concede to Schelling and his compatibilist agenda that undermining depictions of nature in anything like a Newtonian or Laplace's demon fashion is a necessary condition for elaborating a nature-based account of the genesis and existence of autonomous transcendental subjectivity as immanently transcending its natural ground. But, this in/under-determination is only a necessary condition for the self-determination of the free *Cogito*-like subject. By contrast, Schelling's natural self-determination (i.e., *natura naturans* as spontaneous agency) is the necessary and sufficient condition for human self-determination, with human self-determination immediately expressing, nay, being identical to, natural self-determination.

3 Sublating Schelling Today: A Nine-Point Program

I want to bring this chapter to a close with an outline for a contemporary reactualization of a Schellingian compatibilism informed by the criticisms of Schelling I have unfolded throughout the preceding. I will conclude with a series of nine points for a philosophical agenda that perhaps appropriately could be labeled "the latest system-program of German idealism" (in homage to "The Earliest System-Program of German Idealism" of 1796). In the spirit, but not to the letter, of Schelling's *oeuvre*, I too am preoccupied with the task of reconciling a naturalistic fundamental ontology with a transcendentalist theory of subjectivity.

The opening three of these nine programmatic points have to do with Spinoza's *Deus sive natura*. First, Schelling treats this "*sive*" (or) as an inclusive disjunction. In so doing, he allows himself to equivocate between the divine and the natural. Modern scientific sensibilities suggest that Spinoza's "*sive*" should be treated instead as an exclusive disjunction.

Second, these same sensibilities also call for choosing *natura* over *Deus*, especially when the latter abets the infusion of unobservable occult forces and mysterious powers into nature. By contrast with Schelling's pseudo-naturalistic spiritualism (as hylozoism, panpsychism, pantheism, and/or vitalism), any recognizably and properly naturalistic position taking seriously the methodologies and epistemologies, as well as the contents (discoveries, findings, results, etc.), of the empirical, experimental natural sciences must forego appeals to God-the-unexplained-explainer and related notions enshrined in theological dogmas and religious beliefs.

Third, in line with the epistemological-methodological constraints of the modern natural sciences, nature must be understood strictly as *natura naturata*. So as to avoid simply replacing scientific investigation with philosophical visions, nature must not, as Schelling does, be redoubled as a purportedly more fundamental metaphysical *natura naturans*. Schelling's distinction between an "empirical physics" dealing with *natura naturata* as knowable *aposteriori* and a higher "speculative physics" dealing with *natura naturans* knowable *apriori* invites countless flights of fancy projecting themselves onto or eclipsing and disregarding altogether the data and outcomes of lowly non-speculative scientific activities. Schelling himself, especially in his more overtly theosophical later years, is guilty of and epitomizes this danger of the speculative separating from and then interfering with the empirical. Already in the 1804 Würzburg course on the philosophy of nature, Schelling castigates empirical physics for mechanistically de-vitalizing nature, for reducing living, dynamic *natura naturans* to dead, inert *natura naturata*.[68]

Fourth, Schelling's hylozoistic-vitalistic image of Nature in its grand totality as a cosmic mega-organism deserves to be left by the historical wayside. I am sympathetic to his insistence, in the face of the Kant of the *Critique of the Power of Judgment*, that the teleological intentions, plans, and purposes of living beings are not just a Kantian "regulative idea," namely, that final causes really are operative in (organic) *Natur an sich*.[69] But, Schelling here once again falls back on a false dilemma. He pits his universe-as-organism (in which his ontologization of Kant's conception of natural teleology in the third *Critique* is absolutized for nature as a whole) as ostensibly the sole alternative to the Newtonian universe-as-mechanism (with mechanical physics informing the picture of nature integral to Kant's *Critique of Pure Reason*, a picture in which the natural contains efficient but not final causes). This false dilemma readily can be circumvented by recognizing that nature-in-itself actually is composed of varied regions, with certain of its levels and layers being inorganic and others being organic. One need not be compelled to decide between either everything being mechanical or everything being alive. Both of these options deserve to be condemned and dismissed as indefensibly one-sided.

Fifth, nature not only, in line with point four above, is stratified into irreducible-to-each-other dimensions (inorganic, organic, physical, chemical, biological, and so on). This already is to reverse Schelling's tendency to prioritize Identity over Difference. But, through interfacing and secularizing his 1797–1799 philosophy of nature (with its ontologization of the Kant of 1786's *Metaphysical Foundations of Natural Science*) and 1815 *Weltalter* manuscript, one arrives at a reconceptualization of nature according to which, in addition to there being intra-natural non-antagonistic differences, there also are intra-natural antagonistic negativities. This leads to a naturalistic conflict ontology in which various collisions, discrepancies, frictions, oppositions, tensions, and the like configure and agitate material being and its outgrowths (up to and including the sapient human subject as per transcendental idealism[70]).

Schelling's reliance upon Kant's *Anziehungskraft* and *Zurückstossungkraft* often prompts him to depict the intra-natural negativities of a conflict-ontological version of the philosophy of nature as clashing energies and forces. Yet, as Schelling himself readily would admit, nature's inner conflicts are not limited to the level of such inorganic natural phenomena as electricity, gravity, light, and magnetism (i.e., those phenomena of special interest to the young Schelling of the late 1790s in connection with the Kant of *Metaphysical Foundations of Natural Science*). Especially through taking into consideration natural scientific developments post-dating Schelling's death, the domains of organic nature too show themselves to be traversed by conflicts, examples of which include: the evolutionary struggle for survival of a Darwinian "nature red in tooth and claw"; the incompatible jockeying interests and motivations within organisms as divided between, on the one hand, being members of species with these species' genetic determinants and, on the other hand, being somatic (and even psychical) individuals with their own idiosyncratic, particular concerns; tugs-of-war between sexual and self-preservative tendencies as well as between amorous and aggressive inclinations; the discordant interactions between regions and sub-regions of central nervous systems sandwiching together components embodying the influences of multiple distinct evolutionary eras and pressures. Of course, fully embracing such a Schelling-inspired philosophy of nature reworked in the vein of a secular (or even atheistic) conflict ontology (and not a more Spinozist *hen-kai-pan* ontology) entails, among other consequences, repudiating Schelling's own hylozoistic imaginings of Nature in its entirety as the harmonious Whole of a gargantuan super-organism unifying and synthesizing each and every one of its parts.

Sixth, the conflict-ontological philosophy of nature just gestured at in point five is crucial in relation to any compatibilism along the lines of Schelling's Spinozism of freedom seeking to blend a naturalistic ontology with a theory of subjectivity of the sort advanced by transcendental idealism. A not-causally closed, not-thoroughly deterministic nature—this is the idea of nature offered by a philosophy of nature of negativity—is the ultimate material condition of possibility for the (contingent, not predestined) coming to be of *Cogito*-like subjectivity within nature's lone plane of incarnate immanence. There can be nature-emergent free subjects because nature itself does not form inescapable chains of efficient-causal determination precluding in advance the genesis of such freedom.

But, nature's in/under-determination is not itself already the subject's self-determination. The former is a necessary but not sufficient condition for the latter. However, in this essay's companion piece,[71] I show that Schelling again and again, over the many years of his long and winding philosophical journey, directly identifies natural in/under-determination with subjective self-determination. He does so by reducing human freedom to being nothing other than the resurgence of the supposed freedom of *natura naturans*, of Spinoza's *Deus sive natura* as a primordial mega-Subject, within the field of *natura naturata*.

For Schelling, Nature, as φύσις *qua* the ground and producer of everything under the sun, always-already enjoys full-blown self-determination. This divinized *natura* is as much the minded architect of creation as the substantial basis of all beings (in Schellingian parlance, it is the archaic subject-object responsible for reality in its entirety[72]). As Jacques Lacan would phrase this, the rabbit of autonomous *Geist* Schelling pulls out of the hat of heteronomous *Natur* is the one he put there in the first place. Whether this conjuring trick amounts to a bona fide compatibilism is highly questionable. Rather than rendering free Spirit compatible with unfree Nature, Schelling simply makes the latter vanish, replacing it with free Spirit writ large in the guise of *Deus sive natura*.

A real compatibilism inspired by but taking distance from Schelling involves making explicit an implicit distinction between two versions of the unfreedom that could be attributed to an unfree nature. One version, which is likely what springs to most minds when hearing the phrase "unfree nature," is nature as causally closed and thoroughly deterministic. But, another version is nature as plastic and in/under-deterministic. Insofar as in/under-determination is not freedom *qua* self-determination, an in/under-determined and in/under-determining nature still would qualify as unfree. Schelling, once more unwittingly in thrall to the dualistic tendencies he regularly denounces as modernity's cardinal philosophical sin, appears to believe that the only alternative to nature-as-deterministic is nature-as-free, as itself spontaneous, self-determining agency. He does not consider the third possibility I am drawing attention to now, namely, nature-as-unfree-*qua*-in/under-deterministic, a material-objective nature (of *natura naturata* without *natura naturans*) originally lacking but nonetheless allowing for a spiritual-subjective freedom (as full-fledged self-determination).

Seventh, the nature-emergent transcendental subject in its real autonomy, as neither a mere conduit for a divine Spirit nor a sterile and illusory epiphenomenal appearance, must be able to react back upon the natural ground(s) from which it arose. A genuine compatibilism developed in part via an immanent-critical passage through Schelling's Spinozism of freedom should be a non-reductive dialectical naturalism admitting what is nowadays designated as "downward causation." Employing the Spinozist terms utilized by Schelling himself, Schlanger claims that Schelling's thinking posits the power of products (i.e., *natura naturata*) reciprocally to impact, to nudge and alter, the productivity (i.e., *natura naturans*) generating them.[73]

There perhaps are a few moments in Schelling's extensive body of work lending Schlanger's claim a ring of accuracy. But, I would maintain that there are many more other moments therein rendering this claim implausible. The Schelling who regularly reduces subjectivity to *Deus sive natura* and has everything finitely particular (subjects included) amount to unreal expressions or seemings of an infinitely universal One-All forecloses the dialectical movement back-and-forth between upward emergence and downward causation crucial for a non-reductive, compatibilist naturalism. Such movement, for this Schelling, could be only pseudo-movement, the false appearance of different domains interacting, within the motionless One-All of a uniform, homogeneous Absolute Identity. All such dynamics dissolve as mirages for any ontology of *hen kai pan*.

Eighth, if, as per the preceding, one does not posit the end (the emergence of sapient and spontaneous mindedness and like-mindedness) already in the beginning (as the oldest fundamental ontological basis of all beings), then the Absolute, as taking into account everything and leaving out nothing, can be only an Omega and not, *à la* Schelling, also an Alpha. Especially in light of Schelling's (and Hegel's) philosophical sensitivities to historical and temporal dimensions, the Absolute always is shaped and reshaped by what is newest under the sun, by what most lately springs into existence that was not there before. This is because, in order to enjoy absoluteness, the Absolute has to encompass what becomes, and continues to become, as the present unfurls into the future, and not just to encompass what was in the past, "in the Beginning." As Hegel stresses repeatedly, the Absolute is solely a result, coming invariably last and visible exclusively with the hindsight of the Owl of Minerva.

Relatedly, making the Absolute an Omega but not also an Alpha heads off problems about why and/or how an Absolute-as-Alpha ever would take the trouble to appear, dissemble, emanate, express, seem, and so on. Why would an at-one-with-itself homogeneous Infinite disrupt and divide itself so as to give birth to reality as humans know it, namely, as finite, differentiated, individuated, many-faceted, and so on? Having already delved into these sorts of issues earlier in connection with Schelling's relationship with Spinozism and his Spinoza-indebted *hen-kai-pan* ontology, I will not recapitulate all of this here. Suffice it now to say that, even for Schelling himself on certain occasions, the Absolute conceived as a purely self-identical, monochromatic One-All at the origin of all things is a literal non-starter. Nothing starts, nothing proceeds and advances, on the basis of what would be the flat zero level of a sheerly indeterminate, undifferentiated *Ur*-Totality.

Ninth, the Absolute as a result is not, so to speak, a sort of super-moment coming in addition to and merging into a supreme Unity the preceding multitude of moments. The status of "absolute knowing" (*das absolute Wissen*) at the close of Hegel's *Phenomenology of Spirit*, properly interpreted, is the model here. For the Hegel of the *Phenomenology*, the Absolute as absolute knowing is not a final *Gestalt des Geistes* (shape of spirit) unto itself, one wherein the plethora of preceding figures/shapes of consciousness and mind/spirit are dissolved into the pure light of a final and complete One or Whole.

Instead, *das absolute Wissen* is a matter of grasping that the network of one-sided positions and perspectives flowing into each other thanks to each of their dialectics-inducing flaws is the only real Absolute. This network is precisely what Hegel lays out in the main body of the *Phenomenology*, from its opening treatment of "sense certainty" right up to the threshold of absolute knowing. Hegelian *absolute Wissen* amounts to knowing that the sole Absolute is nothing other or more than the patchwork web of inadequate, lop-sided vantage points in which these points struggle to compensate for each other's distortions, errors, and oversights.

Error and falsity are problematic enigmas deeply perplexing and troubling for Schellingian radical monism. By contrast, they are the catalysts sparking and engines powering the speculative dialectics of Hegel's philosophy, in which negativity plays the core role. As it turns out, the solution to the mystery of the always-already-past Absolute becoming epistemically estranged from itself—this is Schelling's great "puzzle of all puzzles" with which I opened this chapter—is to make the always-just-arriving Absolute the latest outcome of a concatenation of preceding estrangements, a chain of prior missteps.

For Schelling, the organic unity of the one true philosophical system is an appropriate subjective mirroring of the organic unity of all objective reality in and of itself.[74] For Hegel, as well as for many inspired by Hegel (myself included), the kaleidoscopic collage of partial conceptions, instances, outlooks, representations, views, and so on assembled by the driving negativity of dialectics fittingly mirrors an existence itself traversed and continually destabilized and disrupted by antagonisms, contradictions, inconsistencies, oppositions, and the like. From this Hegelian perspective, not only do the heterogeneous multiplicity of differences not dissolve in the Absolute as the homogeneous unity of Identity—the Absolute is nothing but the crisscrossing interrelationships between these differences. This heterogeneity displayed by dialectical thinking reflects a heterogeneity inherent to being *an sich*.

These preceding nine points obviously tip my hand so as to show my primarily Hegelian cards. Without revisiting the intricacies of the fraught Schelling-Hegel relationship—doing so would be a book-length undertaking unto itself—I will end by saying a select few words about this relationship. To begin with, I see Hegel as significantly influenced by Schelling, even long after the two of them become alienated from each other following the publication of Hegel's *Phenomenology of Spirit*. To cut a long story short, Hegel, despite his various implicit and explicit criticisms of (especially pre-1809) Schelling, carries forward into his mature works a number of commitments at least partly due to Schelling's influence, including a robust realism affirmed in the teeth of critical transcendental idealism's subjectivist anti-realism; an insistence on the non-negligible importance of nature, naturalism, and the natural sciences for absolute idealism; a view of *Geist* as emerging out of *Natur* through a *Befreiungskampf*; and a compatibilism synthesizing a naturalistic ontology with a theory of spontaneous transcendental subjectivity.

My acknowledgment of these Schelling-indebted features of Hegel's philosophy is at odds with a recent tendency, one featuring prominently in analytic-philosophy-friendly "deflationary" renditions of Hegel, still very popular today. This is a tendency, indefensible on the basis of the historical record, to minimize or deny Schelling's significance for German Idealism in general and Hegel in particular. The deflationists' stories about Hegel require, in order to maintain a veneer of plausibility, revising Schelling (and, along with him, such figures as Spinoza and Hölderlin) out of their narratives about Hegel's formation as a thinker. So as to sustain a dubious rapprochement between Hegel and the anti-naturalism, anti-realism, and subject-centrism of the likes of Kant and Fichte, the deflationists pretend that Schelling has little to no effect on Hegel. This is simply a brazen falsification of intellectual history. It lamentably and irresponsibly sidesteps a philosophically mandatory confrontation with Schelling's and Hegel's multi-pronged critiques of Kant's and Fichte's idealisms.

Yet, acknowledging Schelling's lasting effects on Hegel's philosophizing is wrongly neither to portray the mature Hegel as a Schellingian nor to paper over the many big disagreements between Schelling and Hegel throughout the arc of their careers. As I readily admit, I see Hegel as possessing the upper hand in his debates with Schelling and Hegel's version of post-Kantian, post-Fichtean absolute idealism as more philosophically satisfying than Schelling's various positions staked out over the years of his itinerary as a thinker. Nevertheless, apropos such topics as realism, naturalism, and philosophy of nature, Hegel's advances over Schelling are achieved partly in and through his immanent-critical appropriation of and reckoning with (the early) Schelling's legacy. Indeed, the above nine points outlining a program for a twenty-first-century reactivation of "The Earliest System-Program of German Idealism" signal the relevance of Hegel, Schelling, and the ambivalences both uniting and dividing these two giants of German idealism for contemporary metaphysics in European philosophical traditions—traditions they each continue to shape in myriad ways.

Notes

1. Antonio Gramsci, *Prison Notebooks, Volume Three*, ed. and trans. Joseph A. Buttigieg (New York: Columbia University Press, 2007), 174.
2. Mao Tse-Tung, *Selected Readings* (Peking: Foreign Languages Press, 1971), 502–504.
3. F. W. J. Schelling, *Statement on the True Relationship of the Philosophy of Nature to the Revised Fichtean Doctrine*, trans. Dale E. Snow (Albany, NY: SUNY Press, 2018), 62.
4. Ibid.
5. Ibid., 87.

6. F. W. J. Schelling, *Presentation of My System of Philosophy*, in J. G. Fichte and F. W. J. Schelling, *The Philosophical Rupture between Fichte and Schelling*, trans. and ed. Michael G. Vater and David W. Wood (Albany, NY: SUNY, 2012), 141–225. See Steffen Dietzsch, "Geschichtsphilosophische Dimensionen der Naturphilosophie Schellings," in *Natur und geschichtlicher Prozeß: Studien zur Naturphilosophie F. W. J. Schellings*, ed. Hans Jörg Sandkühler (Frankfurt am Main: Suhrkamp, 1984), 242; Robert J. Richards, *The Romantic Conception of Life: Science and Philosophy in the Age of Goethe* (Chicago: University of Chicago Press, 2002), 181.
7. Dieter Henrich, *Selbstverhältnisse: Gedanken und Auslegungen zu den Grundlagen der klassischen deutschen Philosophie* (Stuttgart: Reclam, 1982), 152.
8. See Adrian Johnston, "Whither the Transcendental?: Hegel, Analytic Philosophy, and the Prospects of a Realist Transcendentalism Today," *Crisis and Critique*, vol. 5, no. 1 (2018), 162–208; Adrian Johnston, "Meta-Transcendentalism and Error-First Ontology: The Cases of Gilbert Simondon and Catherine Malabou," in *New Realism and Contemporary Philosophy*, ed. Gregor Kroupa and Jure Simoniti (London: Bloomsbury, 2020), 145–178.
9. S. J. McGrath, *The Dark Ground of Spirit: Schelling and the Unconscious* (New York: Routledge, 2012), 94.
10. Judith E. Schlanger, *Schelling et la réalité finie: Essai sur la philosophie de la Nature et de l'Identité* (Paris: PUF, 1966), 113.
11. Frederick C. Beiser, *German Idealism: The Struggle Against Subjectivism, 1781–1801* (Cambridge: Harvard University Press, 2002), 466–467.
12. Ibid., 511.
13. Wolfram Hogrebe, *Prädikation und Genesis: Metaphysik als Fundamentalheuristik im Ausgang von Schellings "Die Weltalter"* (Frankfurt am Main: Suhrkamp, 1989), 127–128.
14. Michael Vater, "Schelling's philosophy of identity and Spinoza's *Ethica more geometrico*," *Spinoza and German Idealism*, ed. Eckart Förster and Yitzhak Y. Melamed (Cambridge: Cambridge University Press, 2012), 165.
15. Walter Schulz, *Die Vollendung des deutschen Idealismus in der spätphilosophie Schellings* (Stuttgart: Kohlhammer, 1955), 65.
16. F. W. J. Schelling, *Einleitung in die Philosophie*, ed. Walter E. Ehrhardt (Stuttgart-Bad Cannstatt: Frommann-Holzboog, 1989), 114.
17. F. W. J. Schelling, *Philosophy of Revelation: The 1841–42 Berlin Lectures, Philosophy of Revelation (1841–42) and Related Texts*, trans. Klaus Ottmann (New York: Spring, 2020), 242.
18. F. W. J. Schelling, *The Ages of the World (1811)*, trans. Joseph P. Lawrence (Albany, NY: SUNY, 2019), 158.
19. F. W. J. Schelling, "System of Philosophy in General and of the Philosophy of Nature in Particular," in *Idealism and the Endgame of Theory: Three Essays by F. W. J. Schelling*, trans. Thomas Pfau (Albany, NY: State University of New York Press, 1994), 179.
20. Ibid., 180–181.
21. F. W. J. Schelling, *Ausgewählte Schriften*, vol. 3, ed. Manfred Frank (Frankfurt am Main: Suhrkamp, 1985), 685.
22. Richards, *The Romantic Conception of Life*, 490.
23. F. W. J. Schelling, *Philosophical Investigations into the Essence of Human Freedom*, trans. Jeff Love and Johannes Schmidt (Albany, NY: SUNY, 2006), 23, 36–40.
24. Ibid., 55.
25. Ibid., 62)
26. F. W. J. Schelling, *Clara, or, On Nature's Connection to the Spirit World*, trans. Fiona Steinkamp (Albany: State University of New York Press, 2002), 26–27.
27. F. W. J. Schelling, "Stuttgart Seminars," in *Idealism and the Endgame of Theory*, 232.
28. Ibid., 240.
29. Schelling, *Philosophical Investigations*, 18, 34–35.
30. Schelling, *Philosophical Investigations*, 35.
31. Schelling, *Ausgewählte Schriften*, vol. 4, 403.

32. Schelling, *Philosophy of Revelation*, 60.
33. See Johnston, "Whither the Transcendental?," 162–208; Johnston, "Meta-Transcendentalism and Error-First Ontology," 145–178.
34. Schelling, *Ausgewählte Schriften*, vol. 4, 403.
35. McGrath, *The Dark Ground of Spirit*, 10, 106.
36. Schelling, *Ausgewählte Schriften*, vol. 4, 404–405.
37. See Johnston, "Whither the Transcendental?," 162–208; Johnston, "Meta-Transcendentalism and Error-First Ontology," 145–178.
38. Schelling, *Ausgewählte Schriften*, vol. 4, 403.
39. Ibid., 402–403.
40. F. W. J. Schelling, *The Ages of the World (1815)*, trans. Jason Wirth (Albany, NY: SUNY, 2000), 12, 60, 90.
41. McGrath, *The Dark Ground of Spirit*, 105.
42. Ibid., 143.
43. Xavier Tilliette, *Schelling, une philosophie en devenir*, vol. 1 (Paris: Vrin, 1992), 578.
44. Richards, *The Romantic Conception of Life*, 515.
45. See Beiser, *German Idealism*, 578.
46. Ibid., 506.
47. Ibid., 508–509.
48. Andrew Bowie, "Nature and Freedom in Schelling and Adorno," in *Interpreting Schelling: Critical Essays*, ed. Lara Ostaric (Cambridge: Cambridge University Press, 2014), 191.
49. See Adrian Johnston, *A New German Idealism: Hegel, Žižek, and Dialectical Materialism* (New York: Columbia University Press, 2018), 11–73, 129–186; Adrian Johnston, *Prolegomena to Any Future Materialism, Volume Two: A Weak Nature Alone*, (Evanston: Northwestern University Press, 2019), 15–69; Adrian Johnston, "The Difference Between Fichte's and Hegel's Systems of Philosophy: A Response to Robert Pippin," *Pli*, no. 31 (2019), 1–68.
50. John H. Zammito, *The Gestation of German Biology: Philosophy and Physiology from Stahl to Schelling* (Chicago: University of Chicago Press, 2018), 328–329.
51. Schulz, *Die Vollendung*, 299–300; Bernd-Olaf Küppers, *Natur als Organismus: Schellings frühe Naturphilosophie und ihre Bedeutung für die moderne Biologie* (Frankfurt am Main: Vittorio Klostermann, 1992), 48; Zammito, *The Gestation of German Biology*, 303; Patrick Cerutti, *La philosophie de Schelling: Repères* (Paris: Vrin, 2019), 102.
52. Schlanger, *Schelling et la réalité finie*, 31.
53. G. W. F. Hegel, "The Earliest System-Program of German Idealism," trans. H. S. Harris, in *Miscellaneous Writings of G. W. F. Hegel*, ed. Jon Stewart (Evanston: Northwestern University Press, 2002), 110–112.
54. Adrian Johnston, *Adventures in Transcendental Materialism: Dialogues with Contemporary Thinkers* (Edinburgh: Edinburgh University Press, 2014), 23, 309–312; Johnston, *A New German Idealism*, 13–14, 29, 61, 178; Johnston, *Prolegomena to Any Future Materialism, Volume Two*, 23–29, 68.
55. Rudolf Brandner, *Natur und Subjektivität: Zum Verständnis des Menschseins im Anschluß an Schellings Grundlegung der Naturphilosophie* (Würzburg: Königshausen & Neumann, 2002), 29.
56. Bowie, "Nature and Freedom," 182.
57. Adrian Johnston, "Cake or Doughnut?: Žižek and German Idealist Emergentisms," in *Žižek Responds!: Writing Back to my Critics*, ed. Dominik Finkelde and Todd McGowan (London: Bloomsbury, 2023), 27–51.
58. Baruch Spinoza, *Ethics*, in *Complete Works*, ed. Michael L. Morgan, trans. Samuel Shirley (Indianapolis: Hackett, 2002), 239, 235, 264, 272–5.
59. Ibid., 224–7, 232, 234, 238, 250.
60. Ibid., 217, 224, 227–9, 238–9.
61. Johnston, "Cake or Doughnut?," 27–51.
62. Schelling, *Ideas for a Philosophy of Nature*, 53.

63. Ibid.
64. Ibid.
65. Ibid.
66. Johnston, *Prolegomena to Any Future Materialism, Volume Two*, 39–42.
67. F. W. J. Schelling, *Ages of the World (second draft, 1813)*, trans. Judith Norman, in Slavoj Žižek and F. W. J. Schelling, *The Abyss of Freedom/Ages of the World* (Ann Arbor: University of Michigan Press, 1997), 113, 167.
68. Schelling, *Ausgewählte Schriften*, vol. 3, 275.
69. Richards, *The Romantic Conception of Life*, 518.
70. Johnston, "Cake or Doughnut?," 27–51.
71. Ibid.
72. F. W. J. Schelling, *Der Monotheismus*, in *Sämmtliche Werke*, Div. 2, ed. K. F. A. Schelling (Stuttgart and Augsburg: Cotta, 1857), 5.
73. Schlanger, *Schelling et la réalité finie*, 94.
74. Schelling, *Der Monotheismus*, 5.

Editors' Conclusions: The Past, Present, and Future of the Theory–German Idealism Relation

Tilottama Rajan and Daniel Whistler

1 The Past

When talking about the origins of contemporary theory, one cannot avoid Hegel: much theoretical work was born out of the legacy of his German system mediated via French philosophies of the 1930s and 1940s into Anglophone, and especially North American, Humanities departments.[1] As is well known Alexandre Kojève's lectures on Hegel's *Phenomenology of Spirit* in the 1930s were attended by Jean Hyppolite (who then translated the *Phenomenology* into French in 1939), as well as by Jacques Lacan, Maurice Merleau-Ponty, Georges Bataille, and perhaps Jean-Paul Sartre and Pierre Klossowski.[2] But despite Kojève's legendary status, just as important was Hyppolite (especially because of his position at the École Normale Supérieure),[3] and before him Jean Wahl, who made the unhappy consciousness a "pantragicist" figure for Hegel's thought as a whole.[4] Kojève's different focus on the master-slave relationship—which, after all, went on to inspire Francis Fukuyama[5]—was significant because it provided a blueprint for the complicating of binary oppositions and unleashed death, terror, and negation as intellectual potencies that would ferment and mutate in the environment that also produced Sartre's *Being and Nothingness*.[6] Together, the French Hegelians made the *Phenomenology of Spirit* the paradigmatic Hegelian text, displacing the *Logic*, *Philosophy of Right*, and *Philosophy of Mind* which had dominated the nineteenth-century French reception, as well as a nineteenth-century British reception that used Hegel to control the

T. Rajan (✉)
Centre for Theory and Criticism, University of Western Ontario, London, ON, Canada
e-mail: trajan@uwo.ca

D. Whistler
Department of Philosophy, Royal Holloway, University of London, London, UK
e-mail: daniel.whistler@rhul.ac.uk

© The Author(s), under exclusive license to Springer Nature Switzerland AG 2023
T. Rajan, D. Whistler (eds.), *The Palgrave Handbook of German Idealism and Poststructuralism*, Palgrave Handbooks in German Idealism,
https://doi.org/10.1007/978-3-031-27345-2_23

damage caused by Schelling, whose *Naturphilosophie* put the "I *am*" at risk from the "*It Is*."[7] These thinkers, including Kojève (despite his emphasis on the end of history), also opened a new path for thinking seemingly totalized systems and works as decentered and disturbed from within.

Nevertheless, theory could not but relate to Hegel ambivalently—a relation that was constituted out of two images of Hegel: the post-Kojèvean Hegel of death, difference, unrest and the splitting of consciousness, and the traditional panlogicist Hegel whose totalization of the system left no room for resistance. Thus, in an overlapping reception-history, Hegel began to be displaced and even replaced by a more concertedly radical nineteenth-century philosopher, Nietzsche: more radical insofar as it was the Nietzsche of *The Will to Power* and the death of God who gained traction, rather than the post-Idealist Nietzsche of *The Birth of Tragedy*. The shift from Hegel to Nietzsche is announced in the Introduction to the volume that came out of the Johns Hopkins conference that ushered "theory" into North America[8]; David Allison's 1977 *The New Nietzsche* is less polemical, but still decisive in making Anglophone audiences aware of a French Nietzsche with roots as deep and complex as the French Hegel.[9] As Hegel's star faded, he was once more reduced to a thinker of absolute knowledge, final syntheses, and totalized systems, which is to say that the theorist, under the figure of Nietzsche, was constructed as avant-garde, insurrectionist, and, above all, *anti-idealist*. Nietzsche as a conceptual persona for theory found support not only in Gilles Deleuze's *Nietzsche's Philosophy* (1962), compounded by the accident that his and Félix Guattari's *Anti-Oedipus* (1972) was translated as early as 1983, while the earlier *Difference and Repetition* (1968) and *Logic of Sense* (1969) were not translated until the early 1990s. It also found support in Klossowski's consolidation of a forty-year interest in Nietzsche in *Nietzsche and the Vicious Circle* (1969).[10] Though Klossowski remained untranslated for a long time, his mixture of theory and fiction, of Nietzsche, Sade, Marx, Freud, and Surrealism, was important for Michel Foucault, Deleuze (to whom he dedicated the book on Nietzsche), and Jean-François Lyotard.[11] It is this destructive amalgam of Nietzsche, Sade, Antonin Artaud, and Bataille (who had published a book on Nietzsche in 1945[12]) that Foucault evokes to herald the end of man in *The Order of Things*, and that he takes up in his literary essays in the 1960s on Klossowski, Maurice Blanchot, Bataille, the much earlier proto-anti-humanist writer Raymond Roussel, but also Hölderlin.[13] This was also the period in which theory was often translated in guerilla form in the Semiotext(e) "Foreign Agents" series of pamphlet-like octodecimo-size books.

It is in this context of a postmodernized poststructuralism that we witness a return to Kant that exceeds geographical boundaries,[14] but which also resonates with postwar reconstructionist German philosophies and Anglophone sympathies for pragmatism and analytic philosophy. Kant is a thinker of divisions and boundaries—whether between faculties or disciplines—which he crosses hypothetically but does not transgress. Kant therefore enters the dramaturgy of theory as a restraining force, whose cautionary status is exemplified, methodologically, by critique and, thematically, by the partial but not absolute (de)construction of metaphysics and the subject. While in North America itself the 1980s saw a sharp turn to history and culture and against theory in a philosophical sense,[15] for those who wanted to preserve the latter—for instance, Peter Dews in his 1987 *Logics of Disintegration*—Kant was a path back to a thinking that resists metaphysical totalizations without abandoning rationality, debate, and the subject.[16] Likewise, and also in Britain, Christopher Norris defends Derrida and de Man by aligning them with Kant, while describing Jean Baudrillard as "lost in the funhouse."[17] The opposition between the Nietzschean prolific and Kantian reason also informs Jürgen Habermas's advocacy for a more genuinely "critical" theory against poststructuralism's apocalyptic and avant-garde claims and its "levelling of the genre distinction between philosophy and literature."[18] This renewed Kantianism is not confined to the reception-history that to some extent has co-constituted and redirected "theory," given that the very term, according to Derrida, is a "purely American word and concept"[19]; it also resonates with a return to the Kant of "critique" in the 1980s—in the later work of Derrida, Foucault, to some extent Lyotard (and outside of poststructuralism narrowly conceived, Pierre Bourdieu[20]).

On the one hand, the above Kant-Hegel-Nietzsche triangle re-contains theory in criticism, taming if not denying the speculative. On the other hand, if one takes the far end of this sequence, theory's self-representation through Nietzsche locates its originality outside Idealism, just as, in his analyses of Hegel in the 1960s and 1970s, Derrida[21] (though working with the resources of the textual body) deconstructs it from a more dialectically enlightened outside.[22] However, in the last two decades the balances within this Kant-Hegel-Nietzsche series have shifted by means of a new Kant-Hegel-Schelling sequence in which Schelling has become the radical foil to Hegelian absolutism. It is not that Nietzsche disappears after the 1970s: after *Symbolic Exchange and Death* (1976), Baudrillard, for example, does not follow Lyotard's turn from Nietzsche to Kant in the 1980s.[23] In numerous texts, including *Seduction* (1978), *Fatal Strategies* (1983), *The Evil Demon of Images* (1984), and *The Transparency of Evil* (1990), a Nietzsche-Klossowski axis provides a nihilistic un(der)ground that pulls the cynicism of Baudrillard's end of history in simulation toward a dark implosion into the Real.[24] A more affirmative (if fraught) Nietzscheanism of the end of man has also persisted in such movements as accelerationism, transhumanism, and the fascination with viral networks and metabiotic technologies that take their inspiration from the molecular and nonhuman theories of individuation in Deleuze, especially read alongside the work of Gilles Simondon on individuation.[25] But the important thing for present purposes is that these theoretical strains have disengaged from anything before Nietzsche, thus evacuating an earlier architecture of reception and creating a clearing within which, as Derrida might say, new "possibilities of arrangement or assembling" can emerge to open up the Idealism–theory relation.[26]

For whereas theory under the regime of Nietzsche positioned itself outside Idealism, Schelling reinscribes the end(s) of Idealism within Idealism itself. The return to Schelling occurred after the heyday of poststructuralism,[27] though not without reference to it in the flagship collections that reintroduced him to contemporary philosophy: in *The New Schelling* (2004), whose title echoed the intervention made by *The New Nietzsche*, and in *Schelling Now* (2005).[28] Scholarship on

Schelling often depends on the ethos of theory,[29] whose interdisciplinarity has allowed for the reactivation of non-Hegelian and non-philosophical moments in Schelling's trajectory—particularly his *Naturphilosophie*—that have been seen as implicitly divergent from the progress of Hegelian reason. But this remains notably unstated even in work by thinkers with strong theoretical interests: for instance, in David Farrell Krell's *Contagion* (1999), which reads Novalis, Schelling, and Hegel through Derrida's (then) unpublished seminars on life/death, or his *The Tragic Absolute* (2005), which also reinserts Idealism into the broader context of Romanticism.[30]

What does this silence about theory, whether strategic or accidental, mean for Schelling or Idealism in general? Peter Dews hints at one answer, in already calling for a return to Schelling in the 1990s, as he questions the modernizing limitation of the linguistic turn to post-Nietzschean philosophy, or as Friedrich Kittler calls it, the discourse network of 1900.[31] Dews asks what "Schelling's *Weltalter* speculations explore," if *not* "forms of inconsistency and difference which are prior to the emergence of meaning, rationality, and logic." Accordingly, he sees the linguistic turn as an "idiom" that poststructuralism adopted, but as "mapping—and, in fact, as ultimately identical with—the fissures and diremptions of reality as a whole." That the text and a broader "general text" of reality, consciousness, or being are structurally homologous[32] allows for approaches to these areas that are broadly theoretical without the linguistic credentials of Schelling or Hegel having to be tested at every point. The very belatedness of the Schelling renaissance, in other words, allows for questions to be reintroduced into the reading of both Idealism and theory that were precluded by poststructuralism's ban on metaphysics, which became a bar Idealism could meet only as a precursor or parasite. The lifting of this bar allows a greater scope for what can be taken up as philosophy; and this has also proven true for Hegel: neglected areas of his corpus like the *Philosophy of Nature* or the anthropology section of the *Philosophy of Mind* can now take their place alongside privileged texts like the *Phenomenology* or *Logic*.[33] It may also allow for more engagement with the detailed scholarship of historians of philosophy from Stephen Houlgate onward (or earlier, H. S. Harris),[34] who have opened up the Hegelian system in all its complexity. In the wake of the Nietzschean and Kantian turns, Hegel did not entirely disappear into his caricature, the work of Žižek and Fredric Jameson (even before the 1990s) being counterexamples. But the above more detailed historical scholarship, even against the thrust of its own agendas, adds grain to Jameson's recognition that Hegel's work is "one long critique of premature immediacy… and unreflected unities."[35] Lastly, as a result, Idealism is allowed to speak as a protagonist rather than an antagonist of theory. It becomes a prism for refracting theoretical issues differently, as Krell does in *Contagion* by reversing the direction of the Derridean *pharmakon* of life/death, not to bore downward into unearthing the auto-immunity of Schelling's system but to make this auto-immunity the very basis for reconceiving the project of the absolute.

Finally, Kant can also be seen as gaining a more complex position in theory than previously thought. Recognizing this position is again part of the process seen above of approaching German Idealism from within competing strands inside that movement itself (and often inside the same corpus), and also of reopening traditionally closed-off and systematic philosophies through the detailed work of historical scholarship and heterodox and provocative readings which have become increasingly prominent. In his book on Kant—published a year after the book on Nietzsche—Deleuze invokes "a deeply Romantic Kant" by suggesting that if Kant regulates the borders between faculties by rotating us through different Critiques in which a *determinant* faculty (but always a different one) "impose[s] its rule on others," then "all together" the faculties are "capable of relationships which are free and unregulated."[36] This unbinding of the faculties (whether mental or disciplinary) opens the way for *reflective* relationships between them that allow philosophy to become (in Deleuze's later terms). From this perspective we can go back to Deleuze's own work (especially *Logic of Sense* and *Difference and Repetition*, but even the co-authored *A Thousand Plateaus*) and recognize it as Kantian just as much as Nietzschean. "Kant" reminds us that Deleuze's work is a logic; as Karl Jaspers says, Kant gives us the "forms" of thought, seeing forms as "superior to philosophical embodiment, because, if I think them through, they make me *produce my thought*."[37] Deleuze, then, radically transforms a logic and epistemology concerned with the forms of thought from the neo-Kantian use of epistemology to restrain Hegelian speculative ambitions, but remains Kantian in refusing any historical hypostasis to these new modes of thought, sensing, and practice.

Lyotard also provides a notable instance of the epigenesis of Kant, given that the sheer level of reference to Kant in his work is unparalleled. In moving from Nietzsche in the period of *Libidinal Economy* (1974) to numerous engagements with Kant from 1979 onward,[38] Lyotard did initially turn to the critical Kant, even as he sought, in the spirit of critique, to trace a fine balance between the cognitive and speculative in Kant himself (specifically in Kant's comments on the French Revolution). In this first phase of his Kantian turn (1979–1983), Lyotard was concerned with judgment, with antinomies and differends, and with divisions that could be transgressed by changing phrases only in regulated ways; this description also applies to Kant's presence throughout the analysis of the university in *The Postmodern Condition* and marks Lyotard's submission, during the period of the linguistic turn, to the ubiquity of "discourse" as a determining of thought that can be unsettled only microtactically. But, in his later work with Kant, Lyotard moves in increasingly experimental directions, as he develops the sublime outside of judgment, as a presencing of the unpresentable and of an immaterial, pre-thetic matter. Pursuing the sublime outside the framework of judgment and locating it in art and therefore creativity (which Kant does not do), Lyotard then also extends it back beyond art to rethink Kantian categories of time and space in essays such as "Can Thought Go On Without a Body?" in *The Inhuman*. From Lyotard's perspective these moves, beyond Kant's restraining of a speculative turn that he himself introduces, remain Kantian, insofar as Kant, for Lyotard, is a "sign of history" who can be thought beyond Kant himself.[39] In a sense this was Idealism's wager with Kant,[40] but renewed in a different intellectual milieu. This is to say that German Idealism in all its forms can inspire a more creative thinking "from" and beyond German Idealism itself. Such thinking, to return to the challenge that Dews in 1995 saw

Schelling as posing, "disrupt[s] any homogenizing conception" of Idealism and its "complicity in the exclusion of whatever currently figures as its 'Other.'"[41]

2 The Present

One of the more remarkable phenomena of the 2010s when it comes to the above history is the extent to which theory has turned against itself. Or, more precisely, it reinvented itself in an act of parricide: the "masters" of theory from the 1980s and 1990s were seemingly overthrown for the sake of the new. Hence, while in the Introduction at the beginning of this handbook we wagered that much could be gained from thinking about German Idealism's convergences with and divergences from "poststructuralism" understood in its broadest possible sense, including all "continental" theoretical projects since the 1960s (and we hope the volume itself is evidence that this approach works), when thinking about the present age of the theory-German Idealism relation, it is also worth reflecting on the recent fragmentation of theory to include competing and often hostile "post-poststructuralisms." That is, by disaggregating these different versions of "theory" it becomes possible to reflect on German Idealism's role in constituting, overcoming, or deconstructing various oppositions that have recently emerged within theory.

On 27 April 2007, Ray Brassier, Iain Hamilton Grant, Graham Harman, and Quentin Meillassoux (along with co-organizer, Alberto Toscano) met in a seminar room at Goldsmiths, University of London, to consign certain strands of theory to the past.[42] Or, such is *one story* that managed to gain great traction over the following few years and pass into folklore. The advent of "speculative realism" was taken as the fulfillment of a reversal of much of what theorists had traditionally held dear—a "speculative turn"[43] toward construction away from deconstruction, toward system-building away from textual commentary, and toward metaphysics as first philosophy away from the various turns to ethics, religion, and politics of the 1980s and 1990s. The "speculative realists" saw themselves as opposing a poststructuralist "renunciation of the absolute"[44] and "exacerbated return of the religious"[45]—as opposing, in Harman's words, the "ghetto of human discourse and language and power" in which philosophy had found itself "for the past two hundred and twenty years."[46] Instead, the tendency of the early 2010s was to reactivate a "philosophy in its own name" that did away with commentary, with play and with reading, in the name of a resurrection of thinking[47]—and a thinking, moreover, concerned with "the great outdoors,"[48] beyond the world's relation to humans and beyond subject–object relationality *tout court*. That is, underlying this break with traditional theory is a diagnosis of past thinking as over-obsessed with questions of access, of falling foul of what Meillassoux dubs "the correlation," the seemingly ineluctable axiom that "we cannot represent the 'in itself' without it becoming 'for us.'"[49] So, whether through a return to an early modern mathematicization of intuition (via Alain Badiou), a radicalization of phenomenology, the overthrow of epistemology, or the very death of thinking itself,[50] the various aims of this kind of movement were framed in terms of an overcoming of the various traps, false-moves, and, most generally, limitations in which previous thinking had been stuck. The narrative that emerged was a distinctively heroic one that envisaged the philosopher as an intrepid explorer able to free "himself" from the shackles of poststructuralist ideology and gain unfettered, quasi-Thoreauvian access to an intellectual wilderness.

The speculative-realist narrative was, of course, ultimately little more than a clever piece of marketing—its fictionality clear from its assertion that it marked a reversal, rather than an extension of many tendencies within poststructuralist theories themselves.[51] Nevertheless, whatever the truth of this story, the fact that "speculative realism" itself, as well as, more generally, "new materialisms"[52] and "continental realisms," proved so popular during the 2010s testifies to a perception among a younger generation of theorists of the datedness of many poststructuralist concerns that had seemed so radical only twenty years before. It was a theoretical moment experienced as *supersession*: whether deservedly or not, these movements capitalized on a feeling of the need to move on, to do something new, and to escape the continuous loop of deconstructive readings, *petits récits*, and acknowledgments of alterity. "Poststructuralism" was consigned to the past, notwithstanding the dangers of so consigning a set of theories that had spent so much time developing theories of "mourning," "haunting," and the "pure past."

The role of German Idealism in these debates has been particularly illuminating, for—among both the new realists and the old poststructuralists alike—there is a fundamental ambiguity toward this particular philosophical past. As seen time and time again in this volume, the poststructuralist relation to German Idealism has been a thorny one, heavily appropriating its most radical elements at the expense of what was held to be logocentric, identitarian, or static. The more recent post-poststructuralist responses to German Idealism in many ways repeat this ambivalence and is even more selective in what it explicitly appropriates from its intellectual ancestors. Continental "realisms" have been radically conflicted about German Idealism. On the one hand, all the new "realists" identify forms of German Idealism, especially Kant's, as the very problem to be overcome. Namely, the problem is Kant's classical affirmation of the correlation, in which "we only ever have access to the correlation between thinking and being" and "cannot represent the 'in itself' without it becoming 'for us.'"[53] Harman writes, for example,

> Kant is still the dominant philosopher of our time. Kant's shadow is over everyone, and many of the attempts to get beyond Kant don't get beyond Kant at all. … Obviously, we all think of Kant as a great philosopher. But that doesn't mean he's not a problem. It doesn't mean that Kant is the right inspiration for us, and in fact, I hold that the Kantian alternatives are now more or less exhausted.[54]

It is this Kantian and post-Kantian heritage with which the new realists attempt to break by ultimately returning to a philosophical past more primitive than the Kantian—that is, Kant, Hegel, and Schelling are sometimes bypassed by establishing a new genealogy from Descartes to Badiou.

On the other hand, there are tendencies in recent theory that remain grounded in a substantial appropriation of German Idealist concepts and arguments. That is, while Kantian German Idealism might often be understood as something to be surpassed, this is not always true of other philosophical moments in the German Idealist constellation. Most visibly, the "speculative turn" (however conceived) was in part premised on a return to Schelling and other philosophers of nature in the work of Iain Hamilton Grant. For Grant, "Schelling... takes the opposite direction to Kant,"[55] and this means his whole project of philosophizing from nature works "precisely against the consequences of the Kantian revolution" and initiates "the overthrow of the Copernican revolution."[56] As Grant puts it, "Schelling is not extending but undoing Kant," and hence "completely reinvents a transcendental philosophy."[57] And Schelling achieves this, according to Grant, by a reactivation of the concept of nature for contemporary thought—"the philosophical problem of nature... [as] a springboard for speculation."[58] As Grant sums up, "Schellingianism is resurgent every time philosophy reaches beyond the Kant-inspired critique of metaphysics, its subjectivist-epistemological transcendentalism, and its isolation of physics from metaphysics."[59]

On this basis, one might say: while poststructuralism shares with post-poststructuralist realisms a shared ambivalence toward German Idealism, one of the effects of the latter's break with poststructuralism is, broadly speaking, the separation out of two competing strands of German Idealism—*the critical* and *the speculative* (which are intended to correlate roughly to an "idealist" moment in German Idealism and a "realist" one). The classic evolutionary schema by which German Idealism is narrated—Kant, then Fichte, then Schelling, then Hegel—was thereby overturned and replaced by an agonistic schema, in which later German Idealisms are possibly saved only on condition of turning against their Kantian, "correlationist" origins. And in this complex triangulation of German Idealism, poststructuralism, and post-poststructuralism, poststructuralism was identified as ineradicably Kantian: for Grant, Kant "bequeathed a legacy that has found its ultimate legatee in the avatars of postmodernism."[60] It is the apogee (or, more precisely, nadir) of theoretical interest in subject–object relations and theoretical neglect of "the great outdoors" of speculation. Poststructuralism becomes *past* by being *critical*, a thinking-through of *the wrong strand of German Idealism*.

Grant is, however, not the only theorist working in the wake of a post-poststructuralist "turn" who attends once more to German Idealism. Even Meillassoux grounds his project in dialogue with Fichte, understanding Fichte's 1794 *Wissenschaftslehre* as "the chef-d'oeuvre of such a correlationism... the most rigorous expression of the correlationist challenge opposed to any realism."[61] Meillassoux, that is, begins his anti-correlationism only by means of an undoing of the seeming hegemony of an arch-correlationism inaugurated by Fichte, for whom "the *Science of Knowledge* destroys any attempt at realism by proving it is always and immediately self-contradictory in a pragmatic way."[62] More positively, a whole series of realist theorists making productive use of German Idealism can be identified, including those working on Hegel—a post Žižekian, post-Meillassouxian Hegel, in particular—such as Rebecca Comay, Claire Colebrook, Markus Gabriel, Adrian Johnston, and Frank Ruda[63]; those working on Schelling after Grant, such as Gabriel (again) and Ben Woodard[64]; or those retrieving other members of the

German Idealist constellation in a constructive mode, such as Eugene Thacker's uses of Schopenhauer,[65] or even Michael Burns' and Steven Shakespeare's speculative juxtaposing of Hegel and Schelling with a metaphysical Kierkegaard.[66]

In many ways, one of the trends emerging in this body of literature is a more conciliatory attitude to the tools and methods of traditional "theory" from a position beyond any "speculative turn." In other words, what is starting to emerge here is a contemporary synthesis of the poststructuralist and the post-poststructuralist. Rebecca Comay's and Frank Ruda's collaborations in *The Dash—The Other Side of Absolute Knowing* mark one highpoint of this "present moment," a synthesis of attention to textuality in its details and ambitious constructive philosophizing beyond the limits of the text. There is something here of the best parts of reading Derrida, Deleuze, Meillassoux, and Grant all brought together in an attempt to think the stakes of German Idealism anew. However, perhaps the most exemplary figure and paragon of this new synthetic, post-speculative landscape for theory is Catherine Malabou. Her concern to make use of her Derridean heritage to think the new constructively was already present in *The Future of Hegel* (1996). And what is most significant about her early work is precisely how baldly she states the continuing and unsettling relevance of German Idealism for theory, that is, in how she contests the idea that "we often, perhaps always, have lived, for many decades, in the reassuring certainty that the Hegelian legacy is over and done with."[67] And, even though her Hegel book was originally published in 1996, Malabou achieves the above in a way that speaks to many concerns that only came to the foreground in the Anglophone world in the 2010s (e.g., the insistence that "Hegelian philosophy assumes as an absolute fact the emergence of the random in the very bosom of necessity"[68]).

It is, though, Malabou's more recent work on Kant and the "relinquishing of the transcendental" in post-Meillassouxian realisms that speak most pertinently to the "present moment" of the theory–German Idealism relationship. Hence, on the one hand, more than anyone else, it is Malabou who has drawn attention to the anti-Kantianism of the "speculative turn"—the beginnings of "a farewell," "a break with Kant… in the works in contemporary continental philosophy."[69] Previously, she notes, theorists ("however violent their reading of Kant, however radical their critique of the transcendental") have ended up "always preserv[ing] or maintain[ing] something… calling it 'quasi transcendental,'"[70] and, to this extent, "the destruction or the critique of the transcendental has… only been a readjustment."[71] But she continues, focusing particularly on Meillassoux's claim "to relinquish the transcendental,"[72] what has happened since 2007 "is something way more radical than these destructive-deconstructive-critical re-elaborations. It is something much more abrupt, adamant, dangerous—the idea of an absolute abandonment of the transcendental."[73] Malabou is clear then that something of a break has occurred—and theory is now experiencing something new: "This is the first time that the authority of Kant—the guarantor, if not the founder, of the identity of continental philosophy— has been so clearly up for discussion, from within this same philosophical tradition."[74] Malabou's response, moreover, is to return to a transformative reading of Kant's Critiques themselves. She answers "the question of what to do with Kant,"[75] with a call to return to Kant's texts, to read him afresh, and to think through the implications of the critical project in daring, heterodox but compelling ways. She writes, "What I am saying is that *the relinquishing of Kant must be negotiated with him, not against him*... In Kant himself we find, at the heart of the *Critique*, the orchestration of an encounter between the transcendental and that which resists it."[76] Malabou aims to find "another logic of foundation"[77] *through* Kant, *through* his texts, and *through* attention to the textual and conceptual logics that propel his philosophy forward. What emerges is a new Kant, a Kant whose transcendental structures "grow, develop, transform and evolve,"[78] a Kant who is full of "life."

What this ultimately ends up demonstrating is that poststructuralism and its potential relationships with German Idealism are more complex than can be accounted for by any narrative of supersession. The "theory" that emerged in the 1960s can be seen as monolithically critical and negative, rather than speculative, only if it is limited to the linguistic turn and the paradigm of "representation" questioned by Deleuze and Lyotard. If representation binds thought to correlation, often negatively as that which is lacking, if it thus remains anthropocentric where the new realisms want to think "after life" (as Eugene Thacker puts it[79]), Foucault's speculations in *The Order of Things* on the end of man and Blanchot's *The Writing of the Disaster* are also part of poststructuralism and deconstruction. In "The Ends of Man" Derrida had already cautioned against thinking deconstruction in overly ruptural terms[80]; and similarly, the "post" of post-poststructuralism is not entirely (dis)continuous with poststructuralism. This is the point made by collections such as *Theory and the Disappearing Future, Telemorphosis: Theory in the Age of Climate Change*,[81] and work by Tom Cohen. At the cost of critiquing the "good" deconstruction of Derrida, Cohen has recently directed himself toward recovering "de Man," but not as the object of the monumental history pursued by earlier generations of de Man's sometimes hagiographic followers; rather, de Man is a "cipher," a "toxic asset"[82] whose spirit propels thinking in directions he himself could not have foreseen. As such de Man becomes a "plastic," rather than "linguistic signifier" (to evoke a distinction made by Lyotard in 1971 to describe a signifier or name that is "libidinal" rather than representational),[83] but also to evoke Malabou's more recent use of "plasticity" to suggest the epigenetic and future potential of earlier thinkers like Kant as their concepts are adapted to new milieus.

In a similar vein we hope that the present volume has interrogated the narrative of poststructuralism's supersession by furnishing a much richer conception of its relationship to German Idealism, as well as offering insights into how this relationship can be reactivated in the contemporary theoretical landscape. The chapters in this volume attempt this in at least three ways: (1) by showing that the story of German Idealism's persistence in the present is more complicated than is always admitted—thus, with reference to the speculative-realist challenge, Tom Moynihan's chapter traces a path from *Naturphilosophie* to speculative realism and discourses of extinction; (2) by showing the ways in which poststructuralism is an ally for many contemporary theoretical projects, despite the above story of its outmodedness—arguably a goal of the chapters by Kirill Chepurin and Lenka Vráblíková; and (3) by showing what resources poststructuralism—especially through conversations it catalyzes with German Idealism—can bring that supplement and/or resist the shape of the current theoretical landscape. Joel Faflak's chapter provides an example, again with reference to the speculative-realist challenge described above, as he concludes by imagining how Schopenhauer might think now, how his deconstruction of representation and his broader pessimism might be reactivated today to converge with the realities of extinction and thinking "after life."

3 The Future

Short of prophecy or futurology, there is evidently much less to say at present about the future of the theory–German Idealism relationship. This relationship (and the works that sustain it) could, of course, soon become irrelevant or outmoded in an even more radical manner than was promised by the speculative turn of fifteen years ago. However, this is not the only, or even the likeliest, scenario. The current volume suggests another outcome, as does the increasingly detailed work which is currently being done on connecting the two areas by reading Idealism and extending its margins in ways possible only after theory. For, as mentioned above, the Idealism-theory conjunction has increasingly established itself as a field in its own right, allowing not just for studies of influences or parallels, but also for more experimental synergies and feedback loops in which one field is read transversally across the other, and in which contemporary issues are mediated through the resources that both areas (which are, in turn, further remediated through the challenges and openings created by new realisms) can bring to bear. It is in this vein that we wish to end with some brief suggestions that emerge from this volume about how poststructuralism and German Idealism still matter to each other in 2023.

First, what unites many of the diverse approaches in this volume—and marks these essays as written in the wake of deconstruction and poststructuralism—is their emphasis on the words of philosophers, on the value of textual detail, and on reading as philosophical method. This is something that runs against the grain of both orthodox conceptions of German Idealism and post-poststructuralist realisms: these philosophies have tended to avoid understanding themselves in terms of reading practices and have instead envisioned a thinking emancipated from texts. Contemporary realists and German Idealists alike (at least as they were approached before "theory") try to move beyond words to concepts, beyond texts to systems, and beyond readers to thinkers. Among many examples, one might take, on the one hand, the non-discursive and almost apophatic nature of Schelling's very early method of intellectual intuition as philosophical organ[84] (a method he quickly complicates and surpasses, it should be emphasized); and, on the other hand, there is Meillassoux's book on Mallarmé, which is far more concerned with counting words than reading them.[85] On the contrary, many of the chapters in this volume tend to experience the philosophical past via the poststructuralist imperative: "Read better!" By this phrase we understand a range of practices from the intensive focus on language in the work of the early Derrida and Nancy exemplified in this volume by Kristina Mendicino's chapter on Hegel; to a broader reading of "works" (or entire systems) as "texts," which opens restricted into general economies (as undertaken in Tilottama Rajan's chapter); to, finally, tarrying with "the great indoors" of the philosophical tradition, rather than using it solely for the purpose of "abandoning" it, in Malabou's term (as set out in the previous section). This is the imperative that leads Daniela Voss to turn to Maimon or leads Oriane Petteni and Daniel Whistler to Goethe, among others. Reading as the epigenesis of the tradition was, after all, first theorized as an orientation to the future as well as a philological activity in Romanticism itself,[86] and constitutes the touchstone around which the futures of the poststructuralism–German Idealism relationship will keep on revolving. Moreover, it is in this moment when writing and reading are inter-implicated that the critical reader crosses over into the speculative thinker (and back again), in ways that make poststructuralism into more than just a negative philosophy.

Secondly, if the Idealism-poststructuralism intersection has become a field in its own right, one consequence is that this new area exceeds the contemporary disciplinary borders of philosophy and provides a warrant for more than just philosophers and historians to be interested in reconstructing and reusing German Idealisms. Theory calls for engagements with German Idealism beyond constraining disciplinary norms and practices, indeed beyond the discipline of "theory" itself. We must now recognize, for example, that work done on the history of biology in its intersections with Idealism,[87] even if it does not use theoretical language, unearths a past whose interstices harbor issues about "life" from which theory can think further. The above inter-discipline, in other words, can spark new work in other areas: fields such as art history and aesthetics are also due for a theoretical engagement with the historical record that is speculative as well as documentary and critical.[88] Thus a further consequence of constituting the Idealism-poststructuralism intersection as a field is to approach the past in terms of *densification*, rather than supersession; or to approach it by reading between figures in the general economy of Idealism so as to articulate what is yet to be said between them. Such interactions are one part of what can be encompassed under Derrida's term "New Humanities": a confrontation with philosophical material, or material that is philosophically thinkable, which exceeds the walls of the disciplines and methods through which it has traditionally been channeled.

Derrida uses the term "New Humanities" in an essay on the "unconditional" university,[89] a word that itself goes back to Schelling. Schelling's *On University Studies* wants to think knowledge "unconditionally" and sketches a virtual university without "conditions" (*Bedingungen*), which consists in an array of fields that he does not compose into a Kantian architectonic but projects through what Derrida will later call "Titles" and "Sendoffs."[90] If Derrida elsewhere criticizes this text for being transcendentally holistic, Schelling also uses the word "*unbedingt*" in his much more scientifically granular *First Outline* to introduce a radical and (transcendentally) *empirical* epistemology that leads fields of knowledge back to their unthought: "[E]very science that is *science* at all," Schelling writes, "has its unconditioned" which precedes its hypostasis as a discipline.[91]

The "New Humanities" provides an envelope for thinking the encyclopedic goals of German Idealism more nomadically, freed from any remaining suspicion of panlogicism. But this move from "royal" to "nomad" science[92] had already been made in Novalis's *Notes for a Romantic Encyclopedia*, considered as a limit-text in the German tradition.[93] As with Deleuze's notion that the rotating hegemony of Kant's different faculties allows for them to be unbound and enter into relationships that are free and unregulated, in Novalis' text disciplines and fields enter into what Derrida calls "transversal, horizontal, heterogeneous relations" that unsettle the "*univerticality*" of knowledge,[94] even allowing for the invention of new areas. So, to conclude, one should also point out that the above reflections push back against Derrida's own relatively conservative sense of the German University—even "its 'liberal variant'" at the University of Berlin[95]—as logocentric: a dismissal shared by other theorists such as Lyotard, who sees the German university as organized by a "metasubject" who "links the sciences together as moments in the becoming of spirit," or Bill Readings, for whom the German university has two stages: the Kantian university of "reason" and the post-Kantian university of "culture."[96] Our reflections here aim, by contrast, to open up the "university" of German philosophy to a more plural, fractious, and poststructuralist moment. The body of material that Idealism/Romanticism offers us to think from—especially in the extended form we sketch in the Introduction—makes possible a new institutional configuration, a new university, and a new ownership of philosophy beyond the philosophers.

Notes

1. It is worth recalling at this point that the current volume (and so the current set of conclusions) does not cover the relations of French feminism or Frankfurt School (and post-Frankfurt School) critical theory to German Idealism, as these are being treated in separate volumes. For current purposes, we also leave aside the thorny issue of the tacit interrelations that might hold between Italian theory and bio-philosophy and the German Idealist tradition.
2. Alexandre Kojève, *Introduction to the Reading of Hegel: Lectures on the Phenomenology of Spirit*, assembled by Raymond Queneau (1947), trans. James Nichols (Ithaca: Cornell University Press, 1969). A partial list of those who attended these lectures can be found in Michael Roth, *Knowing and History: Appropriations of Hegel in Twentieth-Century France* (Ithaca: Cornell University Press, 1988), 225–7.
3. Jean Hyppolite, *Genesis and Structure of Hegel's Phenomenology of Spirit* (1946), trans. Samuel Cherniak and John Heckman (Evanston: Northwestern University Press, 1974).
4. Jean Wahl, *Le Malheur de la conscience dans la philosophie de Hegel* (Paris: Presses Universitaires de France, 1929/1951). The resonances of this view can be seen in Paul Ricoeur's "Hegel and Husserl on Intersubjectivity," in *From Text to Action: Essays in Hermeneutics II* (1986), trans. Kathleen Blamey and John B. Thompson (Evanston: Northwestern University Press, 1991), 227–245.
5. Francis Fukuyama, *The End of History and the Last Man* (Harmondsworth: Penguin, 1992).
6. Jean-Paul Sartre, *Being and Nothingness: An Essay in Phenomenological Ontology* (1943), trans. Hazel E. Barnes (New York: Washington Square Press, 1993). For the mid-century French reception of Hegel, see Judith Butler, *Subjects of Desire: Hegelian Reflections in Twentieth-Century France* (New York: Columbia University Press, 1987); Roth, *Knowing and History*; Bruce Baugh, *French Hegel From Surrealism to Postmodernism* (New York: Routledge, 2003); Gary Gutting, "French Hegelianism and anti-Hegelianism in the 1960s: Hyppolite, Foucault, and Deleuze," in *The Impact of Idealism: The Legacy of Post-Kantian*

German Thought, vol. 1: *Philosophy and the Natural Sciences*, ed. Karl Ameriks (Cambridge: Cambridge University Press, 2013), 246–271. Both Baugh (*French Hegel*, 1–7) and Gutting ("French Hegelianism," 247) take the view that Kojeve's importance has been exaggerated.
7. These are the terms S. T. Coleridge uses to explain his turn away from Schelling, as he found Schelling's *Naturphilosophie* exceeding its promised containment within transcendental philosophy (*Collected Letters*, ed. E.L. Griggs, 6 vols. [Oxford: Clarendon, 1956–1971], 4.874). On the nineteenth-century French reception of Hegel, see Kirill Chepurin et al. (eds), *Hegel and Schelling in Early Nineteenth-Century France* (Dordrecht: Springer, forthcoming 2023).
8. Richard Macksey and Eugenio Donato (eds.), *The Structuralist Controversy: The Languages of Criticism and the Sciences of Man* (Baltimore: Johns Hopkins University Press, 1971), x–xiii.
9. David B. Allison (ed.), *The New Nietzsche: Contemporary Styles of Interpretation* (New York: Dell Publishing, 1977). At a time when little French theory had been translated into English—Derrida's *Speech and Phenomena* and *Of Grammatology* and no major work by Deleuze—Allison's collection included essays by Alphonso Lingis, Deleuze, Klossowski, Maurice Blanchot, and Derrida, as well as Martin Heidegger, Eric Blondel, and Sarah Kofman.
10. Pierre Klossowski, *Nietzsche and the Vicious Circle* (1969), trans. Daniel W. Smith (Chicago: University of Chicago Press, 1997).
11. Michel Foucault, "The Prose of Actaeon" (1964), trans. Robert Hurley, in Foucault, *Aesthetics, Method, and Epistemology*, ed. James D. Faubion (New York: New Press, 1998), 123–35; Gilles Deleuze, *Logic of Sense* (1969), trans. Charles Stivale and Constantin Boundas (New York: Columbia University Press, 1990), 280–301; Jean-François Lyotard, *Libidinal Economy* (1974), trans. Iain Hamilton Grant (Bloomington: Indiana University Press, 1993), 67–84.
12. Georges Bataille, *On Nietzsche* (1945), trans. Bruce Boone (St. Paul, MN: Paragon House, 1992).
13. Michel Foucault, *The Order of Things: An Archaeology of the Human Sciences* (1966), n. trans. (New York: Vintage, 1970), 327; Foucault, *Language, Counter-Memory, Practice: Selected Essays and Interviews*, trans. Donald F. Bouchard and Sherry Simon (Ithaca: Cornell University Press, 1977); *Death and the Labyrinth: The World of Raymond Roussel* (1963), trans. Charles Ruas (Berkeley: University of California Press, 1984).
14. See, for example, Luc Ferry and Alain Renaut, *French Philosophy of the Sixties: An Essay on Antihumanism*, trans. Mary H. Cattani (Amherst: University of Massachusetts Press, 1990). See also François Cusset, *French Theory: How Foucault, Derrida, Deleuze & Co., Transformed the Intellectual Life of the United States*, trans. Jeff Fort (Minneapolis: University of Minnesota Press, 2008), 316.
15. See Frank Lentricchia, *After the New Criticism* (Chicago: University of Chicago Press, 1980), especially Chapter 5 ("History or the Abyss: Post-structuralism") and Chapter 8 ("Paul de Man: The Rhetoric of Authority"); John Guillory, *Cultural Capital: The Problem of Literary Canon Formation* (Chicago: University of Chicago Press, 1993), especially Chapter 4 on de Man.
16. Peter Dews, *Logics of Disintegration: Post-structuralist Thought and the Claims of Critical Theory* (London: Verso, 1987), xi–xvii.
17. Christopher Norris, *What's Wrong with Postmodernism: Critical Theory and the Ends of Philosophy* (Baltimore: Johns Hopkins University Press); see especially Chapter 5 on "Kant and Derrida" and the preceding one on Baudrillard, "Lost in the Funhouse." Norris also devotes much of the "Introduction" to positioning Paul de Man, whose *Allegories of Reading: Figural Language in Rousseau, Nietzsche, Rilke and Proust* (New Haven: Yale University Press, 1979) has three chapters on Nietzsche as a thinker of critique. De Man, according to Norris, resists a "Romantic" misappropriation of Kant that risks leading to Hegel in favor of a "vigilant awareness of the dangers" of not "respect[ing] the powers and limits of the various faculties (19–21).
18. Jürgen Habermas, *The Philosophical Discourse of Modernity: Twelve Lectures* (1985), trans. Frederick Lawrence (Cambridge, Mass.: MIT Press, 1987), 185. Habermas is not uncritical of

Kant, wanting to go in a more intersubjective direction; but his emphasis on the public sphere and on modernity as rationality is aligned with a broadly Kantian-Hegelian axis, against the kind of thinking that follows in the wake of Nietzsche (i.e., Heidegger, Bataille, Derrida).
19. Jacques Derrida, "Deconstructions: The Im-possible," in *French Theory in America*, ed. Sylvère Lotringer and Sande Cohen (New York: Routledge, 2001), 16.
20. Pierre Bourdieu, *Distinction: A Social Critique of the Judgment of Taste* (1979), trans. Richard Nice (Cambridge: Harvard University Press, 1984). Bourdieu is in dialogue with Kant at many other points, but, whatever their differences in terms of Bourdieu not subscribing to the universalism of the Enlightenment, Bourdieu's project is broadly speaking one of practical reason.
21. Many of the essays in *Margins of Philosophy* (trans. Alan Bass [Chicago: University of Chicago Press, 1972]) are on, or include, Hegel. In particular, "The Ends of Man" (1968) moves through a long Idealist tradition (Hegel–Husserl–Heidegger), but culminates in Nietzsche and is framed throughout by a Nietzschean rhetoric of thresholds, change, and rebirth.
22. This is Paul de Man's criticism of Derrida's reading of Rousseau, in *Blindness and Insight: Essays in the Rhetoric of Contemporary Criticism* (New York: Oxford University Press, 1971). One can later make the same criticism of de Man himself, but at this stage literature for him is its own deconstruction and begins "on the far side of this knowledge" (ibid., 17). Hence one cannot bracket the "question of the author's knowledge of his own ambivalence" (ibid., 119), as it is not the text that needs to be deconstructed but the first commentaries on it (ibid., 139–141).
23. Jean Baudrillard, *Symbolic Exchange and Death* (1976), trans. Iain Hamilton Grant (London: Sage, 1993); *Forget Foucault* (1977), trans. H. Beitchmann and M. Polizotti (New York: Semiotext(e), 1987); *The Ecstasy of Communication* (1987), trans. B. and C. Schutze (New York: Semiotext(e), 1988), 97. For Nietzsche's influence, see *Fragments: Conversations with François L'Yvonnet* (2001), trans. Chris Turner (London: Routledge, 2004), 1–6, 22, 40.
24. Jean Baudrillard, *Seduction* (1979), trans. Brian Singer (New York: St. Martin's Press, 1990); *Fatal Strategies* (1983), trans. Philip Beitchman and W.G.J. Niesluchowski (New York: Semiotext(e), 1990); *The Evil Demon of Images* (Sydney: Power Institute, 1987); *The Transparency of Evil: Essays on Extreme Phenomena* (1990), trans. James Benedict (London: Verso, 1993).
25. See, for example, Keith Ansell Pearson, *Viroid Life: Perspectives on Nietzsche and the Transhuman Condition* (London: Routledge, 1997); *Germinal Life: The Difference and Repetition of Deleuze* (London: Routledge, 1999). For Gilles Simondon, see *Individuation in Light of Notions of Form and Information* (2005), trans. Taylor Adkins (Minneapolis: University of Minnesota Press, 2020). Parts of this work had appeared between 1964 and 1989.
26. Jacques Derrida, *Points ... Interviews 1974–1994*, ed. Elisabeth Weber, trans. Peggy Kamuf et al. (Stanford: Stanford University Press, 1995), 212.
27. That is, from the mid- to late 1990s onward, the expansion of the corpus of poststructuralism and, more broadly, theory has been largely due to the belated recovery of numerous further theorists and texts beyond the canonical ones introduced in the 1970s and 1980s.
28. Judith Norman and Alistair Welchman (eds.), *The New Schelling* (London: Continuum, 2004), and Jason M. Wirth (ed.) *Schelling Now* (Bloomington: Indiana University Press, 2005). The first collection contained essays by Iain Hamilton Grant, Alberto Toscano, Žižek, Habermas, and Manfred Frank (on Schelling and Sartre); the second included essays by Žižek, Martin Wallen (on Schelling and Deleuze), David Farrell Krell, and a section on Schelling and contemporary philosophy that takes up Emmanuel Levinas and Nancy, as well as Heidegger.
29. See the essays in Tilottama Rajan and Sean McGrath (eds.), *Schelling After Theory*, special issue of *Symposium: Canadian Journal of Continental Philosophy* 19:1 (2015), 1–197.
30. David Farrell Krell, *Contagion: Sexuality, Disease, and Death in German Idealism and Romanticism* (Bloomington: Indiana University Press, 1998); *The Tragic Absolute: German Idealism and the Languishing of God* (Bloomington: Indiana University Press, 2005). In connection with Krell's *Contagion*, see Jacques Derrida, *Life Death*, ed. Pascale-Anne Brault and

Peggy Kamuf, trans. Pascale Anne-Brault and Michael Nass (Chicago: University of Chicago Press, 2020).
31. Friedrich Kittler, *Discourse Networks 1800/1900* (1985), trans. David Wellbery (Stanford: Stanford University Press, 1990). Kittler proposes two discourse networks *(Aufschreibesysteme)*: the logocentric one of 1800 figured by the hand and voice, and one of 1900, figured by the prosthesis of the typewriter as a figure for writing and introduced by Nietzsche's trauma over technology.
32. Peter Dews, *The Limits of Disenchantment: Essays on Contemporary European Philosophy* (London: Verso, 1995), 139–143.
33. The influence of Werner Hamacher's readings of Hegel (as well as Friedrich Schlegel) cannot be overestimated here; see *Pleroma—Reading in Hegel*, trans. Nicholas Walker and Simon Jarvis (Stanford: Stanford University Press, 1998); *Premises: Essays on Philosophy from Kant to Celan*, trans. Peter Fenves (Cambridge, MA: Harvard University Press, 1997). On the anthropology (or specifically madness), see, for example, Daniel Berthold-Bond, *Hegel's Theory of Madness* (Albany: SUNY Press, 1995); Kirill Chepurin, "Subjectivity, Madness, and Habit: Forms of Resistance in Hegel's Anthropology," in *Hegel and Resistance: History, Politics and Dialectics*, ed. Bart Zantvoort and Rebecca Comay (London: Bloomsbury, 2018), 101–16; On the *Philosophy of Nature* (including medicine), see Tilottama Rajan, "(In)digestible Material: Illness and Dialectic in Hegel's *Philosophy of Nature*," in *Cultures of Taste/ Theories of Appetite: Eating Romanticism*, ed. Timothy Morton (Basingstoke: Palgrave Macmillan, 2004), 217–236 and "Hegel's Irritability," *European Romantic Review* 32: 5–6 (2021), 499–517; Wesley Furlotte, *The Problem of Nature in Hegel's Final System* (Edinburgh: Edinburgh University Press, 2018).
34. E.g., Stephen Houlgate, *An Introduction to Hegel: Freedom, Truth, and History* (Oxford: Blackwell, 2005); H.S. Harris, *Night Thoughts (1801–1806)* (Oxford: Oxford University Press, 1983).
35. Fredric Jameson, *The Political Unconscious: Narrative as a Socially Symbolic Act* (Ithaca: Cornell University Press, 1981), 26. Despite unusual and illuminating comments on the *Aesthetics*, for example, Jameson himself does not discuss anything but the *Phenomenology* in detail.
36. Gilles Deleuze, *Kant's Critical Philosophy: The Doctrine of the Faculties* (1963), trans. Hugh Tomlinson and Barbara Habberjam (Minneapolis: University of Minnesota Press, 1990), xi–xiii.
37. Karl Jaspers, *Kant*, trans. Ralph Manheim (New York: Harcourt, 1957), 45–46; our emphasis.
38. In order of publication Lyotard's significant engagements with Kant are in: "The Sign of History" (1982), in *The Lyotard Reader*, ed. Andrew Benjamin (Oxford: Blackwell, 1989), 393–411; *The Differend: Phrases in Dispute* (1983), trans. Georges Van den Abbeele (Minneapolis: University of Minnesota Press, 1988), which takes up Kant at many points but also folds in a version of "The Sign of History" (151–181); "Judicieux dan le Différend," in Jacques Derrida, Vincent Descombes et al., *La Faculté de Juger* (Paris: Les Editions de Minuit, 1985), 195–236; *Enthusiasm: The Kantian Critique of History* (1986), trans. Georges Van Den Abbeele (Stanford: Stanford University Press, 1991); "Sensus Communis" (1986), *Paragraph* 11:1 (1988), 1–23; "The Interest of the Sublime" (1988), in *Of the Sublime: Presence in Question*, trans. Jeffrey S. Librett (Albany: SUNY Press, 1993), 109–132; *Lessons on the Analytic of the Sublime* (1991), trans. Elizabeth Rottenberg (Stanford: Stanford University Press, 1994); and several essays taking up the sublime in *The Inhuman: Reflections on Time* (1988), trans. Geoffrey Bennington and Rachel Bowlby (Stanford: Stanford University Press, 1991). Mentions of Kant are also to be found throughout Lyotard and Jean-Loup Thébaud, *Just Gaming* (1979), trans. Wlad Godzich (Minneapolis: University of Minnesota Press, 1984); and *The Postmodern Condition: A Report on Knowledge* (1979) is guided by the Kantian motif of the contest of faculties (trans. Geoff Bennington and Brian Massumi [Minneapolis: University of Minnesota Press, 1984]).
39. Lyotard, *The Differend*, 161–171.

40. Thus, Coleridge, following a Romantic tradition of "understanding the author better than he understood himself," comments on "The Letter vs. the Spirit of Kant": "I could never believe, it was possible for him to have meant no more by his Noumenon,... than his mere words express" (*Biographia Literaria or Biographical Sketches of my Literary Life and Opinions* [1817], ed. James Engell and Walter Jackson Bate [Princeton: Princeton University Press, 1983], 155).
41. Dews, *Logics of Disenchantment*, 143.
42. A transcript of the workshop appears in Ray Brassier et al., "Speculative Realism," *Collapse* vol. 3 (2012), 307–450.
43. See Levi Bryant et al., *The Speculative Turn: Continental Realism and Materialism* (Melbourne: Re Press, 2011); see further, for example, Lee Braver, "A Brief History of Continental Realism," in *Continental Philosophy Review* vol. 45 (2012), 261–89.
44. Quentin Meillassoux, *After Finitude: An Essay on the Necessity of Contingency* (2006), trans. Ray Brassier (London: Continuum, 2009), 42.
45. Ibid., 45. It is these two properties that lead to Meillassoux's diagnosis of late twentieth-century European philosophy as "fideist."
46. Graham Harman in Brassier et al., "Speculative Realism," 381.
47. See, particularly, Alberto Toscano's contributions to Brassier et al., "Speculative Realism," *passim*.
48. Meillassoux, *After Finitude*, 7. The full quote gives a sense of the topological imaginary at stake in this project: "Contemporary philosophers have lost the *great outdoors*, the *absolute* outside of pre-critical thinkers: that outside which was not relative to us … that outside which thought could explore with the legitimate feeling of being on foreign territory—of being entirely elsewhere" (ibid.).
49. Ibid., 4–5. Meillassoux defines the correlation as follows, "By 'correlation' we mean the idea according to which we only ever have access to the correlation between thinking and being, and never to either term considered apart from the other" (ibid., 5).
50. These four options very crudely correspond to the projects outlined by, respectively, Meillassoux, Harman, Grant, and Brassier.
51. The "turn" imagery persists even when much of this trend is under scrutiny (particularly for its awkward relation to gender); see Katerina Kolozova and Eileen Joy (eds), *After the "Speculative Turn": Realism, Philosophy and Feminism* (New York: Punctum, 2016).
52. See, canonically, Jane Bennett, *Vibrant Matter: A Political Ecology of Things* (Durham, NC: Duke University Press, 2010).
53. Meillassoux, *After Finitude*, 4–5.
54. Harman in Brassier et al., "Speculative Realism," 368.
55. Iain Hamilton Grant, "The Chemistry of Darkness." *Pli* vol. 9 (2000), 45. Grant had previously translated Baudrillard's *Symbolic Exchange and Death* and Lyotard's *Libidinal Economy* as part of the "Nietzschean moment" in theory narrated above. However, the relation of these earlier forays into theory to his work on Schelling and, indeed, the extent to which these earlier translations or, for that matter, this brief "speculative realist" alliance matter for understanding the trajectory of Grant's thinking is not yet clear.
56. Iain Hamilton Grant, *Philosophies of Nature after Schelling* (London: Continuum, 2006), 3, 6.
57. Ibid., 61, 158.
58. Iain Hamilton Grant, "Schellingianism and Postmodernity: Towards a Materialist *Naturphilosophie*," available at: www.bu.edu/wcp/papers/cult/cultgran.htm. Grant concludes elsewhere, "The enemy in all of this is *all* post-Cartesian European philosophy's elimination of the concept, even the existence, of nature, a deficiency common equally to Kant and the postkantians" (*Philosophies of Nature*, x).
59. Grant, *Philosophies of Nature*, 5.
60. Grant, "Schellingianism and Postmodernity."
61. Quentin Meillassoux in Brassier et al., "Speculative Realism," 409–10.

62. Ibid., 412. Meillassoux continues, "To be a contemporary realist means, in my view, to efficiently challenge the Fichtean fatality of pragmatic contradiction; not exactly to challenge the very thesis of the *Science of Knowledge*, but the mode of refutation which is therein invented" (ibid., 413).
63. As well as the contributors included in this volume, see Rebecca Comay, *Mourning Sickness: Hegel and the French Revolution* (Stanford: Stanford University Press, 2010); Rebecca Comay and Frank Ruda, *The Dash—The Other Side of Absolute Knowing* (Cambridge, MA: MIT Press, 2018); Markus Gabriel, *Fields of Sense: A New Realist Ontology* (Edinburgh: Edinburgh University Press, 2015); Markus Gabriel, *Transcendental Ontology: Essays in German Idealism* (London: Bloomsbury, 2011); Frank Ruda, *Hegel's Rabble: An Investigation into Hegel's Philosophy of Right* (London: Bloomsbury, 2011).
64. In addition to the previous note, see Markus Gabriel and Slavoj Žižek, *Mythology, Madness and Laughter: Subjectivity in German Idealism* (London: Continuum, 2009); Ben Woodard, *On an Ungrounded Earth: Towards a New Geophilosophy* (New York: Punctum, 2012); *Schelling's Naturalism: Motion, Space and the Volition of Thought* (Edinburgh: Edinburgh University Press, 2019).
65. For example, his introduction to Arthur Schopenhauer, *On the Suffering of The World*, ed. Eugene Thacker (New York: Repeater, 2020).
66. Michael C. Burns, *Kierkegaard and the Matter of Philosophy: A Fractured Dialectic* (London: Rowman and Littlefield, 2015); Steven Shakespeare, *Kierkegaard and the Refusal of Transcendence* (Basingstoke: Palgrave Macmillan, 2015).
67. Catherine Malabou, *The Future of Hegel: Plasticity, Temporality and Dialectic* (1996) (London: Routledge, 2005), xviii.
68. Ibid., 163.
69. Catherine Malabou, *Before Tomorrow: Epigenesis and Rationality* (2014), trans. Carolyn Shread (Cambridge: Policy, 2015), xiii.
70. Catherine Malabou, "Can We Relinquish the Transcendental?," in *The Journal of Speculative Philosophy* vol. 28, no. 3 (2014), 245–6.
71. Ibid., 246.
72. Meillassoux, *After Finitude*, 27.
73. Malabou, "Relinquish the Transcendental," 246. Meillassoux's word is actually "*abandon*" (ibid., 243)
74. Malabou, *Before Tomorrow*, 2.
75. Ibid., 3.
76. Ibid., 15.
77. Ibid., 19.
78. Ibid., xiv.
79. Eugene Thacker, *After Life* (Chicago: University of Chicago Press, 2010).
80. Jacques Derrida, "The Ends of Man" (1968), in *Margins of Philosophy*, 134–136.
81. Tom Cohen, Claire Colebrook and J. Hillis Miller, *Theory and the Disappearing Future: On de Man, On Benjamin* (New York: Routledge, 2012); Tom Cohen, *Telemorphosis: Theory in the Era of Climate Change, Vol. 1* (Ann Arbor: Open Humanities Press, 2012).
82. Tom Cohen, "Interview," 5 November, http://noise-admiration.blogspot.ca/2012/11/the-interview-22012-tom- (last accessed: 2 July 2016); Cohen, "Toxic Assets: de Man's Remains and the Ecocatastrophic Imaginary (An American Fable)," in *Theory and the Disappearing Future*, 107.
83. Jean-Francois Lyotard, *Discourse, Figure* (1971), trans. Antony Hudek and Mary Lydon (Minneapolis: University of Minnesota Press, 2011), 4, 7, 15, 71.
84. According to the Schelling of 1795, intellectual intuition is beyond words, concepts, philosophical articulation, or any form of determination whatsoever. See F. W. J. Schelling, *The Unconditional in Human Knowledge: Four Early Essays*, ed. and trans. Fritz Marti. (Lewisburg: Bucknell University Press, 1980), 78, 85, 110.
85. Quentin Meillassoux, *The Number and the Siren: A Decipherment of Mallarmé's Coup de dès*, trans. Robin Mackay (Falmouth: Urbanomic, 2012). The title alone testifies to the above point: Meillassoux eschews the more obvious "reading [*lecture*]", in favor of "*déchiffrage*."

86. See, for example, Friedrich Schlegel's notion of "progressive universal poetry" (*Athenaeum Fragments* [1798], in *Philosophical Fragments*, trans. Peter Firchow [Minneapolis: University of Minnesota Press, 1991], 31–32); or Friedrich Schleiermacher's concept, possibly influenced by Schlegel, of understanding an author better than he understands himself through a "divinatory" reading ("The Hermeneutics: The Outline of the 1819 Lectures," trans. Jan Wocjik and Roland Haas, *New Literary History* vol. 10 [1978], 9).

87. We refer to a tradition that runs from Georges Canguilhem (obviously a direct influence on Foucault and Derrida) to several non-theoretical studies that take up Kant, Schelling, and a range of work in the life sciences that is in dialogue with them. See Canguilhem, *Knowledge of Life* (1965), trans. Stefanos Geroulanos and Daniela Ginsburg (New York: Fordham University Press, 2008); see also, among many others, Timothy Lenoir, *The Strategy of Life: Teleology and Mechanics in Nineteenth-Century German Biology* (Dordrecht: Reidel, 1982); Robert Richards, *The Romantic Conception of Life: Science and Philosophy in the Age of Goethe* (Chicago: University of Chicago Press, 2002); Philippe Huneman (ed.), *Understanding Purpose: Kant and the Philosophy of Biology* (Rochester: University of Rochester Press, 2007); and John Zammito, *The Gestation of German Biology: Philosophy and Physiology from Stahl to Schelling* (Chicago: University of Chicago Press, 2018).

88. Two studies that have begun to move in this direction in taking up the Kantian and Hegelian inheritance in art history are Mark Cheetham, *Kant, Art, and Art History: Moments of Discipline* (Cambridge: Cambridge University Press, 2001), and Margaret Iversen and Stephen Melville, *Writing Art History: Disciplinary Departures* (Chicago: University of Chicago Press, 2010).

89. Jacques Derrida, "The University Without Condition" (1998) in *Without Alibi*, ed. and trans. Peggy Kamuf (Stanford: Stanford University Press, 2002), 202–9.

90. F. W. J. Schelling, *On University Studies* (1803), trans. E. S. Morgan (Athens: Ohio University Press, 1966), 9, 12, 17. "Titles" and "Sendoffs" are two of the papers written in 1982 for meetings held in connection with GREPH (Groupe de Recherches sur l'Enseignement Philosophique) and included in Derrida's two-volume *Right to Philosophy* (1990). See *Eyes of the University: Right to Philosophy 2*, trans. Jan Plug et al. (Stanford: Stanford University Press, 2004), 195–249. The idea of a university without condition alludes back to the more concrete suggestions made in these papers, which in effect propose an empirically informed transcendental program for the dissemination of philosophy.

91. Jacques Derrida, "Theology of Translation," in *Eyes*, 64–80; F. W. J. Schelling, *First Outline of a System of the Philosophy of Nature*, trans. Keith R. Peterson (Albany: SUNY Press, 2004), 13.

92. Gilles Deleuze and Félix Guattari, *A Thousand Plateaus: Capitalism and Schizophrenia* (1980), trans. Brian Massumi (Minneapolis: University of Minnesota Press, 1987), 367–74.

93. Novalis, *Notes for a Romantic Encyclopedia: das Allgemeine Brouillon* (1798), trans. and ed. David W. Wood (Albany: SUNY Press, 2007). See the chapter by Tilottama Rajan in this volume for elaboration.

94. Derrida, *Eyes of the University*, 213.

95. Ibid., 224.

96. Lyotard, *The Postmodern Condition*, 32–7; Bill Readings, *The University in Ruins* (Cambridge: Harvard University Press, 1996), 54–69.

Correction to: Reading Novalis and the Schlegels

Kirill Chepurin

Correction to:

Chapter 4 in: T. Rajan, D. Whistler (eds.), *The Palgrave Handbook of German Idealism and Poststructuralism*, **Palgrave Handbooks in German Idealism, https://doi.org/10.1007/978-3-031-27345-2_4**

The book was inadvertently published with incorrect affiliation details of the author, Kirill Chepurin, in Chapter 4. This has been updated in the book.

The updated original version for this chapter can be found at
https://doi.org/10.1007/978-3-031-27345-2_4

© The Author(s), under exclusive license to Springer Nature
Switzerland AG 2023
T. Rajan, D. Whistler (eds.), *The Palgrave Handbook of German Idealism and Poststructuralism*, Palgrave Handbooks in German Idealism,
https://doi.org/10.1007/978-3-031-27345-2_24

Index

A
Abjection, xvii, 88, 249
Abraham, Nicholas, 175
Absolute, the
   absolute idealism, 191, 205, 216, 219, 292, 476, 485
   absolute knowledge, knowing, xxi, 132–133, 142n39, 172, 189, 197, 203, 219, 336, 350, 357, 372, 376, 381n37, 430, 432–434, 436, 437, 439, 440, 442, 460, 484, 490
   absolute subject, 74, 203, 217, 222, 223, 235n86, 356
   future absolute, 68
Accelerationism, 491
Adorno, Theodor, xiii, xvii, xxviiin43, 85, 104, 105n5, 112, 120n22, 178, 373, 379n13, 391
Aesthetics, xxii, 4, 5, 14, 15, 85, 86, 90, 110, 114, 170, 171, 180n23, 188, 189, 191, 199–201, 203, 215, 224, 225, 240, 241, 243–246, 248, 249, 251, 253, 254, 296, 333, 429, 500
Affect, 49, 77, 107, 113, 168, 179, 182n49, 182n52, 196, 217, 229–231, 281, 461, 465
Afrofuturism, 73–75, 79
Agamben, Giorgio, xvi, 85, 86, 95, 103, 104, 105n5, 106n24, 111, 119n21
Agassiz, Louis, 273, 274

Aggregate, 42, 63, 187–189, 191, 194, 195, 200, 205, 221, 228, 230
Alienation, 61, 67, 73, 74, 76, 78, 165, 177, 455, 456
Allison, David, 490, 502n9
Alterity, 11, 48, 102, 112, 121n42, 155, 328, 337, 338, 432, 434, 449, 451, 474, 495
Althusser, Louis, xx, 125–134, 136, 139, 140n16, 141n23, 291
Alvarez, Walter, 284, 286
Ancestrality, 177, 178, 261, 266
Angermuller, Johannes, xxviin31
Animal, 5, 12, 13, 177, 194, 196–200, 217, 218, 220, 250, 262–264, 266, 267, 273–275, 279, 282, 283, 285, 296, 393, 450, 455, 460
Animal magnetism, 217–219
Anstoss, 31
Anthropocene, the, 61, 231, 260, 398n64
Anthropology, xxviin17, 6, 23n206, 60, 122n43, 190, 192, 198, 215, 220, 283, 437, 453, 492, 504n33
Apocalypse, xxiii, 260, 361–377
A priori, 17, 23n206, 33, 34, 39, 40, 44, 46, 52, 55n16, 147, 168, 169, 191–194, 329, 386, 388, 424n64
Archetype, 207, 217, 229, 232n5, 232n8, 233n50, 235n95
Architectonic, xvi, xxi, 6, 9, 26, 35n1, 167, 171, 187, 190–192, 194, 202, 203, 294, 500

[1] Note: Page numbers followed by 'n' refer to notes.

© The Author(s), under exclusive license to Springer Nature Switzerland AG 2023
T. Rajan, D. Whistler (eds.), *The Palgrave Handbook of German Idealism and Poststructuralism*, Palgrave Handbooks in German Idealism,
https://doi.org/10.1007/978-3-031-27345-2

Arendt, Hannah, 35n1, 101
Aristotle, 5, 40, 117, 135, 136, 328, 339, 379n13
Artaud, Antonin, 490
Assemblage, *see* Aggregate
Asystasy, 203, 206, 222, 223
Aufhebung, 5, 92, 112, 119n14, 129, 190, 194, 201, 216, 217, 219–221, 223, 226, 227, 231, 235n99, 301, 323, 326, 339, 344, 353, 355, 361, 364, 381n28, 434, 437–439, 445n21, 456, 474
Austin, J. L., 9, 388
Autenrieth, Johann Heinrich, 198
Autonomy, 8, 30, 72, 126, 142n40, 219, 264, 348, 377, 389, 415–417, 419, 420, 461, 469, 471, 476, 477, 482

B

Badiou, Alain, xix, 85, 87, 92, 93, 95–98, 104, 105n5, 299, 328, 341n29, 494, 495
Balibar, Étienne, 130
Barad, Karen, 158
Barthes, Roland, xvi, xxi, 204, 299, 435
Bataille, Georges, xiii, xvii, xxiii, 35n1, 129, 205, 283, 328, 331, 335, 336, 338, 339, 343, 349, 350, 356, 357, 376, 380–381n28, 430, 432–434, 437–439, 442, 489, 490, 503n18
Battersby, Christine, 240, 242–246, 250, 255n20
Baudrillard, Jean, 297, 491, 502n17, 505n55
Baugh, Bruce, 430, 431, 436, 437
Beautiful soul, the, 366
Beauty, 7, 189, 254, 367, 429
Beckett, Samuel, 328, 372
Being-toward-death, 172, 176, 178
Beiser, Frederick, 38, 468, 475, 476
Benjamin, Walter, xvi, xxvi–xxviin24, 86, 95
Bergson, Henri, 50, 58n104, 58n110, 328
Berkeley, George, 44, 56n58, 325
Berman, Antoine, xv, xix, xxvin21
Bersani, Leo, 173
Bertalanffy, Ludwig von, 188
Betrayal, 11, 99, 102, 104, 372
Bichat, Xavier, 197, 198
Biester, Johann Erich, 384, 387, 396n18
Biology, 188, 191, 192, 194, 197, 200, 211n80, 215, 285, 500
Biran, Maine de, 28
Blake, William, 325
Blanchot, Maurice, xvii, xix, xxiii, xxvin23, xxviin29, xxviin30, xxviiin39, 85, 103, 104, 105n5, 122n51, 178, 181n30, 328, 331, 349–357,

358n27, 359n29, 359n30, 359n39, 359n43, 360n60, 360n65, 371, 375, 490, 498
Blumenbach, Johann Friedrich, 262, 266
Blumenberg, Hans, 363, 368, 379n14
Body without organs (BwO), 204, 228, 229, 461
Bohr, Niels, 338
Bohrer, Karl Heinz, 248
Bonaventure, Saint, 275
Bonnet, Charles, 262
Bourdieu, Pierre, 7, 8, 491, 503n20
Bowie, Andrew, 310, 475–478
Braidotti, Rosi, 261
Brassier, Ray, xxi, xxii, xxixn52, 260, 265, 286, 494, 505n50
Brentano, Clemens, 242
Brentano-von Arnim, Bettina, xv, xxi, xxii, xxixn50, 239, 241, 242, 250–254, 257n84, 258n91
  Goethe's Correspondence with a Child, 242, 250
  Günderrode, xxixn50
Breton, André, 430
British poststructuralism, 298–300
Buffon, Georges, 262–264, 266, 275, 277
Butler, Judith, xiii
Butler, Rex, 144, 153, 157, 158

C

Caesar, Julius, 132, 139, 141n24
Caesura, xx, 85, 87, 89, 95, 96, 98, 331, 332, 336
Camper, Petrus, 263, 266, 268
Canguilhem, Georges., xv, xxvin17, 197, 200, 507n87
Cantor, Georg, 67, 81n17
Capitalism, 60, 126, 156, 158, 159, 163n62, 163n71, 181n37, 182n52, 398n64, 455, 456, 460, 461
Caputo, John., xxiii, xxxn58
Catastrophism, 61, 264, 266, 268, 284
Categorical imperative, 13, 14, 17, 156
Causality, 39, 126, 140n4, 176, 287, 332–336, 340
Caygill, Howard, 384, 396n18
Celan, Paul, 98
Chalmers, David, 176
Chance, 14, 112, 121n36, 123n62, 134, 141n24, 181n29, 266, 284, 285, 326, 333–336, 340, 391
Chaos, 52, 59, 63, 67–70, 72, 75–78, 80n6, 95, 99, 146, 147, 204, 248, 271, 279, 292, 325–327, 334, 335, 339, 340, 369, 461

Index

Châtelet, Gilles, xxviiin38
Chemistry, 192, 193, 196, 197, 199, 205, 212n90, 475
Christianity, 5, 71, 135, 148, 151, 361, 380n21
Cixous, Hélêne, xxii, 241, 243, 317n58
Cogito, the, 49, 170, 172, 209n13, 435
Cohen, Tom, 498
Colebrook, Claire, xxiv, 174, 261, 496
Coleridge, Samuel Taylor, 194, 195, 267, 268, 274, 502n7, 505n40
Colonialism, 70
Comay, Rebecca, 109, 112, 115, 119n16, 120n22, 371, 496, 497
Community, xxiv, 75, 79, 100, 129, 262, 278, 357, 370, 391, 422n23, 426n138, 429–444
Concept, the
 in Deleuze and Guattari, xiv, 324, 325
 in Hegel, 112, 118n3, 121n42, 128–133, 135–137, 139, 142n39, 206, 227, 323, 351, 362, 364, 371, 453
Condorcet, Marquis de, 64
Contemplation, 95, 166, 168, 170, 172, 367, 454, 455
Contingency, xx, 61, 65, 75–78, 96, 119n14, 128, 130, 133–136, 139, 144, 156, 157, 167–170, 181n29, 220–222, 260, 271, 283–287, 333, 419
Contradiction (in Althusser), 127–129, 132, 133
Control, 68, 132, 221, 246, 251, 253, 294, 401, 408, 413, 415, 416, 418, 470, 489
Copernican Revolution, 76, 274, 405, 496
Corkhill, Alan, 241
Corngold, Stanley, 167, 172, 179n10
Correlationism, xxi, 150, 177, 204, 230, 496
Cosmopolitanism, xviii, 11
Cosmos, 208, 216, 226, 227, 231, 260, 270, 274, 275, 280, 282, 461, 468
Coward, Rosalind, 298–300
Creation, 44, 47, 49, 65–69, 75, 78, 143, 155, 223, 225, 227, 262, 263, 266, 271–276, 300, 311, 312, 325, 345, 349, 361, 364, 365, 368, 369, 377, 378n4, 402, 411, 456, 459, 461, 463, 468, 470, 471, 482
Crisis, xix, 60–62, 69, 72, 79, 171, 201, 218, 222, 226, 227, 232n5, 310, 348, 389, 397n33, 466
Critique, xix, xx, 4, 6, 10, 13, 17, 26, 30, 37, 39, 48, 62, 63, 70, 71, 104, 128, 129, 133, 134, 145, 152, 155–159, 163n62, 173, 177, 181n37, 188, 193, 204, 216, 222, 227, 230, 232n8, 241, 293, 297, 309, 312, 315, 338, 341n29, 344, 347, 348,
372, 375, 377, 388–391, 397n33, 401–404, 406, 407, 409, 411, 412, 415–420, 421n6, 423n40, 485, 490–493, 496, 497, 502n17
Cuvier, Georges, 263–266, 268, 275, 284, 287
Cybernetics, 67, 293–295, 297, 316n17

D

Darkness, 84, 206, 260, 292, 293, 304, 306–313
Darstellung, 439, 440
Darwin, Charles, 237n146, 261, 276, 277, 283, 285
Death, 12, 13, 71, 73, 77, 89, 90, 92, 132, 166, 172, 173, 175, 177, 178, 180n25, 181n30, 199, 201, 220, 242, 260, 264, 283, 285, 286, 332, 339, 340, 344, 347–356, 358n27, 359n30, 374–376, 381n34, 386, 405, 481, 489, 490, 492, 494
Death drive, 172–174, 220, 225, 339
Death penalty, xviii, 12–14
Decision, xviii, 9–11, 13, 25–28, 31, 33–35, 98, 109, 140n4, 144, 147–149, 153, 155–160, 162n43, 163n62, 172, 173, 206, 207, 332, 356, 372, 386, 391, 407, 410, 411, 415, 417, 440, 441, 474
Deconstruction, xvi–xviii, xx, xxii, xxviin31, xxixn45, 3, 4, 8, 10–13, 75, 143–145, 149, 158, 160n1, 160–161n2, 161n3, 168, 179, 197, 201, 207, 209n13, 260, 300, 361, 364, 371–375, 377, 383, 385–389, 392, 429, 435–437, 442, 443, 454, 462, 494, 498, 499, 503n22
De Luc, Jean-André, 262
Deleuze, Gilles, xiii, xiv, xvi–xix, xxi, xxiii, xxiv, xxvin23, xxviiin43, xxixn55, 4, 37, 39, 46–54, 57n78, 58n103, 58n105, 58n110, 83–85, 87, 95–97, 104, 125, 129, 145, 147, 173, 174, 176, 178, 181n37, 203, 204, 215–217, 227–231, 232n8, 236n116, 236n121, 260, 291–294, 309, 313–314, 316n18, 320n157, 324–328, 330, 334–336, 339, 361, 413, 431, 450–463, 490, 491, 493, 497, 498, 501, 502n9, 503n28
 Anti-Oedipus, xxi, 181n37, 217, 227, 228, 230, 291, 460, 461, 490
 Cinema II, 294, 313, 314
 Difference and Repetition, xxixn55, 37, 46, 129, 228, 236n116, 325, 450, 451, 457, 458, 460, 490, 493

Deleuze, Gilles (*cont.*)
  Kant's Critical Philosophy, 4
  Nietzsche and Philosophy,
    xxviin33, 464n23
  A Thousand Plateaus, 181n37, 460, 493
  What is Philosophy?, 325, 451, 459–461
De Man, Paul, xvii, xix, xxii, 62, 85, 86, 89,
    104, 113, 120n29, 300, 302, 328,
    331–333, 335, 337, 429, 491, 498,
    502n17, 503n22
Democracy, 156, 393, 398n60
D'Entrèves, Maurizio Passerin, 411
Derrida, Jacques, xiii, 3, 35n1, 71, 84, 114,
    149, 178, 189, 219, 243, 260, 294,
    323, 347, 361–365, 383, 430, 436,
    453, 491
  Acts of Religion, xxixn57
  "Demeure," 353, 354, 359n47
  "The Future of the Profession," 390, 393
  The Gift of Death, 10
  Glas, xiii, 5, 6, 12, 115–117, 123n58, 201,
    355, 445n31
  Margins of Philosophy, xxvin23, 5,
    437, 503n21
  "Mochlos," 8, 384, 390–392
  Of Grammatology, xiii, 5, 14, 502n9
  "Pas," 353
  "The Pit and the Pyramid," xvii, xxii, 115,
    201, 295–297, 355, 381n37, 438
  Specters of Marx, 336
  "Theology of Translation," xv, xxviiin43
  The Truth in Painting, 245
  Writing and Difference, 5, 433, 435, 438
Descartes, René, 28, 120n33, 143, 339, 384,
    439, 462, 467, 495
Descombes, Vincent, xvi, xvii
Desire, xvi, xix, 75, 87, 88, 92, 96, 99, 149,
    170, 171, 174, 176, 181n37, 195,
    198, 227–229, 231, 233n50, 249,
    265, 297, 306, 310, 315, 331, 361,
    362, 366–369, 372–376, 379n14,
    381n28, 415, 431, 433–435,
    456, 459–461
Determination-in-the-last-instance (DLI), 28
Deterritorialization, 215, 456, 460
Dews, Peter, 153, 154, 235n93, 491–493
Dialectic, 27, 84–86, 92, 112, 125, 126, 128,
    129, 132, 190, 198, 202, 226,
    235n99, 236n116, 292, 293, 296,
    299, 304, 315, 337, 339, 353, 356,
    360n50, 361, 362, 365, 366, 372,
    373, 377, 379n13, 380n28, 431,
    433, 437, 438, 441, 449–463, 484

Dickinson, Emily, 363, 369, 375, 378n6
Différance, 4, 6, 14, 323–325, 330, 331,
    337–339, 352, 356, 361, 363, 370,
    373, 374, 376, 380n28
Difference, xiv, xviii–xxiii, xxviin31, 5, 6, 11,
    13–16, 29, 32, 33, 36n17, 36n18,
    37, 42, 44–48, 51–54, 94–98,
    100–102, 108–110, 113, 116, 117,
    119n18, 129, 145–147, 150, 151,
    156, 157, 159, 160, 163n62, 166,
    173, 174, 190, 191, 197, 198, 200,
    203, 205, 207, 211n82, 216, 217,
    236n116, 242, 285, 292, 294, 297,
    305, 308, 311, 317n52, 323–340,
    346, 348, 356, 360n69, 362, 363,
    366, 373, 381n37, 393, 401, 407,
    422n25, 431, 432, 449–462, 481,
    484, 490, 492, 503n20
Differentials, xix, 37, 39–54, 55n13, 57n78,
    58n105, 58n107, 66–69, 98, 112,
    144, 181n37, 222, 232n8, 236n116,
    376, 431, 434, 453, 459, 462
Digestion, 198, 199
Disaster, xxi, 168, 175, 178, 279, 280
Disciplines, xix, xxi, 26, 27, 33, 100, 102,
    182n52, 187, 189, 191–197,
    201–205, 230, 231, 240, 326, 392,
    450, 490, 500, 501
Disease, 64, 188, 194, 199–201, 203, 205,
    218–223, 225, 233n50, 348, 412,
    470, 471
Dissociationism, 226
Döblin, Alfred, 278–280
Dolar, Mladen, xvi, xx, 125, 133, 142n39
Domination, 100, 243, 245, 401, 408, 412,
    413, 416, 422n14
Donne, John, 76
Dostoevsky, Fyodor, 358n14
Dreyfus, Albert, 138, 142n40, 432
Drive, 35, 85, 92, 132, 134, 135, 145, 147,
    148, 153, 154, 158, 169, 172–175,
    206, 216, 220, 223, 225, 227, 228,
    232n5, 311, 339, 343, 350, 351,
    368, 399, 400, 403, 408, 409, 411,
    412, 455
Du Bois, W. E. B., 72
Duty, 10, 11, 138, 182n52, 385, 398n65,
    418, 422n24

E
Eagleton, Terry, 170, 180n20, 180n22
Easthorpe, Anthony, 298

Index 513

Eckhart, Meister, 354, 360n50
Ecstasy, 229, 235n86, 349, 357
Ellis, John, 298–300
Emanation, 189, 363, 454
Empiricism, xix, 4, 13, 37, 46–52, 63, 147, 148, 168, 170, 172, 227, 267–269, 392, 431, 452, 459
Encyclopedia, 67, 188–191, 193–195, 198, 201, 202, 204, 219
End of history, the, xx, 133, 135–139, 281, 282, 376, 405, 431, 443, 454, 460, 490, 491
Enlightenment, xix, xxvn9, 27, 38, 63, 155, 170–172, 178, 232n5, 371–373, 376, 384–389, 392, 394–395, 399–420, 421n6, 503n20
Enthusiasm, xxiii, 372, 373, 399, 400, 408–410, 412, 414, 415
Eshun, Kodwo, 73
Esposito, Roberto, 197
Establet, Roger, 130
Eurocentric, xix, 11, 61–63, 68, 70, 76, 79, 429
Event, xvi, xx, xxii, xxiii, xxvin23, 8, 9, 12, 16, 17, 44, 51, 52, 65, 71, 85, 93, 96, 98, 99, 131–135, 138, 139, 145, 148, 149, 151, 154, 177, 178, 218, 261, 265, 276, 280, 281, 284, 287, 296, 306, 332–336, 362, 363, 385, 386, 390, 391, 399, 405, 408, 410, 414, 420, 420n2, 432, 436, 439, 450, 451, 455–460, 473
Evil, 151, 206, 225, 226, 231, 249, 253, 348, 366, 380n22, 458, 460, 461, 469–472
Exteriority, 41, 84, 113, 130, 295, 328, 356, 438, 456, 459
Extinction, xxi, xxii, 175, 177, 259–287, 498, 499

F
Faith, 11, 26, 305, 362, 363, 376, 378n3, 381n29, 390, 393
Fanon, Frantz, 72, 73
Fantasy, xx, 133, 150, 152, 153, 160, 174, 175, 230, 294, 295, 297–299, 303, 315, 389, 405, 472
Feedback, xxi, xxviiin38, 167, 187, 188, 206, 207, 294, 499
Feuerbach, Ludwig, 344
Fichte, J. G., xiii, xiv, xvi, xviii, xxiii, xxviiin37, xxixn48, 25–35, 84, 242, 261, 291, 292, 328, 345, 346, 355, 466, 467, 475–477, 485, 496
Wissenschaftslehre (1794), 27, 29, 496
Wissenschaftslehre nova methodo, 28
Finitude, 5, 14, 16, 31, 145, 172, 177, 201, 220, 344, 346, 348, 366, 404, 405, 443, 444, 473, 475
Flaubert, Gustave, 204, 206
Flecker, James Elroy, 284
Formlessness, 248
Foucault, Michel, xiii, xiv, xvi, xxiii, xxvn9, 4, 34, 35n1, 158, 197, 204, 206, 209n13, 212n84, 260, 286, 291, 337, 352, 399–420, 421n6, 421n7, 422n18, 422n19, 423n39, 423n40, 423n56, 424n72, 425n107, 425n125, 426n142, 427n192, 431, 433, 435, 490, 491, 498, 507n87
The Order of Things, 404, 423n40, 490, 498
"What is Critique?," 400, 421n6, 421n9, 421n10, 427n192
"What is Enlightenment?," 400, 417, 420, 421n6
Fragment, xv, xxii, 6, 59, 60, 62, 64–66, 68, 70, 76–79, 80n6, 94, 96, 99–103, 120n33, 146, 191, 202, 239, 246–248, 256n52, 279, 370, 380n24, 460, 476
Frank, Manfred, 62, 291
Freedom, xxiii, 9, 12, 25–27, 34, 35, 71, 87, 136, 146, 154, 170, 188, 189, 193, 199, 200, 202, 206, 221–226, 271, 287, 295, 313, 330, 345–349, 355, 356, 358n10, 379n11, 385–389, 391, 393, 394, 399–403, 406–411, 415–420, 424n64, 424n72, 459, 469–472, 476–479, 482, 483
Freud, Sigmund, xx, 10, 165, 167, 173–176, 179, 216, 217, 227, 229, 235n95, 237n146, 301, 329, 332, 338, 490
Fuchs, Renata, 251, 252
Fukuyama, Francis, 136, 489
Future, the, xiv, xviii, xxiii, xxiv, 3, 6, 8, 39, 65, 67–69, 73–75, 78, 86, 97, 99, 104, 115, 133, 136, 141n23, 171, 173, 176, 177, 182n52, 201, 207, 208, 218, 221, 226, 227, 259, 260, 268, 274, 277, 278, 280, 285, 334, 336, 351, 352, 370, 374, 385, 386, 389, 390, 392, 393, 399, 400, 407, 410, 412, 414, 432, 462, 469, 483, 489–501

G

Gabriel, Markus, 496
Gadamer, Hans Georg, 145, 344
Gasché, Rodolphe, xiii, 195
Genesis, xv, 50, 66, 89, 90, 92, 94–103,
    106n27, 145, 153, 232n5, 283,
    300–302, 306, 310, 404, 423n40,
    434, 435, 449, 454, 462, 469, 475,
    476, 479, 482
Genius, 63, 221, 239, 241–243, 248–253, 348
Geography, 71, 192, 193, 230
Geology, 195–198, 204, 205, 260, 267,
    268, 270
Geometry, 3, 27, 195, 305, 306
Givenness, 29, 30, 36n12, 36n17, 46, 48, 54,
    89, 177, 452
Globalization, xviii, xix, xxviiin40, 393
Global, the, xix, 26, 60–64, 66, 70–73, 78, 79
Goethe, Johann Wolfgang von, xv, xxii,
    xxvn16, 141n21, 242, 250–253,
    294, 303–309, 313, 315, 363, 500
    Theory of Colors, 294, 303, 305, 307–309
Goodman, Kay, 241
Gould, Stephen Jay, 284–286
Gramsci, Antonio, 465, 466
Grant, Iain Hamilton, xxii, xxixn51, 261, 265,
    286, 287, 288n32, 289n66, 293,
    302, 316n18, 494, 496, 497,
    503n28, 505n50, 505n55, 505n58
Green, Joseph Henry, 195, 196
Greenberg, Gary, 176
Ground, xix, 13, 14, 26, 32, 34, 35, 35n4, 39,
    44, 48–50, 52, 53, 58n117, 65, 84,
    85, 94, 100, 102, 103, 106n30,
    146–148, 152, 154–156, 167, 168,
    192, 193, 206, 208, 222, 224, 225,
    235n93, 263, 266, 271, 279, 306,
    310, 311, 344, 349, 352, 370, 371,
    399, 404, 430, 453, 456–459, 461,
    469–471, 474, 476, 478, 479, 482,
    483, 491, 496
Guattari, Félix, xiv, xvii, xix, xxi, xxvin23,
    173, 174, 176, 178, 181n37, 204,
    215–217, 227–231, 232n8,
    236n121, 260, 291, 324–328, 330,
    334–336, 451, 452, 455–457, 459,
    463, 490
    Anti-Oedipus, xxi, 181n37, 217, 227, 228,
        230, 291, 460, 461, 490
    A Thousand Plateaus, 181n37, 460, 493
    What is Philosophy?, 451, 459–461
    See also Deleuze, Gilles
Guéroult, Martial, 45–47

Günderrode, Karoline von, xv, xxi, xxii,
    xxixn50, 239, 241–248, 254,
    256n37, 256n52, 258n91
Guttman, James, 311

H

Habermas, Jürgen, xxviiin43, 35n1, 143, 391,
    411, 415, 418, 421n6, 423n40, 454,
    491, 502n18, 503n28
Hamacher, Werner, 62, 108, 110, 115, 119n18,
    122n55, 166, 179n6, 504n33
Haraway, Donna, 261
Hard problem of consciousness, 176
Harman, Graham, 494, 495, 505n50
Harris, H.S., 492
Hart, Kevin, xxiii, 359n30
Hartmann, Eduard von, 216
Hayles, Katherine, 297
Hegel, G. W. F., xiii–xxiv, xxvn5, xxvin23,
    xxviiin38, xxviiin39, xxixn56,
    xxxn59, 5, 35n1, 38, 48, 71, 84–87,
    89, 92, 94, 99, 107–117, 125–139,
    143, 145, 148, 162n39, 162n43,
    166–168, 177, 179n6, 179n8,
    179n10, 180n14, 187–203,
    205–208, 210n27, 210n29, 211n80,
    211n82, 215–217, 281, 291–297,
    299–301, 307–309, 311, 312,
    317n52, 317n58, 323, 325–329,
    331, 336, 338, 339, 344–347,
    349–357, 359n30, 359n39, 359n40,
    359n47, 360n50, 360n54, 360n60,
    360n69, 361–377, 378n5, 379n10,
    379n11, 379n13, 379n14, 379n15,
    379n17, 380–381n28, 381n37, 384,
    418, 429–434, 436–443, 445n21,
    445n31, 449–456, 470, 473,
    475–477, 483–485, 489–492, 496,
    497, 499, 501n6, 502n7, 502n17,
    503n21, 504n33
    Aesthetics, xxvn5, 189, 199, 201, 429
    *Encyclopedia of the Philosophical
        Sciences*, xv, xxi, 108, 188, 215
    Faith and Knowledge, 346
    *Lectures on the History of
        Philosophy*, 210n29
    Lectures on the Philosophy of History, 128,
        134, 141n24
    Logic, 219, 220, 292, 339, 489, 492
    Phenomenology of Spirit, 107, 118n1,
        122n48, 128, 129, 132, 133,
        141n27, 292, 308, 327, 346, 352,

Index

359n43, 359n47, 360n69, 364, 431, 437, 484, 489
Philosophy of Mind, xxi, 195, 216, 220, 221, 233n40, 234n55, 295, 489, 492
Philosophy of Nature, 108, 210n32, 219, 220, 223, 293, 295, 296, 308, 492
Philosophy of Right, xxiii, 128, 131–133, 135, 137, 346, 368, 440, 489
Heidegger, Martin, xviii, xix, xxvin23, 4, 5, 9, 10, 13–17, 35n1, 84–87, 89, 95, 104, 143, 145, 324, 325, 328, 331, 337, 338, 343, 345, 349, 350, 354, 358n23, 371, 380n24, 384, 438, 502n9, 503n18, 503n21, 503n28
Hemsterhuis, Françoic, 242
Henry, Michel, 28, 30, 33, 34, 35n1
Heraclitus, 328, 339, 371
Herder, Johann Gottfried, xv, xxvin21, 80n13, 205, 242
Herz, Markus, 38, 57n69
Hierarchy, 15, 70, 71, 195, 197, 295, 298, 391, 392, 436, 441, 442
Historicism, 157, 158
History, xvi, xix–xxi, xxiv, 3, 5, 8, 9, 11, 12, 27, 28, 35n6, 39, 60–65, 67–76, 78, 79, 90, 91, 104, 110, 116, 120n33, 125–139, 157, 158, 188, 190, 192, 193, 195, 197, 202, 203, 205–208, 216, 225–227, 230, 232n5, 245, 251, 254, 259, 261–264, 267, 270, 271, 273–276, 278, 280–282, 285, 286, 291, 294, 298, 305, 310, 325, 327, 328, 335–339, 351, 354, 364, 365, 368, 376, 380n22, 393, 395, 400, 401, 403, 405, 406, 408–413, 415, 416, 418, 420, 423n40, 423n56, 429–431, 449, 450, 452, 454–462, 476, 485, 490, 491, 494, 498, 500, 507n88
Hogrebe, Wolfgang, 310, 468
Hölderlin, Friedrich, xviii, xix, 83–104, 198, 300, 302, 328, 331, 336, 475–477, 485, 490
Honneth, Axel, 35n1
Hospitality, xviii, 11, 17, 388
Houellebecq, Michel, 165
Houlgate, Stephen, 492
Hui, Yuk, 104
Humboldt, Wilhelm von, xxiii, xxvin17, xxxn59, 384
Hume, David, 16, 38, 39, 168, 333
Hunter, William, 262
Husserl, Edmund, xxvin23, 3–5, 9, 27, 301, 452, 462, 503n21

Hutton, James, 268
Hyperbole, 91–94, 98, 102, 106n31, 145
Hyperobject, 176, 230, 231, 237n146
Hyppolite, Jean, xx, xxviin25, 115, 122n43, 122n51, 430, 438, 489, 501n6

I

Ideality, 3, 4, 14, 148, 170, 220, 295, 302, 440
Ideas
  aesthetic ideas, 248
  the Idea, xxii, 3, 17, 38, 41, 43, 45, 48–52, 55n22, 56n48, 58n105, 59, 62, 68, 70, 71, 91, 102, 108, 130, 133, 134, 137, 139, 141n23, 145, 170–172, 179n6, 180n19, 189–191, 193, 194, 196, 199, 216, 217, 219, 220, 228, 243, 245, 247, 248, 271, 274, 276, 284, 287, 293, 299, 304, 315, 317n52, 325, 346, 349, 379n11, 379n13, 388, 389, 415, 425n111, 449, 450, 469, 479, 482, 497, 505n49, 507n90
  ideas of reason, 8, 12, 16, 42, 45, 50, 195, 409, 417
  ideas of understanding, 42, 43
Ideology, xx, 104, 134, 155, 299, 300, 333, 434, 435, 449, 454, 495
Imagination, the, 6, 16, 44, 130, 248
Immanence, xxiv, 28–34, 66, 74, 129, 228, 230, 231, 243, 364, 366, 369, 370, 379n8, 449–452, 455, 456, 460–463, 465–472, 482
Immediacy, 29, 30, 220, 222, 352, 367, 373, 460, 492
Incompleteness, 144, 180n14, 246, 441, 442
Incomprehensibility, 59, 76
Incorporation (*vs.* introjection), 175
Individuation, 51, 196, 225, 226, 231, 232n8, 469–471, 491
Infinitesimals, xix, 40, 41, 43, 45, 55n13, 56n58, 62, 66–68, 338
Infinity, 3, 17, 44, 48, 61, 65, 66, 76, 78, 81n17, 101, 193, 204, 220–222, 244, 272, 328, 346, 347, 378n5, 405, 452, 467, 475
Intellectual intuition, 28, 30, 35n10, 36n14, 36n17, 224, 235n86, 499, 506n84
Intensive magnitude, 41–43, 50, 51, 53, 56n43
Interdisciplinarity, xv, xxi, 492
International College of Philosophy, 383
Intuition, xx, 6, 14, 15, 31, 36n18, 39, 40, 42–46, 50–52, 56n43, 58n107, 77, 215, 240, 295, 296, 345, 353, 454–456, 494

Irigaray, Luce, xxii, 243, 245
Irony, 62, 76–78, 179n6, 180n25, 224, 337, 478

J
Jacobi, Friedrich Heinrich, 118n3, 346, 477
Jameson, Fredric, xiii, 492, 504n35
Janicaud, Dominique, 303
Jaspers, Karl, 280, 281, 493
Johnston, Adrian, xxiv, xxxn60, 496
Joyce, James, 334, 335
Judaism, 5, 361, 362, 370, 371, 378n5, 380n21
Judgment, 94, 101n6, 120n26, 188, 207, 246, 458, 493
  determinant, 493
  Last, 361–362, 367–369, 373, 375, 377
  reflective, 6
Jung, Carl Gustav, xxi, 174, 176, 216, 217, 223, 227–229, 231, 232n8, 233n50, 235n95, 236n112, 236n121

K
Kafka, Franz, 8, 10, 17, 328
Kamuf, Peggy, 393
Kant, Immanuel, xiii, xiv, xvi–xviii, xxi–xxiii, xxvn9, xxviin24, 3–17, 28, 33, 35n1, 37–40, 42–54, 57n69, 61, 80n13, 95, 143, 167, 168, 179n11, 180n19, 187–194, 201, 203, 215, 224, 242, 243, 245–249, 261, 263–266, 269–271, 274, 275, 291, 292, 300, 323, 325, 328–333, 339, 344–347, 349, 361, 366, 372, 383–389, 391–394, 396n18, 399–401, 407–420, 420n1, 420n3, 421n6, 421n7, 422n23, 423n40, 424n64, 424n72, 424n83, 424n86, 425n131, 427n174, 439, 453, 458, 460, 462, 476, 477, 480, 481, 485, 490–493, 495–498, 502n17, 503n18, 503n20, 504n33, 504n36, 504n37, 504n38, 505n40, 505n58, 507n87
  "An Answer to the Question: What is Enlightenment?," 385
  Anthropology from a Pragmatic Point of View, xxvn9, 4, 215, 404
  The Conflict of the Faculties, 8, 384–391, 393, 394, 400, 408, 418
  Critique of Judgment (CJ), 187, 188, 193
  Critique of Practical Reason, 407
  Critique of Pure Reason, 3, 4, 8, 14, 38, 167, 187, 481
  Encyclopedia lectures, 191
  The Metaphysics of Morals, 10, 13
  Opus Postumum, 266
  Physical Geography, 192, 193
  Religion within the Limits of Reason Alone, 386
Kearney, Richard, xxiii
Keats, John, 328, 332, 340
Kielmeyer, Carl Friedrich, xv, xxii, 263, 264, 272, 280
Kierkegaard, Soren, 145, 166, 179n8, 347, 348, 366, 497
Kittler, Friedrich, 492, 504n31
Klee, Paul, 306, 365, 377
Kleist, Heinrich von, 83, 328, 335
Klossowski, Pierre, xvi, xvii, 489, 490
Kojève, Alexandre, xvi, xx, 129, 136, 140n14, 281–283, 297, 343, 349, 380n28, 430, 431, 433, 445n21, 489, 490, 501n2, 502n6
Koyré, Alexandre, 430, 438
Krell, David Farrell, 492, 503n28
Kripke, Saul, xiv
Kristeva, Julia, xxii, xxiii, xxvin23, 173, 249, 293, 298–301, 310, 311, 317n52, 317n53, 317n58
  Revolution in Poetic Language, xxvin23, 293, 299
Kundera, Milan, 252, 253
Kuzniar, Alice, 62

L
Lacan, Jacques, xvi, xx, xxi, xxviiin44, 35n1, 104, 125, 129, 137, 139, 144–146, 148–151, 158, 174, 216, 217, 227, 235n95, 298, 324, 325, 328, 329, 331, 332, 336, 361, 368, 371, 482, 489
Laclau, Ernesto, 159
Lacoue-Labarthe, Philippe, xix, xxii, 60–62, 80n6, 85, 89, 90, 98, 246–248, 435
  The Literary Absolute, 246
Language, xvii, xviii, xxii, xxixn53, 9, 30, 34, 66, 71, 75, 84, 86, 87, 99, 100, 102, 107, 111–117, 119n10, 121n38, 121n40, 122n42, 122n43, 125, 136, 141n38, 145, 194, 217, 231, 239–241, 245, 248–254, 264, 267, 279, 282, 291–315, 336, 337, 340, 351–354, 356, 359n39, 360n60,

Index

369, 389, 390, 435, 436, 439, 440, 454, 457, 460, 474, 494, 499, 500
Lanson, Gustave, xvii
Laruelle, François, xiv, xvii, xviii, xxiii, 25–35, 35n1, 35n10, 36n11, 36n17, 36n18, 36n19, 36n20, 341n29
Principles of Non-Philosophy, xviii, 26
Latour, Bruno, 79, 188
Lawfulness, 39, 40, 103
Lebesgue, Henry, 329
Le Doeuff, Michêle, 292, 306
Lefebvre, Henri, 430
Leibniz, Gottfried Wilhelm, xiv, xvii, xix, 38, 40, 41, 44, 48, 56n58, 57n69, 66, 146, 197, 204, 208, 211n82, 328, 339, 343, 450, 454, 458, 459
Monadology, 197
Lem, Stanislaw, 285
Levinas, Emmanuel, 328, 331, 338, 371, 380n22, 380n28, 430–434, 438, 503n28
Lévi-Strauss, Claude, 283, 304
Lewis, Philip E., 301, 317n58
Life, xv, xxi, xxvin17, 4, 12, 13, 30, 33, 34, 36n15, 36n20, 60, 63, 65, 67, 71, 78, 84, 85, 89, 91, 92, 95, 101, 106n34, 108–110, 112, 118n3, 119n10, 120n26, 121–122n42, 131, 132, 134, 137, 138, 141n21, 145, 147, 151, 152, 155, 162n39, 168, 172–174, 176–178, 180n23, 188, 195–200, 202, 203, 206, 208, 219, 220, 223, 225, 226, 228, 247, 248, 259–261, 263, 264, 267, 270–277, 279, 281, 283–287, 313, 340, 344, 346–349, 351, 352, 366, 370, 371, 373, 375–377, 381n28, 381n34, 384, 393, 400, 403, 411, 423n56, 431, 434, 440, 450–456, 461–463, 470, 479, 492, 498–500, 507n87
Light, 46, 47, 61, 77, 84, 90, 92, 96, 102, 109, 111, 118n1, 119n21, 138, 162n43, 177, 206, 221, 233n50, 235n95, 263, 275, 278–280, 282, 285, 291–294, 296, 301–315, 344, 363, 370–372, 374–376, 381n37, 411, 414, 431, 432, 450, 459–461, 468, 472, 481, 483, 484
Linguistic turn, xiii, xvii, xxi, xxii, 209n13, 217, 230, 492, 493, 498
Ljubljana School, xx, xxviiin44, 137–139
Lovejoy, Arthur, 288n9
Lukács, György, xiii, xxvn5, 85, 86, 90
Lyell, Charles, 268

Lyotard, Jean-François, xiii, xvi, xviii, xxii, xxvin23, xxviin24, 8, 10, 230, 245, 246, 260, 265, 293–296, 305–306, 313, 490, 491, 493, 498, 501, 504n38, 505n55
"Can Thought Go On Without a Body?," 260, 493
The Differend, xxviin24
Discourse, Figure, 295, 296, 305
Lessons on the Analytic of the Sublime, xiii, xxvn9, 8
Libidinal Economy, 230, 493, 505n55
The Postmodern Condition, 493
"The Sublime and the Avant-Garde," 245, 246

M
Macherey, Pierre, 85, 129, 140n16
Magnetic sleep, 217–222, 226, 227
Maillet, Benoit de, 274
Maimon, Salomon, xiv, xv, xviii, xix, 37–58, 500
Essay on Transcendental Philosophy, 37–46, 54n10
Maimonides, Moses, 38, 40, 54n7, 55n22
Malabou, Catherine, xiii, xvii, 115, 132, 201, 497, 498, 500
Mallarmé, Stéphane, 350, 352, 354, 499
Igitur, 350–352, 354
Marcuse, Herbert, xiii, xxvn5
Marion, Jean-Luc, 303
Marx, Karl, 8, 125, 126, 128, 130, 132, 133, 139, 140n16, 141n23, 145, 148, 344, 347, 362, 461, 490
Materialism
  dialectical materialism, 84, 99, 104, 145, 146, 298, 299, 316n34
  semantic materialism, xxii, 293, 298, 301–302, 315, 316n34
Mathematics, xix, 41, 44, 53, 66, 67, 78, 91, 187, 191, 193, 195, 196, 202, 203, 324–327, 329, 331, 341n29
Maturana, Umberto, 71, 188
McGrath, Sean, 152, 153, 155, 162n43, 472–474
Mechanics, xxviiin38, 112, 116, 195, 196, 200, 211n72, 219, 283, 334, 479
Mechanism, 27, 67, 98, 139, 222, 262, 364, 369, 370, 373, 401, 440, 473
Mediation, xv, 54, 70, 85, 86, 89, 100, 104, 108, 112, 190, 198, 199, 221, 303–305, 312, 360n50, 372, 459
  re-mediation, 62–64, 66, 67, 69–71, 75, 79

Medicine, 8, 190, 195, 201, 203, 205, 215, 387, 422n14, 422n24, 504n33
Meillassoux, Quentin, xvii, 150, 177, 260, 261, 265, 286, 287, 494, 496, 497, 499, 505n45, 505n49, 505n50, 506n62, 506n85
Mendelssohn, Moses, 41
Mereau, Sophie, 241, 254
Merleau-Ponty, Maurice, 28, 35n1, 129, 489
Mesmer, Franz Anton, xxi, 217–219
Messianic, the, xxii, xxiii, 95, 102, 103, 106n24, 362, 364, 365, 378n3, 380n21
Metaphysics, v, xvi, 4–7, 15, 17, 37, 52, 84, 85, 129, 135, 176, 207, 215, 218, 226, 242, 243, 256n37, 293, 294, 337, 356, 376, 379n13, 406, 435, 437, 453, 457, 468, 470, 472, 475, 477, 485, 490, 492, 494, 496
Modernity, xix, 61–63, 68–74, 76, 79, 143, 313, 345, 346, 349, 355, 364, 371, 393, 409, 411, 479, 482, 503n18
Monism, 177, 256n37, 465–488
Moral law, 10, 17, 424n64
Morton, Timothy, 176, 230, 237n146
Multiplicities, xiv, xv, 10, 50, 58n103, 58n105, 65, 66, 72, 203, 204, 245, 274, 317n52, 327, 337, 434, 475, 484
Musil, Robert, 328
Mysticism, 77

N
Nancy, Jean-Luc, xiii, xix, xxii, xxiii, 8, 60–62, 66, 80n6, 112, 115, 143, 180n14, 190, 201, 246–248, 292, 355–357, 430, 432, 435–443, 445n41, 499, 503n28
 The Discourse of the Syncope, 8
 Hegel: The Restlessness of the Negative, 180n14, 355, 360n56, 443
 The Inoperative Community, 357
 The Literary Absolute, 246
 The Speculative Remark, xiii, xxii, 115, 292, 438–440
Natural history, 192, 193, 195, 205, 264, 270, 271, 273, 276, 281, 282, 285, 286, 476
Naturalism, xxii, 287, 293, 300, 302, 304, 475, 476, 483, 485
 anti-naturalism, 302, 485
Natural purposes, 194, 196
Naturphilosophie, xxi, xxii, xxiv, 66, 84, 197, 202, 204–206, 216, 222–226, 234n65, 234n83, 261–264, 266–267, 269, 270, 272, 275, 278, 281, 293, 295, 296, 300, 302, 317n52, 467, 470, 472, 474–477, 479–482, 485, 490, 492, 498, 502n7
Negation, xxii, xxiii, 27, 31–33, 42, 71, 113, 129, 225, 226, 296, 298, 304, 309, 313, 323, 344–346, 349–357, 359n39, 364, 373, 374, 377, 432, 434, 438, 439, 442, 450, 451, 453, 454, 456, 458–460, 476, 489
Negative philosophy, xix, 147, 500
Negative, the, xx, 63, 85, 86, 114, 129, 147, 169, 176, 189, 194, 196, 199, 200, 206, 294, 312, 331, 332, 344–347, 349, 353, 356, 357, 361, 364–367, 369, 371, 373, 375, 377, 378n4, 381n28, 431, 434, 438, 443, 453, 460, 472, 498
 labour of the negative, 194
Neoliberalism, 461
Neoplatonism, 303
New humanities, the, xxiv, 71, 390, 393, 500
Newton, Isaac, 41, 56n58, 66, 305, 307, 309
Nietzsche, Friedrich, xiii–xv, xvii, 165, 166, 168, 328, 331, 336–340, 345, 348, 372, 376, 381n36, 401–407, 411, 412, 418, 457, 460, 490, 491, 493, 502n17, 503n18, 503n21, 504n31
 The Birth of Tragedy, 166, 490
Nihilism, 92, 343, 344, 348, 351
1968, xvi, xvii, xxvin23, 14, 37, 60, 79, 129, 134, 284, 437, 490, 503n21
Norris, Christopher, 491, 502n17
Nothing, xviii, xxiii, 15, 40, 42, 44, 47, 52, 64, 92, 107–109, 112, 114, 117, 120n33, 126, 130, 132, 134, 136, 137, 143, 146, 147, 149–153, 157–159, 168, 174, 179, 203, 205, 227, 237n146, 245, 247, 248, 252, 260, 262, 268, 270, 273, 276, 277, 279, 281, 285, 286, 292, 293, 296, 308, 327, 331, 332, 343–357, 362, 366, 375, 377n1, 378n4, 389, 390, 404, 411, 414, 416, 442, 443, 450, 451, 459–461, 465, 469–471, 473, 477, 479, 482–484
Notion, the, 33, 36n15, 40–51, 57n78, 58n104, 58n110, 103, 120n22, 132, 133, 135, 136, 138, 139, 141n23, 153, 162n39, 173, 191, 195–198, 201, 203–205, 240, 246, 362–364, 378n6, 381n28, 436, 449, 463

Noumena, 329–333
Novak-LeChevalier, Agathe, 165
Novalis (Friedrich von Hardenberg), xv, xviii,
    xix, xxvin21, xxviiin39, 59–79,
    187, 191, 240, 242, 246, 247, 250,
    263, 267, 492, 501
  Christianity, or Europe, 71
  Fichte Studies, xv
  *Notes for a Romantic
    Encyclopedia*, xv, 501

O

Objectivity, 3, 122n42, 224, 231, 346, 367,
    369–371, 379n13, 381n28, 467,
    475, 477–479
Object-oriented ontology (OOO), 176, 230
Obscurity, 50, 292, 293, 305, 311, 313, 338,
    440, 443
Ockham, W., 362
Oken, Lorenz, xv, 273, 274
Ontology, xvi, 9, 16, 74, 84, 86, 88, 98, 146,
    149, 156, 161n3, 169, 174, 176,
    199, 208, 222, 231, 302, 324, 332,
    335, 340, 349, 401, 418, 419, 437,
    438, 453, 468, 469, 471–475, 477,
    480–483, 485
Organism, 169, 171, 187, 188, 194–201, 203,
    205, 212n90, 218, 220, 228, 229,
    232n8, 235n95, 262, 264, 272, 273,
    282, 296, 300, 454, 455, 471, 481
Ørsted, Hans Christian, 275
Overdetermination, 125, 126, 128, 131
Owen, Richard, 276

P

Paley, William, 262
Panlogicism, 501
Panpsychism, 475, 479, 480
Pantheism, 68, 77, 78, 206, 475, 479, 480
Paradox, 5, 11, 62, 83, 125–127, 137, 145,
    169, 171, 304, 329, 350, 351, 441
Parergon, 7
Parmenides, 120n33, 328, 343
Parousia, 133
Parrēsia, 403, 406, 407
Patriarchy, 241, 344
Paul, Jean, 76
Pauli, Wolfgang, 231
Pessimism, 86, 168, 175, 178, 422n26, 499
Petitot, Jean, 98, 319n97
Pharmakon, 220, 223, 225, 374, 375, 492

Phenomenology, xvii, 3, 9, 28, 34, 86, 90, 189,
    195, 209n13, 260, 303, 343, 437,
    452, 460, 462, 494
Phillips, John, 276
Philology, 191
Philosophy of nature, *see Naturphilosophie*
Photology, 293, 303
Physics, xxviiin38, 188, 195, 196, 204, 207,
    212n90, 216, 222, 302, 334, 335,
    340, 475, 479–481, 496
Physiology, xxi, 191, 194, 196–201, 205
Pindar, xix, 90, 93, 94, 96, 98–100, 102
Pinkard, Terry, xxxn60, 118n1
Pippin, Robert, xxxn60, 358n16
Planetary, the, 60, 61, 78, 79, 80n12, 200, 274
Plant, 187, 196–198, 200, 212n90, 221, 222,
    276, 279, 450, 454, 455, 460
Plasticity, xviii, 86, 115, 133, 190, 191, 201, 498
Plato, 129, 170, 180n19, 325, 328, 333, 339,
    354, 449, 450, 455
Plenitude, 60, 92, 272, 275, 286, 302, 351
Plotinus, 303–305
Poiesis, 59, 217, 230, 231
Point de capiton, xiv, xx, 137
Political theology, xxiii, 362, 364–366, 371,
    372, 377, 378n3
Positive philosophy, 147, 399
Postsecular, 361, 374
Potencies, 197, 202, 204, 207, 216, 224, 226,
    312, 350, 362, 489
Pre-Socratics, the, 325, 333
Principle of sufficient philosophy, 26
Principle of sufficient reason, 45, 46, 49, 50,
    146, 168, 169, 175
Progress, 3, 17, 47, 48, 52, 64, 69, 74, 90, 111,
    113, 136, 139, 179, 251, 265, 277,
    399–401, 409, 410, 414, 415, 418,
    420, 422n23, 439, 440, 492
Protestantism, 366, 368, 443
Pseudo-Dionysius, 354
Psychoanalysis, xviii, xx, xxi, xxvin18, 150,
    155, 157, 167, 172–174, 178, 179,
    181n37, 201, 208, 212n84,
    215–231, 232n5, 232n8
Psychology, xxi, 173, 174, 194, 198, 215–217,
    219, 222, 223, 226, 229, 232n8, 314
Puységur, Marquis de, 217–219, 222

Q

Quantum theory, 334, 335, 340
Quid facti?, 39–40, 52
Quid juris?, 39–40, 42, 44, 52, 452

R

Rajan, Tilottama, xiii, xvi, xx–xxii, xxiv, xxviin31, 115, 119n21, 122n48, 160n1, 160n2, 161n3, 179n5, 180n23, 181n27, 212n119, 219, 220, 232n5, 233n28, 233n36, 235n93, 235n97, 422n25, 427n193, 500
Rancière, Jacques, 130
Raschke, Carl, 145
Rationality, 13, 14, 17, 48, 63, 198, 222, 239–241, 260, 280, 304, 443, 491, 492, 503n18
Reading, xv, xvii–xxiii, xxvin23, 3–17, 25–35, 37–54, 59–79, 83–104, 107–117, 125–139, 143–160, 165–179, 190, 194, 205, 235n93, 254, 269, 295–298, 300, 301, 304, 310, 316n17, 317n52, 323, 328, 331, 335–337, 339, 344, 346, 347, 356, 383–385, 387, 388, 394, 400, 401, 408, 410, 430–434, 436–443, 453, 457, 461, 462, 492–495, 497, 499, 500, 503n22, 504n33, 506n85, 507n86
Readings, Bill, 501
Real-beyond-thinking, the (RBT), 324–336, 338–340
Real, the, xx, xxviiin44, 8, 27, 29–34, 36n20, 42–46, 48, 84, 86, 89–93, 95, 99, 104, 108, 130, 131, 144, 146–148, 150–154, 158, 160, 162n35, 202, 231, 324–333, 371, 491
Recognition, 48, 53, 72, 108, 110, 122n42, 136, 146, 177, 243, 253, 261, 281, 345, 368, 370, 389, 392, 431, 450–453, 455–457, 459–462, 492
Redemption, 370, 371, 377n2, 455, 457, 469, 471
Refraction, 73, 311, 312
Reinhold, Karl Leonhard, 38, 54n11
Repetition, 3, 15, 89, 117, 132, 169, 171, 172, 379n11, 451, 454
Representation(s), xx, xxii, 6, 16, 28, 29, 34, 39, 41–44, 47, 58n117, 89, 91, 92, 98, 111, 114, 119n14, 129, 167–175, 177, 180n23, 181n35, 182n47, 208, 215, 219, 221, 229, 246, 247, 249, 250, 253, 258n91, 264, 296, 301, 302, 324, 325, 328–331, 335, 336, 345, 356, 365, 404–406, 423n40, 450, 452, 454, 455, 458–460, 484, 498, 499
Resistance, xvii, 7, 31, 35n6, 111, 168, 170, 178, 198, 205, 216, 230, 251, 296, 401, 402, 406, 412, 415–418, 422n18, 439, 490
Resnais, Alain, 314
Responsibility, 8, 9, 13, 155, 392, 393, 418
Restraint, xxiii, 88, 361–365, 374, 379n8, 418
Revelation, xxiii, 92, 165, 175, 362–370, 372–376, 378n3
Revolution
  French Revolution, xxiii, xxvin23, 61, 62, 65, 80n12, 364, 379n11, 399, 400, 402, 406, 408–410, 412, 414, 419, 420, 443, 493
  Iranian Revolution, xxiii, 402, 420, 427n192
Rhizome, 204
Ricoeur, Paul, 3, 195, 211n65, 501n4
Riemann, Bernhard, 325
Rimbaud, Arthur, 48
Ritter, J. W., xxvin17
Roetzel, Lisa, 251, 254n5, 254n6, 257n83
Romanticism, xv, xix, xxi, xxii, xxvin21, 59–62, 64, 65, 68–71, 76, 79, 80n6, 239, 248, 250, 456, 492, 500, 501
  Frühromantik, xix, 59, 240–242, 246, 344
Rosenzweig, Franz, xxiii, 9, 362, 364, 365, 369–371, 375, 377, 379n18, 380n21
Rousseau, Jean Jacques, xvii, 5, 406, 503n22
Roussel, Raymond, 490
Ruda, Frank, 109, 112, 115, 119n16, 120n22, 122n44, 496, 497, 506n63
Rupke, Nicolaas, 273

S

Sacrifice, 10, 11, 92, 349, 381n28
Sade, Marquis de, 490
Sartre, Jean-Paul, 35n1, 198, 283, 343, 430–433, 437, 489, 501n6, 503n28
Saussure, Ferdinand de, xvii, 306
Schelling, F. W. J., xiii–xv, xviii–xxiv, xxvn16, xxviiin43, xxixn51, xxxn59, 38, 84–86, 88, 92, 94, 99, 143–160, 187–191, 193–195, 197–208, 210n27, 210n29, 213n123, 214n160, 214n167, 215–217, 222–229, 231, 232n5, 234n65, 234n70, 235n86, 235n87, 235n92, 235n93, 235n99, 236n116, 242, 261, 264, 266, 268–275, 278–281, 287, 291–294, 301, 309–315, 317n52, 321n163, 345, 350, 355,

Index

361, 379n15, 384, 466–485, 490–492, 494–497, 499, 500, 502n7, 503n28, 505n55, 507n87
Ages of the World, 145, 148, 155, 202, 204, 206, 225, 226, 232n5, 235n92, 266, 294, 312–314, 468, 473–475, 481, 492
First Outline of a System of the Philosophy of Nature, xiv, 188, 216, 474
Ideas for a Philosophy of Nature, 472, 474, 478
identity philosophy, 189, 310–312, 466, 467, 472–474
"On the Nature of Philosophy as Science," 202, 222, 235n86
On University Studies, xxviiin43, 189, 500, 507n90
Philosophical Investigations into the Essence of Human Freedom, 224
Philosophy of Art, 201, 210n27, 213n123
Philosophy of Mythology, 201, 235n99, 310
System of Transcendental Idealism, 216, 224, 266, 475
Schematism, 6, 51, 268
Schiller, Friedrich von, xv, xxii, 300, 368, 369, 379n17
Schizoanalysis, 181n37, 227–229, 456
Schlegel, August Wilhelm, 59, 62–64, 66, 68, 72
Schlegel, Friedrich, xv, xix, xxi, xxvin21, xxvin22, xxixn48, 59, 62–66, 68, 71, 75–79, 240, 242, 246, 247, 250, 504n33, 507n86
Schleiermacher, Friedrich, xxiii, xxvin21
Schmitt, Carl, 77, 362–364, 366, 377–378n3
Scholem, Gershom, 370, 371, 377n2, 378n4, 380n19
Schopenhauer, Arthur, xiii, xviii, xx, xxii, xxiii, xxixn45, xxixn46, xxxn59, 165–179, 190, 272, 291, 497
On the Fourfold Root of the Principle of Sufficient Reason, 166
The World as Will and Representation, xx, 166, 179n8, 210n32
Schröter, Manfred, 202, 213n126, 214n167
Scotus Eriugena, J., 343
Searle, John, xxiii
Self-consciousness, 29, 85, 86, 89, 121n42, 171, 198, 220, 224, 270, 281, 345, 347–349, 355, 440
Self-positing, 29, 31, 144

Self, the, 4, 31, 95, 169, 195, 200, 217, 224, 242–244, 246–249, 303, 345–347, 352, 355–357, 367, 400, 403, 416, 423n55, 433
Semiotic, the, 295, 297, 299, 301, 306, 310, 317n52
Sensibility, 14–16, 38, 40, 42, 43, 52, 58n107, 121n42, 198, 343, 412, 471, 475, 479, 480
Serres, Michel, xxviiin38
Sexual difference, 5, 6, 393
Shelley, Percy Bysshe, 270, 328, 332, 339, 340
Simondon, Gilbert, 51, 232n8, 491
Sinclair, Isaac von, 95, 96, 106n30
Sinthome, 174–176
Skepticism, 38, 39, 56n65, 89, 409, 413, 414
Sollers, Philippe, 298, 316n34
Sophocles, 332
Soul, soul-life, xxi, 38, 77, 192, 206, 215, 216, 219–223, 227, 229, 252, 296, 354, 370, 437, 458
Sovereignty, 13, 94, 97, 100, 229, 347, 358n10, 363, 393, 429–444, 470
Speculation, 86, 89, 98–100, 269, 272, 283, 304, 471, 476, 492, 496, 498
Speculative realism, 175–177, 230, 494, 495, 498
Spinoza, Baruch, 38, 129, 136, 140n16, 211n82, 320n157, 328, 339, 413, 460, 467, 468, 473–478, 480, 482, 485
Spivak, Gayatri, 394, 398n65
State, the, 5, 8, 13, 38, 41, 58n105, 86–88, 92, 96, 97, 100–102, 127, 128, 130, 131, 133, 135, 137, 152, 156, 157, 166, 177, 188, 189, 198–200, 208, 218, 221–223, 228, 229, 235n86, 249, 260, 262, 266, 273, 276, 304, 306, 308, 325, 328, 335, 346–347, 350, 354, 358n10, 363, 367, 369, 373, 375, 386–388, 390, 394, 399, 402, 410, 414, 417, 418, 420n3, 422n23, 425n131, 434, 436, 440–442, 451, 454, 455, 466, 497
Steffens, Heinrich, 267, 270
Stephens, Scott, 144, 153, 157
Stiegler, Bernard, 462
Stone, Alison, 194, 196, 317n52
Structuralism, xvi, xvii, xxviin31, 137, 143, 144, 147, 148, 158, 160, 298, 299, 304, 338, 347, 433, 435, 444n17
Stufenfolge, 84, 92, 194, 195, 199, 205, 214n160, 223, 224

Style, xvi, 37, 111, 167, 180n20, 199, 230, 241, 267, 291
Subject, the
 the Black subject, 70, 72, 73
 system as subject, 188, 189
Sublation, *see Aufhebung*
Sublime, the, xxii, 55n22, 126, 239, 242–246, 249, 255n20, 257n84, 278, 454, 493, 504n38
Surrealism, 490
Symbolic, the, xx, xxviiin44, 66, 71, 88, 99–101, 104, 143, 144, 148–155, 157, 158, 160, 162n35, 162n43, 174, 175, 189, 190, 199, 201, 210n27, 228, 230, 241, 249, 250, 301, 311, 312, 331, 332, 434, 435, 461
Synthesis, 27, 36n18, 43, 46, 52, 63, 112, 153, 173, 174, 190, 202, 208, 210n27, 228, 229, 247, 283, 302, 309, 336, 339, 430–434, 436, 438, 439, 441, 443, 445n21, 475, 497
System, xvi, xix, xxi, xxiii, 6, 33, 34, 40, 44, 46, 47, 50, 51, 58n107, 60, 61, 65, 67–70, 76–78, 84, 88, 89, 93, 100, 103, 111, 112, 115, 116, 122n55, 129, 144, 146, 147, 150, 154, 156, 159, 162n39, 162n43, 165, 167, 179n8, 180n22, 181n31, 187–208, 219, 220, 222–225, 227, 234n65, 235n95, 246, 249, 252, 259, 264, 268, 271, 275, 276, 280, 292, 294–296, 298, 299, 311, 329, 330, 334, 339, 344, 346–348, 350, 368, 370, 405, 413, 419, 422n14, 422n18, 429–440, 443, 452, 465, 477, 481, 484, 489, 490, 492, 499, 500
Systems theory, 188, 294, 304

T
Taubes, Jacob, 364, 369, 375, 378n3
Technology, xxviiin38, 188, 280, 297, 491, 504n31
Teleology, 17, 45, 78, 136, 170, 199, 217, 219, 223, 226, 272, 307, 373, 401, 409, 430, 481
Thacker, Eugene, xxi, xxii, xxixn46, xxixn52, 168, 172, 176–178, 179n9, 180n14, 497, 498
Time, xix–xxi, 3–10, 12, 14–17, 30, 35, 38, 40, 42–45, 47–49, 51–53, 60–65, 67–70, 72–78, 80n13, 86–88, 91, 92, 95–99, 101–104, 106n24, 109–111, 113–117, 120n22, 120n26, 121n40, 121n42, 122n43, 128–130, 133, 154, 161n7, 165, 166, 169, 171, 173, 175, 176, 178, 192, 207, 208, 218, 219, 223–227, 239–241, 245, 248, 250–254, 259–262, 266–268, 270–277, 279–284, 287, 291–293, 296, 300, 310, 313, 314, 317n58, 331, 332, 335, 336, 340, 348, 350, 352–356, 358n10, 362, 363, 368–370, 372, 375, 377n2, 377n3, 381n37, 389, 390, 399, 400, 402, 405, 409–413, 415, 417, 419, 420, 421n6, 429, 439, 441, 452, 453, 455, 460–462, 473, 490, 493, 495–497, 502n9
Topography, 193, 392
Torok, Maria, 175
Toscano, Alberto, 494, 503n28
Totalitarianism, xxiv, 430–435
Totality, 48, 50, 60, 64, 84, 91, 127, 131, 132, 147, 152–154, 177, 196, 309, 328, 345, 350, 357, 430, 432–443, 459, 460, 480
Transcendence, 27, 30, 32, 33, 93, 242–244, 282, 364–366, 369, 370, 379n8, 380n28, 449, 451, 455, 456, 460, 463
Transcendental empiricism, xix, 37, 46–52, 147, 227
Transgression, 88, 104, 400–407, 409, 411, 417
Translation, xiii, xv, xvi, xix, xxi, xxvn5, xxvn9, xxixn50, 26, 54n7, 90, 93, 94, 96, 99, 105n19, 117, 118n1, 118n3, 118n7, 118n9, 119n14, 119n17, 120n26, 120n33, 121n38, 121n41, 123n58, 129, 140n15, 140n16, 141n24, 142n40, 161n4, 173, 180n14, 190, 191, 198, 199, 201, 203, 207, 209n14, 258n98, 288n32, 303, 354, 360n55, 377n3, 505n55
Transparency, 292–295, 297, 299, 303, 304, 306, 307, 310, 311, 313–315, 468
Tsimtsum, 362–365, 367–369, 371–375, 377, 378n4, 378n5, 378n6

U
Unconditional, the unconditioned, xxi, 11, 16, 50, 88, 94, 203, 204, 207, 271, 345, 358n10, 372–374, 376, 381n29, 391, 470, 476, 500

Index 523

Unconscious, the, xxi, 46–49, 53, 121n36, 147, 152, 153, 155, 165, 172–174, 176, 181n37, 198, 208, 215–217, 219–231, 234n55, 234n65, 235n95, 236n132, 270, 329, 332, 338, 339
Understanding, the, v, xix, xxiii, xxvin17, xxvin21, 6, 7, 15, 16, 31, 38, 40–49, 53, 54, 55n22, 56n48, 57n69, 59, 61, 64, 71, 73, 76, 80n6, 85, 89, 114, 122n43, 122n55, 130–132, 136, 139, 141n23, 160, 173, 188, 215–217, 224, 225, 231, 247, 252, 259, 261, 274, 282, 299, 302, 312, 323, 326, 346, 349, 357, 362, 363, 385, 386, 390, 406, 407, 416, 422n23, 431–433, 435, 456, 461, 496, 499, 505n40, 505n55, 507n86
Ungrund, 85, 206, 216, 225, 226, 235n93, 271, 279, 350
Unhappy consciousness, 431, 433, 436, 489
Unilateral duality, 28, 33
University, xviii, xxiii, xxxn59, 8, 9, 12, 166, 179n10, 189, 253, 274, 383–395, 397n32, 398n60, 398n64, 493, 500, 501, 507n90
Unthinkable, the, xix, 46–49, 53, 87, 324, 326, 330–332, 336, 338, 339, 352
Unthought, the, 31, 86, 209n13, 217, 219–222, 500
Urgrund, 169
Utopia, 72, 74, 364, 404–406, 412, 413

V

Varela, Francesco, 71, 188
Varnhagen, Rahel, 241, 254
Veit-Schlegel, Dorothea, 241, 254
Violence, 15, 70, 74, 78, 85, 87, 95–97, 99–102, 106n34, 123n58, 154, 207, 217, 220, 223, 231, 245, 399, 400, 402, 412, 414, 422n23, 425n125, 433, 434, 436, 442, 473
Virtual, the, 50, 51, 54, 58n104, 326
Vision, 9, 61, 72, 95, 268, 296, 303, 305, 306, 308, 309, 313, 317n58, 392, 405, 412, 419, 480
Vitalism, 475, 479, 480
Viveiros de Castro, Eduardo, 453
Voegelin, Eric, 364, 372

W

Wahl, Jean, 297, 430–432, 489
Washington, Chris, 176
Westphal, Merold, xxiii
Whewell, William, 268
Whitehead, Alfred North, 328
Will, the, 145, 407–411, 424n86, 471
Will to revolution, xxiii, 400, 402, 403, 407–412, 414, 416, 420, 422n23, 424n86
Wissenschaft, 191, 195
Withdrawal, 295, 332, 362, 365, 378n6, 384, 387, 394, 436, 441
Wittgenstein, Ludwig, 325, 357
Wolff, Christian, 40, 41
Woolf, Virginia, 40, 41
Writing, xv, xvii, xix, xx, xxii, xxiii, xxviin29, xxixn46, xxxn58, 5, 8–11, 38, 62, 66, 73, 79, 85, 107–117, 118n1, 119n10, 119n12, 122n55, 155, 156, 165–167, 175, 176, 178, 179, 179n9, 180n14, 201, 202, 204, 206, 219, 221, 230, 231, 233n50, 239–242, 250, 253, 254, 256n52, 266, 267, 291, 293, 294, 296, 297, 300–304, 309, 312, 315, 331, 336–339, 351, 352, 354, 355, 375, 384, 389, 400, 409, 429, 434, 436, 438, 443, 445n31, 500, 504n31
Wynter, Sylvia, 70–73, 79

Y

Yaeger, Patricia, 243–245
Yale deconstruction, xvi, 300

Z

Zammito, John, 196
Žižek, Slavoj, xiii, xiv, xvii, xx, xxvn9, xxviiin44, 84, 87, 89, 98, 99, 104, 125, 133, 137–139, 142n40, 143–160, 160n1, 161n3, 161n4, 161n7, 162n35, 162n43, 163n62, 163n71, 174, 182n52, 188, 189, 235n93, 310, 311, 314, 321n163, 371, 379n11, 492, 503n28
The Indivisible Remainder, 153, 235n93
Less than Nothing, xxivn3, 161n6, 162n31, 162n33, 163n63, 163n69, 379n11
The Sublime Object of Ideology, 141n38
Zola, Émile, 138

Printed in the United States
by Baker & Taylor Publisher Services